PROSPECTS IN CELL BIOLOGY

PROSPECTS IN CELL BIOLOGY

A volume of reviews to mark 20 years of
Journal of Cell Science

Edited by

A. V. Grimstone, Henry Harris and R. T. Johnson

SUPPLEMENT 4   1986
JOURNAL OF CELL SCIENCE
Published by THE COMPANY OF BIOLOGISTS LIMITED, Cambridge

Typeset, Printed and Published by
THE COMPANY OF BIOLOGISTS LIMITED
Department of Zoology, University of Cambridge, Downing Street,
Cambridge CB2 3EJ

© The Company of Biologists Limited 1986

ISBN: 0 948601 01 9

JOURNAL OF CELL SCIENCE SUPPLEMENTS

All supplements are available free to subscribers to *Journal of Cell Science* or may be purchased separately from The Biochemical Society Book Depot, P.O. Box 32, Commerce Way, Colchester CO2 8HP, UK

PREFACE

This volume celebrates the 20th anniversary of the first appearance of *Journal of Cell Science*. It signals the survival and the good health of the journal. We believe that the occasion is an appropriate one on which to offer some brief comments on our scope and future.

The journal originated as the successor to the *Quarterly Journal of Microscopical Science*, a publication that itself had a distinguished history stretching back for over a century. The new journal was intended from the outset to be devoted to all aspects of cell organization: it was to be concerned with cell biology in the broadest sense. This remains our aim. As was to be expected, certain areas of the subject have from time to time figured more prominently than others in the journal's pages. Topics such as nuclear and chromosomal organization, cell recognition and adhesion, cell junctions, the analysis of malignancy – to name a few examples – have on occasion been notably well represented. We have always been pleased to find such tendencies developing, for they help to give the journal a distinctive character and lead to a flow of good papers in those areas. We should emphasize, however, that as editors we have never consciously set out to steer the journal in any particular limited direction: our aim has been simply to provide a medium for the publication of a wide range of important research on cells. We hope that the composition of our Editorial Board at any time sufficiently reflects what we see as being the scope of the journal.

We believe that there is still a place for a journal with such broad aims. This is not, of course, to say that we wish the journal to go on publishing only the sort of work in cell biology that it has done in the past. Time brings major shifts of emphasis in the directions that research takes, and we should be failing as editors if we did not try to ensure that the journal reflected these. We should certainly like to see more work on the molecular aspects of cell organization in our pages, though we would publish this in addition to, rather than at the expense of, work devoted to more complex levels of organization.

This volume is the fourth of a recently started series of Supplements to the journal. These Supplements, designed to reflect areas of major current interest in cell biology, represent one manifestation of our continued growth. The single volume of *Journal of Cell Science* published in 1966 amounted to just over 400 pages; in 1986 we shall publish close to 3000. We expect that future years will see further increases in size and frequency of publication. The journal has a major advantage in that it is not in any way associated with a commercial publisher. It is owned and managed by The Company of Biologists Limited, a non-profit-making organization run by professional biologists. The needs of the journal's contributors and readers and the role of the journal in the contemporary scientific scene are always the prime considerations of the Company, rather than the profitability of the journal in a financial sense. In the last few years, responding to a suggestion from the editors of this journal, the Company has set up its own printing house, which now gives it total control over the printing quality and speed of production of its publications. We see this as likely to be a major factor in the future of *Journal of Cell Science*.

In deciding how we should celebrate our 20th anniversary, it seemed to us appropriate to look to the future as much as to the past. We invited the contributors to this volume to write not the usual sort of comprehensive review of their field, but an assessment of the present situation there and of what is likely to be done in the near future. Inevitably, space did not allow us to cover cell biology at all comprehensively. We hope, however, that the volume is representative enough of what is going on in the subject at the present time. We take it as a sign of the esteem in which the journal is held and as a good augury for the future that so many distinguished cell and molecular biologists have been willing to write for us on these lines. We are grateful to them for doing so. Collectively, they have produced a volume of much interest. If, in the years to come, the journal can publish material of comparable scope and importance, we shall be well satisfied.

The Editors

PROSPECTS IN CELL BIOLOGY

CONTENTS

J. Cell Sci. Suppl. 4, 1–9 (1986)
Printed in Great Britain © *The Company of Biologists Limited 1986*

PROSPECTS FOR REASSEMBLING THE CELL NUCLEUS

R. A. LASKEY

Cancer Research Campaign Molecular Embryology Group, Department of Zoology, University of Cambridge, Downing Street, Cambridge CB2 3EJ, England

INTRODUCTION

The nucleus is the information centre of the eukaryotic cell. Not only does it synthesize the mRNA for thousands of proteins, but it supplies regulated amounts of each mRNA to the cytoplasm. In addition it must replicate its entire structure accurately each cell cycle. The human genome contains 1·8 m of DNA, so that an average human chromosome contains 40 mm of DNA in which the strands of the double helix intertwine $1·4 \times 10^7$ times. This structure must function in a nucleus of about 6 μm diameter. The structural complexity of a nucleus is more apparent from a scale model enlarged by 10^6 times (Table 1). On this scale DNA would be the diameter of thin string, 2 mm, but the DNA in each chromosome would be 40 km long, and the total DNA of one nucleus would reach from London to Leningrad (Table 1). Nevertheless, this 1800 km of 'string' must all be packaged into a sphere of only 6 m diameter in such a way that the entire structure can replicate accurately and that specific regions must be accessible for efficient and regulated expression. To achieve this the nucleus contains a hierarchy of structural organizations. Most of our knowledge of this organization comes from the structural analysis of partly disrupted

Table 1. *Packing DNA into chromosomes and the nucleus*

	Approx. dimensions	Dimensions $\times 10^6$ (to aid perspective)
DNA diameter	2 nm	2 mm
DNA length in diploid human genome	1·8 m	1800 km
Diameter of nucleus	6 μm	6 m
DNA length in average human chromosome	40 mm	40 km
Length of average human metaphase chromosome (approx.)	4 μm	4 m

Ratios

$$\frac{\text{DNA length in chromosome}}{\text{DNA diameter}} = 2 \times 10^7$$

$$\frac{\text{DNA length in chromosome}}{\text{Length of metaphase chromosome}} = 10^4$$

$$\frac{\text{Length of DNA in genome}}{\text{Diameter of nucleus}} = 3 \times 10^5$$

material. However, an alternative approach is emerging, which offers more promise for elucidating the functional significance of structures in the nucleus. This alternative approach involves reconstituting the structural organization of the nucleus from its components *in vitro*. This paper reviews progress in reconstructing components of the cell nucleus and argues that these approaches will find widespread use in the near future.

RECONSTRUCTING FUNCTIONAL CHROMOSOMES

Isolation and propagation of genes in *Escherichia coli* are becoming increasingly routine techniques, but to reconstitute isolated genes into functional chromosomes requires at least three other elements. These are centromeres, telomeres (chromosome termini), and sequences that allow autonomous replication and that appear to be replication origins. Progress in identifying these elements has been largely confined to yeast. In *Saccharomyces cerevisiae* autonomously replicating sequences (ARS elements) were isolated by their ability to allow the replication of DNA ligated to them (Fig. 1; Stinchcomb, Struhl & Davis, 1979). Mutagenesis has defined the minimal consensus sequence required for ARS function as

$$\underset{T}{A}\ T\ T\ T\ A\ T\ \underset{G}{A}\ T\ T\ T\ \underset{T}{A}$$

(Celniker *et al.* 1984; Kearsey, 1984). There is a shortage of direct evidence that replication initiates at ARS elements, but this remains the most reasonable interpretation of their effects.

Plasmids that contain ARS elements are unstable in yeast and are rapidly lost through mitosis and meiosis. Clarke & Carbon (1980) used this observation as an assay to select centromere sequences that confer mitotic and meiotic stability on circular plasmids (Fig. 1).

Although the combination of an ARS with a centromere can confer mitotic and meiotic stability on a circular plasmid, this combination is not enough for efficient maintenance of linear plasmids. Szostak & Blackburn (1982) selected for DNA sequences that could stabilize segregation of linear plasmids. They started with DNA from the amplified linear minichromosomes that encode ribosomal DNA in *Tetrahymena*, and found that the terminal (telomeric) sequences from *Tetrahymena* ribosomal DNA could function to stabilize linear plasmids in yeast. They then constructed linear plasmids with one cleaved end and one *Tetrahymena* telomere to assay random yeast DNA fragments for their ability to maintain linear plasmids in yeast. This strategy enabled them to isolate and compare functional telomere sequences from both *Tetrahymena* and yeast. The structures they found contain simple repeating sequences of C_4-A_2 in *Tetrahymena* or C_{1-3}-A in yeast, apparently arranged as gapped hairpins (reviewed by Blackburn, 1985; Murray, 1985).

When these three elements (telomeres, centromeres and autonomously replicating sequences) are combined, they enable linear plasmids to behave as autonomous chromosomes (Fig. 1). The efficiency of plasmid maintenance is also seriously affected by the length of DNA. Short plasmids containing these elements are much less stable than long plasmids (Murray & Szostak, 1983; reviewed by Blackburn, 1985; Murray, 1985).

In contrast to the progress in reconstituting functional chromosomes in yeast, there has been little progress in identifying the equivalent functional components from the chromosomes of higher eukaryotes. Unfortunately the yeast assay for centromere sequences does not select centromere sequences from animal DNA. This is not surprising since the attachment of microtubules to the centromere differs between yeast and higher eukaryotes. The assay for autonomously replicating sequences does select sequences from animal DNA that can function in yeast (Stinchcomb *et al.* 1980; Mechali & Kearsey, 1984). Furthermore, sequences selected from *Xenopus* genomic DNA by their ability to support plasmid replication in yeast showed clear sequence homology with the yeast ARS consensus sequence (Kearsey, 1984; Mechali & Kearsey, 1984). This emphasizes the sequence specificity of replication in yeast, but it does not demonstrate that these sequences function as replication origins in the species that they are derived from. At present it is not possible to assess the extent to which these sequences might be replication origins in higher eukaryotes in the absence of a comparable assay. Although it is possible to

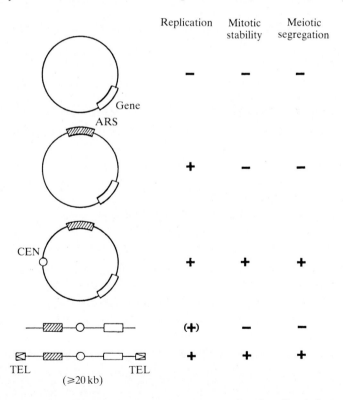

Fig. 1. DNA sequence elements required for reconstructing functional chromosomes in yeast. Note that the stability of linear chromosomes containing centomere and telomere sequences increases with the total length of DNA (Murray & Szostak, 1983). For reviews of the material presented in this figure see Blackburn (1985) and Murray (1985). CEN, centromere; TEL, telomere; kb, 10^3 bases.

observe replication of DNA introduced into frog eggs, it has not been possible to demonstrate sequence specificity of replication (reviewed by Laskey, Kearsey & Mechali, 1985).

There is clearly scope for important advances in future years in identifying and characterizing centromeres, telomeres and replication origins from higher eukaryotes. Already strategies have been devised to isolate replication origins from higher eukaryotes. If these can be combined with effective assays for initiation of replication, then it should be possible to characterize these sequences and to address the puzzling question of why replication initiates at specific DNA sequences. The obvious answers to this question are either that the enzymes of replication might require specific sequences for the initiation mechanism, or that specific initiation sites might be required to coordinate multiple initiations within a single chromosome in such a way that each region replicates once and only once in any cell cycle. However, experiments in which DNA is injected into *Xenopus* eggs show that neither of these mechanisms requires specific DNA sequences (Harland & Laskey, 1980; Mechali, Mechali & Laskey, 1983; Mechali & Kearsey, 1984). An alternative possibility should become accessible to experimental analysis shortly, namely the possibility that site-specific initiation of DNA replication is not required for replication itself, but is required for regulated gene expression, perhaps to define the boundaries of the units of active chromatin (Laskey & Harland, 1981).

REASSEMBLING DNA INTO CHROMATIN

The problem of retaining functional accessibility of 1·8 m of DNA in a 6 μm diameter nucleus was illustrated in Table 1. It is solved by a specific folding hierarchy, which has the nucleosome as its fundamental unit. The levels of compaction of DNA in a metaphase chromosome are summarized in Fig. 2. Reassembling the first level of DNA compaction, the nucleosome core has become relatively simple (reviewed by Laskey & Earnshaw, 1980). Histones and DNA can self-assemble to form nucleosome cores, either by gradient dialysis from 2 M-NaCl or by slow addition of histone dimers and tetramers to an excess of DNA at physiological ionic strength. Alternatively, certain polyanions such as polyglutamic acid or RNA can facilitate rapid assembly at physiological ionic strength (Stein, Whitlock & Bina, 1979; Nelson, Wiegand & Brutlag, 1981). In the case of polyglutamic acid there is evidence that it acts by forming histone octamers in the absence of DNA (Stein *et al.* 1979). Clearly these pathways are unlikely to be accurate guides to the cellular process, particularly as there is evidence that histones H3 and H4 associate with DNA before histones H2A and H2B *in vivo* (Worcel, Han & Wong, 1978; Senshu, Fukada & Ohashi, 1978).

An insight into the cellular process of nucleosome assembly has come from fractionation of a cell-free system derived from *Xenopus* eggs (Laskey, Mills & Morris, 1977). Initial studies of this system revealed that a stored histone pool is complexed to acidic proteins that facilitate nucleosome core assembly *in vitro*. The first of these to be identified and purified is called nucleoplasmin (Laskey, Honda, Mills & Finch, 1978; Earnshaw, Honda, Laskey & Thomas, 1980; Mills, Laskey,

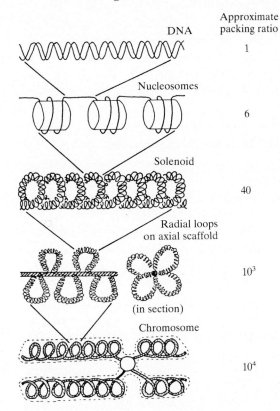

DNA

Approximate packing ratio

1

Nucleosomes

6

Solenoid

40

Radial loops on axial scaffold

10^3

(in section)

Chromosome

10^4

Fig. 2. Summary of structural models for the packing of DNA into a metaphase chromosome (based on Klug *et al.* 1980; Thoma, Koller & Klug, 1979; Paulson & Laemmli, 1977; Rattner & Lin, 1985).

Black & De Robertis, 1980). It is a pentameric heat-stable protein that binds histones *in vitro* and transfers them to DNA. *In vivo* nucleoplasmin is bound to H2A and H2B and to two other proteins, which co-electrophorese with H3 and H4 on sodium dodecyl sulphate–polyacrylamide gels, but with different isoelectric points (Kleinschmidt *et al.* 1985). It is not clear yet if these proteins are modified forms of known histones. Most of the H3 and H4 pool in *Xenopus* eggs and oocytes is complexed to two other acidic proteins called N1 and N2 (Kleinschmidt & Franke, 1982; Kleinschmidt *et al.* 1985).

The existence of these two classes of histone binding factor in *Xenopus* eggs raises several significant questions. First, what is the functional relationship of the factors? Are they solely responsible for transfer of only one class of histones each or do they form a histone-transfer chain? To answer this question we shall need to identify the proteins that resemble H3 and H4 and that are bound to nucleoplasmin. A second question that immediately emerges is whether or not nucleoplasmin and N1 and N2 are only adaptations for managing a stored histone pool or are involved in nucleosome assembly in other types of cell. So far polyclonal antibody studies suggest that nucleoplasmin is distributed widely (Krohne & Franke, 1980*a,b*).

Although several methods are available for reassembling nucleosome cores, it is much more difficult to reconstitute the regular spacing of nucleosomes at intervals of 200 base pairs. Assembly from purified components usually spaces nucleosome cores randomly or at abnormally close intervals. In contrast, extracts of *Xenopus* eggs or oocytes assemble nucleosomes at the physiological spacing of approximately 200 base pairs (Laskey *et al.* 1977; Earnshaw *et al.* 1980; Glikin, Ruberti & Worcel, 1984). The process has not been analysed yet, but there is agreement that ATP and Mg^{2+} are required for accurate nucleosome spacing.

In a few cases it has been possible to assemble nucleosomes at specific sites on DNA (phased nucleosomes) even when starting with purified histones and DNA and reconstituting nucleosomes by salt dialysis (Linxweiler & Horz, 1985; Simpson & Stafford, 1983; Thoma & Simpson, 1985). In the near future, the physiological significance of nucleosome position, if any, should become much clearer.

As described in the following section it is becoming possible to reconstitute whole nuclei from purified DNA. This suggests that higher levels of chromatin structure are also forming and it should permit further progress in studying the structures and their assembly.

In addition, the complexity of the nucleosome assembly pathway emerging from studies of *Xenopus* eggs suggests that much more work will be required before we can fully reproduce the cellular assembly pathway from purified components *in vitro*.

REASSEMBLING THE NUCLEAR ENVELOPE

The hallmark of the eukaryotic cell is the nuclear envelope. It separates the site of transcription from that of translation and determines the exchange of information between the cytoplasm and the nucleus. To reconstruct a functional nucleus it is essential to be able to reassemble a nuclear envelope around chromatin. Two recent advances have made this feasible. First, Lohka & Masui (1983, 1984) have described a cell-free system from eggs of the frog *Rana* that can reconstitute a nuclear envelope around demembranated sperm nuclei. The sperm nuclear membrane is damaged by treatment with lysolecithin before incubation in a low-speed supernatant from *Rana* eggs that have been activated by electric shock and disrupted by centrifugation rather than homogenization. During incubation, nuclear envelope re-forms around the sperm chromatin. It has the conventional structure of a double nuclear membrane containing nuclear pore complexes. After the nuclear envelope is re-formed the chromatin disperses and the nucleus swells (Fig. 3).

A second advance towards reconstructing the nuclear envelope comes from observations of Forbes, Kirschner & Newport (1983), who injected purified phage λ DNA into eggs of *Xenopus laevis* and observed that it becomes assembled into nuclei. These synthetic nuclei composed of phage λ DNA are bounded by double membranes, perforated by numerous nuclear pores and lined by lamins. The results from these experiments indicate that DNA can serve as a signal for enclosure by a nuclear envelope and that envelope formation does not require specific nucleotide sequences.

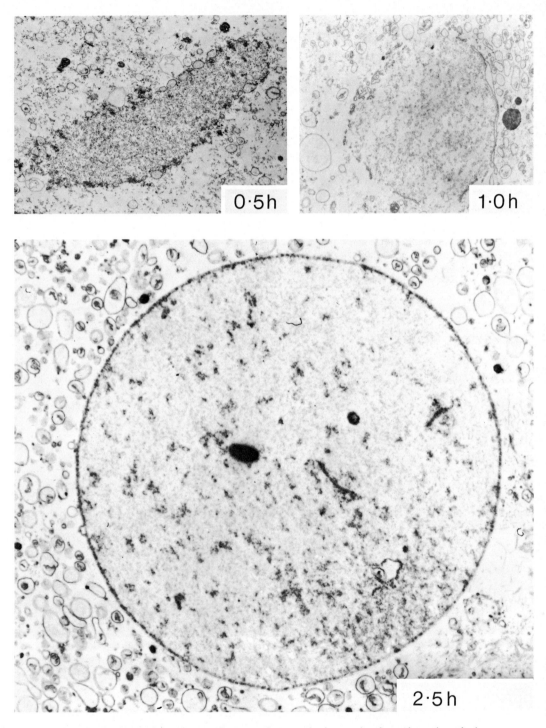

Fig. 3. Re-formation of a nuclear envelope and chromatin decondensation during incubation of demembranated *Xenopus* sperm nuclei in an extract of activated *Xenopus* eggs. Extracts were prepared by a modification of the procedures of Lohka & Masui (1983, 1984) and incubated with nuclei for 0·5, 1·0 and 2·5 h before fixation and sectioning. ×7500. (Micrographs kindly provided by M. P. Rout, J. J. Blow and B. L. Gupta.)

Therefore, it is possible to re-form nuclear envelopes around demembranated nuclei *in vitro*, or around purified DNA after microinjection into intact cells. Clearly the ability to combine these approaches to form nuclei from purified DNA *in vitro* could be important. Several unpublished experiments indicate that this is now possible (Forbes *et al.* 1983, footnote added in press; D. Newmeyer, personal communication; J. J. Blow, personal communication). In each of these cases homogenates of *Xenopus* eggs have been observed to reconstitute nuclei from purified prokaryotic or eukaryotic DNA. This approach has enormous potential for a range of studies such as nuclear envelope assembly itself, protein transport into re-formed nuclei, nuclear disassembly during mitosis, chromosome replication and perhaps synthesis and transport of RNA. Each of these processes can be analysed by fresh experimental approaches using nuclei formed from purified DNA.

I am grateful to Tony Mills and Barbara Rodbard for help with preparation of the manuscript, to Mike Rout, Julian Blow and Brij Gupta for supplying the micrographs in Fig. 3, and to the Cancer Research Campaign for their generous support.

REFERENCES

BLACKBURN, E. H. (1985). Artificial chromosomes in yeast. *Trends Genet.* **1**, 8–12.

CELNIKER, S. E., SWEDER, K., SRIENC, F., BAILEY, J. E. & CAMPBELL, J. L. (1984). Deletion mutations affecting the yeast autonomously replicating sequence ARS1 of *Saccharomyces cerevisiae. Molec. Cell. Biol.* **4**, 2455–2466.

CLARKE, L. & CARBON, J. (1980). Isolation of a yeast centromere and construction of functional small circular chromosomes. *Nature, Lond.* **287**, 504–509.

EARNSHAW, W. C., HONDA, B. M., LASKEY, R. A. & THOMAS, J. O. (1980). Assembly of nucleosomes: the reaction involving *X. laevis* nucleoplasmin. *Cell* **21**, 373–383.

FORBES, D. J., KIRSCHNER, M. W. & NEWPORT, J. W. (1983). Spontaneous formation of nucleus-like structures around bacteriophage DNA microinjected into *Xenopus* eggs. *Cell* **34**, 13–23.

GLIKIN, G. C., RUBERTI, I. & WORCEL, A. (1984). Chromatin assembly in *Xenopus* oocytes: *in vitro* studies. *Cell* **37**, 33–41.

HARLAND, R. M. & LASKEY, R. A. (1980). Regulated replication of DNA microinjected into eggs of *Xenopus laevis. Cell* **21**, 761–771.

KEARSEY, S. (1984). Structural requirements for the function of a yeast chromosomal replicator. *Cell* **37**, 299–307.

KLEINSCHMIDT, J. A., FORTKAMP, E., KROHNE, G., ZENTGRAF, H. & FRANKE, W. W. (1985). Co-existence of two different types of soluble histone complexes in nuclei of *Xenopus laevis* oocytes. *J. biol. Chem.* **260**, 1166–1176.

KLEINSCHMIDT, J. A. & FRANKE, W. W. (1982). Soluble acidic complexes containing histones H3 and H4 in nuclei of *Xenopus laevis* oocytes. *Cell* **29**, 799–809.

KLUG, A., RHODES, D., SMITH, J., FINCH, J. T. & THOMAS, J. O. (1980). A. low resolution model for the histone core of the nucleosome. *Nature, Lond.* **287**, 509–516.

KROHNE, G. & FRANKE, W. W. (1980a). Immunological identification and localisation of the predominant nuclear protein of the amphibian oocyte nucleus. *Proc. natn. Acad. Sci. U.S.A.* **77**, 1034–1038.

KROHNE, G. & FRANKE, W. W. (1980b). A major soluble acidic protein located in nuclei of diverse vertebrate species. *Expl Cell Res.* **129**, 167–189.

LASKEY, R. A. & EARNSHAW, W. C. (1980). Nucleosome assembly. *Nature, Lond.* **286**, 763–767.

LASKEY, R. A. & HARLAND, R. M. (1981). Replication origins in the eucaryotic chromosome. *Cell* **24**, 283–284.

LASKEY, R. A., HONDA, B. M., MILLS, A. D. & FINCH, J. T. (1978). Nucleosomes are assembled by an acidic protein which binds histones and transfers them to DNA. *Nature, Lond.* **275**, 416–420.

LASKEY, R. A., KEARSEY, S. E. & MECHALI, M. (1985). Analysis of chromosome replication with eggs of *Xenopus laevis*. In *Genetic Engineering, Principles and Methods*, vol. 7 (ed. J. K. Setlow & A. Hollaender). New York, London: Plenum.

LASKEY, R. A., MILLS, A. D. & MORRIS, N. R. (1977). Assembly of SV40 chromatin in a cell-free system from *Xenopus* eggs. *Cell* **10**, 237–243.

LINXWEILER, W. & HORZ, W. (1985). Reconstitution experiments show that sequence-specific histone–DNA interactions are the basis for nucleosome phasing on mouse satellite DNA. *Cell* **42**, 281–290.

LOHKA, M. J. & MASUI, Y. (1983). Formation *in vitro* of sperm pronuclei and mitotic chromosomes by amphibian ooplasmic components. *Science* **220**, 719–721.

LOHKA, M. J. & MASUI, Y. (1984). Roles of cytosal and cytoplasmic particles in nuclear envelope assembly and sperm pronuclear formation in cell-free preparations from amphibian eggs. *J. Cell Biol.* **98**, 1222–1230.

MECHALI, M. & KEARSEY, S. E. (1984). Lack of specific sequence requirement for DNA replication in *Xenopus* eggs compared with high sequence specificity in yeast. *Cell* **38**, 55–64.

MECHALI, M., MECHALI, F. & LASKEY, R. A. (1983). Tumor promoter TPA increases initiation of replication on DNA injected into *Xenopus* eggs. *Cell* **35**, 63–69.

MILLS, A. D., LASKEY, R. A., BLACK, P. & DE ROBERTIS, E. M. (1980). An acidic protein which assembles nucleosomes *in vitro* is the most abundant protein in *Xenopus* oocyte nuclei. *J. molec. Biol.* **139**, 561–568.

MURRAY, A. W. (1985). Chromosome structure and behaviour. *Trends Biochem. Sci.* **10**, 112–115.

MURRAY, A. W. & SZOSTAK, J. W. (1983). Construction of artificial chromosomes in yeast. *Nature, Lond.* **305**, 189–193.

NELSON, T., WIEGAND, R. & BRUTLAG, D. (1981). Ribonucleic acid and other polyanions facilitate chromatin assembly *in vitro*. *Biochemistry* **20**, 2594–2601.

PAULSON, J. R. & LAEMMLI, U. K. (1977). The structure of histone-depleted metaphase chromosomes. *Cell* **12**, 817–828.

RATTNER, J. B. & LIN, C. C. (1985). Radial loops and helical coils co-exist in metaphase chromosomes. *Cell* **42**, 291–296.

SENSHU, T., FUKADA, M. & OHASHI, M. (1978). Preferential association of newly synthesized H3 and H4 histones with newly synthesized replicated DNA. *J. Biochem., Tokyo* **84**, 985–988.

SIMPSON, R. T. & STAFFORD, D. W. (1983). Structural features of a phased nucleosome core particle. *Proc. natn. Acad. Sci. U.S.A.* **80**, 51–55.

STEIN, A., WHITLOCK, J. P. JR & BINA, M. (1979). Acidic polypeptides can assemble both histones and chromatin *in vitro* at physiological ionic strength. *Proc. natn. Acad. Sci. U.S.A.* **76**, 5000–5004.

STINCHCOMB, D. T., STRUHL, K. & DAVIS, R. W. (1979). Isolation and characterization of a yeast chromosomal replicator. *Nature, Lond.* **282**, 39–43.

STINCHCOMB, D. T., THOMAS, M., KELLY, J., SELKER, E. & DAVIS, R. W. (1980). Eukaryotic DNA segments capable of autonomous replication in yeast. *Proc. natn. Acad. Sci. U.S.A.* **77**, 4559–4563.

SZOSTAK, J. W. & BLACKBURN, E. H. (1982). Cloning yeast telomeres on a yeast linear plasmid. *Cell* **29**, 245–255.

THOMA, F., KOLLER, T. H. & KLUG, A. (1979). Involvement of histone H1 in the organisation of the nucleosome and of the salt-dependent superstructures of chromatin. *J. Cell Biol.* **83**, 403–427.

THOMA, F. & SIMPSON, R. T. (1985). Local protein–DNA interactions may determine nucleosome positions on yeast plasmids. *Nature, Lond.* **315**, 250–252.

WORCEL, A., HAN, S. & WONG, M. L. (1978). Assembly of newly replicated chromatin. *Cell* **15**, 969–977.

J. Cell Sci. Suppl. 4, 11–28 (1986)
Printed in Great Britain © The Company of Biologists Limited 1986

COMPUTER ANALYSIS OF THE DISTRIBUTION OF NUCLEAR ANTIGENS: STUDIES ON THE SPATIAL AND FUNCTIONAL ORGANIZATION OF THE INTERPHASE NUCLEUS

N. RINGERTZ[1,*], G. HADLACZKY[1], H. HALLMAN[1], U. NYMAN[1], I. PETTERSSON[2] AND G. C. SHARP[2,3]

[1]*Department of Medical Cell Genetics, Medical Nobel Institute, and* [2]*Department of Immunology, Karolinska Institutet, Box 60400, S-104 01 Stockholm, Sweden*

[3]*Departments of Medicine and Pathology, University of Missouri-Columbia, Columbia, Missouri 65212, USA*

INTRODUCTION

The higher-order organization of DNA in chromosomes, and the degree of ordering of chromosomes in interphase chromatin and during mitosis have not yet been elucidated. The problems have, however, been debated in the cytogenetic literature since the early observations of Rabl (1885) and Boveri (1909) (for reviews, see Avivi & Feldman, 1980; Bennett, 1984). Using plant cells, Rabl noted that during anaphase the centromeres are the leading part and telomeres the trailing ends, as daughter chromosomes migrate away from each other. He also made observations on postmitotic cells, suggesting that this chromosome orientation was maintained during interphase with centromeres clustered at one pole of the nucleus and telomeres at the opposite pole in the newly formed nuclei (the 'Rabl orientation'). This chromosome arrangement has also been observed in other plant cells (Ashley, 1979; for a review, see Avivi & Feldman, 1980) and in insect cells (Foe & Alberts, 1985). The situation in animal cells, however, is far from clear (for a review, see Comings, 1980).

In recent years questions concerning the topology of chromosomes in interphase nuclei have been studied by laser-beam microirradiation techniques (Cremer *et al.* 1982*a,b*), optical sectioning and three-dimensional reconstruction of micrographs (Agard & Sedat, 1983), by *in situ* hybridization (Rappold *et al.* 1984), by analysing prematurely condensed chromosomes in fused cells (Sperling & Luedke, 1981), by statistical analysis of the distribution of specific chromosomes in metaphase spreads (Heneen & Nichols, 1972), and by studies of the frequency of chromatid and chromosome aberrations (Hager, Schroeder-Kurth & Vogel, 1982). The evidence accumulated to date suggests that chromosomes are non-randomly distributed both in interphase nuclei and during mitosis (for reviews, see Comings, 1980; Cook & Laskey, 1984). In plant cells and in certain types of insect cells, e.g. in salivary gland cells of *Drosophila*, homologous chromosomes are closely associated in somatic cells.

---

* Author for correspondence

Whether this is so in mammalian cells is not known. Evidence summarized by Comings (1980) indicates that a number of different factors, e.g. association with the nuclear envelope, tendency of nucleolus-organizing regions (NOR) of different chromosomes to aggregate, aggregation of heterochromatin and stickiness of chromosome ends, play a role in determining the topology of chromosomes in the interphase nucleus.

Another aspect of the organization of eukaryotic genomes is the possibility that interphase chromatin may be organized into functional domains differing in transcription and RNA-processing activities. In some types of nuclei it is also clear that nuclear domains engaged in DNA replication differ from non-replicating chromatin regions in both ultrastructure and protein composition (Gall, 1959; Prescott & Kimball, 1961; Ringertz & Hoskins, 1965; Ringertz, Ericsson & Nilsson, 1967).

At the ultrastructural level, analysis of isolated chromatin fibres and nuclei subjected to drastic extraction and, or digestion procedures have revealed at least three levels of organization: nucleosomes, 30 nm solenoids and DNA loops (for a review, see Cook & Laskey, 1984). Autoradiographic studies of sectioned, intact nuclei have shown that dispersed chromatin regions (euchromatin) are transcriptionally active, while condensed chromatin (hererochromatin) is inactive (for a review, see Brown, 1966; Alberts, Worcel & Weintraub, 1977; Igo-Kemenes *et al.* 1982). Condensed chromatin is usually found around the nuclear periphery and close to the nucleolus, while dispersed chromatin occupies a central position surrounding the nucleoli. Several lines of evidence show that interphase chromatin is attached to the nuclear envelope, and to a scaffold consisting of the nuclear pore complexes and a nuclear matrix (for a review, see Lewis, Lebkowski, Daly & Laemmli, 1984). The molecular biology and functional significance of these structures are not yet understood.

Between the molecular and the light microscopic level there is a wide gap in our knowledge of eukaryotic genome organization. Among the questions that remain to be answered are: to what extent are chromosomes randomly entangled in each other during interphase, and to what extent do they occupy distinct chromosomal territories? Other questions concern topological relationships, i.e. whether chromosomes are randomly dispersed within the nucleus or occupy specific positions relative to each other. Related to this question is the functional significance of chromosome topology and the possibility that chromatin may be organized into functional domains involving combinations of genes located on several different chromosomes. Indications that such levels of organization may exist has come from immunofluorescence studies of nuclear antigens and from the fact that ribosomal DNA loci on several different chromosomes may participate in the organization of a single nucleolar domain (for references, see Comings, 1980).

The aim of this review is to summarize some of our own data indicating that the double immunofluorescence technique, when combined with well-defined antibodies to nuclear antigens, and computer analysis of immunofluorescence images can provide new information about the functional and spatial organization of the interphase nucleus. We will illustrate this approach with data concerning the intranuclear localization of complexes between small nuclear RNA and proteins (snRNP), and findings concerning the intranuclear distribution of centromeric antigens. The former type of antigen most probably defines functional domains, while the latter type of antigen provides information about the intranuclear topology of chromosomes. For references to the literature on the higher-order structure of the interphase nucleus the reader is referred to a recent supplement published by this journal (Cook & Laskey, 1984). The literature on human and mouse anti-nuclear antibodies has been reviewed by Tan (1982) and by Sharp & Alspaugh (1985). The technique of digital image analysis has been covered in several monographs, e.g. those edited by Ekström (1984) and Gonzalez & Wintz (1977).

ANTIBODIES TO NUCLEAR ANTIGENS

Autoantibodies to nuclear antigens are common in certain human autoimmune diseases as well as in some inbred mouse strains. The antibodies may be directed against DNA, histones, RNA–protein complexes (RNP) and a variety of other macromolecules. Species-specific antibodies have been very useful in studies of nucleocytoplasmic protein exchange in interspecific heterokaryons (Ringertz, Carlsson, Ege & Bolund, 1971; Ringertz & Savage, 1976; Scheer *et al.* 1983; Nyman, Lanfranchi, Bergman & Ringertz, 1984). Immunofluorescence staining of mammalian cells with sera from patients with various connective tissue diseases often gives a characteristic staining of different nuclear structures.

Some sera produce speckled nuclear patterns (Fig. 1). Two major specificities that produce speckled patterns are known as Sm and RNP. These autoantibodies occur primarily in systemic *lupus erythematosus* (SLE), mixed connective tissue disease (MCTD) and less frequently in other connective tissue diseases. Autoantibodies analogous to those seen in SLE have also been found in NZB×NZW and MRL mouse strains, which develop autoimmune conditions similar to those in man. Lymphocytes from these mouse strains have been used to obtain hybridomas producing monoclonal antibodies to Sm and RNP antigens (Lerner, Lerner, Janeway & Steitz, 1981; Billings, Barton & Hoch, 1985).

Sm and RNP antigens

Antibodies directed against the Sm and RNP antigens selectively precipitate ribonucleoprotein complexes containing small nuclear RNAs (Lerner & Steitz, 1979; Hinterberger, Pettersson & Steitz, 1983; Mimori, Hinterberger, Pettersson & Steitz, 1984; Pettersson *et al.* 1984). These complexes are sometimes referred to as 'snurps' or snRNPs. Sm antibodies precipitate complexes containing U1, U2, U4, U5 and U6 RNAs (Fig. 2A) and some 10 different polypeptides. RNP antibodies precipitate complexes containing U1 RNA and at least nine polypeptides.

Immunoblotting experiments (Fig. 2B) have shown that the antigenic determinants are located on specific peptides. In the case of Sm antibodies the epitopes are located on the B/B', D and E peptides, while RNP antibodies react with the A, C or $68 \times 10^3 M_r$ peptide. The fact that snRNP particles containing U1 RNA only can be

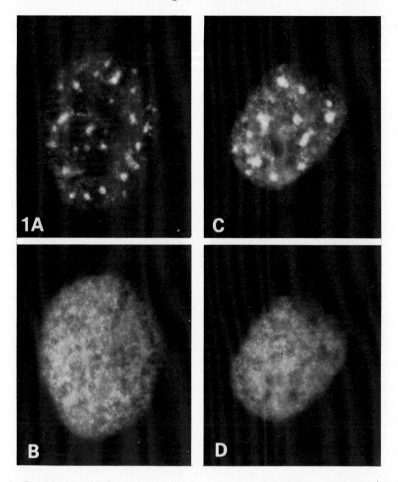

Fig. 1. Double immunofluorescence staining of human fibroblasts of the 253/79 line with a monoclonal anti-Sm (Y12) antibody and a human autoantiserum (HA) directed against the La $50 \times 10^3 M_r$ peptide. Only the nuclei show immunofluorescence. There is a striking difference in the fluorescence patterns obtained with the mouse Sm antibodies (A,C) and the human anti-La (B,D) antibodies. The La antigen is evenly distributed while the Sm antigenicity is concentrated in speckles. The immunofluorescence patterns shown in A,B were examined by digital image analysis in an IBAS computer as illustrated in Fig. 3D,E.)

immunoprecipitated separately by RNP antibodies suggests that the U1 snRNP particles are not strongly associated, physically or chemically, with the other snRNPs. The report of an anti-U2-snRNP antiserum permits the same conclusion to be drawn concerning the U2 snRNPs. In the case of U4 and U6, it has also been shown that, most probably, they form a distinct complex.

Possible role of snRNP complexes in RNA processing

Evidence concerning the biological function of snRNPs is more circumstantial but points to an important role in the post-transcriptional regulation of gene expression (for a review, see Busch, Reddy, Rothblum & Choi, 1982). Consistent observations indicate that some members of this class of complexes play a role in the processing of polymerase II transcripts. U1 snRNPs are thought to participate in heterogeneous nuclear RNA splicing (Lerner, Boyle, Hardin & Steitz, 1980; Mount *et al.* 1983; Padgett, Mount, Steitz & Sharp, 1983) and both U1 and U4/U6 snRNPs could be involved in polyadenylation (Moore & Sharp, 1984). Recently, Birnstiel, Busslinger & Strub (1985) have obtained evidence in sea urchins suggesting that Sm-precipitated U7 snRNPs may be involved in the production of correct 3′ ends from primary

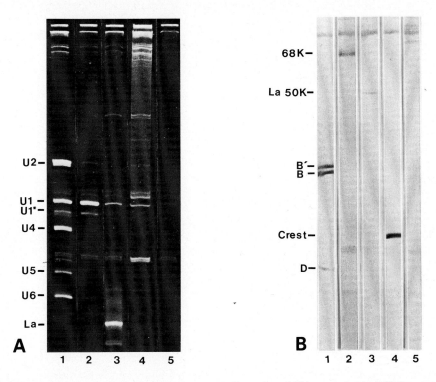

Fig. 2. Characterization of antibodies to small nuclear RNA–protein (snRNP) complexes by RNA and protein electrophoresis (from Nyman *et al.* 1986). A. Polyacrylamide gel fractionation of immunoprecipitated RNAs. Precipitates were obtained using an extract from a human cell line, Jurkat, and antibodies from a mouse anti-Sm hybridoma Y12 (lane 1), and human autoimmune sera (lanes 2–5). The following autoimmune specificities were represented: anti-RNP serum, CL (lane 2), anti-La serum, HA (lane 3), anti-centromere serum, LU (lane 4), and anti-Scl-70 serum, PE (lane 5). The anti-RNP serum (lane 2) immunoprecipitates U1 snRNA, while the mouse (Y12) anti-Sm antibodies immunoprecipitate U1, U2, U4, U5 and U6 snRNA. These RNAs are RNA polymerase II transcripts and part of snRNP complexes involved in the splicing and processing of hnRNA to mRNA. U1* is a degradation product of U1 snRNA. The anti-La-serum (lane 3) immunoprecipitates a mixture of 4·5 S and 5 S RNAs (polymerase III transcripts) and a small amount of U1 RNA. B. Immunoblotting of sodium dodecyl sulphate/polyacrylamide gel-fractionated human (Jurkat) cell proteins. A mouse monoclonal antibody, human autoimmune sera and normal human sera were used. (For nomenclature for snRNP proteins, see Pettersson *et al.* 1984.) The nitrocellulose strips with the transferred proteins were reacted with the following antibodies: mouse anti-Sm monoclonal Y12 (strip 1), anti-RNP serum CL (strip 2), anti-La serum HA (strip 3), anti-centromere serum LU (strip 4) and anti-Scl-70 serum PE (strip 5). $K = 10^3 M_r$.

histone transcripts (premessenger RNA). It seems quite possible that snRNP complexes could modify mRNA production at several different levels. One such level would be alternative splicing of a given primary transcript to generate more than one mRNA, another would be influencing the differential use of alternative poly(A) sites, and a third could be the production of correct 3' termini and stabilization of processed transcripts (Birnstiel *et al.* 1985).

Questions concerning the possible colocalization of Sm and RNP antigens with other nuclear antigens

The speckles seen with Sm and RNP antibodies most probably represent transcriptionally active nuclear domains in which there is an accumulation of snRNP complexes because of active processing of RNA polymerase II transcripts. In polytene chromosomes immunological studies show that both RNA polymerase II (Kabisch & Bautz, 1983) and Sm/RNP antigens (Sass & Pedersen, 1984) are concentrated in transcriptionally active regions. As several different snRNP complexes exist, an interesting question is whether all the snRNA species and all the antigens detected by Sm and RNP antisera are present in the same intranuclear domains.

In addition to the Sm and RNP antibodies commonly found in SLE and MCTD there are other autoantibodies that also produce speckled nuclear immunofluorescence patterns. Among these are autoantibodies to the La antigen (Tan, 1982) in Sjögrens' syndrome illustrated in Fig. 1B,D, the Scl-70 antigen in progressive systemic sclerosis also known as scleroderma (Douvas, Achten & Tan, 1979), and the centromeric antigens in the CREST form of scleroderma (Moroi *et al.* 1980; Cox, Schenk & Olmsted, 1983). Of these antibodies, those directed against the La antigen are most relevant to the present study since they are directed against a $50 \times 10^3 M_r$ peptide transiently (Hendrick *et al.* 1981; Rinke & Steitz, 1982) associated with RNA polymerase III early transcripts (5 S RNA and tRNA species). The type of speckles obtained with this antibody, therefore, may represent a different type of functional domain from those detected by Sm and RNP antibodies.

Figs 3, 4. Digital images (pseudocolours) of immunofluorescence patterns obtained by double immunostaining flat human fibroblasts (253/79) with two different anti-nuclear antibodies.

Fig. 3 Intensely fluorescing regions detected by: A, mouse anti-Sm (Y12) antibodies; B, human anti-RNP (CL) antiserum; and c, computer comparison of images A,B. The anti-Sm antibody immunoprecipitates snRNP complexes containing U1, U2, U4, U5 and U6 RNA and reacts in immunoblots with the B/B' and D peptides of these complexes. This particular anti-RNP serum (CL) immunoprecipitates only U1 RNA and reacts with a $68 \times 10^3 M_r$ peptide. (For details about the specificity of the antisera used in Figs 3, 4, see Nyman *et al.* 1986.) Overlapping regions of high immunofluorescence intensity are represented by white areas in the computer-generated image (c). A very good correlation exists between the antigens detected by the anti-Sm and the anti-RNP serum. To the right are shown images recorded with: D, mouse anti-Sm (Y12) antibodies; E, human anti-La (HA) antiserum; and a computer comparison (F) of patterns D,E. The two patterns differ but there is a partial overlap (white areas in F). Photographs corresponding to images 3D,E are shown in Fig. 1A,B, respectively.

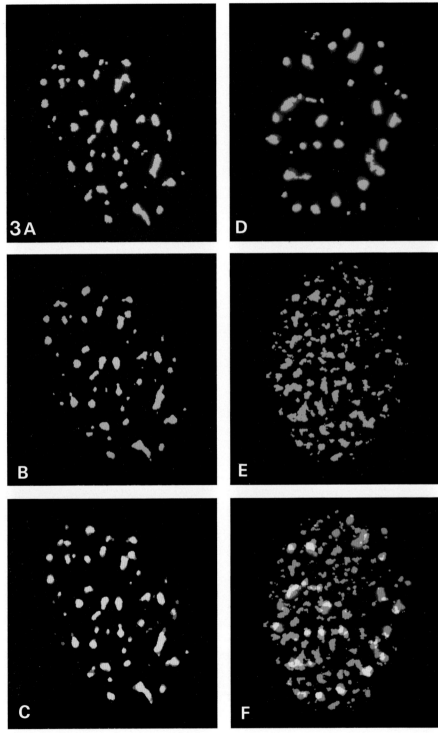

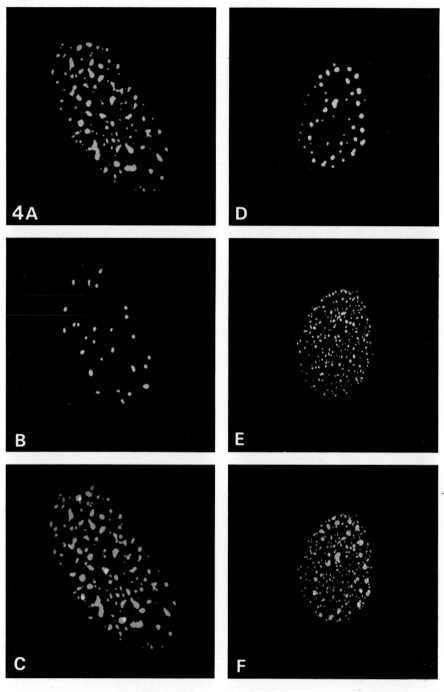

In order to analyse questions concerning the intranuclear localization of different snRNP antigens we have used the double immunofluorescence technique and digital image analysis (Nyman *et al.* 1986). Comparisons have been made between the distribution of Sm antigens detected by an Sm monoclonal antibody and the distribution of different RNP antigens and non-RNP antigens detected by human autoantibodies. Second antibodies were conjugated with, respectively, fluorescein (FITC) and rhodamine (TRITC). This technique makes it possible to compare the distribution of two different antigens in one and the same nucleus. The biochemical specificity of the antisera used for the digital image studies has recently been described by Nyman *et al.* (1986).

DIGITAL IMAGE ANALYSIS

A silicon-intensified-target video camera (Siemens) was used to register immuno-fluorescence patterns. The images were digitized using an analogue-to-digital converter, and then stored and analysed in a Kontron/Zeiss IBAS computer. The images were stored as an array of picture elements (pixels) each having a grey level assigned to it (usually in the range of 0–255). A commonly used size of array has been 512×512 pixels. Using filters, two images were recorded, one representing the FITC and one representing the TRITC fluorescence. Using the computer, the FITC and TRITC images were then compared. This technique has so far only been used for image cross-correlation studies aimed at recording the degree of overlap between TRITC and FITC fluorescent speckles, contrast enhancement and other rather simple operations. It is clear, however, that this method can also be used for more sophisticated forms of analysis, e.g. pattern analysis. By performing mathematical operations on Fourier-transformed images, it will also be possible to analyse optically sectioned nuclei and to make three-dimensional reconstructions of the immune fluorescence patterns. As will be discussed in more detail below, this type of operation may be a help in deducing the ordering of chromosomes on the basis of centromere-specific fluorescence patterns.

COLOCALIZATION ANALYSIS OF Sm, RNP AND La ANTIGENS

Fig. 3 shows the patterns obtained with a human anti-RNP (Fig. 3B) and a mouse monoclonal anti-Sm serum (Fig. 3A). The anti-RNP serum reacts with the $68 \times 10^3 M_r$ peptide and the anti-Sm antiserum with the B/B' and D peptides of snRNP complexes. In spite of this difference, the immunofluorescence patterns are strikingly similar. The extent of colocalization of antigens can be expressed in

Fig. 4. Intensely fluorescing regions detected by: A, mouse anti-Sm (Y12) antibodies; B, human anti-centromere (LU) antiserum; and C, a computer-based comparison of A,B. To the right: D, mouse anti-Sm antibodies; E, anti-Scl-70 antiserum; and F, a computer comparison of D,E. The nuclear immunofluorescence patterns recorded with anti-centromere and anti-Scl-70 antibodies are completely different from those recorded with anti-Sm antibodies (no white areas).

quantitative terms as the degree of overlap between the two patterns. It is illustrated in Fig. 3C by a computer-generated image in which overlapping speckles have been assigned a white pseudocolour. Since anti-RNP sera immunoprecipitate only one of the anti-Sm-reactive complexes it was conceivable that, correspondingly, only a subgroup of Sm speckles would also contain the RNP antigen. The speckles seen with the individual anti-RNP sera, however, agreed very well with those obtained with the mouse anti-Sm monoclonal antibodies. All Sm-reactive regions also contain the RNP antigen. In terms of the intranuclear distribution of the snRNP complexes this implies that the Sm-reactive U2, U4, U5 and U6 RNA–protein complexes are localized in the same nuclear domains as the Sm- and RNP-reactive U1 RNA–protein complexes.

Comparisons between the distribution of mouse anti-Sm speckles with the speckled patterns obtained with anti-La antiserum (Fig. 1A,B; Fig. 3D–F) showed marked differences. The La antigen is much more evenly distributed throughout the nucleus than the Sm/RNP antigens. There is, however, a partial overlap (white areas in Fig. 3F) between the two patterns. Although the La antigen is primarily associated with RNP polymerase III transcripts (Hendrick *et al.* 1981; Rinke & Steitz, 1982), Madore, Wieben & Pederson (1984) reported that La antisera also immunoprecipitate some U1 snRNPs.

The speckled patterns obtained with antibodies to Scl-70 (Fig. 4C), a unique nuclear peptide antigen in scleroderma (Douvas *et al.* 1979), and centromeric antigens (see below), on the other hand, were completely different from the Sm/RNP patterns.

INTRANUCLEAR DISTRIBUTION OF CENTROMERE ANTIGENS

Human autoantibodies to centromeric antigens were used to detect the localization of individual centromeres, and indirectly chromosomes, in interphase nuclei. Autoantibodies that specifically stain the centromere region of metaphase chromosomes have previously been described by Moroi *et al.* (1980), Brenner *et al.* (1981) and Cox *et al.* (1983). When these antibodies are used to immunostain interphase nuclei they give a speckled pattern, the number of spots agreeing with the number of chromosomes (Brenner *et al.* 1981). Brinkley, Valdivia, Tousson & Brenner (1984) also showed that the centromere spots doubled during DNA replication.

In our own work (Hadlaczky, Went & Ringertz, 1986) we have used polyclonal human autoantibodies from a patient suffering from the CREST syndrome. In immunoblotting experiments the antibodies give a strong reaction with an $18 \times 10^3 M_r$ peptide and a faint reaction with several other peptides (Hadlaczky *et al.* 1986). Antibodies eluted from $18 \times 10^3 M_r$ bands of electrophoretic gels specifically stained centromere regions on metaphase chromosomes.

The pattern of fluorescent speckles obtained with centromere-specific antibodies is quite different (Fig. 4B) from that observed with Sm and RNP antibodies (Fig. 4A). The number of centromere speckles observed in human nuclei approximates to that expected from diploid human cells, if all focal planes are added together. Detailed studies of the localization of centromeres in human interphase cells proved difficult because of the fairly high chromosome number and the three-dimensional distribution of fluorescent spots.

In order to test the possibility of performing three-dimensional mapping of centromeres in human nuclei we have instead used cells from animals that have low chromosome numbers. In what follows we will discuss results (Hadlaczky *et al.* 1986) obtained with cell lines from Indian muntjac and rat kangaroo. These cells turned out to be exceptionally flat. In most cases all centromeres could be accounted for in photographs taken at two or three different optical planes.

The karyotype of the Indian muntjac cells has previously been reported by Fredga (1971), while details about the chromosome constitution of the rat kangaroo can be found in papers by Levan, Nichols, Peluse & Coriell (1966), Levan (1970) and Sekiguchi, Shelton & Ringertz (1978).

In the rat kangaroo ($2n = 13$) as well as in the Indian muntjac ($2n = 7$) many cells could be found in which the expected diploid number of centromere speckles could be detected. G_2 cells had double speckles compared to G_1 cells (Fig. 5), thus confirming the observations of Brinkley *et al.* (1984). In the rat kangaroo line we found that in more than 20 % of the cells the centromere spots showed a paired arrangement (Figs 5, 6). The most plausible explanation for this phenomenon was that homologous chromosomes were close to one another. This conclusion was also supported by observations on the distribution of chromosomes in metaphase spreads, where homologous chromosomes were often found close to each other (Fig. 7). Clearly, however, statistical analysis is required to evaluate the significance of these observations. Homologue associations in metaphase spreads have previously been observed by Heenen & Nichols (1972) in Indian muntjac cells and by Gibson (1970) in rat kangaroo cells. Sperling & Lüdke (1981), on the other hand, found no evidence for association of homologous chromosomes after induction of premature chromosome condensation by fusing interphase Indian muntjac cells with mitotic HeLa cells.

Both the preparation of metaphase spreads and slides with prematurely condensed chromosomes involve a number of steps that may disturb chromosome topology. In both cases rounded cells are drastically flattened by the preparative procedure. It would be desirable, therefore, to study the distribution of chromosomes in interphase nuclei which retain, as far as possible their normal shape.

In the present study, the flat shape of the Indian muntjac cells and the different morphology of individual muntjac centromeres in G_1 cells (Hadlaczky *et al.* 1986) made it possible to identify individual centromeres in some 20 % of the cells (Fig. 8B). In cells representing other cell cycle stages the centromeres were too decondensed to permit identification. In those cells in which identification was possible, homologous chromosomes occupied adjacent territories in about one-third of the cells. Although intriguing, these data do not allow us to settle the controversy concerning the topology of homologous chromosomes in interphase chromatin. Further progress may, however, be possible by recording the three-dimensional coordinates of individual centromeres using digital image analysis of optically sectioned nuclei and, or, by confocal laser scanning microscopy. The analysis would also be greatly facilitated by using synchronized G_1 cells that are strictly diploid.

In 16 % of rat kangaroo nuclei, interphase centromeres showed a higher-order arrangement, evidently forming non-random configurations. Centromeres were usually positioned in two or three focal planes. In those cases in which all centromeres were visible in one plane, 38 % of the centromere configurations proved to be highly symmetrical or 'mirror-like' (Fig. 9).

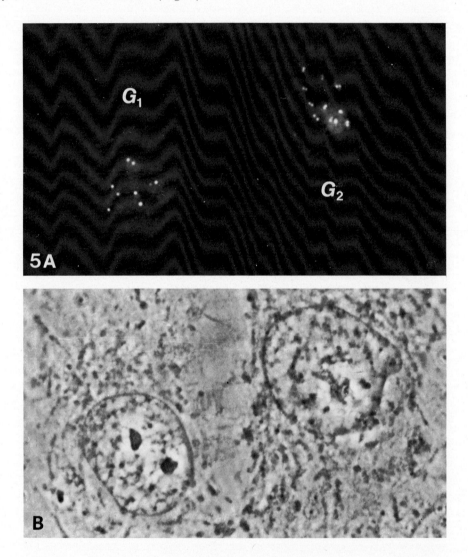

Fig. 5. Interphase centromeres in a G_1 (left) and a G_2 (right) nucleus of a rat kangaroo cell line (PTO). A. Immunofluorescence after staining with human autoantibodies (LU) to centromeric antigens; B, same cells in phase contrast. The number of centromere spots equals the number of chromosomes (modal number = 13) if all optical planes are added together. Centromere spots in G_2 nuclei are double. G_1 centromere spots are single *but arranged in pairs*.

Another type of non-random pattern was seen in a small number of cells where all the centromeres were clustered at one pole of the nucleus. This is highly suggestive of the Rabl orientation. The reason why only a minority of nuclei showed this pattern could be that the nucleus can rotate freely in relation to the plane of the cytoplasm and the substratum.

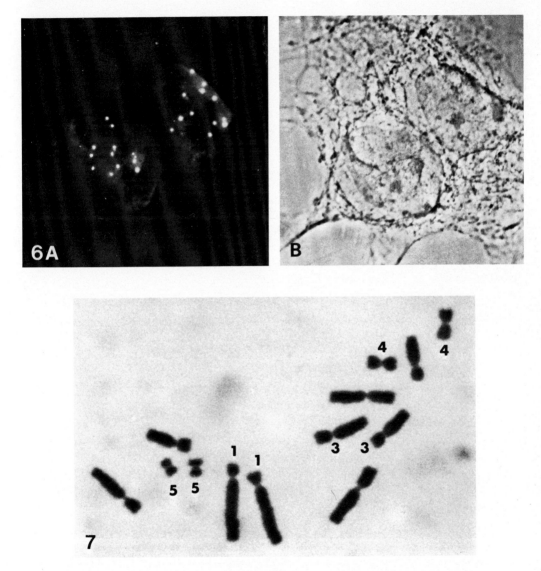

Fig. 6. A. Immunofluorescence staining of PTO interphase centromeres; and B, phase-contrast picture of nuclei in A. The single spots in G_1 nuclei are arranged in pairs (see also G_1 nucleus in Fig. 5), suggesting that homologous chromosomes occupy adjacent territories within the interphase nucleus (from Hadlaczky *et al.* 1986).

Fig. 7. Metaphase plate of a PTO cell showing a non-random arrangement of chromosomes. Homologous chromosomes are often found close to each other.

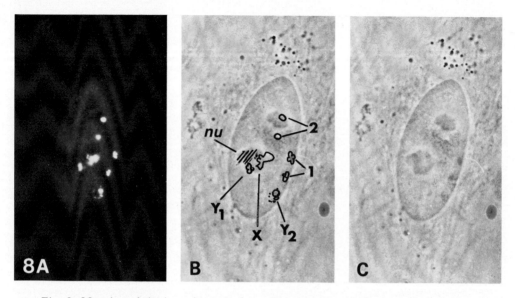

Fig. 8. Mapping of the interphase topology of centromeres of all seven chromosomes present in a somatic nucleus of an Indian muntjac cell. The centromeres of chromosomes 1, 2, X, Y1 and Y2 differ considerably in morphology during interphase also. *nu*, nucleolus. (From Hadlaczky *et al.* 1986.)

OTHER TYPES OF FUNCTIONAL DOMAINS

The fact that antibodies to Sm/RNP, La and RNA polymerase I (Scheer & Rose, 1984; Scheer *et al.* 1983) produce distinctly different immunofluorescence patterns suggests that immunological tools will be powerful in defining nuclear domains differing in type and intensity of transcription. Since centromeric regions have been found to be transcriptionally inactive compared to other types of chromatin, domains reacting with centromere antibodies may also be regarded as functionally inactive regions and not just as a marker of chromosome topology.

Some types of nuclei show a highly organized pattern of DNA replication. In the ciliate *Euplotes* the zones of DNA replication can be identified easily and distinguished from non-replicating chromatin (Gall, 1959; Prescott & Kimball, 1961; Ringertz & Hoskins, 1965; Ringertz *et al.* 1967). Using antibodies to DNA polymerase alpha or other parts of the replication complex it may well be possible to identify replicating domains in animal cell nuclei.

Further examples of speckled nuclear immunofluorescence have been obtained with antibodies to a variety of nuclear antigens (see Table 1). Among these are antibodies to snRNA cap structures (2,2,7-trimethylguanosine, m3G). Their intranuclear binding correlates well with the distribution of Sm/RNP antigens (Reuter *et al.* 1984). A speckled immunofluorescence pattern is obtained also with antisera reacting with components of the nuclear matrix, viral proteins, microtubule-associated proteins, oncogene-coded proteins etc. (for references, see Table 1).

It appears that double immune staining and cross-correlation studies of the immunofluorescence patterns of these different antigens by digital image analysis will contribute to a better understanding of the functional organization of the eukaryotic genome and the interphase nucleus of animal cells.

CONCLUDING REMARKS

The finding of a marked colocalization between Sm and different RNP antigens is interesting in view of the fact that, biochemically, these antigens appear to be associated with different snRNP particles. These particles, therefore, appear to be concentrated in the same nuclear domains. Since both U2 and U2 snRNPs have been

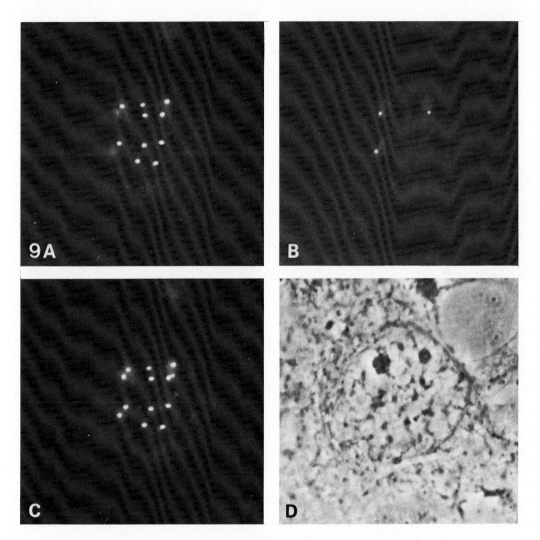

Fig. 9. Indications of higher-order arrangement of centromeres in a PTO nucleus ($n = 13$). A,B. Two different optical planes; C, a projection, which is the sum of A,B; D, the corresponding phase-contrast image. Centromeres are arranged in pairs, which together form a non-random pattern in the centre of the nucleus (from Hadlaczky *et al.* 1986).

Table 1. *Some nuclear antigens showing a speckled distribution in the interphase nucleus*

Antigen	Reference
Sm/RNP	Tan (1982); Sharp & Alspaugh (1985)
Nuclear matrix proteins	Smith *et al.* (1985); Habets *et al.* (1983); Fritzler *et al.* (1984); Chaly *et al.* (1984)
Microtubule-associated proteins	Izant *et al.* (1982); Asai *et al.* (1985); Bonifacio *et al.* (1985)
Ankyrin	Bennett & Davis (1981)
Cyclin (PCNA)*	Celis & Celis (1985)
BA DNA-binding protein	Bennett & Yeoman (1985)
SV40 T cross-reacting cellular protein ($68 \times 10^3 M_r$)	Lane & Hoeffler (1980)

* Proliferating cell nuclear antigen.

implicated in the processing of RNA polymerase II transcripts, it appears most likely that the speckles seen in the immunofluorescence pictures represent regions of intense RNA polymerase II transcription. The La antigen, on the other hand, shows a different pattern that only partially overlaps the Sm/RNP pattern. The La antigen is believed to be a peptide associated with RNA polymerase III transcripts (5 S RNA, tRNA). It therefore seems likely that most of the La immunofluorescence pattern reflects this type of transcription.

The Scl-70 and centromere immunofluorescence patterns are clearly not related to the Sm/RNP pattern. Of these two patterns, the second can be interpreted as showing the interphase distribution of centromeres.

The main result obtained with the CREST anti-centromere antibodies was that in a large proportion of cells, the centromeres were non-randomly distributed. In both Indian muntjac and rat kangaroo cells the centromeres often appeared to form pairs, while in other cases, centromeres were clustered at one pole of the nucleus. The former pattern may reflect somatic associations of homologous chromosomes while the clustering, most probably, is a consequence of mitosis (Rabl configuration). Some cells (Fig. 9) show centromere distributions that suggest even higher orders of genome organization. Clearly these patterns need to be analysed in three dimensions using digital image analysis and statistical methods. The results of such studies must be related to cell cycle stages and the topology of other chromosome markers to provide information about the organization of chromosomes in the interphase nucleus. Existing evidence (Comings, 1980) strongly supports the notion that chromosomes are non-randomly organized in interphase chromatin. Exactly how the chromosomes are ordered, and the degree of order, are questions that remain to be answered. Computer analysis of immunofluorescence images is likely to be a useful technique in gathering the additional information that is needed.

This work was supported by grants from the Swedish Medical Research Council to N.R.R. (13U-5951), H.H. (12P-7309) and I.P. (16X-7173), and by grant USPHS 2RO1 AM20305 to

G.C.S. Additional research support for this work came from a grant awarded to U.N. from the Swedish National Association against Rheumatism and to H.H. from M. Bergvalls Foundation, G.H. is the recipient of a fellowship from the Swedish Academy of Science.

REFERENCES

AGARD, D. A. & SEDAT, J. W. (1983). Three dimensional architecture of a polytene nucleus. *Nature, Lond.* **302**, 676–681.

ALBERTS, B., WORCEL, A. & WEINTRAUB, H. (1977). On the biological implications of chromatin structure. In *The Organization and Expression of the Eukaryotic Genome* (ed. E. M. Bradbury & K. Javaherian), pp. 165–191. New York: Academic Press.

ASAI, D. J., THOMPSON, W. C., WILSON, L., DRESDEN, C. F., SCHULMAN, H. & PURICH, D. L. (1985). Microtubule-associated proteins (MAPs): A monoclonal antibody to MAP1 decorates microtubules *in vitro* but stains stress fibres and not microtubules *in vivo*. *Proc. natn. Acad. Sci. U.S.A.* **82**, 1434–1438.

ASHLEY, T. (1979). Specific end-to-end attachment of chromosomes in *Ornithogalum virens*. *J. Cell Sci.* **38**, 357–367.

AVIVI, L. & FELDMAN, M. (1980). Arrangement of chromosomes in the interphase nucleus of plants. *Hum. Genet.* **55**, 281–295.

BENNETT, F. C. & YEOMAN, L. C. (1985). Co-localization of non-histone protein BA with U-snRNPs to the same regions of the cell nucleus. *Expl Cell Res.* **157**, 379–386.

BENNETT, M. D. (1984). Towards a general model for spatial law and order in nuclear and karyotypic architecture. In *Chromosomes Today* (ed. M. D. Bennett, A. Gropp & U. Wolf), vol. 8, pp. 190–202. London: George Allen & Unwin.

BENNETT, V. & DAVIS, J. (1981). Erythrocyte ankyrin: Immunoreactive analogues are associated with mitotic structures in cultured cells and with microtubules in brain. *Proc. natn. Acad. Sci. U.S.A.* **78**, 7550–7554.

BILLINGS, P. B., BARTON, J. R. & HOCH, S. (1985). A murine monoclonal antibody recognizes the 13,000 molecular weight polypeptide of the Sm small nuclear ribonucleoprotein complex. *J. Immun.* **135**, 428–432.

BIRNSTIEL, M. L., BUSSLINGER, M. & STRUB, K. (1985). Transcription termination and 3′ processing: The end is in site! *Cell* **41**, 349–359.

BONIFACIO, J. S., KLAUSNER, R. D. & SANDOVAL, I. V. (1985). A widely distributed nuclear protein immunologically related to the microtubule associated protein MAP1 is associated with the mitotic spindle. *Proc. natn. Acad. Sci. U.S.A.* **82**, 1146–1150.

BOVERI, T. (1909). Die Blastomerenkerne von *Ascaris megalocephala* und die Theorie der Chromosomenindividualität. *Arch. exp. Zellforsh.* **3**, 181–268.

BRENNER, S., PEPPER, D., BERNS, M. W., TAN, E. & BRINKLEY, B. R. (1981). Kinetochore structure, duplication and distribution in mammalian cells: analysis of human autoantibodies from scleroderma patients. *J. Cell Biol.* **91**, 95–102.

BRINKLEY, B. R., VALDIVIA, M. M., TOUSSON, A. & BRENNER, S. L. (1984). Compound kinetochores of the Indian muntjac. Evolution by linear fusion of unit kinetochores. *Chromosoma* **91**, 1–11.

BROWN, S. W. (1966). Heterochromatin. *Nature, Lond.* **151**, 417–425.

BUSCH, H., REDDY, R., ROTHBLUM, L. & CHOI, Y. C. (1982). SnRNAs, snRNPs, and RNA processing. *A. Rev. Biochem.* **51**, 617–654.

CELIS, J. E. & CELIS, A. (1985). Cell cycle-dependent variations in the distribution of the nuclear protein cyclin proliferating cell nuclear antigen in cultured cells: Subdivision of S-phase. *Proc. natn. Acad. U.S.A.* **82**, 3262–3266.

CHALY, N., BLADON, T., SETTERFIELD, G., LITTLE, J. E., KAPLAN, J. G. & BROWN, D. L. (1984). Changes in distribution of nuclear matrix antigens during the mitotic cycle. *J. Cell Biol.* **99**, 661–671.

COMINGS, D. E. (1980). Arrangement of chromatin in the nucleus. *Hum. Genet.* **53**, 131–143.

COOK, P. R. & LASKEY, R. A. (eds) (1984). *Higher Order Structure in the Nucleus. J. Cell Sci. Suppl. 1.*

Cox, J. V., Schenk, E. A. & Olmsted, J. B. (1983). Human anticentromere antibodies: distribution, characterization of antigens and effect on microtubule organization. *Cell* **35**, 331–339.

Cremer, T., Cremer, C., Baumann, H., Luedtke, E.-K., Sperling, K., Teuber, V. & Zorn, C. (1982*a*). Rabl's model of the interphase chromosome arrangement tested in Chinese hamster cells by premature chromosome condensation and laser UV-microbeam experiments. *Hum. Genet.* **60**, 46–56.

Cremer, T., Cremer, C., Schneider, T., Baumann, H., Hens, L. & Kirsch-Volders, M. (1982*b*). Analysis of chromosome positions in the interphase nucleus of Chinese hamster cells by laser–UV–microirradiation experiments. *Hum. Genet.* **62**, 201–209.

Douvas, A. S., Achten, M. & Tan, E. M. (1979). Identification of a nuclear protein (Scl-70) as a unique target of human antinuclear antibodies in scleroderma. *J. biol. Chem.* **254**, 10514–10522.

Ekström, M. P. (ed.) (1984). *Digital Image Processing Techniques.* New York: Academic Press.

Foe, V. E. & Alberts, B. M. (1985). Reversible chromosome condensation induced in *Drosophila* embryos by anoxia: visualization of interphase nuclear organization. *J. Cell Biol.* **100**, 1623–1636.

Fredga, K. (1971). Idiogram and fluorescence pattern of the chromosomes of the Indian muntjac. *Hereditas* **68**, 332–337.

Fritzler, M. J., Ali, R. & Tan, E. M. (1984). Antibodies from patients with mixed connective tissue disease react with heterogeneous nuclear ribonucleoprotein or ribonucleic acid (hnRNP/RNA) of the nuclear matrix. *J. Immun.* **132**, 1216–1222.

Gall, J. G. (1959). Macronuclear duplication in the ciliated protozoan *Euplotes.* *J. biophys. biochem. Cytol.* **5**, 295–308.

Gibson, D. A. (1970). Somatic homologous association. *Nature, Lond.* **227**, 164–165.

Gonzalez, R. C. & Wintz, P. (1977). *Digital Image Processing.* Reading MA, USA: Addison-Wesley.

Habets, W. J., De Rooij, D. J., Salden, M. H., Verhagen, A. P., Van Eekelen, C. A., Van de Putte, L. B. & Van Venrooij, W. J. (1983). Antibodies against distinct nuclear matrix proteins are characteristic for mixed connective tissue disease. *Clin. exp. Immun.* **54**, 265–276.

Hadlaczky, G., Went, M. & Ringertz, N. R. (1986). Direct evidence for the non-random localization of mammalian chromosomes in the interphase nucleus. *Expl Cell Res.* (in press).

Hager, H. D., Schroeder-Kurth, T. M. & Vogel, F. (1982). Position of chromosomes in the human interphase nucleus. An analysis of nonhomologous chromatid translocations in lymphocyte cultures after trenimon treatment and from patients with Fanconi's anemia and Bloom's syndrome. *Hum. Genet.* **61**, 342–356.

Heenen, W. K. & Nichols, W. W. (1972). Nonrandom arrangement of metaphase chromosomes in cultured cells of the Indian muntjac, *Muntiacus muntjac.* *Cytogenetics* **11**, 153–164.

Hendrick, J., Wolin, S. L., Rinke, M. R., Lerner, M. R. & Steitz, J. A. (1981). Ro small cytoplasmic ribonucleoproteins are a subclass of La ribonucleoproteins: Further characterization of the Ro and La small ribonucleoproteins from uninfected mammalian cells. *Molec. Cell Biol.* **1**, 1138–1149.

Hinterberger, M., Pettersson, I. & Steitz, J. A. (1983). Isolation of small nuclear ribonucleoproteins containing U1, U2, U4, U5 and U6 RNAs. *J. biol. Chem.* **258**, 2604–2613.

Igo-Kemenes, T., Hörz, W. & Zachau, H. G. (1982). Chromatin. *A. Rev. Biochem.* **51**, 89–121.

Izant, J. G., Weatherbee, J. A. & McIntosh, J. R. (1982). A microtubule-associated protein in the mitotic spindle and the interphase nucleus. *Nature, Lond.* **295**, 248–250.

Kabisch, R. & Bautz, E. K. F. (1983). Differential distribution of RNA polymerase B and nonhistone chromosomal proteins in polytene chromosomes of *Drosophila melanogaster.* *EMBO J.* **2**, 395–402.

Lane, D. P. & Hoeffler, W. K. (1980). SV40 large T shares an antigenic determinant with a cellular protein of molecular weight 68,000. *Nature, Lond.* **288**, 167–170.

Lerner, E. A., Lerner, M. R., Janeway, L. A. & Steitz, J. A. (1981). Monoclonal antibodies to nucleic acid containing cellular constituents: Probes for molecular biology and autoimmune disease. *Proc. natn. Acad. Sci. U.S.A.* **78**, 2737–2741.

Lerner, M. R., Boyle, J. A., Hardin, J. A. & Steitz, J. A. (1980). Are snRNPs involved in splicing? *Nature, Lond.* **283**, 220–224.

LERNER, M. R. & STEITZ, J. A. (1979). Antibodies to small nuclear RNAs complexed with proteins are produced by patients with systemic lupus erythematosus. *Proc. natn. Acad. Sci. U.S.A.* **76**, 5495–5499.

LEVAN, A., NICHOLS, W. W., PELUSE, M. & CORIELL, L. L. (1966). The stemline chromosomes of three cell lines representing different vertebrate classes. *Chromosoma* **18**, 343–358.

LEVAN, G. (1970). Contributions to the chromosomal characterization of the PTK 1 rat-kangaroo cell line. *Hereditas* **64**, 85–96.

LEWIS, C. D., LEBKOWSKI, J. S., DALY, A. K. & LAEMMLI, U. K. (1984). Interphase nuclear matrix and metaphase scaffolding structures. *J. Cell Sci. Suppl. 1,* 102–122.

MADORE, S. J., WIEBEN, E. D. & PEDERSON, T. (1984). Eukaryotic small ribonucleoproteins. Anti-La human autoantibodies react with U1 RNA protein complexes. *J. biol. Chem.* **25**, 1929–1933.

MIMORI, T., HINTERBERGER, M., PETTERSSON, I. & STEITZ, J. A. (1984). Autoantibodies to the U2 small nuclear ribonucleoprotein in a patient with scleroderma myositis overlap syndrome. *J. biol. Chem.* **259**, 560–565.

MOORE, C. H. & SHARP, P. A. (1984). Site-specific polyadenylation in a cell-free reaction. *Cell* **36**, 581–591.

MOROI, Y., PEEBLES, C., FRITZLER, M. J., STEIGERWALD, J. & TAN, E. M. (1980). Autoantibody to centromere (kinetochore) in scleroderma sera. *Proc. natn. Acad. Sci. U.S.A.* **77**, 1627–1631.

MOUNT, S. M., PETTERSSON, M., HINTERBERGER, A., KARMAS, A. & STEITZ, J. A. (1983). The U1 small nuclear RNA protein complex selectively binds a 5' splice site *in vitro*. *Cell* **33**, 509–518.

NYMAN, U., HALLMAN, H., HADLACZKY, G., PETTERSSON, I., SHARP, G. & RINGERTZ, N. R. (1986). Intranuclear localization of snRNP antigens. *J. Cell Biol.* **102**, 137–144.

NYMAN, U., LANFRANCHI, G., BERGMAN, M. & RINGERTZ, N. R. (1984). Changes in nuclear antigens during reactivation of chick erythrocyte nuclei in heterokaryons. *J. cell. Physiol.* **120**, 257–262.

PADGETT, R. A., MOUNT, S. M., STEITZ, J. A. & SHARP, P. A. (1983). Splicing of messenger RNA precursors is inhibited by antisera to small nuclear ribonucleoproteins. *Cell* **35**, 101–107.

PETTERSSON, I., HINTERBERGER, M., MIMORI, T., GOTTLIEB, E. & STEITZ, J. A. (1984). The structure of mammalian small nuclear ribonucleoproteins: Identification of multiple protein compounds reactive with anti-(U1)RNP and anti-Sm autoantibodies. *J. biol. Chem.* **259**, 5907–5914.

PRESCOTT, D. M. & KIMBALL, R. F. (1961). Relation between RNA, DNA and protein synthesis in the replicating nucleus of *Euplotes. Proc. natn. Acad. Sci. U.S.A.* **47**, 686–693.

RABL, C. (1885). Über Zellteilung. *Morph. Jb.* **10**, 214–330.

RAPPOLD, G. A., CREMER, T., HAGER, H. D., DAVIES, K. E., MÜLLER, C. R. & YANG, T. (1984). Sex chromosome positions in human interphase nuclei as studied by in situ hybridization with chromosome specific DNA probes. *Hum. Genet.* **67**, 317–325.

REUTER, R., APPEL, B., BRINGMANN, P., RINKE, J. & LÜHRMANN, R. (1984). 5'-terminal caps of snRNAs are reactive with antibodies specific for 2,2,7-trimethylguanosin in whole cells and nuclear matrices. *Expl Cell Res.* **154**, 548–560.

RINGERTZ, N. R., CARLSSON, S.-A., EGE, T. & BOLUND, L. (1971). Detection of human and chick nuclear antigens in chick erythrocyte nuclei during reactivation in heterokaryons with HeLa cells. *Proc. natn. Acad. Sci. U.S.A.* **68**, 3228–3232.

RINGERTZ, N. R., ERICSSON, J. L. E. & NILSSON, O. (1967). Macronuclear chromatin structure in *Euplotes. Expl Cell Res.* **48**, 97–117.

RINGERTZ, N. R. & HOSKINS, G. C. (1965). Cytochemistry of macronuclear reorganization. *Expl Cell Res.* **38**, 160–179.

RINGERTZ, N. R. & SAVAGE, R. E. (1976). *Cell Hybrids*. Monograph. New York: Academic Press.

RINKE, J. & STEITZ, J. A. (1982). Precursor molecules of both human 5S ribosomal RNA and transfer RNAs are bound by cellular proteins reactive with anti-La lupus antibodies. *Cell* **29**, 149–159.

SASS, T. & PEDERSEN, T. (1984). Transcription-dependent localization of U1 and U2 small nuclear ribonucleoproteins at major sites of gene activity in polytene chromosomes. *J. molec. Biol.* **180**, 911–926.

SCHEER, U., LANFRANCHI, G., ROSE, K. M., FRANKE, W. W. & RINGERTZ, N. R. (1983). Migration of rat RNA polymerase I into chick erythrocyte nuclei undergoing reactivation in chick–rat heterokaryons. *J. Cell Biol.* **97**, 1641–1643.

SCHEER, U. & ROSE, K. (1984). Localization of RNA polymerase I in interphase cells and mitotic chromosomes by light and electron microscopic immunocytochemistry. *Proc. natn. Acad. Sci. U.S.A.* **81**, 1431–1435.

SEKIGUCHI, T., SHELTON, K. & RINGERTZ, N. R. (1978). The DNA content of microcells prepared from rat-kangaroo and mouse cells. *Expl Cell Res.* **113**, 247–258.

SHARP, G. C. & ALSPAUGH, M. A. (1985). Autoantibodies to nonhistone nuclear antigens: their immunobiology and clinical relevance. In *Immunology of Rheumatic Diseases* (ed. S. Gupta & N. Talal), pp. 197–219. New York: Plenum.

SMITH, H. C., SPECTOR, D. L., WOODCOCK, L. F., OCHS, R. L. & BHORJEE, J. (1985). Alterations in chromatin conformation are accompanied by reorganization of nonchromatin domains that contain U-snRNP protein p28 and nuclear protein p107. *J. Cell Biol.* **101**, 560–567.

SPERLING, K. & LUEDKE, E. K. (1981). Arrangement of prematurely condensed chromosomes in cultured cells and lymphocytes of the Indian muntjac. *Chromosoma* **83**, 541–553.

TAN, E. M. (1982). Autoantibodies to nuclear antigens (ANA): their immunobiology and medicine. *Adv. Immun.* **33**, 167–280.

J. Cell Sci. Suppl. 4, 29–43 (1986)
Printed in Great Britain © The Company of Biologists Limited 1986

MEIOSIS: SOME CONSIDERATIONS

HERBERT STERN

Department of Biology, University of California, San Diego, La Jolla,
California 92093, USA

INTRODUCTION

Our understanding of meiosis is sturdily rooted in the well-established relationship between chromosome mechanics and genetic transmission. Yet, despite the firmness of that understanding, very little is known about the molecular mechanisms underlying the meiotic process. Such disparity is an outcome of the uneven growth in knowledge between the cytogenetics (including ultrastructure) of meiocytes and their physiology. On *a priori* grounds it would seem that anyone searching for an ideal experimental system to probe mechanisms of chromosome behaviour would at once turn to meiosis. The well-defined structural changes that chromosomes undergo during the process, the excellent correlation between those changes and genetic transmission, and the relatively long time interval during which the changes occur are all highly inviting targets for study. Yet even a brief survey of the field is sufficient to reveal that relatively little progress has been made in molecular studies of meiosis over the past 20 years. The intense and highly fruitful penetrations of molecular biology into a broad variety of cellular phenomena have not yet occurred in studies of meiosis. The theoretical attractiveness of the system, reinforced by the many well-characterized meiotic mutants, is not matched by a corresponding experimental attractiveness for molecular study. Available materials for molecular studies of meiosis have not been inviting, and it is this feature that has discouraged investigations. The situation will undoubtedly change because the rapid advances in experimental techniques will render the phenomenon wide open to molecular analysis.

A BACKGROUND TO CURRENT STUDIES OF MEIOSIS

A relatively brief but pithy chapter on meiosis written by Rhoades (1961) clearly delineated the cytological features of meiosis while also defining certain fundamental issues concerning the mechanism of synapsis and its relationship to recombination. No substantive changes have since been made in the cytological description of meiosis and, at best, no more than a partial answer has been provided concerning the process of recombination. The biggest and most fruitful contribution made during the past 20 years to our understanding of meiosis has been through use of the electron microscope. That understanding has been enriched by the identification of a variety of meiotic mutants (Baker *et al.* 1976) and by the application of radioautography and related techniques to the intracellular localization of different meiotic components

(Zickler, 1984). The centrepiece of the electron microscope contribution is the discovery and description of the synaptonemal complex (SC). The early studies of Moses (Moses, Dresser & Poorman, 1984) laid the groundwork for subsequent investigations. The intensive studies of von Wettstein and colleagues (von Wettstein, Rasmussen & Holm, 1984) provided a detailed account of SC structure while the distinctive studies of Carpenter (1984) brought major attention to a small but critical SC-associated structure, the recombination nodule (Rasmussen & Holm, 1984). The significant outcome of these contributions has been the recognition that chromosome synapsis involves the formation of an elaborate intranuclear structure, one that is conserved in its organization across the phylogenetic spectrum.

To assess the contributions made in recent years to all aspects of meiosis is well beyond the reach of the writer and the scope of this volume. I cannot usefully dwell on the micromanipulation studies by Nicklas and co-workers (Nicklas, 1977) concerning the mechanics of chromosome disjunction in meiocytes; they have provided important insights into the interactions between bivalents and spindle body. It would also be over-reaching to consider the many meiotic mutants described and to relate them to the mechanics of meiosis. I would rather raise the same broad questions discussed by Rhoades (1961), and consider how current studies relate to them. Because my orientation is towards the biochemical or molecular aspects of the process, most of the studies to be considered will be based on meiosis in *Lilium*. These can probably be extrapolated to other organisms but adequate evidence for such extrapolation is lacking.

In considering meiosis as a distinctive cellular event, three broad questions can be raised about its nature. The first of these concerns the intracellular factors that alter chromosome behaviour upon entry of a cell into meiosis. On entering premeiotic interphase, a meiocyte is the product of a clone of cells that have proliferated by mitosis. It is important to identify the mechanism that alters the behaviour of the chromosomes from a mitotic to a meiotic pattern. That mechanism is of particular interest because irreversible commitment to meiosis does not occur until close to the termination of S-phase (Ninneman & Epel, 1973). It is also of interest because the alteration is from a pattern of chromosome behaviour that has occurred repeatedly over many cell generations to a pattern that will occur but once.

The second question concerns the mechanism whereby homologous chromosomes are aligned for synapsis. That question cannot be answered in simplistic molecular terms, because the synapsis of chromosomes is not a large-scale synapsis of complementary DNA strands. In most, if not all, eukaryotes a very small fraction of chromosomal DNA is directly involved in synapsis, a situation very different from the pairing of polytene chromosomes in the salivary glands of *Drosophila*. In considering the mechanism of meiotic chromosome pairing, the role of synapsis in meiosis needs also to be considered. Synapsis is generally viewed as a juxta-positioning of chromosomes to facilitate crossing-over. There is, however, clear evidence that synapsis regulates certain metabolic activities during meiotic prophase. The possibility that synapsis is primarily addressed to the needs of a reductional division rather than crossing-over has also been proposed (Grell, 1973). These different, but not mutually exclusive, roles of synapsis in meiosis determine the context within which the mechanism of homologous alignment should be considered.

The third question that needs to be addressed is the mechanism whereby regularity in meiotic recombination is assured. Exceptions aside, each chromosome pair has at least one chiasma, thus assuring normal reductional disjunction. If crossovers were abundant in each meiotic division, such regularity would be easily explained. However, crossovers are anything but abundant, the frequency per nucleotide being very low in large genomes. The mechanism whereby a meiocyte achieves the regular occurrence of a rare event is a problem that is at least as challenging as the molecular mechanism of recombination itself. Each of these broad questions was posed by Rhoades (1961); the differences are in the phrasing. That some of these questions can now claim a partial answer attests to the fact that some progress has been made during the past 25 years in elucidating the phenomenon of meiosis.

I do not intend to answer each of the questions separately or in the order posed. Indeed, I prefer to deal with the phenomenology of the process and, in doing so, to relate the events of meiotic prophase that have been characterized in biochemical (or molecular) terms to the three questions just raised. I do so because there is little general awareness of the molecular events that are already known to occur during meiosis. Familiarization should provide a needed perspective for assessing the unavoidably speculative answers to the target questions.

PATTERNS OF DNA REPLICATION

The first creative theory providing for a mechanism of meiotic development was proposed by C. D. Darlington (1937). It was called the 'Precocity theory' because it maintained that chromosomes enter prophase precociously and pair before undergoing replication. The theory held that chromosome compaction in the absence of prior replication exposed chromosome pairing surfaces. Because pairing preceded replication, crossing-over could occur simultaneously with replication; such a model was favoured by many. When the radioautographic evidence disclosed that DNA replication preceded meiotic prophase just as it did mitotic prophase (Taylor & McMaster, 1954) the theory had to be abandoned, although the absence of convincing evidence for any DNA synthesis during meiotic prophase made it difficult to associate chromosome synapsis with crossing-over. About 20 years ago, a major issue in meiosis was the apparent absence of DNA synthesis beyond the premeiotic S-phase.

This brief historical account provides an appropriate setting for evaluating current information on DNA synthesis in meiocytes. Darlington was correct in his intuition even if he was incorrect in his doctrine. The meiotic process, unlike the mitotic cycle, is characterized by three distinct intervals of DNA synthesis, and probably a fourth that remains difficult to establish (Hotta & Stern, 1971, 1976). As was made evident by autoradiography, replication of the nuclear genome occurs before the occurrence of meiotic prophase. In this respect, mitosis and meiosis are identical except for a small but significant difference. In the case of meiocytes, replication of the genome is incomplete at the end of the premeiotic S-phase. A small proportion of the genome, previously estimated as being 0·3 % but recently revised to a value lying between 0·1 and 0·2 % (Hotta, Tabata, Stubbs & Stern, 1985a), is not replicated during the premeiotic interval, its replication being delayed until zygotene, in coordination with chromosome synapsis. The apparent singleness of chromosome threads during the initial stages of meiotic prophase that led Darlington to infer an absence of replication may be accounted for by an incompleteness of replication, which leaves sister chromatids tightly apposed. Synthesis of DNA during zygotene has been demonstrated not only by biochemical techniques in lily meiocytes but also by radioautography in both lily microsporocytes (Kurata & Ito, 1978) and mouse spermatocytes (Moses et al. 1984). That synthesis, like the premeiotic DNA synthesis, is semiconservative.

I will return later to the functional role of delayed 'zygDNA' replication. Before doing so, a brief account of the nature of this DNA is appropriate. Unlike the highly repeated DNA sequences in heterochromatin that are replicated late, zygDNA consists mainly of unique or low copy number sequences. Although their precise distribution is unknown, segments of zygDNA, generally ranging from 5×10^3 to 10×10^3 bases in length, are distributed among all the chromosomes and are not localized within any particular chromosomal region (Hotta et al. 1985a). The unusual behaviour of the zygDNA segments is further displayed by their incomplete replication even at the termination of zygotene (Hotta & Stern, 1976). The ends of the newly replicated zygDNA strands are not ligated to the rest of the genome; instead, short gaps remain at the ends of the segments and possibly some interstitial ones. Replication at these sites does not occur until diplotene or later. Undoubtedly, such a pattern of staged replication is unique to meiosis. Presumptive meiocytes that are stimulated to revert to mitosis replicate their zygDNA before entering mitotic prophase. It is inviting to speculate that zygDNA plays a structural role in chromosome behaviour.

The sweep of DNA events that mark meiosis is further punctuated by the occurrence of DNA replication during pachytene. The exit of cells from zygotene and their entry into pachytene is characterized by a striking switch in the pattern of DNA replication. The precise timing of the switch is uncertain, but by early pachytene it is evident that the DNA replication is not semiconservative, nor does it involve the zygDNA sequences. The extended pachytene interval is characterized by repair replication that continues through midpachytene. By the end of pachytene, repair synthesis is no longer detectable (Hotta & Stern, 1971). That such repair is a distinct part of the meiotic program is made evident by the fact that it is initiated by the action of a meiosis-specific endonuclease (Howell & Stern, 1971) and a still unidentified exonuclease that extends the nicks introduced by the endonuclease into short single-stranded gaps. The gaps occur in specific regions of the genome and are all repaired before the termination of pachytene. The point I emphasize here is that the concerns of 20 years ago regarding the apparent absence of DNA synthesis during the prophase interval when crossing-over is presumed to occur have now been replaced by a very different set of concerns. A highly organized pattern of DNA replication occurs after the S-phase and during meiotic prophase. That pattern involves two specific sets of DNA sequences, one being the seat of semiconservative replication and the other the seat of repair replication. Our present set of concerns is to assign these processes specific meiotic functions.

RECOMBINOGENIC PROTEINS: PATTERN OF MEIOTIC BEHAVIOUR

Debates about the timing of meiotic recombination pale before the evidence now accumulated on the behaviour of recombination-related proteins in meiocytes. A most obvious feature of that behaviour is the transient but strong appearance of a number of major proteins during the zygotene–pachytene stages of meiosis and their absence or near-absence during the premeiotic S-phase and the post-pachytene stages (Hotta *et al.* 1985*b*). Put briefly, the entry of meiocytes into zygotene and then pachytene is accompanied by the formation of a group of proteins that act directly on DNA with properties that are relevant to recombination. The conclusion is inescapable that meiocytes are programmed to metabolize DNA during meiotic prophase. Whether all metabolism so programmed is directed at recombination cannot yet be ascertained but it is clearly evident that these metabolic activities are a primary feature of zygotene–pachytene and not of the premeiotic S-phase.

From the standpoint of meiotic function the various recombination-related proteins that are prominent at prophase fall into two classes with respect to their activities during meiosis. One class has just been described; it consists of proteins that are prominent only during the prophase stages. Most of these proteins have not been found in somatic tissues; where their counterparts have been identified in somatic cells, they differ in a number of properties. In general, proteins exclusive to meiotic prophase are meiosis-specific. The second class of recombination-related proteins are not at all exclusive to meiotic prophase. They are similar, if not identical, to their somatic equivalents. They are not necessarily recombination-related; they can and may function in replication. Among the proteins identified are DNA ligase, polynucleotide kinase, DNA polymerase and topoisomerases I and II (Stern & Hotta, 1983). The significant point is that the relatively few meiosis-specific proteins identified to date function in association with numerous broadly distributed DNA-metabolizing proteins. Whether the meiosis-specific proteins are even partly responsible for the unique features of meiotic recombination is a consideration beyond the reach of present information.

The behaviour of meiosis-specific proteins that are recombination-related is such as to settle the question of when recombination occurs in meiocytes. Their respective roles in recombination may be inferred, at least partly, from a brief description of their respective properties. The first enzyme identified was a meiotic endonuclease that introduces the DNA nicks at pachytene as discussed above. The high activity of this protein during early and mid-pachytene points to the probable importance of single-stranded interruptions as potential sites for initiating crossovers. The absence of nicking in the absence of homologous pairing reveals an important regulatory feature of meiosis. Homologous synapsis regulates several of the metabolic activities that are specific to meiotic prophase (Hotta, Bennett, Toledo & Stern, 1979). Although direct evidence for a role of nicking in recombination is lacking, it is difficult to avoid the conclusion that the programmed introduction of nicks at pachytene and its dependence on homologous pairing are an essential step in at least one of the several meiotic recombination mechanisms.

Two of the other meiosis-specific proteins act on the secondary structure of DNA. One of these, the 'U-protein', unwinds DNA in the presence of ATP so as to yield single-stranded tails at nicked sites (Hotta & Stern, 1978). Such tails could function either in aligning chromosomes for synapsis or in the formation of heteroduplexes for recombination. The other protein, the 'R-protein' has the property of catalysing the formation of duplex DNA from complementary single strands (Hotta & Stern, 1979). The combination of endonuclease, U-protein and R-protein would, at least in theory, be sufficient to mediate the formation of heteroduplex regions for recombination. Evidence from recent studies, however, removes the need to speculate on the actual role of this group of proteins in mediating the recombination process. The evidence concerns recA-like proteins and still unfractionated extracts that effect genetic recombination *in vitro* (Hotta *et al.* 1985*b*).

The critical role of the *Escherichia coli* recA protein in general recombination is well-established. Similar proteins have been found in other bacteria and also in the eukaryote, *Ustilago farfara*. Recently, the presence of a recA-like protein has been demonstrated in tissues of mouse and lily. In both species, rec proteins have been identified in meiocytes and in somatic tissues. The proteins differ in a number of respects; those derived from somatic cells are referred to as 's-rec' and those from meiocytes as 'm-rec' proteins. In both mouse and lily, s-rec proteins have molecular weights in the neighbourhood of 70×10^3 whereas the m-rec proteins are in the range of 45×10^3. Tissues of the mouse lend themselves to an instructive comparison with respect to the activities of the two protein types at different temperatures. Mouse spermatocytes normally undergo meiosis at about 33 °C, in contrast with the other tissues that function at 37 °C. In all tests performed, the m-rec protein functioned optimally at 33 °C whereas the s-rec protein functioned more effectively at 37 °C. When m-rec protein was tested at 37 °C its activity was very much lower than at 33 °C. Parallel behaviour was observed in comparing the two rec proteins of lily. The activity of m-rec protein was highest at 23–25 °C whereas the s-rec protein could function effectively at temperatures as high as 30 °C. Pollen formation is known to be defective in lilies maintained at temperatures above 25 °C. It is apparent that the m-rec proteins are designed to function at temperatures different from those that are optimal for the s-rec proteins. In addition to these physiological differences, which point to the uniqueness of m-rec protein to meiotic cells, the behaviour of m-rec protein during meiosis demonstrates its importance to the process. There is virtually no m-rec or s-rec protein in microsporocytes during the premeiotic *S*-phase. The m-rec protein begins to rise during late leptotene and early zygotene, reaching its highest level in early pachytene and declining to its original base level after termination of pachytene. The point to be emphasized is that the m-rec protein, which can be designated as a direct agent of recombination, is a virtually exclusive property of the zygotene–pachytene stages.

Even more impressive in terms of timing recombination activity in meiosis is the behaviour of extracts that are capable of effecting recombination between mutant plasmids, each mutant being defective in a different region of the tetracycline resistance gene. Recombination between the two mutants confers tetracycline resistance in bacteria transformed by the recombinant plasmid. The assay is unambiguous and is highly relevant about the timing of recombination in yeast, mouse and lily. In the case of yeast (*Saccharomyces cerevisiae*), the recombination activity in extracts of cells induced to undergo meiosis increases 100-fold. In mouse spermatocytes the increase on entry into meiosis is about 500-fold. In lily microsporocytes, the increase is 700-fold but, in this case, it can be shown that the peak of activity occurs at late zygotene–early pachytene. The broad spectrum of recombination-related proteins described above coupled with the recombination activity of cell extracts provide an overwhelming argument for the occurrence of the ultimate molecular steps of recombination during the zygotene–pachytene of meiosis. The evidence thus provided neatly affirms the conclusion of most cytogeneticists that meiotic recombination follows chromosome synapsis. More complex and less tractable issues must now be addressed.

REGULATION OF MEIOTIC EVENTS

In an important sense the uniqueness of meiosis is derived not so much from the novelty of its special components as from the distinctiveness of its regulation. Synapsis occurs in somatic cells of the Diptera; recombination is a property of somatic cells in general and of certain cells, like those of the immunogenic system, in particular. Chromosome separation occurs by essentially the same mechanism in mitotic and meiotic cells. From a regulatory standpoint, however, the differences between these two activities are very apparent. Meiotic pairing, unlike somatic pairing, is transient and secured by a proteinaceous structure. Recombination in meiotic cells is not randomized as in mitotic ones and, in meiosis, it occurs with matchless regularity. Reductional separation of chromosomes is an essential feature of meiosis and an unacceptable one for mitosis. The principal issue in my mind is how the different components of the meiotic process are regulated in their behaviour; the individual components of meiosis and mitosis, the SC excepted, do not by themselves provide an explanation. What I would like to do is to link the different meiotic components discussed above to schemes of regulation. The linkage is bound to be in error but it is also bound to point to some new directions.

Initiation of meiosis

The conditions under which meiosis is initiated are exceedingly diverse. In animals, the germline is set aside very early in development and is the only source of meiocytes in the organism. In mammals, female meiosis is initiated in the foetus following a characteristic level of oogonial proliferation. In the males, meiosis is regularly and repeatedly induced following continuous cycles of spermatogonial proliferation. Even so, ectopically located germ cells in the region of the adrenal gland in a male foetus initiate meiosis on the female schedule (Zamboni & Upadhyay, 1983). In higher plants, apical meristems are the source of all cell types, germ cells included. In many fungi meiosis is induced under adverse conditions, nitrogen starvation in *S. cerevisiae*, for example. In the fungus, *Neottiella rutilans*, the zygotic cell enters the prophase of meiosis immediately following a fusion of gametes that have already separately completed their premeiotic DNA replication (Rossen & Westergaard, 1966). There is no single extracellular stimulus that is a universal inducer of meiosis, but it is reasonable to suppose that the respective actions of different stimuli converge at the intracellular level to initiate the complex development resulting in meiosis. In so stating the issue, I am not taking into account the developmental state of the cells thus stimulated; that state may well determine the effectiveness of the meiotic inducer.

Microsporocytes of *Lilium*, as discussed earlier, become irreversibly committed to meiosis near the end of the premeiotic S-phase. At this time, the zygDNA segments are unreplicated and it is in relation to their replicative behaviour that a regulatory scheme can be imagined. The failure to replicate during the premeiotic S-phase is due to the suppressive action of a recently described L-protein or leptotene protein (Hotta, Tabata & Stern, 1984). The protein, apart from its being meiosis-specific, has at least three distinctive features that make it a likely factor in the regulation of meiotic induction. It selectively inhibits the replication of zygDNA, although its ability to do so in mitotic S-phases has not been demonstrated. zygDNA in duplex form has a specific binding affinity for L-protein, an affinity that is due to a subset of zygDNA sequences that are probably no more than 90 bp in length and that are believed to be present in each of the zygDNA segments. If ATP is added to the L-protein:zygDNA complex, the L-protein introduces a single nick in one strand only, presumably in the vicinity of the binding region. When the experiment is performed with a plasmid bearing a zygDNA insert and the plasmid is then denatured, the result is one circular single strand and one linear strand, both of similar length. This does not occur if the zygDNA segment lacks the binding region, nor has it been observed to occur with any other form of DNA. If the timing of L-protein formation and disappearance is taken into account, the different properties of the L-protein can be fitted into a regulatory scheme. L-protein becomes detectable in meiocytes at the time that cells become irreversibly committed to meiosis, which is also close to the end of the premeiotic S-phase. Because L-protein formation appears to occur near the end of S-phase, it may be inferred that during premeiotic S-phase zygDNA replication is either not initiated or is repressed by a factor other than L-protein. An attractive speculation is that zygDNA is regularly replicated at the end of S-phase in mitotic systems, the late replication being required by the special role of zygDNA in chromosome behaviour as would be the case if it were part of the axial element of chromosomes. In so functioning, zygDNA could signal the completion of sister chromatid formation and initiate entry into the G_2 phase of the mitotic cell cycle.

If unreplicated zygDNA segments are a precondition for synapsis, the suppressive action of the L-protein makes possible the formation of those components essential to stabilized synapsis before zygDNA replication is initiated. If this is so, the induction of L-protein synthesis must be accompanied by an induction of other essential meiotic components. L-protein formation thus marks a critical point in meiotic induction, one for which much necessary information is lacking. Perturbation of cells during the interval between *S*-phase and zygotene has been found by some to affect chiasma formation, a finding that is consistent with the scheme just described (Church & Wimber, 1971). Presumably, the irreversibility of meiotic commitment at the time of L-protein appearance is due to the irreversibility of its suppressive effect until zygotene is reached.

Regulation of synapsis

The tentative nature of meiotic synapsis has become fully evident in the past few years. The occurrence of non-homologous pairing in meiocytes with apparently normal SCs was demonstrated in the sixties. It is now apparent that synapsis has dynamic properties even under conditions of genetic homology. In a number of situations it has been found that, following recombination, requirements for homologous synapsis may be relaxed, leading to 'synaptic adjustment' (Moses *et al.* 1984). In such cases, for example, the strains of inversion loops that do not house a chiasma are altered to a linear arrangement resulting in non-homologous pairing. Homoeologous pairing has also been shown to precede homologous pairing in hexaploid wheat, a process that is designed to accommodate the homoeologies between the three chromosome sets (von Wettstein *et al.* 1984). It may be concluded that homologous alignment of chromosomes is a process that is separate from synapsis. The components of the synaptonemal complex appear to be indifferent to homology but capable of securing chromosome pairs. Homologous synapsis probably occurs because of the temporal coordination between homologous alignment and SC formation.

zygDNA segments may be viewed as serving the process of homologous alignment. The nicking action of the L-protein may be a mechanism whereby the resultant single-stranded DNA tails lead to the formation of duplexes from complementary strands furnished by pairs of homologous chromosomes. In this way transient alignment is achieved. It may be significant that the R-protein, which catalyses duplex formation, is located in the nuclear membrane, as is the L-protein, and that the level of R-protein is depressed in the absence of homologous pairing. Regions of nuclear lipoprotein may provide advantageous sites for collisions between complementary DNA strands. With the onset of zygDNA replication, the alignment capacity of the DNA is lost; the association must then be secured by the SC. In this speculation the components of the SC that interact with the chromosomes to maintain synapsis are not the components that effect alignment. It may well be, however, that zygDNA segments furnish sites of attachment for proteins of the SC regardless of DNA homology.

The process by which homologous synapsis is secured is probably more complex than the scheme proposed indicates. Not only is zygDNA nicked by L-protein but at least 1–2 % of the zygDNA sequences undergo transcription in coordination with the pairing process (Hotta *et al.* 1985*a*). The zygRNA thus formed is short-lived. The surge of poly(A)$^+$ zygRNA in lily begins in late leptotene and reaches its peak in early zygotene, at which time it constitutes 40 % of poly(A)$^+$ RNA in the meiocytes. Its span of formation and disappearance is the narrowest thus far found in meiosis. Its level is tied to homologous pairing. It is very low in an achiasmatic hybrid. The fact that in mouse about 5 % of the poly(A)$^+$ RNA from prophase spermatocytes, but not from the germ cells at other stages, hybridize to lily zygDNA makes it probable that the transcription of zygDNA is a common feature of the meiotic pairing process. We have no information on whether the transcripts are translated but it is obviously an essential piece of information. It is indeed difficult to escape the conclusion that zygDNA segments have a critical and special role in chromosome function. The delayed replication followed by delayed ligation, the site-specific nicking, the brief meiosis-specific transcription, and its apparent localization in the region of the synaptonemal complex point to a unique chromosomal component with a unique function. That function appears to be both structural and at least partly informational.

Regulation of recombination

It is generally recognized that the genetically determined distance between genes and the physical distance between them do not necessarily correspond. Heterochromatin in *Drosophila* has been found to have no genetic distance, a reflection of the fact that crossing-over is virtually absent in heterochromatic stretches even though these may occupy a considerable length of the chromosome. Numerous cytological studies point to the non-random distribution of chiasmata (Jones, 1984). The case for selectivity in meiotic crossing-over is strong. The selectivity applies not only to the limitation in sites at which crossing-over may occur, but it also applies to the restriction in the number of chiasmata that may form in any one chromosome arm, the so-called 'positive interference'. Selectivity and regularity are the principal features in regulation of meiotic recombination. The selectivity must have a molecular basis and the regularity must be achieved by metabolic design.

A sweeping statement can be made about the metabolic design of meiosis that accounts for the regularity, but not for the selectivity, of recombination. The components required for effecting recombination are present in overwhelming abundance. The huge excess in germ cell and gamete production over the number required for fertilization provides an attractive analogy with the situation underlying recombination at meiotic prophase. The number of nicks introduced at pachytene is about 10 000 times that required to initiate the actual number of crossovers. Although quantification is difficult, it is almost certain that the concentration of recombinogenic proteins is far in excess of what is required for the process. It is only the component or complex of components that governs the ultimate site of recombination that is limiting, but its effective action is virtually ensured by the abundance of all the other essential components. Given the likelihood that the recombination nodule is the limiting factor, its molecular nature is a choice target for future research.

The selectivity of recombination is, at least in its initial stages, regulated by the sites in which nicking is localized. These are the P-DNA regions and their subsets of PsnDNA regions. If the latter have functions other than serving as sites for pachytene nicking and gap formation, the functions remain undisclosed. The very high degree of sequence conservation of PsnDNA within the *Lilium* genome (Bouchard & Stern, 1980) and the presence of similar sequences in the diverse plant species tested (Friedman, Bouchard & Stern, 1982) make it highly probable that the primary, if not the sole, role of the P-DNA segments is to limit the sites at which meiotic recombination may be initiated. An immediate problem is to determine the location of P-DNA sites with respect to transcribed regions, and a more challenging problem is to determine what events, if any, occur in an actual crossover. It is of interest that in their radioautographic studies of mouse spermatocytes Moses and collaborators found about 60 % of the pachytene DNA label to be present in the region of the synaptonemal complex (Moses *et al.* 1984). This observation makes it probable that the pattern of pachytene chromosome compaction is such as to locate P-DNA segments close to the SC. Such an arrangement raises the question of the structural relationship between the P-DNA and the zygDNA segments. Preliminary evidence from analyses of lily microsporocytes indicates that the two groups of sequences are not randomly distributed with respect to one another and that they are more closely positioned than randomness would allow. If so, it would have to be concluded that among the various features of intrachromosomal DNA sequence organization, one is specifically addressed to chromosome pairing and crossing-over.

The selectivity in sites of pachytene nicking cannot be simply explained by the moderately repeated character of PsnDNA sequences. Obviously, a mechanism must be present that localizes nicking activity in those sequences. The only established characteristics of specificity in meiotic endonuclease behaviour are its exclusive action on duplex DNA and its introduction of nicks that have 3′ phosphoryl and 5′ OH termini (Howell & Stern, 1971). To date there is no evidence for sequence preference by the enzyme. On the other hand, the evidence is unambiguous in favour of chromatin structure determining site-specificity in pachytene nicking (Hotta & Stern, 1981). PsnDNA regions are housed in a distinctive chromatin structure. Most, if not all, of the histones are replaced by a non-basic protein conveniently referred to as 'Psn-protein'. That protein renders the PsnDNA segments accessible to the endonuclease and also to a variety of other enzymes. The protein is deficient in achiasmatic cells and has not been detected at stages other than zygotene–pachytene. It renders all PsnDNA segments accessible to the endonuclease during pachytene. In the meiocytes, the endonuclease is ineffective if administered to isolated nuclei that lack the Psn-protein. It may be inferred that the general organization of chromatin at meiosis is such as to limit endonucleolytic activity to selected regions of the genome.

The mechanism whereby PsnDNA regions alone are simultaneously rendered accessible to the endonuclease is partly understood. Site selectivity is determined by a small nuclear RNA termed PsnRNA. This RNA consists of as many families as there are families of PsnDNA. Chromatin segments housing PsnDNA and Psn-protein also house PsnRNA. Moreover, whereas the PsnDNA does not have a selective binding affinity for Psn-protein, PsnRNA does. Isolated pachytene nuclei from achiasmatic cells can be rendered susceptible to endonuclease activity by incubating the nuclei with relatively high concentrations of PsnRNA in the presence of a partially purified preparation of proteins from chiasmatic cells and ATP. A source of energy is essential to the pretreatment. The regulatory model proposed is one in which certain genes serve as sites of transcription of the various families of PsnRNA. Transcription of these genes is initiated at some time during pachytene, probably in coordination with the transcription of the gene or genes for Psn-protein. There is thus a mechanism for regulating the simultaneous initiation of recombination activity in diverse but selected regions of the genome at a specific stage of meiosis. The mechanism may serve as another example of maximizing the possibilities for initiating recombination in order to ensure regularity in large genomes where the frequency of recombinants per nucleotide is very low.

A PERSPECTIVE

Providing a perspective on the course of future research in the molecular and biochemical mechanisms of meiosis is, at best, a doubtful venture. The data underlying the models and interpretations discussed in this presentation have a very narrow experimental base. That base is vanishingly narrow when compared with the cytogenetic and electron microscopy data on meiosis. The molecular mechanisms for synapsis and recombination that have been encountered in studies of lily and, to a lesser extent, of mouse may be exclusive to large genomes; different mechanisms may prevail in smaller genomes. In both species, too, the data obtained are derived almost entirely from studies of male gametogenesis. These limitations should be borne in mind when considering the significance of the generalized comments made below.

The need for determining the molecular composition of the principal extra-chromosomal structures – the SC and the recombination nodule – is too well recognized and too obvious to merit further comment. What is less obvious is what may be considered to be the fundamental issues in explaining the mechanism of meiosis. I believe that the biochemical and/or molecular descriptions outlined above settle a few basic questions even as they introduce many others. The dilemma of DNA synthesis being confined to the premeiotic S-phase has been disposed of; DNA synthesis is a distinct feature of meiotic prophase. Similarly, the question of whether meiotic recombination can be separated from the process of genome replication is also settled; the overwhelming presence of recombinogenic mechanisms during meiotic prophase along with the occurrence of repair replication puts that issue to rest. I also believe that the search for some general force for homologous chromosome pairing can be replaced by a more sophisticated view of synapsis as a multicomponent process involving the coordination of a number of separate mechanisms.

I believe that there are at least three broad issues towards which future studies should be directed. The first of these is the organization of chromosomal DNA for meiosis. Genic properties aside, I doubt that chromosomes are passive substrates for a highly organized system of disjuction and recombination. Beyond a certain size (lower limit unknown) the DNA of chromosomes requires an internal organization to make possible the structural events that chromosomes undergo in the course of meiosis. Some of the events have their counterparts in the mitotic process. Whether zygDNA and P-DNA segments are elements of that organization in one or both processes is part of the question that needs to be answered.

The second broad issue is a resolution of the events that occur at the termination of the premeiotic S-phase and direct chromosomes into a pattern of meiotic behaviour. L-protein synthesis must be one of the events coordinated with the formation of the lateral elements along the leptotene chromosomes. I believe that all the critical events during the preleptotene interval must involve accessory components of chromosome structure. It is chromosome behaviour that is at the core of meiotic differentiation. In thus stating the issue it is important to bear in mind that the highly coordinated meiotic processes are not necessarily integrally regulated. An outstanding example of this is the dissociability of the induction of the metabolic system for recombination from the occurrence of homologous synapsis. Pachytene DNA nicking, but not meiotic endonuclease, is suppressed in the absence of homologous pairing. Similarly, recombination but not recombinogenic protein formation is suppressed even in the absence of meiotic induction as occurs in yeast. Dissociable regulation of highly coordinated processes very probably reflects still unrecognized cellular needs. Whether or not this is the case, the need to identify the critical factors that operate at the termination of the premeiotic S-phase remains.

A third general issue is the tying together of homologous synapsis with the recombinational mechanisms that seemingly saturate meiotic prophase. We know that homologous pairing not only juxtaposes homologues for recombination, but also has pronounced effects on some of the metabolic events concerned with recombination. The low levels of R-protein, PsnRNA, Psn-protein and zygRNA all indicate that there is a device by which the homologously paired chromosomes can signal their state to the metabolic apparatus of the meiocyte. We lack a conceptual approach to the dependence of metabolic activity on chromosome pairing, a relation that probably also holds in the cases of somatic pairing. It is a fundamental relation that begs resolution.

Because meiosis is a highly conserved process, the essential proteins, and also the critical DNA sequences, may be expected to show a high degree of conservation. By itself this situation would have limited significance to future studies. However, the experimental possibilities are enormously enlarged by techniques available for gene selection and cloning, and also for ultrastructural localizations with immunochemical agents. Many meiotic mutants are known and many others can be found. Even if serendipity is discounted, it is very likely that the molecular mechanisms of meiosis will lose their obscurity by virtue of the rich technology that has been made available to contemporary cell biology. The biochemical virtues of lily meiosis may well grace the findings in genetically more tractable organisms.

I express special thanks to my longtime colleague, Dr Yasuo Hotta, who has been the major source of creativity in our studies of meiosis. I can only repeat the recognition acknowledged in previous publications to the National Science Foundation, the American Cancer Society, and the National Institutes of Health for their generous financial support of our research.

REFERENCES

BAKER, B. S., CARPENTER, A. T. C., ESPOSITO, M. S., ESPOSITO, R. E. & SANDLER, L. (1976). The genetic control of meiosis. *A. Rev. Genet.* **10**, 53–134.

BOUCHARD, R. A. & STERN, H. (1980). DNA synthesized at pachytene in *Lilium*: A non-divergent subclass of moderately repetitive sequences. *Chromosoma* **81**, 349–363.

CARPENTER, A. T. C. (1984). Recombination nodules and the mechanism of crossing-over in *Drosophila*. In *Symp. Soc. exp. Biol.*, vol. 38 (ed. C. W. Evans & H. G. Dickinson), pp. 233–244. Cambridge: The Company of Biologists Limited.

CHURCH, K. & WIMBER, D. E. (1971). Meiosis in *Ornithogalum virens*. II. Univalent production by preprophase cold treatment. *Expl Cell Res.* **64**, 119–124.

DARLINGTON, C. D. (1937). *Recent Advances in Cytology*. Philadelphia, Pennsylvania: Blakiston.

FRIEDMAN, B. E., BOUCHARD, R. A. & STERN, H. (1982). DNA sequences repaired at pachytene exhibit strong homology among distantly related higher plants. *Chromosoma* **87**, 409–424.

GRELL, R. F. (1973). DNA replication and recombination in the *Drosophila* oocyte. In *Chromosomes Today,* vol. 4 (ed. J. Wahrman & K. R. Lewis), pp. 149–160. New York: John Wiley and Sons.

HOTTA, Y., BENNETT, M. D., TOLEDO, L. A. & STERN, H. (1979). Regulation of R-protein and endonuclease activities in meiocytes by homologous chromosome pairing. *Chromosoma* **72**, 191–201.

HOTTA, Y. & STERN, H. (1971). Analysis of DNA synthesis during meiotic prophase in *Lilium*. *J. molec. Biol.* **55**, 337–355.

HOTTA, Y. & STERN, H. (1976). Persistent discontinuities in late replicating DNA during meiosis in *Lilium*. *Chromosoma* **55**, 171–182.

HOTTA, Y. & STERN, H. (1978). DNA unwinding protein from meiotic cells of *Lilium*. *Biochemistry* **17**, 1872–1880.

HOTTA, Y. & STERN, H. (1979). The effect of dephosphorylation on the properties of a helix-destabilizing protein from meiotic cells and its partial reversal by a protein kinase. *Eur. J. Biochem.* **95**, 31–38.

HOTTA, Y. & STERN, H. (1981). Small nuclear RNA molecules that regulate nuclease accessibility in specific chromatin regions of meiotic cells. *Cell* **27**, 309–319.

HOTTA, Y., TABATA, S., BOUCHARD, R. A., PINON, R. & STERN, H. (1985b). General recombination mechanisms in extracts of meiotic cells. *Chromosoma* (in press).

HOTTA, Y., TABATA, S. & STERN, H. (1984). Replication and nicking of zygotene DNA sequences: Control by a meiosis-specific protein. *Chromosoma* **90**, 243–253.

HOTTA, Y., TABATA, S., STUBBS, L. & STERN, H. (1985a). Meiosis-specific transcripts of a DNA component replicated during chromosome pairing: homology across the phylogenetic spectrum. *Cell* **40**, 785–793.

HOWELL, S. H. & STERN, H. (1971). The appearance of DNA breakage and repair activities in the synchronous meiotic cycle of *Lilium*. *J. molec. Biol.* **55**, 357–378.

JONES, G. H. (1984). Control of chiasma distribution. In *Symp. Soc. exp. Biol.,* vol. 38 (ed. C. W. Evans & H. G. Dickinson), pp. 293–320. Cambridge: The Company of Biologists Limited.

KURATA, N. & ITO, M. (1978). Electron microscope autoradiography of ^{3}H-thymidine incorporation during the zygotene stage in microsporocytes of lily. *Cell Struct. Funct.* **3**, 349–356.

Moses, M. J., Dresser, M. E. & Poorman, P. A. (1984). Composition and role of the synaptonemal complex. In *Symp. Soc. exp. Biol.,* vol. 38 (ed. C. W. Evans & H. G. Dickinson), pp. 245–270. Cambridge: The Company of Biologists Limited.

Nicklas, R. B. (1977). Chromosome distribution: experiments on cell hybrids and *in vitro. Phil. Trans. R. Soc.* B **277**, 267–276.

Ninnemann, H. & Epel, B. (1973). Inhibition of cell division by blue light. *Expl Cell Res.* **79**, 318–326.

Rasmussen, S. W. & Holm, P. B. (1984). The synaptonemal complex, recombination nodules, and chiasmata in human spermatocytes. In *Symp. Soc. exp. Biol.,* vol. 38 (ed. C. W. Evans & H. G. Dickinson), pp. 271–292. Cambridge: The Company of Biologists Limited.

Rhoades, M. M. (1961). Meiosis. In *The Cell,* vol. 3 (ed. J. Brachet & A. E. Mirsky), pp. 1–75. New York: Academic Press.

Rossen, J. M. & Westergaard, M. (1966). Studies on the mechanism of crossing over. II. Meiosis and the time of meiotic chromosome replication in the Ascomycete *Neottiella rutilans. C.r. Trav. Lab. Carlsberg* **35**, 233–260.

Stern, H. & Hotta, Y. (1983). Meiotic aspects of chromosome organization. *Stadler Symp.,* vol. 15 (ed. J. P. Gustafson), pp. 25–41.

Taylor, J. H. & McMaster, R. D. (1954). Autoradiographic and microspectrophotometric studies of desoxyribonucleic acid during microgametogenesis in *Lilium longiflorum. Chromosoma* **6**, 489–521.

von Wettstein, D., Rasmussen, S. W. & Holm, P. B. (1984). The synaptonemal complex in genetic segregation. *A. Rev. Genet.* **18**, 331–413.

Zamboni, L. & Upadhyay, S. (1983). Germ cell differentiation in mouse adrenal glands. *J. exp. Zool.* **228**, 173–193.

Zickler, D. (1984). Données récentes sur la prophase I de meiose. *Annls Sci. nat. (Bot.), Paris* **6**, 177–197.

J. Cell Sci. Suppl. 4, 45–70 (1986)
Printed in Great Britain © The Company of Biologists Limited 1986

CELL SURFACE CARBOHYDRATES: MOLECULES IN SEARCH OF A FUNCTION?

GEOFFREY M. W. COOK

Department of Pharmacology, University of Cambridge, Hills Road, Cambridge CB2 2QD, UK

INTRODUCTION

"Many knowledgeable biologists would say, almost reflexly, that complex carbohydrates probably play a pivotal role in determining the specificity of many biological recognition phenomenon" (Marchesi, Ginsburg & Robbins, 1978). So states the preface to an authorative symposium volume on surface carbohydrates. However, 16 years previously it was possible, in the light of contemporary knowledge, for a discussant at an equally authorative symposium to state, in relation to the recognition of self and non-self, "At the cell level it is possible that carbohydrate may play a part, carbohydrate is always present, but I know of no clear evidence yet to indicate that it plays a role in the mechanism by which cells discriminate between their closer and more distant relatives" (Davies, 1963). Clearly over this period, which incidentally corresponds very closely with the establishment of the *Journal of Cell Science*, a considerable development in the study of surface carbohydrates has taken place, though interestingly there is still a need for definitive evidence for the role of carbohydrates in cell discrimination.

Rothstein (1978) drew attention to the fact that when the membrane literature was reviewed in the *Annual Review of Physiology* in 1968 about 400 of an estimated 600 published references were used, among which papers on glycoproteins, *per se*, were not a recognizable category. However, between 1968 and 1976 the annual rate of production of papers on membranes jumped from about 600 to 3000, of which in 1976, 300 papers were identifiable as being concerned with proteins and glycoproteins. The pace of research into glycoproteins in particular continues unabated, with Sharon quoting in 1984 that since 1976 over 20 000 papers have been published on these compounds. In being invited to make a contribution to this twentieth anniversary volume of the Journal it is perhaps appropriate to step back and look at the way in which an interest in surface carbohydrates has developed and to examine the body of work started in the 1960s, which has resulted in this quantum jump in endeavour, before going on to speculate on the direction that this area of research is likely to take in the next 20 years.

CHEMISTRY OF CELL SURFACE CARBOHYDRATES

For the general reader it may be helpful to give some details as to the type of compound that comes within the scope of the description 'Cell Surface Carbohydrates'.

The carbohydrates of the surface of animal cells can be considered to fall into two groups, namely those molecules that are components of the 'extracellular matrix' and those that are integral to the plasma membrane. While the former group may be said to have an ephemeral association with the plasma membrane during their bio-synthesis and secretion, the latter group constitute a definite part of the plasma membrane. This is not to suggest that the division into these two groups is absolute but it does constitute a working basis on which to consider these compounds. The former group of molecules comprise glycoproteins and proteoglycans/glycosaminoglycans, and their relationship to the cell surface has recently been reviewed by Yamada (1983). In the case of the second group, glycolipids are an important additional component.

'Glycoprotein' as a term has often been used to describe any macromolecule containing carbohydrate and protein, and as such would encompass molecules that are more properly defined as proteoglycans. For the purposes of this article the term glycoproteins will be used to describe those molecules in which, covalently at-tached to a protein backbone, there are one or more hetero-oligosaccharide chains. These chains are usually branched and can contain the neutral sugars D-galactose, D-mannose, L-fucose, the basic monosaccharides 2-amino-2-deoxy-D-glucose and 2-amino-2-deoxy-D-galactose (the basic residues are invariably N-acetylated), and the sialic acids. The latter are a family of nine-carbon sugars based on 5-amino-3,5-dideoxy-D-glycero-D-galacto-2-nonulosonic acid; the nomenclature of Blix, Gottschalk & Klenk (1957) in which the unsubstituted parent compound is re-ferred to as 'neuraminic acid', whilst sialic acid is used as a generic term for all the acylated neuraminic acids, will be used here, though other terminology has been proposed more recently (Scott, Yamashina & Jeanloz, 1982). Two major types of carbohydrate–peptide linkages occur in the glycoproteins, namely N- and O-glycosidically linked sequences and these structures are shown in more detail in Fig. 1.

In the proteoglycans there is a group of molecules in which carbohydrate is again covalently linked to protein, though the underlying pattern of a disaccharide repeating unit is quite different from that encountered with the 'glycoproteins'. These compounds are the only source of hexuronic acid in animals and may carry sulphate ester groups. The term 'glycosaminoglycan' refers purely to the poly-saccharide portion of the proteoglycans; the term 'mucopolysaccharide' is now obsolete.

In the case of the glycolipids in animal cells one is dealing with derivatives of long-chain bases related to sphingosine. The group of sphingolipids formed by attaching long-chain fatty acids via amide linkage to sphingosine are given the generic name of ceramides. Glycosphingolipids are those groups of molecules in which carbohydrate is attached via a glycosidic linkage to the terminal hydroxyl group of the ceramide residue and include the gangliosides, which contain sialic acids in their carbohydrate moieties.

EVIDENCE FOR CARBOHYDRATE AT THE CELL PERIPHERY

Electrokinetic studies

It is interesting that the classical models (Gorter & Grendel, 1925; Danielli & Davson, 1934) of plasma membranes, with their emphasis on the lipid nature of the structure, continued to influence an understanding of the chemical nature of the cell surface well into the 1960s. These models of membrane structure, which completely ignore the carbohydrates, were accepted as a basis for understanding the molecular nature of the cell surface, even though the work of Morgan & Watkins (Watkins & Morgan, 1952; Morgan & Watkins, 1959) in the 1950s had drawn attention to the carbohydrate nature of the blood-group substances. In 1952, Watkins & Morgan, in noting that simple sugars could neutralize the anti-H agglutinins in eel serum, suggested that such observations "can have practical significance"; even then they were careful to point out that the simple sugar "need not be even a constituent of the hapten or antigen but merely possess a close structural relationship to a component in these complexes". However, seven years later Morgan & Watkins (1959) were able to write that "the weight of evidence obtained from different laboratories and by

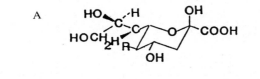

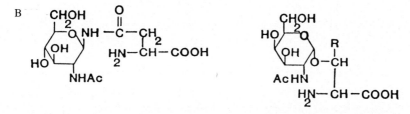

Fig. 1. A. Structure of the sialic acids (in the pyranose form as represented by Reeves). *N*-acetylneuraminic acid (R=CH$_3$CO.HN) and *N*-glycolylneuraminic acid (R= HO.CH$_2$CO HN) are trivial names accepted in biochemical and biological nomenclature; in the nomenclature of Blix *et al.* (1957) 'neuraminic acid' (R=H$_2$N) is the unsubstituted structure 5-amino-3,5-dideoxy-D-glycero-α-D-galacto-2-nonulopyranonic acid-^{1}C$_4$ whilst the various acylated derivatives (e.g. *N*-acetylneuraminic acid) are collectively known as the sialic acids. The carboxyl group of free *N*-acetyl neuraminic acid has a pK_α = 2·6 and it is this ionogenic group that is responsible for a significant proportion of the electrokinetic charge on animal cells. In sialylated materials the glycosidic linkage between the sialic acid residue and the partner sugar is in the α anomeric configuration; the hydrolysis of this bond being catalysed by neuraminidase. B. Structure of carbohydrate–protein linkages present in glycoproteins. On the left-hand side of the figure is 2-acetamido-*N*-(L-aspart-4-oyl)-2-deoxy-β-D-glucopyranosylamine. The asparagine residue, as part of an extended polypeptide chain, forms the point of attachment of what are classified as *N*-glycans. As regards *O*-glycans the linkage structure of this type most commonly found in higher organisms is depicted on the right-hand side of the figure; *N*-acetylgalactosaminyl serine (R=H)/threonine (R=CH$_3$). The sugar residues are depicted as 'Haworth formulae' and for convenience only the configuration of non-hydrogen substituents on the sugar rings are indicated.

different techniques therefore indicates that: (1) the specificity of the A, B, H and Le[a] substances resides in the carbohydrate portion of the mucopolysaccharide molecules". These authors (Morgan & Watkins, 1959) went on to point out that in the blood-group substances, "although it is the carbohydrate structures which determine specificity" the orientation of these structures necessary for full serological activity was brought about by their polypeptide moieties.

As the human erythrocyte has been used as the classic model in plasma membrane studies it is surprising that the results of immunochemistry had little impact on those of membrane biophysics. The answer to this apparent discrepancy probably lies in the fact that the biochemical studies at that time on blood-group substances were confined to tissue fluids and body secretions, in which the blood-group substances occur in water-soluble form. Certainly, as Morgan & Watkins (1959) pointed out, red blood cells are "the most obvious materials from which to attempt to isolate the blood-group substances", but they drew attention to the particular difficulties associated with solubilizing serologically active material from this source. This fact, coupled with the need to use mild methods of isolation and purification for obtaining biologically active material, indicates why biochemical studies in blood-group active materials largely ignored the erythrocyte and consequently probably accounts for the lack of impact of immunochemistry on membrane studies at that time.

The need to consider the role of carbohydrates at the cell surface received the necessary impetus from two sources, namely cell electrophoresis and, subsequently, microscopical observations. The electrophoresis of cells is a particularly valuable technique, as it enables one to study those molecules that are ionogenic or in which a charged group may be introduced by appropriate chemical modification, into the outer periphery of the cell, in a non-destructive manner. The electrophoresis of cells has been pursued actively for over 50 years, the method having been pioneered at the turn of the century, though it was only in the 1960s that this technique was fully exploited as regards the chemical nature of the cell surface. It is not intended to give here a detailed historical review of the electrokinetic studies performed on cells, but rather, to highlight those contributions that were instrumental in influencing scientific opinion towards considering carbohydrate at the cell surface. In particular, the red blood cell, so often the prototype in plasma membrane studies, received particular attention from this technique. All animal cells studied by the cell electrophoresis technique have been shown to possess a net negative surface charge, and in the case of the human red blood cell it had long been realized that this charge arises from strongly acidic groups (see Seaman, 1975, for a more detailed review). With the all-pervasive influence of the classical models of membrane structure, with their emphasis on the phospholipid nature of the plasmalemma, it is not surprising that this charge was ascribed to phosphate groups. Even the demonstration by Ponder in 1951 that, following the action of the proteolytic enzyme trypsin on the human erythrocyte the surface charge was lowered, corresponding to an approximately 30 % decrease in the net negative surface charge density, failed to have any impact on the view that biological surfaces were phospholipid in nature. Three years later, Pondman & Mastenbroek (1954), confirming Ponder's earlier observations, went so far as to suggest that trypsin was cleaving P—N bonds with a resultant loss of phospholipid from the red blood cell membrane. Re-examining the question in 1960 Seaman & Heard were unable to find any significant release of lipid-bound phosphate from the human erythrocyte by trypsin treatment and suggested that the changes in the electrokinetic properties of the cell could be explained in two ways, either by the fission of peptide bonds and a general "structural loosening up" without any loss of material from the cell membrane or, alternatively, fission resulting in the direct loss of carboxyl groups associated with amino acid elements in a polypeptide chain, or phosphate or sulphate groups from a protein–phospholipid or protein–carbohydrate complex. This explanation was a significant attempt to explain the electrokinetic phenomena on the basis of the known properties of trypsin without being completely dominated by the classical membrane models.

Following the above work, Cook, Heard & Seaman (1960) examined the tryptic degradation products released from the intact, saline-washed, human erythrocyte. Using paper chromatography they were able to demonstrate that the decrease in the electrophoretic mobility of the erythrocytes, following trypsin treatment, was accompanied by the release of a sialoglycopeptide into the medium. These analytical results enabled the authors to provide an explanation of the specific action of trypsin on intact cells as opposed to stroma. However, more importantly, as the authors (Cook *et al.* 1960) had made concomitant electrokinetic measurements, it enabled, for the first time, a sialic-acid-containing moiety to be localized at the periphery of a cell. This work was rapidly followed by a detailed description of the action of the specific glycosidase, neuraminidase, on the electrokinetic properties of the human erythrocyte (Cook, Heard & Seaman, 1961) and a wide range of erythrocytes from different animals (Eylar, Madoff, Brody & Oncley, 1962), which conclusively demonstrated that the carboxyl group of sialic acids is a dominant charge-determining species at the surface of the red cell. It was shown that, following neuraminidase treatment, the much reduced electrophoretic mobility was a result of the release of free sialic acids and not of the generation of any significant number of cationic groups. Similar experiments followed in rapid succession with a variety of other cell types, so that by the end of the decade it had become clear that sialic acids are to varying degrees ubiquitous components of the surfaces of animal cells, and consequently the species bearing these residues (glycoproteins and possibly glycolipids) must be taken into account in any complete model of the plasma membrane.

Twenty-five years on, the decision to test the effect of neuraminidase on the electrokinetic properties of cells seems not only entirely logical, in view of the results obtained with trypsin, but a relatively easy step to take; the latter viewpoint, if indeed it is held, completely belies the facts. At the time that these experiments were in progress both purified neuraminidase and authentic sialic acid samples were not readily available commercially and a sensitive method for the estimation of sialic acids only became available in 1959 (Warren); indeed the structure of these materials had only recently been elucidated (see Ledeen & Yu, 1976, for a review). Work on the purification of neuraminidase, particularly from *Vibrio cholerae*, had received attention from Ada & French (1959), who were conscious of the increasing interest in the biological and chemical properties of compounds containing *N*-acetyl neuraminic acid and who made samples available to Cook *et al.* (1961). Earlier, Gottschalk (1957) had investigated what was then termed receptor destroying enzyme (RDE) and had shown that the terminal neuraminic acid "in its mono or diacetyl form" was split off the well-defined substrate neuramin–lactose. Gottschalk (1957), from this work, proposed the term neuraminidase and defined its action "as the hydrolytic cleavage of the glycosidic bond joining the keto group of neuraminic acid to D-galactose or D-galactosamine and possibly to other sugars". The effect of RDE on the ability of erythrocytes to adsorb haemoglobin had been investigated in the same year by Piper (1957), who had suggested that enzymes split off relatively strongly acid anionic groups, which determine the electrophoretic pattern of normal erythrocytes. Working with stroma, as opposed to intact erythrocytes, Klenk and his colleagues (Klenk & Lempfrid, 1957; Klenk & Uhlenbruck, 1958) had found that RDE liberates acylated neuraminic acids from a number of mammalian species. These latter studies no doubt led Klenk (1958) to make the suggestion that one may assume that the negative charge of the erythrocyte is due to an acylated neuraminic acid. However, even at this stage Klenk's suggestion was largely hypothetical, no direct measurements having been made to test this supposition. Indeed, investigators who would have been in a position to test experimentally the relationship of sialic acids to surface charge were firmly of the view that the negative charge of the erythrocyte arose from phosphate groups of phospholipids. That Bateman, Zellner, Davis & McCaffrey (1956) had previously suggested the decrease in the electrophoretic mobility of erythrocytes treated with the PR8 strain of influenza virus was caused by the appearance of cationic groups no doubt further complicated the picture, as did Curtain's (1953) studies on a urinary mucoprotein inhibitor of viral haemagglutination. In these latter studies Curtain (1953) showed that following the treatment of this inhibitor with RDE it possessed cationic groups of about pK11. Throughout the 1950s the idea that the surface charge on cells was due to groups other than the phosphate groups of phospholipids met with little enthusiasm and the central importance of lipids remained firmly entrenched.

Microscopic demonstration of cell surface carbohydrates

At the time that electrokinetic studies on intact cells were revealing the presence of sialic acid-containing materials at the surfaces of an increasing variety of cell types, concomitant histochemical studies, at the level of both the light and the electron microscope, did much to confirm the ubiquitous presence of carbohydrate at the cell periphery. A burgeoning body of histochemical data on surface carbohydrates had its beginning in the 1960s, initially with the application of the periodic acid–Schiff (PAS) reaction to the study of the cell surface. It would be inappropriate to review here all the many contributions to this important aspect of the subject but rather attention will be focused on those papers that have made a particular impact on our understanding of the structural organization of plasma membrane. For those requiring detailed information on the development of the study of the histochemical aspects of surface carbohydrates, the reviews of Martinez-Palomo (1970) and

Rambourg (1971) would be especially useful. The mechanism of PAS staining had been investigated earlier by Leblond and his colleagues (Leblond, Glegg & Eidinger, 1957), who stressed that once glycogen had been removed from the specimen, by treatment with amylase, the technique is specific for carbohydrate–protein complexes.

As pointed out by Rambourg & Leblond (1967) "In 1962, Gasic provided the first direct histochemical evidence of a carbohydrate-rich layer at the surface of some mammalian cells". Gasic & Gasic (1962*a*) examining in ascitic tumour cells the chemical nature and formation of what they referred to as "cell coating" showed that it was PAS-positive and susceptible to digestion with proteolytic enzymes. In addition, Gasic & Gasic (1962*a*,*b*) suggested that the Hale stain, introduced in 1946 for acid mucopolysaccharides, was particularly appropriate as a method for detecting sialic acids at the cell surface and quickly adapted this method for use with the electron microscope (Gasic & Berwick, 1963). It is perhaps a pity that Gasic's laboratory did not examine a wider range of cell types for, as Rambourg & Leblond (1967) suggest, "because his work was chiefly done with ascites tumour cells, the opinion arose that surface carbohydrates are a feature of malignant cells". This is another illustration of how the entrenched view that membranes were largely lipid in nature had such a lasting effect on our understanding of the biochemical composition of the cell surface. When evidence in favour of surface carbohydrate emerged it is easy to understand how the contemporary prejudice would have been to regard it as a specific feature of malignant cells. Indeed, as pointed out subsequently (Rambourg & Leblond, 1967) "this opinion persisted in spite of a few dissenting voices, such as that of Kalckar (1965) who thought that carbohydrates may be 'as abundant, if not more so, in normal cells' as in tumor cells".

Cationic colloids have also been used to visualize sialic acid residues and a particularly important advance in our understanding of membrane structure stemmed from the application of this methodology, and was published in the second volume of this Journal by Benedetti & Emmelot (1967) (Fig. 2). These authors used colloidal iron hydroxide (CIH) at pH 1·7 to study the ultrastructural localization of sialic acid residues in plasma membranes isolated from rat liver and transplanted rat hepatoma. They showed that CIH-reactive neuraminidase-sensitive groups were always asymmetrically distributed in the membranes studied. Because Benedetti & Emmelot (1967) had used membrane preparations in which the junctional complexes were preserved they were able easily to distinguish the outer surface from the cytoplasmic side of the plasmalemma and were able to make the very important observation that sialic acid was exclusively located in the outer leaflet of the plasma membrane. Four years later this aspect of the subject was extended by the introduction of ferritin-labelled lectins, by Nicolson & Singer (1971), as reagents for studying the distribution of sugar residues within membranes. Nicolson & Singer (1971) examined double membrane thick erythrocyte ghosts spread flat on carbon–colloidin-coated grids. In such preparations the upper membrane is occasionally broken and folded back, revealing the inner surface of the lower membrane. Using ferritin-labelled concanavalin A (ConA), these authors demonstrated that the

G. M. W. Cook

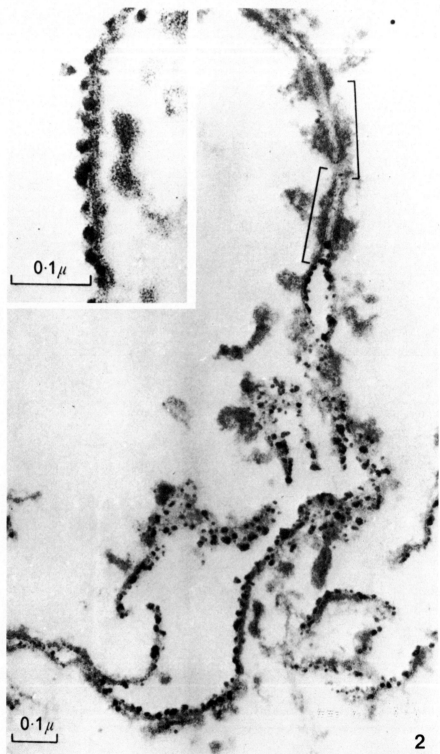

0.1 μ

0.1 μ

2

conjugate binds specifically to the outer surface but not the inner surface of the erythrocyte plasma membrane. Acknowledging that earlier electrokinetic studies, coupled with the work of Benedetti & Emmelot (1967), pointed to the essentially exclusive location of sialic acids at the outer surface of the cell membrane, the work of Nicolson & Singer (1971) had the advantage of extending localization studies to other sugar residues, though for differentiating between outer and inner surfaces of the membrane they had to rely on differential adsorbancies of their micrographs. The fact that the asymmetric distribution of saccharides was a feature of plasma membranes of cells in general, rather than the erythrocyte in particular, was further strengthened by the work of Hirano *et al.* (1972), who extended the use of ferritin-labelled lectins with their specificity for particular saccharides (conjugates of ConA and *Ricinus communis* agglutinin were used) to membrane fragments from a myeloma cell homogenate. Confirming that saccharide residues are uniformly localized to a single surface of each membrane fragment, Hirano *et al.* (1972) stated that the asymmetric distribution of saccharide residues previously found for the plasma membrane holds for the rough endoplasmic reticulum membranes and probably other intracellular smooth membranes as well. The latter was impossible to ascertain unambiguously as some suitable ultrastructural marker would have to be used, and unlike Benedetti & Emmelot (1967) these authors (Hirano *et al.* 1972) were faced with a subcellular fraction markedly enriched in rough membrane elements but containing some smooth-membrane fragments and vesicles. However, with the first of these structures it was possible to show that ferritin–ConA bound exclusively to the internal side of membrane fragments of the rough endoplasmic reticulum.

A particularly interesting and important aspect of the paper by Hirano *et al.* (1972) was their consideration of the implications of the ultrastructural localization of saccharides as regards understanding the biogenesis of membranes. In essence, they suggested that an intracellular membrane 'assembly line' exists that leads penultimately to the formation of precursor vesicles, with oligosaccharides exclusively localized at the inner surface of the vesicle membrane. These vesicles are then considered to fuse with previously existing plasma membrane, thereby accounting for the exclusive localization of sugars at the outer surface of the plasma membrane. Drawing on studies performed on the biosynthesis of glycoproteins in various laboratories (see section on Biosynthesis of Surface Carbohydrates, for details), Hirano *et al.* (1972) pictured the initial sugar residues as being incorporated in the rough endoplasmic reticulum, with additional residues being added in the smooth-membrane elements, probably in the Golgi zone, leading to the formation of the precursor vesicle. This scheme has undoubtedly had a profound influence on thinking as regards the biogenesis of membrane heterosaccharides and, though

Fig. 2. This figure, originally published in the Journal by Benedetti & Emmelot (1967) shows isolated rat-liver plasma membranes stained with colloidal iron hydroxide. Note that the electron-dense granules are restricted to the outer leaflet of the membranes (insert). Junctional complexes (brackets) are not stained. The figure is republished by kind permission of Dr E. L. Benedetti.

subject to modifications of detail, it continues to dominate this area of research activity.

No précis of the key contributions of histochemistry to the acceptance of carbo-hydrate as an important constituent of cell surfaces would be complete without reference to the work of Leblond and his colleagues. Rambourg, Neutra & Leblond (1966), working with the PAS and colloidal iron–Prussian blue techniques, surveyed in the light microscope some 50 different cell types from the rat and concluded "not only that the presence of a 'cell coat' is a common feature of vertebrate cells, but also that this coat is rich in carbohydrates". This deduction was rapidly confirmed by Rambourg & Leblond (1967), who extended their studies to the level of the electron microscope and went on to suggest that "a 'cell coat' exists at the surface of most, if not all, cells" and that it contains carbohydrates that "may play a role in holding cells together and in controlling the interactions between cells and environment".

Lectins and cell surfaces

Certainly one of the major growth areas in the study of cell surface carbohydrates has been the use of plant agglutinins, lectins; as will be apparent in the concluding sections of this article, attention has now moved beyond the plant lectins to the endogenous carbohydrate-binding proteins of animal cells.

Though lectins have been known since the turn of the century, the contemporary interest in these materials as regards the study of cell surfaces can be traced to the work of Aub, Tieslau & Lankester (1963). These authors, who were interested in using enzymes to identify alterations that occur in cell surfaces during neoplasia, described an impurity in a wheat germ lipase preparation that acted as a preferential agglutinin for tumour cells. Aub *et al.* (1963) showed that the cell agglutinating and lipolytic activities appeared to be separable and suggested that they might be dealing with a plant agglutinin, though they were unable to find precedents in the literature for such a molecule with a specific reactivity towards tumour cells. No doubt the apparent specificity for tumour cell surfaces was the key factor in stimulating a renewed interest in the plant agglutinins. Interestingly, two years previously, Ambrose, Dudgeon, Easty & Easty (1961), studying the action of a number of different enzyme preparations on the adhesiveness of ascites tumour cells to glass, had shown that of the various enzymes tested wheat germ lipase was the only enzyme preparation to show a selective action on tumour cells. In view of the dominant interest at that time in lipids in membrane structure it is not surprising that Ambrose *et al.* (1961) interpreted their results as showing that the altered surface properties of tumour cells are associated with an altered lipid structure of the cell membrane. However, Aub *et al.* (1963) were aware of the contemporary histochemical studies that "implicated mucopolysaccharides in cellular interactions and adhesions" and hoped that their finding would help in understanding the changes in cell membranes taking place during neoplasia. The proof that a lectin was indeed involved came in 1967, when Burger & Goldberg isolated and characterized the agglutinin in wheat germ lipase as a glycoprotein that interacted with surface sites containing N-acetylglucosamine. Since then work on the plant lectins has increased astronomically for, though there appears to be no simple relationship between malignant trans-formation and lectin-mediated agglutinability, these agglutinins have found use as cell mitogens, probes for glycoconjugate structure, in the investigation of membrane dynamics and asymmetry as well as for glycoconjugate, cell and virus purifications. Without these tools the study of surface carbohydrates would not have advanced to the extent that it has today. Certainly, the work accomplished with these materials is well beyond the scope of this present article and the reader wishing to delve further into the subject would be well advised to consult one of the classic reviews, such as that by Nicolson (1974) or one of the more recent papers on lectins, such as that by Lis & Sharon (1984).

BIOSYNTHESIS OF SURFACE CARBOHYDRATES

At the time that electrokinetic and histochemical studies were demonstrating that carbohydrates are present at the cell surface attention was beginning to be directed to the question of how and where the cell synthesizes these structures. The question that this article will address is how far has the study of surface carbohydrates progressed? In answer one should observe that, historically, work on the biosynthesis of membrane glycoproteins and glycolipids can really be divided into two main periods of activity: starting in 1965 a number of investigators approached the problem by following the incorporation of ^{14}C-labelled sugars and amino sugars into cell particulates; and this was rapidly followed by elegant autoradiographic studies, which identified the initial cellular site of incorporation of the various mono-saccharide precursors. All of this work clearly demonstrated the importance of the Golgi apparatus in the glycosylation process. The second period of activity started with the demonstration by Caccam, Jackson & Eylar (1969) that [1-^{14}C]mannose incubated with various mammalian tissues is incorporated into a lipid having the characteristics of a mannosyl-1-phosphoryl polyisoprenoid compound, reminiscent of the type of compound shown to be involved in the biosynthesis of bacterial cell walls. Since then an enormous amount of work has been directed towards lipid intermediates in the biosynthesis of N-glycosidically linked sugar moieties, as a result of which the biochemistry of the synthesis of these structures is known in considerable detail.

Throughout the study of surface glycoproteins it has been tacitly accepted that the polypeptide chains of these molecules are synthesized in an identical manner to the non-glycosylated proteins. As a number of the early electrokinetic (Cook, Heard & Seaman, 1962; Wallach & Eylar, 1961) and histochemical studies (Gasic & Gasic, 1962a,b) were performed with ascites tumour cells, it is not surprising that these cells were used in the initial studies of the incorporation of radioactive sugars. Initially it was shown that inhibitors of protein synthesis have a much more marked effect on the synthesis of the polypeptide component of plasma membranes than on the carbohydrate portion (Cook, Laico & Eylar, 1965; Molnar, Lutes & Winzler, 1965), suggesting that there is a pool of protein precursors that need only glycosylation for completion and incorporation into the membrane. In an attempt to amplify information gained from studies on whole cells, especially with regard to the site of synthesis of the oligosaccharide units of membrane glycoproteins, Eylar & Cook (1965) returned to the Ehrlich ascites carcinoma cell to develop the first cell-free system for the study of a glycoprotein. Eylar & Cook (1965) were able to demonstrate that the enzymes responsible for incorporating glucosamine and galactose (the latter sugar was shown to be incorporated from UDP-galactose) into soluble and membrane glycoproteins were present in a smooth membrane fraction obtained from the post-microsomal supernatant fluid; this fraction was inactive as regards protein synthesis. As expected, membranes bearing ribosomes actively supported protein synthesis but were found to be inactive in the synthesis of oligosaccharides. Eylar & Cook (1965) made the suggestion that the smooth membranes active in mediating glycosylation in their cell-free system were derived from the Golgi apparatus and considered that this suggestion was entirely plausible, particularly as it has been suggested from cytochemical evidence that the Golgi apparatus is a site of surface glycoprotein synthesis (Gasic & Gasic, 1963). It is a pity that the French pressure cell, the method used by Eylar & Cook (1965) for producing the cellular homogenate, destroyed the morphology of the Golgi apparatus. The first reports on the isolation of the Golgi apparatus from animal cells were not to appear for another four or five years and then success was confined mainly to mammalian sources such as liver, fractions enriched in Golgi apparatus being notoriously difficult to isolate from transformed cells (see Cook, 1982; Morré & Creek, 1982, for discussion of this problem).

Further progress in our understanding of the way in which cells synthesize glycoproteins came with the autoradiographic studies of Neutra & Leblond (1966) on the synthesis of the carbohydrate of mucus by the goblet cells of rats. Killing animals at various times up to 20 min, following the administration of [3H]glucose, they were able to show that the vast majority of autoradiographic grains were localized over the Golgi region. Further work by Leblond and his colleagues (Whur, Herscovics & Leblond, 1969), on the radioautographic visualization of the incorporation of [3H]galactose and [3H]mannose in relation to the synthesis of thyroglobulin by rat thyroid epithelial cells, demonstrated that the addition of core sugars ([3H]mannose) to the peptide takes place in the rough endoplasmic reticulum; the precursors then migrate to the Golgi apparatus where the addition of terminal sugars ([3H]galactose) is effected. While these studies were aimed at soluble glycoproteins it is clear, from the use of L-[3H]fucose by Bennett, Leblond & Haddad (1974) with a wide range of cell types from the rat, that the Golgi saccules are the site of incorporation of terminal sugars destined for the cell surface.

The role of the Golgi apparatus in the cell has been reviewed by a number of investigators, and in particular, more recently by Farquhar & Palade (1981) and Dauwalder (1984), and they give considerably more detail on the importance of the Golgi apparatus in the glycosylation of glycoproteins (and of glycolipids) than is possible or appropriate here. However, both these groups of reviewers draw attention to the fluctuating status of the Golgi apparatus as a *bona fide* cell organelle, a point that is relevant to this present article, which attempts to review the major lines of enquiry that have led to our present understanding of surface carbohydrates. Farquhar & Palade (1981) split the study of the Golgi apparatus historically into four main periods; the Light microscope era (before 1854), the Renaissance (1954–1963), The Modern Period (1964–1973) and the Current Period (1973 to the Present). The 'Modern Period' was characterized by the application of such techniques as autoradiography and the development of procedures for isolating Golgi fractions by Morré & Mollenhauer (1964), Fleischer, Fleischer & Ozawa (1969), Morré, Merlin & Keenan (1969) and Schachter *et al.* (1970), the latter being particularly important in providing detailed biochemical evidence for the involvement of Golgi membranes in the addition of terminal hexose residues to glycoproteins. No doubt the arrival of this Modern Period in the study of the Golgi apparatus came at an opportune moment from the standpoint of establishing carbohydrates as components of the cell periphery.

The addition of sugar to the appropriate acceptor is catalysed by the glycosyl-transferases, a group of enzymes that utilize sugar nucleotides as donor molecules (see Leloir, 1964). Until 1970 it was considered that all carbohydrate units of glycoproteins were synthesized by the direct transfer of monosaccharide from sugar nucleotide to the appropriate amino acid residue in the polypeptide chain, or saccharide residue in the growing oligosaccharide. This view was radically changed as regard *N*-glycosides, by the demonstration that lipid-linked sugars are important intermediates in their biosynthesis. Reference has been made to the contribution in this regard made by Eylar's laboratory (Caccam *et al.* 1969); this group rather surprisingly did not follow up their original observations and many reviewers of this subject have perhaps not surprisingly failed to cite their contribution. Undoubtedly, Leloir's laboratory (see Behrens & Leloir, 1970) did much to establish the importance of saccharide–lipids in the synthesis of glycoproteins, and this area of research (reviewed by Struck & Lennarz, 1980) has received considerable attention from the laboratories of Jeanloz, Kornfeld, Lennarz, Robbins and Spiro; so active has interest been in this field that one commentary (Sharon & Lis, 1981) has described this topic as "perhaps the single most crowded area in glycoprotein research". As a result of all this effort it is now known that a major structure, $(Glc)_3$ $(Man)_9$ $(GlcNAc)_2$ attached to dolichol pyrophosphate, is the direct precursor of *N*-glycans, and that this oligosaccharide is transferred *en bloc* to asparagine residues in the polypeptide acceptor. It is also known that after transfer to polypeptide the complete oligosaccharide undergoes modification *via* a complex series of reactions known as 'processing', which converts the glycosylated high-mannose structure to the complex oligosaccharides found on a number of mature glycoproteins. The details of processing go beyond the scope of this article. However, it is relevant to point out that a group of drugs that can inhibit processing are finding use as new tools in an effort to understand more of the biological role of glycoproteins (see Schwarz & Datema, 1984). Certainly, enormous advances in our understanding of the biosynthesis of *N*-glycosides have taken place over the last 15 years, almost to the point that *O*-glycosidically linked carbohydrate groups have been ignored.

THE FUNCTIONAL SIGNIFICANCE OF SURFACE CARBOHYDRATES

For well over a hundred years it has been recognized that the plasma membrane of the cell acts as a permeability barrier. Armed with a presumed knowledge of the function of this organelle, investigators have then proceeded to elucidate the molecular structure and biosynthesis of biological membranes. However, in the case of the surface carbohydrates this sequence of events has been reversed. Since the early 1960s, when the need to consider carbohydrates as constituents of plasma membranes became apparent, an enormous body of information has been built up on the localization and biosynthesis of surface heterosaccharides, together with an increasing amount on the structure of these materials (see Kobata, 1984). All of this information has been gained without our understanding why carbohydrates are ubiquitous components of the surfaces of animal cells. This is not to suggest that attempts have not been made to determine the function of surface sugars, but rather that the state of knowledge in this area is disproportionately less than in the structural and biosynthesis aspects of the subject, and that what evidence is available on function is often circumstantial. Indeed surface heterosaccharides are very much molecules 'in search of a function'.

Certainly glycosylation is an expensive enterprise from the cell's point of view, requiring a large amount of genetic information, the synthesis of several enzymes and cofactors, as well as intermediates. No doubt much of the motivation for the work on biosynthesis and structure has rested on the view that every structure in nature has a function or otherwise it would not have persisted throughout evolution, and that in due course the function would be elucidated: indeed important clues regarding function would be likely to come from a fuller understanding of structure and biosynthesis. The problem of the functional aspects of surface carbohydrates is likely to remain as the major challenge over the next 20 years to investigators committed to the study of surface carbohydrates. Before speculating on how this work will develop it seems appropriate to highlight what progress has been made to date on the relationship of carbohydrates to recognition.

For those people studying the role of carbohydrates at the cell surface there is a working hypothesis that heterosaccharides serve as important recognition markers at the cell periphery and as such may be an essential component of the mechanisms by which cells recognize other cells and large ligands. When talking of recognition phenomena there is still a strong prejudice towards thinking only in terms of proteins, even though the classical work of Kabat (1985) has shown that pure polysaccharides are able to elicit immunological recognition and it is well established that sugars are specific determinants of blood group activity. The classical blood group determinants illustrate well the dual molecular nature of carbohydrate receptors at the cell surface: these determinants may be present as glycoproteins or glycolipids or both, clearly demonstrating the importance of the carbohydrate in providing the recognition marker. The view that heterosaccharides at the cell periphery serve a recognition function is not just based upon their advantageous location at the cell surface, with their carbohydrate groups directed entirely at the external environment, but upon the enormous potential for structural diversity possible in these compounds, which makes them ideal candidates for carrying biological information. With polypeptides and oligonucleotides information content is confined to the number of different monomeric units present and the sequence in which these are arranged. In the carbohydrate groups of heterosaccharides not only is it possible for structural diversity to be generated on the basis of the number of different monosaccharides present and their sequence, but also by the anomeric configuration of the glycosidic linkage and the ability to form branched structures. As a consequence of these structural features oligosaccharides have the potential for carrying more information per weight than proteins and nucleic acids. This latter point may be illustrated by a simple example: with three different monosaccharides it is theoretically possible to construct 1056 different trisaccharides, though with three different amino acids only six tripeptides are possible. Clamp (cited by Sharon, 1974) has made some interesting calculations for a typical carbohydrate group: assuming a composition of three residues each of mannose, N-acetylglucosamine and sialic acid all linked to a single N-acetylglucosamine, Clamp has estimated a figure of 10^{24} possible binding arrangements. Even with the known restraints of sequence it is still possible to form 6×10^6 isomeric forms.

One of the earliest studies on the function of surface heterosaccharides was the work of Gesner & Ginsburg (1964) on the effect of glycosidases on the fate of transfused lymphocytes. They suggested that the integrity of the sugars on lymphocytes is necessary for the cells to traverse their unique route through the body, by acting as sites recognized by complementary structures on the surface of endothelial cells in the post-capillary vessels of lymphoid tissue. This paper is not only interesting as an example of an early attempt to assign a physiological function to surface carbohydrate, but because the authors (Gesner & Ginsburg, 1964) draw attention to the general absence of glucose residues in surface heterosaccharides and argue that the efficiency of a recognition surface based on D-glucosyl residues would be impaired by free D-glucose, in the same way that haptens interfere with antigen–antibody interactions. Gesner & Ginsberg (1964) suggested that evolutionary selection against this impairment, however slight, would tend to eliminate D-glucose as a component of cell surfaces.

Over the last two decades a substantial body of information has been built up from studies on the mating of yeast, fertilization, non-immune phagocytosis and cell differentiation, all of which point to cell surface carbohydrates playing a role in intercellular adhesion. However, the evidence for the role of sugars in adhesive recognition in these systems is at the best circumstantial. A well-defined role for carbohydrate in recognition phenomena has, however, come from a different approach. The first definitive evidence of a role for carbohydrate in recognition phenomena came from studies by Morell *et al.* (1968) on the disappearance of asialoceruloplasmin from the circulatory system of the rabbit. Previously, Morell, Van Den Hamer, Scheinberg & Ashwell (1966) had prepared a radioactive form of ceruloplasmin, to probe the role of this glycoprotein in the regulation of copper metabolism. By removing terminal sialic acid residues from ceruloplasmin with neuraminidase and treating the exposed galactosyl residues with galactose oxidase it was possible to introduce a tritium atom into the galactose residue, by reducing the resulting aldehyde with tritiated borohydride. As the half-life of ceruloplasmin in rabbits is several hours, Morrell *et al.* (1968) were surprised to find that the asialoproduct disappeared from the circulation in minutes. The unique role of the terminal galactosyl residues in this phenomenon was demonstrated by the removal of these residues by treatment with β-galactosidase or their modification by galactose oxidase. It appears that the exposed galactosyl residues of a number of glycoproteins are recognized by the liver cells, which rapidly take up and catabolize asialglyco-proteins. The hepatic receptor for galactose-terminated glycoproteins has been purified (Hudgin *et al.* 1974) and characterized (Kawasaki & Ashwell, 1976). Since then a number of clearance systems in which carbohydrates other than galactose act as recognition determinants have been identified and a comprehensive review published by Neufeld & Ashwell (1980). In this context mannose 6-phosphate, the 'common recognition marker' of lysosomal enzymes, deserves particular mention as an important finding in this field. Although the mannose 6-phosphate recognition marker on these enzymes owes its discovery to the fact that fibroblasts express an uptake (pinocytosis) receptor for this determinant on their cell surface, it is now known that the major function of this marker is to provide an intracellular transport system for the specific delivery of enzymes to lysosomes (see Sly, 1982). Clearly, the case for considering the role of carbohydrate in biological recognition phenomena is well founded, though the extent to which such recognition is generally operative at the cell surface is still open to question and likely to be an outstanding problem for the next few years.

If carbohydrate is providing the cell periphery with recognition properties, then molecules capable of recognizing such structures should also be present at cell surfaces. Much attention has been given to this subject and one proposal made by Roseman (1970), that ectoglycosyltransferases are involved, has generated consider-able debate: proponents of the idea (Shur & Roth, 1975) and arguments against it (Keenan & Morré, 1975) have stimulated much experimentation. Briefly, Roseman (1970) proposed that glycosyltransferases present at the cell surface (ectoglycosyl-transferases) recognizing appropriate sugar residues on an apposing cell could, as a consequence of the formation of an enzyme–substrate complex, result in intercellular adhesion. Should the appropriate sugar donor become available then transglycosyl-ation would take place, together with dissociation of the enzyme–substrate complex, providing a ready explanation of mutable cell–cell adhesions. The development of this idea and its degree of acceptability by the scientific community have perhaps been best summed up by Ivatt (1984), who pointed out that the argument has shifted from, "Are they really on the outer surface of intact, healthy cells?" to "Are they really active when on the outside of cells?", and then finally to, "So they are out-side and potentially active but is there any functional importance to them?". This change in attitude has depended on proponents of the hypothesis demonstrating that glycosylation is not the result of acceptor being internalized or of broken cells being a source of accessible enzyme. In addition, it has been necessary to control for radiolabelled sugar released by hydrolysis of sugar nucleotide and internalized. Certainly, with the known dynamic properties of membranes and the inter-relationship between Golgi membranes and cell surfaces, the demonstration that ectoglycosyltransferases exist is not surprising, though the idea that they represent a general mechanism for the recognition of surface sugars is perhaps not one that would find wide acceptance, though it remains an option for specific cases.

As an alternative to considering ectoglycosyltransferases as candidates for the recognition of surface carbohydrates, attention has been turning to the non-immune and enzymically inactive carbohydrate-binding proteins, the lectins. The subject has been reviewed in detail by Barondes (1981) and an increasing number of lectins associated with cells is being described. Sharon (1984) has summarized evidence from various laboratories that carbohydrate–lectin interactions serve as the molecular basis for recognition in non-immune phagocytosis. No doubt studies on animal lectins will continue to receive increasing attention and in the next 20 years we should be in a position to ascertain whether lectin–carbohydrate interactions play a pivotal role in cellular interactions. In view of the diversity of structure possible in the carbohydrate moieties of surface glycoconjugates, the range of lectins detected is perhaps disproportionately low if, indeed, the recognition of surface carbohydrate is *via* a lectin-mediated mechanism. As inevitably the presence of lectins is determined by haemagglutination assay one may be artificially limiting the number detected by the cell used in these assays. In a re-evaluation of the function of the carbohydrate moieties of glycoproteins, Olden, Parent & White (1982) pointed out that an important lesson has been learned from the work on the mannose 6-phosphate binding lectin and lysosomal enzyme localization: the identification of an efficient lectin-mediated uptake of glycoconjugates at the cell surface does not necessarily mean that the primary function of the lectin within the cell is at the cell periphery. These authors (Olden *et al.* 1982) have presented a model for carbohydrates having a more general localization function than just being restricted to lysosomal enzymes. Their model envisages the oligosaccharide moiety functioning as a 'sorting signal', which specifies where glycoproteins will travel in the cell; the mechanism of interpreting the sorting signal would depend upon an array of membrane-bound lectins with different sugar specificities. These lectins, available within the lumen of the internal membrane system, would then bind and concentrate glycoproteins with the appropriate carbohydrate moiety into discrete membrane areas, which bud off to form vesicles. In their model, Olden *et al.* (1982) do not envisage the 'language' that specifies the route that the vesicles will traverse as depending on carbohydrates or lectins but rather on cytoskeletal components. Certainly, a number of the lectins currently being implicated in cell–cell interaction phenomena are present in sizeable quantities within the cell and this is in accord with the suggestions of Olden *et al.* (1982). The next 20 years should resolve whether animal lectins have a primary function either within the cell or at the cell surface as part of a recognition system, or whether they have a dual function.

PROSPECTS

Undoubtedly, the next two decades will continue to produce considerable methodological advances in the study of surface carbohydrates, for example high-resolution proton nuclear magnetic resonance is already being used to give important information on anomeric configuration and position of linkages in oligosaccharides. However, the central problem of the biological function of surface sugars will remain and must present the major challenge to those working in this area of cell biology. In an effort to try and predict how the field will develop it is probably instructive to look at those systems that are being studied at the moment from the standpoint of the biological functions of carbohydrates.

One approach to understanding carbohydrate function is to produce cell lines resistant to various lectins (see Stanley (1980) for a comprehensive review) and to see if such glycosylation-deficient mutants bearing alterations on surface oligosaccharide structures can be correlated with alterations in cellular properties. Hughes and his colleagues (see Edwards, Dysart & Hughes, 1976) have used this approach effectively in the study of cellular adhesion, and no doubt such systems will continue to be particularly important in the study of cell–cell adhesions.

One of the early attempts to correlate carbohydrate structure with recognition phenomena in cellular interactions was the work of Gesner & Ginsburg (1964) on lymphocyte homing; they observed a transient sequestration of lymphocytes in the liver after neuraminidase treatment. In a recent review of new directions in research, Hooghe & Pink (1985) have come back to this phenomenon as having important ramifications for the development of ideas on the homing of normal and, indeed, neoplastic cells. Pointing out that the phenomena described by Gesner & Ginsburg (1964) may be explained by the removal of sialic acid from the lymphocyte surface generating terminal galactosyl residues, which probably interacted with the liver galactose receptor described by Morell, Ashwell and their colleagues (see Morell *et al.* 1968), Hooghe & Pink (1985) suggest that hyper-sialylation as has been reported for some tumour cells (see the pioneering studies of Warren, Fuhrer & Buck, 1972) will have the opposite effect and prevent their removal and destruction. Certainly, there is good evidence that the increased sialylation of surface glycoconjugates may confer resistance to NK-mediated lysis of tumour cells (Yogeeswaran *et al.* 1981; Young *et al.* 1981), though whether this is as a consequence of electrostatic repulsion by sialic acid-bearing molecules close to the binding site or modification of the binding site itself is a matter requiring further investigation. These reviewers (Hooghe & Pink, 1985) point out that the elucidation of the molecular biology of lymphocyte homing has greatly benefited from the introduction of an *in vitro* test for measuring the interaction between lymphocytes and post-capillary high endothelium venules, the site of lymphocyte exit from the blood stream. This test has been particularly useful for showing that not any lymphocyte binds to every high endothelium venule and that some lymphoma cells bind preferentially to Peyer's patch high endothelium venules, whilst others adhere to the high endothelium venule from lymph nodes (Gallatin, Weissman & Butcher, 1983). A glycoprotein has been isolated from rat lymph that blocks the interaction between lymphocytes and high endothelium venules (Chin *et al.* 1983); this material is much more abundant on those lymphocytes that bind to high endothelium vesicles than on thymocytes, which do not bind. A different high endothelial adhesion glycoprotein has been described on lymphocytes migrating to Peyer's patches (Chin, Rasmussen, Cakiroglu & Woodruff, 1984). Citing this and other relevant studies, Hooghe & Pink (1985) are of the view that there is evidence supporting a role in homing and recirculation for membrane glycoproteins and, or, glycolipids, and that the study of the homing of normal or neoplastic cells, involving as it does the exit from one tissue, movement in extracellular spaces and arrest at another site, "is only beginning". How quickly this type of study will develop is difficult to ascertain for, as Smets & Van Beek (1984) point out, "today oncogenes clearly dominate the scene of fundamental cancer research" though they stress that, "it is evident that changes at the genetic level must become expressed in cellular sites and organelles crucial to the control of normal proliferation and cell behaviour", and in this respect the cell surface and surface carbohydrates are of particular interest. Stressing that, "the most urgent task now is to provide direct proof that a specific alteration in a single class of membrane glycoproteins is directly responsible for a characteristic biological response", Smets & Van Beek (1984) suggested that there is an urgent need for compounds that can modulate protein glycosylation to yield normal and neoplastic phenotypes with minimal side-effects. They suggest that molecular biology may make this attainable; the genes for putatively involved glycosytransferases could be cloned and transferred to normal cells whilst assumed regulator genes could be introduced into neoplastic cells to see if cancer-related glycosylation changes result from altered control on the editing of normal genetic information.

In many respects cancer cells resemble undifferentiated, rapidly growing cells. No doubt much of the interest in cancer cells and surface carbohydrates will continue to be centred on tumour-associated changes *per se*, though these molecules, with their potential for structural diversity may also be important as receptors of regulators of cell growth and differentiation. Glycopeptides released from cell surfaces by mild proteolysis inhibit protein synthesis (Fisher & Koch, 1976, 1977) and inhibit mitogenic stimulation of human lymphocytes (Kalvelage & Koch, 1982). More recently, membrane glycoproteins and a mannose-binding lectin isolated from the plasma membrane of GH_3 cells have been immobilized on glass, tested as substrates for cell culture and been shown to be involved in density-dependent growth regulation (Weiser & Brunner, 1983). In a more recent paper Yaoi (1984) described growth-inhibiting glycopeptides in which the carbohydrate moiety is essential for inhibitory activity. Feizi & Childs (1985) raise the exciting possibility that the receptor for epidermal growth factor (EGF) contains carbohydrate chains that are receptors for other endogenous regulators that modulate the cellular response to the growth factor. In the scheme (see Fig. 3) that they put forward, to stimulate ideas, they suggest that an endogenous carbohydrate-binding protein (a lectin) might interact with carbohydrate on the EGF receptor and other components (glycoproteins/glycolipids) of the membrane to form a macromolecular complex through which the receptor glycoprotein may be linked to other extra- and

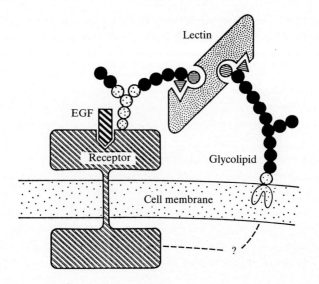

Fig. 3. Diagram of a cell membrane depicting the glycoprotein receptor for epidermal growth factor carrying an N-glycosidically linked carbohydrate chain (the various monosaccharide residues are represented diagrammatically by circular and triangular symbols, the triangle and circle with cross-hatching depict fucose and N-acetylgalactosamine, respectively, which constitute the blood group A determinant). The carbohydrate group contains sequences that may be shared by other glycoproteins and membrane glycolipids. In this scheme Feizi & Childs (1985) suggest that a hypothetical endogenous lectin with blood group A-related specificity could be responsible for linking the receptor to other extra- and intracellular signalling systems. This scheme, which was first published in *Trends in Biochemical Sciences*, was intended to stimulate thoughts on the way carbohydrate structures shared between the receptor and other glycoproteins (and glycolipids) of the cell surface might interact and is reproduced here by kind permission of Dr T. Feizi and the publisher.

intracellular signalling systems. There is evidence from the immunochemical analysis of the EGF receptor, purified by EGF-affinity chromatography from the human epidermoid carcinoma cell line, A431, that blood-group-active carbohydrate chains are present (Childs *et al.* 1984). Certain lectins inhibit EGF binding (Carpenter & Cohen, 1977) and anti-receptor antibodies known to bind carbohydrate structures may elicit stimulatory or inhibitory effects on growth (Schreiber *et al.* 1983; Gregoriov & Rees, 1984). Carding, Thorpe, Thorpe & Feizi (1985) have shown that in transformed and mitogen-stimulated lymphocytes there is an increased level of proteins antigenically related to mammalian β-galactoside-binding lectin, posing again the possibility that this family of lectin-related proteins may be somehow involved in the regulation of growth control. It will be interesting to see over the coming years whether this postulated role for surface carbohydrate and endogenous lectins in growth control is substantiated.

Undoubtedly, another area in which surface carbohydrates will attract increasing attention is in regard to embryonic development and differentiation. This aspect of the subject typifies another approach to understanding the function of glycan moieties in complex carbohydrates, namely the use of inhibitors of glycosylation.

Using tunicamycin with the developing sea-urchin embryo, Heifetz & Lennarz (1979) have shown that N-glycosylation is required for gastrulation. Compactin, a potent inhibitor of polyisoprenoid synthesis, causes a substantial inhibition of the synthesis of N-linked glycoproteins and prevents normal embryonic development beyond the mesenchyme blastula stage (Carson & Lennarz, 1979). Subsequently, Carson & Lennarz (1981) have demonstrated that a qualitative increase in *de novo* synthesis of dolichol and dolichol phosphate occurs just prior to gastrulation.

The anticipation that monoclonal antibodies might be used to reveal unique cell surface antigens during embryogenesis, differentiation and oncogenesis has been replaced by the realization that such antigens as are detected by these antibodies are principally carbohydrate structures that occur in the glycoproteins and glycolipids of many cell types. Feizi (1985) has reviewed this area, pointing out that while monoclonal antibodies have not revealed a much-sought-after unique antigen marker of embryonic stage or neoplastic state, there are strong indications that these carbohydrate structures have a role as receptors for regulation of cell growth and differentiation. This reviewer (Feizi, 1985) makes the important point that while much progress is being made in the structural analysis of glycoconjugates by physicochemical techniques, these procedures are unlikely to supercede the sensitivity of monoclonal antibodies for visualizing the *in situ* disposition of the diverse oligosaccharide sequences in individual cells.

Other workers (e.g. see Currie, Maylié-Pfenninger & Pfenninger, 1984) have used lectin-labelling techniques to show that surface carbohydrates are developmentally regulated and that differences in plasmalemmal glycoconjugates may be related to developmental control mechanisms. Manasek & Cohn (1977) had previously suggested that one might expect to find, "within each differentiating cell line, an ontogeny of surface glycopeptides that reflect its degree of functional specialization". Whilst even minor quantitative differences in the expression of carbohydrates may be important in recognition, Finne (1985) makes the point that a tissue-specific pattern of distribution or developmental regulation would be more indicative of a biological role and then proceeds to put forward polysialic acid as a novel carbohydrate structure that seems to fulfil these latter two criteria. One may confidently predict that interest in surface carbohydrates and differentiation will continue to expand. For as Ivatt (1984) states in a chapter devoted to glycoproteins in early mammalian embryogenesis, we are now entering an exciting phase that makes the transition from molecular description to function assignment.

REFERENCES

Ada, G. L. & French, E. L. (1959). Purification of bacterial neuraminidase (receptor-destroying enzyme). *Nature, Lond.* **183**, 1740–1741.

Ambrose, E. J., Dudgeon, J. A., Easty, D. M. & Easty, G. C. (1961). The inhibition of tumour growth by enzymes in tissue culture. *Expl Cell Res.* **24**, 220–227.

Aub, J. C., Tieslau, C. & Lankester, A. (1963). Reactions of normal and tumour cell surfaces to enzymes. 1. Wheatgerm lipase and associated mucopolysaccharides. *Proc. natn. Acad. Sci. U.S.A.* **50**, 613–619.

BARONDES, S. H. (1981). Lectins: their multiple endogenous cellular functions. *A. Rev. Biochem.* **50**, 207–231.

BATEMAN, J. B., ZELLNER, A., DAVIS, M. S. & McCAFFREY, P. A. (1956). The electrophoretic properties of red blood cells after reaction with influenza virus hemagglutinin. *Archs Biochem. Biophys.* **60**, 384–391.

BENEDETTI, E. L. & EMMELOT, P. (1967). Studies on plasma membranes. IV. The ultrastructural localisation and content of sialic acid in plasma membranes isolated from rat liver hepatoma. *J. Cell Sci.* **2**, 499–512.

BENNET, G., LEBLOND, C. P. & HADDAD, A. (1974). Migration of glycoprotein from the Golgi-apparatus to the surface of various cell types as shown by radioautography after labelled fucose-injection into rats. *J. Cell Biol.* **60**, 258–284.

BEHRENS, N. H. & LELOIR, L. F. (1970). Dolichol monophosphate glucose: an intermediate in glucose transfer in liver. *Proc. natn. Acad. Sci. U.S.A.* **66**, 153–159.

BLIX, F. G., GOTTSCHALK, A. & KLENK, E. (1957). Proposed nomenclature in the field of neuraminic and sialic acids. *Nature, Lond.* **179**, 1088.

BURGER, M. M. & GOLDBERG, A. R. (1967). Identification of a tumour-specific determinant on neoplastic cell surfaces. *Proc. natn. Acad. Sci. U.S.A.* **57**, 359–366.

CACCAM, J. F., JACKSON, J. J. & EYLAR, E. H. (1969). The biosynthesis of mannose-containing glycoproteins: A possible lipid intermediate. *Biochem. Biophys. Res. Commun.* **35**, 505–571.

CARDING, S. R., THORPE, S. J., THORPE, R. & FEIZI, T. (1985). Transformation and growth related changes in levels of nuclear and cytoplasmic proteins antigenically related to mammalian β-galactoside-binding lectin. *Biochem. Biophys. Res. Commun.* **127**, 680–686.

CARPENTER, G. & COHEN, S. (1977). Influence of lectins on the binding of ^{125}I-labelled EGF to human fibroblasts. *Biochem. Biophys. Res. Commun.* **72**, 1229–1236.

CARSON, D. D. & LENNARZ, W. J. (1979). Inhibition of polyisoprenoid and glycoprotein biosynthesis causes abnormal embryonic development. *Proc. natn. Acad. Sci. U.S.A.* **76**, 5709–5713.

CARSON, D. D. & LENNARZ, W. J. (1981). Relationship of dolichol synthesis to glycoprotein synthesis during embryonic development. *J. biol. Chem.* **256**, 4679–4686.

CHILDS, R. A., GREGORIOV, M., SCUDDER, P., THORPE, S. J., REES, A. R. & FEIZI, T. (1984). Blood group-active carbohydrate chains on the receptor for epidermal growth factor of A431 cells. *EMBO J.* **3**, 2227–2233.

CHIN, Y.-H., CAREY, G. D. & WOODRUFF, J. J. (1983). Lymphocyte recognition of lymph node endothelium. V. Isolation of adhesion molecules from lysates of rat lymphocytes. *J. Immun.* **131**, 1368–1374.

CHIN, Y.-H., RASMUSSEN, R., CAKIROGLU, A. G. & WOODRUFF, J. J. (1984). Lymphocyte recognition of lymph node high endothelium. VI. Evidence of distinct structures mediating binding to high endothelial cells of lymph nodes and Peyer's patches. *J. Immun.* **133**, 2961–2965.

COOK, G. M. W. (1982). Isolation of Golgi apparatus: Problems in adapting normal cell methods to leukaemic cells. In *Cancer-cell Organelles* (ed. E. Reid, G. M. W. Cook & D. J. Morré), pp. 299–309. Chichester: Ellis Horwood.

COOK, G. M. W., HEARD, D. H. & SEAMAN, G. V. F. (1960). A sialomucopeptide liberated by trypsin from the human erythrocyte. *Nature, Lond.* **188**, 1011–1012.

COOK, G. M. W., HEARD, D. H. & SEAMAN, G. V. F. (1961). Sialic acids and the electrokinetic charge of the human erythrocyte. *Nature, Lond.* **191**, 44–47.

COOK, G. M. W., HEARD, D. H. & SEAMAN, G. V. F. (1962). The electrokinetic characterisation of the Ehrlich ascites carcinoma cell. *Expl Cell Res.* **28**, 27–39.

COOK, G. M. W., LAICO, M. T. & EYLAR, E. H. (1965). Biosynthesis of the Ehrlich ascites carcinoma cell membranes. *Proc. natn. Acad. Sci. U.S.A.* **54**, 247–252.

CURRIE, J. R., MAYLIÉ-PFENNINGER, M.-F. & PFENNINGER, K. H. (1984). Developmentally regulated plasmalemmal glycoconjugates of the surface and neural ectoderm. *Devl Biol.* **106**, 109–120.

CURTAIN, C. C. (1953). Nature of the bond split by the influenza-virus enzyme. *Aust. J. exp. Biol. med. Sci.* **31**, 623–630.

DANIELLI, J. F. & DAVSON, H. (1934). A contribution to the theory of permeability of thin films. *J. cell. comp. Physiol.* **5**, 495–508.

DAUWALDER, M. (1984). The Golgi apparatus. In *Membrane Structure and Function*, vol. 6 (ed. E. E. Bittar), pp. 174–216. New York: John Wiley.

DAVIES, D. A. L. (1963). In *The Structure and Function of the Membrane and Surfaces of Cells. Biochem. Soc. Symp.*, no. 22 (ed. D. J. Bell & J. K. Grant), p. 51. Cambridge University Press.

EDWARDS, J. G., DYSART, J. McK. & HUGHES, R. C. (1976). Cellular adhesiveness reduced in ricin-resistant hamster fibroblasts. *Nature, Lond.* **264**, 66–68.

EYLAR, E. H. & COOK, G. M. W. (1965). The cell-free biosynthesis of the glycoprotein of membranes from Ehrlich ascites carcinoma cells. *Proc. natn. Acad. Sci. U.S.A.* **54**, 1678–1685.

EYLAR, E. H., MADOFF, M. A., BRODY, O. V. & ONCLEY, J. L. (1962). The contribution of sialic acid to the surface charge of the erythrocyte. *J. biol. Chem.* **237**, 1992–2000.

FARQUHAR, M. G. & PALADE, G. E. (1981). The Golgi apparatus (complex) – (1954–1981) – from artifact to centre stage. *J. Cell. Biol.* **91**, 77s–103s.

FEIZI, T. (1985). Demonstration by monoclonal antibodies that carbohydrate structures of glycoproteins and glycolipids are onco-developmental antigens. *Nature, Lond.* **314**, 53–57.

FEIZI, T. & CHILDS, R. A. (1985). Carbohydrate structures of glycoproteins and glycolipids as differentiation antigens, tumour associated antigens and components of receptor systems. *Trends Biochem. Sci.* **10**, 24–29.

FINNE, J. (1985). Polysialic acid – a glycoprotein carbohydrate involved in neural adhesion and bacterial meningitis. *Trends Biochem. Sci.* **10**, 129–132.

FISHER, L. E. & KOCH, G. (1976). Inhibition of protein synthesis by HeLa cell surface peptides. *Biochem. biophys. Res. Commun.* **72**, 1229–1236.

FISHER, L. E. & KOCH, G. (1977). Partial characterisation and proposed mode of action of inhibitory HeLa cell surface polypeptides. *Biochim. biophys. Acta* **470**, 113–120.

FLEISCHER, B., FLEISCHER, S. & OZAWA, H. (1969). Isolation and characterisation of Golgi membranes from bovine liver. *J. Cell Biol.* **43**, 59–79.

GALLATIN, W. M., WEISSMAN, I. L. & BUTCHER, E. C. (1983). A cell-surface molecule involved in organ-specific homing of lymphocytes. *Nature, Lond.* **304**, 30–34.

GASIC, G. & BERWICK, L. (1963). Hale stain for sialic acid-containing mucins. Adaptation to electron microscopy. *J. Cell Biol.* **19**, 223–228.

GASIC, G. & GASIC, T. (1962a). Removal and regeneration of the cell coating in tumour cells. *Nature, Lond.* **196**, 170.

GASIC, G. & GASIC, T. (1962b). Removal of sialic acid from the cell coat in tumour cells and vascular endothelium, and its effects on metastasis. *Proc. natn. Acad. Sci. U.S.A.* **48**, 1172–1177.

GASIC, G. & GASIC, T. (1963). Origin of the surface sialomucins in free tumour cells. *Proc. Am. Assoc. Cancer Res.* **4**, 22.

GESNER, B. M. & GINSBURG, V. (1964). Effect of glycosidases on the fate of transfused lymphocytes. *Proc. natn. Acad. Sci. U.S.A.* **52**, 750–755.

GORTER, E. & GRENDEL, F. (1925). On bi-molecular layers of lipoids on the chromocytes of the blood. *J. exp. Med.* **41**, 439–443.

GOTTSCHALK, A. (1957). Neuraminidase: the specific enzyme of influenza virus and *Vibrio cholerae. Biochim. biophys. Acta* **23**, 645–646.

GREGORIOV, M. & REES, A. R. (1984). Properties of a monoclonal antibody to epidermal growth factor receptor with implications for the mechanism of action of EGF. *EMBO J.* **3**, 929–937.

HEIFITZ, A. & LENNARZ, W. J. (1979). Biosynthesis of N-glycosidically linked glycoproteins during gastrulation of sea urchin embryos. *J. biol. Chem.* **254**, 6119–6127.

HIRANO, H., PARKHOUSE, B., NICOLSON, G. L., LENNOX, E. S. & SINGER, S. J. (1972). Distribution of saccharide residues on membrane fragments from a myeloma-cell homogenate: its implications for membrane biogenesis. *Proc. natn. Acad. Sci. U.S.A.* **69**, 2945–2949.

HOOGHE, R. J. & PINK, J. R. L. (1985). The role of carbohydrate in lymphoid cell traffic. *Immun. Today* **6**, 180–181.

HUDGIN, R. L., PRICER, W. E. JR, ASHWELL, G., STOCKERT, R. S. & MORELL, A. G. (1974). The isolation and properties of a rabbit liver binding protein specific for asialoglycoproteins. *J. biol. Chem.* **249**, 5536–5543.

IVATT, R. J. (1984). Role of glycoproteins during early mammalian embryogenesis. In *The Biology of Glycoproteins* (ed. R. J. Ivatt), pp. 95–181. New York, London: Plenum.

KABAT, E. A. (1985). Antibody combining sites past, present and future. In *Investigation and Exploitation of Antibody Binding Sites, Methodological Surveys in Biochemistry and Analysis*, vol. 15 (B) (ed. E. Reid, G. M. W. Cook & D. J. Morré). New York, London: Plenum.

KALCKAR, H. M. (1965). Galactose metabolism and cell "Sociology". *Science* **150**, 305–318.

KALVELAGE, B. & KOCH, G. (1982). Inhibition of mitogenic stimulation of human lymphocytes by protease released membrane glycopeptides. *Eur. J. Cell Biol.* **28**, 238–242.

KAWASAKI, T. & ASHWELL, G. (1976). Chemical and physical properties of a hepatic membrane protein that specifically binds asialoglycoproteins. *J. biol. Chem.* **251**, 1296–1302.

KEENAN, T. W. & MORRÉ, D. J. (1975). Glycosyltransferases: Do they exist on the surface membrane of mammalian cells? *FEBS Lett.* **55**, 8–13.

KLENK, E. (1958). In *The Chemistry and Biology of Mucopolysaccharides* (ed. G. E. W. Wolstenholme & M. O'Connor), p. 311. London: J. & A. Churchill.

KLENK, E. & LEMPFRID, H. (1957). Nature of the cell-receptor for the influenza virus. *Hoppe-Seyler's Z. physiol. Chem.* **307**, 278–283.

KLENK, E. & UHLENBRUCK, G. (1958). A mucoprotein containing neuraminic acid from the stroma of bovine erythrocytes. *Hoppe-Seyle's Z. physiol. Chem.* **311**, 227–233.

KOBATA, A. (1984). The carbohydrates of glycoproteins. In *Biology of Carbohydrates*, vol. 2 (ed. V. Ginsburg & P. W. Robbins), pp. 87–161. New York: John Wiley.

LEBLOND, C. P., GLEGG, R. E. & EIDINGER, D. (1957). Presence of carbohydrates with free 1,2-glycol groups in sites stained by the periodic acid-Schiff technique. *J. Histochem. Cytochem.* **5**, 445–458.

LEDEEN, R. W. & YU, R. K. (1976). Chemistry and analysis of sialic acid. In *Biological Roles of Sialic Acid* (ed. A. Rosenberg & C.-L. Schengrand), pp. 1–57. New York, London: Plenum Press.

LELOIR, L. F. (1964). The biosynthesis of polysaccharides. In *Proc. Plenary Sessions Sixth Int. Congr. Biochem.* I.U.B., vol. 33, pp. 15–29. Washington: Fed. Am. Socs Exp. Biol.

LIS, H. & SHARON, N. (1984). Lectins: properties and applications to the study of complex carbohydrates in solution and on cell surfaces. In *Biology of Carbohydrates*, vol. 2 (ed. V. Ginsburg & P. W. Robbins), pp. 1–85. New York: John Wiley.

MANASEK, F. J. & COHEN, A. M. (1977). Anionic glycopeptides and glycosaminoglycans synthesised by embryonic neural tube and neural crest. *Proc. natn. Acad. Sci. U.S.A.* **74**, 1057–1061.

MARCHESI, V. T., GINSBURG, V. & ROBBINS, P. W. (1978). Preface. In *Cell Surface Carbohydrates and Biological Recognition. Prog. Clin. biol. Res.*, vol. 23 (ed. V. T. Marchesi, V. Ginsberg, P. W. Robbins & C. F. Fox), p. 13. New York: Alan R. Liss.

MARTINEZ-PALOMO, A. (1970). The surface coats of animal cells. *Int. Rev. Cytol.* **29**, 29–75.

MOLNAR, J., LUTES, R. A. & WINZLER, R. J. (1965). The biosynthesis of glycoproteins. V. Incorporation of glucosamine-1-^{14}C into macromolecules by Ehrlich ascites carcinoma cells. *Cancer Res.* **25**, 1438–1445.

MORELL, A. G., IRVINE, R. A., STERLIEB, I., SCHEINBERG, I. H. & ASHWELL, G. (1968). Physical and chemical studies on ceruloplasmin. V. Metabolic studies on sialic acid-free ceruloplasmin *in vivo. J. biol. Chem.* **243**, 155–159.

MORELL, A. G., VAN DEN HAMER, C. J. A., SCHEINBERG, I. H. & ASHWELL, G. (1966). Physical and chemical studies on ceruloplasmin. IV. Preparation of radioactive, sialic acid-free ceruloplasmin labelled with tritium on terminal D-galactose residues. *J. biol. Chem.* **241**, 3745–3749.

MORGAN, W. T. J. & WATKINS, W. M. (1959). Some aspects of the biochemistry of human blood-group substances. *Br. med. Bull.* **15**, 109–112.

MORRÉ, D. J. & CREEK, K. H. (1982). Isolation of Golgi apparatus from hepatomas and cultures cells. In *Cancer-cell Organelles* (ed. E. Reid, G. M. W. Cook & D. J. Morre), pp. 321–334. Chichester: Ellis Horwood.

MORRÉ, D. J., MERLIN, L. M. & KEENAN, T. W. (1969). Localisation of glycosyl transferase activities in a Golgi apparatus-rich fraction isolated from rat liver. *Biochem. biophys. Res. Commun.* **37**, 813–819.

MORRÉ, D. J. & MOLLENHAUER, H. H. (1964). Isolation of the Golgi apparatus from plant cells. *J. Cell Biol.* **23**, 295–305.

NEUFELD, E. F. & ASHWELL, G. (1980). Carbohydrate recognition systems for receptor mediated pinocytosis. In *Biochemistry of Glycoproteins and Proteoglycans* (ed. W. J. Lennarz), pp. 241–266. New York, London: Plenum.

NEUTRA, M. & LEBLOND, C. P. (1966). Synthesis of the carbohydrate of mucous in the Golgi complex as shown by electron microscope radioautography of goblet cells from rats injected with glucose-^{3}H. *J. Cell Biol.* **30**, 119–136.

NICOLSON, G. L. (1974). The interactions of lectins with animal cell surfaces. *Int. Rev. Cytol.* **39**, 90–190.

NICOLSON, G. L. & SINGER, S. J. (1971). Ferritin-conjugated plant agglutinins as specific saccharide stains for electron microscopy: Applications to saccharides bound to cell membranes. *Proc. natn. Acad. Sci. U.S.A.* **68**, 942–945.

OLDEN, K., PARENT, J. B. & WHITE, S. L. (1982). Carbohydrate moieties of glycoproteins a re-evaluation of their function. *Biochim. biophys. Acta* **650**, 209–232.

PIPER, W. (1957). Untersuchungen uber die wirkung des 'Receptor-destroying-enzyme' auf menschliche erythrocyten. *Acta haemat.* **18**, 414–428.

PONDER, E. (1951). Effects produced by trypsin on certain properties of the human red cell. *Blood* **6**, 350–356.

PONDMAN, K. V. & MASTENBROEK, G. G. A. (1954). On some properties of the red cell membrane. *Vox Sang.* **4**, 98–107.

RAMBOURG, A. (1971). Morphological and histochemical aspects of glycoprotein at the surface of animals cells. *Int. Rev. Cytol.* **31**, 57–114.

RAMBOURG, A. & LEBLOND, C. P. (1967). Electron microscope observations on the carbohydrate-rich cell coat present at the surface of cells in the rat. *J. Cell Biol.* **32**, 27–53.

RAMBOURG, A., NEUTRA, M. & LEBLOND, C. P. (1966). Presence of a 'cell coat' rich in carbohydrate at the surface of cells in the rat. *Anat. Rec.* **154**, 41–72.

ROSEMAN, S. (1970). The synthesis of complex carbohydrates by multiglycosyltransferase systems and their potential function in intercellular adhesion. *Chem. Phys. Lipids* **5**, 270–297.

ROTHSTEIN, A. (1978). The cell membrane: A short historical perspective. In *Current Topics in Membranes and Transport,* vol. 11 (ed. R. L. Juliano & A. Rothstein), pp. 1–13. New York, London: Academic Press.

SCHACHTER, H., JABBAL, I., HUDGIN, R. L., PINTERIC, L., McGUIRE, E. J. & ROSEMAN, S. (1970). Intracellular localisation of liver sugar nucleotide glycoprotein glycosyltransferases in a Golgi-rich fraction. *J. biol. Chem.* **245**, 1090–1100.

SCHREIBER, A. B., LIBERMANN, T. A., LAX, L., YARDEN, Y. & SCHLESSINGER, J. (1983). Biological role of epidermal growth factor-receptor clustering; investigation with monoclonal anti-receptor antibodies. *J. biol. Chem.* **258**, 846–853.

SCHWARTZ, R. T. & DATEMA, R. (1984). Inhibitors of trimming: new tools in glycoprotein research. *Trends Biochem. Sci.* **9**, 32–34.

SCOTT, J. E., YAMASHINA, I. & JEANLOS, R. W. (1982). A proposal for a terminology of sialic acid derivatives. *Biochem. J.* **207**, 367–369.

SEAMAN, G. V. F. (1975). Electrokinetic behaviour of red cells. In *The Red Blood Cell*, vol. II (ed. D. McN. Surgenor), pp. 1135–1229. New York, London: Academic Press.

SEAMAN, G. V. F. & HEARD, D. H. (1960). The surface of the washed human erythrocyte as a polyanion. *J. gen. Physiol.* **44**, 251–268.

SHARON, N. (1974). Glycoproteins. *Scient. Am.* **230**, 78–86.

SHARON, N. (1984). Glycoproteins. *Trends Bioch. Sci.* **9**, 198–202.

SHARON, N. & LIS, H. (1981). Glycoproteins: research booming on long-ignored, ubiquitous compound. *Chem. Eng. News* **59**, 21–44.

SHUR, B. D. & ROTH, S. (1975). Cell surface glycosyl transferases. *Biochim. biophys. Acta* **415**, 473–512.

SLY, W. S. (1982). The uptake and transport of lysosomal enzymes. In *The Glycoconjugates,* vol. IV (ed. M. I. Horowitz), pp. 3–25. New York, London: Academic Press.

SMETS, L. A. & VAN BEEK, W. P. (1984). Carbohydrates of the tumor cell surface. *Biochim. biophys. Acta* **738**, 237–249.

STANLEY, P. (1980). Surface carbohydrate alterations of mutant mammalian cells selected for resistance to plant lectins. In *The Biochemistry of Glycoproteins and Proteoglycans* (ed. W. J. Lennarz), pp. 161–189. New York, London: Plenum.

STRUCK, D. K. & LENNARZ, W. J. (1980). The function of saccharide-lipids in synthesis of glycoproteins. In *The Biochemistry of Glycoproteins and Proteoglycans* (ed. W. J. Lennarz), pp. 35–83. New York, London: Plenum.

WALLACH, D. F. H. & EYLAR, E. H. (1961). Sialic acid in the cellular membranes of Ehrlich ascites-carcinoma cells. *Biochim. biophys. Acta* **52**, 594–596.

WARREN, L. (1959). The thiobarbituric acid assay for sialic acids. *J. biol. Chem.* **234**, 1971–1975.

WARREN, L., FUHRER, J. P. & BUCK, C. A. (1972). Surface glycoproteins of normal and transformed cells: A difference determined by sialic acid and a growth-dependent sialyl transferase. *Proc. natn. Acad. Sci. U.S.A.* **69**, 1838–1842.

WATKINS, W. M. & MORGAN, W. T. J. (1952). Neutralization of the anti-H agglutinin in eel serum by simple sugars. *Nature, Lond.* **169**, 825–826.

WEISER, R. & BRUNNER, G. (1983). Initiation of contact-inhibition by substrate-bound plasma membrane glycoprotein and lectin in serum-free hormone-supplemented cultures of GH_3 cells. *Expl Cell Res.* **147**, 23–30.

WHUR, P., HERSCOVICS, A. & LEBLOND, C. P. (1969). Radioautographic visualisation of the incorporation of galactose-^{3}H and mannose-^{3}H by rat thyroids in *in vitro* in relation to the stages of thyroglobulin synthesis. *J. Cell Biol.* **43**, 289–311.

YAMADA, K. M. (1983). Cell surface interactions with extracellular materials. *A. Rev. Biochem.* **52**, 761–799.

YAOI, Y. (1984). Growth inhibitory glycopeptides obtained from the cell surface of cultured chick embryo fibroblasts. *Expl Cell Res.* **154**, 147–154.

YOGEESWARAN, G., GRONBERG, A., HANSSON, M., DALIANIS, T., KIESSLING, R. & WELSH, R. M. (1981). Correlation of glycosphingolipids and sialic acid in YAC-1 lymphoma variants with their sensitivity to natural killer-cell-mediated lysis. *Int. J. Cancer* **28**, 517–526.

YOUNG, W. W. JR, DURDIK, J. M., URDALL, D., HAKOMORI, S. & HENNEY, C. S. (1981). Glycolipid expression in lymphoma cell variants: Chemical quantity immunologic reactivity and correlation with susceptibility to NK cells. *J. Immun.* **126**, 1–6.

J. Cell Sci. Suppl. 4, 71–88 (1986)
Printed in Great Britain © The Company of Biologists Limited 1986

THE MEMBRANE-ASSOCIATED 'CORTEX' OF ANIMAL CELLS: ITS STRUCTURE AND MECHANICAL PROPERTIES

DENNIS BRAY, JULIAN HEATH* AND DIANA MOSS

MRC Cell Biophysics Unit, 26 Drury Lane, London WC2B 5RL, UK

INTRODUCTION

We often think of the plasma membrane as a physically separable part of the cell. It is chemically distinct: a thin oily film of lipids and hydrophobic proteins that is immiscible with the water-based cytoplasm it encloses. In questions of cell physiology and metabolism the outer membrane is conveniently regarded as an isolated permeability barrier controlling the entry and egress of ions and small molecules. However, when we come to consider the mechanical properties of cells and their movements, any attempt to segregate the plasma membrane from the rest of the cell is misleading. It is true that the forces necessary for motile phenomena such as locomotion and mitosis are generated mainly in the cytoplasm, by a system of protein filaments known collectively as the cytoskeleton. But the cytoskeleton does not move within the flexible enclosure of the plasma membrane like a cat in a bag. There are extensive and substantial links between the two that give the cell surface appreciable strength and make it an important structural element in cell movements.

Perhaps the most conspicuous form taken by the membrane-associated cytoskeleton is that of a cell 'cortex'. Early studies of free-living amoebae, later extended to echinoderm eggs and macrophages, revealed a peripheral layer of gelated cytoplasm closely associated with the inner face of the plasma membrane. This appeared to be a major determinant of cell form and was at one time thought to be responsible for many kinds of cell movements including those of vertebrate cells. More recent work has shown that contacts between the cytoskeleton and the membrane in vertebrate cells are mainly confined to discrete regions, such as intercellular junctions and microvilli, each of which has a distinctive structure and complement of proteins. At first sight this seems at variance with the idea of a uniform, and universal, cortex.

Our plan in this short essay is to describe the layer of peripheral cytoplasm associated with the plasma membrane of animal cells and to compare the uniform thick cortex found in amoebae and echinoderm eggs with the much thinner layer present in the cells of vertebrate tissues. Since the function of the cortex is to give rigidity and form to the cell surface, we will also consider the cellular mechanics of the cortex and speculate on its role in cell movements. For reasons of space and

---

* Present address: Department of Biology, University of Pennsylvania, Philadelphia, PA 19104, USA.

fluency we will give only a short selection of references. However, a number of recent reviews are cited that will provide greater access to the very extensive literature relating to the cell cortex.

STRUCTURE OF THE MEMBRANE-ASSOCIATED CORTEX

Amoebae and echinoderm eggs

The earliest indication of a peripheral layer of cytoplasm associated with the outer cell membrane came from studies of large freshwater amoebae of the *Amoeba proteus* type. These organisms have been studied by microscopists for more than 200 years, and the differentiation of their cytoplasm into regions of distinct organelle content and physical consistency was one of the earliest features to be noted (see Allen & Kamiya, 1964; Jeon, 1973; Chambers & Chambers, 1961). Already, by 1926, Mast was able to summarize more than a century of observation and debate in his classical account of movement in *A. proteus* (Mast, 1926). Incorporating concepts of sol and gel states of cytoplasm, he named the central, relatively fluid region the plasmasol and the tube of stiffer cytoplasm that encloses it the plasmagel (two regions now also known as endoplasm and ectoplasm, respectively). Outside the plasmagel and between it and the plasma membrane, Mast described a clear layer of variable thickness known as the hyaline layer or hyaline cortex; this was continuous with a much larger cap of similar appearance at the tip of a pseudopod (the hyaline cap) (Fig. 1).

The hyaline layer of large amoebae is therefore the doyen of cell membrane cortices. By the early 1970s this layer had been shown to contain many thin filaments and evidence had been obtained that these were probably actin (Pollard & Ito, 1970; Comly, 1973). However, as far as we are aware there have been no further investigations of its precise nature and, moreover, there is reason to believe that it is not essential for cell movements. As noted by Mast, and corroborated by many subsequent observers, the material of the hyaline layer and cap is relatively fluid; the cell surface on one side of this layer slips easily over the plasmagel on the other side, with little if any permanent attachment between the two. When the outer membrane

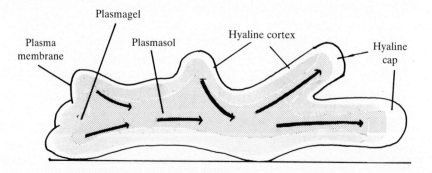

Fig. 1. Schematic diagram of *A. proteus* crawling over a solid substratum showing the regional differentiation of the cytoplasm discussed in the text. The migration is accompanied by streaming movements in the inner plasmasol region, as indicated.

is physically removed from the cell, the denuded cytoplasm remains able to carry out streaming movements similar to those seen in intact pseudopodia (Allen, Cooledge & Hall, 1960; Taylor & Condeelis, 1979). In a sense, therefore, *A. proteus* does move as a 'cat in a bag', although the 'bag' in this case includes both the plasma membrane and a tightly associated actin-rich cytoskeleton.

In other types of amoeba the structure of the cortex is better understood. In an early study, isolated membrane fragments from the relatively minute protozoa *Acanthamoeba* were found to be associated with large numbers of actin filaments (Pollard & Korn, 1973). In the electron microscope these appeared as a series of filaments attached end-on to the inner surface of the plasma membrane, like a fur lining. A similar layer appears to exist beneath the membrane of the amoeboid form of the slime mould *Dictyostelium discoideum* and has been the subject of detailed biochemical studies of the actin–membrane association (Bennett & Condeelis, 1984). Isolated membrane fragments, freed of their extrinsic protein by treatment with 0·1 M-NaOH, will bind to purified actin filaments in a controlled and specific fashion, and several membrane proteins involved in this binding have been identified (Luna, Goodloe-Holland & Ingalls, 1984; Goodloe-Holland & Luna, 1984; Stratford & Brown, 1984). Interestingly, actin filaments are able to bind not only end-on but also laterally, and are evidently able to form a feltwork of actin filaments beneath the cell surface. A lateral association of this kind could occur through the binding of actin filaments to a large number of membrane proteins each with relatively low affinity.

Probably the most conspicuous and certainly the best-studied example of a membrane cortex is found in sea-urchin eggs. These cells are spherical, usually about 100 μm in diameter, and have a distinct gelated layer of cytoplasm about 3–4 μm thick associated with their inner surface (Hiramoto, 1957). The presence of this cortical layer, and the fact that it is firmly attached to the plasma membrane, were established in a series of delicate micromanipulation studies. For example, Hiramoto, by introducing fine glass needles into sea-urchin eggs, showed that the inner contents of the cytoplasm have the consistency of an easily stirred fluid while the peripheral layer 3–5 μm from the surface is more gel-like (Hiramoto, 1957). Attempts to push through this outer layer from the inside resulted in the deformation of the surface (Fig. 2). The existence of a cortex in these and other types of cell can also be demonstrated by allowing portions of the cell surface to stick to an adhesive coverslip and then washing the remainder of the cell away with a stream of fluid. The exposed inner surface of the cortex can then be visualized directly and its composition examined using antibodies and other specific reagents (see, e.g., Spudich & Spudich, 1979).

From studies of this kind it appears that echinoderm eggs, in common with the eggs of frogs and fruit-flies, have cortices composed of a thick actin-rich network. Before fertilization, the echinoderm cortex is relatively poorly ordered and contains less extensively polymerized actin. Shortly after fertilization, the surface of the egg becomes covered with numerous fine microvilli, each of which contains a bundle of actin filaments similar to those described below for the intestinal epithelial cells (Schroeder & Stricker, 1983).

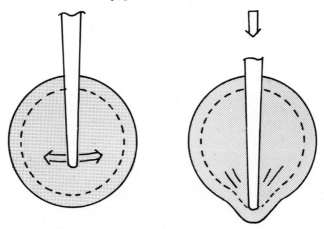

Fig. 2. Experiment demonstrating the presence of a gelated cortex in sea-urchin eggs (Hiramoto, 1957). The glass needle inserted into the egg encounters mechanical resistance only when it comes within 3–5 μm of the egg plasma membrane.

Vertebrate cells

Any attempt to relate the echinoderm egg cortex to the membrane-associated cytoskeleton of vertebrate cells encounters problems of scale. A layer 3–5 μm thick would occupy most, if not all, of the contents of a fibroblast or an epithelial cell (Fig. 3).

Nevertheless, parallels have been drawn. In 1939, for example, Lewis compared the migration of leucocytes with that of giant freshwater amoebae and interpreted

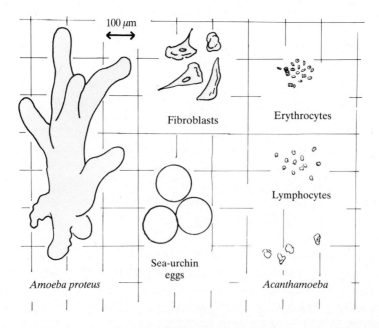

Fig. 3. Comparative sizes of some of the cells discussed in the text. Note that the fibroblasts appear to be relatively large since they are depicted as though flattened onto a culture substratum.

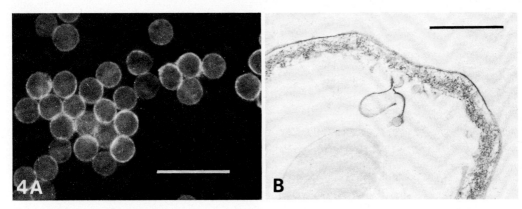

Fig. 4. A. Neutrophils stained with rhodamine/phalloidin to reveal actin filaments. Note the intensity of the fluorescence in the region beneath the plasma membrane. Bar, 20 μm. B. Transmission electron micrograph of a neutrophil showing the actin feltwork beneath the residual plasma membrane. Bar, 1 μm. (Courtesy of Peter Sheterline.)

them in terms of a contractile layer of peripheral cytoplasm. Unfortunately, as we have seen, the layer of cytoplasm that generates movements in *A. proteus* is not firmly attached to the plasma membrane and the membrane cortex has no direct role in cell locomotion. But with regard to the membrane-associated cytoskeleton of leucocytes, Lewis's ideas have been shown to be essentially correct. There is indeed a distinct layer of specialized cytoplasm beneath the plasma membrane of macrophages, neutrophils and lymphocytes (see reviews by Stossel, Hartwig & Yin, 1981; Oliver & Berlin, 1982; Loor, 1981; Hartwig, Niederman & Lind, 1985). In electron micrographs this appears as an amorphous inner coat of fine filaments from which other cytoplasmic organelles are excluded (Fig. 4). Evidence of several kinds shows that these filaments are composed largely of actin.

To learn more about the biochemistry of the cortex we would like ideally to obtain it in large quantities entirely free of other cell components. While this is difficult, it is feasible to obtain membrane fragments in reasonable amounts that consist of both plasma membrane and associated cytoskeleton. As we saw with regard to the *Dictyostelium* and *Acanthamoeba* cortices, preparations of this kind enable the links between actin filaments and integral membrane proteins to be analysed. A further step in purification used with a number of vertebrate cells is to isolate from a membrane preparation a residual cytoskeleton by detergent extraction. This results in a membrane shell, which has been extensively characterized in the case of the red blood cell, as described below, but is clearly more complex in the case of tissue cells (Apgar, Herrmann, Robinson & Mescher, 1985; Moss, 1983).

The primary source of information on the nature of the cortex itself, as distinct from its linkage to the plasma membrane, comes from studies of actin-rich gels. If sea-urchin eggs, macrophages or indeed, any of a wide range of other animal cell types are homogenized at low temperatures in buffers lacking Ca^{2+}, watery extracts are obtained that turn into a semi-solid gel upon warming. Subsequent manipulation of the Ca^{2+} concentration then causes regional liquefaction and contraction, and even a form of directed streaming (Taylor & Condeelis, 1979).

Biochemical analysis of the gels permits identification of the proteins that 'conspire' with actin to produce the changes in physical state. These include a class of long flexible protein molecules, such as filamin, that are able to link adjacent actin filaments together whatever their relative orientation; even in small proportions, such proteins cause a solution of actin filaments to turn into a gel. Also present is a class of actin-fragmenting proteins, such as gelsolin, which can sever actin filaments in response to small increases in the concentration of Ca^{2+}, and a number of other calcium-sensitive actin-binding proteins. The collective action of these proteins on an actin filament gel is to generate a precipitous fall in viscosity analogous to a gel-to-sol conversion. Finally, the gelating extracts from echinoderm eggs and macrophages contain myosin and associated control proteins, which enable it to produce a Ca^{2+}-stimulated contraction of the actin filaments in a gel and, under the right conditions, a form of streaming (Weeds, 1982; Geiger, 1983).

Reconstituted gels resemble in their ultrastructure and physical properties the cortical layer of cytoplasm of large cells, and several of the gel-forming proteins have a predominantly peripheral location in the cytoplasm. They are probably not unique to the cortex, since similar sets of actin-binding proteins can be isolated from vertebrate tissue cells that lack a conspicuous membrane cortex, and even from the extruded, membrane-free cytoplasm of giant amoebae. It is clear, however, that without actin-binding proteins no cortex could be formed.

Motile cells such as neutrophils and macrophages are similar to amoeboid protozoa in the sense that they persue a 'free-living' existence, albeit within the confines of the animal body. The other cells of the multicellular tissues of the body, such as endothelial cells, lung alveolar cells and lens epithelial cells, have a more anisotropic environment, being in contact in some regions with neighbouring cells and in other regions with the extracellular matrix. Possibly for this reason, the layer of actin and other proteins associated with the plasma membrane is more variable in thickness and in composition. Connections with the plasma membrane still exist, but they are most prominent in regions of specialized function (Geiger, 1983). We will now consider briefly the nature of the actin–membrane association in these regions.

Microvilli are found in large numbers on the luminal surface of epithelial cells in the intestine and in other tissues. Each intestinal microvillus has a core of actin filaments arranged in a parallel bundle; and a number of proteins that crosslink the actin filaments together and link them to the membrane have been identified. Lateral association with the plasma membrane seems to be due to a series of regularly spaced, $7\,nm \times 20\,nm$ bridges composed of a $110\,000\,M_r$ actin-activated ATPase, which is tightly associated with calmodulin. The ends of the actin filaments appear, in the electron microscope, to be embedded in a plaque of dense material at the tip of the microvillus. Evidently the ends of the filaments are still accessible, since incubation of isolated brush-border preparations in actin solutions results in the growth of filaments at their distal, membrane-associated ends (Mooseker, Pollard & Wharton, 1982).

It may be noted in passing that growth of actin filaments at their membrane-associated ends seems to occur elsewhere. In the almost explosive extension of the actin-based acrosomal process of *Thyone* sperm, the kinetics of elongation are consistent with the diffusion-limited addition of actin monomers to the distal, membrane-associated end (Tilney & Inoué, 1982). In the far slower morphogenesis of the bundle of actin in the *Limulus* sperm acrosomal process, there is also ultrastructural evidence that growth occurs at the membrane-associated ends (Tilney, Bonder & DeRosier, 1981). More generally, in essentially every situation in which the polarity of actin filaments attached to membranes has been examined by myosin decoration, they have been found to be attached by the end that, in isolated actin preparations, is the preferred end for growth.

One further similarity between the peripheral cytoplasm of echinoderm eggs and that of vertebrate tissue cells lies in the specialized structure formed in the course of cell division. In most, if not all, animal cells, a circumferential band of actin filaments and associated proteins known as the contractile ring forms around the equator of the cell in the final stages of mitosis. This produces a mechanical force by its constriction, which, in turn, causes a furrow to form in the cell surface and eventually pinches the cell into two. In echinoderm eggs the contractile ring is clearly part of the submembrane cortex: indeed, the more centrally located cytoplasm can be disrupted or even removed entirely without arresting the progress of the cleavage furrow. The contractile rings of vertebrate tissue cells are smaller, but otherwise closely similar to those of echinoderm eggs. Evidently, they are also closely associated with the plasma membrane, since surface receptors directly or indirectly associated with the actin filaments align with the cleavage furrow during cytokinesis (Rogalsky & Singer, 1985).

Actin filaments are also attached to the plasma membrane at sites at which the cell as a whole is anchored to external features such as another cell, the extracellular matrix or a tissue culture substratum. These sites include tight junctions and zonulae adherens between epithelial cells, neuronal synapses and the advancing margins of fibroblasts crawling in tissue culture (Fig. 5). The latter cells also form attachment points, or adhesion plaques, to the culture substratum on more proximal regions of their lower surface. In the adhesion plaque, a bundle of parallel actin filaments lying close to the lower surface of the cell, known as a stress fibre, appears to terminate at a specialized region of the plasma membrane. Here the actin filaments are mechanically linked to the membrane and through it to components of the extracellular matrix, such as fibronectin. Several of the proteins involved in his linkage have been identified, such as vinculin, talin and integral membrane proteins involved in binding to fibronectin (see, e.g., Chen *et al.* 1985; Damsky *et al.* 1985; Mangeat & Burridge, 1984). At present, however, we do not have a detailed understanding of their arrangement within the adhesion plaque.

The extracellular matrix also affects the membrane-associated cytoskeleton in lens epithelial cells. In this case actin filaments lie in bundles approximately 0.2μm thick parallel to the basal membrane creating the characteristically smooth and quiescent lower surface. Experiments with cultured epithelial cells have shown that the organization of this actin-rich layer depends on extracellular matrix components. The attachment of these actin bundles to the plasma membrane is less well

5

Fig. 5. Transmission electron micrograph of a vertical section through the leading edge of a well-spread fibroblast. Note the thick dorsal and ventral cortical layers of aligned microfilaments. ×32 000.

characterized than in the case of the adhesion plaques or microvilli; however, an integral membrane heparan sulphate proteoglycan as well as specific receptors for laminin and collagen may be involved (Hay, 1985).

Away from these regions of specialized function the cortex of vertebrate tissue cells, if it exists at all, is certainly less conspicuous and harder to detect. Transmission electron microscopy sometimes shows a thin region of amorphous material from which other cytoplasmic organelles are excluded (Ben Ze'ev, Dueer, Solomon & Penman, 1979). Techniques such as fast-freeze, deep-etch electron microscopy sometimes reveal fine filaments extending between the inner surface of the plasma membrane and the lateral surfaces of actin filaments (Tilney, 1983; Hirokawa, 1982). It is possible that these crosslinks are easily lost in the course of preparation for electron microscopy and that they are more widely distributed than is generally recognized.

A thinner and more specialized type of membrane-associated cortex is found in circulating erythrocytes and may be an example of a structure common to all cells. The skin of the red blood cell consists of a bimolecular leaflet of lipid and a number of glycoproteins. Attached to its inner surface is a very thin layer of protein, perhaps 10 nm in thickness (Fig. 6). The make-up of this thin two-dimensional layer is fairly well understood (Bennett, 1985). A transmembrane protein, 'band 3', is bound to a cytoplasmic protein, ankyrin, which in turn is bound to spectrin. Spectrin itself is a long flexible protein, which forms a complex with another protein termed 'band 4.1', and short oligomeric lengths of actin filament stabilized by tropomyosin, thereby building an extended two-dimensional network (Byers & Branton, 1985). A notable feature of this arrangement is that actin is not attached directly to the membrane but

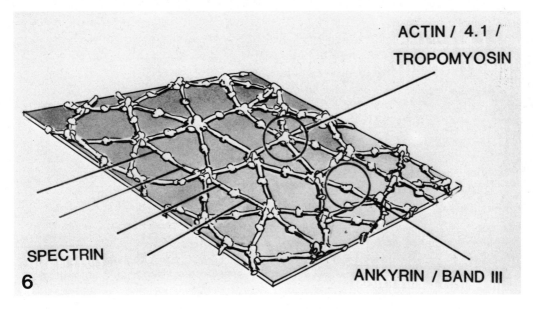

Fig. 6. Schematic diagram of the two-dimensional network of spectrin and other proteins on the inner face of the plasma membrane of the mammalian red blood cell (see Byers & Branton, 1985).

through a series of intermediate molecules. Indeed this is also the case in microvilli and probably in stress fibres, and may be a general feature of the association of actin with membranes in vertebrate cells.

Spectrin-like and ankyrin-like proteins have been detected in most types of vertebrate cells (Bennett, 1985). They are closely similar to their erythrocyte counterparts and presumably can form a cortical network similar to that in the red blood cell. However, the situations are not precisely the same. At least in fibroblastic cells in culture, the spectrin family of proteins are not uniformly distributed around the entire cell cortex. They are excluded from certain regions of specialized function, such as adhesion plaques, and are detectable in the cytoplasm. While neurones appear to possess a relatively uniform peripheral layer of ankyrin and spectrin in association with actin, the particular isoforms of spectrin and ankyrin found in the axon differ from those in the perikarya and dendrites (Lazarides & Nelson, 1985). The significance of these regional differences and, indeed, the function of spectrin and ankyrin in non-erythroid cells is not known.

To summarize the points raised thus far: a membrane-associated cortex is a conspicuous feature of certain very large cells, such as giant freshwater amoebae and echinoderm eggs. In these cells the cortex consists of an actin-rich gel visible in the light microscope and mechanically distinct from the rest of the cytoplasm. In contrast, in vertebrate cells a uniform, mechanically strong cortex is only rarely found. A thin layer of this kind is evident in macrophages and neutrophils. But in most tissue cells the association between the plasma membrane and the cytoskeleton is variegated: conspicuous in certain specialized regions, such as in the core of surface extensions (microspikes and microvilli) and intercellular adhesions but weaker and transitory elsewhere. Even in regions of vertebrate tissue cells that appear to lack a well-defined cortex there may be a thin layer of spectrin and actin similar to the network underlying the membrane of mammalian red blood cells.

MECHANICAL PROPERTIES OF THE CELL CORTEX

To paraphrase a comment made by Wilhelm His a century ago, cell biology "cannot proceed independently of all reference to the general laws of matter – to the laws of physics and mechanics" (His, 1887). Certainly, until we know how cells produce and respond to physical forces we will not fully understand how they move and maintain their shape. But in turning to the mechanical properties of the cell surface we enter a grey area between whole cells and molecules in which we lack not only experimental data but also adequate concepts. Experimental difficulties exist because cells are small, and generally irregular and changing in shape. The interpretation of any parameters that one succeeds in measuring is often complicated by the variable contribution made by the cytoskeleton tightly associated with the plasma membrane and by internal contents, such as the nucleus and major organelles. Most fundamentally, it is extremely difficult to relate mechanical parameters such as moduli of elasticity and bending to molecular composition.

The mammalian red blood cell, in many ways ideal for such analysis, illustrates the state of the art. Many attempts have been made to give a mechanical explanation for its ability to adopt discoid, cup-shaped or echinocytic shapes under different conditions (see, e.g., Stokke, Mikkelson & Elgsaeter, 1986). But even in this stripped-down shell of a cell we cannot predict emergent shape or mechanical properties from the molecular details of the membrane.

But we must start somewhere. To simplify both the measurement of material properties and their interpretation in terms of cellular structures most experiments in 'cell mechanics' have used cells that are: (1) relatively large, (2) smooth-contoured, or (3) have a well-defined cortex (notably sea-urchin eggs and mammalian erythrocytes). They have also involved a number of ingenious devices by which small forces of known magnitude can be applied to the surfaces of cells and the resulting deflection measured. Three principal methods of applying force have been used. Those in which cells are: (1) squashed beneath a flat plate, (2) sucked in a small pipette, or (3) depressed by a small probe (Fig. 7).

The earliest estimates of the resistance to deformation of the cell surface, some of which go back to the nineteenth century, were based on the compression of sea-urchin eggs by a constant weight. As reviewed by Hiramoto (1981), a cluster of eggs are sandwiched between the lower floor of a microscope chamber, on which they rest, and a glass plate is placed on their upper surface. The decrease in vertical diameter as the eggs are squashed then indicates the ease with which their surface can be deformed (the interpretation of such results is discussed below). A closely similar experimental method was recently used to follow changes in surface properties following fertilization (Schroeder, 1981). An important modification of this

Fig. 7. Experimental approaches to the mechanical properties of the cell surface. The deformation produced in these experiments is a measure of the rigidity of the cell surface. A. The cell is squashed beneath a plate of known mass, such as a fragment of glass coverslip. B. A portion of the cell surface is sucked into the tip of a micropipette using a negative pressure of known value. C. The cell is indented by a flexible probe the bending of which indicates the force exerted.

technique, enabling the weight applied to the cells to be varied was devised by Cole in 1932. He used a thin gold beam, 6 μm thick, 180 μm wide and 3 mm long, which could be lowered onto a cell. The force applied was then calculated from the bending of the beam.

A different apparatus was used by Mitchison & Swann (1954). Called a 'cell elastimeter', this caused a bulge to be sucked from the surface of an echinoderm egg with a small pipette. From the size of the bulge, and the negative pressure needed to produce it, a parameter termed the surface 'stiffness' could be estimated. Micro-aspiration experiments of this kind have been used extensively. They have been used to follow the post-fertilization changes in sea-urchin eggs mentioned above (Wolpert, 1966). More recently, they have been used to measure the increase in the surface tension of erythrocytes following exposure to lectins (Evans & Leung, 1984; Smith & Hochmuth, 1982).

By far the most delicate and precise instrument used to date to investigate cell surface mechanics is that devised by Elson and colleagues (see Pasternak & Elson, 1985). The cell is depressed locally by a small glass probe mounted on a flexible steel wire or (more recently) on a glass beam. The wire is moved through a cyclic waveform by a piezoelectric motor and optical sensors monitor the deflections of the tip motor and of the probe. Since the tip of the probe is only 2 μm in diameter, and displacements of under 0·1 μm can be detected, the apparatus is able to measure the properties of very small cells, such as lymphocytes. It is even able to compare values in different regions of the same cell (Petersen, McConnaughey & Elson, 1982).

The raw data obtained in the experiments described above consist in every case of a distance, or 'strain' (depression of the surface or size of a bulge in a pipette or change in cell diameter), produced by a force, or 'stress', of known magnitude. For many purposes this empirical relationship between stress and strain is sufficient, e.g. when the properties of different kinds of cells, or of the same cell under different conditions, are to be compared. Calculation of intrinsic elastic moduli from such data is more complicated. It depends on the detailed geometry of the apparatus and of the cell; also on the time taken in the measurement, since the cell surface, in common with many biological materials, shows viscoelastic behaviour. Analysis, therefore, requires a number of simplifying assumptions.

The first assumption, without which analysis would indeed be difficult, is that the mechanical properties of the cell are dominated by its outer 'skin', that is, by the plasma membrane and its tightly associated cortex. As we have seen, this is probably true for echinoderm eggs and mammalian erythrocytes. Resistance to deformation in such a cell then arises from the flexural rigidity of the cortex and from its resistance to stretching (see, e.g., Taber, 1983). In a similar way, a car tyre resists deformation because it is made of thick rubber, which is difficult to bend, and because inflation with air has generated tension in the surface, which resists further areal expansion. Mitchison and Swann, in the experiments already mentioned, made an attempt to distinguish between the contributions of these two components, reaching the conclusion that flexural rigidity made a major contribution to the observed stiffness. However, this conclusion has been criticized on theoretical grounds (Wolpert, 1966; Yoneda, 1973), and other investigators have also assumed that the resistance to bending forces is negligible.

The latter view, at least, has the virtue that it makes analysis simpler. If resistance to bending is negligible, then the surface becomes a 'thin shell' in mechanical terms: one in which the only important forces are those in the plane of the membrane (Calladine, 1983). Two kinds of surface tension are then relevant: interfacial tension, arising from the phase boundary between the hydrophobic membrane components and their water-based surroundings, and the elasticity of the plasma membrane and its associated cortex.

The difference between these two types of surface tension is illustrated by two physical models of a flexible shell or skin: that of a soap bubble and that of a rubber balloon. In the soap bubble, tension in the skin and, hence, the inward pressure it exerts on the enclosed volume of air are direct consequences of the interfacial surface tension between soap solution and air. So long as an adequate reserve supply of soap solution exists, then the interfacial surface tension will be the same at all regions of the bubble surface independently of its size. The surface tension of a rubber balloon, in contrast, is a measure of the Hookean elasticity of the rubber of which the skin is made. As the balloon is inflated, the rubber stretches and the tension it generates increases.

Returning to the surface of the cell, we know that this must possess an area-independent interfacial surface tension similar to that seen in a soap bubble. (One might, for example, draw parallels between the incorporation of new membrane into the surface by exocytosis to the recruitment of fresh soap solution into the skin of the soap bubble.) Yet the contribution of this interfacial tension to the overall tension of the cell is probably minor. In the original study by Cole (1932), the response of the cell to compression appeared to be dominated by a large elastic component. Even though this viewpoint has been questioned (Yoneda, 1973), most subsequent investigators have, similarly, agreed that elasticity (or more accurately viscoelasticity) is the most important characteristic of the cell surface (Evans & Hochmuth, 1978).

It will be apparent from the foregoing that we are at present a long way from making secure and objective measurements of the moduli of elasticity and bending of the cell surface. Similarly, it is not yet possible to compare, rigorously, measurements made on different types of cells with different types of apparatus. However, measurements that have been made reveal such large variations in mechanical properties that we have been tempted to make an order-of-magnitude comparison. We have therefore listed in Table 1 approximate values of 'cell stiffness' based on the forces found necessary to deform the surface of the cell by $1 \mu m$, regardless of the methods used, and ignoring questions of the origins of the resistance to deformation.

Conspicuous in this table is the very small, essentially unmeasurable, value for a bimolecular leaflet of phospholipid compared to that at the surface of real cells. The lipid component of the plasma membrane seems to be of negligible strength and, by itself, unlikely to provide the motive force for cell movements in amoebae or fibroblasts (although such a role has been proposed; Bretscher, 1984). It should be noted, however, that plasma membranes also contain a variable complement of integral proteins, and where these reach high concentrations, or even form crystalline arrays as in gap junctions, the plasma membrane may contribute to cell surface stiffness.

A second salient feature in Table 1 is the large difference between the values for the red blood cell and a fibroblast. Evidently the spectrin-rich network associated with the plasma membrane is much weaker than a fully developed actin-rich cortex. Indeed, it may be weak enough to be influenced by the lipid bilayer, and there is evidence that the shape of the mammalian erythrocyte is affected by the composition of the phospholipid bilayer (Kuypers *et al.* 1984). Finally, it may be noted in Table 1 that, as expected, surface stiffness increases with the thickness of the cortical cytoskeleton.

Possibly the most interesting recent findings in cell mechanics concern changes in the surface stiffness of a cell with physiological activities. In the sophisticated measurements made by Elson and associates referred to above, the properties of

Table 1. *Mechanical 'stiffness' of the animal cell surface*

Type of cell	Cortical thickness (μm)	Stiffness (mdyne μm^{-1})	Reference
Sea-urchin egg	3–5	100	Schroeder (1981)
Cultured fibroblast	≈ 0.2	0.6	Petersen *et al.* (1982)
Lymphocyte	0.1–0.2	0.15	Pasternak & Elson (1985)
Red blood cell	0.01–0.02	10^{-3}	Evans (1973)
Phospholipid bilayer	0	$<10^{-3}$	Evans & Hochmuth (1978)

Representative, order-of-magnitude values obtained in surface indentation or microaspiration experiments. As emphasized in the text, stiffness is an empirical parameter incorporating both bending and stretching moduli of elasticity, and values are not strictly comparable between different experimental situations. Citations are to recent determinations or reviews.

lymphocytes were found to change in response to various kinds of treatment. Exposure of the cell to lectins or antibodies caused aggregation of receptors on the cell surface and produced a large increase in surface tension and decrease in receptor mobility (Edelman, 1976). Both responses occurred even if crosslinking was confined to one small region of the cell surface, so that it was not considered due simply to the formation of a rigid 'crust' on the cell surface. Here, as in studies of the fertilization of sea-urchin eggs, the membrane cortex seems capable of a profound reorganization, almost a change of state.

Besides their relevance to lymphocyte capping, phenomena of this kind are of great interest from the point of view of the response of cells to solid surfaces (which can act, in a sense, rather like crosslinking agents). A change in the cortex in response to contact with a surface is likely to be of major importance in cell locomotion and possibly also in the substrate dependence of cell growth shown by most freshly explanted animal tissue cells.

The surface stiffness of sea-urchin eggs shows interesting temporal and regional changes following fertilization. There is initially a global increase in tension (which may be related to the tendency of even small vertebrate cells to round-up before division) followed by focal relaxation at the two opposite poles. In the circumferential band midway between the poles, at the site of the forming contractile ring, surface stiffness or tension remains high throughout the second phase of general relaxation.

White & Borisy (1983) have discussed these changes of surface tension in a theoretical paper, using them as the basis of a model for cytokinesis. In their hypothesis, the surface tension is produced by linear contractile elements in the plane of the surface – a metaphor for the membrane-associated actin-rich cortex. As changes in surface tension occur (mediated, in the White–Borisy model, by influences spreading from the two mitotic spindles) the linear contractile elements move from regions of lower to regions of higher surface tension, changing as they do so from a random orientation to alignment with the equator of the cell. A suitable physical analogy might be that of an elastic net stocking drawn tightly around the cell, which is loosened at either pole by cutting some of the threads. The tension of the remaining network will automatically draw the remaining strands together around the middle of the cell while at the same time changing their orientation until they are circumferentially aligned (Fig. 8).

Although a sea-urchin egg is much larger than a vertebrate cell, and designed to survive in a very different environment, we suspect that the changes described above may be of widespread significance. Certainly, cytokinesis follows a similar course in most kinds of animal cells, so that even if we cannot at present measure such small-scale changes, it is not unreasonable to think that they exist. Moreover, the concept of regional changes in surface tension produced by the internal cytoskeleton, and especially microtubules, seems to fit several kinds of vertebrate cell movement.

Take fibroblast migration as an example. At the leading edge of the cell a highly motile flexible surface produces lamellipodia and microspikes while at the sides of the cell the surface is quiescent and smoothly rounded. As noted by Vasiliev (1982),

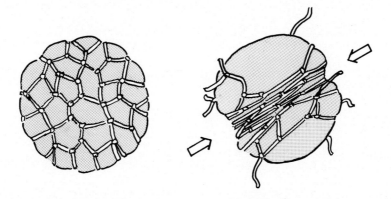

Fig. 8. Mechanical analogy for the changes in surface tension accompanying cytokinesis. The 'cell' on the left is enclosed in a network of elastic threads. Cutting some of these threads in the polar regions causes the remainder of the network to migrate to the equatorial region (right). Note that the threads will also tend to adopt an equatorial orientation.

these regional differences correspond to the distribution of microtubules, which in general tend to lie parallel to the long axis of the cell; and regional differences are lost when the microtubules break down in response to colchicine treatment. Furthermore, microspikes and lamellipodia, as well as particles on the cell surface and submembrane assemblies of actin filaments known as arcs (Heath, 1983), all flow backwards from the leading edge of the cell to the smoother more quiescent regions. Evidently, cycles of actin-containing structures occur in such cells, probably carrying with them other membrane components.

It seems reasonable to us to see this rearward flow of surface material as arising from regional variations in surface tension in the membrane and associated cyto-skeleton. The movements on the surface of a fibroblast would then conform to a pattern similar to that described above for a dividing echinoderm egg with certain modifications (for example, it must involve compensatory flow of membrane and cytoskeletal components through the cytoplasm to the advancing 'low tension' end of the cell). A very similar picture can be painted for the surface movements that occur on the growth cone at the advancing tip of a growing nerve axon (Bray & Chapman, 1985). In this case the surface at the actively moving (putatively low-tension) region of the growth cone moves back to the axonal cylinder, where it appears to be stabilized by interactions with the longitudinally aligned microtubules and neurofilaments.

We thank Elliot Elson and Tom Pollard for their helpful comments on this article.

REFERENCES

ALLEN, R. D., COOLEDGE, J. W. & HALL, P. J. (1960). Streaming in cytoplasm dissociated from the giant amoeba, *Chaos chaos. Nature, Lond.* **187**, 896–899.

ALLEN, R. D. & KAMIYA, N. (1964). *Primitive Motile Systems in Cell Biology*. New York, London: Academic Press.

APGAR, J. R., HERRMANN, S. H., ROBINSON, J. M. & MESCHER, M. F. (1985). Triton X-100 extraction of P185 humour cells: evidence for a plasma membrane skeleton structure. *J. Cell Biol.* **100**, 1369–1378.

BENNETT, H. & CONDEELIS, J. (1984). Decoration with myosin subframent-1 disrupts contacts between microfilaments and the cell membrane in isolated *Dictyostelium* cortices. *J. Cell Biol.* **99**, 1434–1440.

BENNETT, V. (1985). The membrane skeleton of human erythrocytes and its implication for more complex cells. *A. Rev. Biochem.* **54**, 273–304.

BEN ZE'EV, A., DUEER, N., SOLOMON, F. & PENMAN, S. (1979). The outer boundary of the cytoskeleton: Lamina derived from plasma membrane probes. *Cell* **17**, 859–865.

BRAY, D. & CHAPMAN, K. (1985). Analysis of microspike movements on the neuronal growth cone. *J. Neurosci.* **5**, 3204–3213.

BRETSCHER, M. S. (1984). Endocyosis: relation to capping and cell locomotion. *Science* **224**, 681–686.

BYERS, T. J. & BRANTON, D. (1985). Visualization of the protein associations in the erythrocyte membrane skeleton. *Proc. natn. Acad. Sci. U.S.A.* **82**, 6153–6157.

CALLADINE, C. R. (1983). *Theory of Shell Structures*. Cambridge University Press.

CHAMBERS, R. & CHAMBERS, E. L. (1961). *Explorations into the Nature of the Living Cell*. Cambridge, Mass.: Harvard University Press.

CHEN, W. T., HASEGAWA, E., HASEGAWA, T., WEINSTOCK, C. & YAMADA, K. M. (1985). Development of cell surface linkage complexes in cultured fibroblasts. *J. Cell Biol.* **100**, 1103–1114.

COLE, K. S. (1932). Surface forces of *Arbacia* eggs. *J. cell. comp. Physiol.* **1**, 1–19.

COMLY, L. T. (1973). Microfilaments in *Chaos carolinensis*: Membrane association, distribution and heavy meromyosin binding in the glycerinated cell. *J. Cell Biol.* **58**, 230–237.

DAMSKY, C. H., KNUDSEN, K. A., BRADLEY, D., BUCK, C. A. & HORWITZ, A. F. (1985). Distribution of cell substratum attachment (CSAT) antigen on myogenic and fibroblastic cells in culture. *J. Cell Biol.* **100**, 1528–1539.

EDELMAN, G. H. (1976). Surface modulation in cell recognition and cell growth. *Science* **192**, 218–226.

EVANS, E. A. (1973). New membrane concept applied to the analysis of fluid shear- and micropipette-deformed red blood cells. *Biophys. J.* **13**, 941–954.

EVANS, E. A. & HOCHMUTH, R. M. (1978). Mechanochemical properties of membranes. *Int. Rev. Cytol.* **10**, 1–64.

EVANS, E. A. & LEUNG, A. (1984). Adhesivity and rigidity of erythrocyte membrane in relation to wheat germ agglutinin binding. *J. Cell Biol.* **98**, 1201–1208.

GEIGER, B. (1983). Membrane–cytoskeleton interaction. *Biochim. biophys. Acta* **737**, 305–341.

GOODLOE-HOLLAND, C. M. & LUNA, E. J. (1984). A membrane cytoskeleton from *Dictyostelium discoideum*. III. Plasma membrane fragments bind predominantly to the sides of actin filaments. *J. Cell Biol.* **99**, 71–78.

HARTWIG, J. H., NIEDERMAN, R. & LIND, S. E. (1985). Cortical actin structures and their relationship to mammalian cell movements. In *Subcellular Biochemistry* (ed. D. B. Roodyn), vol. 11, pp. 1–49. New York: Plenum Press.

HAY, E. D. (1985). Matrix–cytoskeletal interactions in the developing eye. *J. cell. Biochem.* **27**, 143–156.

HEATH, J. P. (1983). Behaviour and structure of the leading lamella in moving fibroblasts. I. Occurrence and centripetal movement of arc-shaped microfilament bundles beneath the dorsal cell surface. *J. Cell Sci.* **60**, 331–354.

HIRAMOTO, Y. (1957). The thickness of the cortex and the refractive index of the protoplasm in sea urchin eggs. *Embryologia* **3**, 361–374.

HIRAMOTO, Y. (1981). Mechanical properties of dividing eggs. In *Mitosis/Cytokinesis* (ed. A. M. Zimmerman & A. Forer), pp. 398–418. New York: Academic Press.

HIROKAWA, N. (1982). Cross-linker system between neurofilaments, microtubules and membranous organelles in frog axons revealed by the quick-freeze, deep-etching method. *J. Cell Biol.* **94**, 129–142.

HIS, W. (1887–88). On the principles of animal morphology. *Proc. R. Soc. Edinb.* **15**, 287–298.

JEON, K. W., editor (1973). *The Biology of* Amoeba. New York, London: Academic Press.

KUYPERS, F. A., ROELOFSEN, B., BERENDSEN, W., OP DEN KAMP, J. A. F. & VAN DEENEN, L. L. M. (1984). *J. Cell Biol.* **99**, 2260–2267.

LAZARIDES, E. & NELSON, W. J. (1985). Expression and assembly of the erythroid membrane-skeleton proteins ankyrin (globin) and spectrin in the morphogenesis of chicken neurons. *J. cell. Biochem.* **27**, 423–441.

LEWIS, W. H. (1939). The role of a superficial plasmagel layer in changes of form, locomotion and division of cells in tissue cultures. *Arch. exp. Zellforsch.* **23**, 1–7.

LOOR, F. (1981). Cell surface–cell cortex transmembranous interactions with special reference to lymphocyte functions. *Cell Surf. Rev.* **7**, 253–335.

LUNA, E. J., GOODLOE-HOLLAND, C. M. & INGALLS, H. M. (1984). A membrane cytoskeleton from *Dictyostelium discoideium*. II. Integral proteins mediate the binding of plasma membranes to F-actin affinity beads. *J. Cell Biol.* **99**, 58–70.

MANGEAT, P. & BURRIDGE, K. (1984). Actin–membrane interaction in fibroblasts: What proteins are involved in this association? *J. Cell Biol.* **99**, 955–1035.

MAST, S. O. (1926). Structure, movement, locomotion and stimulation of amoeba. *J. Morph. Physiol.* **41**, 347–425.

MITCHISON, J. M. & SWANN, M. M. (1954). The mechanical properties of the cell surface. I. The cell elastimeter. *J. exp. Biol.* **31**, 443–460.

MOOSEKER, M. S., POLLARD, T. D. & WHARTON, K. A. (1982). Nucleated polymerisation of actin from the membrane-associated ends of microvillar filaments in the intestinal brush border. *J. Cell Biol.* **95**, 223–233.

MOSS, D. J. (1983). Cytoskeleton-associated glycoproteins from chicken sympathetic neurons and chicken embryo brain. *Eur. J. Biochem.* **135**, 291–297.

OLIVER, J. M. & BERLIN, R. D. (1982). Mechanisms that regulate the structural and functional architecture of cell surfaces. *Int. Rev. Cytol.* **74**, 55–94.

PASTERNAK, C. & ELSON, E. L. (1985). Lymphocyte mechanical response triggered by cross-linking surface receptors. *J. Cell Biol.* **100**, 860–872.

PETERSON, N. O., MCCONNAUGHEY, W. B. & ELSON, E. L. (1982). Dependence of locally measured cellular deformability on position on the cell, temperature and cytochalasin B. *Proc. natn. Acad. Sci. U.S.A.* **79**, 5327–5331.

POLLARD, T. D. & ITO, S. (1970). Cytoplasmic filaments of *Amoeba proteus*. I. The role of filaments in consistency changes and movement. *J. Cell Biol.* **46**, 267–289.

POLLARD, T. D. & KORN, E. D. (1973). Electron microscopic identification of actin associated with isolated amoeba plasma membranes. *J. biol. Chem.* **248**, 448–450.

ROGALSKI, A. A. & SINGER, S. J. (1985). An integral glycoprotein associated with the membrane attachment sites of actin microfilaments. *J. Cell Biol.* **101**, 785–801.

SCHROEDER, T. E. (1981). The origin of cleavage forces in dividing eggs. A mechanism in two steps. *Expl Cell Res.* **134**, 231–240.

SCHROEDER, T. E. & STRICKER, S. A. (1983). Morphological changes during maturation of starfish oocytes: surface ultrastructure and cortical actin. *Devl Biol.* **98**, 373–384.

SMITH, L. & HOCHMUTH, R. M. (1982). Effect of wheat germ agglutinin on the viscoelastic properties of erythrocyte membrane. *J. Cell Biol.* **94**, 7–11.

SPUDICH, A. & SPUDICH, J. A. (1979). Actin in Triton-treated cortical preparations of unfertilised and fertilised sea urchin eggs. *J. Cell Biol.* **82**, 212–226.

STRATFORD, C. A. & BROWN, S. S. (1984). Isolation of an actin-binding protein from membranes of *Dictyostelium discoideum*. *J. Cell Biol.* **100**, 727–735.

STOKKE, B. T., MIKKELSEN, A. & ELGSAETER, A. (1986). The human erythrocyte membrane skeleton may be an ionic gel. *Eur. biophys. J.* (in press).

STOSSEL, T. P., HARTWIG, J. H. & YIN, H. L. (1981). Actin gelation and the structure of and movement of cortical cytoplasm. In *Cytoskeletal Elements and Plasma Membrane Organization. Cell Surface Rev.*, vol. 7, pp. 138–168. Amsterdam: North-Holland.

TABER, L. A. (1983). Compression of fluid-filled spherical shells by rigid indenters. *J. appl. Mech.* **50**, 717–722.

TAYLOR, D. L. & CONDEELIS, J. S. (1979). Cytoplasmic structure and contractility. *Int. Rev. Cytol.* **56**, 57–144.

TILNEY, L. G. (1983). Interactions between actin filaments and membranes give spatial organization to cells. *Modern Cell Biol.* **2**, 163–199.

TILNEY, L. G., BONDER, E. M. & DEROSIER, D. J. (1981). Actin filaments elongate from their membrane associated ends. *J. Cell Biol.* **90**, 485–494.

TILNEY, L. G. & INOUÉ, S. (1982). The acrosomal reaction of *Thyone* sperm. II. The kinetics and possible mechanism of acrosomal process elongation. *J. Cell Biol.* **93**, 820–827.

VASILIEV, J. M. (1982). Spreading and locomotion of tissue cells: factors controlling the distribution of pseudopodia. *Phil. Trans. R. Soc. Lond.* B **299**, 159–167.

WEEDS, A. (1982). Actin-binding proteins: regulators of cell architecture and motility. *Nature, Lond.* **296**, 811–816.

WHITE, J. G. & BORISY, G. G. (1983). On the mechanism of cytokinesis in animal cells. *J. theor. Biol.* **101**, 289–316.

WOLPERT, L. (1966). The mechanical properties of the membrane of the sea urchin egg during cleavage. *Expl Cell Res.* **41**, 385–396.

YONEDA, M. (1973). Tension at the surface of sea urchin eggs on the basis of 'liquid drop' concept. *Adv. Biophys.* **4**, 153–190.

J. Cell Sci. Suppl. 4, 89–102 (1986)
Printed in Great Britain © The Company of Biologists Limited 1986

CELL MOTILITY

EDWIN W. TAYLOR

Department of Molecular Genetics & Cell Biology, The University of Chicago, 920 E. 58th Street, Chicago, IL 60637, USA

INTRODUCTION

A review of progress in a field as broad as cell motility will be a selection of topics that reflects the interest of the reviewer. I will restrict the subject even further by concentrating on a single problem, the progress in our understanding of the physical-chemical basis of motility. One measure of progress in cell biology is the extent to which the description of a phenomenon is replaced by a chemical mechanism. An understanding of the mechanisms of individual processes studied in isolation still comes far short of a science of cell biology, which must deal with the integration of processes into a description of the cell as a functional unit. Considerable progress has been made in the understanding of individual processes but their integration in the cell remains a problem to be studied over the next 20 years.

Studies on a wide variety of cells and tissues have led to the important concept that the vast majority of the examples of motile behaviour can be accounted for by a small number of basic mechanisms for the conversion of chemical energy into mechanical work. Although there are a few exceptions, such as spasmonemes (Amos, 1975) and myonemes (Huang & Pitelka, 1973), motile behaviour can generally be ascribed to the action of actin and myosin or microtubules plus an enzyme such as dynein or kinesin. In both cases the source of energy is the hydrolysis of ATP. The fundamental questions are how is chemical energy converted into force or movement and whether the underlying mechanisms are similar in the different systems.

Striated muscle provides the best model for the understanding of an actomyosin-based motile system and the concepts developed in the studies of muscle have been the basis for an understanding of motility in non-muscle cells. The major advantage of striated muscle is the high degree of order, which provides the possibility of determining the structural change that leads to force development, and of correlating the structural change with biochemical steps in the enzyme mechanism. However, much of the structure is a specialization for the particular problem for which the muscle was designed and we wish to extract from the mechanism the properties of the minimum motile system that can serve as the basis for cell functions.

Myosins from a variety of organisms ranging from amoeba to mammals have similar properties and it is reasonable to infer that the energy conversion mechanism is essentially the same in all organisms. A possible exception is the presence in some amoebae of two types of myosin, the normal two-headed myosin and a second myosin having a single head (Pollard & Korn, 1973).

THE ACTOMYOSIN SYSTEM OF MUSCLE

Progress in the study of the mechanism of muscle contraction has been the subject of numerous reviews (Goody & Holmes, 1982; Webb & Trentham, 1983). The structural elements of the sarcomere are an array of actin filaments of the same polarity in each half sarcomere and a bipolar myosin thick filament. The mechanism can be discussed in terms of a single myosin cross-bridge and a single actin filament, since the bridges appear to act independently as tension generators (Huxley & Simmonds, 1971). A mechanochemical scheme was put forward in the early seventies based on structural, mechanical and biochemical evidence (Huxley, 1969; Huxley & Simmonds, 1971; Lymn & Taylor, 1971). It was proposed that the acto-myosin complex (AM) could exist in two states in which the cross-bridge head is bound to actin at an angle of 45° or 90°. Rotation of the head from the 45° to the 90° (rigor) orientation produces a relative sliding of the filaments or stretches a spring in the myosin molecule if the filaments are held at fixed length. The three important properties of the enzyme reaction are: (1) nucleotide binding to AM alters the conformation, leading to a very rapid dissociation of the protein complex, $AM + ATP \rightarrow A + M \cdot ATP$; (2) the nucleotide is hydrolysed fairly rapidly by myosin but the products dissociate slowly from the enzyme site, $M \cdot ATP \rightarrow M \cdot ADP \cdot P_i \rightarrow M + ADP + P_i$; (3) actin activates myosin ATPase by increasing the rate of product dissociation, $AM \cdot ADP \cdot P_i \rightarrow AM + ADP + P_i$. It was proposed that reaction (1) corresponds to the dissociation of the cross-bridge at the end of the force-generating step, that the hydrolysis step alters the structure of the free bridge in reaction (2) so that it binds at a 90° orientation, and that release of products in reaction (3) is coupled to rotation to the 45° state to complete the cycle. This simple model was important in the development of the subject since it appeared to provide a simple explanation of the structural changes in the contraction cycle and to answer the question of how ATP hydrolysis could be coupled to movement.

During the last dozen years extensive studies have been devoted to testing the assumptions and predictions of this model. It is evident that the actual mechanism is more complex. Studies by X-ray diffraction of muscle and by spectroscopy using fluorescence and spin-labels (Huxley *et al.* 1983: Yanigita, 1981; Cooke, Crowder & Thomas, 1982; Burghardt, Ando & Borejdo, 1983) have failed to provide clear evidence for a 90° orientation of the cross-bridge. The results of these studies are not in agreement and in only one case (Burghardt *et al.* 1983) has any difference in angle been obtained for active *versus* rigor muscle. The large rotation was based on the mechanical evidence that the cross-bridge range was of the order of 10 nm and the head was about 10 nm long; consequently, a 45° rotation is required. A 90° orientation of the cross-bridge was also inferred from the diffraction pattern of relaxed muscle (Huxley & Brown, 1967), but this interpretation has not been confirmed. Recent evidence from crystals of myosin (Winkelmann, Mekeel & Rayment, 1985) indicates that the head has a length of 16 nm. The minimum range of the elastic element is 4 nm; larger ranges are model-dependent conclusions (Ford, Huxley & Simmonds, 1977). Consequently, the actual rotation may be only 15° to

20° (Huxley & Kress, 1985) and it has so far escaped detection. The head is also considerably bent in shape and may not rotate as a rigid body attached to a spring. The head may bend in the region distal to the sites to which fluorescence or spin-labels have been attached since these labels generally fail to detect any rotation of the head. In this case the spring is part of the globular head. A satisfactory answer has not been obtained to the question of whether the head rotates or bends and by how much.

The biochemical model has also become more complex with the finding of additional intermediate states in the mechanism. More important is the evidence that the equilibrium constant of the hydrolysis step is small, and that hydrolysis in solution can occur without dissociation of actomyosin at a comparable or somewhat slower rate than for myosin (Stein, Chock & Eisenberg, 1984; Rosenfeld & Taylor, 1984). The weakly bound $M \cdot ATP$ and $M \cdot ADP \cdot P_i$ states attach and detach rapidly on the time scale of the cycle, hence they are essentially in equilibrium with the corresponding bound states. The same situation is probably the case in muscle. Thus, the reaction cannot be described by a simple cycle. In its simplest form the reaction is:

$$AM+T \; \rightleftharpoons \; AM \cdot T \; \rightleftharpoons \; AM \cdot D \cdot P \; \rightleftharpoons \; AM \cdot D \; \rightleftharpoons \; AM$$
$$\updownarrow \qquad\qquad \updownarrow \qquad\qquad \updownarrow \qquad\qquad \updownarrow \qquad\qquad \updownarrow$$
$$M+T \; \rightleftharpoons \; M \cdot T \; \rightleftharpoons \; M \cdot D \cdot P \; \rightleftharpoons \; M \cdot D \; \rightleftharpoons \; M$$

where, T, D and P refer to ATP, ADP and inorganic phosphate, respectively.

In the absence of structural evidence it is not clear how the biochemical states are to be assigned to cross-bridge orientations. A better model of the cycle is to regard the weakly attached states, $M \cdot T$ and $M \cdot D \cdot P$, as a pool of bridges that are in rapid equilibrium with the corresponding attached states. Since these states can change actin sites rapidly they exert negligible force and whether they have the same or different orientation has little effect on the properties of the system. The $AM \cdot D \cdot P$ state is still equivalent to the 90° state of the original model and the strongly bound states $AM \cdot D$ and AM correspond to the 45° orientation (Eisenberg & Greene, 1980). The behaviour is illustrated in Fig. 1. The cross-bridge enters the pool by the rapid detachment by ATP. The rate of transit through the pool is determined by the rate of the hydrolysis step and the attached bridge leaves the pool by the transition from $AM \cdot D \cdot P$ to $AM \cdot D$ with a change in orientation or deformation. The model retains most of the features of the original scheme but we have no information on the relative orientation of the weakly bound states. Consequently, we can no longer assign a change in the orientation of binding to a structural effect of the hydrolysis step.

A problem with contraction models is that the significance of two heads has not been explained. It is generally assumed that the heads act independently. A single-headed myosin prepared by proteolytic digestion can form threads with actin that exert the same tension per head as normal myosin (Cooke & Franks, 1978). The single-headed myosin of *Acanthamoeba* produces bead movement in the model system described below (Albanesi *et al.* 1985). Although the evidence suggests that a single-headed myosin is sufficient to produce movement, the efficiency of such

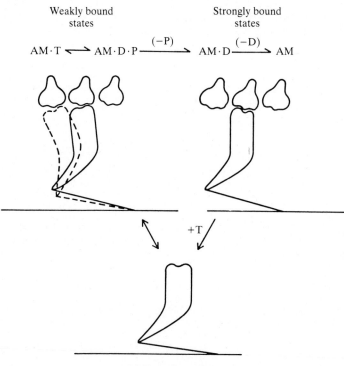

Weakly bound states | Strongly bound states

$$AM \cdot T \rightleftharpoons AM \cdot D \cdot P \xrightarrow{(-P)} AM \cdot D \xrightarrow{(-D)} AM$$

$$+T$$

$$M \cdot D \cdot P \rightleftharpoons M \cdot T$$

Fig. 1. Representation of the cross-bridge cycle. The strongly bound AM·D and AM states correspond to the 45° orientation of the myosin head. The AM state is very rapidly detached by the binding of ATP but M·T can re-attach rapidly to give a weakly bound state (AM·T). Hydrolysis can occur in either the M·T or AM·T states and M·D·P is also weakly bound to actin. The AM·T and AM·D·P states rapidly detach and possibly re-attach to different actin units. This fluctuation is symbolized by drawing the same head in continuous and broken outlines attached to different actins in a different orientation. It is not known whether the hydrolysis step effects the preferred orientation of attachment of the weakly bound states. The interaction of actin with the structure of the head accelerates the disociation of phosphate and the head rotates to the strongly bound orientation. 'Rotation' is drawn as a movement of the whole head but it could involve a deformation of the tapered region; a change in orientation of actin units might also occur in the cycle.

systems is unknown. The special requirements of muscle for high energy-conversion efficiency and the development of large forces may necessitate a more subtle mechanism involving interaction of the two heads. At present we do not understand why myosin and dynein have at least two heads.

THE MICROTUBULE–DYNEIN SYSTEM OF CILIA

Cilia and flagella are discussed by Brokaw in this volume but we are concerned with the relationship between the mechanisms of force generation in the microtubule–dynein and actomyosin systems. This problem has been the subject of a recent review (Johnson, 1985) and only the main conclusions need be repeated here.

Dynein, isolated from various organisms, is a two- or three-headed molecule. It consists of two (or three) heavy chains with molecular weights in the $300\,000\,M_r$ range, two (or three) intermediate chains of $70\,000$ to $100\,000\,M_r$ and three or four light chains in the $15\,000$ to $20\,000\,M_r$ range. The globular heads are connected by flexible strands to a root-like base that appears to bind to the A tubule. The heads interact with the B tubule in the enzyme cycle. Thus, dynein has a superficial resemblance to myosin and the heads may undergo a cycle of attachment, movement and detachment.

The three properties of actomyosin ATPase discussed in the last section are also properties of the microtubule–dynein system. The heads are rapidly detached from the microtubule by the binding of ATP, the free dynein has a relatively rapid hydrolysis step followed by a slower release of products, although the rate is much faster than with myosin, and microtubules can activate dynein ATPase in solution. As discussed in detail by Johnson (1985), the similarities in kinetic properties suggest that the nucleotide-binding and hydrolysis steps have similar functions in driving the microtubule–dynein and actomyosin systems.

CONSTRUCTING A MOTILE SYSTEM

What is the minimum structure necessary to produce movement? In smooth muscle the thick and thin filaments are not arranged in a regular lattice, yet the muscle can exert a tension comparable to striated muscle. In muscle the thick filament is a bipolar structure, which normally interacts with two actin filament bundles of opposite polarity. The heads of myosin are able to rotate about the base of the globular region, including an axial rotation, since the two curved heads of heavy meromyosin are observed in a parallel orientation in the actin–heavy meromyosin complex (Craig *et al.* 1980). Since the molecule is a dimer, a relative axial rotation of the two heads must occur. Although there may be some constraint on this rotation, which reduces the probability of interaction of heads with actin filaments of the wrong polarity at short sarcomere lengths, it is primarily the polarity of the actin filament that determines the direction of sliding. An array of myosin molecules that are not organized into a bipolar filament may be expected to act additively in generating a force in a given direction determined by the polarity of actin filaments. The polarity of actin filaments relative to a Z line, dense body or membrane is defined by the direction specified by decoration of the filaments with myosin, which gives an arrowhead structure. The arrow points away from the Z line. The opposite or barbed end is referred to as the plus end because it has a higher rate of elongation in the polymerization reaction. Thus, myosin molecules or thick filaments move toward the plus end of actin filaments.

Movement has been demonstrated in reconstituted actomyosin mixtures. Individual thick filaments slide along polarized bundles of actin filaments (Higashi-Fujime, 1982). A rotary motor was constructed by polymerizing actin filaments on the trailing surface of four paddles arranged at right angles. The addition of myosin fragments and ATP caused a rotation of the paddles (Yano, Yamomoto & Shimizu, 1982). A more interesting model, suitable for quantitative studies, was constructed by covalent attachment of myosin to small beads. The coated beads moved along polarized actin filament bundles obtained from *Nitella* (Sheetz & Spudich, 1983; Sheetz, Chasan & Spudich, 1984). The velocity of movement corresponded closely to the velocity of unloaded shortening of the sarcomeres of the muscles used as the source of the myosin. Although there is some uncertainty as to movement produced by heavy meromyosin from muscle, the single-headed myosin will function in the bead system (Albanesi *et al.* 1985), and endogenous vesicles of *Acanthamoeba*, which have the myosin bound to them, are also transported by actin filaments (Adams & Pollard, 1985). The important conclusion from these studies is that the minimum motile system consists of a polarized bundle of actin filaments and independent myosin molecules attached to a suitable substrate.

Various authors have been intrigued by the possibility that a microtubule–dynein-like system might be acting in intracellular movement. Although the cilium uses a doublet microtubule that is not found in cytoplasm, the enzyme of cilia will bind to cytoplasmic microtubules (Johnson, 1985). Dynein-like molecules have been isolated from cytoplasm (Pratt, 1980; Hisanga & Sakai, 1983) but convincing evidence for the participation of these components in a motile system has not been obtained. Recently, the movement of vesicles along single microtubules has been observed using extracts of axoplasm (Allen *et al.* 1985; Vale *et al.* 1985*a*; Lasek & Brady, 1985) and a protein that is necessary for this movement has been purified (Vale *et al.* 1985*b*; Brady, 1985). The protein, named kinesin, binds to microtubules and to vesicles or to carboxylated latex beads. It is dissociated from microtubules by ATP. Although the enzymic activity is very low the properties of the protein suggest that it may be the component of the system responsible for motility. It appears to be distinct from ciliary dynein, since the M_r is about 600 000 and it lacks the heavy polypeptide chains characteristic of dynein. Although it is too soon to evaluate this important discovery it appears that a motile system can consist of a single microtubule and an enzyme, presumably kinesin, attached to a suitable substrate. So, cells contain two motile systems capable of producing the movement of organelles and the order that is required for unidirectional movement is provided by the polarity of the microtubule or actin filament.

CONTRACTION AND MOTILITY IN CELLS

The wide variety of the motile behaviour of cells is divided into three classes for the purpose of discussion. Hopefully the classes correspond to distinguishable differences in mechanism. (1) Organelle movements, including the movement of vesicles in axons, possibly secretory processes in cells, melanophores and some aspects of chromosome movements; (2) changes in cell shape, spreading and cleavage; (3) streaming and amoeboid locomotion.

The classification is not based on whether the movement is caused by an actomyosin or a microtubule system, because the mechanism of a minimum motile system is likely to be the same for both cases.

Organelle movements

In some respects this category may be the simplest to understand. The movements of vesicles and chromosomes at velocities of a few μm per second require a very low rate of energy production to overcome viscous drag (Taylor, 1964). The summation of the action of a small number of myosin molecules is sufficient to meet the energy requirement. The experiments with coated beads show that binding of myosin or other enzymes to the beads does not require a specific structural arrangement of the myosin. The direction of movement is determined by the polarity of the actin filament or microtubule. The properties of the actomyosin system are well suited to this type of movement. A small number of myosin molecules positioned to interact with actin, probably between 10 and 100, are sufficient to maintain the attachment by summation of weak interactions of M·ATP and M·ADP·P states. The rapid detachment of these weakly bound states does not impede the movement. Hydrolysis of ATP at an appreciable rate occurs only for the myosins that interact with actin to complete the hydrolysis cycle. In muscle the activation factor is 500–1000; consequently, the system is reasonably efficient if only a small fraction of the myosins on the surface of the bead are able to interact with actin. Cytoplasmic myosin is activated by calcium binding to a calmodulin-dependent kinase, which phosphorylates a myosin light chain; consequently, the system is controlled by calcium.

This system accounts for organelle movement in a plant cell such as *Nitella* but it has not been shown to be responsible for vesicle movements in animal cells. The axon provides the most useful system for the study of vesicle movement in animal cells (Schliwa, 1984) and in this case the movement depends on a microtubule system. Fast transport occurs at a rate of $2-3 \mu m\,s^{-1}$, which is comparable to the velocity of sliding of filaments in a muscle. Beads or foreign synaptic vesicles injected into an axon are transported at comparable rates, indicating the presence of a soluble factor (Adams & Bray, 1983; Schroer, Brady & Kelly, 1985). The motion of beads and axoplasmic vesicles has been demonstrated in a reconstituted system consisting of synthetic microtubules and the protein kinesin prepared from the soluble fraction of extracts of brain axoplasm (Vale *et al.* 1985*b*). Velocities of movement of particles along single microtubules are comparable to the rate of fast transport in axons.

Movements in the reconstituted system are unidirectional along a particular microtubule but in axons different classes of vesicles are transported in both directions. In axons the microtubules appear to be unipolar (Burton & Paige, 1981), with the plus end pointing down the axon as expected from the polarity of microtubule growth from the centrosome. This poses a problem, since the direction of movement is expected to be determined by the polarity of the microtubule. In crude extracts of axoplasm bidirectional movement of vesicles was observed along a single microtubule (Allen *et al.* 1985; Vale *et al.* 1985*a*). It is difficult to imagine a mechanism of bidirectional movement produced by a single enzyme, which makes it necessary to suppose that two different enzymes are involved.

The movement of chromosomes in mitosis has obvious similarities to the movement of vesicles in axons by a microtubule system. Saltatory movements of particles along astral rays and along the surface of the mitotic spindle are commonly observed in cells (Taylor, 1964). This phenomenon may be explained by the same mechanism as axon transport if the particle dissociates from the microtubule at the end of the saltation.

The mechanism of chromosome movement has long been debated in spite of the absence of evidence. Recent observations, aided by improvements in fluorescence microscopy, have begun to provide important evidence on chromosome movements (Mitchison & Kirschner, 1985*a,b*). The kinetochore region of the metaphase chromosome is able to capture a microtubule and the plus end of the microtubule points toward the chromosome. In the presence of ATP the chromosome moves toward the plus end as the microtubule elongates by polymerization. The nature of the enzyme is unknown but a kinesin-like factor is an obvious candidate. Although the authors of this exciting work registered some disappointment that the chromosome moves away from the pole, the results suggest an explanation for much of the movement that occurs in mitosis, the movement of chromosomes to the metaphase plate and the oscillation of chromosomes on the plate during metaphase. A second enzyme could be involved in movement to the pole, as in the axon system.

The striking progress in the study of organelle movement promises to provide a biochemical explanation for some of the outstanding problems of cell biology within the next few years.

Cell shape

Immunofluorescence microscopy has revealed the complex arrangement of actin filaments, microtubules and intermediate filaments in the cytoplasm of the cell. A prominent feature of cells, particularly when spread on a surface, is the network of stress fibres (Byers, White & Fujiwara, 1984). The fibres consist of bundles of actin filaments, which in some cases show periodic staining with anti-α-actinin and anti-tropomyosin. Staining with anti-myosin showed a periodicity of $0.5\,\mu\text{m}$ (Herman & Pollard, 1981). Thus, some stress fibres have a sarcomere-like structure. Active shortening of stress fibres has not been commonly observed *in vivo*, although contraction can be induced by ATP in isolated fibres (Isenberg *et al.* 1976).

Stress fibres often terminate at or near focal contacts of the cell with the underlying substrate, which serve to anchor the cell (Izzard & Lochner, 1976). The inner plaque of the adherens junction contains α-actinin, which binds to actin, and vinculin, which is implicated in attachment to membranes (Geiger, Zafrira, Kreis & Schlessinger, 1984). Although there is some uncertainty as to the arrangement of these proteins in the plaque, the structure appears to be responsible for attachment of the stress fibre to the junction. Thus, the stress fibres appear to provide a set of connections among the points of attachment of the cell to the surface. Although there does not appear to be direct evidence that the fibres maintain a state of tension, this would act to stiffen the connections (Byers *et al.* 1984).

The stress fibre, among the various arrangements of these proteins in cells, comes closest to reproducing the muscle-like organization of actomyosin and it is surprising that it appears to have a structural rather than a contractile function in the cell. However, a structure resembling a stress fibre may function indirectly in cell motility. Moving fibroblasts often taper down to a tail-like projection at the trailing end of the cell. The tail appears to be anchored to the substrate and is pulled off the surface by what appears to be an active contraction of a stress fibre. Retraction requires ATP and activation of the myosin by phosphorylation by myosin light-chain kinase (Yenna & Goldman, 1978; Yenna, Askoy, Hartshorn & Goldman, 1978). Thus, breaking of focal contacts by contraction of a stress fibre may be necessary for movement in cells making strong contacts with the substrate but this contraction does not generate the force for movement.

Cell cleavage can be considered to be a sarcomere-type contraction mechanism. Myosin and a ring of actin filaments are found in the cleavage furrow (Fujiwara & Pollard, 1978). Bundles of actin filaments project at intervals from the membrane and appear to interact with myosin thick filaments (Sanger & Sanger, 1980). This arrangement corresponds to the bipolar sarcomere structure and would act like a draw-string.

Thus, actin and myosin can be arranged in a sarcomere-like structure in the cell but the function of this is in maintaining and changing cell shape, rather than in locomotion. In addition to stress fibres, actin filaments occur in small bundles and in a more or less random orientation, suggesting a gel structure. This type of organization is found adjacent to the plasma membrane and is particularly prominent in the leading lamella of migrating fibroblasts. It is this type of organization, rather than the stress fibre, that is associated with cell movement.

Amoeboid locomotion and streaming

Movement by protoplasmic streaming is exhibited by amoeboid cells and slime moulds and is probably the most difficult to understand of the three classes. The motive force is undoubtedly generated by actomyosin, but the lack of any well-defined structure suggests only a negative conclusion, that a highly ordered structure is not necessary. Small actin filament bundles are observed in the cortex and associated with the membrane but actin is rather uniformly distributed throughout the ectoplasmic gel and streaming sol (Taylor, Wang & Heiple, 1980a). We are left with the conclusion that force is generated by the contraction of a relatively uniform three-dimensional gel of actomyosin. A further difficulty is that the gel must dissolve and be transported in the stream, and again re-form a gel in order to continue the motion in one direction. This would require a fine balance of the factors controlling both contraction and the sol–gel transformation. This double requirement is the basis of the solation–contraction hypothesis, which stresses that contraction and solation are linked reactions (Taylor, Hellewell, Virgin & Heiple, 1979).

The more difficult problem is not the contraction but the control of the state of actin and myosin in the cell. Progress in understanding streaming has come from the extensive studies on the state of actin and myosin in cells.

Myosins of smooth muscle and non-muscle cells, including the macrophage, a typical amoeboid cell, have similar properties. Activation by actin is controlled by phosphorylation of a myosin light chain. Phosphorylation also favours the formation of thick filaments (Suzuki, Onishi, Takahashi & Watanabe, 1978; Trybus, Huiatt & Lowey, 1982; Craig, Smith & Kendrick-Jones, 1983). The tail of myosin folds around the head in the unphosphorylated state and inhibits filament formation. Thus, myosin is soluble at the ionic strength present in a cell and individual myosin molecules are very weakly bound to actin at this ionic strength in the presence of ATP. Thick filament formation can occur in regions of the cell that have a sufficiently high calcium concentration to activate the kinase. In a region of lower calcium concentration, filaments would break down by being dephosphorylated by a phosphatase.

A striking development over the last few years is the isolation of a large number of proteins that interact with actin and control its state of aggregation in the cell. In the earlier studies of muscle actin it was recognized that α-actinin was bound at or near the barbed end of actin filaments and that β-actinin affected filament length (Maruyama, 1971), but the significance of these proteins was not appreciated. A variety of proteins have been isolated from non-muscle cells that bind to the barbed end, the pointed end and preferentially to actin monomers and thus determine the degree of polymerization of cellular actin. Other proteins induce the formation of bundles of filaments, the formation of three-dimensional gels and breakage of filaments (lists are given by Shliwa, 1981; Craig & Pollard, 1982). The polymerization of pure actin as studied in the test tube may not be relevant to what happens in the cell, but recent studies of actin polymerization call attention to an interesting property. The rates of addition of monomers differ by a factor of about 10 for the two ends (Pollard & Mooseker, 1981) and the coupling of ATP hydrolysis to polymerization leads to treadmilling in the steady state. What may be more important is that the rate of dissociation of subunits is larger for an end unit containing bound ADP than bound ATP; consequently, at a steady state some filaments can depolymerize while others protected by an actin·ATP cap can continue to grow (Pantaloni, Carlier & Korn, 1985). This effect (dynamic instability) is more dramatic for microtubules (Mitchison & Kirschner, 1984) but may also be important for actin filaments.

In order to deal with the bewildering list of proteins that interact with actin it is assumed that proteins with similar properties, which keep turning up in a variety of organisms, are probably important in controlling the state of actin, even though they may have different names. Proteins with similar functions may differ in details such as molecular weight but they will be considered to be essentially the same protein. The types of proteins found in different organisms are: (1) a barbed-end capping protein, which nucleates polymerization and requires calcium to bind to actin. It reduces the length of actin filaments by preventing reannealing of broken filaments or actively breaks filaments and immediately seals the new barbed end. (2) A large flexible dimeric protein, which cross-links actin filaments to yield a three-dimensional gel (in which every actin filament is connected to at least one other actin filament). It does not require calcium. (3) A smaller protein, which forms bundles or weak gels with actin. A pointed-end capping protein, requiring calcium, has been described in macrophages (Southwick, Tatsumi & Stossel, 1982). Although it may be important, pointed-end capping proteins have not been described in other cells except for muscle β-actinin. In the macrophage (1) and (2) are gelsolin and actin-binding proteins, respectively. In the sea urchin they are the $45000 M_r$ capping protein (Wang & Spudich, 1984) and the $200000 M_r$ protein (Bryan & Kane, 1978). The corresponding proteins have been described in smooth muscle, *Acanthamoeba, Physarum* and *Dictyostelium* (Schliwa, 1981; Craig & Pollard, 1982).

The capping and cross-linking proteins can function to produce a calcium-dependent sol–gel transformation (Stossel, 1983). In a region of low calcium concentration the cross-linking protein forms a three-dimensional gel with actin. At a higher calcium concentration the capping protein binds to barbed ends and the filament length is reduced by dissociation of actin from the pointed end and by preventing end-to-end association. It may also cut filaments. As the filament length is reduced the three-dimensional gel breaks down into small aggregates of capped filaments connected by the cross-linking protein. Myosin molecules form small thick filaments and interact with actin to bring about contraction of the aggregate. The loose gel of actomyosin, and possibly a bundling protein, probably breaks up into smaller aggregates as contraction proceeds and enters the streaming region. In the amoeba, *Chaos carolinensis*, the calcium concentration is relatively high in the tail region, where the force of contraction is probably developed, and the concentration decreases toward the head (Taylor, Blinks & Reynolds, 1980b). As the actomyosin aggregates are moved forward by the stream, the thick filaments dissociate and the actin re-forms a three-dimensional gel as the capping protein is released. This description, as given by Stossel, Taylor and their collaborators, is certainly incomplete but it is the beginning of a molecular description of this complex phenomenon.

SUMMARY

Approximately 20 years have passed since the first isolation of tubulin, dynein and non-muscle actomyosin. During this period actomyosin, microtubule–dynein or microtubules plus other ATPases (kinesin) have been implicated in almost all cellular motile phenomena. A possible exception is that polymerization of actin in a preferred direction could be responsible for extending the leading edge of a fibroblast. We now tend to look for an explanation of a motile process in terms of the cross-bridge cycle or some variation on this general mechanism. It will be of considerable interest to determine whether the new system for organelle movement fits this concept.

In spite of great progress in identifying the basis of motility, fundamental problems remain unsolved. The nature of the conformation change of actomyosin in the cross-bridge cycle is still unknown and the solution of this problem may require the determination of the three-dimensional structure of the actin–myosin–nucleotide complex. We are still at the stage of classifying proteins that bind to actin and microtubules. The control of the dynamic state of actin and the microtubules in the cell is still poorly understood. Recent studies give hope that it will be possible to understand the mechanism of mitosis, but the biochemical study of this problem has only just begun.

This work was supported by Program Project grant HL 20592 of the Heart, Lung and Blood Institute of the National Institutes of Health and by the Muscular Dystrophy Society of America.

REFERENCES

ADAMS, R. J. & BRAY, D. (1983). Rapid transport of foreign particles microinjected into crab axons. *Nature, Lond.* **303**, 718–720.

ADAMS, R. J. & POLLARD, T. D. (1985). Organelle movements on actin bundles. *J. Cell Biol.* **101**, 389a.

ALBANESI, J. P., FUJISAKI, H., HAMMER, J. A., KORN, E. D., JONES, R. & SHEETZ, M. P. (1985). Monomeric acanthamoeba myosin I supports movement *in vitro*. *J. biol. Chem.* **260**, 8649–8652.

ALLEN, R. D., WEISS, D. E., HAYDEN, J. H., BROWN, D. T., FIJISAKI, H. & SIMPSON, M. (1985). Gliding movement of and bidirectional organelle transport along single native microtubules. *J. Cell Biol.* **100**, 1736–1752.

AMOS, W. B. (1975). Contraction and calcium binding in the vorticelled ciliates. In *Molecules and Cell Movement* (ed. S. Inoue & P. E. Stephens), pp. 411–436. New York: Raven Press.

BRADY, S. T. (1985). Novel brain ATPase with properties expected for a fast axonal transport motor. *Nature, Lond.* **317**, 73–75.

BRYAN, J. & KANE, R. E. (1978). Separation and interaction of the major components of sea urchin actin gel. *J. molec. Biol.* **175**, 207–244.

BURGHARDT, T. P., ANDO, T. & BOREJDO, J. (1983). Evidence for cross bridge order in contraction of glycerinated skeletal muscle. *Proc. natn. Acad. Sci. U.S.A.* **80**, 7515–7519.

BURTON, P. R. & PAIGE, J. L. (1981). Polarity of axoplasmic microtubules in the olfactory nerve of the frog. *Proc. natn. Acad. Sci. U.S.A.* **78**, 3269–3273.

BYERS, H. R., WHITE, G. E. & FUJIWARA, K. (1984). Organization and function of stress fibers in cells. In *Cell and Muscle Motility* (ed. J. W. Shay), vol. 5, pp. 83–125. New York: Plenum Press.

COOKE, R., CROWDER, M. S. & THOMAS, D. D. (1982). Orientation of spin-labels attached to cross-bridges in contracting muscle fibers. *Nature, Lond.* **300**, 776–778.

COOKE, R. & FRANKS, K. (1978). Generation of force by single-headed myosin. *J. molec. Biol.* **120**, 361.

CRAIG, S. W. & POLLARD, T. D. (1982). Actin binding proteins. *Trends Biochem. Sci.* **7**, 88–92.

CRAIG, R., SMITH, R. & KENDRICK-JONES, J. (1983). Light-chain phosphorylation controls the conformation of vertebrate non-muscle and smooth muscle myosin molecules. *Nature, Lond.* **302**, 436–439.

CRAIG, R., SZENT-GYÖRGYI, A. G., BEASE, L., FLICKER, P., VIBERT, P. & COHEN, C. (1980). Electron microscopy of thin filaments decorated with a Ca-regulated myosin. *J. molec. Biol.* **140**, 35–55.

EISENBERG, E. & GREENE, L. E. (1980). Relation of muscle biochemistry to muscle physiology. *A. Rev. Physiol.* **42**, 293–309.

FORD, L. E., HUXLEY, A. F. & SIMMONDS, R. M. (1977). Tension responses to sudden length change in stimulated frog muscle fibres near slack length. *J. Physiol.* **269**, 441–515.

FUJIWARA, K. & POLLARD, T. D. (1978). Fluorescent antibody localization of myosin in the cytoplasm, cleavage furrow and mitotic spindle of human cells. *J. Cell Biol.* **71**, 848–875.

GEIGER, B., ZAFRIRA, A., KREIS, T. E. & SCHLESSINGER, J. (1984). Dynamics of cytoskeletal organization in areas of cell contact. *Cell and Muscle Motility* (ed. J. W. Shay), vol. 5, pp. 195–224. New York: Plenum Press.

GOODY, R. S. & HOLMES, K. C. (1983). Cross-bridges and the mechanism of muscle contraction. *Biochim biophys. Acta* **726**, 13–39.

HERMAN, I. M. & POLLARD, T. D. (1981). Electron microscopic localization of cytoplasmic myosin. *J. Cell Biol.* **88**, 346–351.

HIGASHI-FUJIME, S. (1982). Active movement of bundles of actin and myosin filaments from muscle. *Cold Spring Harbor Symp. quant. Biol.* **46**, 69–75.

HISANGA, S. & SAKAI, H. (1983). Cytoplasmic dynein of the sea urchin egg. *J. Biochem.* **93**, 87–98.

HUANG, B. & PITELKA, D. (1973). Contractile process in the ciliate, *Stentor coerulens*. Role of microtubules and filaments. *J. Cell Biol.* **57**, 704–722.

HUXLEY, A. F. & SIMMONDS, R. M. (1971). Proposed mechanisms of force generation in striated muscle. *Nature, Lond.* **233**, 533–538.

HUXLEY, H. E. (1969). Mechanism of muscle contraction. *Science* **164**, 1356–1366.

HUXLEY, H. E. & BROWN, W. (1967). Low angle X-ray diagram of vertebrate striated muscle. *J. molec. Biol.* **30**, 383–434.

HUXLEY, H. E. & KRESS, M. (1985). Cross-bridge behavior during muscle contraction. *J. Muscle Res. Cell Motil.* **6**, 153–164.

HUXLEY, H. E., SIMMONDS, R. M., FARUQI, A. R., KRESS, M., BORDES, J. & KOCH, M. H. J. (1983). Changes in X-ray reflections from contracting muscle during rapid mechanical transients. *J. molec. Biol.* **169**, 469–506.

ISENBERG, G., RATHKE, P. C., HULSMANN, N., FRANKE, W. W. & WOHLFARTH-BOTTERMANN, K. E. (1976). Cytoplasmic actomyosin fibrils in tissue culture cells. *Cell Tiss. Res.* **166**, 427–443.

IZZARD, C. S. & LOCHNER, L. R. (1976). Cell to substrate contacts in living fibroblasts. *J. Cell Sci.* **21**, 129–159.

JOHNSON, K. A. (1985). Pathway of the microtubule-dynein ATPase and the structure of dynein. *A. Rev. biophys. biophys. Chem.* **14**, 161–188.

LASEK, R. J. & BRADY, S. T. (1985). Attachment of transported vesicles to microtubules in axoplasm is facilitated by AMPPNP. *Nature, Lond.* **316**, 645–646.

LYMN, R. W. & TAYLOR, E. W. (1971). Mechanism of adenosine triphosphate hydrolysis by actomyosin. *Biochemistry* **10**, 4617–4624.

MARUYAMA, K. (1971). A study of β-actinin. *J. Biochem. Tokyo* **69**, 369–375.

MITCHISON, T. & KIRSCHNER, M. (1984). Microtubule dynamics and cellular morphogenesis. In *Molecular Biology of the Cytoskeleton* (ed. G. G. Borisy, D. W. Cleveland & D. B. Murphy), pp. 27–44. New York: Cold Spring Harbor Laboratory Press.

MITCHISON, T. J. & KIRSCHNER, M. W. (1985a). Properties of kinetochore *in vitro*. I. *J. Cell Biol.* **101**, 755–765.

MITCHISON, T. J. & KIRSCHNER, M. W. (1985b). Properties of kinetochore *in vitro*. II. *J. Cell Biol.* **101**, 766–777.

PANTALONI, D., CARLIER, M. & KORN, E. D. (1985). Interaction between ATP-actin and ADP-actin. *J. biol. Chem.* **260**, 6572–6578.

POLLARD, T. D. & KORN, T. D. (1973). *Acanthamoeba* myosin. *J. biol. Chem.* **248**, 4682–4690.

POLLARD, T. D. & MOOSEKER, M. S. (1981). Direct measurement of actin polymerization rate constants by electron microscopy. *J. Cell Biol.* **88**, 654–659.

PRATT, M. M. (1980). The identification of a dynein ATPase in unfertilized sea urchin eggs. *Devl Biol.* **74**, 364–378.

ROSENFELD, S. S. & TAYLOR, E. W. (1984). ATPase mechanism of skeletal and smooth muscle actosubfragment-1. *J. biol. Chem.* **259**, 11 908–11 919.

SANGER, J. M. & SANGER, J. W. (1980). Banding and polarity of actin filaments in interphase. *J. Cell Biol.* **86**, 568–575.

SCHLIWA, M. (1981). Proteins associated with cytoplasmic actin. *Cell* **25**, 587–590.

SCHLIWA, M. (1984). Mechanisms of intracellular organelle transport. In *Cell and Muscle Motility* (ed. J. W. Shay), vol. 5, pp. 1–66. New York: Plenum Press.

SCHROER, T. A., BRADY, S. T. & KELLY, R. B. (1985). Fast transport of foreign synaptic vesicles in squid axoplasm. *J. Cell Biol.* **101**, 568–572.

SHEETZ, M. P., CHASAN, R. & SPUDICH, T. A. (1984). ATP-dependent movement of myosin *in vitro*: Characterization by a quantitative assay. *J. Cell Biol.* **99**, 1867–1871.

SHEETZ, M. P. & SPUDICH, J. A. (1983). Movement of myosin-coated fluorescent beads on actin cables *in vitro*. *Nature, Lond.* **303**, 31–35.

SOUTHWICK, F. S., TATSUMI, N. & STOSSEL, T. P. (1982). Acumentin, an actin modulating protein of pulmonary macrophages. *Biochemistry* **21**, 6321–6326.

STEIN, L. A., CHOCK, P. B. & EISENBERG, E. (1984). Rate-limiting step in the actomyosin ATPase cycle. *Biochemistry* **23**, 1555–1563.

STOSSEL, T. P. (1983). Spatial organization of cortical cytoplasm in macrophages. In *Modern Cell Biology* (ed. J. R. McIntosh), vol. 2, pp. 203–224. New York: Alan R. Liss.

SUZUKI, H., ONISHI, H., TAKAHASHI, K. & WATANABE, S. (1978). Structure and function of chicken gizzard myosin. *J. Biochem. Tokyo* **84**, 1529–1542.

TAYLOR, D. L., BLINKS, J. R. & REYNOLDS, G. (1980*b*). Aequorin luminescence during amoeboid movement, endocytosis and capping. *J. Cell Biol.* **86**, 599–607.

TAYLOR, D. L., HELLEWELL, S. B., VIRGIN, H. W. & HEIPLE, J. (1979). The solation–contraction coupling hypothesis of cell movements in cell motility: molecules and organization (ed. S. Matano, H. Ishikawa & M. Sato), pp. 363–377. Tokyo: University of Tokyo Press.

TAYLOR, D. L., WANG, Y. & HEIPLE, J. M. (1980*a*). Distribution of fluorescently-labelled actin in living amoebas. *J. Cell Biol.* **86**, 590–598.

TAYLOR, E. W. (1964). Brownian and saltatory movements of cytoplasmic granules and the movement of anaphase chromosomes. *Proc. 4th Int. Conf. Rheol.* pp. 175–191. New York: J. Wiley.

TRYBUS, K. M., HUIATT, T. W. & LOWEY, S. (1982). A bent monomeric conformation of myosin from smooth muscle. *Proc. natn. Acad. Sci. U.S.A.* **79**, 6151–6155.

VALE, R. D., REESE, T. S. & SHEETZ, M. P. (1985*b*). Identification of a novel free-generating protein, kinesin, involved in microtubule-based motility. *Cell* **42**, 39–50.

VALE, R. D., SCHNAPP, B. J., REESE, T. S. & SHEETZ, M. P. (1985*a*). Movement of organelles along filaments dissociated from axoplasm of squid giant axon. *Cell* **40**, 449–454.

WANG, L. & SPUDICH, J. A. (1984). A 45,000 mol. wt. protein from unfertilized sea urchin eggs severs actin filaments in a calcium-dependent manner. *J. Cell Biol.* **99**, 844–851.

WEBB, M. F. & TRENTHAM, D. R. (1983). Chemical mechanism of myosin catalyzed ATP hydrolysis. In *Handbook of Physiology: Skeletal Muscle* (ed. L. D. Peachey, H. Adrian & S. R. Geiger), pp. 237–255. Baltimore: Waverley Press.

WINKELMANN, D. A., MEKEEL, H. & RAYMENT, I. (1985). Packing analysis of crytalline myosin sub-fragment-1. *J. molec. Biol.* **181**, 487–501.

YANIGITA, T. (1981). Angles of nucleotides bound to cross bridges in glycerinated muscle fibers. *J. molec. Biol.* **146**, 539–560.

YANO, M., YAMAMOTO, Y. & SHIMIZU, H. (1982). An actomyosin motor. *Nature, Lond.* **299**, 557–559.

YENNA, M., AKSOY, M., HARTSHORN, D. J. & GOLDMAN, R. D. (1978). BHK-21 myosin. Isolation, biochemical characterization and intracellular localization. *J. Cell Sci.* **31**, 411–429.

YENNA, M. & GOLDMAN, R. D. (1978). Ca sensitive regulation of actin and myosin interaction in cultured BHK-21. *J. Cell Biol.* (Abstr.) **79**, 274a.

J. Cell Sci. Suppl. 4, 103–113 (1986)
Printed in Great Britain © The Company of Biologists Limited 1986

FUTURE DIRECTIONS FOR STUDIES OF MECHANISMS FOR GENERATING FLAGELLAR BENDING WAVES

CHARLES J. BROKAW

Division of Biology, California Institute of Technology, Pasadena, CA 91125, USA

INTRODUCTION

The modern era of research on cilia and flagella of eukaryotic cells began in the early 1950s with the discovery of the $9+2$ structure of the axoneme, quickly followed by the demonstration of flagellar ATPase activity, the demonstration of ATP-reactivated motility of membrane permeabilized flagella, and the classic study of the morphology of movement of the sea-urchin sperm flagellum by Professor Sir James Gray (1955; see Gibbons, 1981, for other references). During the past two decades, the idea that the bending of flagella and cilia is caused by active sliding between the outer doublet microtubules of the axoneme has become firmly established (Gibbons, 1981). The active sliding process derives energy from the dephosphorylation of MgATP, and this ATPase activity is associated with the dynein arms, which are attached at their basal ends to the A-tubules of the outer doublet microtubules and interact transiently with the B-tubules of the outer doublet microtubules. Since uniform activity of dynein arms distributed around the ring of outer doublet microtubules will not effectively generate bending, it has been concluded that there must be a control process that modulates the generation of active sliding by dynein arms. When planar bending is being generated, this control process should ensure that the dynein arms on one side of the axoneme are inactive while the arms on the other side of the axoneme are active. The regular propagation of bends along a flagellum then requires a regular alternation of activity of these different subsets of the dynein arms at every point along the length of the axoneme.

Cilia and flagella can be viewed as oscillators. Any pattern of oscillatory bending could be generated just by programming an appropriate oscillatory pattern of dynein arm activation. Alternatively, the characteristics of the oscillation could be established by physical parameters such as flagellar elasticity, with the activity of dynein arms serving only to overcome viscous damping of the oscillation. Flagella resemble more familiar physical oscillators in having elastic resistances that tend to restore an equilibrium configuration of the flagellum in the absence of internal activity. The magnitudes of these elastic resistances can be determined by measurements of the bending resistance of inactive flagella (Okuno, 1980). These measurements have demonstrated that the elastic resistances are large enough to play a significant role in the balance of active and resistive forces on a moving flagellum. Unlike the most familiar physical oscillators, flagella have no significant inertia because they operate at very low Reynolds numbers, where inertial forces are negligible in comparison with viscous resistances. Oscillation requires that instead of a physical inertia, there must be an effective 'inertia' that results from the control of dynein arm activity, such that dynein arm activity continues, and does not fall to zero, when the flagellum reaches the equilibrium configuration determined by elastic resistances. The behaviour of a flagellum as an oscillator thus involves a balancing of elastic, viscous and active forces, or bending moments. The mathematical tools for analysing the moment balance have been developed and used in several studies of possible control mechanisms (Machin, 1958; Brokaw, 1972a; Hines & Blum, 1978). The most thoroughly explored proposal is the idea that some result of active sliding, such as the curvature of the flagellum, is involved in controlling the active sliding. This establishes a 'feedback loop' that can lead to oscillatory bending (Machin, 1958; Brokaw, 1971, 1972b). Computer simulations have been used to demonstrate that flagellar models containing a mechanism for control of active sliding by the curvature of the flagellum will oscillate and propagate bending waves (Brokaw, 1972a). However, many of the types of behaviour of real flagella have not yet been successfully duplicated by these models.

CONTROL OF ACTIVE SLIDING BY FLAGELLAR CURVATURE

Recent kinetic studies of dynein ATPase and the interactions of dynein with microtubules reveal a complex, multi-step ATP hydrolysis cycle with many similarities to actomyosin ATPase (Johnson, 1985). Models of active shear generation by dynein cross-bridges have relied heavily on ideas proposed for muscle cross-bridges (Huxley, 1957; Eisenberg & Hill, 1985). For many purposes it is convenient to describe our ideas about dynein–microtubule interactions in terms of two states. One state, called the detached state, may actually encompass several detached states and weakly bound states in rapid equilibrium with detached states. In this state dynein neither drives nor restricts sliding between tubules. The second state is a strongly bound attached state. Dynein can enter this state in a non-equilibrium position, thus establishing a force that tends to cause sliding as the dynein changes to an equilibrium configuration that produces zero force. While the strongly bound state remains in the equilibrium configuration, it can restrict sliding between tubules, even if it is not generating force. Binding of ATP by the dynein is required to destabilize the strongly bound equilibrium state and return the dynein to the detached state. ATP hydrolysis then restores the dynein to a form in which it can re-enter the strongly bound state. In muscle, there is evidence that the transition to the strongly bound state is the phosphate-release step in the ATPase cycle, and that this step may be regulated by the troponin–tropomyosin control system.

It is easy to imagine that distortion of the microtubule surface lattice accompanying flagellar bending could modify dynein binding activity, and thus provide a mechanism for the control of active sliding (Douglas, 1975). A change in dynein binding affinity of sites on the B-tubule of an outer doublet requires an energy input analogous to the energy input provided to the actomyosin control system in muscle by Ca^{2+} binding to troponin C. A possible source of this energy is the work done in bending the microtubule. The energy put into controlling active sliding by this mechanism will then contribute to the bending resistance of the microtubule. A preliminary estimate (Brokaw, 1982) suggested that the flagellar bending resistance required by such a mechanism would be too high. This question deserves more thorough treatment.

A recent estimate suggests that the bending resistance of an individual doublet microtubule is about $E = 0.02 \times 10^9 \, pN \, nm^2$ (Omoto & Brokaw, 1982). Assuming that the additional bending resistance that might result from a mechanism for controlling dynein–microtubule interaction is comparable in magnitude, the energy per unit length stored in a bent microtubule will then be approximately $E \times (\text{curvature})^2$. If there is one dynein arm for every 12 nm of length, the energy stored per dynein arm when the microtubule is bent to a curvature of 0.0002 $rad \, nm^{-1}$ is $10 \, pN \, nm$. How does this compare with the amount of energy needed to control active sliding?

In the worst case, where every tubulin monomer (69 per 12 nm of doublet length) is a potential dynein binding site, and where the energy of bending is uniformly distributed among all of the tubulin monomers, the energy per site in the bent doublet is less than $0.2 \, pN \, nm$. This is negligible compared to the free energy difference of $8.7 \, pN \, nm$ that is required for a 10-fold reduction in the affinity of dynein (or any ligand) for a binding site. If the site is larger, and located in a region of the doublet that undergoes relatively large strain when the flagellum bends, the energy per site can be larger, but it is still going to be only a fraction of the total bending energy of $10 \, pN \, nm$.

For comparison, it is instructive to look at the system for regulation of the actomyosin contractile system in skeletal muscle, as described by Hill (1983). With three myosin molecules (6 heads) per $14.3 \, nm$ of myosin filament, two troponin complexes per $38.5 \, nm$ of actin filament, and two actin filaments per myosin filament, the troponin:myosin ratio is approximately 0.5. If a change in Ca^{2+} concentration from $10^{-7} \, M$ to $10^{-5} \, M$ causes the binding of two Ca^{2+} per troponin, this corresponds to a free-energy change of $17 \, pN \, nm$ per myosin. In the actomyosin system, cooperativity between adjacent tropomyosin molecules plays a significant role in enhancing the degree of regulation of myosin cross-bridge activity that can be achieved by this free-energy change (Hill, 1983). An important point is that the energy requirement could not have been deduced just from thermodynamic principles. It is necessary to know that an efficient system has evolved in which potential myosin binding sites on seven actin monomers are covered by one tropomyosin molecule and therefore regulated by one troponin complex. It is also necessary to know about the cooperativity of tropomyosin in order to know the extent of the regulation that can be obtained from Ca^{2+} binding.

In flagella, this information is lacking. Therefore, it is not possible to rule out *a priori* the possibility that the energy to control the active sliding is obtained directly from bending, and represented in the flagellar bending resistance.

However, this idea has an important experimental consequence. The regulation of actomyosin by Ca^{2+} binding to troponin C can be expressed as an increase in the stability of strongly bound attached cross-bridges, generated by an increase in the rate constant for entering the strongly bound state (Hill, 1983). If microtubule bending regulates in a similar manner the stability of dynein attachment to sites on the microtubule, then dynein binding to these sites should change the configuration of the microtubule. The more efficient the system, in terms of regulating many dynein binding sites by a small amount of energy introduced by bending the microtubule, the larger should be the effect of dynein binding on the configuration of the microtubule. Experiments designed to examine the effects of dynein concentration on the configurations of outer doublet microtubules in solution might be the most effective means of testing the hypothesis that the active sliding process is regulated directly by flagellar bending in this manner.

If this version of the hypothesis is not correct, what are the alternatives? One possibility is that the information in flagellar bending is amplified with energy from another source to provide the energy needed to regulate the dynein cross-bridge cycle. This energy might be provided by ATP dephosphorylation, perhaps by one of the several dynein ATPase molecules present in each dynein arm. The direct approach to this question probably requires perfection of methods for reassembly of dynein molecules into functional arms. If this can be achieved, it may be possible to incorporate non-functional A_α or A_β dyneins into an arm, and test which ones are required to be functional in order to cause sliding disintegration of dynein-depleted axonemes, as in the recombination experiments of Yano & Miki-Noumura (1981), or to cause an increase in the beat frequency of demembranated flagella as in the experiments of Gibbons & Gibbons (1976). This experimental method should in principle be able to identify a dynein ATPase that is not required for active sliding, but is required for flagellar oscillation and bend propagation. If these experimental techniques for *in vitro* reconstitution cannot be perfected, the alternative may be to construct dynein arms with non-functional dynein ATPases by genetic engineering in *Chlamydomonas*. However, the transformation techniques that are required for such constructions are not yet perfected.

Comparison with the troponin–tropomyosin control system in muscle may be misleading. In muscle, which must remain in a turned-off state for long periods of time, the method of choice may be a mechanism that alters the stability of actin–myosin interactions. However, to generate flagellar bending waves, it is only necessary to suppress dynein activity for short periods – approximately half a beat cycle. This could be done with a *catalytic* mechanism, as is more common in controlling cellular biochemistry, in which both the forward and reverse rates of a reaction step are altered by the same amount and no changes in the free energy of states in the reaction sequence are required. For example, both forward and reverse rates of a phosphate-release step might be reduced to turn off cross-bridge activity.

How could this alternative be detected experimentally? In principle, methods involving changes in free-energy levels of cross-bridge states should work independently of the beat frequency. On the other hand, a mechanism involving rate control that was optimized for normal beat frequencies might not function well at very low beat frequencies. Such a mechanism could conceivably be responsible for the threshold effect that is seen when demembranated sea-urchin sperm flagella are reactivated at low ATP concentrations (Brokaw, 1975*b*), but this hypothesis is difficult to evaluate because low ATP concentration will directly affect other steps in the cross-bridge cycle.

ALTERNATIVES TO CURVATURE-CONTROLLED SLIDING

The final alternatives would be mechanisms that do not depend at all upon information about the curvature of the flagellum. I have suggested (Brokaw, 1975*a*, 1976) that a decrease in sliding velocity might provide a signal for switching between alternative cross-bridge systems, and presented cross-bridge models that auto-matically respond in this way when a resistance to sliding is encountered. Support for this idea has been provided by observations of oscillatory sliding during measure-ments of sliding forces in disintegrating axonemes (Kamimura & Takahashi, 1981), and by observations that very short regions of a flagellum can oscillate, showing oscillatory sliding with little obvious bending in the active region (Brokaw & Gibbons, 1973). However, extensive computations of the behaviour of flagellar models incorporating velocity-regulated active sliding systems have revealed that these models can produce stable oscillation and bend propagation in the absence of external viscous resistances, but that the behaviour becomes unstable when realistic values for the external viscous resistance are used.

In a propagating bending wave on a sea-urchin sperm flagellum, the pattern of new bend initiation involves minimal sliding in more distal portions of the flagellum (Goldstein, 1975, 1976). Consequently, in propagating bends, regions of high sliding velocity travel along the flagellum in phase with regions of high curvature. One might expect, therefore, that models in which either curvature or sliding velocity control the active sliding process would be rather similar. Results of computations with such models show that this is not the case, and that there are significant differences between results obtained with these two types of models. On the other hand, these two parameters are similar enough that models that use various linear combinations of these two parameters to control the active sliding process show no new properties.

These two parameters, curvature and sliding velocity, by no means exhaust the possibilities for parameters that might control the active sliding process. Another obvious possibility is the shear displacement, which will be out of phase with curvature and sliding velocity. *A priori*, one might expect this not to be a very useful control parameter. In a short flagellum, regions near the distal end of the flagellum will be the first to attain the values of shear displacement that might be required for switching between active sliding systems. As a consequence, the switching event, and the bending waves, would be expected to propagate towards the basal end of the flagellum rather than towards the tip.

Other control parameters might be the rate of bending, and the rate of change of curvature with length. These parameters will also be out of phase with curvature and sliding velocity. A control paradigm that used a combination of curvature and rate of change of curvature might be ideal for generating active shear moment with components in phase with both viscous and elastic resistances.

These possibilities are enumerated largely to show that many theoretical possibilities remain to be explored by detailed computer modelling, just to examine the formal relationships to control parameters without even considering the detailed mechanisms. An important, if not the most important, reason for this exploration is to determine whether there are differences between the behaviour of these various models that could be distinguished experimentally.

A serious impediment to progress with these modelling investigations of alternative control mechanisms has been realized as a result of recent studies of a simple curvature-controlled model (Brokaw, 1985). This work demonstrates that specifying the control of the active sliding process by curvature is not sufficient to determine the behaviour of a flagellar model. At low viscosities, the parameters of the bending waves generated by this curvature-controlled model were found to be very sensitive to minor variations in the details of bend initiation at the base of the flagellum. At high viscosities, these models tend to choose bending wave parameters that give an integral number of waves on the flagellum, because this facilitates the satisfaction of boundary conditions for moments at the ends of the flagellum. However, these properties can be over-ridden by forcing the flagellar model to operate at a designated frequency. These insights demonstrate that other control properties of a flagellum, in addition to control of active sliding by a parameter such as curvature, strongly influence the bending behaviour. It is therefore difficult to evaluate the various possibilities for controlling the active sliding process unless the other control properties are known, or at least considered.

MORE THAN ENOUGH DATA?

Over the past two decades, a lot of detailed quantitative information about the behaviour of cilia and flagella has accumulated. Some of this has exploited the usefulness of ATP-reactivated, demembranated flagella, particularly those of sea-urchin spermatozoa; other work has benefited from the availability of *Chlamydomonas* mutants with altered flagellar behaviour. These data should contain important clues to help us deduce the internal control mechanisms of flagella. (1) The basic bending wave parameters – frequency, mean bend angle and wavelength – of sea-urchin sperm flagella are invariant when the asymmetry and, therefore, the curvatures of the bends of the bending waves are manipulated by changing the Ca^{2+} concentration (Brokaw, 1979). Similarly, the beat frequency of reactivated ctenophore comb-plate cilia is independent of Ca^{2+} concentration changes, which can induce ciliary reversal (Nakamura & Tamm, 1985). (2) The frequency of flagellar oscillation is sensitive to mechanical loading, such as changes in viscosity (Brokaw, 1966; Mulready & Rikmenspoel, 1984). The wavelength of flagellar bending waves is especially sensitive to viscosity, and can be changed even under conditions where viscosity has little effect on beat frequency (Brokaw, 1975*b*). (3) Several situations are known in which changes in beat frequency are accompanied by inverse changes in bend angle, indicating that sliding velocity is an invariant parameter under these conditions (Brokaw, 1980; Okuno & Brokaw, 1979; Brokaw & Luck, 1985). However, in other situations, bend angle and sliding velocity can be reduced, with frequency remaining relatively constant (Brokaw & Simonick, 1976; Asai & Brokaw, 1980). (4) Flagella containing 'rigor bends' can be produced in various ways (Gibbons & Gibbons, 1974; Brokaw & Simonick, 1976). When conditions for bend propagation are restored, these bends resume propagation in the normal direction. This suggests that information about the control status of the active sliding process is stored during rigor, either in the bent configuration of the flagellum or by some other mechanism.

Missing from this list are statements about the *shapes* of flagellar bending waves, which are commonly thought to be a direct indicator of the underlying forces responsible for generating the bending waves. This remains an area of controversy. New methods for enhancement and analysis of microscopic images of beating flagella, combined with computerized management of the large amount of data provided by these methods, will probably revolutionize this area in the next decade.

RADICAL NEW IDEAS?

Most of the ideas mentioned in the above discussion have been around in various forms for the past 20 years. Perhaps our failure to understand flagellar bending-wave generation by now indicates a need to think about flagella in quite new and different ways. Two recent observations may serve as useful stimulants for new ways of thinking about flagella.

Allen *et al.* (1985) have used high-resolution video-enhanced light microscopy to demonstrate the gliding movements of native microtubules in extruded squid nerve axoplasm. When the forward gliding of a microtubule is impeded by an obstruction at its forward end, the microtubule remains in place and can generate regular, propagated, bending waves with a striking similarity to the bending waves generated by highly organized flagellar axonemes (Fig. 1). I have performed computer simulations of this phenomenon, using appropriately modified versions of the computer programs developed for analysis of flagellar bending wave propagation (Brokaw, 1972*a*, 1985). These simulations demonstrate that the generation of propagated bending waves by a microtubule does not require any control or modulation of the mechanism for longitudinal translation and force generation along the axis of the microtubule. The bending waves arise because the curvature of the microtubule causes the force generated along the length of the microtubule to produce bending moments. The curvature therefore enters into the generation of bending moments in a manner analogous to its role in curvature-controlled models for flagellar bending waves.

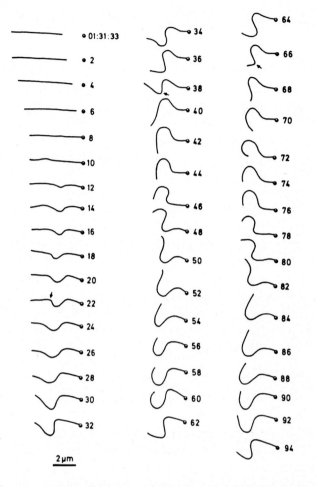

Fig. 1. The sequence of straight and serpentine shapes assumed by a gliding microtubule (length 4·8 μm) before and after it encounters an obstacle. Times are in seconds. (Reproduced from *The Journal of Cell Biology* (1985) **100**, 1736–1752, with copyright permission of the Rockefeller University Press.)

Could this elementary property of microtubules have been exploited in the early stages of the evolution of the eukaryotic flagellum, with the major evolutionary trend being the increasing organization of the force-producing molecules (dyneins) to produce higher forces and velocities? Does appreciation of such a possible scenario help us in thinking about the mechanism for bending wave generation by flagella? These are new questions, and the answers are not yet clear.

Another recent observation, from my own laboratory, suggests that the organization of the eukaryotic flagellar axoneme may be more subtle than previously suspected. Direct visualization of active sliding by flagellar outer doublet microtubules has most often made use of digestion by elastase or trypsin to eliminate structural constraints that prevent sliding beyond the range associated with normal oscillatory bending (e.g. see Summers & Gibbons, 1970). However, axonemes of

Tetrahymena cilia frequently disintegrate by sliding without protease digestion, especially at low ATP concentrations (Warner & Zanetti, 1980). At low ATP concentrations, sea-urchin sperm flagella will also show partial sliding disintegration without protease digestion, when bending is prevented by attachment of part of the axoneme to the microscope slide surface. This disintegration typically begins by a bulging out of a bundle of doublets from the side of the axoneme, thus allowing sliding in the more distal region of the axoneme. This sliding would normally produce a principal bend near the base of the flagellum, but this bending is prevented by attachment of the basal region of the flagellum to the slide surface. In a few cases, the restriction on bending has been transitory, and the separated bundle of doublets has been able to reassociate with the remainder of the axoneme and restore its original appearance. In the most dramatic case observed, the 'bulge' of separated doublets appeared to be driven off the end of the flagellum by bending and reassociation of doublets in the basal portion of the flagellum. For a brief instant, the distal third of the flagellum appeared as a 'brush' of three or more separated microtubule bundles. These bundles then reassociated, and the flagellum resumed normal beating, looking

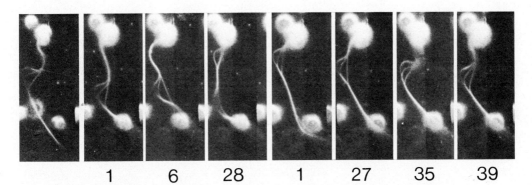

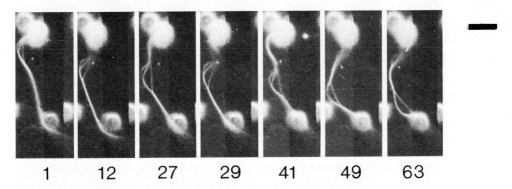

Fig. 2. Selected images from a series of records showing weak beating, partial disintegration, and reassembly of a demembranated sea-urchin spermatozoon (*Arbacia punctulata*) reactivated at low ATP concentration in the presence of 2 mM-ADP. For methods, see Brokaw (1986). Photographed on moving film with flashes at 100 Hz. Relative image numbers within each record are indicated. The beat frequency was approximately 8 Hz.

just like other flagella in the preparation. Unfortunately, this event was not photographed, but Fig. 2 shows another case, of a flagellum that underwent repeated dissociation and reassociation of microtubule bundles over a period of several minutes.

These observations, although difficult to reproduce and record, suggest that the structural constraints that maintain the axoneme are not permanent, unbreakable linkages. The observations are more consistent with the view of interdoublet linkages suggested by the observations of Warner (1983) than with earlier views of the 'nexin' links as permanent, highly elastic, linkages.

Taken together, these new observations suggest that the flagellum could have arisen as, and may still be, a loosely associated bundle of microtubular elements retaining and enhancing the capability for bending wave generation that is seen with individual axoplasmic microtubules. Whether this new view of the flagellum will turn out to be correct, or even helpful, remains to be tested.

Preparation of this paper has been supported by an NIH research grant, no. GM 18711.

REFERENCES

ALLEN, R. D., WEISS, D. G., HAYDEN, J. H., BROWN, D. T., FUJIWAKE, H. & SIMPSON, M. (1985). Gliding movement of and bidirectional transport along single native microtubules from squid axoplasm: Evidence for an active role of microtubules in cytoplasmic transport. *J. Cell Biol.* **100**, 1736–1752.
ASAI, D. J. & BROKAW, C. J. (1980). Effects of antibodies against tubulin on the movement of reactivated sea urchin sperm flagella. *J. Cell Biol.* **387**, 114–123.
BROKAW, C. J. (1966). Effects of increased viscosity on the movements of some invertebrate spermatozoa. *J. exp. Biol.* **45**, 113–139.
BROKAW, C. J. (1971). Bend propagation by a sliding filament model for flagella. *J. exp. Biol.* **55**, 289–304.
BROKAW, C. J. (1972a). Computer simulation of flagellar movement. I. Demonstration of stable bend propagation and bend initiation by the sliding filament model. *Biophys. J.* **12**, 564–586.
BROKAW, C. J. (1972b). Flagellar movement: a sliding filament model. *Science* **178**, 455–462.
BROKAW, C. J. (1975a). Molecular mechanism for oscillation in flagella and muscle. *Proc. natn. Acad. Sci. U.S.A.* **72**, 3102–3106.
BROKAW, C. J. (1975b). Effects of viscosity and ATP concentration on the movement of reactivated sea urchin sperm flagella. *J. exp. Biol.* **62**, 701–719.
BROKAW, C. J. (1976). Computer simulation of flagellar movement. IV. Properties of an oscillatory two-state cross-bridge model. *Biophys. J.* **16**, 1029–1041.
BROKAW, C. J. (1979). Calcium-induced asymmetrical beating of Triton-demembranated sea urchin sperm flagella. *J. Cell Biol.* **82**, 401–411.
BROKAW, C. J. (1980). Elastase digestion of demembranated sperm flagella. *Science* **207**, 1365–1367.
BROKAW, C. J. (1982). Models for oscillation and bend propagation by flagella. *Symp. Soc. exp. Biol.* **35**, 313–338.
BROKAW, C. J. (1985). Computer simulation of flagellar movement. VI. Simple curvature controlled models are incompletely specified. *Biophys. J.* **48**, 633–642.
BROKAW, C. J. (1986). Sperm motility. In *Echinoderm Gametes and Embryos* (ed. T. A. Schroeder) *Methods in Cell Biology*, vol. 27. New York: Academic Press. (in press).
BROKAW, C. J. & GIBBONS, I. R. (1973). Localized activation of bending in proximal, medial and distal regions of sea-urchin sperm flagella. *J. Cell Sci.* **13**, 1–10.
BROKAW, C. J. & LUCK, D. J. L. (1985). Bending patterns of *Chlamydomonas* flagella. III. A radial spoke deficient mutant and a central pair deficient mutant. *Cell Motil.* **5**, 195–208.

BROKAW, C. J. & SIMONICK, T. F. (1976). CO_2 regulation of the amplitude of flagellar bending. In *Cell Motility* (ed. R. Goldman, T. Pollard & J. Rosenbaum), pp. 933–940. New York: Cold Spring Harbor Laboratory.

DOUGLAS, G. (1975). Sliding filaments in sperm flagella. *J. theor. Biol.* **53**, 247–252.

EISENBERG, E. & HILL, T. L. (1985). Muscle contraction and free energy transduction in biological systems. *Science* **227**, 999–1006.

GIBBONS, I. R. (1981). Cilia and flagella of eukaryotes. *J. Cell Biol.* **91**, 107s–124s.

GIBBONS, B. H. & GIBBONS, I. R. (1974). Properties of flagellar "rigor waves" produced by abrupt removal of adenosine triphosphate from actively swimming sea urchin sperm. *J. Cell Biol.* **63**, 970–985.

GIBBONS, B. H. & GIBBONS, I. R. (1976). Functional recombination of dynein 1 with demembranated sea urchin sperm partially extracted with KCl. *Biochem. biophys. Res. Commun.* **73**, 1–6.

GOLDSTEIN, S. F. (1975). Morphology of developing bends in sperm flagella. In *Swimming and Flying in Nature* (ed. T. Y. Wu, C. Brennan & C. J. Brokaw), pp. 127–132. New York: Plenum.

GOLDSTEIN, S. F. (1976). Form of developing bends in reactivated sperm flagella. *J. exp. Biol.* **64**, 173–184.

GRAY, J. (1955). The movement of sea urchin spermatozoa. *J. exp. Biol.* **32**, 775–801.

HILL, T. L. (1983). Two elementary models for the regulation of skeletal muscle contraction by calcium. *Biophys. J.* **44**, 383–396.

HINES, M. & BLUM, J. J. (1978). Bend propagation in flagella. I. Derivation of equations of motion and their simulation. *Biophys. J.* **23**, 41–58.

HUXLEY, A. F. (1957). Muscle structure and theories of contraction. *Prog. Biophys.* **7**, 255–318.

JOHNSON, K. A. (1985). Pathway of the microtubule-dynein ATPase and the structure of dynein: A comparison with actomyosin. *A. Rev. Biophys. biophys. Chem.* **14**, 161–188.

KAMIMURA, S. & TAKAHASHI, K. (1981). Direct measurement of the force of microtubule sliding in flagella. *Nature, Lond.* **293**, 566–568.

MACHIN, K. E. (1958). Wave propagation along flagella. *J. exp. Biol.* **35**, 796–806.

MULREADY, D. E. & RIKMENSPOEL, R. (1984). Time course of the motion of bull sperm flagella. *Cell Motil.* **4**, 387–401.

NAKAMURA, S. & TAMM, S. (1985). Calcium control of ciliary reversal in ionophore-treated and ATP-reactivated comb plates of ctenophores. *J. Cell Biol.* **100**, 1447–1454.

OKUNO, M. (1980). Inhibition and relaxation of sea urchin sperm flagella by vanadate. *J. Cell Biol.* **85**, 712–725.

OKUNO, M. & BROKAW, C. J. (1979). Inhibition of movement of Triton-demembranated sea-urchin sperm flagella by Mg^{2+}, ATP4$^-$, ADP and P_i. *J. Cell Sci.* **38**, 105–123.

OMOTO, C. K. & BROKAW, C. J. (1982). Structure and behaviour of the sperm terminal filament. *J. Cell Sci.* **58**, 385–409.

SUMMERS, K. E. & GIBBONS, I. R. (1971). Adenosine-triphosphate-induced sliding of tubules in trypsin-treated flagella of sea urchin sperm. *Proc. natn. Acad. Sci. U.S.A.* **68**, 3092–3096.

WARNER, F. D. (1983). Organization of interdoublet links in *Tetrahymena* cilia. *Cell Motil.* **3**, 321–332.

WARNER, F. D. & ZANETTI, N. C. (1980). Properties of microtubule sliding disintegration in isolated *Tetrahymena* cilia. *J. Cell Biol.* **86**, 436–445.

YANO, Y. & MIKI-NOUMURA, T. (1981). Recovery of sliding ability in the arm-depleted flagellar axonemes after recombination with extracted dynein 1. *J. Cell Sci.* **48**, 223–239.

J. Cell Sci. Suppl. 4, 115–135 (1986)
Printed in Great Britain © The Company of Biologists Limited 1986

MOLECULAR AND CELL BIOLOGY OF PLANT CELLS*

D. H. NORTHCOTE

Department of Biochemistry, University of Cambridge, Tennis Court Road,
Cambridge CB2 1QW, UK

INTRODUCTION

In a review that supposedly incorporates prospects of the subject the most that can be done is to indicate what is going on at present, and to select and postulate in a limited number of areas what will happen in the short-term, i.e. over the next 1–2 years. The important advances in the subject matter will arise as a result of novel approaches or ideas, which will revolutionize both the possibilities for research and our ideas on the subject. This type of advance is impossible to predict.

What has been attempted in this review, therefore, is to give an account of some of the exciting areas that are being extensively studied at present and to suggest in a limited way the problems encountered by the use of present techniques and the possible ways in which the work might be extended.

PLANT CELL GROWTH AND DIFFERENTIATION

The growth of a plant cell is dependent upon a supply of nutrients, which are for the most part supplied by the autotrophic activity of the plant. There is usually, therefore, no shortage of carbon compounds. The restrictions on plant growth involve supplies of light, water and salts; most of the other material is derived from an unlimited supply of carbon dioxide.

Some of the organic compounds synthesized as minor nutrients such as the vitamins and growth factors, have an influence upon the growth, development and physiology of the plant when their supply, which is necessary only in small amounts, is varied. This can be brought about either by alterations in the amounts synthesized, control of transport to particular tissues, metabolic conversion and turnover, or by an exogenous supply of the material to the plant tissue. The effect of variation in the supply of any one nutrient is related to the relative amounts of other growth factors and the major nutrients as a whole.

The techniques of molecular biology are now being used to elucidate the function and role of the growth factors at the level of gene control and protein synthesis. In this way the mechanisms whereby they produce their dramatic effects on the whole plant can be explored and the work is influencing the ideas on the control of the read-out of the plant genome during development.

*This paper is dedicated to Dr Luis Leloir on the occasion of his 80th birthday.

The work is directed at exploring the changes in transcription and translation of particular proteins during a developmental process that is influenced by the growth factor and that takes place over a controlled particular time-course. Amongst the systems that are being actively worked on at present and that can be expected to yield important results in the near future are: (1) seed germination, (2) seed formation and development, (3) fruit ripening, (4) cell wall formation and its differentiation during xylem and phloem formation, (5) wounding and other stress responses, and (6) organelle development.

The general techniques for investigating these systems are: (1) measurement of the increase in the activity of a particular enzyme over the time course, e.g. isocitrate lyase during castor-bean germination. (2) Purification of the enzyme. (3) Establishment of a method for detecting and measuring the amount of the protein rather than its biological activity. This is usually accomplished by immunological techniques. (4) Preparation of a messenger RNA fraction for the particular protein. (5) Preparation of a complementary DNA clone for the protein. (6) Preparation of a genomic clone. (7) Identification and measurement of the mRNA for the protein over the time course by means of the DNA probes. (8) Identification and measurement of the mRNA directly from isolated nuclei of the cells or by the use of 4-thiouridine on the intact tissue (Cramer, Ryder, Bell & Lamb, 1984). These techniques establish the controlling steps for the production of the specific protein during the developmental sequence and enable the action of the growth factors on the process, both *in vitro* and *in vivo*, to be ascertained.

In addition to the direct information that is given by experimental procedures, the isolation of the DNA clones makes it possible to sequence the genes and the cDNA so that reading frames and control sequences of the genome can be explored. Almost incidentally the amino acid sequence of the active protein is obtained and the identification of active sites of the enzyme together with transit sequences for localization of the protein into cellular organelles may become possible. These very powerful approaches to biological problems will undoubtedly be exploited and expanded over the next decade.

Specific examples of the applications of the methods will be described below so that variations, difficulties and expansions of the technique and approach can be more clearly seen.

Seed germination

Seed germination can be controlled so that it takes place over a definite time course and the food reserve of the seed is mobilized. The food reserves can be stored as starch, lipid or protein in the endosperm or cotyledons of the seed. Two types of seed will be discussed here.

Grain seeds. These seeds store starch in the endosperm. This is mobilized by the production of α-amylase from the specific aleurone layer of cells at the periphery of the seed. The α-amylase production of the aleurone cells is greatly influenced by the application of gibberellic acid and abscisic acid (Jacobsen, 1984). The system is complicated because of the existence of at least four to eight isoenzymes (set A isoenzymes 1 and 2; set B isoenzymes 3 and 4) (Rogers, 1985). There are at least two different sets of structural genes and the loci for the two different sets of isoenzymes are on different chromosomes (Brown & Jacobsen, 1982). Generally, gibberellic acid stimulates an increase in α-amylase activity, which is inhibited by abscisic acid (Higgins, Jacobsen & Zwar, 1982). Experiments have been designed using cDNA probes to mRNAs that are regulated by application of gibberellic acid. These probes have been used with the intact seeds, isolated aleurone cells, protoplasts and nuclei isolated from the protoplasts of aleurone cells (Baulcombe & Buffard, 1983; Chandler *et al.* 1984; Jacobsen & Beach, 1985; Jacobsen, Zwar & Chandler, 1985). It has been shown that type A mRNAs are present in relatively large amounts in unstimulated aleurone cells and increase about 20-fold after stimulation with gibberellic acid. In contrast, type B mRNA is present at very low levels in unstimulated cells but increases at least 100-fold after gibberellic acid treatment (Rogers, 1985). Some other mRNA species are reduced in amount by the application of gibberellic acid. There is evidence for a less specific control whereby a large number of mRNA species are generally increased, i.e. a general increase in poly(A)$^+$RNA per seed on the application of gibberellic acid. This general effect may account for the action of gibberellic acid on the type A isoenzymes of α-amylase. These effects of gibberellic acid are reversed by the application of abscisic acid. The work on gene transcription in isolated nuclei shows that the effects of growth factors on protein and mRNA levels are also apparent at the level of transcription. There is also some evidence for another action of gibberellic acid at the translational level (Higgins *et al.* 1982; Mozer, 1980), and Ca^{2+}, which affects secretion of the α-amylase from the aleurone cells, may also be necessary for translation of the B-type isoenzymes or for post-translational processing (Deikman & Jones, 1985). However, these latter mechanisms may also be dependent on continual secretion of the enzymes from the cells. It is known that precursor proteins occur that carry a signal peptide that probably functions in the transport of the enzymes (Higgins *et al.* 1982; Chandler *et al.* 1984).

Lipid-storing seeds. In these seeds the fat is mobilized by a set of enzymes (those for β-oxidation of fatty acids and the enzymes of the glyoxylate cycle) contained within an organelle (the glyoxysome) that develops during germination. Gibberellic acid stimulates the activity of the β-oxidation enzymes and those of the glyoxylate cycle; abscisic acid has the reverse effect. A study of the molecular biology of the control by growth factors will therefore not only indicate the control of the plant genome, but also how a particular organelle and its complement of enzymes is derived, i.e. how the proteins synthesized in the cytoplasm are directed and trans-located to a particular membrane-bound cell compartment (Trelease, 1984). At a later stage in seedling development the glyoxysome may be transformed to a peroxisome with a different enzyme complement. Modern methods permit an experimental approach to the problem of whether the glyoxysome is converted to a peroxisome or whether the peroxisome is generated independently.

The enzymes that have been studied in some detail are isocitrate lyase and malate synthase. These proteins have been purified and antibodies raised against them, and clones corresponding to the mRNAs have been prepared (Weir *et al.* 1980; Martin & Northcote, 1982; Dommes & Northcote, 1985*b*).

During germination the activities of the enzymes in the endosperm of the seed increase from near zero to a peak value after about 6–7 days. The action of gibberellic acid is to speed up and stimulate the process (Martin & Northcote, 1982, 1983). This it seems to accomplish by a general effect on protein synthesis, which is manifested by an earlier appearance of ribosomal RNA and poly(A)$^+$RNA in seeds treated with gibberellic acid compared with untreated seeds. With these seeds there seems to be no specific stimulation of the synthesis of particular mRNA species and, in particular, no stimulation of the specific transcription of the mRNAs for isocitrate lyase and malate synthase (Martin & Northcote, 1982; Martin, Beeching & Northcote, 1984). No evidence can be obtained for an action of gibberellic acid on translation other than that on the increased production of RNA. Recruitment of isocitrate lyase mRNA is not specifically stimulated into polysomes by the application of gibberellic acid. Using cDNA clones prepared from castor-bean endosperm, one of which is complementary to isocitrate lyase mRNA, it can be shown that gibberellic acid non-specifically stimulates the production of transcripts from the genome (Martin, Beeching & Northcote, 1984). The action of gibberellic acid in these seeds may therefore occur either by a synchronization of cellular activity, so condensing the time scale for the developmental changes that occur without altering the rate of activity in any particular cell, or modifying the rate of transcription in each cell.

The action of abscisic acid on castor-bean seeds is the same as in grain seeds, i.e. to negate the action of gibberellic acid (Dommes & Northcote, 1985*a,b*). However, the application of abscisic acid does, unlike that of gibberellic acid, show some specific effects in addition to its action in inhibiting the overall accumulation of rRNA and total mRNA. Some mRNAs are stimulated by the growth factor; in particular the major mRNA stored in the dry seed, coding for a polypeptide of M_r 25 600, normally disappears in untreated seeds during 12 h of germination but is maintained for periods up to 7 days in the presence of abscisic acid (Dommes & Northcote, 1985*a,b*; Quatrano *et al.* 1983). This mRNA might be specific for maturation of the seed before it is allowed to germinate, it might code for a storage protein, or it may be involved in the mechanism whereby abscisic acid acts on other metabolic events. Whatever its function, this is a significant observation about the action of abscisic acid in seed development and will undoubtedly be investigated further. Generally, however, the action of abscisic acid is to inhibit the accumulation of most endosperm proteins, some enzymes possibly being more affected than others. This inhibition is achieved mainly by a general inhibition of transcription or the consequence of an acceleration of RNA turnover. There is little evidence at present for an action of abscisic acid at the level of translation.

Targeting of cytoplasmic proteins to organelles

The preparation of cDNA complementary to the specific enzymes of the glyoxylate cycle has made it possible to sequence the enzymes, and comparisons of the sequences of the enzymes as unprocessed polypeptides makes it possible to investigate transit sequences for entry of the proteins into the glyoxysome. In addition, chimaeric genes carrying the transit sequence can be prepared and introduced into plant tissue to show the entry of a foreign marker polypeptide into the organelle.

This technique has been well illustrated by the elegant experiments carried out using the nuclear gene for the small subunits of ribulose 1,5-bisphosphate carboxylase and the Ti plasmid of *Agrobacterium tumefaciens*. A deleted portion of the T-DNA was replaced by pBR322, which provided homology for insertional recombination of a pBR322 derivative mobilized from *Escherichia coli* (see section on Ti plasmid below). The constructions of the plasmids were of three types. (1) The light-inducer promoter sequence from pea – the transit peptide coding sequence of the chloroplast-located ribulose bisphosphate carboxylase – the first intron and coding sequence of the first 22 amino acids of the small subunit of ribulose 1,5-bisphosphate carboxylase from pea, fused to the coding sequence of neomycin phosphotransferase 11 from *E. coli* transposon Tn*5* (Schreier, Seftor, Schell & Bohnert, 1985). (2) The coding sequence for the transit peptide fused to the coding sequence of neomycin phosphotransferase 11 under the control of the pea ss 3·6 promoter, which directs expression of the chimaeric gene in plant cells. (3) Similar to (2) but under the control of the *lac* UV5 promoter (Broeck *et al.* 1985). Using these plasmid constructs *in vivo* and *in vitro*, experiments were carried out that showed that the chimaeric gene was induced by light and the fused protein was located and processed within the chloroplast. The processing of the peptide was carried out by a stromal protease of the chloroplast. An *in vitro* preparation of chloroplasts could take up the fused peptide prepared in *E. coli* from the construct described in (3) above and it was processed in the chloroplast. Since in this latter experiment there were no additional plant cytoplasmic factors present in the *in vitro* experiment, it could be deduced that these were not required for the translocation mechanism. The experiments showed clearly that all of the sequence information required for translocation into the chloroplast was present in the transit peptide of some 57 amino acids as an amino-terminal extension.

These experiments, while providing important information in their own right, can act as a model system for future work. It is now possible to envisage the procedures for the introduction of foreign gene products into specific plant organelles and to contemplate the different mechanisms for the movement of material between the various specific compartments of the cell and, into and within the membrane systems.

Other experimental systems concerned with gene regulation

There are a number of other fields of investigation that are being developed on the lines indicated above, but in some of these particular problems arise that make a modification of the approach necessary. These fields therefore invite speculation to indicate how they will develop during the next few years.

Cell wall differentiation. The enzyme induction that occurs during the development of the cambial primary wall of dicotyledons into the secondarily thickened, lignified wall of xylem is now well documented, and the increase in activity of phenylalanine ammonia lyase, S-adenosyl methionine:caffeic acid 3-O-methyl transferase, cinnamic 4-hydroxylase and xylan synthase, and the decrease in activity of arabinan and polygalacturonan synthases, have been clearly shown by direct measurements (Northcote, 1984). This differentiation is controlled in tissue cultures by the application of particular ratios of auxin and cytokinin. The polysaccharide synthases are membrane-bound at the Golgi apparatus and are difficult to purify, so that a direct preparation of antibodies is at present not possible (Northcote, 1985a). This restricts development of the work, which would involve the preparation of cDNA probes for the measurement of the mRNA of these enzymes, the subsequent elaboration for the sequencing of the enzyme and the mechanism of their localization at the Golgi apparatus. That the increase in activities is consequent on the synthesis of increased amounts of enzyme can be shown by the careful use of inhibitors of transcription and translation (Jones & Northcote, 1981; Bolwell & Northcote, 1983). However, the major problems are being overcome by the use of isolated membranes and the preparation from these of monoclonal antibodies, which in one case at least seems to have yielded a clone with an antibody to arabinan synthase (Bolwell & Northcote, 1984). If and when cDNA clones, complementary to specific synthases, can be identified, then their initial selection will be considerably helped by *in vitro* systems such as that for *Zenia* mesophyll cells, where up to 30 % of the cells can be caused to differentiate synchronously to xylem (Kohlenbach & Schmidt, 1975; Fukuda & Komamine, 1980a,b).

The influence of auxin and cytokinin on the differentiation of plant tissue cultures and cell elongation has prompted investigations of the effect of these growth factors on gene expression during the response. With the tissue cultures the induction of phenylalanine ammonia lyase by the two growth factors can be separated in time, so that it is possible that they may act at different sites within the cell to bring about differentiation. Auxin added at the time of subculture of the tissue changed the pattern of cell protein synthesis by changing the transcription pattern of the mRNA after 2 h. Kinetin does not have this effect (Bevan & Northcote, 1981a,b). The rapidity of the auxin effect suggests that this growth factor can directly modulate the possible transcription of certain mRNA molecules. More direct evidence for the specific effect of auxin on the expression of a set of genes has been obtained by Walker, Legocka, Edelman & Key (1985) (see also Walker & Key, 1982), who have used cloned cDNAs to two auxin-responsive mRNAs produced during cell elongation in soybean. Neither fusicoccin nor ethylene enhanced the expression of these two mRNAs, whereas during auxin-stimulated cell elongation the mRNAs are accumulated.

Fruit ripening. Grierson and his co-workers (Grierson, Slater, Spiers & Tucker, 1985) have clearly demonstrated that ripening of tomatoes is a developmental process involving regulation of gene expression, so that a group of mRNAs are transcribed during fruit growth and then decline during maturation, while another group increase at the onset of ripening; one of them probably being partly controlled by the growth factor ethylene. One of the enzymes produced during ripening has been shown to be polygalacturonase. This enzyme has been purified and an antibody raised to it and this has permitted the identification of one of the ripening mRNAs as the one coding for polygalacturonase production. The next steps will presumably be the isolation and identification of DNA probes for the mRNA, the identification of more specific enzymes concerned with ripening and the study of the control of the genome to produce these enzymes, which may be mediated by ethylene.

Stress responses. In these responses a set of proteins is synthesized in response to an external stress such as wounding or heat shock (Burke, Hatfield, Klein & Mullet, 1985; Ohashi & Matsuoka, 1985). The environmental stress has an effect on gene expression (Shirras & Northcote, 1984; Key *et al.* 1985). Although there may be some similarities in the responses to the various stresses that are applied to the tissues there is no evidence yet that they are the same. In some instances, however, it has been shown that at least one protein is stimulated by a variety of stress conditions (Heikkila, Papp, Schultz & Bewley, 1984). This type of reaction of the plant to the environment is of importance in the coordination of the defensive mechanism of the plant in response to attack by parasites such as bacteria and fungi.

The work on the investigations of wound and other stress responses in plants is therefore connected with recent research on plant pathology. The plant in some instances responds to the attack of the parasite by the production of phytoalexins, which are induced by elicitors. Phytoalexins are antimicrobial compounds of low molecular weight synthesized and accumulated by plant cells in the immediate vicinity of the site of fungal or bacterial attack (Darvill & Albersheim, 1984). It is probable that the synthetic system that is necessary to produce the various phytoalexins is induced by the elicitor by regulation of gene expression in the plant cells (Cramer *et al.* 1984). The elicitors, therefore, which are present in some bacteria and fungi, and which can also be produced by degradation of the plant cell wall, are interesting compounds for the study of gene regulation. Some of these elicitors have been characterized and shown to be oligosaccharides, such as a neutral, branched hepta-β-glucoside isolated from a partially degraded cell of *Phytophthora megasperm* (Ayers, Ebel, Valent & Albersheim, 1976; Darvill & Albersheim, 1984), acidic oligogalacturonides isolated from degraded plant cell walls (Hahn, Darvill & Albersheim, 1981), or glycopeptides extracted from *Colletatrichum lagenarium* (Toppan & Esquerré-Tugaye, 1984) and *Fulvia fulva* (De Wit & Roseboom, 1980).

Generally, the difficulty with research on a stress response at the molecular level is that although the response permits the isolation of cDNA clones that correspond to the mRNAs that are stimulated by the stress, the individual proteins that are synthesized by the mRNAs are, for the most part, not known. Nevertheless, the work can be used to identify genomic clones, transcription of which is stimulated by the external stimuli and this opens up the possibility of the study of a regulated coordinated gene response to a specific stimulus. In this way, after sequencing of the DNA, chimaeric marker-genes can be constructed, introduced by an appropriate vehicle into a plant and their response noted. This type of experiment should then give information about the regulation of gene expression.

In wound response of carrot cells, one particular and interesting protein has been identified. This is the hydroxyproline-rich glycoprotein that is eventually deposited as insoluble material in the cell wall. Using the wound response, a cDNA and a genomic clone to the unmodified polypeptide precursor of this glycoprotein have been prepared (Chen & Varner, 1985, 1986). This work has now opened up the possibility of exploring the signal sequence and the total sequence of this protein, the mechanism of its deposition in the wall, which may be developmentally regulated (Cassab *et al.* 1985), and its possible relationship to other glycoproteins that carry hydroxyproline. It is also possible that the function of these proteins, which has given rise to considerable speculation in the last two decades, may be understood as the control of their synthesis is elucidated.

Recently, it has been shown that elicitors of phytoalexins from various fungal origins induce the synthesis of ethylene from plant tissues (Toppan & Esquerré-Tugaye, 1984). The fungal elicitors from *C. lagenarium* and *P. megasperm* at low concentrations ($0 \cdot 1$–$0 \cdot 3$ mg Glc equiv. ml^{-1}) also increased the amount of synthesis of hydroxyproline-rich glycoprotein in melon and soybean hypocotyls; at higher concentrations its production was inhibited, as was general protein synthesis. A crude endogenous elicitor prepared from melon cell walls also stimulated the production of ethylene and the synthesis of hydroxyproline-rich glycoprotein in melon petioles (Roby, Toppan & Esquerré-Tugaye, 1985). These endogenous elicitors might be important in tissue wounded by an environmental stress that is not caused by a parasite attack (e.g. mechanical breakage). The results show that there is a relationship between the production of the hydroxyproline-rich glycoprotein and the production of ethylene. It also seems as if the elicitors can bring about a stimulation of glycoprotein synthesis in the same way as they elicit production of phytoalexins (Cramer *et al.* 1984; Showalter *et al.* 1985). These observations open up the possibility of investigating the responses between parasite and host tissue, and the action of the plant growth substance, ethylene, in addition to their obvious relevance to the mechanisms of gene regulation and cell–cell interactions in terms of surface receptors for the elicitors.

PLANT BREEDING

Information gained from plant molecular biology may have a possible application in altering the plant genome to meet particular requirements. Prospects for genetic engineering of the plant cell are now very great. The subject will be discussed in two sections: (1) the introduction of foreign DNA into plant cells and its expression, and (2) the use of tissue cultures and the regeneration of plants from them.

The introduction of foreign DNA into plant cells and its expression

The Ti plasmid. One of the most promising vectors for the introduction of foreign genes into the plant genome is the Ti plasmid of *Agrobacterium*. The DNA transformation that is mediated by this plasmid has in recent years been extensively studied and several important transformations have been obtained by the use of suitably constructed Ti plasmids.

The use of the Ti plasmid depends on investigations that have enabled a genetic map of the various functional loci of the 150 000–200 000 base-pairs of the plasmids to be made. A 20 000–23 000 base-pair fragment, the T-DNA (some 10 % of the plasmid), is transferred to the plant chromosomes. The fragment carries various genes depending upon the type of plasmid (e.g. octopine or nopaline type) but essentially it carries regions that can transcribe for opine synthesis (either *ocs* or *nos*), loci for the control of the levels of plant growth regulators (oncogenes) in the tumour cells that arise from the infection, and various promoter and stop codons (Howell, 1982; Glover, 1984). The whole fragment is flanked by T-DNA border regions (Hooykaas & Schilperoort, 1985). The definition of the boundaries of the T-DNA is important, since these control the transfer of the DNA and it is possible to increase the size of the T-DNA fragment by insertion of foreign DNA without affecting transfer. These boundary regions include sequences adjacent to the ends of the fragment and are required for the integration of the DNA into the plant nucleus. They also include appropriate transcriptional control elements.

For the genetic engineering of plants the Ti plasmid has been modified. The constructions have involved the deletion of the internal oncogenes of the T-DNA, together with other selected regions such as the gene for nopaline synthase (*nos*) in a nopaline Ti plasmid and insertion of the foreign DNA under the control of the *nos* promoter left intact upstream from the insert (Caplan *et al.* 1983; Herra-Estrella *et al.* 1983*a,b*). In some experiments the promoter region from known eukaryotic or prokaryotic genes has been inserted between the border regions of the T-DNA and the foreign gene (see section on targeting of cytoplasmic proteins, above). The insertion of the foreign DNA has usually been accomplished by the use of an intermediate plasmid, such as pBR322. The pBR322 is first inserted in the deleted region of the T-DNA and then the foreign DNA is cloned in pBR322 and trans-formed into the Ti plasmid by homologous recombination with the pBR322-DNA insert in the modified Ti plasmid (De Block, Schell & van Montagu, 1985). An additional antibiotic resistance marker gene inserted into the intermediate pBR plasmid carrying the foreign DNA can be used for selection of the recombination process (Bevan, Flavell & Chilton, 1983).

Outside the T-DNA region the Ti plasmid carries virulence regions, which are thought to control the integration of the T-DNA into the plant genome. The T-DNA and virulence regions can act as physically self-contained units, so that the possibility arises whereby genetic engineering is accomplished by the use of two small plasmids, one carrying the T-DNA border regions plus promoter sequences and foreign DNA, while the virulence regions are carried on a second small constructed plasmid. This goal has recently been realized to a considerable extent by An *et al.* (1985), who have prepared wide host-range vectors that contain T-DNA border sequences flanking multiple restriction sites. The vectors can be used to clone foreign DNA in *E. coli* and then the replicons can be directly transferred to *Agrobacterium*, where they are stably maintained *in trans* with wild-type Ti plasmid.

Thus these vectors do not require homologous recombination for their stable maintenance in *Agrobacterium tumefaciens*. The cloned DNA in the shuttle vector can be transferred to plant cells by means of the natural transformation system of the helper (Ti) plasmid, of the *Agrobacterium*.

In the earlier experiments it was shown that the promoter sequence of the nopaline synthase gene permitted the transcription of bacterial and other genes in the plant cell nuclei when transformation was achieved (Herra-Estrella *et al.* 1983*a,b*). The 5′ untranslated leader sequence of the nopaline synthase gene does not contain a Shine–Dalgarno sequence and this probably explains why the gene is not expressed in *Agrobacterium*. The chimaeric genes on the other hand, constructed from bacteria and inserted into the T-DNA, are expressed in *E. coli* and *A. tumefaciens* and do carry the Shine–Dalgarno sequences derived from the bacterial genes, so that the *nos* promoter can be functional in prokaryotes (De Block *et al.* 1985).

A chimaeric gene consisting of the promoter region of the nopaline synthase gene fused to a DNA fragment coding for chloramphenicol acetyl transferase and re-combined into a non-oncogenic acceptor Ti plasmid was expressed in chloroplasts after being transformed into tobacco protoplasts by co-cultivation (De Block *et al.* 1985). This construct had in its promoter region the Shine–Dalgarno sequences derived from the bacterial acetyl transferase, as well as sequences from the promoter region of the nopaline synthase gene. The experiment clearly indicated that the *Agrobacterium* Ti plasmid vector system could be used to introduce genes into chloroplasts. The system is therefore being developed in a spectacular way and the progress in the next few years should have a great impact, not only on the practical aspects of plant breeding, but on the fundamental problems of gene control.

The type of information that indicates possible ways in which the control of gene transcription operates during a developmental process has been hinted at by the work of Murai *et al.* (1983). These workers have constructed a Ti plasmid that carries the DNA coding for phaseolin, the bean-seed storage protein. The gene was fused so that it came under the control of the octopine synthase gene promoter. These engineered plasmids were used in *Agrobacterium* to transform sunflower plants. The gall tissue that resulted showed that phaseolin was made and that, interestingly, the intervening sequences (introns) present in the gene for phaseolin were excised in the sunflower cells to yield a functional mRNA. No introns are present in T-DNA in the wild-type Ti plasmid. When the whole phaseolin gene plus its promoter was inserted in the sunflower genome, the level of transcript expressed was significantly lower than when the gene was controlled by the octopine synthase promoter. This result is probably an indication of the type of gene control that occurs during development, since in bean seeds the phaseolin is produced at a particular stage of seed formation. These results have been extended further by the introduction of the β-phaseolin gene *via* a Ti plasmid of *A. tumefaciens* into tobacco stem tissue. The stem segments were subsequently regenerated into whole plants and seeds were obtained from them. The phaseolin gene was present in their genome. It was transcribed during tobacco seed germination and the phaseolin was localized in the embryonic tissues, which included the cotyledons (Sengupta-Gopalan *et al.* 1985).

The Ti plasmid system is being actively developed and extended and its use has resulted in some very promising transformations in plants. The potential of the system for the introduction of genes to improve and alter plants is very great. However, the system has one major limitation in that the Ti plasmid vectors are specific for dicotyledons. Transformation of some important crop plants such as the cereals is therefore not yet possible with this vector.

Virus vectors. There are two groups of plant virus that contain DNA (Howell, 1982; Hull & Davies, 1983). These are being studied and adapted for carrying foreign DNA into their host tissues. Caulimoviruses contain double-stranded DNA and have a narrow host range, infecting a limited range of dicotyledons, such as species of Cruciferae and some Compositae. Sites have been found on the virus genome at which short lengths of foreign DNA can be inserted or removed without destroying the infectivity of the virus. The virus in its linearized form can be cloned into the bacterial plasmid pBR322, where it might be possible to manipulate it and then reintroduce it into the plant. The virus can easily be introduced into the plant by rubbing the DNA on leaves with an abrasive; once introduced the virus spreads throughout the plant. The virus probably replicates in the nucleus but does not become integrated into the plant genome, so that the vehicle and passenger DNA are produced in high copy number in the infected plant cell. Integration into the nucleus is not so essential in plant tissue that can be vegetatively propagated and the high copy number could be useful for the formation of some engineered products by the plant.

In the last few years the Geminiviruses have attracted some attention as possible vehicles for plant genetic engineering. These viruses contain single-stranded DNA. They infect some important crop plants, both monocotyledons, including maize and wheat, and dicotyledons such as bean and tomato. They have, however, some serious limitations, not the least of which is their method of transmission to plant cells, which is *via* white-flies and leaf-hoppers. Once in the plant they tend to be confined to the phloem elements of the vascular system, although infection of plant proto-plasts has been achieved.

Transposable elements. The research that is currently being carried out on the transposable elements of higher plants (Freeling, 1984; Saedler & Nevers, 1985), bacteria (Shapiro, 1979) and *Drosophila* (Spradling & Rubin, 1982) has directed attention to the use of transposons as vehicles for introduction of new DNA into the plant genome. The sequences of several transposable elements have been determined and the terminal inverted repeat sequences identified. Short duplications are generated in the host DNA upon insertion and these have also been identified (Doring & Starlinger, 1984). The transposable elements that have been studied in detail are usually inserted at sites on the chromosome characterized by the presence of different direct duplications of 6–10 base-pairs. It is possible that the product encoded by the element for transposition (the transposase) recognizes these short duplications as insertion sites. With this type of information, transformation vectors may well be constructed from the transposons, which could be injected into embryos for the introduction of new genes into the plant chromosomes. Similar experiments have already been done with *Drosophila*.

Tissue cultures and protoplasts

Liposomes and cell fusion. Direct insertion of new DNA into plant cells can be achieved by cell fusion of protoplasts or by the packaging of DNA into liposomes (Szoka & Papahadjopoulos, 1978) and the fusion of these with protoplasts (Uchimiya, 1981). Direct injection of DNA into protoplast nuclei can also be carried out (Morikawa & Yamada, 1985). The foreign DNA that is introduced is in some cases integrated and expressed in the new plant genome. The limitations on the method are: (1) the haphazard nature of the DNA integration and its stability in the genome; (2) the low level of fusion that can be achieved; (3) the difficulty of the selection procedures for transformed cells; (4) the need for regeneration of plants from the protoplasts *via* the formation of a tissue culture.

Over the last few years a new method for cell fusion (and liposome/cell fusion) has been elaborated (Zimmermann & Vienken, 1982). This involves subjecting the cells to a non-uniform alternating electrical field between two electrodes so that the cells align as chains between the electrodes (dielectrophoresis). Adjustment of the electrical field can bring about close contact between the cells covering an area of the surface of each cell. The membranes of the aligned cells at the sites of contact are then reversibly broken down by the application of a brief single d.c. pulse of high intensity. The breakdown of the membrane results in fusion of the cells as the membrane bilayers reform in continuity with one another at the edge of the contact zone. By controlling the density of the protoplasts between the electrodes, the distance between the electrodes and their arrangement, the frequency of the a.c. electrical field and the strength of the d.c. pulse, optimum conditions are found for high yields of fused cells for a particular mixture of protoplasts (Verhoeka-Köhler, Hampp, Ziegler & Zimmermann, 1983; Bates, 1985; Kohn, Schieder & Schieder, 1985; Tempelaar & Jones, 1985). The major difficulties with the method after fusion has been achieved are the selection of the fused heterokaryons and the regeneration process to obtain plants from protoplasts.

Plant regeneration. The regeneration of the plants is a major obstacle in these experiments. Usually, in experiments that involve protoplasts as a model system to accept foreign DNA, either by cell fusion or with Ti plasmids and other vectors, tobacco protoplasts are used. These experiments are often suggested to be systems capable of extension for general application to a wide variety of plants. The protoplasts of nearly all species can usually be cultivated to re-form a cell wall, so that a tissue culture or callus may be obtained. It is at this stage that tobacco is fairly unusual, in that plants can easily be regenerated from this callus. The manipulation of growth factors (auxin and cytokinin), so well documented for the totipotent cells of tobacco callus (Murashige, 1963; Binns, Sciaky & Wood, 1982), does not produce the desired differentiation response in the calluses of a large number of important crop plants. It is not possible in a great many cases to regenerate even differentiated tissue such as roots or nodules of xylem and phloem from the tissue culture cells, especially if they have been cultured for several transfers in a maintenance medium. At present this problem is being approached at an empirical level by the use of various ratios of growth factors in an attempt to obtain a differentiating medium for the particular cell culture. However, the continued use of protoplasts as recipient cells for DNA in order to obtain plants with desirable and engineered properties has a serious limitation at this practical stage. Maybe it implies that more basic investigations of the totipotency of plant cells and their ageing in culture need to be made along the lines of work with animal cells (Hayflick, 1984).

THE MECHANISMS OF PLANT CELL WALL FORMATION

The formation of the plant cell wall involves synthesis of polysaccharide, glycoprotein and lignin, transport and targeting of material in the cell, vesicle formation and membrane fusion, location of synthases and other enzymes in membrane compartments, and specific transport processes across membranes (Northcote, 1985b). All these topics are being investigated in plant, animal and bacterial tissues and they are areas where new information and ideas are continually being put forward and evaluated. Some of these topics will be discussed below.

Polysaccharide synthesis

The polysaccharides, like the glycoproteins, are synthesized within the membrane system (endoplasmic reticulum, Golgi apparatus, plasma membrane). The sugars are assembled from donor nucleoside diphosphate sugar compounds and, since the assembly is carried out in the lumen of the membrane system, specific transporting mechanisms are necessary to get these compounds, formed on the cytoplasmic side of the membrane, across to the synthases on the other side of the membrane. In the case of the asparagine-linked glycoproteins, where the oligosaccharide is assembled on a dolicol diphosphate acceptor, before transfer to the protein, it has been suggested either that the initial sugars are transferred to the lipid acceptor on the cytoplasmic side of the membrane and, or, that there is a transglycosylation–transport process involving the dolicol phosphate (Kornfeld & Kornfeld, 1985). Later processing and further glycosylations take place in the Golgi apparatus and at this compartment specific transporters of the nucleoside diphosphate sugars occur (Dixon & Northcote, 1985).

The synthesis of the cell wall polysaccharides, although occurring within the membrane system, does not seem to involve polyisoprenoid lipid carriers but to involve a more direct transfer of sugars from the nucleoside diphosphate sugar to the growing polysaccharide. However, using *in vitro* systems of membrane preparations, the yield of polysaccharide formed from the donor sugar compound is low and the rates of synthesis are not high, so that other factors or steps in the synthesis need to be elucidated. It seems fairly clear, however, from negative evidence that polyisoprenoid–phosphate–sugar intermediates are not formed in polysaccharide synthesis (Bolwell & Northcote, 1981). This can be assumed because of the lack of their isolation during synthesis *in vitro*, the lack of stimulation of polysaccharide synthesis by the addition of dolicol phosphate and the failure of inhibitors such as bacitracin and tumicamycin to interfere with polysaccharide formation. (There is, however, some evidence that lipid intermediates may be found in cellulose synthesis (Hopp, Romero, Daleo & Pont Lezica, 1978; Datema, Schwartz, Rivas & Pont Lezica, 1983).)

The control of polysaccharide synthesis within the endomembrane system is obviously first initiated by the control of the transport of the nucleoside diphosphate sugars across the membrane. This could not only control the rate of synthesis but be qualitatively important and determine the type of polysaccharide that is formed at a particular membrane compartment. Once in the lumen of the membrane compartment the transfer of the sugar from the donor to the growing polymer is determined by the activity of the synthase. These synthases are synthesized and inserted through the membrane from the cytoplasm, and the induction of their synthesis is determined by the regulation of gene expression during the development of the cell (see above). The activity of the synthases is also dependent on the level of available energy in the cell, so that the synthases are modulated by the level of mono- and diphospho-nucleosides by direct feed-back inhibition (Northcote, 1985a). Many aspects of the control of the formation of sugar polymers, either as polysaccharides or glyco-proteins, are related one to another because they involve control of membrane synthesis, membrane fusion and the secretion process of the cell. These important cell functions will be understood only in terms of the control of their integrated mechanisms.

The endomembrane system

The work on the synthesis of animal glycoproteins has shown that the cisternae of the Golgi apparatus can be divided into *cis*, medial and *trans* regions and that different transglycosylases identified by immunochemistry are located in the differ-ent regions (Roth & Berger, 1982; Dunphy, Brands & Rothman, 1985). It is also apparent that during the packaging and export of material from the Golgi apparatus it is almost certainly sequestered in particular cisternae and perhaps even in par-ticular parts of a cisternum (Griffiths *et al.* 1982; Griffiths, Quinn & Warren, 1983; Deutscher, Creek, Merion & Hirschberg, 1983). The lysosomal enzymes, which are glycoproteins and are synthesized within the endoplasmic reticulum and Golgi apparatus, become specifically labelled so that they can be separated from other glycoproteins carrying mannose oligosaccharides. The recognition markers are phosphate esters on the mannose, put there by two enzymes, *N*-acetylglucosaminyl-phosphotransferase and *N*-acetylglucosamine-1-phosphodiester-α-*N*-acetylglucosa-minidase (Kornfeld *et al.* 1982). It is probable that the transferase recognizes the protein of the lysomal enzymes and distinguishes them from the other mannose-carrying glycoproteins (Lang *et al.* 1984). These results indicate the types of sorting processes that might be more generally applicable to plant polysaccharides during wall formation. However, similar mechanisms have not yet been found in plants (Gaudreault & Beevers, 1984), although it is apparent that during the growth of the wall different polysaccharides are deposited at different times in particular locations around the wall. In addition to the recognition markers that may be found for the polymers contained within the vesicles and other compartments of the membrane system, the movement of the secretory vesicles within the cell and the mechanisms of vesicle formation and their fusion as shuttle vehicles between the various parts of the membrane system are important areas of research. The large amount of membrane incorporated into the plasma membrane during the secretion of the cell wall polymers must entail a recycling pathway to retrieve the membrane and return it to the cytoplasm. Although coated vesicles and coated pits in the plasma membrane have been noted in plant tissues, the functions of these in the endocytotic pathways by which material could be taken into the plant cell have not been established (Lang *et al.* 1984; Mersey, Griffing, Rennie & Fawke, 1985). While in animal cells, clathrin-coated vesicles have been shown to be concerned with the internalization of material and to be related to intermediate compartments (endosomes or recepto-somes) and the Golgi apparatus, this is by no means so clear in plant tissues. The importance of Ca^{2+} for membrane fusion and the possible control of secretion by adjustment of the Ca^{2+} concentration at the plasma membrane seems to be indicated by several experimental approaches (Baydoun & Northcote, 1980; Dieter, 1984). These control mechanisms and the relationship of the secretory vesicles to the distribution of microtubules for movement to particular areas of the plasma membrane can now be explored by sensitive cytological methods involving immunology, radioimmunology, fluorescently labelled antibodies and the binding of fluorescent compounds (specific inhibitors, e.g. phenothiazines) (Hausser, Herth & Reiss, 1984)) to tubulin (Wick *et al.* 1981; Muto, 1982) and calmodulin.

Cellulose synthesis

The synthesis and distribution of cellulose within the wall needs special discussion. The synthesis of cellulose is not by any means understood. There are several major problems that arise with the use of *in vitro* membrane systems for the study of cellulose synthesis, one of which is that damaged cells synthesize callose β-$(1 \rightarrow 3)$ glucan at a rapid rate. This callose synthase is present at the plasma membrane, as is the cellulose synthase (Northcote, 1985*a*). Usually, therefore, the products of the *in vitro* synthetic activity of the membranes contain both β-$(1 \rightarrow 3)$ and β-$(1 \rightarrow 4)$ glucans, either as separate polymers or as a mixed polymer (heteropolyglucan) containing both linkages. Callose arises as a wound response; it is used to plug the lesion and it can be rapidly removed, probably by a hydrolytic or phosphorolytic system. The rate of β-$(1 \rightarrow 4)$ glucan synthesis in isolated membranes *in vitro* is usually much lower than that *in vivo*, whereas callose synthesis is nearly always much greater in preparations *in vitro* than it is *in vivo*. It has also been shown that the glucose incorporated into callose can be found subsequently in cellulose, so that it has been suggested that callose is a possible precursor of cellulose (Meier, Bucks, Buchala & Homewood, 1981; Pillonel & Meier, 1985). These observations can all be reconciled if due importance is given to the membrane at which the synthetic activity occurs. It is possible that the same enzyme carried on the membrane can synthesize both β-$(1 \rightarrow 3)$ and β-$(1 \rightarrow 4)$ links and that the particular polymer that is formed depends on the orientation of the donor and acceptor molecules in relation to the enzymes on the organized membrane (Jacob & Northcote, 1985). In this way the hydroxyl on position C-3 or C-4 (even on occasion C-2) of the glucose becomes available for glycosylation. The specificity of the transglucosylase (the synthase) for the particular hydroxyl group on C-3, C-4 or C-2 depends upon the nature of the organized enzyme system: wounding (damage of the membrane) automatically allows the β-(1→3) glucan plug to be formed. Callose synthesis might also occur to a limited extent when organized cellulose microfibrils are being formed. If it is postulated that it is continually being degraded then it is possible to show how the glucose of callose comes, subsequently, to be incorporated into cellulose (Jacob & Northcote, 1985). The scheme permits an experimental approach for investigating cellulose synthesis and indicates possible extensions to other types of polysaccharide synthesis and membrane-bound synthetic processes. The synthesis of cellulose, besides involving the biosynthesis of β-(1→4) glucan chains, also necessitates the control of processes that bring about the aggregation of these chains (crystallization) into discrete microfibrils and their orientation within the wall in definite directions. Freeze-etch studies of the plasma membrane of higher plants and some algae have revealed that there is an abundance of rosettes of particles (Emons, 1985) and terminal globules in regions of high production of cellulose, for example, regions of secondary thickening during xylem formation (Herth, 1985). The rosettes of six particles arranged in hexagonal arrays (25 nm diameter, each particle 8 nm diameter) are seen at the E face, while the rather larger terminal globules (single particles 12 nm diameter) are found on the P face. It is postulated that the rosettes and globules form a complex across the membrane and that this constitutes an enzymic array for the formation of a microfibril (one rosette plus globule forms one fibril, 3·5 nm in diameter, formed of 36 glucan chains). The whole complex is thought to be mobile in the surface of the plasma membrane, guided by some direct or indirect association with microtubules in the cytoplasm. The motive force for the movement may be provided by the cytoskeletal elements of the cell or by the crystallization of the glucan chains into organized microfibrils (Heath & Seagull, 1982). The rosettes may be labile or incorporated back into the cytoplasm for recycling and this may make difficult the isolation of a membrane-bound enzymic system that can mimic the activity of the system *in vivo*. However, the relationship of the particles by biochemical enzymic complexes for cellulose formation remains to be studied and is an area where work is in progress and important results are possible.

REFERENCES

AN, G., WATSON, B. D., STACHEL, S., GORDON, M. P. & NESTER, E. W. (1985). New cloning vehicles for transformation of higher plants. *EMBO J.* **4**, 277–284.

AYERS, A. R., EBEL, J., VALENT, B. & ALBERSHEIM, P. (1976). Host–pathogen interactions. X. Fractionation and biological activity of an elicitor isolated from the mycelial walls of *Phytophthora megasperma* var. sojae. *Pl. Physiol.* **57**, 760–765.

BATES, G. W. (1985). Electrical fusion for optimal formation of protoplast heterokaryons in *Nicotiana. Planta* **165**, 217–224.

BAULCOMBE, D. C. & BUFFARD, D. (1983). Gibberellic-acid-regulated expression of α-amylase and six other genes in wheat aleurone layers. *Planta* **157**, 493–501.

BAYDOUN, E. A.-H. & NORTHCOTE, D. H. (1980). Measurement and characteristics of fusion of isolated membrane fractions from maize root tips. *J. Cell Sci.* **45**, 169–186.

BEVAN, M. W., FLAVELL, R. B. & CHILTON, M. D. (1983). A. chimaeric antibiotic resistance gene as a selectable marker for plant cell transformation. *Nature, Lond.* **304**, 184–187.

BEVAN, M. & NORTHCOTE, D. H. (1981a). Subculture-induced protein synthesis in tissue cultures of *Glycine max* and *Phaseolus vulgaris*. *Planta* **152**, 24–31.

BEVAN, M. & NORTHCOTE, D. H. (1981b). Some rapid effects on mRNA levels in cultured plant cells. *Planta* **152**, 32–35.

BINNS, A., SCIAKY, D. & WOOD, H. N. (1982). Variation in hormone automony and regenerative potential of cells transformed by strain A66 of *Agrobacterium tumefaciens*. *Cell* **31**, 605–612.

BOLWELL, G. P. & NORTHCOTE, D. H. (1981). Control of hemicellulose and pectin synthesis during differentiation of vascular tissue in bean (*Phaseolus vulgaris*) callus and in bean hypocoytyl. *Planta* **152**, 225–233.

BOLWELL, G. P. & NORTHCOTE, D. H. (1983). Induction by growth factors of polysaccharide synthases in bean cell suspension cultures. *Biochem. J.* **210**, 509–515.

BOLWELL, G. P. & NORTHCOTE, D. H. (1984). Demonstration of a common antigenic site on endomembrane proteins of *Phaseolus vulgaris* by a rat monoclonal antibody. Tentative identification of arabinan synthase and consequences for its regulation. *Planta* **162**, 139–146.

BROECK, G. V., TIMKO, M. P., KAUECH, A. P., CASHMORE, A. R., VAN MONTAGU, M. & HERRA-ESTRELLA, L. (1985). Targeting of a foreign protein to chloroplasts by fusion to the transit peptide from the small subunit of ribulose 1,5-biphosphate carboxylase. *Nature, Lond.* **313**, 358–363.

BROWN, A. H. D. & JACOBSEN, J. V. (1982). Genetic basis and natural variation of α-amylase isoszymes in barley. *Genet. Res.* **40**, 315–324.

BURKE, J. J., HATFIELD, J. L., KLEIN, R. R. & MULLET, J. E. (1985). Accumulation of heat shock proteins in field-grown cotton. *Pl. Physiol.* **78**, 394–398.

CAPLAN, A., HERRA-ESTRELLA, L., INZE, D., VAN HAUTE, E., VAN MONTAGU, M., SCHELL, J. & ZAMBRYSKI, P. (1983). Introduction of genetic material into plant cells. *Science* **222**, 815–821.

CASSAB, G. I., NIETO-SOTELA, J., COOPER, J. B., VAN HOLST, G-J. & VARNER, J. E. (1985). A developmentally regulated hydroxyproline-rich glycoprotein from the cell walls of soybean seed coats. *Pl. Physiol.* **77**, 532–535.

CHANDLER, P. M., ZWAR, J. A., JACOBSEN, J. V., HIGGINS, T. J. V. & INGLIS, A. S. (1984). The effects of gibberellic acid and abscisic acid on amylase mRNA levels in barley aleurone layers using an α-amylase cDNA clone. *Pl. molec. Biol.* **3**, 407–418.

CHEN, J. & VARNER, J. E. (1985). Isolation and characterization of cDNA clones for carrot extensin and a proline-rich 33 kd protein. *Proc. natn. Acad. Sci. U.S.A.* **82**, 4399–4403.

CHEN, J. & VARNER, J. E. (1986). An extracellular matrix protein in plants: Characterization of a genomic clone for carrot extensin. *EMBO J.* (in press).

CRAMER, C. L., RYDER, T. B., BELL, J. N. & LAMB, C. J. (1984). Rapid switching of plant gene expression induced by fungal elicitor. *Science* **227**, 1240–1243.

DARVILL, A. G. & ALBERSHEIM, P. (1984). Phytoalexins and their elicitors: a defence against microbial infection in plants. *A. Rev. Pl. Physiol.* **35**, 243–275.

DATEMA, R., SCHWARZ, R. T., RIVAS, L. A. & PONT LEZICA, R. (1983). Inhibition of β1,4-glucan biosynthesis by deoxyglucose. The effect on the glucosylation of lipid intermediates. *Pl. Physiol.* **71**, 76–81.

DE BLOCK, M., SCHELL, J. & VAN MONTAGU, M. (1985). Chloroplast transformation by *Agrobacterium tumefaciens*. *EMBO J.* **4**, 1367–1372.

DEIKMAN, J. & JONES, R. L. (1985). Control of α-amylase mRNA accumulation by gibberellic acid and calcium in barley aleurone layers. *Pl. Physiol.* **78**, 192–198.

DEUTSCHER, S. L., CREEK, K. E., MERION, M. & HIRSCHBERG, C. B. (1983). Subfractionation of rat liver Golgi apparatus: separation of enzyme activities involved in the biosynthesis of the phosphomannosyl recognition marker in lysosomal enzymes. *Proc. natn. Acad. Sci. U.S.A.* **80**, 3938–3942.

DE WIT, P. J. G. M. & ROSEBOOM, P. H. M. (1980). Isolation, partial characterization and specificity of glycoprotein elicitors from culture filtrates, mycelium & cell walls of *Cladosporium fulvum* (syn *Fulvia fulva*). *Physiol. Pl. Path.* **16**, 391–408.

DIETER, P. (1984). Calmodulin and calmodulin-mediated processes in plants. *Pl. Cell & Environ.* **7**, 371–380.

DIXON, W. T. & NORTHCOTE, D. H. (1985). Plant cell secretory processes. In *Developments in Cell Biology: Secretory Processes* (ed. R. T. Dean, & P. Stahl), pp. 77–98. London: Butterworths.

DOMMES, J. & NORTHCOTE, D. H. (1985a). The action of exogenous abscisic and gibberellic acids on gene expression in germinating castor beans. *Planta* **165**, 513–521.

DOMMES, J. & NORTHCOTE, D. H. (1985b). The action of exogenous abscisic acid on malate synthase synthesis in germinating castor bean seeds. *Planta* **166**, 550–556.

DORING, H. P. & STARLINGER, P. (1984). Barbara McClintock's Controlling elements: now at the DNA level. *Cell* **39**, 253–259.

DUNPHY, W. G., BRANDS, R. & ROTHMAN, J. E. (1985). Attachment of terminal N-acetylglucosamine to asparagine-linked oligosaccharides occurs in central cisternae of the Golgi stock. *Cell* **40**, 463–472.

EMONS, A. M. C. (1985). Plasma-membrane rosettes in root hairs of *Equisetum hyemale*. *Planta* **163**, 350–359.

FREELING, M. (1984). Plant transposable elements and insertion sequences. *A. Rev. Pl. Physiol.* **35**, 277–298.

FUKUDA, H. & KOMAMINE, A. (1980a). Establishment of an experimental system for the study of tracheary element differentiation from single cells isolated from the mesophyll of *Zinnia elegans*. *Pl. Physiol.* **65**, 57–60.

FUKADA, H. & KOMAMINE, A. (1980b). Direct evidence for cytodifferentiation to tracheary elements without intervening mitosis in a culture of single cells isolated from the mesophyll of *Zinnia elegans*. *Pl. Physiol.* **65**, 57–60.

GAUDREAULT, P.-R. & BEEVERS, L. (1984). Protein bodies and vacuoles as lysosomes. Investigations into the role of mannose 6-phosphate in intracellular transport of glycosidases in pea cotyledons. *Pl. Physiol.* **76**, 228–232.

GLOVER, D. M. (1984). The mechanics of DNA manipulation. In *Gene Cloning*. London: Chapman & Hall.

GRIERSON, D., SLATER, A., SPIERS, J. & TUCKER, G. A. (1985). The appearance of polygalacturononase mRNA in tomatoes; one of a series of changes in gene expression during development and ripening. *Planta* **163**, 263–271.

GRIFFITHS, G., BRANDS, R., BURKE, B., LOUVARD, D. & WARDEN, G. (1982). Viral membrane proteins acquire galactose in trans-Golgi cisternae during intracellular transport. *J. Cell Biol.* **95**, 781–792.

GRIFFITHS, G., QUINN, P. & WARREN, G. (1983). Dissection of the Golgi complex. 1. Monensin inhibits the transport of viral membrane proteins from medial to trans Golgi cisternae in baby hamster kidney cells infected with Semliki forest virus. *J. Cell Biol.* **96**, 835–850.

HAHN, M. G., DARVILL, A. G. & ALBERSHEIM, P. (1981). Host–pathogen interactions. XIX. The endogenous elicitor, a fragment of a plant cell wall polysaccharide that elicits phytoalexin accumulation in soybeans. *Pl. Physiol.* **68**, 1161–1169.

HAUSSER, I., HERTH, W. & REISS, H.-D. (1984). Calmodulin in tip-growing plant cells, visualised by fluorescing calmodulin-binding phenothiazines. *Planta* **162**, 33–39.

HAYFLICK, L. (1984). Intracellular determinants of cell ageing. *Mech. Ageing Dev.* **28**, 177–185.

HEATH, I. B. & SEAGULL, R. W. (1982). Oriented cellulose fibrils and the cytoskeleton: A critical comparison of models. In *The Cytoskeleton in Plant Growth and Development* (ed. C. W. Lloyd), pp. 163–182. London: Academic Press.

HEIKKILA, J., PAPP, J. E. T., SCHULTZ, G. A. & BEWLEY, J. D. (1984). Induction of heat shock protein messenger RNA in maize mesocotyls by water stress, abscisic acid and wounding. *Pl. Physiol.* **76**, 270–274.

HERERRA-ESTRELLA, L., DE BLOCK, M., MESSENS, E., HERNALSTEENS, J. P., VAN MONTAGU, M. & SCHELL, J. (1983a). Chimaeric genes as dominant selectable markers in plant cells. *EMBO J.* **2**, 987–995.

HERERRA-ESTRELLA, L., DEPICKER, A., VAN MONTAGU, M. & SCHELL, J. (1983*b*). Expression of chimaeric genes transferred into plant cells using a Ti-plasmid derived vector. *Nature, Lond.* **303**, 209–213.

HERTH, W. (1985). Plasma-membrane rosettes involved in localized wall thickening during xylem vessel formation of *Lepidium sativum. Planta* **164**, 12–21.

HIGGINS, T. J. V., JACOBSEN, J. V. & ZWAR, J. A. (1982). Gibberellic and abscisic acids modulate protein synthesis and mRNA levels in barley aleurone layers. *Pl. molec. Biol.* **1**, 191–215.

HOOYKAAS, P. J. J. & SCHILPEROORT, R. A. (1985). The Ti-plasmid of *Agrobacterium tumefaciens*: a natural genetic engineer. *Trends Biochem. Sci.* **10**, 307–309.

HOPP, H. E., ROMERO, P. A., DALEO, G. R. & PONT LEZICA, R. (1978). Synthesis of cellulose precursors. The involvement of lipid-linked sugars. *Eur. J. Biochem.* **84**, 561–571.

HOWELL, S. H. (1982). Plant molecular vehicles: potential vectors for introducing foreign DNA into plants. *A. Rev. Pl. Physiol.* **33**, 609–650.

HULL, R. & DAVIES, J. W. (1983). Genetic engineering with plant viruses and their potential as vectors. *Adv. Virus Res.* **28**, 1–33.

JACOB, S. R. & NORTHCOTE, D. H. (1985). *In vitro* glucan synthesis by membranes of celery petioles: the role of the membrane in determining the type of linkage formed. *J. Cell Sci. Suppl.* **3**, 1–11.

JACOBSEN, J. V. (1984). Regulation of protein synthesis in aleurone cells by gibberellin and abscisic acid. In *The Biochemistry and Physiology of Gibberellins*, vol. 2 (ed. A. Crozier), pp. 159–187. New York: Praeger.

JACOBSEN, J. V. & BEACH, L. R. (1985). Control of transcription of α-amylase and rRNA genes in barley aleurone protoplasts by gibberellin and abscisic acid. *Nature, Lond.* **316**, 275–277.

JACOBSEN, J. V., ZWAR, J. A. & CHANDLER. P. M. (1985). Gibberellic-acid responsive protoplasts from mature aleurone of Himalaya barley. *Planta* **163**, 430–438.

JONES, D. H. & NORTHCOTE, D. H. (1981). Induction by hormones of phenylalanine ammonia-lyase in bean-cell suspension cultures. Inhibition and superinduction by actinomycin D. *Eur. J. Biochem.* **116**, 117–125.

KEY, J. L., KIMPEL, J. A., VIERLING, E., LIN, C. Y., NAGAO, R. T., CZARNECKA, E. & SCHOFFL, F. (1985). *Changes in Eukaryotic Gene Expression in Response to Environmental Stress* (ed. B. G. Alkinson & D. B. Walden), pp. 327–348. New York: Academic Press.

KOHLENBACK, H. W. & SCHMIDT, B. (1975). Cytodifferensierung in Form einer direkten. Umwandlung isolierter Mesophyllzellen zu Tracheiden. *Z. PflPhysiol.* **75**, 369–374.

KOHN, H., SCHIEDER, R. & SCHIEDER, O. (1985). Somatic hybrids in tobacco mediated by electrofusion. *Pl. Sci.* **38**, 121–128.

KORNFELD, R. & KORNFELD, S. (1985). Assembly of asparagine-linked oligosaccharides. *A. Rev. Biochem.* **54**, 631–664.

KORNFELD, S., REITMAN, M. L., VARKI, A., GOLDBERG, D. & GABEL, C. A. (1982). Steps in the phosphorylation of the high-mannose oligosaccharides of lysomal enzymes. In *Membrane Recycling, Ciba Fdn Symp.* vol. 92 (ed. D. Evered & G. M. Collins), pp. 138–156. London: Pitman.

LANG, L., REITMAN, M., TANG, C. J., ROBERTS, R. M. & KORNFELD, S. (1984). Lysosomal enzyme phosphorylation. Recognition of a protein-dependent determinant allows specific phosphorylation of oligosaccharides present on lysosomal enzymes. *J. biol. Chem.* **25**, 14663–14671.

MARTIN, C., BEECHING, J. R. & NORTHCOTE, D. H. (1984). Changes in levels of transcripts in endosperms of castor beans treated with exogenous gibberellic acid. *Planta* **162**, 68–76.

MARTIN, C. & NORTHCOTE, D. H. (1982). The action of exogenous gibberellic acid on isocitrate lyase-mRNA in germinating castor bean seeds. *Planta* **154**, 174–183.

MARTIN, C. & NORTHCOTE, D. H. (1983). The action of exogenous gibberellic acid on polysome formation and translation of mRNA in germinating castor-bean seeds. *Planta* **158**, 16–26.

MEIER, H., BUCKS, L., BUCHALA, A. J. & HOMEWOOD, T. (1981). $(1\rightarrow3)$-β-D-glucan (callose) is probable intermediate in biosynthesis of cellulose of cotton fibres. *Nature, Lond.* **289**, 821–822.

MERSEY, B. G., GRIFFING, L. R., RENNIE, P. J. & FAWKE, L. C. (1985). The isolation of coated vesicles from protoplasts of soybean. *Planta* **163**, 317–327.

MORIKAWA, H. & YAMADA, Y. (1985). Capillary microinjection into protoplasts and intranuclear localization of injected materials. *Pl. Cell Physiol.* **26**, 229–236.

MOZER, T. J. (1980). Control of protein synthesis in barley aleurone layers by the plant hormones gibberellic acid and abscisic acid. *Cell* **20**, 479–485.

MURAI, N., SUTTON, D. W., MURRAY, M. G., SLIGHTOM, J. L., MERLO, D. J., REICHERT, N. A., SENGUPTA-GOPALAN, C., STOCK, C. A., BARKER, R. F., KEMP, J. D. & HALL, T. C. (1983). Phaseolin gene from bean is exposed after transfer to sunflower via tumor-inducing plasmid vectors. *Science* **222**, 476–482.

MURASHIGE, T. (1963). The role of gibberellin in shoot differentiation in tobacco tissue cultures. In *Proc. Int. Conf. Pl. Tiss. Culture* (ed. P. R. White & A. R. Grove), pp. 321–330. Berkeley CA, USA: McCrutchan Pub. Co.

MUTO, S. (1982). Distribution of calmodulin within wheat leaf cells. *FEBS Lett.* **147**, 161–167.

NORTHCOTE, D. H. (1984). Control of cell wall assembly during differentiation. In *Structure, Function and Biosynthesis of Plant Cell Walls* (ed. W. M. Dugger & S. Bartricke-Garcia), *Proc. 7 Symp. Bot. U.C. Riverside*, pp. 222–234. Am. Soc. Pl. Physiol.

NORTHCOTE, D. H. (1985a). Control of cell wall formation during growth. *Soc. exp. Biol. Sem. Series* **28** (ed. C. Brett & Hillman), pp. 177–197. Cambridge University Press.

NORTHCOTE, D. H. (1985b). Cell organelles and their function in biosynthesis of cell wall components: Control of cell wall assembly during differentiation. In *Biosynthesis and Biodegradation of Wood Components* (ed. T. Higuchi), pp. 87–108. Orlando, U.S.A.: Academic Press.

OHASHI, Y. & MATSUOKA, M. (1985). Synthesis of stress proteins in tobacco leaves. *Pl. Cell Physiol.* **26**, 473–480.

PILLONEL, CH. & MEIER, H. (1985). Influence of external factors on callose and cellulose synthesis during incubation *in vitro* of intact cotton fibres with [^{14}C]sucrose. *Planta* **165**, 76–84.

QUATRANO, R. S., BALLO, B. L., WILLIAMSON, J. D., HAMBLIN, M. T. & MANSFIELD, M. (1983). ABA controlled expression of embryo-specific genes during wheat grain development. In *Plant Molecular Biology. UCLA Symp. molec. cell. Biol*, New Series, vol. 12 (ed. R. B. Goldberg), pp. 343–353. New York: A. R. Liss.

ROBY, D., TOPPAN, A. & ESQUERRÉ-TUGAYE, M.-T. (1985). Cell surfaces in plant–microorganism interactions. V. Elicitors of fungal and of plant origin trigger the synthesis of ethylene and of cell wall hydroxyproline-rich glycoprotein in plants. *Pl. Physiol.* **77**, 700–704.

ROGERS, J. C. (1985). Two barley α-amylase gene families are regulated differently in aleurone cells. *J. biol. Chem.* **260**, 3731–3738.

ROTH, J. & BERGER, E. G. (1982). Immunocytochemical localization of galactosyltransferase in HeLa cells; Codistribution with thiamine pyrophosphatase in trans-Golgi cisternae. *J. Cell Biol.* **93**, 223–229.

RUBIN, G. M. & SPRADLING, A. C. (1982). Genetic transformation of *Drosophila* with transposable element vectors. *Science* **218**, 348–353.

SAEDLER, H. & NEVERS, P. (1985). Transposition in plants: a molecular model. *EMBO J.* **4**, 585–590.

SCHREIER, P. H., SEFTOR, E. A., SCHELL, J. & BOHNERT, H. J. (1985). The use of nuclear-encoded sequences to direct the light-regulated synthesis and transport of a foreign protein into plant chloroplasts. *EMBO J.* **4**, 25–32.

SENGUPTA-GOPALAN, C., REICHERT, N. A., BAKER, R. F., HALL, T. C. & KEMP, J. D. (1985). Developmentally regulated expression of bean β phaseolin gene in tobacco seed. *Proc. natn. Acad. Sci. U.S.A.* **82**, 3320–3324.

SHAPIRO, J. A. (1979). Molecular model for the transposition and replication of bacteriophage Mu and other transposable elements. *Proc. natn. Acad. Sci. U.S.A.* **76**, 1933–1937.

SHIRRAS, A. D. & NORTHCOTE, D. H. (1984). Molecular cloning and characterisation of cDNAs complimentary to mRNAs from wounded potato (*Solanum tuberosum*) tuber tissue. *Planta* **162**, 353–360.

SHOWALTER, A. M., BELL, J. N., CRAMER, C. L., BAILEY, J. A., VARNER, J. E. & LAMB, C. J. (1986). Accumulation of hydroxyproline-rich glycoprotein mRNAs in response to fungal elicitor and infection. *Proc. natn. Acad. Sci. U.S.A.* (in press).

SPRADLING, A. C. & RUBIN, G. M. (1982). Transposition of cloned elements into *Drosophila* germ line chromosomes. *Science* **218**, 341–347.

Szoka, F. & Papahadjopoulos, D. (1978). Procedure for preparation of liposomes with large internal aqueous space and high capture by reverse-phase evaporation. *Proc. natn. Acad. Sci. U.S.A.* **75**, 4194–4198.

Tempelaar, M. J. & Jones, M. G. K. (1985). Fusion characteristics of plant protoplasts in electric fields. *Planta* **165**, 205–216.

Toppan, A. & Esquerré-Tugaye, M. T. (1984). Cell surfaces in plant–microorganism interactions. IV. Fungal glycopeptides which elicit the synthesis of ethylene in plants. *Pl. Physiol.* **75**, 1133–1138.

Trelease, R. N. (1984). Biogenesis of glyoxysomes. *A. Rev. Pl. Physiol.* **35**, 321–347.

Uchimiya, H. (1981). Parameters influencing the liposome-mediated insertion of fluorescein diacetate into plant protoplasts. *Pl. Physiol.* **67**, 629–632.

Verhoek-Köhler, B., Hampp, R., Ziegler, H. & Zimmermann, U. (1983). Electro-fusion of mesophyll protoplasts of *Avenia sativa. Planta* **158**, 199–204.

Walker, C. & Key, J. L. (1982). Isolation of cloned cDNAs to auxin-responsive poly(A)$^+$ RNAs of elongating soybean hypocotyl. *Proc. natn. Acad. Sci. U.S.A.* **79**, 7185–7189.

Walker, J. C., Legocka, J., Edelman, L. & Key, J. L. (1985). An analysis of growth regulator interactions and gene expression during auxin-induced cell elongation using cloned cDNAs to auxin-responsive mRNAs. *Pl. Physiol.* **77**, 847–850.

Weir, E. M., Riezman, H., Grienenberger, J. M., Becker, W. M. & Leaver, C. J. (1980). Regulation of glyoxysomal enzymes during germination of cucumber. Temporal changes in translatable mRNAs for isocitrate lyase and malate synthase. *Eur. J. Biochem.* **112**, 469–477.

Wick, S. M., Seagull, R. W., Osborn, M., Weber, K. & Gunning, B. E. S. (1981). Immunofluorescence microscopy of organised microtubule arrays in structurally-stabilised meristematic plant cells. *J. Cell Biol.* **89**, 685–690.

Zimmermann, U. & Vienken, J. (1982). Electric field-induced cell to cell fusion. *J. Membr. Biol.* **67**, 165–182.

J. Cell Sci. Suppl. 4, 137–153 (1986)
Printed in Great Britain © The Company of Biologists Limited 1986

CELL SIGNALLING THROUGH PHOSPHOLIPID METABOLISM

MICHAEL J. BERRIDGE

AFRC Unit of Insect Neurophysiology and Pharmacology, Department of Zoology, University of Cambridge, Downing Street, Cambridge CB2 3EJ, UK

INTRODUCTION

An early event in evolution was the development of cell membranes, which served to encapsulate small microenvironments in which biochemical processes could occur with much greater efficiency. The presence of a hydrophobic barrier created problems with regard to gaining nutrients and eliminating waste products, which led to the development of numerous transport mechanisms to cope with this two-way traffic across the cell surface. In addition, this early cell had to be able to respond to changes in the environment and there probably was considerable selective advantage in developing receptor mechanisms for detecting external signals. The impermeability of the surface membranes imposed serious difficulties in transmitting information into the cell and this problem was solved in two quite separate ways. Certain chemicals, such as the steroid hormones, are hydrophobic and can pass through membranes *en route* to receptor sites within the nucleus. By far the majority of chemicals that influence cellular activity, however, are hydrophilic and must exert their effects without entering the cell. Their action depends on elegant transduction processes within the cell membrane, which detect external signals and transduce the information into a limited repertoire of internal signals (second messengers). This article deals with a newly discovered transduction mechanism, based on inositol lipids, which is responsible for controlling many aspects of cell function including, it seems, the crucial decision about whether or not to grow.

SECOND MESSENGER SYSTEMS

Cyclic AMP and calcium are the two major second messenger systems in cells and they share a number of interesting similarities with regard to the transduction mechanisms in the cell membrane responsible for generating these signals (Fig. 1). The concept of a second messenger arose from the discovery of cyclic AMP, which mediated the action of certain hormones in liver. Upon arriving at the cell surface, hormones such as glucagon interact with a receptor, which in turn stimulates an enzyme (adenylate cyclase) located on the inside of the cell membrane, which uses ATP as a precursor to generate cyclic AMP, which diffuses into the cell to bring about the breakdown of glycogen. In this way, the first message (glucagon) is transduced into the second messenger (cyclic AMP) responsible for relaying information into the cell. It soon became apparent that cyclic AMP was fairly ubiquitous,

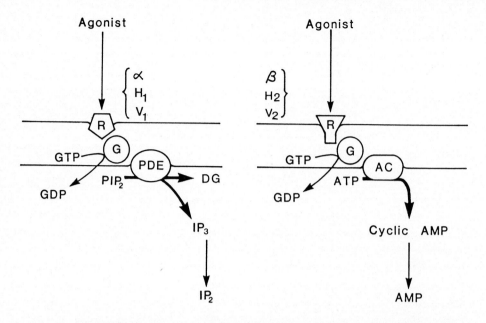

Fig. 1. Comparison of signal transduction through the inositol lipid and cyclic AMP pathways. In the former, a highly phosphorylated lipid, phosphatidylinositol 4,5-bisphosphate (PIP_2) is the substrate used to generate the second messengers diacylglycerol (DG) and inositol trisphosphate (IP_3). In contrast, ATP is used to form cyclic AMP. In both cases a GTP-binding protein (G) functions to couple surface receptors (R) to the underlying amplification units of PIP_2 phosphodiesterase (PDE) and adenylate cyclase (AC).

but as we learnt more about control mechanisms it gradually became apparent that the main action of this second messenger was to modulate calcium, which appears to be the primary regulator of cell function. Consequently, there is now much interest in finding out how external signals bring about the increase in intracellular calcium responsible for triggering the activity of many different cellular processes. The problem is to understand how such external signals induce either entry of external calcium or the release of calcium from an internal reservoir.

In excitable cells such as nerve and muscle, changes in calcium permeability usually arise by membrane depolarization, which will open voltage-dependent calcium channels in the plasma membrane and will trigger the release of calcium from internal stores. For most cells, however, such calcium fluxes are brought about by the arrival of a chemical signal such as a hormone or a neurotransmitter, thus necessitating the requirement of a transduction mechanism. These external signals use one of the phospholipids in the membrane as a precursor to generate not one, but at least two, second messengers (Fig. 1). During transduction the lipid is cleaved into two parts: the hydrophobic diacylglycerol (DG) portion remains within the membrane while the water-soluble inositol phosphate head group is released into the cytoplasm.

INOSITOL TRISPHOSPHATE AND DIACYLGLYCEROL AS SECOND MESSENGERS

The first indication that inositol lipids might play a role in hormone action occurred in 1953 when Hokin & Hokin discovered that acetylcholine stimulated the incorporation of radioactive phosphorus into phosphatidylinositol (PI) in pancreas. While this observation could be repeated in many different cell types, its function remained a mystery until Michell (1975) suggested that it might play a role in calcium mobilization. The relationship between inositol lipids and calcium signalling is still not fully resolved but an important breakthrough occurred with the discovery that inositol trisphosphate (IP_3) was a second messenger responsible for mobilizing calcium from intracellular stores (Berridge, 1983, 1984; Streb, Irvine, Berridge & Schulz, 1983; Berridge & Irvine, 1984). A unique aspect of PI is that it can be further phosphorylated to give the polyphosphoinositides. Addition of a phosphate at the 4-position gives phosphatidylinositol 4-phosphate (PIP), which, in turn, can be phosphorylated on the 5-position to give phosphatidylinositol 4,5-bisphosphate (PIP_2) (Fig. 2). Of these three inositol lipids, which are located within the inner leaflet of the plasma membrane, it is the PIP_2 that is the precursor used by the receptor to generate second messengers (Figs 1, 2). A component of the hydrophobic barrier is used as a precursor to produce a bifurcating signal system that is highly

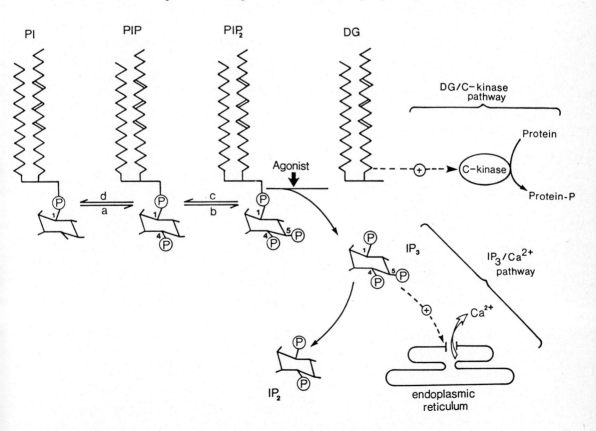

Fig. 2. Basic biochemical features of the inositol-lipid signal pathway.

versatile and flexible. Before speculating on how this control system operates in some specific cell types, it is necessary to provide a little more detail of the two signal pathways.

The IP_3 released into the cytoplasm functions as a second messenger to mobilize calcium from intracellular reservoirs. One wonders why such an elaborate mechanism was devised when the cell is surrounded by an infinite reservoir of calcium, which it could use simply by allowing it to flood in from the outside. Indeed such a mechanism is used by some cells but they tend to be small cells where the effector system being controlled by calcium is close to the cell surface, e.g. synaptic endings, smooth muscle and mast cells. For larger cells, however, there appears to be a problem in using external calcium, probably because this ion has a very slow diffusion rate in cytoplasm. The diffusion of calcium is restricted by internal organelles such as the endoplasmic reticulum and mitochondria, which are constantly sequestering this ion to ensure that cytoplasmic levels remain low. IP_3 acts on one of these stores, the endoplasmic reticulum, to release calcium within local regions of the cell. The picture that emerges, therefore, is that cells carry within themselves local pools of calcium, the IP_3 limb of the pathway is responsible for releasing this calcium and this represents a primary signal pathway to control many different cellular processes.

The function of diacylglycerol (DG), the other member of the bifurcating signal pathway, is still somewhat obscure. Its reputation as a putative second messenger rests on the observation that it can activate a protein kinase (now known as C-kinase) capable of phosphorylating specific proteins (Nishizuka, 1984). Considerable excitement was generated by the dicovery that phorbol esters, which are potent tumour-promoting agents, could mimic the action of the natural messenger DG in activating C-kinase (Castagna *et al.* 1982). Indeed, the latter turns out to be the cellular receptor for the phorbol esters (Niedel, Kuhn & Vandenbark, 1983; Leach, James & Blumberg, 1983). Another way of activating C-kinase is to apply oleoyl-acetyl-diacylglycerol (OAG) (Nishizuka, 1984). Addition of either OAG or the phorbol esters results in the phosphorylation of a similar set of proteins to those phosphorylated by natural agonists (Garrison, Johnsen & Campanile, 1984). In addition, agonists will phosphorylate another set of proteins by activating the IP_3/Ca pathway. The problem we face, therefore, is to unravel how these two sets of proteins contribute to the final response.

Everything we know about the action of DG suggests that it functions more as a modulator rather than as a direct activator of specific cellular processes. This modulatory action of C-kinase is not only restricted to the inositol lipid mechanism but it extends to other signal pathways such as the EGF receptor and the cyclic AMP system (Fig. 3). The EGF receptor is a dumb-bell-shaped molecule; an extracellular domain that binds EGF is linked through a membrane-spanning region to a cytoplasmic domain that has tyrosine kinase activity. At the interface between the membrane-spanning and cytoplasmic domains there is a threonine residue at position 654 that is specifically phosphorylated by C-kinase. As a consequence of this phosphorylation the receptor is converted from a high to a low affinity state.

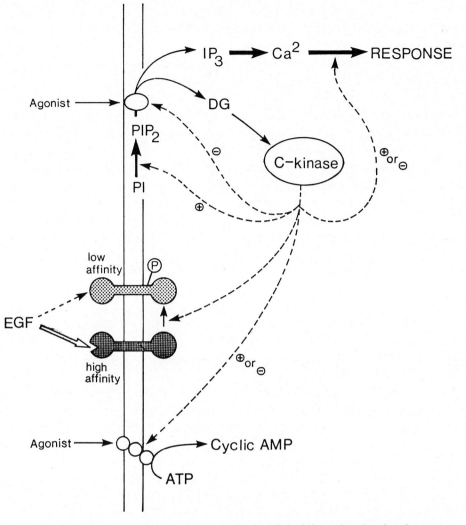

Fig. 3. A hypothesis to account for the contribution of the bifurcating signal pathway to cell regulation. The IP_3/Ca^{2+} pathway is considered to exert primary control over cellular responses, whereas the DG/C-kinase pathway functions mainly as a signal modulator. Not only does DG/C-kinase modulate the operation of the IP_3/Ca^{2+} pathway but it can adjust the flow of information through other signal pathways.

Activation of receptors that stimulate the hydrolysis of PIP_2 and so activate the DG/C-kinase pathway results in a marked reduction in the affinity of the EGF receptor (Brown *et al.* 1984). The DG/C-kinase pathway can also alter the generation of cyclic AMP both positively and negatively. A good example of positive modulation has been described in the pineal gland where stimulation of cyclic AMP formation through β-receptors is enormously enhanced by phorbol esters (Sugden *et al.* 1985).

In addition to modulating these other receptor mechanisms, the DG/C-kinase pathway has effects on its own receptor mechanism including the supply of PIP_2, the breakdown of PIP_2 and the operation of the IP_3/Ca pathway. Effects of the DG/C-kinase pathway on the supply of substrate have been studied in some detail in brain where the activity of PIP kinase responsible for converting PIP to PIP_2 appears to be regulated by the state of phosphorylation of a specific B50 protein (Jolles *et al.* 1980; Aloyo, Zwiers & Gispen, 1983). Dephosphorylated B50 is active but is converted to the inactive state by being phosphorylated by C-kinase (Fig. 3). A particularly intriguing possibility is that ACTH, which is known to have a variety of behavioural effects, may act by inhibiting C-kinase and will thus enhance the supply of the PIP_2 required by calcium-mobilizing receptors (Jolles *et al.* 1981; Zwiers *et al.* 1982). A completely opposite effect of C-kinase on PIP_2 formation has been described in thymocytes and blood platelets where phorbol esters stimulate the incorporation of label into both PIP and PIP_2 (De Chaffoy de Courcelles, Roevens & van Belle, 1984; Taylor *et al.* 1984; Halenda & Feinstein, 1985). In many other cells, however, pretreatment with phorbol esters causes a profound inhibition of agonist-dependent PIP_2 breakdown and calcium signalling (Sagi-Eisenberg, Lieman & Pecht, 1985; Orellana, Solski & Brown, 1985; Watson & Lapetina, 1985; MacIntyre, McNicol & Drummond, 1985).

It is evident that this bifurcating signal pathway is under stringent negative feedback control through the DG/C-kinase limb, which severely limits the activity of this receptor mechanism. Another example of such negative feedback regulation has been uncovered in pituitary cells where the DG/C-kinase pathway seems to reduce the calcium signal by promoting the pump mechanisms that remove this ion from the cytosol (Drummond, 1985). A characteristic feature of the output signals (IP_3, Ca^{2+} and DG) from these receptors is that they invariably are phasic in nature, i.e. they increase rapidly upon stimulation but then after a short period return close to the resting level where they remain for the rest of the stimulation period. During the initial stimulation period, therefore, there is an enormous overproduction of second messenger but this may be the price the cell must pay in order to have a messenger system that responds rapidly. The rate of second messenger production is initially very fast leading to an overshoot, which is then reduced when the DG/C-kinase negative feedback loop begins to dampen down the breakdown of PIP_2 or begins to enhance the extrusion of calcium.

The final and perhaps the most important modulatory effect of the DG/C-kinase pathway is to alter the responsiveness of a variety of processes controlled through the IP_3/Ca^{2+} pathway. This phenomenon may well explain the synergistic relationship that exists between the two limbs of the bifurcating signal pathway as originally described in blood platelets (Nishizuka, 1984). This synergism was demonstrated by devising ways of activating each pathway independently of the other. Conventional calcium ionophores were employed to raise intracellular calcium and so bypass the action of IP_3, while phorbol esters were used to mimic the action of DG in stimulating C-kinase. Threshold doses of these two agents, which have no effect when given separately, induce a maximal release of serotonin from blood platelets when applied in combination (Nishizuka, 1984). A clue to the physiological basis of this synergism emerged from studies using the fluorescent dye Quin 2 to measure the level of intracellular calcium (Rink, Sanchez, & Hallam, 1983). A threshold dose of ionomycin caused a small increase in internal calcium without triggering exocytosis but the subsequent addition of a phorbol ester induced near maximal secretion without any further change in intracellular calcium. Very similar observations were reported for the release of dopamine from cultured neurosecretory cells (Pozzan *et al.* 1984). These remarkable observations seemed to indicate that the DG/C-kinase pathway was capable of stimulating secretory processes independently of any change in intracellular calcium. A possibility exists, therefore, that this limb of the bifurcating pathway might be capable of switching on complex physiological processes independently of the IP_3/Ca^{2+} pathway. Alternatively, the DG/C-kinase pathway may function indirectly by modulating the sensitivity of physiological processes to the action of calcium. Evidence for such a mechanism has come from measuring calcium activation curves in permeabilized adrenal cells (Knight & Baker, 1983) and blood platelets (Knight & Scrutton, 1984). Once the cells are permeabilized they become accessible to external agents and as the concentration of calcium is elevated above 10^{-7}M they begin to release their granules, so giving a characteristic dose-response curve to calcium. If such permeabilized cells are pretreated with a phorbol ester there is a large leftward shift in the dose-response curve indicating that the secretory process has become much more sensitive to calcium. Such modulation of calcium sensitivity by the DG C-kinase pathway may not be restricted to the control of exocytosis but may extend to other calcium-dependent processes and to other aspects of calcium homeostasis.

A GENERAL HYPOTHESIS OF CELLULAR CONTROL THROUGH INTERACTIONS BETWEEN IP_3/Ca^{2+} AND DG/C-KINASE-SENSITIVE PATHWAYS

On the basis of the evidence presented above it is possible to construct a simple hypothesis to account for the way in which the bifurcating inositol-lipid signal pathway functions to regulate a whole variety of cellular processes. The two signal pathways appear to have quite separate functions, with the IP_3/Ca^{2+} pathway having a primary role in triggering the final response whereas the DG/C-kinase limb seems to be primarily concerned with modulating not only this primary calcium pathway but possibly also other signal pathways (e.g. the cyclic AMP system) (Fig. 3). Some of these modulatory effects of the DG/C-kinase pathway were described earlier and others will become apparent as we consider how this inositol lipid receptor mechanism functions in various specific cell types. Perhaps the most remarkable aspect of this receptor mechanism is that it appears to play a role in almost every aspect of cell function during the entire life history of a cell, ranging from early steps in development (maturation, fertilization and cell growth) to a whole host of cell functions in fully differentiated adult cells (contraction, secretion and metabolism). Some specific examples will illustrate just how ubiquitous this receptor mechanism is in cell regulation.

OOCYTE MATURATION AND FERTILIZATION

Recent experiments on oocytes from both invertebrates and vertebrates offer a fascinating glimpse into the possible role of the inositol lipid pathway in the control of early development. Much of the work has been done on *Xenopus* oocytes where the animal and vegetal poles are clearly delineated by the dark pigment granules surrounding the former. In the immature oocyte, the animal pole also differs from the vegetal pole in several physiological parameters. Using a vibrating electrode, Robinson (1979) demonstrated an electrical current that flowed in at the animal pole and out at the vegetal pole. The precise function of this current, which is carried by chloride and regulated through calcium, is unknown but it may segregate specific molecules along the animal–vegetal axis, so helping to organize early development. Another mystery concerns the origin of this current but it might be linked to the existence of acetylcholine receptors, which are particularly concentrated around the animal pole (Kusano, Miledi & Stinnakre, 1982). Addition of acetylcholine leads to membrane depolarization due to the opening of chloride channels. Similar channels are opened when oocytes are injected with calcium, suggesting the existence of calcium-dependent chloride channels (Cross, 1981; Miledi & Parker, 1984). Of particular interest was the finding that calcium was more effective when injected into the animal rather than the vegetal pole, thus pointing to another physiological difference between the two regions.

Regulation of the chloride channel by acetylcholine is mediated through IP$_3$ (Oron, Dascal, Nadler & Lupu, 1985). Addition of acetylcholine results in the formation of IP$_3$ while the injection of IP$_3$ can exactly mimic the membrane currents induced by acetylcholine. In the absence of acetylcholine, some oocytes show spontaneous fluctuations, which are sometimes cyclic in nature, and it was proposed that they may represent 'transient accumulation of the channel gating substance' (Kusano *et al.* 1982). It is tempting to suggest that this 'channel gating substance' might be IP$_3$.

As cells mature in response to progesterone they loose their sensitivity to acetyl-choline but they retain all the elements of the inositol-lipid signal pathway, which is now re-employed to carry out some of the early events of fertilization. The first indication that IP$_3$ may play a role in fertilization was obtained in sea-urchin oocytes where injection of this second messenger stimulated the release of cortical granules to form a typical fertilization membrane (Whitaker & Irvine, 1984). Exactly the same phenomenon occurs in *Xenopus* oocytes where, in addition to stimulating the formation of the fertilization membrane, IP$_3$ injection also induces a typical activation potential (Busa & Nuccitelli, 1985; Busa *et al.* 1985). When an egg is fertilized, the membrane potential suddenly depolarizes from about $-40\,\text{mV}$ to approximately $0\,\text{mV}$ where it remains for up to 20 min (Cross, 1981). This activation potential has all the hallmarks of the acetylcholine-induced depolarization that exists in the immature oocyte: the only site of sperm entry is the animal pole; the activation potential can be induced by injecting calcium and again one finds that the animal pole is much more sensitive than the vegetal pole; the change in potential is the result of opening calcium-dependent chloride channels. Apart from the acetylcholine receptor, which disappears during maturation, the remaining signalling system that existed in the immature oocyte appears to be carried through maturation and is then employed to mediate the early events of fertilization.* The implication is that the fusion of an egg with a sperm is analogous to a hormone interacting with a receptor in that it triggers a breakdown of PIP_2. There already is evidence for a change in PIP_2 metabolism following fertilization in sea urchin eggs (Turner, Sheetz & Jaffe, 1984), to give the IP_3 that initiates these early membrane events.

The IP_3-induced increase in intracellular calcium levels at fertilization may also be important in egg *activation*, i.e. in initiating the sequence of events that culminate in DNA synthesis. Another important ionic requirement for activation is alkalinization of the cytoplasm and it has been known for a long time that following fertilization eggs begin to extrude protons, sometimes referred to as fertilization acid. Proton extrusion is carried out by a Na^+/H^+ exchanger, which appears to be regulated through the DG/C-kinase limb of the signal pathway (Berridge, 1984; Berridge & Irvine, 1984). The two major events associated with the initiation of DNA synthesis at fertilization are regulated separately by the two limbs of the bifurcating signal pathway: IP_3 gives the calcium signal, whereas the DG/C-kinase pathway increases intracellular pH.

CONTROL OF CELL GROWTH

The inositol lipid transduction mechanism, which has served so well during maturation and fertilization, may continue to be employed during subsequent cell growth. Just how cell growth is controlled during embryogenesis is still something of a mystery and most attention has been focused on the way in which growth factors stimulate DNA synthesis in postembryonic cells using lymphocytes or cultured cells as model systems. Swiss 3T3 cells respond to certain growth factors (PDGF, bombesin, vasopressin, $PGF_{2\alpha}$) by hydrolysing inositol lipids to give IP_3 and DG. The latter then induce the same ionic changes just described for fertilization, i.e. IP_3 mobilizes calcium while DG activates the Na^+/H^+ exchanger to increase intracellular pH. The action of these growth factors thus depends upon the inositol lipid mechanism to induce exactly the same ionic events as those that occur at fertilization.

Other growth factors such as EGF and insulin apparently do not operate through the inositol lipid pathway, implying that there are additional messenger pathways responsible for initiating DNA synthesis. A similar conclusion has been reached from studies on lymphocytes in which a combination of a calcium ionophore and phorbol ester was incapable of stimulating DNA synthesis unless the cells were also stimulated either with interleukin II (Truneh, Albert, Goldstein & Schmitt-

---

*This reutilization of a pre-existing transduction system can also be demonstrated experimentally in *Xenopus* by injecting them with brain mRNA, which results in the insertion of new receptors into the cell surface. When one of the newcomers is a 5-hydroxytryptamine (5-HT) receptor, the addition of 5-HT induces a physiological response identical to that normally given by acetylcholine (Gundersen, Miledi & Parker, 1984). It appears as if the newly inserted 5-HT receptor can hijack the pre-existing transduction mechanism.

Verlulst, 1985) or with phytohaemagglutinin (Kaibuchi, Takai & Nishizuka, 1985). Lymphocytes seem to require some additional information derived from these receptors apart from the changes in intracellular calcium and pH. What is lacking is a clear understanding of which of the possible second messenger candidates is ulti- mately responsible for initiating DNA synthesis. An important step forward oc- curred when it was discovered that certain growth factors and phorbol esters could stimulate, within minutes, the appearance of mRNA of both the *myc* and *fos* genes (Kelly, Cochran, Stiles & Leder, 1983; Greenberg & Ziff, 1984). For the first time, there was a specific link between transduction events at the cell membrane and transcriptional events within the nucleus. To what extent these early transcriptional events involving *myc* and *fos* are related to the onset of DNA synthesis many hours later remains to be established. Nevertheless, it is becoming increasingly apparent that the inositol-lipid receptor mechanism plays an important role in controlling certain aspects of growth especially some of the early transcriptional events.

CONTROL OF DIFFERENTIATION

At a certain stage during development cells opt out of the cycle of growth and begin to differentiate into specialized cell types. This decision to stop growing and to begin to perform some specific function is a unique event in the life history of a cell in that the process is often irreversible. In some cases, however, cells retain the option of returning to the cell cycle as part of adaptive responses, as occurs in the immune response or during the hyperplasia seen in various organs such as salivary glands, brown fat cells and liver. Little is known about how cells decide when to stop growing and to begin to express their programme of differentiation. Phorbol esters are potent pharmacological agents that can induce differentiation in many cells, which is most puzzling because these agents are traditionally associated with the stimulation of growth since they are tumour-promoting agents. This paradox is unresolved, but a possible solution might be found in the nature of the feedback relationships described earlier, particularly the negative feedback control excercised on PIP_2 breakdown through the DG/C-kinase pathway. If an increase in intra- cellular calcium is an important signal for growth then it might be argued that low calcium levels may prevent growth and permit cells to differentiate. On the basis of this calcium-switching hypothesis, phorbol esters might work by inhibiting the breakdown of PIP_2, so removing one of the signal pathways for supplying calcium. Suppressing the intracellular level of calcium during the critical period early in G_1 may be an important part of the switch from growth to differentiation.

CONTROL OF CELLULAR PROCESSES IN DIFFERENTIATED CELLS

As part of the differentiation programme cells develop signalling mechanisms that enable them to respond to a whole host of external signals. The inositol lipid mechanism, which plays such an important role in growth, is re-employed to regulate an enormous variety of cellular processes. A few specific examples will serve to illustrate the versatility of this uniquely flexible signalling system.

Secretory cells

The role of IP_3 as a second messenger for mobilizing calcium was first uncovered in studies on secretory tissues such as the insect salivary gland (Berridge, 1983; Berridge, Downes & Hanley, 1982) and mammalian pancreas (Streb, Irvine, Berridge & Schulz, 1983). Such secretory cells were known to use internal calcium for signalling especially during early periods of stimulation so it was necessary to explain how secretagogues acting on the cell surface could trigger a release of calcium from intracellular reservoirs. There is now overwhelming support for the idea that these secretagogues stimulate a hydrolysis of PIP_2 to release IP_3 which then diffuses into the cytoplasm to release calcium. This agonist-induced IP_3/Ca^{2+} pathway seems to control secretion in many other cell types including macrophages (Hirata *et al.* 1984), blood platelets (O'Rourke, Halenda, Zavoico & Feinstein, 1985), neutrophils (Prentki, Wollheim & Lew, 1984), insulinoma cells (Biden *et al.* 1984), pituitary (Gershengorn, Geras, Purrello & Rebecchi, 1984) and adrenal glomerulosa (Kojima, Kojima, Kreutter & Rasmussen, 1984). For many of these secretory systems, the action of the IP_3/Ca^{2+} pathway is augmented by the DG/C-kinase pathway as described earlier.

Contractile cells

The increase in calcium responsible for triggering contraction may also be controlled through inositol lipids. An obvious example is pharmaco-mechanical coupling in smooth muscle. All the neurotransmitters that can induce cells to contract do so by triggering the breakdown of PIP_2, and the IP_3 produced then releases the calcium for contraction. A more interesting possibility is that IP_3 may function in skeletal muscle (Vergara & Tsien, 1985; Volpe, Salviati, Di Virgilio & Pozzan, 1985). Excitation–contraction (E–C) coupling is one of the major unsolved physiological problems, which concerns the way in which a depolarization of the T-tubule membrane triggers the release of calcium from the sarcoplasmic reticulum. Somehow information is transferred across the 20 nm gap that separates the two membrane systems. An exactly analogous problem exists at synapses where information has to traverse a similar gap separating the pre- and post-synaptic membranes and we now know that information is relayed by neurotransmitters diffusing across the synaptic cleft. A similar chemical transmission mechanism may be responsible for E–C coupling in skeletal muscle, where IP_3 may function as the transmitter to relay information from the T-tubule to the sarcoplasmic reticulum. In this case, the transmitter is not stored in vesicles, as it is in the synapse, but exists as an inert precursor (PIP_2) within the sarcolemma. During the brief instant in which the T-tubule membrane is depolarized, a small fraction of the precursor may be cleaved to IP_3, which then diffuses across the narrow gap to excite the sarcoplasmic reticulum.

Control of metabolism

Control of glycogen metabolism by the liver provides an excellent example of cellular control through the inositol-lipid receptor pathway (Williamson, Cooper, Joseph & Thomas, 1985). Hormones such as vasopressin and α_1-agonists stimulate a rapid hydrolysis of PIP_2 to give both IP_3 and DG. The former acts on the sarcoplasmic reticulum to release calcium, which then stimulates phosphorylase kinase to begin the enzyme cascade that culminates in the hydrolysis of glycogen. This control of glycogen metabolism through IP_3/Ca^{2+} seems to occur independently of the DG/C-kinase pathway and the latter also has no effect on calcium fluxes across the plasma membrane (Williamson *et al.* 1985). However, the DG/C-kinase pathway does exert some effects in liver cells, but these are mostly modulatory in nature and so conform to the hypothesis outlined earlier. Of particular interest is the finding that phorbol esters markedly inhibit the effects of α_1-agonists while having little or no effect on vasopressin receptors. The DG/C-kinase pathway thus exerts a specific down-regulation of α_1-receptors and is an example of a negative feedback effect on the calcium signalling pathway.

The nervous system

One of the challenging problems for the future is to understand the role of inositol-lipid receptor mechanisms in neural function. With the introduction of the lithium amplification technique (Berridge *et al.* 1982) it has been possible to identify a whole host of neurotransmitters (acetylcholine, norepinephrine, substance P, neurotensin, 5-hydroxytryptamine, histamine, vasopressin, bradykinin) that use this transduction mechanism. Of all the tissues in the body, the brain is the richest source of C-kinase, thus supporting the view that this receptor mechanism plays a central role in neural processing. Although we are still a long way from understanding how these receptors operate in the nervous system, there are sufficient clues to see how they might operate in both pre- and post-synaptic events.

Release of transmitter from synaptic endings is usually triggered by the arrival of an action potential, which causes a temporary opening of voltage-dependent calcium gates, which allow calcium to flow into the cell to stimulate exocytosis (Fig. 4). It seems unlikely that pre-synaptic calcium-mobilizing receptors will be involved in providing an independent signal pathway for triggering the release of neurotransmitter. However, there are two ways this pathway could play an important role in modulating transmitter release brought about by the voltage-dependent calcium channels. Firstly, the formation of IP_3 could mobilize intracellular calcium and so contribute to facilitation by adjusting the resting level of calcium. Nerring & McBurney (1984) have described a labile intracellular store of calcium in mammalian neurones that can be released by caffeine and could represent a possible site of action for IP_3. The most likely candidate for this store are the subsurface cisternae of endoplasmic reticulum that lie close to the neuronal plasma membrane (Henkart, Landris & Reese, 1976). Stimulation of a neurosecretory cell line (PC12) with carbachol results in rapid IP_3 formation and elevation of intracellular calcium

(Vicentini *et al.* 1985). The parallel DG/C-kinase pathway could contribute to such facilitation by enhancing the sensitivity of exocytosis as has been described in neurosecretory cells (Pozzan *et al.* 1984). In a neuroblastoma × glioma hybrid cell line that can form synapses with striated muscle cells, there is evidence that bradykinin may induce facilitation (as measured by an increase in mepp, miniature end-plate potentials) by stimulating the hydrolsysis of PIP_2 (Yano, Higashida, Inoue & Nozawa, 1984). This study on cultured cells supports the idea that calcium-mobilizing receptors may function presynaptically to modulate transmitter release.

By carrying out lesions in the hippocampal regions of the brain it has been concluded that cholinergic-induced hydrolysis of inositol lipids could occur at post-synaptic sites (Agranoff, 1983). It remains to be seen what the bifurcating signal pathway does at such sites and the function is likely to vary depending on the neurone in question. In the case of hippocampal pyrimidal neurones, which have calcium-activated potassium channels, any increase in calcium will stimulate an outflow of potassium leading to membrane hyperpolarization. As the membrane hyperpolarizes it ceases to initiate action potentials, a phenomenon known as accommodation. Activation of muscarinic receptors, which stimulate the hydrolysis of PIP_2, can alleviate such accommodation through a mechanism that seems to be controlled

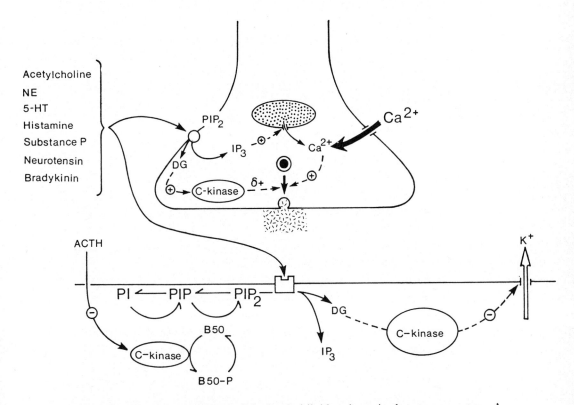

Fig. 4. Some possible functions of the inositol lipid pathway in the nervous system. A large number of transmitters are now known to stimulate the hydrolysis of PIP_2 to release IP_3 and DG at both pre- and post-synaptic sites.

through the DG/C-kinase pathway (Baraban, Snyder & Alger, 1985). When such hippocampal neurones are treated with a phorbol ester there is a marked reduction in the flow of potassium through the calcium-activated channels, thus providing another example of how the DG/C-kinase pathway acts to modulate the effects of calcium. Another example of channel modification through the DG/C-kinase pathway occurs in *Aplysia* bag cells where calcium action potentials are enhanced following stimulation with phorbol esters (De Riemer *et al.* 1985).

On an even more speculative note one can envisage that the inositol-lipid signal pathway might play a role in neuronal plasticity that covers numerous adaptive changes in neurones including growth and the long-term storage of information underlying memory. An interesting model for the latter is long-term potentiation (LTP) in the hippocampus, which is associated with an increase in the phosphorylation of specific proteins (Akers & Routtenberg, 1985). One of these proteins (protein F_1) seems to be identical to growth-associated protein (GAP43), which is particularly concentrated in growth cones, thus raising the possibility that the same protein may function in both growth and the stabilization of synaptic pathways. A link with inositol lipids comes with the realization that F_1 and GAP43 may also be identical to protein B50, which has been identified in brain (Jolles *et al.* 1980, 1981). As discussed earlier, B50 appears to function as a regulator of PIP kinase. Although the link with inositol lipids is somewhat tenuous, it is appealing to imagine that some of the long-term changes that occur in the nervous system might be accomplished through alterations in the performance of the transduction mechanism that generates IP_3 and DG.

CONCLUSION

From one instant to another the behaviour of all cells is governed by signalling systems that translate external information into a limited repertoire of internal second messengers. A ubiquitous and perhaps the major signalling system in cells is based on the cleavage of an inositol lipid to give two key second messengers. Inositol trisphosphate (IP_3) is released to the cytosol where it interacts with the endoplasmic reticulum to mobilize calcium, whereas diacylglycerol remains within the plasma membrane where it activates protein kinase C to phosphorylate various proteins. It is argued that the IP_3/Ca^{2+} limb of this signal pathway is directly responsible for activating a whole variety of cellular processes whereas the DG/C-kinase limb functions primarily as a modulatory pathway. This universal signalling system operates during all stages of the life history of a cell. It is present in immature oocytes and persists during maturation to be used during fertilization. There is reason to believe that it plays a role in regulating cell growth and it finally comes into its own in controlling the activity of cells once they have differentiated. The role of this receptor mechanism in certain cells such as the liver and pancreas is well-established and there now are exciting suggestions that this transduction mechanism might explain other phenomena such as excitation–contraction coupling in skeletal muscle and some of the plastic changes that underlie higher brain function.

REFERENCES

AGRANOFF, B. W. (1983). Biochemical mechanisms in the phosphatidylinositol effect. *Life Sci.* **32**, 2047–2054.

AKERS, R. F. & ROUTTENBERG, A. (1985). Protein kinase C phosphorylates a 47 M_r protein (F_1) directly related to synaptic plasticity. *Brain Res.* **334**, 147–151.

ALOYO, V. J., ZWIERS, H. & GISPEN, W. H. (1983). Phosphorylation of B-50 protein by calcium-activated, phospholipid-dependent protein kinase and B-50 protein kinase. *J. Neurochem.* **41**, 649–653.

BARABAN, J. M., SNYDER, S. H. & ALGER, B. E. (1985). Protein kinase C regulates ionic conductance in hippocampal pyramidal neurones: Electrophysiological effects of phorbol esters. *Proc. natn. Acad. Sci. U.S.A.* **82**, 2538–2542.

BERRIDGE, M. J. (1983). Rapid accumulation of inositol trisphosphate reveals that agonists hydrolyse polyphosphoinositides instead of phosphatidylinositol. *Biochem. J.* **212**, 849–858.

BERRIDGE, M. J., DOWNES, C. P. & HANLEY, M. R. (1982). Lithium amplifies agonist-dependent phosphatidylinositol responses in brain and salivary glands. *Biochem. J.* **206**, 587–595.

BERRIDGE, M. J. & IRVINE, R. F. (1984). Inositol trisphosphate, a novel second messenger in cellular signal transduction. *Nature, Lond.* **312**, 315–321.

BIDEN, T. J., PRENTKI, M., IRVINE, R. F., BERRIDGE, M. J. & WOLLHEIM, C. B. (1984). Inositol 1,4,5-trisphosphate mobilizes intracellular Ca^{2+} from permeabilized insulin-secreting cells. *Biochem. J.* **223**, 467–473.

BROWN, K. D., BLAY, J., IRVINE, R. F., HESLOP, J. P. & BERRIDGE, M. J. (1984). Reduction of epidermal growth factor receptor affinity by heterologous ligands; evidence for a mechanism involving the breakdown of phosphoinositides and the activation of protein kinase C. *Biochem. biophys. Res. Commun.* **123**, 377–384.

BUSA, W. B., FERGUSON, J. E., JOSEPH, S. K., WILLIAMSON, J. R. & NUCCITELLI, R. (1985). Activation of frog (*Xenopus laevis*) eggs by inositol trisphosphate. I. Characterization of Ca^{2+} release from intracellular stores. *J. Cell Biol.* **101**, 677–682.

BUSA, W. B. & NUCCITELLI, R. (1985). An elevated free cytosolic Ca^{2+} wave follows fertilization in eggs of the frog, *Xenopus laevis. J. Cell Biol.* **100**, 1325–1329.

CASTAGNA, M., TAKAI, Y., KAIBUCHI, K., SANO, K., KIKKAWA, U. & NISHIZUKA, Y. (1982). Direct activation of calcium-activated, phospholipid-dependent protein kinase by tumour-promoting phorbol esters. *J. biol. Chem.* **257**, 7847–7851.

CROSS, N. L. (1981). Initiation of the activation potential by an increase in intracellular calcium in eggs of the frog *Rana pipiens. Devl Biol.* **85**, 380–384.

DE CHAFFOY DE COURCELLES, D., ROEVENS, P. & VAN BELLE, H. (1984). 12-0-Tetradeca-noylphorbol 13-acetate stimulates inositol lipid phosphorylation in intact human platelets. *FEBS Lett.* **173**, 389–393.

DE RIEMER, S. A., STRUNG, J. A., ALBERT, K. A., GREENGARD, P. & KACZMAREK, L. K. (1985). Enhancement of calcium current in *Aplysia* neurones by phorbol ester and protein kinase C. *Nature, Lond.* **313**, 313–316.

DRUMMOND, A. H. (1985). Bidirectional control of cytosolic free calcium by thyrotropin-releasing hormone in pituitary cells. *Nature, Lond.* **315**, 752–755.

GARRISON, J. C., JOHNSEN, D. E. & CAMPANILE, C. P. (1984). Evidence for the role of phosphorylase kinase, protein kinase C, and other Ca^{2+} sensitive protein kinase in the response of hepatocytes to angiotensin II and vasopressin. *J. biol. Chem.* **259**, 3283–3292.

GERSHENGORN, M. C., GERAS, E., PURRELLO, V. S. & REBECCHI, M. J. (1984). Inositol trisphosphate mediates thyrotropin-releasing hormone mobilization of nonmitochondrial calcium in rat mammatropic pituitary cells. *J. biol. Chem.* **259**, 10 675–10 681.

GREENBERG, M. E. & ZIFF, E. B. (1984). Stimulation of 3T3 cells induces transcription of the c-*fos* proto-oncogene. *Nature, Lond.* **311**, 433–438.

GUNDERSON, C. B., MILEDI, R. & PARKER, I. (1984). Messenger RNA from human brain induces drug- and voltage-operated channels in *Xenopus* oocytes. *Nature, Lond.* **308**, 421–424.

HALENDA, S. P. & FEINSTEIN, M. B. (1984). Phorbol myristate acetate stimulates formation of phosphatidylinositol 4-phosphate and phosphatidylinositol 4,5-bisphosphate in human platelets. *Biochem. biophys. Res. Commun.* **124**, 507–513.

HENKART, M., LANDIS, D. M. D. & REESE, T. S. (1976). Similarity of junctions between plasma membranes and endoplasmic reticulum in muscle and neurons. *J. Cell Biol.* **70**, 338–347.

HIRATA, M., SUEMATSU, E., HASHIMOTO, T., HAMACHI, T. & KOGA, T. (1984). Release of Ca^{2+} from a non-mitochondrial store site in peritoneal macrophages treated with saponin by inositol 1,4,5-trisphosphate. *Biochem. J.* **223**, 229–236.

HOKIN, M. R. & HOKIN, L. E. (1953). Enzyme secretion and the incorporation of ^{32}P into phospholipids of pancreas slices. *J. biol. Chem.* **203**, 967–977.

JOLLES, J., ZWIERS, H., DEKKER, A., WIRTZ, K. W. A. & GISPEN, W. H. (1981). Corticotropin-(1-24)-tetracosapeptide affects protein phosphorylation and polyphosphoinositide metabolism in rat brain. *Biochem. J.* **194**, 283–291.

JOLLES, J., ZWIERS, H., VAN DONGEN, C. J., SCHOTMAN, P., WIRTZ, K. W. A. & GISPEN, W. H. (1980). Modulation of brain polyphosphoinositide metabolism by ACTH-sensitive protein phosphorylation. *Nature, Lond.* **286**, 632–625.

KAIBUCHI, K., TAKAI, Y. & NISHIZUKA, Y. (1985). Protein kinase C and calcium ion in mitogenic response of macrophage-depleted human peripheral lymphocytes. *J. biol Chem.* **260**, 1366–1369.

KELLY, K., COCHRAN, G. H., STILES, C. D. & LEDER, P. (1983). Cell-specific regulation of the c-*myc* gene by lymphocyte mitogens and platelet-derived growth factor. *Cell* **35**, 603–610.

KNIGHT, D. E. & BAKER, P. F. (1983). The phorbol ester TPA increase the affinity of exocytosis for calcium in 'leaky' adrenal medullary cells. *FEBS Lett.* **160**, 98–100.

KNIGHT, D. E. & SCRUTTON, M. C. (1984). Cyclic nucleotides control a system which regulates Ca^{2+} sensitivity of platelet secretion. *Nature, Lond.* **309**, 66–68.

KOJIMA, I., KOJIMA, K., KREUTTER, D. & RASMUSSEN, H. (1984). The temporal integration of the aldosterone secretory response to angiotensin occurs via two intracellular pathways. *J. biol. Chem.* **259**, 14 448–14 457.

KUSANO, K., MILEDI, R. & STINNAKRE, J. (1982). Cholinergic and catecholaminergic receptors in the *Xenopus* oocyte membrane. *J. Physiol.* **328**, 143–170.

LEACH, K. L., JAMES, M. L. & BLUMBERG, P. M. (1983). Characterization of a specific phorbol ester aporeceptor in mouse brain cytosol. *Proc. natn. Acad. Sci. U.S.A.* **80**, 4208–4212.

MACINTYRE, D. E., MCNICOL, A. & DRUMMOND, A. H. (1985). Tumour-promoting phorbol esters inhibit agonist-induced phosphatidate formation and Ca^{2+} flux in human platelets. *FEBS Lett.* **180**, 160–164.

MICHELL, R. H. (1975). Inositol phospholipids and cell surface receptor function. *Biochim. biophys. Acta* **415**, 81–147.

MILEDI, R. & PARKER, I. (1984). Chloride current induced by injection of calcium into *Xenopus laevis* oocytes. *J. Physiol.* **357**, 173–183.

NERRING, J. R. & MCBURNEY, R. N. (1984). Role for microsomal Ca storage in mammalian neurones? *Nature, Lond.* **309**, 158–160.

NIEDEL, J. E., KUHN, L. J. & VANDENBARK, G. R. (1983). Phorbol ester receptor copurifies with protein kinase C. *Proc. natn. Acad, Sci. U.S.A.* **80**, 36–40.

NISHIZUKA, Y. (1984). The role of protein kinase C in cell surface signal transduction and tumor promotion. *Nature, Lond.* **308**, 693–697.

ORELLANA, S. A., SOLSKI, P. A. & BROWN, J. H. (1985). Phorbol ester inhibits phosphoinositide hydrolysis and calcium mobilization in cultured astrocytoma cells. *J. biol. Chem.* **260**, 5236–5239.

ORON, Y., DASCAL, N., NADLER, E. & LUPU, M. (1985). Inositol 1,4,5-trisphosphate mimics muscarinic response in *Xenopus* oocytes. *Nature, Lond.* **313**, 141–143.

O'ROURKE, F. A., HALENDA, S. P., ZAVOICO, G. B. & FEINSTEIN, M. B. (1985). Inositol 1,4,5-trisphosphate release Ca^{2+} from a Ca^{2+}-transporting membrane vesicle fraction derived from human platelets. *J. biol. Chem.* **260**, 956–962.

POZZAN, T., GATTI, G., DOZIO, N., VICENTINI, L. M. & MELDOLESI, J. (1984). Ca^{2+}-dependent and -independent release of neurotransmitters from PC12 cells: a role for protein kinase C activation? *J. Cell Biol.* **99**, 628–638.

PRENTKI, M., WOLLHEIM, C. B. & LEW, P. D. (1984). Ca^{2+} homeostasis in permeabilized human neutrophils characterization of Ca^{2+}-sequestering pools and the action of inositol 1,4,5-trisphosphate. *J. biol. Chem.* **259**, 13 777–13 782.

RINK, T. J., SANCHEZ, A. & HALLAM, T. J. (1983). Diacylglycerol and phorbol ester stimulate secretion without raising cytoplasmic free calcium in human platelets. *Nature, Lond.* **305**, 317–319.

ROBINSON, K. R. (1979). Electrical currents through full-grown and maturing *Xenopus* oocytes. *Proc. natn. Acad. Sci. U.S.A.* **76**, 837–841.

SAGI-EISENBERG, R., LIEMAN, H. & PECHT, I. (1985). Protein kinase C regulation of the receptor-coupled calcium signal in histamine secreting rat basophilic leukaemia cells. *Nature, Lond.* **313**, 59–60.

STREB, H., IRVINE, R. F., BERRIDGE, M. J. & SCHULZ, I. (1983). Release of Ca^{2+} from a nonmitochondrial intracellular store in pancreatic acinar cells by inositol-1,4,5-trisphosphate. *Nature, Lond.* **306**, 67–69.

SUGDEN, D., VANECEK, J., KLEIN, D. C., THOMAS, T. P. & ANDERSON, W. B. (1985). Activation of protein kinase C potentiates isoprenaline-induced cyclic AMP accumulation in rat pinealocytes. *Nature, Lond.* **314**, 359–361.

TAYLOR, M. V., METCALFE, J. C., HESKETH, T. R., SMITH, G. A. & MOORE, J. P. (1984). Mitogens increase phosphorylation of phosphoinositides in thymocytes. *Nature, Lond.* **312**, 462–465.

TRUNEH, A., ALBERT, F., GOLDSTEIN, P. & SCHMITT-VERLULST, A.-M. (1985). Early steps of lymphocyte activation bypassed by synergy between calcium ionophores and phorbol ester. *Nature, Lond.* **313**, 318–320.

TURNER, P. R., SHEETZ, M. P. & JAFFE, L. A. (1984). Fertilization increases the polyphosphoinositide content of sea urchin eggs. *Nature, Lond.* **310**, 414–415.

VERGARA, J. & TSIEN, R. Y. (1985). Inositol trisphosphate induced contactures in frog skeletal muscle fibers. *Biophys. J.* **47**, 351a.

VICENTINI, L. M., AMBROSINI, A., DI VIRGILIO, F., POZZAN, T. & MELDOLESI, J. (1985). Muscarinic receptor-induced phosphoinositide hydrolysis at resting cytosolic Ca^{2+} concentration in PC12 cells. *J. Cell Biol.* **100**, 1330–1333.

VOLPE, P., SALVIATI, G., DI VIRGILIO, F. & POZZAN, T. (1985). Inositol 1,4,5-trisphosphate induces calcium release from sarcoplasmic reticulum of skeletal muscle. *Nature, Lond.* **316**, 347–349.

WATSON, S. P. & LAPETINA, E. G. (1985). 1,2-Diacyglycerol and phorbol ester inhibit agonist-induced formation of inositol phosphates in human platelets: possible implications for negative feedback regulation of inositol phospholipid hydrolysis. *Proc. natn. Acad. Sci. U.S.A.* **82**, 2623–2626.

WHITAKER, M. & IRVINE, R. F. (1984). Inositol 1,4,5-trisphosphate microinjection activates sea urchin eggs. *Nature, Lond.* **312**, 636–639.

WILLIAMSON, J. R., COOPER, R. H., JOSEPH, S. K. & THOMAS, A. P. (1985). Inositol trisphosphate and diacylglycerol as intracellular second messengers in liver. *Am. J. Physiol* **248**, C203–C216.

YANO, K., HIGASHIDA, H., INOUE, R. & NOZAWA, Y. (1984). Bradykinin-induced rapid breakdown of phosphatidylinositol 4,5-bisphosphate in neuroblastoma × glioma hybrid NG 108-15 cells. *J. biol. Chem.* **259**, 10201–10207.

ZWIERS, H., JOLLES, J., ALOYO, V. J., OESTREICHER, A. B. & GISPEN, W. H. (1982). ACTH and synaptic membrane phosphorylation in rat brain. *Prog. Brain Res.* **56**, 405–417.

J. Cell Sci. Suppl. 4, 155–170 (1986)
Printed in Great Britain © The Company of Biologists Limited 1986

CELL CYCLE REGULATION IN YEAST

JACQUELINE HAYLES AND PAUL NURSE

Imperial Cancer Research Fund, PO Box 123, Lincoln's Inn Fields,
London WC2A 3PX, UK

INTRODUCTION

The study of cell cycle control is entering a new and exciting phase. The classical physiological and cytological approaches to investigating the cell cycle have been supplemented with the powerful techniques of molecular biology and genetics. This is particularly the case for the budding yeast *Saccharomyces cerevisiae* and the fission yeast *Schizosaccharomyces pombe*. As yeasts are simple eukaryotes, cell cycle regulation is less likely to be confused with the controls involved in growth and differentiation, which are required in multicellular organisms. Thus they provide excellent systems in which to study the basic mechanism of cell cycle regulation and represent good models for understanding eukaryotic cell cycle control.

The ease of classical genetic analysis in the two yeasts has resulted in the isolation of mutants in many genes that are required for the cell cycle. Study of such mutants has been useful for formulating hypotheses about how the cell cycle might be controlled and for identifying genes that have a role to play in those controls. These abstract studies have then been followed up using the tools of molecular biology to determine the biochemical basis of the controls involved. In this paper we shall concentrate on one particular gene function, that of *cdc28* from *S. cerevisiae* and the analogous gene *cdc2* from *Schiz. pombe*. This gene function has a pivotal position in cell cycle control. We shall review work that establishes that the *cdc2/cdc28* gene function is required in G_1 to commit cells to S phase and the rest of the mitotic cell cycle, and then again in G_2, where it determines the cell cycle timing of mitosis. Isolation and characterization of the *cdc2* and *cdc28* genes have shown that they encode protein kinases that may be regulated by phosphorylation. This has led to the hypothesis that phosphorylation of a specific set of proteins may control the transition from G_1 into S phase and from G_2 into mitosis. The hypothesis has obvious similarities to several models being developed for control of the cell cycle in other eukaryotic cells. However, before considering these matters we want to discuss briefly what we mean by the cell cycle and its control, in order to define more precisely the problems that we think are important to investigate.

THE CELL CYCLE AND ITS CONTROL

The cell cycle is made up of the events and processes that take place between the birth of the cell and its subsequent division into two daughters. In steady-state growth the mass of the cell will also double during the cell cycle. Therefore, taken literally, cell cycle events and processes will include all those that are required for cellular growth as well as those for direct reproduction of the cell. Such a literal interpretation is rather unfocused since it will include processes such as protein and RNA synthesis, which are only indirectly relevant to cell reproduction. So we shall confine our attention to those cell cycle events and processes that are specifically required for cell reproduction and not for cellular growth. This distinction has not always been fully appreciated. For example, the changes that occur when quiescent cells are stimulated are often assumed to be cell-cycle-specific. But, as well as being stimulated to enter into the cell cycle, such cells are also being stimulated to grow. Consequently, many of the changes observed will be associated with the growth of the cell rather than with the cell cycle itself. The two major processes that are specifically required for cell reproduction are S phase and mitosis. These ensure the replication and segregation of the chromosomes and are found in all eukaryotic cell cycles.

When considering cell cycle control we run into the problem that the term 'control' can mean very different things to different people. It may be used in the sense of 'required for'. In this sense, any event that is necessary for successful completion of the cell cycle can be considered part of its control. We do not think that this is a very useful way to look at the problem. For us, implicit in the term 'control' is the idea of regulation, and we want to identify events that are important for regulation. Three useful ways of identifying regulatory events are to find those acting at: (1) initiation steps, (2) rate-limiting steps and (3) commitment steps. We shall consider each of these in turn.

An initiation event is simply the first event that is specifically required for the process under consideration. The difficulty here is knowing when the first event has been found, as there may always be an earlier event that has not been identified. In cell cycle terms we are interested in the initiation events of the whole cell cycle, of S phase and of mitosis.

A rate-limiting step is an event that makes a major contribution to the overall rate at which a process is completed. Any event necessary for the cell cycle will become rate-limiting if it is inhibited, but that does not mean that it is normally rate-limiting. It is more informative to speed up an event than inhibit it, since in these circumstances only genuinely rate-limiting steps will advance the whole process. Various treatments such as the use of mutants, medium shifts and addition of cell extracts have been used to advance cells through the cell cycle into S phase and mitosis in order to identify major rate-limiting steps.

A commitment step is more difficult to identify. It can be defined as a point of no return beyond which no alternative developmental pathways can be initiated until the cell cycle in progress has finished. Thus practical identification of a commitment step requires developmental fates as alternatives to the mitotic cell cycle; then, as cells progress through the cell cycle their ability to undergo these alternatives can be assessed. Problems arise because the various alternatives may become excluded at different times during the cycle, making it difficult to define the true point of no return.

From our discussion so far it would seem that we are dealing with quite different controls. However, this need not be the case. For example, a point of commitment to the cell cycle in G_1 might also be a major rate-limiting step of the cell cycle and an initiation event for S phase. Indeed if this were the case we would feel encouraged that, imperfect as our individual views of control are, together they are leading us generally in the right direction. As we shall show, this does seem to be the case from studies with the yeasts.

MITOTIC CELL CYCLES OF THE YEASTS

The first parts of the cell cycle of both yeasts are similar to each other and to those of other eukaryotic cells. There is a G_1 period that becomes much expanded at very low growth rates. After G_1 there is a discrete S phase during which DNA replication takes place using multiple replicons (Newlon, Petes, Hereford & Fangman, 1974). However, the second part of the cell cycle differs between the two yeasts (Nurse, 1985a). Fission yeast is more typically eukaryotic, with a G_2 period and mitosis. During mitosis a microtubular spindle forms, chromosomes visibly condense and the cell divides by medial fission. The condensation of *Schiz. pombe* chromosomes has been dramatically demonstrated by Yanagida and co-workers using a mutant strain defective in tubulin (Umesono, Hiraoka, Toda & Yanigida, 1983). In budding yeast there is no real G_2 period. A short mitotic spindle is formed during S phase and the cell becomes arrested in mid-mitosis for the rest of the cycle. The spindle then elongates, mitosis is completed and the cell divides by budding. No visible chromosome condensation takes place. Both yeasts differ from most eukaryotes in that the nuclear membrane does not break down during mitosis. As we shall see later the difference in the organization of the two cell cycles is also reflected in their mitotic controls.

CELL CYCLE GENES OF THE YEASTS

A large number of conditionally lethal cell cycle mutants have been isolated in the two yeasts that are unable to complete the cell cycle (Hartwell, Mortimer, Culotti & Culotti, 1973; Nurse, Thuriaux & Nasmyth, 1976; Reed, 1980; Nasmyth & Nurse, 1981). Most of these mutants are heat-sensitive although some are cold-sensitive (Moir, Stewart, Osmond & Botstein, 1982; Hiraoka, Toda & Yanigida, 1984). The mutants fall into two classes: those that continue growth and macromolecular synthesis at their restrictive temperature and those that do not. Following our earlier discussion, we consider only those mutants that can continue growth and macro-molecular synthesis as being specifically defective in cell cycle progress. By this criterion, about 50 *cdc* genes have been identified in budding yeast and about 40 genes in fission yeast. These genes define functions that are specifically required for successful completion of the cell division cycle, but only a few can be expected to be involved in cell cycle control.

G_1 'START' CONTROL

The major cell cycle control in budding yeast is located in G_1 at start. 'Start' was originally identified by the pioneering work of Hartwell, Pringle and co-workers. It is the earliest gene-controlled event of the cell cycle identified to date and, therefore, may be the point of initiation (Pringle & Hartwell, 1981). Traverse of start results in commitment to the cell cycle with respect to the alternative developmental pathway of conjugation (Hartwell, 1974). After start is passed conjugation is not possible until the cell cycle in progress has been completed. The start event does not take place until cells have attained a critical size: at low growth rates daughter cells are smaller at division and so cells must grow for a longer period before passing start (Hartwell & Unger, 1977; Carter & Jagadish, 1978: Lord & Wheals, 1980). Therefore, under these conditions traverse of start is a major rate-limiting step of the cell cycle. We can see that all three ways of identifying regulatory control events can be applied to start.

Start gene functions have been investigated by Reed and his co-workers. Four gene functions, *cdc28, -36, -37* and *-39*, are required to traverse start (Reed, 1980). It has been claimed that mutants in other genes also block at or before start but in these cases it has not been firmly established that the mutants can still undergo cellular growth. For this reason they may not be defective specifically in cell cycle progress. The mating pheromones α and **a** factor also arrest cells at start to prepare them for conjugation (Bucking-Throm, Duntze, Hartwell & Manney, 1973). Mutants in *cdc36* and *-39* appear to be constitutive for mating pheromone response. In cells that are unable to mate, e.g. **a**/α diploids, the *cdc36* and *-39* mutants do not show cell cycle arrest. *cdc36* and *-39* mutants also allow certain *ste* (*ste*rile) mutants to mate that are normally unable to do so (Shuster, 1982). This evidence suggests that these two genes are involved in the mating pheromone response pathway that arrests cells at start. Mutants in the other two start genes *cdc28* and *-37* are not influenced by the mating system and so appear to be more central to the start control system.

A start control has also been identified in the fission yeast. Mutants in two genes, *cdc2* and *cdc10*, block at a point in the cell cycle during G_1 where cells are still able to conjugate if challenged to do so (Nurse & Bissett, 1981; Aves, Durkacz, Carr & Nurse, 1985). But once past this point cells are committed to the mitotic cycle and are unable to conjugate. Traverse of start in fission yeast also appears to be a major rate-limiting step (Fantes, 1977; Nurse & Thuriaux, 1977; Nasmyth, Nurse & Fraser, 1979). In mutants that divide at a reduced cell size, the G_1 period before start becomes expanded. A similar expansion is seen when growth rate is reduced by growing cells in chemostat cultures (Nasmyth, 1979). As with budding yeast, passage of start also requires growth to a critical cell size.

The *cdc2* start gene in fission yeast is functionally similar to the *cdc28* start gene in budding yeast (Beach, Durkacz & Nurse, 1982). When the *cdc28* gene is introduced into mutants of *cdc2* these cells are able to divide and grow at the restrictive temperature. This suggests that the *cdc2* and *cdc28* genes are functionally interchangeable and therefore perform essentially similar functions within the two organisms. Both genes have been sequenced (Lorincz & Reed, 1984; Hindley & Phear, 1984) and a comparison of their predicted amino acid sequences shows that they are identical at 62% of their amino acid positions. This suggests that the two genes are related by common descent. The two yeasts are not closely related: sequence comparisons suggest that they may have diverged as much as 1000 million years ago, close to the origin of eukaryotic life (Huysmans, Dams, Vandenberghe & de Wachter, 1983). Therefore, any function that is conserved in both yeasts is likely to be found in other organisms and it is possible that a similar control mechanism exists in all eukaryotic cells.

G_2 MITOTIC CONTROL

A second major cell cycle control has been identified in the fission yeast (Nurse, 1975). This acts during the G_2 period and determines the cell cycle timing of mitosis. The control was identified as the major rate-limiting step in G_2 by isolating 'wee' mutants, which are advanced through G_2 and undergo mitosis and cell division prematurely at a reduced size. The mutants define two genes *wee1* and *cdc2* (Nurse & Thuriaux, 1980). The *cdc2* gene is required twice during the cell cycle, in G_1 at start, as discussed earlier, and then in G_2 at the mitotic control. Recessive temperature-sensitive lethal *cdc2* mutants become blocked in G_1 or G_2, depending on where they are in the cell cycle when shifted to the restrictive temperature (Nurse & Bissett, 1981). In contrast, dominant wee *cdc2* and partially recessive *wee1$^-$* mutations advance cells through G_2. The *wee1* gene codes for an inhibitor and the *cdc2* gene for an activator in the mitotic control (Nurse & Thuriaux, 1980).

Changes in the medium or growth rate of the cells modulate the mitotic control. Shifting cells into poor medium transiently advances cells through G_2 as do wee mutants (Fantes & Nurse, 1977). This can be explained if a critical cell size is required before the mitotic control can be passed, which is modulated downwards in poor growth medium. As a consequence, cells undergo cell division at a small size and are too small to pass start in the subsequent cell cycle. The G_1 period therefore becomes expanded before the start point of commitment. With further nutrient deprivation these uncommitted cells will undergo conjugation and sporulation or enter stationary phase.

In budding yeast there does not appear to be an equivalent of this control because as explained earlier there is no G_2 period. The *cdc28* gene is required for mitosis (Piggott, Rai & Carter, 1982) but its mitotic function is completed very soon after start, consistent with the early initiation of mitosis. There is an approximately constant time from S phase to the completion of mitosis and thus a certain period of time may be required to complete all the events of mitosis (Carter & Jagadish, 1978). It is this that determines when mitosis is completed.

THE *cdc2*/*cdc28* GENE FUNCTION

The *cdc2*/*cdc28* gene has a remarkable role in cell cycle control of the two yeasts. It is involved in the G_1/S phase transition at start and then again at the G_2/M transition of the mitotic control in fission yeast. Several powerful molecular biological techniques have been used to investigate this gene and we shall now summarize what these recent studies have shown concerning the molecular role of this gene function in the cell.

Plasmids containing the *cdc2* and *cdc28* genes have been isolated from gene banks by virtue of their ability to allow mutants of *cdc2* and *cdc28* to grow at their restrictive temperatures (Nasmyth & Reed, 1980; Beach *et al.* 1982). The sequence of the *cdc28* gene reveals that it contains a single open reading frame encoding a protein of 298 amino acids (Lörincz & Reed, 1984). A similar protein of 297 residues is predicted from the sequence of the *cdc2* gene, although in this case four introns have to be postulated (Hindley & Phear, 1984). The two proteins have a 20% identity with the *src* family of oncogene products and with cyclic-AMP-dependent protein kinase. Most of this similarity can be accounted for by the presence of two active sites within the protein: an ATP-binding site of the sort found in protein kinases and a phosphorylation site (Nurse, 1985a). Therefore, it is likely that the *cdc2/28* gene function is a protein kinase that can become phosphorylated. Because of its similarity to the *src* family of oncogenes the *cdc2/28* gene could be considered a primitive oncogene. We do not think that this is likely since most of the similarity is due to the presence of the two active sites, and once these sites are removed from the comparison there is very little further similarity.

Antibodies have been raised against a *cdc28*–β-galactosidase fusion, which identifies a budding yeast protein of the correct relative molecular mass (M_r) of 36 000 (Reed, 1984). This protein has been shown to be the product of the *cdc28* gene, since in strains containing the *cdc28* gene on a multicopy number plasmid the protein is increased in amount (Reed, Hadwiger & Lörincz, 1985). The *cdc28* gene product is phosphorylated and also has protein kinase activity. Exponentially growing cells labelled with $^{32}PO_4$ incorporate the isotope into the p36 protein. The protein kinase activity has been assayed by following the transfer of phosphate to a protein of $M_r = 40\,000$, which is co-immunoprecipitated with the *cdc28* gene product. The 40 000 M_r protein may be the natural substrate for the *cdc28* protein kinase. Extracts made from temperature-sensitive *cdc28* mutants also have temperature-sensitive activity *in vitro*, proving that the protein kinase activity is definitely associated with the *cdc28* gene product. The protein kinase activity is magnesium-dependent and apparently zinc-activated.

Antibodies have also been raised against the *cdc2* gene product by using synthetic peptides (V. Simanis & P. Nurse, unpublished data). These identify a protein from fission yeast with a relative molecular mass of 34 000. This protein is overproduced in cells with an increased level of *cdc2* transcripts produced by fusion of the *cdc2* gene with the strong alcohol dehydrogenase (*adh*) promoter. The protein is phosphorylated like the *cdc28* gene product and also has protein kinase activity. The kinase activity is divalent-cation-dependent but in contrast with *cdc28* is not activated by zinc. These data confirm that the *cdc2/cdc28* gene product is indeed a protein kinase that becomes phosphorylated.

The *cdc2* gene is not regulated at the level of transcription (Durkacz, Carr & Nurse, 1986). No changes in steady-state transcript level are seen during the cell cycle or when cells undergo the transition from rapid growth into quiescence. Nor are there any changes at the level of RNA processing; all four introns appear to be used all the time. Therefore, changes in *cdc2* transcript level or its processing do not appear to be responsible for regulating either progress through the cell cycle or the transition between rapid proliferation and quiescence. Even when *cdc2* transcription is increased 30-fold over normal there is no disturbance of normal regulation of the mitotic cycle.

The *cdc2* antibody has been used to monitor changes in protein level and phosphorylation state of the *cdc2* gene product (V. Simanis & P. Nurse, unpublished data). Surprisingly, no changes in either steady-state protein level or overall phosphorylation state are found during the cell cycle. However, a dramatic change is observed when cells become quiescent upon shift into nitrogen starvation conditions. The level of *cdc2* protein does not change, but it becomes rapidly dephosphorylated and there is a dramatic reduction in the level of its protein kinase activity. Therefore, exit of cells from the mitotic cell cycle into a quiescent state may well be regulated by modulating the *cdc2* protein kinase activity by changes in phosphorylation. The reduction in protein kinase activity would then prevent the cell from initiating any further mitotic cell cycles. The regulation of the phosphorylation state of the *cdc2* gene product may be the key to understanding how the cell cycle is initiated. Also, identification of substrates should be revealing about what the *cdc2/28* gene protein does and how it mediates the G_1/S phase transition at start and the G_2/M transition at the mitotic control (Dudani & Prasad, 1984).

GENES INTERACTING WITH THE *cdc2/28* GENE FUNCTION

Gene products that interact with the *cdc2/28* gene function are potential regulators and substrates. Two gene functions that interact closely with the *cdc2* function at the mitotic control point are those of *wee1* and *cdc25* (Fantes, 1979; Nurse & Thuriaux, 1980; Fantes, 1983). The *wee1* gene codes for an inhibitor in the mitotic control as discussed earlier. The *cdc25* gene has been implicated in the control because mutants in *wee1* and wee mutants of *cdc2* are able to suppress a defective *cdc25* gene function (Fantes, 1979). Normally, mutants of *cdc25* are unable to undergo mitosis but in a wee mutant background they are able to do so. The suppressor effects on *cdc25* suggest a close relationship between *cdc25*, *wee1* and *cdc2*, and several models have been proposed to account for their close interaction. Direct evidence in favour of *cdc25* being involved in the mitotic control has recently been obtained after cloning the gene (Russell & Nurse, 1986). When the *cdc25* gene is fused behind the strong *adh* promoter, thus increasing its transcription, cells are advanced through G_2 into mitosis and cell division at a reduced size. This establishes that the *cdc25* gene function can be rate-limiting for the timing of mitosis. The *cdc25* gene function is also completely dispensable in a *wee1* mutant background. Deletion of the chromosomal copy of the *cdc25* gene using recombinant DNA procedures is lethal in a *wee1*$^+$ strain whereas a *wee1*$^-$ strain is still viable. The similarity of the phenotype of *cdc2* wee mutants, *wee1* mutants and of overproducing *cdc25* suggests that the *wee1* and *cdc25* gene products are regulators of the *cdc2* protein kinase. The *cdc25* gene codes for an inducer and the *wee1* gene for an inhibitor. If *cdc25* is overproduced in a *wee1* mutant then the mitotic control is grossly disturbed, leading to various mitotic catastrophes and cell death. These data are all consistent with the following model. The *cdc2* gene product is considered to be in two states, an active one and an inactive one. The *cdc25* gene product converts the inactive form into the active form and the *wee1* gene product converts the active form into the inactive form. The balance of these two gene product activities determines when the *cdc2* gene product becomes sufficiently active to initiate mitosis.

Another gene product appears to interact directly with the *cdc2* protein at both its G_1 and its G_2 points of action. This gene, called *suc1* (for *suppressor of cdc2*) was identified by mutants that allow temperature-sensitive lethal mutants of *cdc2* to grow at their restrictive temperature (Hayles, Beach, Durkacz & Nurse, 1986). The gene has been cloned by exploiting the fact that overproduction of *suc1*$^+$ transcripts from a high copy-number plasmid enables certain *cdc2* mutants to divide. The suppression is also seen when the *suc1*$^+$ gene is fused to the strong *adh* promoter. Overproduction of the *suc1*$^+$ transcript, and therefore presumably of the *suc1*$^+$ gene product, in a *cdc2*$^+$ strain causes a delay of mitosis. This suggests that the *suc1*$^+$ gene product has a direct effect in its own right upon cell cycle progress and may physically interact with the *cdc2* protein. Further evidence in favour of this hypothesis is that *suc1* suppression of *cdc2* mutants is allele-specific. The role that the *suc1* gene product may play is as yet unclear but it is an obvious candidate for a protein that directly interacts with the *cdc2* protein.

Various classes of mutants appear to act at a similar time to the start genes already mentioned. They include *cdc37* in budding yeast and *cdc10* in fission yeast. The *whi1* and *whi2* (Sudbery, Goodey & Carter, 1980) mutants in budding yeast are advanced into start at a reduced cell size so these may be important for regulating *cdc28* gene function. Mutants of the *ran1/pat1* gene (Nurse, 1985b; Iino & Yamamoto, 1985a,b) in fission yeast may also function close to the *cdc2* point of action at start. These mutants undergo conjugation and sporulation in conditions under which cells should be progressing through the mitotic cell cycle. They appear to be defective in the monitoring process that determines whether a cell should become committed to conjugation and sporulation or mitosis. Study of all these various mutants may turn out to be revealing about how *cdc2/28* gene function is regulated.

ANALOGOUS CONTROLS IN OTHER EUKARYOTES

The work we have described indicates that there are two major cell cycle controls in the yeasts that both involve the *cdc2/28* protein kinase function: a commitment control acting at the G_1/S boundary and, at least in fission yeast, a mitotic control acting at the G_2/M boundary. We will now consider whether there are any analogous controls present in other eukaryotic cells.

Many workers studying animal cells have proposed that the major point of cell cycle regulation occurs in late G_1 (Pardee, Dunbrow, Hamlin & Kletzien, 1978). These proposals have been based mainly on the observations that arresting cell proliferation by using a variety of conditions such as serum starvation, nutrient depletion or high cell density leads to G_1 arrest. A good example of this type of analysis is provided by the work of Pardee and his co-workers (Pardee, 1974), who put forward the hypothesis that there is a restriction point, R, in late G_1, which can only be passed in conditions favourable for cell proliferation. When conditions are not favourable cells become arrested at the R point and cannot enter the mitotic cycle. Transformed cells may be defective in R point control, failing to arrest correctly in unfavourable conditions.

Such an R point in G_1 has obvious similarities to the start commitment control in the yeasts. There are other features about G_1 arrest points in animal cells that also show similarities. It has been shown that in certain cases of differentiation cells leave the mitotic cycle from a specific point in G_1 (Scott, Florine, Willie & Yun, 1982). In an *in vitro* adipocyte differentiation system, cells become committed to differentiation from a point in G_1 called G_D. Once past this point they are unable to differentiate until they have completed the mitotic cycle in progress. However, it is unlikely that a general argument of this sort can be made, since many cell types undergoing differentiation still continue to proliferate. Traverse of a G_1 arrest point is also rate-limiting for entry into S phase in certain growth conditions; the G_1 period usually becomes much extended at low growth rates (Darzynkiewicz, Traganos & Melamed, 1980). The major rate-limiting step may be the attainment of a critical cell size as in the yeasts, but the evidence for mammalian cells is conflicting and if there is a relationship between cell size and entry into the mitotic cycle it must be of a much looser kind and easily dissociated (Shields *et al.* 1978). What is clear from cell fusion experiments, though, is that factors accumulate during the G_1 period that determine the rate at which cells initiate S phase (Rao, Sunkara & Wilson, 1977; Rao & Johnson, 1974).

Mitotic controls have received much less attention in mammalian cells, although some cell types do become arrested at some point in G_2 (Gelfant, 1962; Pederson & Gelfant, 1970). These cells are only a small proportion of the total population, but when stimulated to divide they undergo mitosis without first entering S phase. Mammalian cell fusion experiments also suggest that there are inhibitory factors that can block cells in G_2 before mitosis (Rao & Johnson, 1974). There have been more extensive studies of mitotic control in the slime mould *Physarum plasmodium*. Fusion of naturally synchronous plasmodia at different times of G_2 have indicated that mitotic inducing factors accumulate during the G_2 period (Rusch, Sachsenmaier, Behrens & Gruter, 1966). Such factors have been purified and found to advance nuclei into mitosis (Loidl & Gröbner, 1982). The factors can be mimicked by Ehrlich ascites cell extracts containing protein kinase activity able to phosphorylate histone H1 *in vitro* (Inglis *et al.* 1976), suggesting a role for protein phosphorylation in the mitotic control. A formally similar approach has been used recently by Kirschner and his co-workers to investigate mitotic control in *Xenopus* eggs. They have investigated the role of maturation promoting factor (MPF) in mitosis and meiosis. MPF was first identified as a factor required for maturation of *Xenopus* oocytes; the maturation process involves the transition of G_2-arrested oocytes into meiotic nuclear division. MPF also varies cyclically during the mitotic cycle in early *Xenopus* embryos, peaking at mitosis (Gerhart, Wu & Kirschner, 1984; Newport & Kirschner, 1984). This suggests that MPF may be a component of a regulatory system controlling the initiation of mitosis. Preparations containing MPF activity have been isolated from a variety of organisms including mitotically arrested yeast and mammalian cells (Weintraub *et al.* 1982; Sunkara, Wright & Rao, 1979), and so this regulatory system may be widespread amongst eukaryotic cells. It is also possible that MPF may involve phosphorylation, since its activity is stabilized by phosphatase inhibitors, and a fraction that is 20-fold enriched in MPF has protein kinase activity (Wu & Gerhart, 1980).

Other evidence also indicates that protein phosphorylation may play an important role in regulating progress through the eukaryotic cell cycle. A number of proteins have been identified that only become phosphorylated during mitosis (Sahasrabuddhe, Adlakha & Rao, 1984; Davis, Tsao, Fowler & Rao, 1983; Vandre, Davis, Rao & Borisy, 1984). Antibodies have been raised against these proteins and a subset of these have been shown to be associated with microtubular organizing centres, which are responsible for organizing the mitotic spindle. A variety of other proteins including histones also undergo changes in phosphorylation during the cell cycle (Ottaviano & Gerace, 1985; Piras & Piras, 1975; Bradbury, Inglis & Matthews, 1974; Gurley, Walters, Barham & Deaven, 1978: Yamashita, Nishimoto & Sekiguchi, 1984).

Taken together these data establish that there are G_1 and G_2 control points in other eukaryotic cells, including mammalian cells, which may be analogous to the two controls identified in the two yeasts. Furthermore, phosphorylation has been implicated in certain cases, suggesting that protein kinases that are possibly similar to that encoded by *cdc2/28* may have an important role to play in the controls.

REGULATION OF THE *cdc2/28* FUNCTION

We conclude this review by speculating on the molecular basis of the *cdc2/28* function and its regulation. The best clue for regulation obtained so far is the observation that phosphorylation and protein kinase activity of the *cdc2* protein is much reduced when cells become quiescent and accumulate before start. Therefore phosphorylation and activation of the *cdc2* protein kinase may regulate entry into the mitotic cycle and the transition from G_1 into S phase. This raises the question of how the phosphorylation of the *cdc2/28* protein is controlled. One exciting possibility is provided by recent studies of the *ras* oncogene homologues and cyclic-AMP-dependent protein phosphorylation in budding yeast. Mutants with reduced levels of cyclic-AMP-dependent protein phosphorylation accumulate in G_1 before start (Matsumoto, Uno, Oshima & Ishikawa, 1982). These observations have led to the model that cyclic-AMP-dependent protein phosphorylation may regulate the initiation of the mitotic cell cycle. Furthermore, the control of phosphorylation may be determined by the *ras* oncogene homologues modulating adenylate cyclase activity and thus cyclic AMP levels in the cell (Toda *et al.* 1985). An obvious candidate for activation by this phosphorylation system is the *cdc2/28* function, which could then proceed to initiate the cell cycle. This is an intriguing possibility since it would provide a direct link between the *ras* oncogene and the control of cell proliferation.

However, the situation may be more complex than this. The mutants defective in cyclic-AMP-dependent protein phosphorylation that accumulate in G_1 are also defective in overall growth of the cell (Matsumoto *et al.* 1982). As explained earlier, cells that grow at a reduced rate often accumulate in G_1. Therefore, the G_1 block point of these mutants may simply be a pleiotropic effect very distant from the initial biochemical defect. The critical experiment in these studies concerns the *bcy1* gene, mutants of which result in a deficiency of the regulatory subunit of cyclic-AMP-dependent protein kinase. These mutants have a cyclic-AMP-dependent protein kinase, which is now cyclic-AMP-independent, and consequently have a constitutive kinase activity. If the model is correct these mutants should undergo cell proliferation even when conditions are not appropriate, for example under nutrient deprivation. Mutants that behave in this way do exist, for example *whi2* mutants, continue to proliferate even when they have run out of nutrients. They continue to bud and divide and produce very small cells. *bcy1* mutants do not seem to have this phenotype. It has been claimed that on starvation *bcy1* mutants continue budding and eventually arrest in a budded state (Matsumoto, Uno & Ishikawa, 1983). However, if the results are examined more carefully it appears that cells do not continue to bud, they simply fail to complete the mitotic cycle that is in progress when shifted into nutrient starvation conditions. This can be seen by the low increase in cell number observed in these mutants when shifted into nutrient starvation conditions. They fail to complete the cell cycle in progress and thus arrest as budded cells. Therefore, an alternative interpretation of the data is that the cells are sick and are unable to complete the cell cycle in progress in starvation conditions. Until these points are clarified the roles of cyclic AMP and the *ras* gene product in cell cycle regulation, and thus their effects on the *cdc2/28* gene function and overall phosphorylation, will remain uncertain.

Overall phosphorylation of the *cdc2/28* protein is unlikely to be responsible for regulating the mitotic control since phosphorylation levels are unchanged during G_2 and mitosis. Of course, it is possible that there may be a more subtle change in phosphorylation not detected to date, such as different amino acid residues becoming modified. Alternatively, the *cdc2/28* gene function could be regulated by substrate availability. Changes in compartmentation of the *cdc2/28* protein or its substrates may be responsible for determining the cell cycle timing of mitosis.

MOLECULAR BASIS OF THE *cdc2/28* FUNCTION

What could the single *cdc2/28* gene function be doing that facilitates both the transitions from G_1 into S and from G_2 into M? Many different changes occur as cells progress through the cell cycle and it is difficult to identify those processes that may be important. We suggest that the most important processes that occur are those central to DNA replication and chromosome segregation. One such process is a change in the chromatin condensation state. Chromatin must decondense to become available for replication at S phase, and then condense in mitosis to permit segregation of the chromosomes. The hypothesis has been suggested that there is a cycle of chromatin condensation and decondensation (Mazia, 1963): when chromatin is maximally decondensed S phase occurs and when it is maximally condensed mitosis takes place. Decondensation of chromatin may make the DNA available to a constantly present replication apparatus giving rise to a discrete S phase (Newport & Kirschner, 1984).

A second important process concerns alterations in the cytoskeleton. Changes occur in the cytoskeleton during the cell cycle, the most dramatic being the disappearance of cytoplasmic microtubules at the G_2/M transition and the formation of a mitotic spindle, which is necessary for accurate segregation of the sister chromatids. A transient disassembly of microtubules has also been suggested as a necessary requirement for the initiation of S phase (Otto *et al.* 1979; Friedkin, Legg & Rozengurt, 1979; Crossin & Carney, 1981; Thyberg, 1984). Therefore, there may well be changes in both chromatin and cytoskeletal organization at the G_1/S and G_2/M transitions, and we suggest that these changes may be brought about by the *cdc2/28* protein kinase phosphorylating specific proteins. Obvious candidates for these proteins are those associated with chromatin and the cytoskeleton; for example, both histones and microtubular associated proteins (MAPs) are believed to be important for organization of chromatin and the cytoskeleton. Several of the histones undergo substantial changes in phosphorylation during the cell cycle and may be partly responsible for the state of chromatin condensation (Dolby, Belmont, Borun & Nicolini, 1981; Gurley *et al.* 1978; Bradbury *et al.* 1974; Hanks, Rodriquez & Rao, 1983). Both MAPs 1 and 2 can become phosphorylated (Herrmann, Dalton & Wiche, 1985) and their level of phosphorylation may be important for levels of microtubular disassembly.

The *cdc2/28* protein when activated could phosphorylate a series of proteins within the cell which could bring about changes in chromatin and cytoskeletal organization. The reason for the different behaviour at G_1/S and G_2/M is not clear but could be due to different availability of substrates. The *cdc2/28* protein at the apex of a protein phosphorylation cascade can potentially control the two major transitions involved in cell cycle control. We propose that this is how the cell cycle is regulated in yeast and knowledge gained from these studies may provide a useful framework for studying cell cycle regulation in higher eukaryotes.

We thank Steve Aves, Tony Carr, Iain Hagan, Pete Magee, Paul Russell and Viesturs Simanis for helpful discussions and for supplying unpublished data.

REFERENCES

AVES, S. J., DURKACZ, B. W., CARR, A. & NURSE, P. (1985). Cloning, sequencing and transcriptional control of the *Schizosaccharomyces pombe cdc10* "start" gene. *EMBO J.* **4**, 457–463.

BEACH, D., DURKACZ, B. & NURSE, P. (1982). Functionally homologous cell cycle control genes in budding and fission yeast. *Nature, Lond.* **300**, 706–709.

BRADBURY, E. M., INGLIS, R. J. & MATTHEWS, H. R. (1974). Control of cell division by very lysine rich histone (F1) phosphorylation. *Nature, Lond.* **247**, 257–261.

BUCKING-THROM, E., DUNTZE, W., HARTWELL, L. H. & MANNEY, T. R. (1973). Reversible arrest of haploid yeast cells at the initiation of DNA synthesis by a diffusible sex factor. *Expl Cell Res.* **76**, 99–110.

CARTER, B. L. A. & JAGADISH, M. N. (1978). The relationship between cell size and cell division in the yeast *Saccharomyces cerevisiae*. *Expl Cell Res.* **112**, 15–24.

CROSSIN, K. L. & CARNEY, D. H. (1981). Evidence that microtubule depolymerization early in the cell cycle is sufficient to initiate DNA synthesis. *Cell* **23**, 61–71.

DARZYNKIEWICZ, Z., TRAGANOS, F. & MELAMED, M. R. (1980). New cell cycle compartments identified by multiparameter flow cytometry. *Cytometry* **1**, 98–109.

DAVIS, F. M., TSAO, T. Y., FOWLER, S. K & RAO, P. N. (1983). Monoclonal antibodies to mitotic cells. *Proc. natn. Acad. Sci. U.S.A.* **80**, 2926–2930.

DOLBY, T. W., BELMONT, A., BORUN, T. W & NICOLINI, C. (1981). DNA replication, chromatin structure and histone phosphorylation altered by theophylline in synchronised HeLa S3 cells. *J. Cell Biol.* **89**, 78–85.

DUDANI, A. K. & PRASAD, R. (1984). A hypothesis for the possible involvement of microtubules and protein kinase in the mechanism of action of *cdc28* gene product of *Saccharomyces cerevisiae*. *FEBS Lett.* **172**, 139–141.

DURKACZ, B., CARR, A. & NURSE, P. (1986). Transcription at the *cdc2* cell cycle control gene of the fission yeast *Schizosaccharomyces pombe*. *EMBO J.* **5** (in press).

FANTES, P. A. (1977). Control of cell size and cycle time in *Schizosaccharomyces pombe*. *J. Cell Sci.* **24**, 51–67.

FANTES, P. A. (1979). Epistatic gene interactions in the control of division in fission yeast. *Nature, Lond.* **279**, 428–430.

FANTES, P. A. (1983). Control of timing of cell cycle events in fission yeast by the *wee1*[+] gene. *Nature, Lond.* **302**, 153–155.

FANTES, P. & NURSE, P. (1977). Control of cell size in fission yeast by a growth modulated size control over nuclear division. *Expl Cell Res.* **107**, 377–386.

FRIEDKIN, M., LEGG, A. & ROZENGURT, E. (1979). Antitubulin agents enhance the stimulation of DNA synthesis by polypeptide growth factors in 3T3 mouse fibroblasts. *Proc. natn. Acad. Sci. U.S.A.* **76**, 3909–3912.

GERHART, J., WU, M. & KIRSCHNER, M. W. (1984). Cell cycle dynamics of a M phase specific cytoplasmic factor in *Xenopus laevis*. *J. Cell Biol.* **98**, 1247–1255.

GELFANT, S. (1962). Initiation of mitosis in relation to the cell division cycle. *Expl Cell Res.* **26**, 395–403.

GURLEY, L. R., WALTERS, R. A., BARHAM, S. S. & DEAVEN, L. L. (1978). Heterochromatin and histone phosphorylation. *Expl Cell Res.* **111**, 373–383.

HANKS, S. K., RODRIQUEZ, L. V. & RAO P. N. (1983). Relationship between histone phosphorylation and premature chromosome condensation. *Expl Cell Res.* **148**, 293–302.

HARTWELL, L. H. (1974). *Saccharomyces cerevisiae* cell cycle. *Bact. Rev.* **38**, 164–198.

HARTWELL, L. H., MORTIMER, R. K., CULOTTI, J. & CULOTTI, M. (1973). Genetic control of cell division in yeast: Genetic analysis of *cdc* mutants. *Genetics* **74**, 267–286.

HARTWELL, L. H. & UNGER, M. W. (1977). Unequal division in *Saccharomyces cerevisiae* and its implications for the control of cell division. *J. Cell Biol.* **75**, 422–435.

HAYLES, J., BEACH, D., DURKACZ, B. & NURSE, P. (1986). The fission yeast cell cycle control gene *cdc2*: isolation of a sequence *suc1* that suppresses *cdc2* mutant function. *Molec. gen. Genet.* (in press).

168 *J. Hayles and P. Nurse*

HERRMANN, H., DALTON, J. M. & WICHE, G. (1985). Microheterogeneity of microtubule associated proteins MAP1 and MAP2 and differential phosphorylation of individual subcomponents. *J. biol. Chem.* **260**, 5797–5803.

HINDLEY, J. & PHEAR, G. A. (1984). Sequence of the cell division gene *CDC2* from *Schizosaccharomyces pombe*; patterns of splicing and homology to protein kinases. *Gene* **31**, 129–134.

HIRAOKA, Y., TODA, T. & YANAGIDA, M. (1984). *NDA3* gene of fission yeast encodes β tubulin: a cold sensitive *nda3* mutation reversibly blocks spindle formation and chromosome movement in mitosis. *Cell* **39**, 349–358.

HUYSMANS, E., DAMS, E., VANDENBERGHE, A. & DE WACHTER, R. (1983). The nucleotide sequences of the 5S RNAs of four mushrooms and their use in studying the phylogenetic positions of basidiomycetes among the eukaryotes. *Nucl. Acids Res.* **11**, 2871–2880.

IINO, Y. & YAMAMOTO, M. (1985a). Mutants of *Schizosaccharomyces pombe* which sporulate in the haploid state. *Molec. gen. Genet.* **198**, 416–421.

IINO, Y. & YAMAMOTO, M. (1985b). Negative control for the initiation of meiosis in *Schizosaccharomyces pombe*. *Proc. natn. Acad. Sci. U.S.A.* **82**, 2447–2451.

INGLIS, R. J., LANGAN, T. A., MATTHEWS, H. R., HARDIE, D. G. & BRADBURY, E. M. (1976). Advance of mitosis by histone phosphokinase. *Expl Cell Res.* **97**, 418–425.

LOIDL, P. & GRÖBNER, P. (1982). Acceleration of mitosis induced by mitotic stimulators of *Physarum polycephalum*. *Expl Cell Res.* **137**, 469–472.

LORD, P. G. & WHEALS, A. E. (1980). Asymmetrical division of *Saccharomyces cerevisiae*. *J. Bacteriol.* **142**, 808–818.

LÖRINCZ, A. T. & REED, S. I. (1984). Primary structure homology between the product of yeast cell division control gene *CDC28* and vertebrate oncogenes. *Nature, Lond.* **307**, 183–185.

MATSUMOTO, K., UNO, I. & ISHIKAWA, T. (1983). Control of cell division in *Saccharomyces cerevisiae* mutants defective in adenylate cyclase and cAMP dependent protein kinase. *Expl Cell Res.* **146**, 151–161.

MATSUMOTO, K., UNO, I., OSHIMA, Y. & ISHIKAWA, T. (1982). Isolation and characterisation of yeast mutants deficient in adenylate cyclase and cAMP-dependent protein kinase. *Proc. natn. Acad. Sci. U.S.A.* **79**, 2355–2359.

MAZIA, D. (1963). Synthetic activities leading to mitosis. *J. cell. comp. Physiol.* **1** (suppl. 1), 123–140.

MOIR, D., STEWART, S. E., OSMOND, B. C. & BOTSTEIN, D. (1982). Cold-sensitive cell division cycle mutants of yeast: Isolation, properties and pseudoreversion studies. *Genetics* **100**, 547–563.

NASMYTH, K. (1979). A control acting over the initiation of DNA replication in the yeast *Schizosaccharomyces pombe*. *J. Cell Sci.* **36**, 215–233.

NASMYTH, K. & NURSE, P. (1981). Cell division cycle mutants altered in DNA replication and mitosis in the fission yeast *Schizosaccharomyces pombe*. *Molec. gen. Genet.* **182**, 119–124.

NASMYTH, K., NURSE, P. & FRASER, R. S. S. (1979). The effect of cell mass on the cell cycle timing and duration of *S*-phase in fission yeast. *J. Cell Sci.* **39**, 215–233.

NASMYTH, K. A. & REED, S. I. (1980). Isolation of genes by complementation in yeast: Molecular cloning of a cell cycle gene. *Proc. natn. Acad. Sci. U.S.A.* **77**, 2119–2123.

NEWLON, C. S., PETES, T. D., HEREFORD, L. M. & FANGMAN, W. L. (1974). Replication of yeast chromosomal DNA. *Nature, Lond.* **247**, 32–35.

NEWPORT, J. W. & KIRSCHNER, M. W. (1984). Regulation of the cell cycle during early *Xenopus* development. *Cell* **37**, 731–742.

NURSE, P. (1975). Genetic control of cell size at cell division in yeast. *Nature, Lond.* **256**, 547–551.

NURSE, P. (1985a). Cell cycle control genes in yeast. *Trends Genet.* **1**, 51–55.

NURSE, P. (1985b). Mutants of the fission yeast *Schizosaccharomyces pombe* which alter the shift between cell proliferation and sporulation. *Molec. gen. Genet.* **198**, 497–502.

NURSE, P. & BISSETT, Y. (1981). Gene required in G_1 for commitment to cell cycle and in G_2 for control of mitosis in fission yeast. *Nature, Lond.* **292**, 558–560.

NURSE, P. & THURIAUX, P. (1977). Controls over the timing of DNA replication during the cell cycle of fission yeast. *Expl Cell Res.* **107**, 365–375.

NURSE, P. & THURIAUX, P. (1980). Regulatory genes controlling mitosis in the fission yeast *Schizosaccharomyces pombe*. *Genetics* **96**, 627–637.

NURSE, P., THURIAUX, P. & NASMYTH, K. (1976). Genetic control of cell division cycle in fission yeast *Schizosaccharomyces pombe*. *Molec. gen. Genet.* **146**, 167–178.

OTTAVIANO, Y. & GERACE, L. (1985). Phosphorylation of nuclear lamins during interphase and mitosis. *J. biol. Chem.* **1**, 624–632.

OTTO, A. M., ZUMBE, A., GIBSON, L., KUBLER, A. M. & DE ASUA, L. J. (1979). Cytoskeleton-disrupting drugs enhance effect of growth factors and hormones on initiation at DNA synthesis. *Proc. natn. Acad. Sci. U.S.A.* **76**, 6435–6438.

PARDEE, A. B. (1974). A restriction point for control of normal animal cell proliferation. *Proc. natn. Acad. Sci. U.S.A.* **71**, 1286–1290.

PARDEE, A. B., DUNBROW, R., HAMLIN, J. L. & KLETZIEN, R. F. (1978). Animal cell cycle. *A. Rev. Biochem.* **47**, 715–750.

PEDERSON, T. & GELFANT, S. (1970). G_2-population cells in mouse kidney and duodenum and their behaviour during the cell division cycle. *Expl Cell Res.* **59**, 32–36.

PIGGOTT, J. R., RAI, R. & CARTER, B. L. A. (1982). A bifunctional gene product involved in two phases of the yeast cell cycle. *Nature, Lond.* **298**, 391–394.

PIRAS, R. & PIRAS, M. M. (1975). Changes in microtubule phosphorylation during cell cycle of HeLa cells. *Proc. natn. Acad. Sci. U.S.A.* **72**, 1161–1165.

PRINGLE, J. R. & HARTWELL, L. H. (1981). The *Saccharomyces cerevisiae* cell cycle. In *The Molecular Biology of the Yeast* Saccharomyces – *Life Cycle and Inheritance* (ed. J. N. Strathern, E. W. Jones & J. R. Broach), pp. 97–142. New York: Cold Spring Harbor Laboratory Press.

RAO, P. N. & JOHNSON, R. T. (1974). Regulation of cell cycle in hybrid cells. In *Control of Proliferation in Animal Cells, Cold Spring Harbor Conf. Cell Prolif.* (ed. B. Clarkson & R. Baserga), vol. 1, pp. 785–800. New York: Cold Spring Harbor Laboratory Press.

RAO, P. N., SUNKARA, P. S. & WILSON, B. A. (1977). Regulation of DNA synthesis: age dependent cooperation among G_1 cells upon fusion. *Proc. natn. Acad. Sci. U.S.A.* **74**, 2869–2873.

REED, S. I. (1980). The selection of *S. cerevisiae* mutants defective in the start event of cell division. *Genetics* **95**, 561–577.

REED, S. I. (1984). Preparation of product specific antisera by gene fusion: antibodies specific for the product of yeast cell division cycle gene *CDC28*. *Gene* **20**, 255–265.

REED, S. I., HADWIGER, J. A. & LÖRINCZ, A. T. (1985). Protein kinase activity associated with the product of the yeast cell division cycle gene *CDC28*. *Proc. natn. Acad. Sci. U.S.A.* **82**, 4055–4059.

RUSCH, H. P., SACHSENMAIER, W., BEHRENS, K. & GRUTER, V. (1966). Synchronization of mitosis by the fusion of the plasmodia of *Physarum polycephalum*. *J. Cell Biol.* **31**, 204–209.

RUSSELL, P. & NURSE, P. (1986). *cdc25*[+] functions as an inducer in the mitotic control of fission yeast. *Cell* (in press).

SAHASRABUDDHE, C. G., ADLAKHA, R. C. & RAO, P. N. (1984). Phosphorylation of non-histone proteins associated with mitosis in HeLa cells. *Expl Cell Res.* **153**, 439–450.

SCOTT, R. E., FLORINE, D. L., WILLIE, J. J. JR & YUN, K. (1982). Coupling of growth arrest and differentiation at a distinct state in the G_1 phase of the cell cycle: G_D. *Proc. natn. Acad. Sci. U.S.A.* **79**, 845–849.

SHIELDS, R., BROOKS, R., RIDDLE, P. N., CAPELLARO, D. F. & DELIA, D. (1978). Cell size, cell cycle and transition probability in mouse fibroblasts. *Cell* **15**, 469–474.

SHUSTER, J. R. (1982). Mating-defective *ste* mutations are suppressed by cell division cycle start mutations in *Saccharomyces cerevisiae*. *Molec. Cell Biol.* **2**, 1052–1063.

SUDBERY, P. E., GOODEY, A. R. & CARTER, B. L. A. (1980). Genes which control cell proliferation in the yeast *Saccharomyces cerevisiae*. *Nature, Lond.* **288**, 401–404.

SUNKARA, P. S., WRIGHT, D. A. & RAO, P. N. (1979). Mitotic factors from mammalian cells induce germinal vesicle breakdown and chromosome condensation in amphibian oocytes. *Proc. natn. Acad. Sci. U.S.A.* **76**, 2799–2802.

TODA, T., UNO, I., ISHIKAWA, T., POWERS, S., KATAOKA, T., BROCK, D., CAMERON, S., BROACH, J., MATSUMOTO, K. & WIGLER, M. (1985). In yeast RAS proteins are controlling elements of adenylate cyclase. *Cell* **40**, 27–36.

THYBERG, J. (1984). The microtubular cytoskeleton and the initiation of DNA synthesis. *Expl Cell Res.* **155**, 1–8.

UMESONO, K., HIRAOKA, Y., TODA, T. & YANAGIDA, M. (1983). Visualisation of chromosomes in mitotically arrested cells of the fission yeast *Schizosaccharomyces pombe*. *Curr. Genet.* **7**, 123–128.

VANDRE, D. D., DAVIS, F. M., RAO, P. N. & BORISY, G. G. (1984). Phosphoproteins are components of mitotic microtubule organising centres. *Proc. natn. Acad. Sci. U.S.A.* **81**, 4439–4443.

WEINTRAUB, H., BUSCAGLIA, M., FERREZ, M., WEILLER, S., BOULET, A., FABRE, F. & BAULIEU, E. E. (1982). Mise en evidence d'une activité "MPF" chez *Saccharomyces cerevisiae*. *C.R. hebd. Séanc. Acad. Sci., Paris* (series III) **295**, 787–790.

WU, M. & GERHART, J. C. (1980). Partial purification and characterisation of Maturation Promoting Factor from eggs of *Xenopus laevis*. *Devl Biol.* **79**, 465–477.

YAMASHITA, K., NISHIMOTO, T. & SEKIGUCHI, M. (1984). Analysis of proteins associated with chromosome condensation in Baby Hamster kidney cells. *J. biol. Chem.* **259**, 4667–4671.

J. Cell Sci. Suppl. 4, 171–180 (1986)
Printed in Great Britain © The Company of Biologists Limited 1986

REGULATION OF CELL PROLIFERATION AT THE ONSET OF DNA SYNTHESIS

ARTHUR B. PARDEE, DONALD L. COPPOCK AND
HENRY C. YANG

*Department of Pharmacology, Harvard Medical School and Division of Cell Growth and
Regulation, Dana-Farber Cancer Institute, 44 Binney St, Boston, MA 02115, USA*

INTRODUCTION

General outlines are now emerging as to how cellular proliferation is regulated. Growth factors provide external signals that govern proliferation. These factors interact with their receptors to set in motion intracellular signals, sometimes called second messages, which in turn activate specific genes including oncogenes and initiate key biochemical events.

Duplication of all of a cell's initial components furnishes the substance for eventual cell duplication. These components come together to permit the readily observed biochemical events, such as the onset of DNA synthesis at the beginning of S phase and morphological terminal events of nuclear and cellular divisions. Relatively few growth-factor-regulated biochemical processes are critical for cell proliferation, amongst this myriad of events during the cell cycle. All present evidence suggests that these controlling events occur in only one part of the cycle, G_1, that culminates in the onset of DNA synthesis. All that follows – in S, G_2, M and cytokinesis – proceeds and goes to completion independently of extracellular regulatory factors. Homeostatic control mechanisms must balance the events in the different phases, as well as those in G_1 itself. However, these controls are secondary in contrast to the few primary regulations of the most critical processes, of which onset of DNA synthesis is a major one. In this essay, the control of onset of DNA synthesis will be discussed. We will discuss primarily results obtained with some fibroblastic rodent lines such as 3T3.

PROLIFERATION CONTROL IN RELATION TO THE CELL CYCLE

Arrest of proliferating cells selectively in any part of the cell cycle other than G_1 is not possible by manoeuvres that are dependent on physiological agents (as opposed to inhibitory drugs). Furthermore, cessation of growth under physiological conditions stops cells in intact animals or in culture with unduplicated DNA contents. That is, arrested cells exist in the quiescent (G_0) state before they can make DNA. Furthermore, the derangements of proliferation control found in neoplastic cells are all G_0/G_1-related. These pieces of information focus attention on the G_0/G_1 condition when proliferation and its derangements are considered.

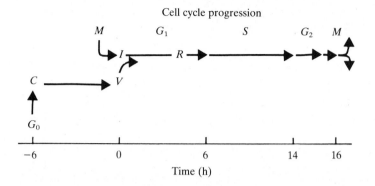

Fig. 1. Progression through the cell cycle. Stages of the cell cycle and major regulatory points are indicated at times representing the fastest proliferating mouse 3T3 cells. Note that duration of G_1 period before R is highly variable in a population and depends on growth conditions. The diagram also indicates convergence of pathways from mitosis by cycling cells and recovery of initially quiescent cells.

This topic is described conventionally (Baserga, 1985) in the framework of a temporal sequence leading from quiescent cells into and through the cell cycle. The interval from G_0 to the onset of DNA synthesis (S) can now be divided into four subsections, as shown in Fig. 1. Cells are stimulated to emerge from quiescence into a competent state (C), which has been studied in most detail with fibroblastic 3T3 cells (Stiles, 1983). Then during a period of about 6 h they come to a point (V), at which they are similar to cycling cells that have just completed mitosis (M). Following V (or M) cells usually require several more hours in G_1 to prepare for DNA synthesis. They then reach a control point (R), beyond which neither growth factors nor transcription and rapid translation are required (Yang & Pardee, 1986). Between R and the onset of DNA synthesis (start of S phase) is a period for organization of the machinery for DNA synthesis. Once DNA synthesis has started, the rest of the cycle – S, G_2, M and cytokinesis – follows independently of external physiological controls. Cells that have started DNA synthesis will reach the next G_1 phase, and then will either proceed through another cycle if conditions are adequate, or fall back into quiescence (G_0) from which they will emerge only when restimulated.

Hydroxyurea and aphidicolin, which block ribonucleotide reductase and DNA polymerase, respectively, prevent the synthesis of DNA, and the events that follow, such as mitosis and cytokinesis. Similarly, blocking cells in mitosis with agents such as colcemid also prevents cytokinesis. These results suggest that each event is dependent upon prior events in the cycle. But there is no method for stopping cells in S, G_2 or M specifically that depends upon normal physiological conditions such as growth factors or high cell density.

Although these statements are based mostly on studies with fibroblasts, similar events have been described for other kinds of cells such as lymphocytes (for a recent review, see Baserga, 1985). Not every factor required for cell growth is a physiological regulator. Many components are needed for growth, but all do not normally regulate it. For example, removal of extracellular phosphate or potassium ions causes cells to stop growing, but there is little likelihood that these ions are crucial to controlling the decision as to whether or not a cell will grow. It is much more likely that the levels of factors such as platelet-derived growth factor and somatomedin C are critical for determining whether or not normal cells will grow. The same factors seem to be less essential for cancer cells, thereby permitting neoplastic growth.

Various sorts of events are under study during each of these successive steps, as listed in Table 1. We cannot in this brief essay begin to summarize all of this information, and how they relate to each of the half-dozen parts of the cell cycle. We will discuss some that are involved in the onset of DNA synthesis, in particular during the interval between the termination of cell division (M) (or the V point) and the beginning of S phase. We will work progressively backwards from each effect to its prior event.

THE ONSET OF DNA SYNTHESIS

DNA synthesis begins suddenly, many hours after a quiescent cell is stimulated or a cycling cell has completed mitosis. The remainder of the cell cycle then proceeds according to a quite exact time schedule, compared to the highly variable G_0 to S interval. The onset of DNA synthesis is usually measured by determining incorporation of radioactive thymidine into trichloracetic acid insoluble material (DNA). This method is subject to numerous possible errors, particularly if quantified as counts incorporated rather than by autoradiography, which determines whether or not a cell is incorporating thymidine. The amount of thymidine incorporated depends upon factors such as intracellular pools, activity of the thymidine transport mechanism, and activities of enzymes including thymidine kinase; but it is still by far the most convenient and most frequently used method. If one exposes an exponentially growing population of cells to thymidine, about half the cells are observed to incorporate radioactivity immediately, as shown by autoradiography (Fig. 2). These are the cells initially in S phase and synthesizing DNA. Thereafter, more cells become labelled, as they enter S phase. So as time progresses the curve measures transit into S of cells from earlier parts of the cycle, initially from G_1 and later from G_2. G_1 cells constitute the majority of this remaining population, as can be shown in studies in which colcemid is added to prevent eventual entry of the G_2 and M cells into S phase.

Table 1. *Cell proliferation components*

1.	Growth factors
2.	Membrane receptors
3.	Second messengers
4.	Activated genes
5.	Messenger RNAs
6.	Proteins
7.	Enzymes

What event is it that suddenly permits a cell to start making DNA? Many of the required enzymes are present in G_1 cells; and the availability of DNA precursors does not seem to be limiting, since when these are supplied to cells made permeable to deoxynucleoside triphosphates new DNA only appears in the same time frame as in intact cells (Castellot, Miller & Pardee, 1978), which must make their own deoxynucleoside triphosphates through a series of enzyme-catalysed events starting with the ribonucleoside diphosphates.

The final incorporation of deoxynucleotides into DNA depends upon at least a dozen enzymes and other proteins, as demonstrated with lower organisms primarily by Kornberg (1980) and co-workers. In higher organisms a multiprotein 'replitase' complex contains many of the known enzymes that are required for DNA synthesis (Reddy & Pardee, 1980). Such a complex with a molecular weight of about 5×10^6 has been purified about 10-fold and shown to contain nascent DNA as well as a considerable number of enzymes involved in DNA synthesis (Noguchi, Reddy & Pardee, 1983). Until these enzymes and associated proteins are assembled the complex should not function. A reasonable hypothesis is that the final step leading to onset of DNA synthesis is production of one of these enzymes or proteins. Indeed, a number of enzymes rise dramatically at the same time as DNA synthesis starts (Coppock & Pardee, 1985; Szyf *et al.* 1985). Their appearance is not dependent on DNA synthesis, unlike histones, which are made coordinately with DNA (Sariban, Wu, Erickson & Bonner, 1985). However, none of these has been demonstrated

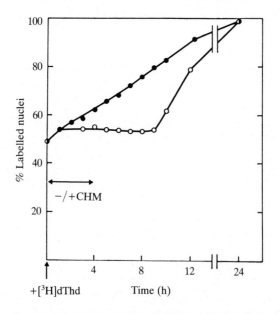

Fig. 2. Entry of an exponential population of cells into *S* phase. Exponential populations of 3T3 cells received [³H]thymidine ([³H]dThd) at time zero. Half also received $0.1 \,\mu g \, ml^{-1}$ cycloheximide (CHM), which was removed after 4 h (○). The other culture did not receive cycloheximide (●). Samples were taken for autoradiography at intervals as shown. The data are plotted as percentage of cells with labelled nuclei. (Modified data from Campisi & Pardee (1984).)

to provide the essential final element for incorporation of deoxynucleotides into DNA.

Interestingly, this complex was not found in G_1 phase cells, but only in S phase cells; its appearance correlated with the time at which DNA synthesis started (Reddy & Pardee, 1980). Formation of this complex from its components could thus be the signal that is required to trigger DNA synthesis. Remarkably, enzymes of the complex were not even found in the nuclei of pre-S cells, but rather in their cytoplasm; they were located in the nuclei only after DNA synthesis had begun (Reddy & Pardee, 1980). Possibly the nucleus permits facilitated diffusion of these enzymes shortly before DNA synthesis starts. An alternative and simpler hypothesis, however, is that the enzymes can penetrate freely into the nucleus but they are trapped there only when they are able to assemble into the multienzyme complex (see Feldherr, 1985). The assembly of enzymes into the nucleus just at the time when DNA synthesis starts requires explanation.

Studies *in vivo* also suggest interaction of enzymes required for DNA synthesis. Remarkably, an inhibitor of one of the enzymes blocks the activity of another within the intact cell, although not inhibiting this second enzyme in extracts. Thus, aphidicolin, which is an inhibitor of solubilized DNA polymerase but not of thymidylate synthase, strongly inhibited both of these activities in intact cells. Hydroxyurea, a specific inhibitor of ribonucleotide reductase and novobiocin, a preferential inhibitor of topoisomerase, similarly also blocked thymidylate synthase within the intact cell (Reddy & Pardee, 1983). The degree of thymidylate synthase inhibition has been found by others (Chiba, Bacon & Chiba, 1984; Nicander & Reichard, 1985) to be slightly less than that of the primarily inhibited enzyme. This partial inhibition was under different experimental conditions, and in both cases it was very considerable.

Possible explanations for this cross-inhibition *in vivo* are: (1) the enzymes are all associated in a multienzyme complex and inhibition of one allosterically affects another, as modulated by protein conformational changes (Reddy & Pardee, 1983). (2) The inhibitor of one enzyme modulates various deoxynucleotide pools, with inhibitory effects upon thymidylate synthase. There is, however, no evidence for large modifications of pool components, or of inhibition by any such components on thymidylate synthase.

Another sort of data supporting the idea of a multienzyme complex for DNA synthesis is a phenomenon called channelling (Reddy & Pardee, 1982). Labelled ribonucleoside diphosphate was preferentially incorporated into trichloroacetic acid-insoluble material relative to the incorporation of deoxynucleoside triphosphate, the proximal DNA precursor. One explanation for this is that enzymes of the pathway to DNA, from ribonucleoside diphosphate reductase may be so closely coupled that only a molecule of ribonucleoside diphosphate entering this sequence is able to be incorporated.

Although such a preferential incorporation into TCA-insoluble material of permeabilized cells has been demonstrated (Reddy & Pardee, 1982), it has been argued that the product formed is RNA rather than DNA, in which case it is not surprising that deoxy-triphosphates do not interfere (Spyrou & Reichard, 1983). More recent work (Reddy, Klinge & Pardee, 1986) shows that the product formed by these cells, which must be permeabilized in order to permit entry of labelled and charged compounds, is not RNA but actually a co-polymer of ribo- and deoxynucleotides. Although this is an artifactual product and not authentic DNA, neither is it RNA. Furthermore, incorporation of ribonucleoside diphosphate into only the deoxy-nucleotides of this product clearly showed selective chanelling. The concept that the enzymes leading from the ribo-precursors into DNA are closely coupled is thus supported.

Tight coupling (exclusion of deoxytriphosphates) can be demonstrated with permeabilized cells, but this can be loosened so as to allow incorporation of both precursors (Reddy & Pardee, 1980). Various experiments with intact cells clearly demonstrate both formation of deoxynucleotide pools (important in regulation of ribonucleotide reductase) and their incorporation into DNA, and therefore leaky channelling (Nicander & Reichard, 1983).

Further work is required in order to demonstrate the degree of channelling in intact cells, and that it is *via* a multienzyme complex involving all of the enzymes from ribonucleoside diphosphate reductase to DNA polymerase. Many data are, however, very hard to explain without this hypothesis. The sudden onset of DNA synthesis is plausibly accounted for by assembly of some or all of these enzymes into a replitase complex at the time DNA synthesis starts.

THE RESTRICTION POINT

The G_1 (M to S) interval and the latter part of the considerable longer interval from G_0 to S is bipartite. Before the restriction (R) point, which is located about 2 h before the onset of DNA synthesis, cells require transcription and rapid protein synthesis as well as somatomedin C in order to move on and start DNA synthesis. In contrast, cells beyond the R point are independent of growth factors, of transcription and of rapid protein synthesis. An illustration of this phenomenon is seen (Fig. 2) after addition of the translational inhibitor cycloheximide to a population of exponentially growing cells. Cells continued to enter S for approximately 2 h (Campisi *et al.* 1982). Cells originally located earlier in the cycle were blocked. A variety of experiments show timing corresponding to a critical R point event being reached at about 2 h before onset of DNA synthesis, and also a good correlation between loss of requirement for the growth factor somatomedin C and loss of transcriptional inhibition (80 %) by 5,6-dichlororibofuranosylbenzimidazole (DRB) (Yang & Pardee, 1986). Cells became independent of translation, as determined using inhibitors of protein synthesis an hour later (but they are not independent of an isoleucine requirement until S phase starts) (Wynford-Thomas, La Montagne, Marin & Prescott, 1985). These results are generally consistent with transcriptional events that are completed 2 h before S, leading to translations completed an hour later.

De novo synthesis of several enzymes such as thymidylate synthase and thymidine kinase occurs after R (Coppock & Pardee, 1985), and is apparently under the same control as onset of DNA synthesis.

The important point here is that cells initiated DNA synthesis after a period of an hour during which neither rapid transcription nor (rapid) translation were important. This result suggests that morphological changes, possibly associated with rearrangements of the DNA synthetic apparatus, were occurring during this considerable time interval. As described above, enzymes for DNA synthesis both move from cytoplasm to nucleus and assemble into a readily sedimented high molecular weight complex at about this time.

It should be noted that the interval following R is not subject to physiological regulation of cell proliferation. The extracellular factors have lost their ability to stimulate or block progression of cells into the cycle by the time the cells have reached the R point, but protein synthesis inhibitors such as cycloheximide are useful for further fractionation of this last part of the pre-S phase.

Das (1981) has reported that cells held at the G_1/S interface with hydroxyurea lose ability to make DNA when released, with a half-life of about 5 h. The loss is kinetically consistent with a prereplicative state that is lost as a unit. In general, cells that are arrested in their cycle are in a dynamic state. They do not long remain so, unlike an electric clock that has been detached from its power source. Molecules are in dynamic states of varying stabilities. So, after a stimulus necessary for progression in the cycle is removed some molecules are degraded, and time is later required for their resynthesis. Other synthetic processes go on at the same time, resulting in a different balance of cell components. This instability of certain cell components makes interpretations of position in the cycle on the basis of interrupted timing of events quite complex and difficult to interpret.

REGULATION BEFORE THE RESTRICTION POINT

A major process for control of cell proliferation is located in G_1 before the restriction point. During this interval of several hours somatomedin C is the only factor required by 3T3 cells (Leof, Van Wyck, O'Keefe & Pledger, 1984; Campisi & Pardee, 1984). Somatomedin C like insulin autophosphorylates a tyrosine in its cell membrane receptor. Little is known regarding the biochemical events triggered by somatomedin C beyond the relevance of rates of protein synthesis and degradation.

The *ras* oncogene is activated during this same interval, as shown by increases in its mRNA (Campisi *et al.* 1984). The relationship between growth factors and this oncogene remains to be unravelled. The timing of *ras* activation is very different from the timing of activation of *fos* and *ras* oncogenes, which occurs shortly after cells in quiescence are stimulated, and thus half a dozen hours before activation of *ras*. Transcriptional events are required during this earlier part of G_1, up to the R point (Yang & Pardee, 1986). A few mRNAs are made specifically during this same interval (Linzer & Nathans, 1983). Since mRNAs for enzymes such as thymidine kinase appear at the end of G_1 phase (Stuart, Ito, Stewart & Conrad, 1985), some of these messages possibly correspond to proteins required for DNA synthesis.

Not only is transcription required for transit through the early part of G_1 phase, but rapid translation is also important. Concentrations of cycloheximide that incompletely block total protein synthesis nearly completely block transit specifically through this part of the cell cycle. We have proposed that this is because a particular protein is required, i.e. one that is quite labile and hence must be synthesized rapidly in order to increase in amount in the face of its continued degradation (Rossow, Riddle & Pardee, 1979; Campisi, Medrano, Morreo & Pardee, 1982). Remarkably, this requirement for rapid protein synthesis was absent in a variety of cells transformed either with carcinogens or with RNA viruses (Campisi *et al.* 1982). These results suggest that stabilization of such a protein has an important role in the loss of growth control in cancer cells.

Having postulated an important regulatory protein that must be made in G_1, that is unstable in normal cells, and that is stabilized in tumour cells, we initiated a search for it using two-dimensional electrophoresis gels. One such protein was identified, of M_r 68 000 and isoelectric point 6·3 (Croy & Pardee, 1983). This protein is made in larger amounts by tumour cells, and appears to be more stable. Its functional role is unknown, but it is being studied further with regard to its genetics, location and activity.

Not only does the onset of DNA synthesis depend differently upon rapid protein synthesis in normal *versus* transformed cells, presumably of an unstable protein such as p68, but also the activities of enzymes such as thymidine kinase, which appear at this time, are similarly controlled (Stuart *et al.* 1985; Coppock & Pardee, 1985). A regulatory mechanism that is dependent upon this labile protein appears to trigger a set of events including the appearance of new enzymes as well as the onset of DNA synthesis.

EVENTS LEADING QUIESCENT CELLS INTO THE CYCLE

Up to this point, we have discussed events culminating in the onset of DNA synthesis and initiated after M phase, by cycling cells. Quiescent cells are in a state (G_0) that is different from the G_1 state of cycling cells, even though the latter have the same unduplicated DNA content as do G_0 cells. Extra biochemical events are required for cells to emerge from quiescence, and these require extra time. G_0 cells essentially need, as a first step, to reactivate their machinery for making proteins, including stimulation of messenger RNA enzymology, and this requires a period of several hours. Cycling G_1 cells already have active protein and mRNA synthetic machinery after they emerge from mitosis, and so they prepare more quickly for events that lead to synthesis of DNA. To activate these quiescent cells and bring them back into the cycle occupies half a dozen hours, during which the synthesis of RNA and protein can increase considerably, and higher activities of various systems for transporting metabolites into cells can appear (see Baserga, 1984).

Activation of quiescent cells is another highly controlled event, dependent upon different factors such as platelet-derived and epidermal growth factors, and possibly insulin. Furthermore, a number of genes are activated, as shown by the appearance of new mRNAs, including those coded by oncogenes such as *myc* and *fos*. It is important here to note that the whole cast of characters for activation of quiescent cells is quite different from the corresponding factors, oncogenes and proteins such as p53 (see Baserga, 1985), involved in the preparation of cells to begin DNA synthesis. The events required for this activation have recently been reviewed (Stiles, 1983) and will not be discussed here. There now appear to be two critical regulatory processes required to bring quiescent cells into full proliferation: (1) those involved in initial activation; (2) those involved in the later onset of DNA synthesis. The relative importance of these two processes for cancer in its various stages remains to be elucidated.

In conclusion, clearly a great deal has been learned during the past dozen years about the relation of the cell cycle and its control to cell proliferation. Discoveries of growth factors, their receptors, oncogenes, new messages and new proteins, to say nothing of enzymes such as protein kinases have led to a much deeper understanding of the proliferation of normal cells and the derangement of cells that have become neoplastic.

This work was aided by a USPHS grant no. GM24571. The authors are indebted to Marjorie Rider for preparing the manuscript.

REFERENCES

BASERGA, R. (1984). Growth in size and cell DNA replication. *Expl Cell Res.* **151**, 1–5.

BASERGA, R. (1985). *The Biology of Cell Reproduction.* Cambridge, MA: Harvard University Press.

CAMPISI, J., GRAY, H. E., PARDEE, A. B., DEAN, M. & SONENSHEIN, G. E. (1984). Cell-cycle control of c-*myc* but not c-*ras* expression is lost following chemical transformation. *Cell* **36**, 241–247.

CAMPISI, J., MEDRANO, E. E., MORREO, G. & PARDEE, A. B. (1982). Restriction point control of cell growth by a labile protein: Evidence for increased stability in transformed cells. *Proc. natn. Acad. Sci. U.S.A.* **79**, 436–440.

CAMPISI, J. & PARDEE A. B. (1984). Post-transcriptional control of the onset of DNA synthesis by an insulin-like growth factor. *Molec. cell. Biol.* **4**, 1807–1814.

CASTELLOT, J. J. JR, MILLER, M. R. & PARDEE, A. B. (1978). Animal cells reversibly permeable to small molecules. *Proc. natn. Acad. Sci. U.S.A.* **75**, 351–355.

CHIBA, P., BACON, P. E. & CORY, J. G. (1984). Studies directed toward testing the "Channeling" hypothesis – ribonucleotides -> DNA in leukemia L1210 cells. *Biochem. biophys. Res. Commun.* **123**, 656–662.

COPPOCK, D. L. & PARDEE, A. B. (1985). Regulation of thymidine kinase activity in the cell cycle by a labile protein. *J. cell. Physiol.* **124**, 269–274.

CROY, R. G. & PARDEE, A. B. (1983). Enhanced synthesis and stabilization of M_r 68,000 protein in transformed BALB/c-3T3 cells: Candidate for restriction point control of cell growth. *Proc. natn. Acad. Sci. U.S.A.* **80**, 4699–4703.

DAS, M. (1981). Initiation of nuclear DNA replication: evidence for formation of committed prereplicative cellular state. *Proc. natn. Acad. Sci. U.S.A.* **78**, 5677–5681.

FELDHERR, C. M. (1985). The uptake and accumulation of proteins by the cell nucleus. *BioEssays* **3**, 52–55.

KORNBERG, A. (1980). *DNA Replication.* San Francisco: W. H. Freeman.

LEOF, E. G., VAN WYK, J. J., O'KEEFE, E. J. & PLEDGER, W. J. (1984). Epidermal growth factor (EGF) is required only during the traverse of early G_1 in PDGF stimulated density-arrested Balb/c-3T3 cells. *Expl Cell Res.* **14**, 202–208.

LINZER, D. I. H. & NATHANS, D. (1983). Growth-related changes in specific mRNAs of cultured cells. *Proc. natn. Acad. Sci. U.S.A.* **80**, 4271–4275.

NICANDER, B. & REICHARD, P. (1983). Dynamics of pyrimidine deoxynucleoside triphosphate pools in relationship to DNA synthesis in 3T6 mouse fibroblasts. *Proc. natn. Acad. Sci. U.S.A.* **80**, 1347–1351.

NICANDER, B. & REICHARD, P. (1985). Relations between synthesis of deoxyribonucleotides and DNA replication in 3T6 fibroblasts. *J. biol. Chem.* **260**, 5376–5381.

NOGUCHI, H., REDDY, G. P. V. & PARDEE, A. B. (1983). Rapid incorporation of label from ribonucleoside diphosphates into DNA by a cell-free high molecular weight fraction from animal cell nuclei. *Cell* **32**, 443–451.

REDDY, G. P. V., KLINGE, E. M. & PARDEE, A. B. (1986). Ribonucleotides are channeled into a mixed DNA–RNA polymer by permeabilized hamster cells. *Biochem. biophys. Res. Commun.* (in press).

REDDY, G. P. V. & PARDEE, A. B. (1980). Multienzyme complex for metabolic channeling in mammalian DNA replication. *Proc. natn. Acad. Sci. U.S.A.* **77**, 3312–3316.

REDDY, G. P. V. & PARDEE, A. B. (1982). Coupled ribonucleoside diphosphate reduction, channeling. & incorporation into DNA of mammalian cells. *J. biol. Chem.* **257**, 12526–12531.

REDDY, G. P. V. & PARDEE, A. B. (1983). Inhibitor evidence for allosteric interaction in the replitase multienzyme complex. *Nature, Lond.* **304**, 86–88.

ROSSOW, P. W., RIDDLE, V. G. H. & PARDEE, A. B. (1979). Synthesis of labile, serum-dependent protein in early G_1 controls animal cell growth. *Proc. natn. Acad. Sci. U.S.A.* **76**, 4446–4450.

SARIBAN, E., WU, R. S., ERICKSON, L. C. & BONNER, W. C. (1985). Inter-relationships of protein and DNA syntheses during replication of mammalian cells. *Molec. cell. Biol.* **5**, 1279–1286.

SPYROU, G. & REICHARD, P. (1983). Ribonucleotides are not channeled into DNA in per-meabilized mammalian cells. *Biochem. biophys. Res. Commun.* **115**, 1022–1026.

STILES, C. D. (1983). The molecular biology of platelet-derived growth factor. *Cell* **33**, 653–655.

STUART, P., ITO, M., STEWART, C. & CONRAD, S. E. (1985). Induction of cellular thymidine kinase occurs at the mRNA level. *Molec. cell. Biol.* **5**, 1490–1497.

SZYF, M., KAPLAN, F., MANN, V., GILOH, H., KEDAR, E. & RAZIN, A. (1985). Cell cycle-dependent regulation of eukaryotic DNA methylase level. *J. biol. Chem.* **260**, 8653–8656.

WYNFORD-THOMAS, D., LAMONTAGNE, A., MARIN, G. & PRESCOTT, D. M. (1985). Location of the isoleucine arrest point in CHO and 3T3 cells. *Expl Cell Res.* **158**, 525–532.

YANG, H. C. & PARDEE, A. B. (1986). Insulin-like growth factor I regulation of transcription and DNA replicating enzyme induction necessary for S phase entry. *J. cell. Physiol.* (in press).

J. Cell Sci. Suppl. 4, 181–200 (1986)
Printed in Great Britain © The Company of Biologists Limited 1986

CELLULAR ASPECTS OF CIRCADIAN RHYTHMS

HANS-GEORG SCHWEIGER, ROMANA HARTWIG

Max-Planck-Institut für Zellbiologie, Ladenburg bei Heidelberg, Federal Republic of Germany

AND MANFRED SCHWEIGER

Institut für Biochemie, Universität Innsbruck, Austria

What is summarized under the term life is necessarily linked to the vector time; in other words, it is subject to dynamics. This is manifested by the fact that perpetual changes are an essential feature of living organisms. The changes involve metabolism, morphogenesis, motility and many other phenomena. On the other hand, cells make efforts to keep changes to a minimum, as illustrated by metabolic reactions that keep the milieu interieur constant.

Among the best-studied examples of dynamics in biology are development and rhythms. In our view differential gene expression must play a central role in developmental processes. The work done in this field in the last three decades has demonstrated that the mechanisms underlying gene expression offer a large number of possibilities for regulation. However, even today uncertainty predominates concerning the role played by any individual regulatory step.

Another example of dynamic processes in living organisms is the different types of rhythms. Their periods range from small fractions of a second up to one or several years (Hildebrandt, 1967). It is interesting to note that at least some of them have periods resembling environmental rhythms, e.g. day, month and year. The corresponding biological periodicities are circadian, circalunar and circannual rhythms, where the prefix 'circa' is to indicate that we are dealing with a range of frequencies rather than an exact frequency (Halberg, 1960). The frequencies of these endogenous rhythms are likely to reflect evolutionary adaptation to corresponding exogenous rhythms. In contrast to these three rhythms there are a number of other biological oscillations without any recognizable relationship to any given exogenous temporal structure.

A good example in this connection is that of the circaseptan rhythms, which were unknown until a couple of years ago, and it was not until recently that these rhythms attracted major interest (Halberg *et al.* 1974; Schweiger & Halberg, 1982; Hayes, Halberg, Cornelissen & Shankaraiah, 1985). They occur in multicellular as well as in unicellular organisms. The fact that no relationship could be recognized between circaseptan rhythms and any exogenous rhythm does not necessarily mean that there are no such relationships. However, the apparent lack of such a relationship raises the question of how such rhythms could emerge. An interesting explanation is based on the observation that living organisms are apparently capable of multiplying and demultiplying frequencies (Hildebrandt, 1967), resulting in periodicities in which the ratio of two frequencies is an integer even under changing conditions. Although rhythms have been investigated in many different organisms, very little is known about the underlying mechanism, and to date only circadian rhythms have been studied in any detail. Therefore, this paper will be concerned exclusively with circadian rhythms.

Circadian rhythms have been known for a long time. Their features have been described in numerous, some very thorough, studies (for references, see Chovnick, 1960; Aschoff, 1965a; Sweeney, 1969; Menaker, 1971; Bierhuizen, 1972; Bünning, 1973; Mills, 1973; Hastings & Schweiger, 1976; Schweiger & Schweiger, 1977; Scheving & Halberg, 1980; Moore-Ede, Sulzman & Fuller, 1982; Reinberg & Smolensky, 1983; Goto, Laval-Martin & Edmunds, 1985; Rensing & Jaeger, 1985). The major feature of these rhythms is that they are endogenous and the oscillation is retained even under constant conditions (Aschoff, 1960). The period of these rhythms is about 24 h, ranging from about 18 to 32 h. These rhythms can be entrained, i.e. they can be adapted to an exogenous rhythm or Zeitgeber (Bruce, 1960). Chemical and physical pulses can shift the phase of circadian rhythms in a characteristic way. The results from a number of pulses can be summarized in a phase-response curve (Aschoff, 1965b). Another important feature of circadian rhythms is that they can be inherited in a biparental way (Bünning, 1973). This indicates that expression of nuclear genes is involved and that translation of the products of these genes is performed on 80 S ribosomes. Last, but not least, it should be mentioned that these rhythms are temperature compensated, i.e. in a physiological temperature range the period will change to a small extent only (Sweeney & Hastings, 1960). In a number of cases an increase in temperature even results in a lengthening of the period. One would not expect such behaviour if the rhythm were based on a simple chemical reaction.

Circadian rhythms have been shown to occur in numerous animals and plants and, although it cannot be proved, the assumption seems to be justified that in all organisms at least some functions are subjected to circadian rhythms. Apparent exceptions are the prokaryotes, since to date no hard evidence has been presented that circadian rhythms occur in prokaryotes. This might be of importance for the discussion of the underlying mechanism and will be considered later in connection with differences in the gene expression systems of eukaryotes and prokaryotes.

Circadian rhythms are also exhibited by unicellular eukaryotic organisms. It need not be laboured that for studies on the molecular mechanisms underlying circadian rhythms unicellular organisms may be advantageous. Among the circadian rhythms demonstrated in unicellular organisms are bioluminescence, glow, photosynthesis and cell-division rhythms in *Gonyaulax* (Hastings, 1970), a photoaccumulation rhythm in *Chlamydomonas* (Bruce, 1970, 1974), a motility (Brinkmann, 1966) and a photoaccumulation (Pohl, 1948) rhythm in *Euglena*, and photosynthesis (Sweeney & Haxo, 1961; Schweiger, Wallraff & Schweiger, 1964a; Van den Driessche & Hars, 1966), chloroplast migration (Broda, Schweiger, Koop, Schmid & Schweiger, 1979) and an electrical potential rhythm (Novak & Sironval, 1976; Broda & Schweiger,

1980) in *Acetabularia*. In addition relevant results were obtained from studies on circadian rhythms in *Neurospora* (Feldman & Hoyle, 1973), *Aplysia* (Eskin, 1972; Jacklet, 1977) and *Drosophila* (Konopka & Benzer, 1971).

The fact that not only higher animals and plants but also unicellular organisms exhibit circadian rhythms rules out the possibility that this phenomenon is restricted to multicellular structures. In this context a fundamental question is whether a single unicellular organism is capable of expressing a circadian rhythm. Early experiments performed by Sweeney & Haxo (1961) indicated that in an individual cell of the unicellular and uninucleate marine green alga *Acetabularia* the oxygen production exhibits an endogenous rhythm. Later on, this early finding was confirmed and extended to other parameters by monitoring in one individual cell the oxygen evolution (Mergenhagen & Schweiger, 1973; and Fig. 1), the intracellular chloroplast migration (Broda *et al.* 1979; and Fig. 2) and the electrical potential (Broda & Schweiger, 1980; and Fig. 3).

The observation that an individual cell is capable of expressing circadian rhythms prompted the question of where in the cell the regulatory principle of a circadian rhythm could be. This question has been answered by fragmentation experiments performed in *Acetabularia*. In these experiments a cell was cut into two fragments, one with and one without a nucleus. It was shown unequivocally that the oxygen evolution rhythm is retained in both fragments (Mergenhagen & Schweiger, 1975*a*). Two conclusions could be drawn from this result. First, it is not possible to locate a specific site for the origin of the rhythm in the cell. Secondly, the possibility was ruled out that the rhythm originates in the nucleus. This idea has been favoured for many years by a number of authors (for references, see Ehret & Trucco, 1967). The

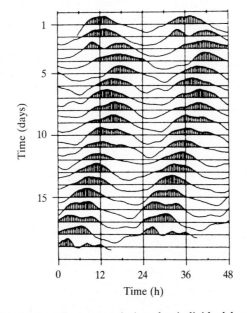

Fig. 1. Circadian rhythm of oxygen evolution of an individual *Acetabularia* cell. Data are presented as a double-phase plot (Wallraff *et al.* 1977).

fragmentation experiment suggested rather that the rhythmicity is a feature of the cytoplasm.

The fragmentation experiment also leads to the admittedly simplified question of whether there is one or more than one clock in a cell. One answer comes from the observation that the rhythm is retained in all fragments, even if a cell is cut into three pieces. This result indicates that a circadian rhythm is an inherent feature of the cytoplasm and that it can even be expressed in small pieces of cytoplasm. This leads to the question of how small a cytoplasmic fragment can be without losing the capability of performing a circadian rhythm. Of course, this is only a theoretical consideration, but an answer might be that there is an elementary unit of minimum size fulfilling the requirements of expressing a circadian oscillation, which one might

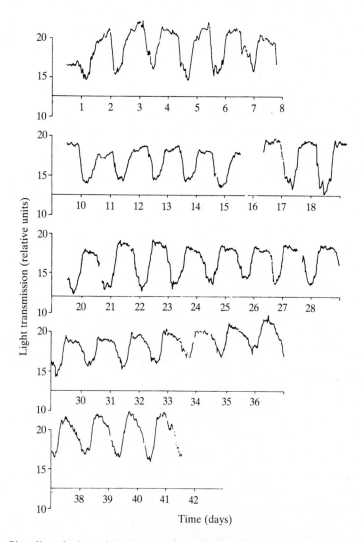

Fig. 2. Circadian rhythm of chloroplast migration in an individual *Acetabularia* cell. The cell was kept under constant conditions for 41 days (Schweiger, 1980).

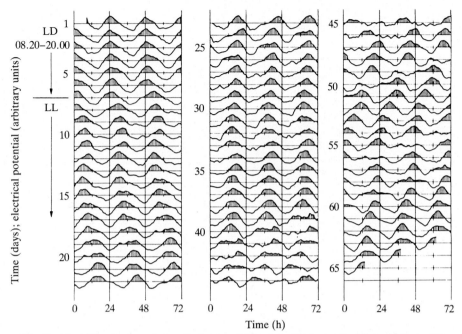

Fig. 3. Circadian rhythm of electrical potential in an individual cell of *Acetabularia*. The first 7 days were under light:dark (12 h:12 h) conditions (LD). From day 8 to 65 the cell was kept under constant conditions (LL) (Broda & Schweiger, 1981).

call a 'chronon'. Nothing is known about its characteristics, which are supposed to be functional rather than structural.

The question whether there is one or more than one clock in one cell may also lead to the question whether there is more than one oscillating parameter in one cell and if so whether these parameters are independent of each other. The fact that in *Acetabularia* at least three parameters, oxygen evolution, chloroplast migration and electrical potential, oscillate might indicate that there is more than one clock in one cell. A definite answer to this question, however, is hard to get if the different parameters oscillate in phase. This could either mean that there is only one clock governing three parameters or that there are three different oscillations tightly coupled to each other.

The development of methods that permit simultaneous monitoring of oxygen evolution and chloroplast migration (Schweiger, Broda, Wolff & Schweiger, 1983) or chloroplast migration and electrical potential, or even all three parameters (Broda & Schweiger, 1981) in one cell, made this problem accessible. Experiments in which pairs of parameters were measured simultaneously revealed that the two parameters under consideration were in a close phase relationship (Schweiger, unpublished data; and Fig. 4). This is a striking result considering the observation that in an individual *Acetabularia* cell the period of a circadian rhythm is not as stable (Wallraff *et al.* 1977; and Fig. 1) as it is in a multicellular organism (Aschoff, 1970; and Fig. 5), and this means that it is subject to slow changes. A stable phase

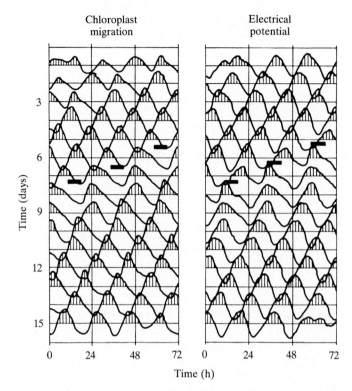

Fig. 4. Simultaneous measurement of chloroplast migration and electrical potential in an individual cell of *Acetabularia*. The cell was kept under constant conditions. An 8 h dark pulse was given on day 7.

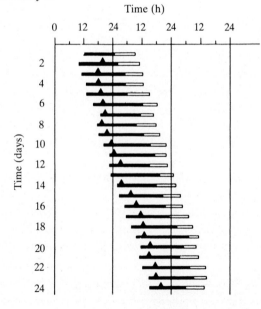

Fig. 5. Circadian rhythms in a human being. The person was kept under conditions of isolation and constant light (Aschoff, 1970). Activity (■■■■), rest (☐☐☐) and maximum of rectal temperature (—▲—) are presented. Note the constancy of the periods.

relationship between two parameters was also found in experiments in which the cells were exposed to temperature shifts or to dark pulses (Fig. 4). Both treatments resulted in characteristic phase shifts whose size varied depending on the timing of the pulse. In these experiments also, the phase relationship was unequivocally retained.

However, these results did not enable us to distinguish between the two possibilities, that we are either dealing with a hierarchy in which a pace-maker (master clock; Pittendrigh, 1981) directs several slave clocks or with two equal-ranking clocks closely coupled to each other. For obvious reasons the distinction between these alternatives would only be possible if we were dealing with two clocks and the phase relationship could be suspended. In fact, among a large number of experiments in which two parameters were monitored simultaneously a few definite cases were found in which, after a dark pulse, the phase was shifted in one but not in the other parameter. After the shift the new phase relationship was retained (Schweiger, unpublished data). These experiments demonstrate that we are dealing with two different clocks whose phases are closely coupled to each other.

From the experiments on anucleate cell fragments it follows that the cytoplasm is capable of expressing a rhythm. However, these experiments do not definitely rule out the possibility that in nucleate cells the nucleus is capable of affecting the rhythm. In order to study this problem nuclear exchange experiments were performed. In these experiments the nuclei from two cells out of phase by 180° were isolated and reimplanted crosswise. These experiments demonstrated that the phase of the rhythm of oxygen evolution could be shifted by a nucleus originating from a cell that was out of phase (Schweiger, Wallraff & Schweiger, 1964*b*; and Fig. 6). They also indicated that there are major differences in the expression of a circadian rhythm in the absence compared with the presence of the nucleus.

Moreover, the nuclear exchange experiments shed some light on the molecular mechanisms underlying circadian rhythms. On the one hand the nuclear effect on the phase indicated that gene expression is involved in the manifestation of circadian rhythms. On the other hand the persistence of the rhythm after enucleation and the ability of the nucleus to shift the phase resembled the behaviour of mRNA, which in *Acetabularia* has been shown to be more stable in the absence than in the presence of the nucleus (Kloppstech & Schweiger, 1982). Recent experiments on *Acetabularia* have extended these results and demonstrated that the different degrees of stability in nucleate compared with anucleate cells also characterize individual mRNAs (Li-Weber & Schweiger, 1985).

In order to test the hypothesis that gene expression is involved in the basic mechanism underlying the clock, the effects of a number of inhibitors of both transcription and translation on the rhythm of oxygen evolution were investigated. These experiments demonstrated that in an *Acetabularia* cell inhibitors like cycloheximide and anisomycin affecting translation on 80 S ribosomes or puromycin affecting translation on both 80 S and 70 S ribosomes suspended the circadian rhythm, while rifampicin and chloramphenicol, which are known to inhibit specifically transcription and translation of mitochondria and chloroplasts, respectively,

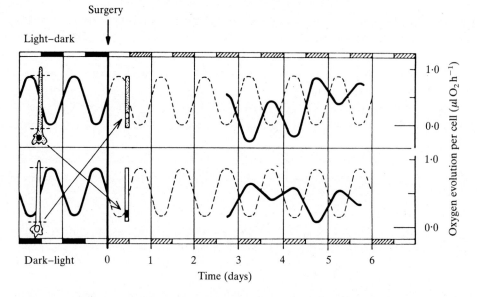

Fig. 6. Nuclear exchange experiment. Two cells of *Acetabularia* entrained to phases different by 180°C were subjected to nuclear exchange on day 0. The periodicity predicted from the data before day 0 is presented by the broken line, experimental data by the bold line (Schweiger *et al.* 1964*b*).

did not produce any effect on the rhythm (Mergenhagen & Schweiger, 1975*b*). The inhibitory effect of cycloheximide and the absence of effect of enucleation, or rifampicin and of chloramphenicol are in agreement with the assumption that if gene expression is involved in the clock it must be at the level of translation on 80 S ribosomes, while the 70 S ribosomes of chloroplasts and mitochondria do not appear to play an essential part in circadian rhythms (Fig. 7).

The observed effect of cycloheximide on the clock does not necessarily mean that it is due to specific inhibition of translation. However, the specificity of the effect was demonstrated by two types of experiments. In the first G418, a translation inhibitor closely related to kanamycin and neomycin, was shown to inhibit the oscillation and,

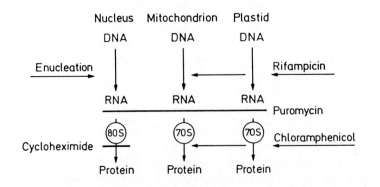

Fig. 7. Effect of different treatments on the circadian photosynthesis rhythm in *Acetabularia*. Bold lines represent inhibition, thin lines no effect.

if given as a pulse, to shift the phase of the circadian rhythm of the oxygen evolution like cycloheximide does. *Acetabularia* cells transformed by a gene construction coding for a neomycin-phosphorylating phosphotransferase served as controls. Transformation was performed by microinjection of the gene construction into an isolated nucleus and reimplantation of the loaded nucleus into an anucleate fragment. Cells were checked for antibiotic resistance by using the antibiotic G418, and for the effect of G418 on the circadian rhythm. In the transformed antibiotic-resistant cells G418 did not affect the rhythm of oxygen evolution while non-transformed cells exhibited the characteristic effect (Schweiger, unpublished data; and Fig. 8). This means that the enzymic phosphorylation of G418 inactivates the effect of the antibiotic on translation as well as on the rhythm.

Another set of experiments was aimed at answering the question whether cycloheximide affects the basic mechanism of the clock or rather the hands. In these experiments pulses of cycloheximide or anisomycin were given at different times in the circadian cycle (Karakashian & Schweiger, 1976*a*,*b*). These pulses resulted in phase shifting. The extent of the phase-shifting effect depended on the time in the cycle when the pulse was given. From these results it was concluded that the antibiotic in fact hits the central mechanism of the clock rather than the hands, and that the central mechanism of the clock has something to do with translation on 80 S ribosomes. Moreover, these experiments have shown that only a limited number of the proteins synthesized on 80 S ribosomes are essential for the clock. This follows from the fact that the phase-shifting effect of the cycloheximide is observed only in a distinct part of the cycle while the rate of synthesis of most of the proteins does not oscillate.

Many experiments on multicellular and also on unicellular organisms suggest that membranes also play a role in the central mechanism of the clock (Eskin, 1972; Sweeney, 1974*a*). This prompted us to suggest the coupled translation–membrane model (Schweiger & Schweiger, 1977; and Fig. 9), which combines the effects

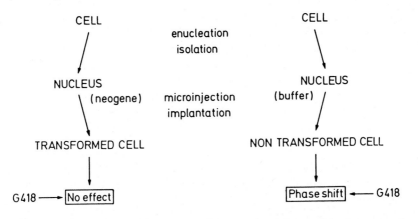

Fig. 8. Expression of antibiotic resistance and the effect of G418 on the circadian photosynthesis rhythm. Transformation of *Acetabularia* cells was performed by micro-injection of a gene coding for an antibiotic-specific phosphotransferase into the isolated nucleus and reimplantation of the loaded nucleus into the cytoplasm.

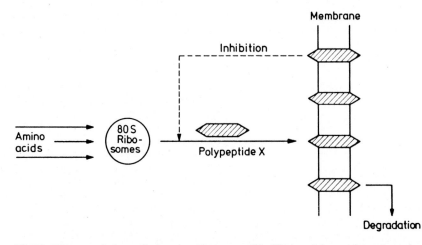

Fig. 9. The coupled translation–membrane model. The model postulates the existence of a polypeptide that is synthesized on 80 S ribosomes and integrated into a membrane. The integrated polypeptide affects the function of the membrane, resulting in inhibition of the production of the polypeptide. Owing to degradation of the essential protein the inhibition is suspended and the polypeptide is synthesized again.

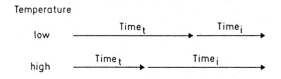

Fig. 10. Temperature compensation and the coupled translation–membrane model. The compensation is based on the fact that at low temperature the time needed for translation (Time$_t$) is longer, the time needed for integration (Time$_i$) is shorter. At high temperature the situation is reversed.

observed for membranes with the translation on 80 S ribosomes described above. This model postulates that one or a few proteins are translated on 80 S ribosomes and are then integrated into a membrane. The integrated protein affects the features of the membrane, in particular permeability and transport, and thereby, perhaps, the concentration of certain ions at the site of translation. This change in the milieu interieur then results in a suspension of the synthesis of the essential protein. The essential protein integrated into the membrane is subjected to turnover, and as soon as a critical threshold is reached the translation of the essential protein is resumed.

The coupled translation–membrane model is in full agreement with relevant results from a number of different experiments. Moreover, it also presents an explanation of how an essential characteristic of circadian rhythms, i.e. temperature compensation, works. The model suggests that two processes are involved that exhibit temperature dependence in opposite ways (Schweiger & Schweiger, 1977; and Fig. 10). The translation of the essential protein on 80 S ribosomes is assumed to be temperature dependent as any normal chemical reaction is known to be, i.e.

within a certain range increasing temperature will increase the rate of synthesis. On the other hand, for the second process, i.e. the integration of the essential protein into the membrane, an increase in temperature would result in a decrease in the rate of integration. This could be due to the fact that the degree of order in the membrane is lower at high temperature. The combination of the two processes would then result in a temperature coefficient near unity. In fact in some cases it is even smaller.

What is the evidence for the coupled translation–membrane model? The role of membranes in the expression of a circadian rhythm has been discussed by a number of authors. In particular, experiments on *Neurospora* have suggested that unsaturated fatty acids play a major role in this phenomenon (Brody & Martins, 1979; Brody, Dieckmann & Mikolajczyk, 1985). On the basis of a variety of experiments, membrane models have been suggested (Njus, Sulzman & Hastings, 1974; Sweeney, 1974*b*). Their major disadvantage is that hardly any experiments can be designed that can prove or disprove the hypothesis. In contrast, the coupled translation–membrane model suggests a clearly circumscribed metabolic pathway as an essential part of the clock and it attributes a definite role to the membranes. Designing experiments is also facilitated because the coupled translation–membrane model does not postulate that the expression of a circadian rhythm is bound to total protein synthesis but rather to the translation of one or a few proteins. These proteins are translated on 80 S ribosomes of the cytosol and are considered to be essential for the clock. Based on all these features, the coupled translation–membrane model permits reasonable experiments to be performed.

Since circadian rhythms represent a ubiquitous phenomenon one may assume that they follow similar rules, i.e. that the underlying mechanisms are similar in different organisms. This assumption is supported by numerous experiments showing that in quite different organisms the basic features of circadian rhythms are similar if not identical (Bünning, 1973). This assumption was corroborated by more recent experiments designed to answer the question whether in other organisms inhibitors of the translation on 80 S ribosomes affect the expression of a circadian rhythm as they do in *Acetabularia*. A second question was whether in these organisms pulses of cycloheximide or similar inhibitors also shift the phase in a characteristic way. In fact, such experiments have been performed in *Aplysia* (Jacklet, 1977), *Gonyaulax* (Dunlap, Taylor & Hastings, 1980; Stahr, Holzapfel & Hardeland, 1980) and also in *Neurospora* (Nakashima, Perlman & Feldman, 1981). They unequivocally demonstrated that in these organisms antibiotics exhibit effects like those observed in *Acetabularia*. These results are in agreement with the assumption that the mechanism underlying circadian rhythms is similar in different organisms.

If the coupled translation–membrane model is correct then there should be one or a few essential proteins that fulfil the requirements of the model, and it should be possible to find a protein whose synthesis exhibits rhythmic changes under constant conditions. This protein should be translated on 80 S ribosomes and the phase of its synthesis should be shifted by cycloheximide pulses in a characteristic way.

In the chloroplast fraction of *Acetabularia* a protein (P 230) has been found that fulfils these requirements (Hartwig, Schweiger, Schweiger & Schweiger, 1985). It has the following characteristics: in sodium dodecyl sulphate (SDS)/polyacrylamide gel electrophoresis the apparent molecular weight of this protein is 230000. Its translation oscillates with a period of about 24 h and reaches a maximum about 3 h after illumination (Fig. 11). The synthesis rhythm can be demonstrated for a number of cycles. The high molecular weight in the presence of SDS suggests that P 230 does not consist of subunits but rather represents a single polypeptide chain. The location of P 230 is not fully understood. Although it is isolated from the stroma fraction it could originate in the membranes of the chloroplasts, as the preparation of this protein includes repeated freezing and thawing steps, which are known to dissolve a number of membranes or membrane-bound proteins.

The oscillatory synthesis of P 230 is in contrast to the behaviour of practically all other proteins in the same preparation. Quantitative measurements of *in vivo* labelling with [^{35}S]methionine were performed by comparing P 230 with other bands obtained by one-dimensional SDS/polyacrylamide gel electrophoresis and autoradiography (Hartwig *et al.* 1985). In two-dimensional polyacrylamide gel electrophoresis, in addition to P 230 whose rate of synthesis reaches a maximum 3 h after illumination, two other proteins were found whose syntheses oscillated and were highest 15 h after illumination. The molecular weights of these proteins were significantly lower than 230000.

If one compares the course of the synthesis of P 230 with the rate of oxygen evolution it appears that the synthesis of P 230 reaches its maximum 3–6 h earlier than the photosynthesis rhythm. It is striking that this difference corresponds quite well to the time predicted for integrating the essential protein into a corresponding membrane (Schweiger & Schweiger, 1977).

The oscillatory synthesis of P 230 could be simulated by differences in the rate of its degradation. Preliminary experiments, however, have indicated that the rate of degradation does not depend on the time in the cycle.

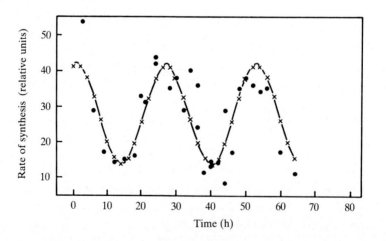

Fig. 11. Circadian rhythm of the synthesis of P 230 in *Acetabularia*. Experimental data (●) and the best-fitting cosine curve (×——×) are given. The rhythmicity is statistically significant (for details, see Hartwig *et al.* 1985).

A fundamental question is how circadian variations in the rate of synthesis of P 230 emerge. Two major possibilities should be considered. They may be caused by regulation at either the transcription or the translation level. Experiments with enucleated cells of *Acetabularia*, however, have demonstrated that the circadian rhythm of the synthesis of P 230 is retained after removal of the nucleus (Hartwig & Schweiger, unpublished data). Therefore, we conclude that the translation of the message for P 230 is rhythmically switched on and off. This is also in accordance with the inhibitor studies discussed above.

It will be of general importance to find out how this regulation is achieved. By using species-specific complementary DNA clones it has been shown that in an anucleate *Acetabularia* cell there is a cytoplasmic storage-pool of mRNA, that the cell is capable of selecting a specific message out of this pool and of putting it onto polysomes (Li-Weber & Schweiger, 1985). It is tempting to assume that once it is positioned on polysomes the mRNA is in fact translated. If so, regulation of translation might occur at the level of selection, transport, binding or initiation.

Similar assumptions could be made for the expression of P 230. Interestingly, such mechanisms might also explain the apparently contradictory results indicating that the cell does not need the nucleus to express a circadian rhythm but that the nucleus is capable of affecting a rhythm. In the light of the capability of the *Acetabularia* cell to perform regulation of gene expression at the translation level (de Groot & Schweiger, 1983), one might assume that in the anucleate cell the message for P 230 originates in the cytoplasmic storage-pool while in the nucleate cell the message is directed to the polysome immediately after transcription (Fig. 12). In both cases, however, the site of regulation would be at the level of selection, transport, binding or initiation.

The fact that the rate of synthesis of P 230 exhibits a circadian rhythm is striking, since essentially all other proteins do not exhibit such oscillations. An important piece of evidence, however, comes from experiments in which pulses of cyclo-heximide were given at different times in the cycle. These experiments demonstrated

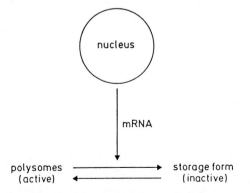

Fig. 12. Two forms of mRNA in the cell. It is suggested that mRNA originating in the nucleus goes onto polysomes or into a storage pool. In the absence of the nucleus mRNA can shuttle between the storage pool and the polysomes (Li-Weber & Schweiger, 1985; Hartwig & Schweiger, unpublished data).

that pulses of cycloheximide can shift the phase and, moreover, that they can also affect the period (Hartwig *et al.* 1985). These effects depended on the timing of the pulse.

Besides P 230, another protein was found in the chloroplast membranes of *Acetabularia* exhibiting peculiar behaviour in the presence and absence of cyclo-heximide and at different temperatures (Leong & Schweiger, 1979). It has an apparent molecular weight of 39000. Its role in the clock is still unknown. The same is true for the enzyme luciferase whose concentration oscillates in a circadian way in the dinoflagellate *Gonyaulax* (Johnson, Roeber & Hastings, 1984).

Genetic studies on circadian rhythms were performed mainly in *Drosophila* (Konopka & Benzer, 1971), *Neurospora* (Feldman & Hoyle, 1973) and *Chlamydomonas* (Bruce, 1974; Mergenhagen, 1980). More recently, the fact that circadian rhythms are inherited has attracted increased attention. Among the features inherited are the ability or inability to express a rhythm, the phase-angle behaviour, and also the length of the period. Since only a limited number, but certainly more than one, gene loci are involved in rhythms (for reviews, see Mergenhagen, 1980; Feldman, 1982) one may conclude that there are only a limited number of gene products. The genes under consideration are nuclear genes since they are inherited biparentally, i.e. in a Mendelian way. An obvious conclusion is that if these genes are translated into proteins this should occur on the 80 S ribosomes of the cytosol. This is in agreement with the coupled translation–membrane model.

Recently, one of the loci involved in the expression of the biological clock in *Drosophila*, the so-called *per* locus (Konopka & Benzer, 1971), has been studied in detail (Bargiello & Young, 1984; Reddy *et al.* 1984). DNA of this locus was prepared by microsurgery and cloned. By introducing DNA sequences of the *per* locus from normal organisms it was possible to convert mutant *Drosophila* with significantly changed periods or arhythmic mutants into insects with normal circadian rhythms (Bargiello, Jackson & Young, 1984; Zehring *et al.* 1984).

If the coupled translation–membrane model is correct and one or only a few essential proteins are directly involved in the basic mechanism of the biological clock, these proteins should be ubiquitous, and with a certain probability their primary structure should be conserved. On the basis of this consideration, DNA sequences from the *per* locus of *Drosophila* were used as probes to search for homologous sequences in other organisms known to exhibit circadian rhythms. Such homology was found in different tissues of a number of animal species (Young, Jackson, Shin & Bargiello, 1985). A striking result was obtained with *Acetabularia* in which homo-logous sequences were also detected (Li-Weber & Schweiger, unpublished data). In this case, however, homologous sequences were not found in the nuclear but in the chloroplast genome. When chloroplast DNA from *Acetabularia* was digested with the restriction enzymes *Eco*RI or *Hind*III, the homologous sequences were found in a band corresponding to 2·0 and $2·5 \times 10^3$ base-pairs, respectively.

The fact that DNA sequences homologous to the nuclear *per* locus of *Drosophila* occur in the chloroplast genome of *Acetabularia* raises the question of how this finding relates to the coupled translation–membrane model. At first glance there seems to be a contradiction as the homologous sequences are not located in the nuclear but in the chloroplast genome. This implies that if these homologous sequences were expressed as proteins, they would be translated on the 70 S ribosomes of the chloroplasts rather than on the 80 S ribosomes of the cytosol. This, of course, is apparently not in agreement with the coupled translation–membrane model and with the results obtained with *Acetabularia*. However, one may ask whether this consideration is conclusive or whether there are any alternative explanations.

A possible resolution of the apparent contradiction between the results obtained with *Acetabularia* and the results obtained with *Drosophila* may lie in the special features of the *Acetabularia* chloroplast genome. The *Acetabularia* plastome is significantly different from other chloroplast genomes, at least those that have been studied to date (Tymms & Schweiger, 1985). This is true not only for plastomes from higher plants but also from algae.

Recent experiments have indicated that the chloroplast genome of *Acetabularia* represents an ancient phase of symbiosis between a eukaryotic host cell and a prokaryotic photosynthesizing and highly autonomous organism, in contrast to the fully integrated chloroplasts of higher plants. The ancient situation is underlined by the size of the chloroplast genome, which in *Acetabularia* is at least four- to fivefold that of the chloroplast genome in higher plants (Woodcock & Bogorad, 1970), but much smaller than the genome of a putative precursor like *Cyanobacterium*. Moreover, there is evidence that during evolution at least one gene has been translocated from the chloroplast to the nuclear genome (de Groot & Schweiger, 1984). In the Dasycladaceae, in particular in *Acetabularia*, we apparently face a situation where these processes have not been completed and where we still find genes in the chloroplast genome that in higher plants are located in the nuclear genome.

The apparent incompatibility of the coupled translation–membrane model and the homology between the *per* locus of *Drosophila* and the chloroplast genome of *Acetabularia* may be overcome in the following way. P 230, which in accordance with the model is supposed to be an essential clock protein and to which a highly specialized function in the membrane is attributed, may be strongly affected by the microenvironment. The two major components of the microenvironment in the membrane are lipids and proteins. As discussed above, the lipid moeity of the membranes may play a substantial role in the expression of circadian rhythms. A change in their composition may affect the putative essential clock protein and may give rise to a change in the period. In a similar way neighbouring proteins could exert an influence on the structure and function of the essential protein. If the putative gene product of the *per* locus is a protein located in the neighbourhood of the essential clock protein a change in the primary sequence, for instance by mutation, might affect the function of the essential protein. Thus a protein like the putative product of the *per* locus without itself being an essential clock protein could affect the clock function. In contrast to the essential protein, such a near-neighbour protein could but does not necessarily have to be coded by the nuclear genome and translated on 80 S ribosomes. In *Acetabularia* such a protein could still be coded in the chloroplast genome, while in *Drosophila* it is coded in the nuclear genome.

At present such considerations are pure speculations, but experiments can be designed that might help us to solve this problem. An important step in this direction would be to determine the exact localization of P 230 in the cell, but this requires purified protein. The problems connected with the purification of an extremely high molecular weight polypeptide from an organism like *Acetabularia* cannot be overestimated. Unfortunately, at present the most reliable way to prove its existence and to study its behaviour is by labelling P 230 with radioactive precursors.

Once P230 is purified it should be possible to raise antibodies to it and at least partially sequence the protein. Antibodies might help to localize the protein in the cell. Antibodies or partial sequences of the protein might permit the separation of the corresponding mRNA. It will also be interesting to clone and perhaps to express the 2·0 or 2·5 $(\times 10^3)$ base-pair DNA fragment of the chloroplast genome of *Acetabularia* homologous to the *per* locus from *Drosophila*. Localization of the putative gene product might answer the question of whether it is in the neighbourhood of P 230.

Over the last few years the molecular mechanism of circadian rhythm has been open to a number of promising experimental approaches. This reflects real progress, as a couple of years ago some experts in the field were not even certain that a molecular basis for this phenomenon existed at all.

There are some practical reasons for trying to understand the phenomenon of circadian rhythms. Although most of the work on the molecular mechanism underlying circadian rhythms has been done on unicellular organisms it should not divert attention from the fact that this phenomenon also occurs in multicellular organisms and in particular in human beings.

As pointed out above, unicellular organisms exhibit a number of circadian rhythms and these rhythms can be demonstrated and studied in an individual cell. Starting from the question of how in an individual cell the different oscillations are coupled to each other, one may ask how this coupling is related to other features of circadian rhythms like the ability to become entrained and whether the characteristic phase-shifting effect of perturbations of the rhythms can be explained by the coupled translation–membrane model, whether cells can communicate with each other in this context (Mergenhagen & Schweiger, 1974) and, if so, how this 'cross-talk' is done.

This type of question should also be extended to multicellular organisms. Again one may ask whether there are special mechanisms, on the basis of cell–cell interactions, that participate in the temporal organization of multicellular organisms and affect biological rhythms. Finally, the role of humoral pathways and neural mechanisms in the expression of biological rhythms in multicellular organisms should also be explored.

Progress in our undertanding of how rhythms work leads to the use of chronobiological approaches to solving numerous problems in biology and medicine. Some of these problems are of extremely practical importance. For example, an important field is chemotherapy. Chemotherapy is usually performed with toxic substances and a major problem is to separate the toxic from the therapeutic effect.

Chronobiology may be able to separate the two effects at the temporal level. Evidence is accumulating that toxicity of drugs oscillates in a circadian way (Scheving, 1980). The same is true for therapeutic effects (Reinberg, 1983). On the basis of this knowledge, many drugs are now being studied in order to find a time in the cycle when the ratio of the therapeutic to the toxic effects reaches its maximum. With that knowledge it should be possible to increase the dose without increasing the risk, and decrease the risk without decreasing the therapeutic effect. Manipulation of the rhythm, for example by entrainment and, or, phase shifting based on the knowledge of the mechanisms underlying circadian rhythms, might develop into a useful tool.

We gratefully appreciate the careful and critical reading of the manuscript by Mrs Barbara Gernert. We thank Mrs Christiane Schardt for typing the manuscript and Dr Gunther Neuhaus for preparing the photographs.

REFERENCES

ASCHOFF, J. (1960). Exogenous and endogenous components in circadian rhythms. *Cold Spring Harbor Symp. quant. Biol.* **25**, 11–28.

ASCHOFF, J., ed. (1965a). *Circadian Clocks.* Amsterdam: North-Holland.

ASCHOFF, J. (1965b). Response curves in circadian periodicity. In *Circadian Clocks* (ed. J. Aschoff), pp. 95–111. Amsterdam: North-Holland.

ASCHOFF, J. (1970). Circadiane Periodik als Grundlage des Schlaf-Wach-Rhythmus. In *Ermüdung, Schlaf, Traum* (ed. W. Baust), pp. 55–98. Stuttgart: Wiss. Verlagsgesellschaft.

BARGIELLO, T. A., JACKSON, F. R. & YOUNG, W. Y. (1984). Restoration of circadian behavioural rhythms by gene transfer in *Drosophila. Nature, Lond.* **312**, 752–754.

BARGIELLO, T. A. & YOUNG, W. Y. (1984). Molecular genetics of a biological clock in *Drosophila. Proc. natn. Acad. Sci. U.S.A.* **81**, 2142–2146.

BIERHUIZEN, J. F. (1972). *Circadian Rhythmicity.* Wageningen: Centre for Agricultural Publishing and Documentation.

BRINKMANN, K. (1966). Temperatureinflüsse auf die circadiane Periodik von *Euglena gracilis* bei Mixotrophie und Auxotrophie. *Planta* **70**, 344–389.

BRODA, H. & SCHWEIGER, H. G. (1980). Long-term measurements of the electrical potential along an *Acetabularia* cell reveals an endogenous diurnal rhythm. *Eur. J. Cell Biol.* **22**, 497.

BRODA, H. & SCHWEIGER, H. G. (1981). Long-term measurements of three rhythmic-parameters in *Acetabularia. Protoplasma* **105**, 352–353.

BRODA, H., SCHWEIGER, G. KOOP, H. U., SCHMID, R. & SCHWEIGER, H. G. (1979). Chloroplast migration; a method for continuously monitoring a circadian rhythm in a single cell of *Acetabularia.* In *Developmental Biology of Acetabularia* (ed. S. Bonotto, V. Kefeli & S. Puiseux-Dao), pp. 163–168.

BRODY, S., DIECKMANN, C. & MIKOLAJCZYK, S. (1985). Circadian rhythms in *Neurospora crassa*: the effects of point mutations on the proteolipid portion of the mitochondrial ATP synthetase. *Mol. gen. Genet.* **200**, 155–161.

BRODY, S. & MARTINS, S. A. (1979). Circadian rhythms in *Neurospora crassa*: effects of unsaturated fatty acids. *J. Bact.* **137**, 912–915.

BRUCE, V. G. (1960). Environmental entrainment of circadian rhythms. *Cold Spring Harbor Symp. quant. Biol.* **25**, 29–48.

BRUCE, V. G. (1970). The biological clock in *Chlamydomonas reinhardi. J. Protozool.* **17**, 328–334.

BRUCE, V. G. (1974). Recombinants between clock mutants of *Chlamydomonas reinhardi. Genetics* **77**, 221–230.

BÜNNING, E. (1973). *The Physiological Clock. Circadian Rhythms and Biological Chronometry.* Berlin: Springer-Verlag.

CHOVNIK, A. (1960). Biological clock. *Cold Spring Harbor Symp. quant. Biol.* **25**, 1–514.

DE GROOT, E. J. & SCHWEIGER, H. G. (1983). Thymidylate kinase from *Acetabularia*. II. Regulation during the life cycle. *J. Cell Sci.* **64**, 27–36.

DE GROOT, E. J. & SCHWEIGER, H. G. (1984). Possible translocation of a gene for thymidylate kinase from the chloroplast to the nuclear genome during evolution. *J. Cell Sci.* **72**, 15–21.

DUNLAP, J. C., TAYLOR, W. & HASTINGS, J. W. (1980). The effect of protein synthesis inhibitors on the *Gonyaulax* clock. I. Phase-shifting effects of cycloheximide. *J. comp. Physiol.* **138**, 1–8.

EHRET, C. F. & TRUCCO, E. (1967). Molecular models for the circadian clock. *J. theor. Biol.* **15**, 240–262.

ESKIN, A. (1972). Phase shifting a circadian rhythm in the eye of *Aplysia* by high potassium-pulses. *J. comp. Physiol.* **80**, 353–376.

FELDMAN, J. F. (1982). Genetic approaches to circadian clocks. *A. Rev. Pl. Physiol.* **33**, 583–608.

FELDMAN, J. F. & HOYLE, M. N. (1973). Isolation of circadian clock mutants of *Neurospora crassa*. *Genetics* **75**, 605–613.

GOTO, K., LAVAL-MARTIN, D. L. & EDMUNDS, L. N. (1985). Biochemical modeling of an autonomously oscillatory circadian clock in *Euglena*. *Science* **228**, 1284–1288.

HALBERG, F. (1960). Temporal coordination of physiologic function. *Cold Spring Harbor Symp. quant. Biol.* **25**, 289–310.

HALBERG, F., RATTE, J., KÜHL, J. F.W., NAJARIAN, J., POPOVIC, V., SHIOTSUKA, R., CHIBA, Y., CUTKOMP, L. & HAUS, E. (1974). Rhythmes circaseptidiens – environ 7 jours – synchronisés ou non avec la semaine sociale. *C.r. hebd. Séanc. Acad. Sci., Paris* **278**, 2675–2678.

HARTWIG, R., SCHWEIGER, R., SCHWEIGER, M. & SCHWEIGER, H. G. (1985). Identification of a high molecular weight polypeptide that may be part of the circadian clockwork in *Acetabularia*. *Proc. natn. Acad. Sci. U.S.A.* **82**, 6899–6902.

HASTINGS, J. W. (1970). Cellular–biochemical clock hypothesis. In *The Biological Clock* (ed. F. A. Brown, Jr, J. W. Hastings, & J. D. Palmer), pp. 63–91. New York: Academic Press.

HASTINGS, J. W. & SCHWEIGER, H. G. (1976). *The Molecular Basis of Circadian Rhythms*. Berlin: Dahlem Konferenzen.

HAYES, D. K., HALBERG, F., CORNELISSEN, G. & SHANKARAIAH, K. (1986). Frequency response of the face fly (*Musca autumnalis, Diptera muscidae*) to lighting schedule shifts after varied intervals. *Ann. ent. Soc. Am.* (in press).

HILDEBRANDT, G. (1967). Die Koordination rhythmischer Funktionen beim Menschen. *Verh. dt. Ges. inn. Med.* **73**, 921–941.

JACKLET, J. (1977). Neuronal circadian rhythms: phase shifting by a protein synthesis inhibitor. *Science* **198**, 69–71.

JOHNSON, C. H., ROEBER, J. F. & HASTINGS, J. W. (1984). Circadian changes in enzyme concentration account for rhythm of enzyme activity in *Gonyaulax*. *Science* **223**, 1428–1430.

KARAKASHIAN, M. W. & SCHWEIGER, H. G. (1976a). Evidence for a cycloheximide-sensitive component in the biological clock of *Acetabularia*. *Expl Cell Res.* **98**, 302–312.

KARAKASHIAN, M. W. & SCHWEIGER, H. G. (1976b). Temperature dependence of cycloheximide-sensitive phase circadian cycle in *Acetabularia mediterranea*. *Proc. natn. Acad. Sci. U.S.A.* **73**, 3216–3219.

KLOPPSTECH, K. & SCHWEIGER, H. G. (1982). Stability of poly(A)$^+$ RNA in nucleate and anucleate cells of *Acetabularia*. *Pl. Cell Rep.* **1**, 165–167.

KONOPKA, R. J. & BENZER, S. (1971). Clock mutants of *Drosophila melanogaster*. *Proc. natn. Acad. Sci. U.S.A.* **68**, 2112–2116.

LEONG, T. Y. & SCHWEIGER, H. G. (1979). The role of chloroplast-membrane-protein synthesis in the circadian clock. Purification and partial characterization of a polypeptide which is suggested to be involved in the clock. *Eur. J. Biochem.* **98**, 187–194.

LI-WEBER & SCHWEIGER, H. G. (1985). Evidence for and mechanism of translational control during cell differentiation in *Acetabularia*. *Eur. J. Cell Biol.* **38**, 73–78.

MENAKER, M. (1971). *Biochronometry*. Washington, DC: National Academy of Sciences.

MERGENHAGEN, D. (1980). Circadian rhythms in unicellular organisms. *Curr. Top. Microbiol. Immun.* **90**, 123–147.

MERGENHAGEN, D. & SCHWEIGER, H. G. (1973). Recording the oxygen production of a single *Acetabularia* cell for a prolonged period. *Expl Cell Res.* **81**, 360–364.

MERGENHAGEN, D. & SCHWEIGER, H. G. (1974). Circadian rhythmicity: does intercellular synchronization occur in *Acetabularia*? *Sci. Lett.* **3**, 387–389.

MERGENHAGEN, D. & SCHWEIGER, H. G. (1975*a*). Circadian rhythm of oxygen evolution in cell fragments of *Acetabularia mediterranea. Expl Cell Res.* **92**, 127–130.

MERGENHAGEN, D. & SCHWEIGER, H. G. (1975*b*). The effect of different inhibitors of transcription and translation on the expression and control of circadian rhythm in individual cells of *Acetabularia. Expl Cell Res.* **94**, 321–326.

MILLS, J. N. (1973). *Biological Aspects of Circadian Rhythms.* London: Plenum Press.

MOORE-EDE, M. C., SULZMAN, F. M. & FULLER, C. A. (1982). *The Clocks That Time Us.* Cambridge, MA: Harvard University Press.

NAKASHIMA, H., PERLMAN, J. & FELDMAN, J. F. (1981). Cycloheximide-induced phase shifting of circadian clock of *Neurospora. Am. J. Physiol.* **241**, R31–R35.

NJUS, D., SULZMAN, F. M. & HASTINGS, J. W. (1974). Membrane model for the circadian clock. *Nature, Lond.* **248**, 116–120.

NOVAK, B. & SIRONVAL, C. (1976). Circadian rhythm of the transcellular current in regenerating enucleated posterior stalk segment of *Acetabularia mediterranea. Pl. Sci. Lett.* **6**, 273–283.

PITTENDRIGH, C. S. (1981). Circadian systems: entrainment. In *Handbook of Behavioural Neurobiology*, vol. 4 (ed. J. Aschoff), pp. 95–124. New York: Plenum Press.

POHL, R. (1948). Tagesrhythmus im phototaktischen Verhalten der *Euglena gracilis. Z. Naturf.* **3B**, 367–374.

REDDY, P., ZEHRING, W. A., WHEELER, D. A., PIRROTTA, V., HADFIELD, C., HALL, J. C. & ROSBASH, M. (1984). Molecular analysis of the period locus in *Drosophila melanogaster* and identification of a transcript involved in biological rhythms. *Cell* **38**, 701–710.

REINBERG, A. (1983). Clinical chronopharmacology: an experimental basis for chronotherapy. In *Biological Rhythms and Medicine* (ed. A. Reinberg & M. H. Smolensky), pp. 211–263. New York: Springer.

REINBERG, A. & SMOLENSKY, M. H. (1983). *Biological Rhythms and Medicine.* New York: Springer.

RENSING, L. & JAEGER, N. I. (1985). *Temporal Order.* Berlin: Springer.

SCHEVING, L. E. (1980). Chronotoxicology in general and experimental chronotherapeutics of cancer. In *Chronobiology: Principles and Applications to Shifts in Schedules* (ed. L. E. Scheving & F. Halberg), pp. 455–479. Alphen aan den Rijn: Sijthoff & Noordhoff International Publishers B.V.

SCHEVING, L. E. & HALBERG, F. (1980). In *Chronobiology: Principles and Applications to Shifts in Schedules.* Alphen aan den Rijn: Sijthoff & Noordhoff International Publishers B.V.

SCHWEIGER, H. G. (1980). The role of cytoplasmic control of circadian rhythms. In *Chronobiology: Principles and Applications to Shifts in Schedules* (ed. L. E. Scheving & F. Halberg), pp. 239–247. Alphen aan den Rijn: Sijthoff & Noordhoff International Publishers B.V.

SCHWEIGER, H. G., BRODA, H., WOLFF, D. & SCHWEIGER, G. (1983). A method for the simultaneous long-term recording of oxygen evolution and chloroplast migration in an individual cells of *Acetabularia.* In *Polarographic Oxygen Sensors, Aquatic and Physiological Applications* (ed. E. Ganiger & H. Forstner), pp. 190–194. Berlin: Springer-Verlag.

SCHWEIGER, H. G. & HALBERG, F. (1982). Can a unicell measure the week, an isolated cytoplasm measure half a week? *Notiziario Soc. ital. Biochim. clin.* **6**, 525–526.

SCHWEIGER, H. G. & SCHWEIGER, M. (1977). Circadian rhythms in unicellular organisms: an endeavour to explain the molecular mechanism. *Int. Rev. Cytol.* **51**, 315–342.

SCHWEIGER, E., WALLRAFF, H. G. & SCHWEIGER, H. G. (1964*a*). Über tagesperiodische Schwankungen der Sauerstoffbilanz kernhaltiger und kernloser *Acetabularia mediterranea. Z. Naturf.* **19b**, 499–505.

SCHWEIGER, E., WALLRAFF, H. G. & SCHWEIGER, H. G. (1964*b*) Endogenous circadian rhythm in cytoplasm of *Acetabularia*: influence of the nucleus. *Science* **146**, 658–659.

STAHR, N., HOLZAPFEL, G. & HARDELAND, R. (1980). Phase shifting of the *Gonyaulax* clock by puromycin. *J. Interdiscipl. Cycle Res.* **11**, 277–284.

SWEENEY, B. M. (1969). *Rhythmic Phenomena in Plants.* London: Academic Press.

SWEENEY, B. M. (1974*a*). The potassium content of *Gonyaulax polyedra* and phase changes in the circadian rhythm of stimulated bioluminescence by short exposure to ethanol and valinomycin. *Pl. Physiol.* **53**, 337–342.

SWEENEY, B. M. (1974*b*). A physiological model for circadian rhythms derived from the *Acetabularia* rhythm paradox. *Int. J. Chronobiol.* **2**, 25–33.

SWEENEY, B. M. & HASTINGS, J. W. (1960). Effects of temperature upon diurnal rhythms. *Cold Spring Harbor Symp. quant. Biol.* **25**, 145–148.

SWEENEY, B. M. & HAXO, F. T. (1961). Persistence of a photosynthetic rhythm in enucleated *Acetabularia. Science* **134**, 1361–1363.

TYMMS, M. J. & SCHWEIGER, H. G. (1985). Tandemly repeated non-ribosomal DNA sequences in the chloroplast genome of an *Acetabularia mediterranea* strain. *Proc. natn. Acad. Sci. U.S.A.* **82**, 1706–1710.

VAN DEN DRIESSCHE, T. & HARS, R. (1966). Circadian rhythms in *Acetabularia*: photosynthetic capacity and chloroplast shape. *Expl Cell Res.* **42**, 18–30.

WALLRAFF, H. G., SCHWEIGER, E., CAIRNS, W. C., WOLFF, D. & SCHWEIGER, H. G. (1977). Improved procedure for processing of circadian rhythm data from individual cells of *Acetabularia.* In *Progress in* Acetabularia *Research* (ed. C. L. F. Woodcock), pp. 331–338. New York: Academic Press.

WOODCOCK, C. F. & BOGORAD, L. (1970). Evidence for variation in the quantity of DNA among plastids of *Acetabularia. J. Cell Biol.* **44**, 361–375.

YOUNG, M. W., JACKSON, F. R., SHIN, H. S. & BARGIELLO, T. A. (1985). A biological clock in *Drosophila. Cold Spring Harbor Symp. quant. Biol.* (abstracts) p. 103.

ZEHRING, W. A., WHEELER, D. A., REDDY, P., KONOPKA, R. J., KYRIACOU, C. P., ROSBASH, M., HALL, J. C. (1984). P-element transformation with period locus DNA restores rhythmicity to mutant, arythmic *Drosophila melanogaster. Cell* **39**, 369–376.

J. Cell Sci. Suppl. 4, 201–219 (1986)
Printed in Great Britain © The Company of Biologists Limited 1986

INTER-RELATION OF CELL ADHESION AND DIFFERENTIATION IN *DICTYOSTELIUM DISCOIDEUM*

GÜNTHER GERISCH

Max-Planck-Institut für Biochemie, D-8033 Martinsried, West Germany

INTRODUCTION

During the development of *Dictyostelium discoideum* single cells aggregate to form a multicellular organism. The change from the single cell state to multi-cellularity is mediated by chemotactic cell movement and intercellular adhesion. *Dictyostelium* represents a side branch in the evolution of multicellular organization in eukaryotes. Therefore, the general importance of any work done in *Dictyostelium* will be measured by its applicability to other biological systems. Similarities be-tween the adhesion system of *D. discoideum* and those acting during embryonic development of vertebrates demonstrate that research in a 'simple' microorganism like *Dictyostelium* can provide a basis for studies in more complex organisms. In this survey, the adhesion system of aggregating cells and its regulation during development is taken as a platform from which to outline problems to be solved in the future.

TARGET SITES OF ADHESION BLOCKING Fab: CANDIDATES FOR CELL ADHESION MOLECULES

Several methods have been employed for the identification of cell surface com-ponents that mediate intercellular adhesion. One method is to deplete cells of certain components of the adhesion system, to purify the extracted components, and to reconstitute adhesiveness by readdition of these constituents to the non-adhesive cells (Lilien & Moscona, 1967; Noll *et al.* 1979). This method is easily applicable in cases in which an intercellular material forms a bridge between cells by interacting non-covalently with components anchored in the plasma membrane, and proved to be particularly useful in analysing the species-specific adhesion systems of the marine sponges *Haliclona* and *Microciona* (Humphreys, 1963; Misevic *et al.* 1982). A second principle by which an adhesion system can be analysed is to replace one of the interacting cells with a chemically defined surface. Thus cells will adhere *via* carbohydrate-binding sites on their surfaces to polyacrylamide gels derivatized with specific sugars (Schnaar *et al.* 1978). A third, more indirect method is to produce antisera against cell membrane antigens, to test the adhesion blocking activity of Fab prepared from these sera (Beug *et al.* 1970, 1973), and to purify membrane com-ponents that neutralize the blocking Fab (Huesgen & Gerisch, 1975; Müller &

Gerisch, 1978; for summary of the work on vertebrates, see Edelman, 1985). The target antigens of adhesion blocking Fab are candidates for molecules that mediate cell-to-cell adhesion.

The Fab neutralization method has limitations that relate to the size of the Fab molecule (which is roughly an ellipsoid of 6 nm length and 4 nm diameter), and to the possible cross-reactivity of target sites. Because of its size, Fab is hardly applicable as a probe for those substructures on cell-surface molecules whose interaction is responsible for cell adhesion. Thus it might not be feasible to determine whether oligosaccharide residues of a glycoprotein are directly involved in contact formation. Cross-reactivity between carbohydrate chains linked to different proteins causes another problem. When antisera are used that contain primarily anti-carbohydrate antibodies against a glycoprotein involved in cell adhesion, any other glycoprotein carrying carbohydrate residues with similar epitopes will neutralize the Fab from these antisera.

After having identified candidates for cell adhesion molecules by the Fab neutralization method it is necessary to prove their actual function in cell-to-cell adhesion. This can be done by incorporation of purified proteins into liposomes (Hoffman & Edelman, 1983) or by selecting mutants specifically defective in either these proteins or in carbohydrate residues linked to them. This is easily possible in *D. discoideum*, as will be shown in later sections.

DISTINCT EDTA-STABLE AND EDTA-SENSITIVE CELL ADHESION IN AGGREGATING *D. DISCOIDEUM* CELLS

Growth phase cells of *D. discoideum* form only EDTA-sensitive contacts, whereas aggregation-competent cells form EDTA-stable contacts in addition to the sensitive ones (Gerisch, 1961). At the time of this change in adhesiveness the cells acquire the capacity to aggregate into streams of end-to-end associated cells. Only cells capable of forming the EDTA-stable contacts are capable of sorting out by species-specific adhesion from cells of another species, *Polysphondylium pallidum* (Bozzaro & Gerisch, 1978; Gerisch *et al.* 1980). EDTA-labile as well as EDTA-stable contacts can be blocked independently by Fab of appropriate specificity (Beug *et al.* 1973). It is also possible to block cell adhesion of both types by the same Fab, which is the case if the cell surface components involved carry common epitopes such as carbohydrate structures (M. Yoshida & G. Gerisch, unpublished). From membranes of aggregation-competent cells an $80 \times 10^3 M_r$ glycoprotein, designated contact site A (csA), has been purified that is specifically expressed in aggregation-competent cells. This glycoprotein neutralizes the Fab species that block the EDTA-stable adhesion from polyspecific antisera against total membranes (Müller & Gerisch, 1978). In growth-phase cells a $126 \times 10^3 M_r$ glycoprotein has been identified as a target site of Fab that blocks the EDTA-labile type of cell adhesion (Chadwick & Garrod, 1983).

Results similar to those for *D. discoideum* have been obtained with cell adhesion systems involved in vertebrate embryogenesis. Mouse embryonic and teratocarcinoma cells can simultaneously operate two independent types of intercellular adhesion, a Ca^{2+} requiring and a Ca^{2+} independent one (Takeichi *et al.* 1979). As in

D. discoideum, the two types of cell adhesion differ in their specificity, and one can be blocked independently from the other by Fab of an adequate specificity (Takeichi *et al.* 1981; Shirayoshi *et al.* 1983).

A feature of cell aggregation in *D. discoideum* that is related to the dual nature of its adhesion system is the composite pattern of cell assembly. Specifically, if the EDTA-labile cell adhesion is blocked by Fab, the cells assemble preferentially end-to-end into chains or rosettes (Beug *et al.* 1973). Blockage of the EDTA-stable, csA-mediated cell adhesion results in a more irregular pattern of assembly since the EDTA-labile cell adhesion often causes the cells to associate through lateral extensions (Fig. 1). The restriction of a certain type of cell adhesion to a limited area of the cell surface is comparable to cell adhesion mediated by N-CAM in neurones of the chicken embryo. It is specifically the lateral association of outgrowing nerve fibres that is blocked by Fab against N-CAM (Rutishauser *et al.* 1978).

A problem left for future study is the relationship between cell shape and local cell adhesion. The end-to-end adhesion of the cylindrical aggregating cells is amenable to rapid changes when the polarity of a cell is changed by its reorientation in a cyclic-AMP gradient (Fig. 2). This observation suggests that cell adhesion sites interact, through the membrane, with the cytoskeleton, which determines cell shape, and are regulated in their activity by this interaction. The question of how adhesiveness is regulated is therefore linked to the question of how cell shape and oriented cell movement are controlled. Changes in the degree of myosin phosphorylation (Rahmsdorf *et al.* 1978; Berlot *et al.* 1985), which regulates polymerization of myosin into filaments (Kuczmarski & Spudich, 1980), in the localization of poly-merized myosin within the cell (Yumura & Fukui, 1985), and in the quantity of membrane-associated actin (McRobbie & Newell, 1984), have been observed in cells stimulated with the chemoattractant, cyclic-AMP.

These observations need to be fitted into a consistent picture of how the cytoskeleton is organized and how its local activities are coordinately regulated in a moving amoeboid cell. In this approach mutants will be of great help in reducing complexity. This might be of importance because the cytoskeleton appears to consist of more components than are required for its actual function. In other words, there are non-essential proteins that, like the actin crosslinker α-actinin or the actin-severing protein severin, can be eliminated by mutation without severe effects on cell shape and motility (Wallraff *et al.* 1986). These proteins may serve as 'double insurance' components by supplementing other proteins of similar functions. For the experimental analysis of cell functions double insurance systems are a handicap, since two proteins have to be eliminated together before a functional defect is seen. It should be the aim to create 'minimal complexity' mutants that contain only the proteins absolutely necessary for functioning of the cells under standardized laboratory conditions.

CONSTITUENTS AND BIOSYNTHESIS OF THE CONTACT SITE A GLYCOPROTEIN

The csA glycoprotein with an apparent molecular weight of $80 \times 10^3 M_r$ is modified by phosphorylation at serine residues (Coffman *et al.* 1982; Schmidt & Loomis,

1982) and by fatty acid acylation (Stadler *et al.* 1984). Its carbohydrate moieties contain D-mannose, *N*-acetylglucosamine, L-fucose and probably D-glucose (Müller *et al.* 1979). Two types of carbohydrate residues can be distinguished. Type 2 carbohydrate reacts strongly with wheat germ agglutinin (Yoshida *et al.* 1984), type 1 carbohydrate with concanavalin A (H.-P. Hohmann, unpublished data). Furthermore, type 1 carbohydrate is distinguished from type 2 carbohydrate by its

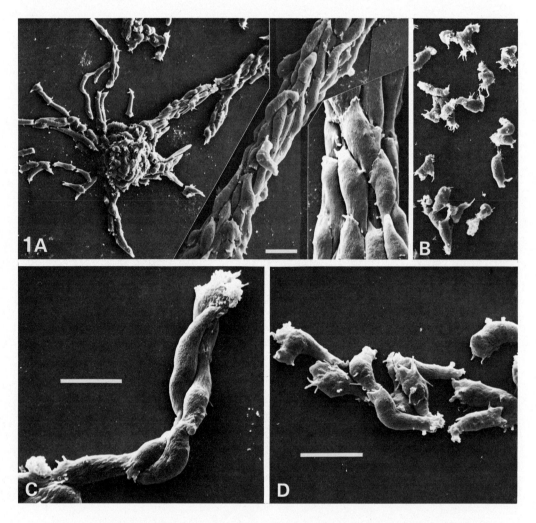

Fig. 1. A. Cells moving towards centres and forming streams during normal aggregation, shown at various powers of magnification. On the right, end-to-end adhesion and adhesion by lateral extensions is clearly seen. B. Cells of the aggregation stage dissociated by polyspecific Fab against total membranes of aggregation-competent cells. C. Cells forming end-to-end adhesions in the presence of Fab against membranes of growth phase cells. D. Cells forming irregular assemblies in the presence of Fab against total membranes of aggregation-competent cells, which has been absorbed with growth-phase cells. This Fab reacts primarily with the developmentally regulated csA glycoprotein (Gerisch *et al.* 1985*a*). Scanning EM photographs by R. Guggenheim, Basel; from Gerisch *et al.* (1980). Bars, 10 μm.

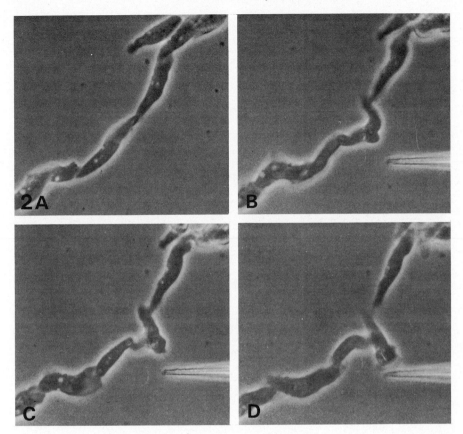

Fig. 2. End-to-end adhesion of aggregating *D. discoideum* cells (A) and subsequent stages of polarity change and disconnection of a cell exposed to a gradient of cyclic AMP (B–D). The chemoattractant has been applied through a micropipette filled with 1×10^{-4} M-cyclic-AMP, according to Gerisch *et al.* (1975a). Experiment performed together with D. Hülser, Stuttgart.

sulphation *in vivo* as well as in a cell-free system (Stadler *et al.* 1983; Hohmann *et al.* 1985). Type 2 carbohydrate is highly immunogenic in rabbits and mice. It is recognized by a series of monoclonal antibodies that cross-react to various extents with other glycoproteins. These different cross-reactivities mean that type 2 carbohydrate of the csA glycoprotein shares various epitopes with quite a number of other glycoproteins, whereas certain other epitopes of the type 2 oligosaccharide chains are more specific for the csA glycoprotein (Bertholdt *et al.* 1985).

In membrane fractions containing rough endoplasmic reticulum or Golgi membranes a glycoprotein that has an apparent molecular weight of $68 \times 10^3 M_r$ is enriched (Fig. 3). This glycoprotein is recognized by monoclonal antibodies against the polypeptide portion of the csA glycoprotein. It carries only type 1 carbohydrate and is degraded by glycosidases F or H into a $53 \times 10^3 M_r$ protein (Hohmann *et al.* 1985). The type 1 carbohydrate appears to be cotranslationally and *N*-glycosidically linked to the protein core. The $68 \times 10^3 M_r$ glycoprotein is a precursor that is converted in the Golgi apparatus into the mature $80 \times 10^3 M_r$ glycoprotein by sulphation of its type 1 carbohydrate residues and by attachment of type 2 carbohydrate. Stability of its linkage to β-elimination suggests that type 2 carbohydrate is N-glycosidically linked, although the Golgi apparatus would be an unusual site for N-glycosylation (H.-P. Hohmann, unpublished data).

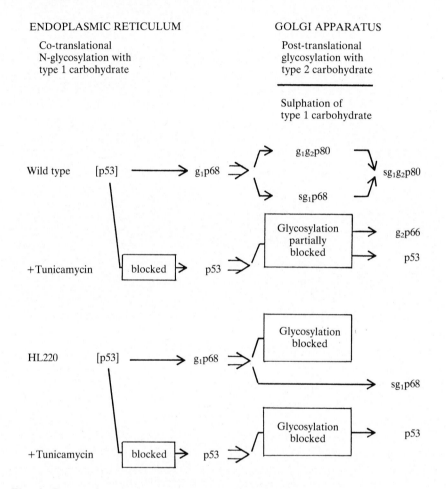

Fig. 3. Proposed steps of glycosylation and sulphation of the csA glycoprotein in wild-type and in mutant HL220 defective in type 2 glycosylation. The blocker of N-glycosylation, tunicamycin, inhibits preferentially type 1 glycosylation. Tunicamycin treated wild-type cells produce a $66 \times 10^3 M_r$ glycoprotein that carries only type 2 carbohydrate and a $53 \times 10^3 M_r$ protein that lacks both type 1 and type 2 carbohydrate. Tunicamycin-treated cells of the mutant produce only the $53 \times 10^3 M_r$ protein. The intermediates and the final product are designated by their apparent molecular masses ($\times 10^{-3}$) with the prefix p for protein and by symbols for their modifications: g_1, glycosylated with type 1 carbohydrate; g_2, glycosylated with type 2 carbohydrate; s, sulphated (on type 1 carbohydrate). The mature contact site A glycoprotein carries all these modifications. The unmodified $53 \times 10^3 M_r$ protein of non-tunicamycin-treated cells is in brackets because it was not detectable by antibody labelling. Slightly modified from Hohmann et al. (1985).

Using monoclonal antibodies against type 2 carbohydrate as a probe, mutants defective in type 2 glycosylation have been selected (Murray *et al.* 1984; Loomis *et al.* 1985). In these mutants the $68 \times 10^3 M_r$ precursor is the end-product of csA biosynthesis (Yoshida *et al.* 1984; Gerisch *et al.* 1985a). These mutants produce relatively little of the $68 \times 10^3 M_r$ glycoprotein as compared to the production of the $80 \times 10^3 M_r$ glycoprotein in the wild type, and labelling of cells with antibodies shows that only a fraction of the $68 \times 10^3 M_r$ glycoprotein appears on the cell surface (H.-P. Hohmann & S. Bozzaro, unpublished data). These results suggest that type 2 carbohydrate is required for effective transport of the protein to the plasma membrane, and they suggest that $68 \times 10^3 M_r$ glycoprotein that has been led astray is degraded intracellularly (H.-P. Hohmann, S. Bozzaro & G. Gerisch, unpublished data). EDTA-stable cell adhesion has been reported to be detectable but weak under conditions in which some $68 \times 10^3 M_r$ glycoprotein is expressed in the mutants (Gerisch *et al.* 1985a), or to be lacking under conditions where the $68 \times 10^3 M_r$ glycoprotein remains undetectable (Loomis *et al.* 1985; West & Loomis, 1985). These results suggest that the protein equipped with type 1 carbohydrate can mediate EDTA-stable cell adhesion in the absence of type 2 carbohydrate, provided it is on the cell surface.

Similarities between the chemical nature of csA from *D. discoideum* and N-CAM from chicken embryos are obvious. Both are integral membrane proteins with negatively charged carbohydrate residues, and both proteins are further modified by acylation and phosphorylation. csA is the most prominently sulphated membrane protein of aggregating cells (Stadler *et al.* 1983). N-CAM is polysialylated (Rothbard *et al.* 1982) and also sulphated (Sorkin *et al.* 1984). The protein moieties of csA are phosphorylated at serine residues (Schmidt & Loomis, 1982), and those of N-CAM at serine and threonine residues (Sorkin *et al.* 1984). The csA glycoprotein is the most strongly labelled lipoprotein in membranes of developing cells that have been incubated with palmitic acid (Stadler *et al.* 1984), and also N-CAM incorporates palmitic acid (Edelman, 1985). Although none of these modifications is unique to cell adhesion molecules, their combination in two typical contact sites from unrelated organisms indicates their importance for the function of these molecules in cell adhesion or its regulation.

The precise functions of the various modifications of the csA glycoprotein remain to be elucidated. It is possible that the glycoprotein is designed not only for its interaction with other cells, but is also endowed with structures required for its transport to and its maintenance at the cell surface. Determining a clear distinction between these two functions should be the subject of future studies.

DEVELOPMENTAL REGULATION OF THE CONTACT SITE A GLYCOPROTEIN IN WILD-TYPE AND IN 'BYPASS' MUTANTS

In growth-phase cells the csA glycoprotein is not detectably expressed; it accumulates after 4–6 h of development. In some strains of *D. discoideum*, including the axenically growing laboratory strains AX2 and AX3, the expression of the glycoprotein is regulated *via* cyclic AMP receptors on the cell surface. Periodic pulses of cyclic AMP are the optimal signals for stimulation of csA expression, apparently because the response to cyclic AMP undergoes adaptation. Pulsatile signals simulate the natural ones, since the cells themselves produce cyclic AMP rhythmically by periodic activation of adenylate cyclase (Roos *et al.* 1977). The pulsatile shape of the signals is maintained in the extracellular space by cell-surface and extracellular phosphodiesterases, which rapidly hydrolyse the cyclic AMP synthesized and released from the cells. The enhancement of csA expression and EDTA-stable cell adhesiveness is clearly seen when cyclic AMP is applied in pulses of 5–20 nM-amplitude every 6 min (Darmon *et al.* 1975; Gerisch *et al.* 1975b; Chisholm *et al.* 1984). In contrast to the stimulating effect of pulses, suppression of csA expression is observed when the same average amounts of cyclic AMP per time are applied in the form of a continuous flux to maintain non-fluctuating steady-state concentrations (Gerisch *et al.* 1984). A similar inhibition of csA expression is obtained in agar plate cultures to which a cyclic AMP analogue, 3′,5′-cyclic-adenosine phosphorothioate (cAMPS) is added (Rossier *et al.* 1978). This analogue acts as an agonist of the cyclic AMP receptors but is largely resistant to phosphodiesterases. The hydrolysis of cAMPS is slow enough to inhibit development completely in agar plate cultures for several days, while aggregation and fruiting body formation proceed in control cultures.

The inhibition of wild-type development by cAMPS can be used to select mutants that develop under conditions in which the normal pulsatile signals of cyclic AMP have been eliminated. Mutants that aggregate in the presence of cAMPS might not need cyclic AMP at all for development, or they might not need pulsatile signals. Mutants of the first class have been called 'bypass mutants' to indicate that the requirement for cyclic AMP as an inducer of development has been bypassed in these strains (Gerisch *et al.* 1985b). Among mutants of the second class non-adapting strains are expected that are stimulated by continuous signals in the same way as the wild type is stimulated by pulsatile signals.

HG302 is one of the strongly cAMPS-resistant mutants that form small but numerous aggregates and fruiting bodies in the presence of 10 μM-cAMPS (Wallraff *et al.* 1984). It is considered to be a bypass mutant and has been chosen for a detailed study and for further mutagenesis. The csA glycoprotein is still stringently regulated in HG302; it is undetectable in growth-phase cells and is expressed with the normal time course during development. This result indicates that cyclic AMP is not the only control factor in development; other control mechanisms exist that do not require cyclic AMP signals for their function. In wild-type cells, these mechanisms are obscured by the cyclic AMP signal system, which dominates the control of development in these cells.

In an attempt to isolate a double bypass mutant, HG302 has been mutagenized and progeny clones have been assayed for aggregation in the presence of nutrient medium. Neither wild-type nor HG302 cells will develop and aggregate when they reach the stationary phase as long as the nutrient medium is not replaced by a non-nutrient buffer. One mutant, HG592, has been selected from HG302 that aggregates

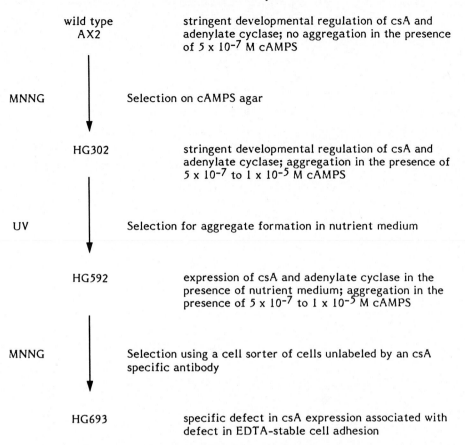

Fig. 4. Scheme of three steps of mutagenesis after which HG693, a mutant specifically defective in csA expression, has been selected. The cells have been mutagenized either with ultraviolet light (UV) or with 1-methyl-3-nitro-1-nitrosoguanidine (MNNG).

in the presence of nutrient medium (Gerisch *et al.* 1985*b*). In HG592 a second control mechanism of development appears to be bypassed in addition to the control by cyclic AMP. Simultaneously, a third control mechanism has been unmasked. This mechanism is responsible for the suppression of the csA glycoprotein during growth of HG592. This mutant expresses the csA glycoprotein when it enters the stationary phase, independent of whether or not nutrient medium is removed (Fig. 4).

Bypass mutants are of interest for two reasons. One is that these mutants permit a step-by-step analysis of the control mechanisms of development. The other reason is that bypass mutants provide a source for the selection of mutants specifically defective in certain developmentally regulated proteins. If wild type is used as a source, most developmental mutants are defective in regulatory genes. These mutants are usually pleiotropic, and the few mutants specifically defective in a single developmentally regulated protein are hard to separate from the pleiotropic ones. Selection of mutants specifically defective in a single protein is less tedious when bypass mutants are used as a source, since defects in regulatory genes that have been bypassed will no longer result in developmental arrest. Consequently, among the mutants that do not express a certain protein, a higher proportion will be specifically defective in that particular protein.

In *D. discoideum* several membrane proteins of aggregating cells are under developmental control: cell-surface cyclic AMP receptors and phosphodiesterase, adenylate cyclase, and the csA glycoprotein. Bypass mutants may be applicable to the selection of structural gene mutants in all these proteins. In the following, the csA glycoprotein is taken as an example to test the usefulness of bypass mutants for mutant selection.

A MUTANT SPECIFICALLY DEFECTIVE IN CONTACT SITE A EXPRESSION

Since the csA glycoprotein is exposed on the cell surface and antibodies are available for fluorescence-activated cell sorting, it is no problem to enrich for mutants defective in the expression of this glycoprotein (Fig. 4). The double bypass mutant HG592 has been mutagenized and a highly specific monoclonal antibody has been used for the selection. This antibody recognizes a portion of the polypeptide chain that is exposed on the cell surface.

Out of more than 50 mutants that do not express the csA glycoprotein one mutant, HG693, has been found that appears to have specifically lost the capability of synthesizing the protein portion of the csA glycoprotein (Noegel *et al.* 1985). The mutant produces type 2 carbohydrate and modifies proteins other than the csA glycoprotein with this oligosaccharide. HG693 is also capable of sulphating carbohydrate residues since glycoproteins other than csA are sulphated in the mutant.

Evidence that HG693 specifically lacks csA has been provided by comparing developmentally regulated transcripts in wild-type and mutant cells by Northern blot analysis. Of the eight cDNA probes used in this study seven have been obtained from poly(A)$^+$ RNA that had been isolated from membrane-bound polysomes. All these seven cDNA probes recognize RNA species that are not or only weakly expressed during the growth phase of AX2 wild-type cells. Their expression increases strongly during the first 6 h of development and is enhanced to various degrees by stimulating wild-type AX2 cells with pulses of cyclic AMP. In mutant HG693 all seven RNA species are expressed, indicating that the mutant does not suffer from a general block in development.

The eighth DNA probe used has been obtained by screening a cDNA expression library with a monoclonal antibody that specifically recognizes the polypeptide moiety of the csA glycoprotein. This cDNA probe recognizes a 1.9×10^3 base-pair transcript in the wild type, expression of which is strongly developmentally regulated and enhanced by cyclic AMP pulses. This transcript is the mRNA for the polypeptide moiety of the csA glycoprotein. In mutant HG693 it is expressed in only trace amounts (Noegel *et al.* 1985). The selective suppression of this transcript suggests that a regulatory region of the csA protein gene is changed in HG693.

Because of its specific defect in csA expression, mutant HG693 has been used to study the function of the csA glycoprotein. Cells of the mutant form almost no

EDTA-stable contacts after 8 h of starvation, the time at which EDTA-stable contact formation reaches its maximum in wild-type AX2 cells. EDTA-sensitive contacts, which are not developmentally regulated, are still observed in the mutant. These results are in accord with the blockage of EDTA-stable cell adhesion by Fab against the csA glycoprotein. In agar plate cultures cells of the mutant still aggregate and form fruiting bodies. The latter result indicates that the csA glycoprotein is not essential at the postaggregative stage of development, which is consistent with observations indicating down-regulation of the csA glycoprotein in the slug stage.

The aggregation of HG693 cells on agar plates shows that in the absence of shear forces the cells can accumulate into aggregates without requiring the csA glycoprotein for the strengthening of intercellular adhesion. It is conceivable that a double insurance system is implemented in the adhesion system of aggregating cells, similar to that discussed earlier for the cytoskeleton. In this connection a $130 \times 10^3 M_r$ protein is of interest; this is developmentally regulated in a similar way to the csA glycoprotein. The carbohydrate residues of the $130 \times 10^3 M_r$ glycoprotein resemble type 1 carbohydrate in being strongly sulphated (Stadler *et al.* 1983), but its polypeptide moiety is not recognized by antibodies against the polypeptide portion of the csA glycoprotein. Mutant HG693 may be used to find out whether or not the $130 \times 10^3 M_r$ glycoprotein can assist and partially replace the csA glycoprotein in mediating intercellular adhesion. The mutant will also help to reveal whether the csA glycoprotein is responsible for the species specificity of cell adhesion, as is observed when aggregating *D. discoideum* cells are mixed with those of a related species, *P. pallidum*.

CARBOHYDRATE MODIFICATION AND CELL AGGREGATION IN *P. PALLIDUM*

P. pallidum forms aggregates similar to those of *D. discoideum*. Sorting out between *D. discoideum* and *P. pallidum* cells is partly due to differences in the chemotactic systems; the attractant of *Polysphondylium* is a peptide rather than cyclic AMP (Shimomura *et al.* 1982). Involvement of cell adhesion in sorting out becomes evident when immobile cells of *D. discoideum* and *P. pallidum* are mixed (Gerisch *et al.* 1980). These cells form separate clusters in gently shaken suspensions, which indicates that the adhesion systems of the two species discriminate between self and non-self. This sorting out has been observed only with aggregation-competent cells of the two species (Bozzaro & Gerisch, 1978). Mixed growth-phase cells adhere indiscriminately to each other; they do not sort out before they reach the stage of aggregation competence. In accord with the proposed involvement of the csA glycoprotein in species-specific cell recognition, Fab specific for aggregation-competent cells of *D. discoideum* blocks the sorting out of the two species (Gerisch *et al.* 1980). This Fab does not block the non-species-specific type of cell adhesion of growth-phase cells.

Although the approach to identifying cell adhesion factors in *P. pallidum* has been similar to the method that has led to the isolation of the csA glycoprotein in *D. discoideum*, the outcome has not been the same. One reason is the strong immunodominance of certain carbohydrate structures of *P. pallidum* glycoproteins. First, a $64 \times 10^3 M_r$ glycoprotein, designated contact site 1 (cs1), has been purified (Bozzaro *et al.* 1981). This single glycoprotein neutralizes most of the adhesion blocking activity of polyclonal Fab from rabbit antisera raised against aggregation-competent cells of *P. pallidum*. However, the adhesion blocking Fab that is neutralized is primarily directed against carbohydrate residues and cs1 is particularly abundant, though not the only protein that carries these carbohydrate chains. Polyclonal antisera and monoclonal antibodies raised against the purified cs1 glycoprotein cross-react with the carbohydrate residues of many other proteins, and anti-carbohydrate Fab prepared from the antisera blocks cell adhesion completely (Toda *et al.* 1984a). These results resemble those obtained by Springer & Barondes (1985) with *D. discoideum*. These authors have obtained adhesion blocking anti-bodies that are neutralized by a series of proteins of different molecular weight. As in the case of *P. pallidum*, the blocking antibodies are apparently directed against carbohydrate residues common to different glycoproteins.

If the target sites of adhesion blocking Fab are carbohydrate epitopes common to several glycoproteins, the Fab neutralization assay is obviously not the method of choice for attributing a function in cell adhesion to a specific protein. There might be a specific glycoprotein involved; however, it cannot be distinguished from other ones that neutralize the same adhesion blocking Fab, independent of whether or not they are involved in adhesion. Alternatively, the carbohydrate residues may play a role in cell adhesion independent of the particular protein to which they are linked. This latter possibility has been followed up in *P. pallidum*.

Fab of one monoclonal antibody, mAb293, has been found to block cell adhesion in growth-phase cells as well as in aggregation-competent cells of *P. pallidum* (Toda *et al.* 1984a). This antibody reacts with the non-reducing ends of oligosaccharide chains that contain L-fucose as the terminal sugar. Binding of the antibody to the cs1 glycoprotein is blocked by free L-fucose (Toda *et al.* 1984b). The epitope recognized by mAb293, termed ep293, is already detectable in exponentially growing cells. Nevertheless, it is not constitutively expressed. During the early exponential growth phase the cells lack ep293, and they acquire it one or two generations before the end of exponential growth (Toda *et al.* unpublished data). Aggregation competence is acquired much later, about 7 h after the beginning of starvation. Although ep293 expression is not immediately followed by cell aggregation, its presence on the cell surface might be a prerequisite for aggregation. Results obtained with mutants are in accord with this possibility, but they do not provide final proof.

Mutants defective in ep293 expression have been obtained by selection with a cell sorter (Francis *et al.* 1985). All of the mutants obtained show disturbed aggregation: most of them form rudimentary aggregates and aberrant fruiting bodies, some are almost non-aggregative. Recombination analysis has proved that the defects in ep293 expression and in morphogenesis are linked to each other, indicating that they are due to the same genetic defect. In most of the mutants, ep293 is not expressed at the normal time but after an extended period of starvation. Simultaneously with ep293 expression the mutant cells begin to aggregate. In a few mutant strains ep293 is expressed only in trace amounts after prolonged starvation and aggregation is almost completely blocked. This coincidence of defects in ep293 expression and in cell aggregation could mean that ep293 is required for cell aggregation, but the possibility remains that ep293 expression and cell aggregation are caused by a common regulatory mechanism by which other cell surface changes are also controlled.

Glycoproteins that are later recognized by mAb293 are present in the cells before. A monoclonal antibody against the polypeptide moiety of the cs1 glycoprotein has been obtained by immunizing mice with antigen that had been treated with anhydrous HF (Mort & Lamport, 1977). This treatment removes the highly immunogenic carbohydrate residues and thus increases the probability of isolating hybridomas that produce antibodies against the polypeptide moiety of the glycoprotein. The anti-polypeptide antibody identifies the protein before ep293 is expressed, during early exponential growth in wild-type cells as well as in starving mutant cells (K. Toda, D. Francis & G. Gerisch, unpublished data). These and other results indicate that it is not the synthesis of the protein but the modification of its carbohydrate residues that is developmentally regulated and is retarded or suppressed in the mutants.

The modification of carbohydrate residues during development requires special attention as a means of modulating cell surfaces without changing the protein cores to which the carbohydrates are linked. Partial desialylation has been observed when the E-CAM of chicken embryos is changed into the A-CAM of adults (Rothbard *et al.* 1982). In *D. discoideum* binding sites for wheat germ agglutinin increase strongly during the later stages of development (Burridge & Jordan, 1979; West & McMahon, 1979). At least some of the newly appearing binding sites seem to be generated by modification of pre-existing glycoproteins (M. Yoshida & G. Gerisch, unpublished data). An increase in the proportion of fucosylated oligosaccharides in the later stages of *D. discoideum* development (Ivatt *et al.* 1984) may also be due to carbohydrate modification rather than to the induction of new specific proteins endowed with a unique carbohydrate structure.

CELL ADHESION AND THE REGULATION OF DEVELOPMENT IN THE
D. DISCOIDEUM SLUG

In nuce, development of the multicellular *Dictyostelium* slug shows all facets of temporal and spatial cell differentiation and its regulation, of differential cell adhesiveness, and morphogenetic cell movements, as they are observed during embryogenesis of higher animals. Not only are the contact sites of aggregating cells subject to developmental regulation, as shown in previous sections, but cell adhesion is in turn a factor that controls development in the slug stage. In this stage differentiation of the cells into prespore and prestalk cells becomes manifest. Differentiation into these two cell types is embedded in a supercellular control system, which determines the correct position (prestalk cells in front and prespore cells behind), the precise proportioning of the two cell types, and also guarantees reversibility of the prespore/prestalk differentiation. Reversibility is a prerequisite of the regulation observed in front and hind pieces of a slug, which, after their separation, readjust the proportions of prespore and prestalk cells (Raper, 1940).

In principle, there are two ways of investigating a system of that complexity. One is to take the system as a whole, to study its behaviour under various conditions, to test its regulatory responses after disturbing its homoeostasis, and to build mathematical models that reproduce the behaviour of the natural system (Meinhardt, 1983). Another way is to simplify the system step-by-step by replacing unknown factors with known experimentally controlled ones, and thus to sort out from the complex system single reactions that can be rigorously analysed down to the molecular level. To arrive at a complete picture of development in a multicellular system such as the *Dictyostelium* slug, a combination of both approaches seems to be indispensable.

In the following sections, recent results are compiled that focus on one facet or the other of the complex cell interactions going on in the slug, and provide starting points for future investigations.

Gene regulation during cell differentiation

As probes for cell-type-specific messages, cDNA clones have been isolated (Barklis & Lodish, 1983; Mehdy *et al.* 1983); and as probes for cell-type-specific proteins, polyclonal and monoclonal antibodies have been raised (Tasaka *et al.* 1983; Krefft *et al.* 1984; Wallace *et al.* 1984). These probes are being used to study gene regulation during and preceding differentiation into the final cell types, spores and stalk cells, and their precursors. One of the major purposes of these studies is to unravel the regulatory DNA sequences and to identify DNA binding proteins responsible for the concerted activation of sets of genes coding for cell-type-specific products. This work will take advantage of the techniques available for transformation of *D. discoideum* cells (Nellen *et al.* 1984) and for genetic engineering.

A group of genes that are activated after slug formation code for a specific class of prespore-specific transcripts, called prespore class II mRNAs (Chisholm *et al.* 1984). These genes are of interest because they are activated in cells kept in suspension cultures by a high concentration of cyclic AMP in combination with tight cell-to-cell adhesion. Several pieces of evidence indicate that cell adhesion in the slug is mediated by cell-surface molecules other than the csA glycoprotein, and that the cell adhesion molecules relevant for prespore differentiation are characteristic of the slug stage (Steinemann & Parish, 1980; Wilcox & Sussman, 1981; Siu *et al.* 1983; Kumagai & Okamoto, 1985).

Replacement or bypassing of cell-to-cell adhesion

The necessity of cell-to-cell adhesion for the activation of cell-type-specific genes limits experimental work to cell aggregates and thus restricts the accessibility of cells to external factors. These limitations have been overcome in different ways. One is simply to replace cell-to-cell contact by the adhesion of single cells to a plastic surface (Mehdy & Firtel, 1985). Expression of the class of prespore-specific mRNAs, which normally requires tight cell-to-cell contact, has been obtained in the presence of both cyclic AMP and a conditioning factor, by plating cells into dishes where they adhere to the bottom. Another method has been used to study differentiation of single cells into spores. To this end mutants have been selected in which cell adhesion as a requirement for sporulation has been bypassed (Kay, 1982). In these sporogenous mutants cyclic AMP acts as non-pathway-specific inducer of differentiation into spores and stalk cells. The important point in this approach is the possibility of manipulating the fate of the cells. The decision whether a cell differentiates into a spore or a stalk cell is determined by a low molecular weight factor produced during the later stages of development. This differentiation-inducing factor (DIF) drives differentiation into the stalk-cell pathway (Kopachik *et al.* 1983). The direction of differentiation is also varied by the extracellular pH (Gross *et al.* 1983), indicating that by this method a variety of factors influencing cell differentiation can be investigated.

Starting cell differentiation from uniform cells

It is one of the peculiarities of *Dictyostelium* that multicellular development starts from an apparently homogeneous population of single cells. However, evidence has been provided that cells differ from each other already before they begin to aggregate, and that they sort out in the slug according to their pre-established differences. It is intriguing that an intrinsic variable is crucial for the fate of the cells. This variable is the cell cycle phase in a non-synchronized cell population (Weijer *et al.* 1984). Cells that are in early G_2 phase at the beginning of starvation tend to become prestalk cells, and cells in late G_2 phase prespore cells. In order to study other factors determining the fate of cells it will be important to start the experiments with synchronized cells. It is not known whether cells from different cell-cycle phases will differ in their adhesiveness, which could be a basis for their sorting-out behaviour.

Control of gene expression by attachment of cells to chemically defined surfaces

A step towards the definition of cell surface components involved in the control of cell differentiation is the replacement of cells by surfaces of known chemical composition as partners of contact interactions. A promising pilot experiment has been performed by attaching cells to polyacrylamide gel surfaces derivatized with specific sugars (Bozzaro *et al.* 1984). The cells interact with the immobilized sugars *via* carbohydrate binding sites on their surfaces. Cell attachment to glucoside-derivatized gels, on which the cells can move and aggregate, results in the blockage of development at a stage following aggregation. The binding to the glucoside-derivatized gel interferes with the expression of genes that are normally turned on when the slug is formed.

Potential use of antibodies to simulate morphogenetic signals

Tools of great potential value in the analysis of cell differentiation and its control by intercellular signals might be monoclonal antibodies against cell surface components that act as receptors for developmental signals. The value of antibodies that bind to specific epitopes of receptors resides not only in their potential activity in blocking the response of a cell to a developmental signal but, more importantly, in their potential capacity to replace the natural signal in activating the receptors. It would be a great help in investigating the molecular mechanisms underlying signal processing from the cell surface to intracellular targets responsible for the activation of specific genes if signals that are normally mediated by intimate cell-to-cell contact could be replaced by an antibody. An observation indicating that cell differentiation in *D. discoideum* can be turned on by antibodies is the production of stalk cells when cells are incubated with a polyspecific Fab preparation that inhibits aggregation (Gerisch, 1980). It might be useful to immobilize the antibodies on a solid surface by a technique similar to the one described in the preceding paragraph, in order to simulate more closely the contact of a cell with the membrane of another cell.

It is to be hoped that in continuing work along the lines summarized above, the approaches originating from different points will merge to provide us with a comprehensive view of cell interactions underlying development in *Dictyostelium*, the simple model of more complicated developmental systems.

REFERENCES

BARKLIS, E. & LODISH, H. F. (1983). Regulation of *Dictyostelium discoideum* mRNAs specific for prespore or prestalk cells. *Cell* **32**, 1139–1148.

BERLOT, C. H., SPUDICH, J. A. & DEVREOTES, P. N. (1985). Chemoattractant-elicited increases in myosin phosphorylation in *Dictyostelium. Cell* **43**, 307–314.

BERTHOLDT, G., STADLER, J., BOZZARO, S., FICHTNER, B. & GERISCH, G. (1985). Carbohydrate and other epitopes of the contact site A glycoprotein of *Dictyostelium discoideum* as characterized by monoclonal antibodies. *Cell Differ.* **16**, 187–202.

BEUG, H., GERISCH, G., KEMPFF, S., RIEDEL, V. & CREMER, G. (1970). Specific inhibition of cell contact formation in *Dictyostelium* by univalent antibodies. *Expl Cell Res.* **63**, 147–158.

BEUG, H., KATZ, F. E. & GERISCH, G. (1973). Dynamics of antigenic membrane sites relating to cell aggregation in *Dictyostelium discoideum. J. Cell Biol.* **56**, 647–658.

BOZZARO, S. & GERISCH, G. (1978). Contact sites in aggregating cells of *Polysphondylium pallidum. J. molec. Biol.* **120**, 265–279.

BOZZARO, S., PERLO, C., CECCARELLI, A. & MANGIAROTTI, G. (1984). Regulation of gene expression in *Dictyostelium discoideum* cells exposed to immobilized carbohydrates. *EMBO J.* **3**, 193–200.

BOZZARO, S., TSUGITA, A., JANKU, M., MONOK, G., OPATZ, K. & GERISCH, G. (1981). Characterization of a purified cell surface glycoprotein as a contact site in *Polysphondylium pallidum. Expl Cell Res.* **134**, 181–191.

BURRIDGE, K. & JORDAN, L. (1979). The glycoproteins of *Dictyostelium discoideum*. Changes during development. *Expl Cell Res.* **124**, 31–38.

CHADWICK, C. M. & GARROD, D. R. (1983). Identification of the cohesion molecule, contact sites B, of *Dictyostelium discoideum. J. Cell Sci.* **60**, 251–266.

CHISHOLM, R. L., BARKLIS, E. & LODISH, H. F. (1984). Mechanism of sequential induction of cell-type specific mRNAs in *Dictyostelium* differentiation. *Nature, Lond.* **310**, 67–69.

COFFMAN, D. S., LEICHTLING, B. H. & RICKENBERG, H. V. (1982). The phosphorylation of membranal proteins in *Dictyostelium discoideum* during development. *Devl Biol.* **93**, 422–429.

DARMON, M., BRACHET, P. & PEREIRA DA SILVA, L. (1975). Chemotactic signals induce cell differentiation in *Dictyostelium discoideum. Proc. natn. Acad. Sci. U.S.A.* **72**, 3163–3166.

EDELMAN, G. M. (1985). Cell adhesion and the molecular processes of morphogenesis. *A. Rev. Biochem.* **54**, 135–169.

FRANCIS, D., TODA, K., MERKL, R., HATFIELD, T. & GERISCH, G. (1985). Mutants of *Polysphondylium pallidum* altered in cell aggregation and in the expression of a carbohydrate epitope on cell surface glycoproteins. *EMBO J.* **4**, 2525–2532.

GERISCH, G. (1961). Zellfunktionen und Zellfunktionswechsel in der Entwicklung von *Dictyostelium discoideum*. V. Stadienspezifische Zellkontaktbildung und ihre quantitative Erfassung. *Expl Cell Res.* **25**, 535–554.

GERISCH, G. (1980). Univalent antibody fragments as tools for the analysis of cell interactions in *Dictyostelium*. *Curr. Top. Devl Biol.* **14**, 243–270.

GERISCH, G., FROMM, H., HUESGEN, A. & WICK, U. (1975*b*). Control of cell-contact sites by cyclic AMP pulses in differentiating *Dictyostelium* cells. *Nature, Lond.* **255**, 547–549.

GERISCH, G., HAGMANN, J., HIRTH, P., ROSSIER, C., WEINHART, U. & WESTPHAL, M. (1985*b*). Early *Dictyostelium* development: Control mechanisms bypassed by sequential mutagenesis. *Cold Spring Harbor Symp. quant. Biol.* **50**.

GERISCH, G., HÜLSER, D., MALCHOW, D. & WICK, U. (1975*a*). Cell communication by periodic cyclic-AMP pulses. *Phil. Trans. R. Soc. Lond.* B. **272**, 181–192.

GERISCH, G., KRELLE, H., BOZZARO, S., EITLE, E. & GUGGENHEIM, R. (1980). Analysis of cell adhesion in *Dictyostelium* and *Polysphondylium* by the use of Fab. In *Cell Adhesion and Motility, 3rd Sym. Br. Soc. Cell Biol.* (ed. A. S. G. Curtis & J. D. Pitts), pp. 293–307. Cambridge University Press.

GERISCH, G., TSIOMENKO, A., STADLER, J., CLAVIEZ, M., HÜLSER, D. & ROSSIER, C. (1984). Transduction of chemical signals in *Dictyostelium* cells. In *Information and Energy Transduction in Biological Membranes*, pp. 237–247. New York: Alan R. Liss.

GERISCH, G., WEINHART, U., BERTHOLDT, G., CLAVIEZ, M. & STADLER, J. (1985*a*). Incomplete contact site A glycoprotein in HL220, a modB mutant of *Dictyostelium discoideum*. *J. Cell Sci.* **73**, 49–68.

GROSS, J. D., BRADBURY, J., KAY, R. R. & PEACEY, M. J. (1983). Intracellular pH and the control of cell differentiation in *Dictyostelium discoideum*. *Nature, Lond.* **303**, 244–245.

HOFFMAN, S. & EDELMAN, G. M. (1983). Kinetics of homophilic binding by embryonic and adult forms of the neural cell adhesion molecule. *Proc. natn. Acad. Sci. U.S.A.* **80**, 5762–5766.

HOHMANN, H.-P., GERISCH, G., LEE, R. W. H. & HUTTNER, W. B. (1985). Cell-free sulfation of the contact site A glycoprotein of *Dictyostelium discoideum* and of a partially glycosylated precursor. *J. biol. Chem.* **260**, 13 869–13 878.

HUESGEN, A. & GERISCH, G. (1975). Solubilized contact sites A from cell membranes of *Dictyostelium discoideum*. *FEBS Lett.* **56**, 46–49.

HUMPHREYS, T. (1963). Chemical dissolution and *in vitro* reconstruction of sponge cell adhesions. I. Isolation and functional demonstration of the components involved. *Devl Biol.* **8**, 27–47.

IVATT, R. L., DAS, O. P., HENDERSON, E. J. & ROBBINS, P. W. (1984). Glycoprotein biosynthesis in *Dictyostelium discoideum*: Developmental regulation of the protein-linked glycans. *Cell* **38**, 561–567.

KAY, R. R. (1982). cAMP and spore differentiation in *Dictyostelium discoideum*. *Proc. natn. Acad. Sci. U.S.A.* **79**, 3228–3231.

KOPACHIK, W., OOHATA, A., DHOKIA, B., BROOKMAN, J. J. & KAY, R. R. (1983). *Dictyostelium* mutants lacking DIF, a putative morphogen. *Cell* **33**, 397–403.

KREFFT, M., VOET, L., GREGG, J. H., MAIRHOFER, H. & WILLIAMS, K. L. (1984). Evidence that positional information is used to establish the prestalk–prespore pattern in *Dictyostelium discoideum* aggregates. *EMBO J.* **3**, 201–206.

KUCZMARSKI, E. R. & SPUDICH, J. A. (1980). Regulation of myosin self-assembly: Phosphorylation of *Dictyostelium* heavy chain inhibits formation of thick filaments. *Proc. natn. Acad. Sci. U.S.A.* **77**, 7292–7296.

KUMAGAI, A. & OKAMOTO, K. (1985). Changes of plasma membrane proteins during prespore differentiation in *Dictyostelium discoideum*. *J. Biochem.* **98**, 1–7.

LILIEN, J. E. & MOSCONA, A. A. (1967). Cell aggregation: its enhancement by a supernatant from cultures of homologous cells. *Science* **157**, 70–72.

LOOMIS, W. F., WHEELER, S. A., SPRINGER, W. R. & BARONDES, S. H. (1985). Adhesion mutants of *Dictyostelium discoideum* lacking the saccharide determinant recognized by two adhesion-blocking monoclonal antibodies. *Devl Biol.* **109**, 111–117.

McRobbie, S. J. & Newell, P. C. (1984). Chemoattractant-mediated changes in cytoskeletal actin of cellular slime moulds. *J. Cell Sci.* **68**, 139–151.

Mehdy, M. C. & Firtel, R. A. (1985). A secreted factor and cyclic AMP jointly regulate cell-type-specific gene expression in *Dictyostelium discoideum*. *Molec. cell. Biol.* **5**, 705–713.

Mehdy, M. C., Ratner, D. & Firtel, R. A. (1983). Induction and modulation of cell-type-specific gene expression in *Dictyostelium*. *Cell* **32**, 763–771.

Meinhardt, H. (1983). A model for the prestalk/prespore patterning in the slug of the slime mold *Dictyostelium discoideum*. *Differentiation* **24**, 191–202.

Misevic, G. N., Jumblatt, J. E. & Burger, M. M. (1982). Cell binding fragments from a sponge proteoglycan-like aggregation factor. *J. biol. Chem.* **257**, 6931–6936.

Mort, A. J. & Lamport, D. T. A. (1977). Anhydrous hydrogen fluoride deglycosylates glycoproteins. *Analyt. Biochem.* **82**, 289–309.

Müller, K. & Gerisch, G. (1978). A specific glycoprotein as the target site of adhesion blocking Fab in aggregating *Dictyostelium* cells. *Nature, Lond.* **274**, 445–449.

Müller K., Gerisch, G., Fromme, I., Mayer, H. & Tsugita, A. (1979). A membrane glycoprotein of aggregating *Dictyostelium* cells with the properties of contact sites. *Eur. J. Biochem.* **99**, 419–426.

Murray, B. A., Wheeler, S., Jongens, T. & Loomis, W. F. (1984). Mutations affecting a surface glycoprotein, gp80, of *Dictyostelium discoideum*. *Molec. cell. Biol.* **4**, 514–519.

Nellen, W., Silan, C. & Firtel, R. A. (1984). DNA-mediated transformation in *Dictyostelium discoideum*: regulated expression of an actin gene fusion. *Molec. cell. Biol.* **4**, 2890–2898.

Noegel, A., Harloff, C., Hirth, P., Merkl, R., Modersitzki, M., Stadler, J., Weinhart, U., Westphal, M. & Gerisch, G. (1985). Probing an adhesion mutant of *Dictyostelium discoideum* with cDNA clones and monoclonal antibodies indicates a specific defect in the contact site A glycoprotein. *EMBO J.* **4**, 3805–3810.

Noll, H., Matranga, V., Cascino, D. & Vittorelli, L. (1979). Reconstitution of membranes and embryonic development in dissociated blastula cells of the sea urchin by reinsertion of aggregation-promoting membrane proteins extracted with butanol. *Proc. natn. Acad. Sci. U.S.A.* **76**, 288–292.

Rahmsdorf, H. J., Malchow, D. & Gerisch, G. (1978). Cyclic AMP-induced phosphorylation in *Dictyostelium* of a polypeptide comigrating with myosin heavy chains. *FEBS Lett* **88**, 322–326.

Raper, K. B. (1940). Pseudoplasmodium formation and organization in *Dictyostelium discoideum*. *J. Elisha Mitchell Sci. Soc.* **56**, 241–282.

Roos, W., Scheidegger, C. & Gerisch, G. (1977). Adenylate cyclase activity oscillations as signals for cell aggregation in *Dictyostelium discoideum*. *Nature, Lond.* **266**, 259–261.

Rossier, C., Gerisch, G., Malchow, D. & Eckstein, F. (1978). Action of a slowly hydrolysable cyclic AMP analogue on developing cells of *Dictyostelium discoideum*. *J. Cell Sci.* **35**, 321–338.

Rothbard, J. B., Brackenbury, R., Cunningham, B. A. & Edelman, G. M. (1982). Differences in the carbohydrate structures of neural cell-adhesion molecules from adult and embryonic chicken brains. *J. biol. Chem.* **257**, 11 064–11 069.

Rutishauser, U., Gall, W. E. & Edelmann, G. M. (1978). Adhesion among neural cells of the chick embryo. IV. Role of the cell surface molecule CAM in the formation of neurite bundles in cultures of spinal ganglia. *J. Cell Biol.* **79**, 382–393.

Schmidt, J. A. & Loomis, W. F. (1982). Phosphorylation of the contact site A glycoprotein (gp80) of *Dictyostelium discoideum*. *Devl Biol.* **91**, 296–304.

Schnaar, R. L., Weigel, P. H., Kuhlenschmidt, M. S., Lee, Y. C. & Roseman, S. (1978). Adhesion of chicken hepatocytes to polyacrylamide gels derivatized with *N*-acetylglucosamine. *J. biol. Chem.* **253**, 7940–7951.

Shimomura, O., Suthers, H. L. B. & Bonner, J. T. (1982). Chemical identity of the acrasin of the cellular slime mold *Polysphondylium violaceum*. *Proc. natn. Acad. Sci. U.S.A.* **79**, 7376–7379.

Shirayoshi, Y., Okada, T. S. & Takeichi, M. (1983). The calcium-dependent cell–cell adhesion system regulates inner cell mass formation and cell surface polarization in early mouse development. *Cell* **35**, 631–638.

SIU, C.-H., DES ROCHES, B. & LAM, T. Y. (1983). Involvement of a cell-surface glycoprotein in the cell-sorting process of *Dictyostelium discoideum*. *Proc. natn. Acad. Sci. U.S.A.* **80**, 6596–6600.

SORKIN, B. C., HOFFMAN, S., EDELMAN, G. M. & CUNNINGHAM, B. A. (1984). Sulfation and phosphorylation of the neural cell adhesion molecule, N-CAM. *Science* **225**, 1476–1478.

SPRINGER, W. R. & BARONDES, S. H. (1985). Protein-linked oligosaccharide implicated in cell–cell adhesion in two *Dictyostelium* species. *Devl Biol.* **109**, 102–110.

STADLER, J., BAUER, G. & GERISCH, G. (1984). Acylation *in vivo* of the contact site A glycoprotein and of other membrane proteins in *Dictyostelium discoideum*. *FEBS Lett.* **172**, 326–330.

STADLER, J., GERISCH, G., BAUER, G., SUCHANEK, C. & HUTTNER, W. B. (1983). *In vivo* sulfation of the contact site A glycoprotein of *Dictyostelium discoideum*. *EMBO J.* **2**, 1137–1143.

STEINEMANN, C. & PARISH, R. W. (1980). Evidence that a developmentally regulated glycoprotein is target of adhesion-blocking Fab in reaggregating *Dictyostelium*. *Nature, Lond.* **286**, 621–623.

TAKEICHI, M., ATSUMI, T., YOSHIDA, C., UNO, K. & OKADA, T. S. (1981). Selective adhesion of embryonal carcinoma cells and differentiated cells by Ca^{2+}-dependent sites. *Devl Biol.* **87**, 340–350.

TAKEICHI, M., OZAKI, H. S., TOKUNAGA, K. & OKADA, T. S. (1979). Experimental manipulation of cell surface to affect cellular recognition mechanisms. *Devl Biol.* **70**, 195–205.

TASAKA, M., NOCE, T. & TAKEUCHI, I. (1983). Prestalk and prespore differentiation in *Dictyostelium* as detected by cell type-specific monoclonal antibodies. *Proc. natn. Acad. Sci. U.S.A.* **80**, 5340–5344.

TODA, K., BOZZARO, S., LOTTSPEICH, F., MERKL, R. & GERISCH, G. (1984a). Monoclonal anti-glycoprotein antibody that blocks cell adhesion in *Polysphondylium pallidum*. *Eur. J. Biochem.* **140**, 73–81.

TODA, K., THARANATHAN, R. N., BOZZARO, S. & GERISCH, G. (1984b). Monoclonal antibodies that block cell adhesion in *Polysphondylium pallidum*: reaction with L-fucose, a terminal sugar in cell-surface glycoproteins. *Eur. J. Biochem.* **143**, 477–481.

WALLACE, J. S., MORRISSEY, J. H. & NEWELL, P. C. (1984). Monoclonal antibodies specific for stalk differentiation in *Dictyostelium discoideum*. *Cell Differ.* **14**, 205–211.

WALLRAFF, E., SCHLEICHER, M., MODERSITZKI, M., RIEGER, D., ISENBERG, G. & GERISCH, G. (1986). Selection of *Dictyostelium* mutants defective in cytoskeletal proteins: use of an antibody that binds to the ends of α-actinin rods. *EMBO J.* **5**.

WALLRAFF, E., WELKER, D. L., WILLIAMS, K. L. & GERISCH, G. (1984). Genetic analysis of a *Dictyostelium discoideum* mutant resistant to adenosine 3′:5′-cyclic phosphorothioate, an inhibitor of wild-type development. *J. gen. Microbiol.* **130**, 2103–2114.

WEIJER, C. J., DUSCHL, G. & DAVID, C. N. (1984). Dependence of cell-type proportioning and sorting on cell cycle phase in *Dictyostelium discoideum*. *J. Cell Sci.* **70**, 133–145.

WEST, C. M. & McMAHON, D. (1979). The axial distribution of plasma membrane molecules in pseudoplasmodia of the cellular slime mold *Dictyostelium discoideum*. *Expl Cell Res.* **124**, 393–401.

WEST, C. M. & LOOMIS, W. F. (1985). Absence of a carbohydrate modification does not affect the level or subcellular localization of three membrane glycoproteins in *mod*B mutants of *Dictyostelium discoideum*. *J. biol. Chem.* **260**, 13 803–13 809.

WILCOX, D. K. & SUSSMAN, M. (1981). Serologically distinguishable alterations in the molecular specificity of cell cohesion during morphogenesis in *Dictyostelium discoideum*. *Proc. natn. Acad. Sci. U.S.A.* **78**, 358–362.

YOSHIDA, M., STADLER, J., BERTHOLDT, G. & GERISCH, G. (1984). Wheat germ agglutinin binds to the contact site A glycoprotein of *Dictyostelium discoideum* and inhibits EDTA-stable cell adhesion. *EMBO J.* **3**, 2663–2670.

YUMURA, S. & FUKUI, Y. (1985). Reversible cyclic AMP-dependent change in distribution of myosin thick filaments in *Dictyostelium*. *Nature, Lond.* **314**, 194–196.

J. Cell Sci. Suppl. 4, 221–237 (1986)
Printed in Great Britain © The Company of Biologists Limited 1986

DESMOSOMES, CELL ADHESION MOLECULES AND THE ADHESIVE PROPERTIES OF CELLS IN TISSUES

D. R. GARROD

Cancer Research Campaign Medical Oncology Unit, University of Southampton, Centre Block, CF99, Southampton General Hospital, Tremona Road, Southampton SO9 4XY, UK

INTRODUCTION

In this article intercellular adhesion of vertebrate tissue cells, especially epithelia, will be discussed. The underlying theme may be expressed by the question 'What cellular adhesive properties are required in order to develop and maintain the organization and structure of normal tissues?' I shall begin by outlining a number of principles and properties of cell adhesions that have been presented previously (Garrod, 1981; Garrod & Nicol, 1981; Garrod, 1985) and can be updated and extended following recent studies on the molecular basis of cell adhesion. Detailed consideration will then be given by the principal adhesive junctions of epithelial cells, desmosomes or maculae adhaerentes, particularly in so far as recent studies illustrate general principles of adhesion. Advances in the study of other cell–cell adhesion mechanisms will also be considered. Cell adhesion has been reviewed recently by Damsky, Knudsen & Buck (1984), and Edelman (1984). It is hoped that the material presented here will be largely complementary to those reviews.

PRINCIPLES OF TISSUE CELL ADHESION

A cell has several adhesion mechanisms

Individual cells of a given type possess a variety of different molecular adhesion mechanisms, some junctional and some non-junctional (Garrod, 1981; Garrod & Nicol, 1981; Garrod, 1985). The most complex situation probably arises in the so-called simple epithelial cell, which is shown in a generalized diagram in Fig. 1. This illustrates five different mechanisms of cell–cell adhesion and six different mechanisms of cell–matrix adhesion. Of the intercellular adhesion mechanisms, the tight junction and gap junction have other well-established functions, occluding the intercellular space and intercellular communication, respectively. These functions depend upon strong intercellular binding, so that the junctions must contribute to the adhesiveness of the cell. Some earlier electron-microscopical observations suggested that, under some experimental circumstances, intercellular bonding at these junctions is more resistant to disruption than that at the other junctional types (Sedar & Forte, 1964; Muir, 1967; Berry & Friend, 1969). The adhesive function of the desmosome and the zonula adhaerens are widely recognized. These, together with non-junctional adhesion molecules, probably constitute the major adhesive

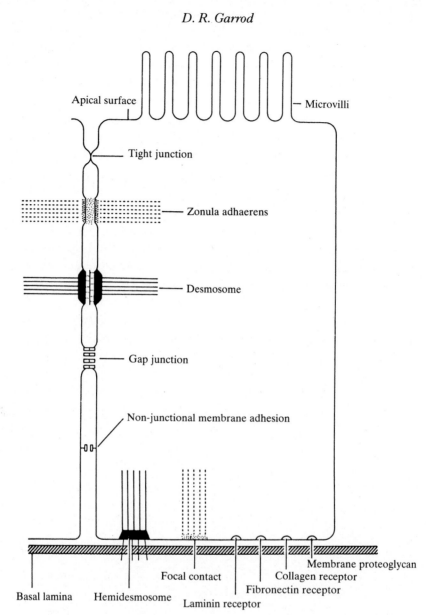

Fig. 1. Diagram showing multiple adhesion mechanisms of epithelial cells. (N.B. This diagram shows a probable maximum number of mechanisms not all of which are present in all epithelial cells.)

mechanisms in most cell types. In a previous review (Garrod, 1985) it was suggested that so-called liver cell adhesion molecule (L-CAM) (Edelman, 1984) might be involved in non-junctional membrane adhesion. However, it has recently been shown that uvomorulin (probably equivalent to L-CAM) is concentrated in the zonula adhaerens of intestinal epithelial cells (Boller, Vestweber & Kemler, 1985). It may therefore be necessary to postulate another molecular adhesion mechanism or mechanisms for non-junctional membranes. In liver, this could be the molecule known as cell CAM-105 (Ocklind & Öbrink, 1982). It is also possible that adhesion molecules that are concentrated at junctions may be present at lower density on other parts of the cell surface, where they may mediate adhesion.

The cell–matrix adhesion mechanisms consist of receptors for matrix components and two 'junctional' types, the hemidesmosome and the focal contact. They have been discussed in a previous review where appropriate references are given (Garrod, 1985).

Epithelial cells possess a number of adhesion mechanisms because they require a range of different adhesive properties in order to maintain their epithelial organization (Garrod, 1985). They need links (desmosomes) between their intermediate filament cytoskeletons in order to provide structural strength and continuity throughout the tissue (Arnn & Staehelin, 1981; Ellison & Garrod, 1984; Docherty, Edwards, Garrod & Mattey, 1984; Garrod, 1985), they need links (zonulae adhaerentes) between their contractile microfilaments (Baker & Schroeder, 1967; Karfunkel, 1971; Burgess, 1982; Garrod, 1985), they need to bind to and interact with their substratum (matrix receptors and hemidesmosomes) and to form links between their actin cytoskeleton and the matrix (focal contacts) to facilitate movement during morphogenesis or wound healing (Billig *et al.* 1982). Each of these functions involves a specialized adhesion mechanism that has evolved in response to the need for its particular function. Simple epithelial cells may possess nine or ten different adhesion mechanisms, in order to fulfil a complex set of adhesive requirements.

This plurality of adhesion mechanisms is not restricted to epithelial cells. Nerve cells may possess a minimum of four mechanisms, the neural cell adhesion molecule (N-CAM) (Thiery, Brackenbury, Rutishauser & Edelman, 1977), the L1 antigen (Rathjen & Schachner, 1984) (now shown to be definitely distinct from N-CAM; Rathjen & Rutishauser, 1984), the calcium-dependent adhesion mechanism recognized by monoclonal antibody NCD-1 (Hatta, Okada & Takeichi, 1985) and the neuron–glial cell adhesion molecule (Ng-CAM) (Thiery, Delouvée, Grumet & Edelman, 1985). They also possess cell–matrix adhesion mechanisms (Cole & Glaser, 1984; Schubert & LaCorbière, 1985).

Fibroblasts are probably less complex than either epithelial cells or neurones but certainly form adhaerens-type junctions (Heaysman & Pegrum 1973), and gap junctions (Pitts, 1978), and possess calcium-dependent and calcium-independent adhesion mechanisms (Takeichi, Atsumi, Yoshida & Okada, 1981) as well as various types of cell–substratum adhesions.

The possession of multiple adhesion mechanisms is the general rule among tissue cells. Any cells that are shown to possess only a simple mechanism will be highly specialized for a particular adhesive function.

Finally, in this context the term *cellular adhesiveness* is sometimes used in a strictly quantitative sense. For example, quantitative differences in adhesiveness have been invoked to explain the experimentally induced phenomenon known as sorting-out (Steinberg, 1964). The present analysis demonstrates that the total adhesiveness of a cell *at a given time in a given situation* receives a quantitative contribution from those of its molecular adhesive mechanisms that are functional *at that time and in that situation*. When we have identified all the molecular adhesive mechanisms in a cell, quantified their expression on the cell surface and determined the strength of the adhesive bonds that they form, we shall be able to compute cellular adhesiveness for that cell type.

CELLS OF DIFFERENT TYPES SHARE ADHESION MECHANISMS

Ultrastructural studies have shown that intercellular junctions are similar in cells of different tissues and different species (McNutt & Weinstein, 1973; Overton, 1974*a*; Staehelin, 1974). It is believed that all epithelia possess desmosomes, except the pigmented epithelium of the eye (Middleton & Pegrum, 1976; Nicol & Garrod, 1982; Docherty *et al.* 1984) and lens epithelium. Moreover, the only non-epithelial tissue that possesses desmosomes is cardiac muscle, where they occur in the intercalated discs. Endothelial cells do not possess desmosomes, except in fish (Cowin, Mattey & Garrod, 1984*a*).

The distribution of cell adhesion molecules (CAMs) has been studied by Edelman and his colleagues (Edelman, 1983, 1984). L-CAM is present in adult animals in the stratum germinativum of the skin, the epithelium of the urinogenital, digestive and respiratory tracts, the lymphoid organs and secretory glands. L-CAM is probably similar or identical to the other calcium-dependent adhesion molecules isolated from other sources by other workers. These include uvomorulin (Hyafil, Morello, Babinet & Jacob, 1980), cell CAM 120/80 (Damsky *et al.* 1983) and cadherin (Yoshida-Noro, Suzuki & Takeichi, 1984) (now called E-cadherin (Hatta *et al.* 1985). These also occur in a wide distribution and in different animal species (mammals and birds). (If these molecules are identical, the name cadherin would seem preferable to the others, which all carry somewhat restrictive connotations with regard to function, distribution or molecular weight.)

N-CAM is present in adult animals in nervous system, testis and cardiac muscle, and has been found in fish, lizard, frog, chick, mouse, rat and human (Edelman, 1984). A very similar tissue distribution to that of N-CAM (which is a calcium-independent mechanism) has been found for the calcium-dependent neural cell adhesion mechanism, N-cadherin (Hatta *et al.* 1985). Ng-CAM, is found exclusively in the nervous system (Thiery *et al.* 1985).

Some adhesion molecules appear to have a fairly restricted distribution. Antibody studies showed that cell CAM-105, first identified in adult rat hepatocytes (Ocklind & Öbrink 1982), was found only in mouse liver, rat liver, rat kidney and rat small intestine (Vestweber *et al.* 1985). However, the survey was rather limited and the failure of antibodies to cross-react does not necessarily mean that the molecule is absent from a tissue.

The general conclusion from study of the distribution of adhesion molecules is that adhesion mechanisms are widely shared between different cell types. In his 'modulation' theory of cell adhesion, Edelman has asserted that, in general, tissues will have only a few cell–cell adhesion molecules, corresponding in number perhaps only to the number of classes of cells and tissues (Edelman, 1983). This formulation is in direct contrast to previous theories, which require a large repertoire of cell type-specific adhesion molecules (Moscona, 1962; Sperry, 1963). We have pointed out that such a large repertoire of molecules is not required in order to account for the adhesive behaviour of cells (Garrod, 1981; Garrod & Nicol, 1981). I believe that there are indeed a limited or restricted number of molecular adhesion mechanisms, in fact far fewer than there are differentiated cell types within the vertebrate body. However, the number of molecules appears to be greater than that suggested by Edelman, because cells of any one tissue class clearly possess a number of mechanisms.

One of the consequences of the sharing of adhesion mechanisms is that cells from a wide variety of tissues and from different animal species exhibit mutual adhesion. A cell has a much greater potential for adhesion to other cell types than it shows in its normal tissue location (Garrod, 1981). Desmosomes (Overton, 1974b; Mattey & Garrod, 1985a; and below), adhaerens type junctions (Armstrong, 1970, 1971) and gap junctions (Epstein & Gilula, 1977) have all been shown to be capable of forming between some different types of cells. Like L-CAM and N-CAM (Edelman, 1984), these junctions probably represent examples of 'homophilic' adhesive binding in which the adhesion molecules bind to the same or similar adhesion sites on the other cell. Thus molecularly specific adhesion binding can give rise to non-specific cell–cell adhesion, and in doing so shows that the adhesion binding sites are conserved between different tissues and different species (see later discussion on desmosomes). Another type of adhesion between different cell types arises from 'heterophilic' binding, in which a CAM recognizes a different molecule on another cell. Examples are Ng-CAM, which is involved in neuron–glial cell adhesion and is present only on neurons (Edelman, 1984; Thiery *et al.* 1985), and the J_1 glycoprotein, which is involved in astrocyte–neuron adhesion and is present only on astrocytes (Kruse *et al.* 1985). In neither case has the complementary molecule been identified.

THE DIFFERING ADHESIVE PROPERTIES OF DIFFERENT CELL TYPES

The fact that cells share adhesion mechanisms, and if confronted experimentally can use these to form mutual adhesions, makes it necessary to list the ways in which the adhesive properties of different cell types can differ from each other.

(a) Cells can possess different combinations of intercellular junctions and CAMs.

(b) Cells can possess different numbers of intercellular junctions and CAMs.

(c) Cells can possess different surface distributions of junctions or CAMs.

(d) Cells can have adhesion mechanisms of different stability, i.e. adhesion may be reversible or irreversible.

Differences in category (a) are qualitative and have been amply illustrated above. Differences in categories (b) to (d) are more subtle. A single adhesion mechanism such as the desmosome, may vary in one or all of these ways between different cell types. I shall now review recent work on desmosomes laying stress on two aspects:

how desmosomes in different tissues resemble each other *and* how desmosomes can give rise to different adhesive properties between different tissues.

DESMOSOMES

Desmosome ultrastructure has been reviewed many times (McNutt & Weinstein, 1973; Overton, 1974*a*; Staehelin, 1974; Skerrow, 1978; Arnn & Staehelin, 1981; Garrod & Cowin, 1985; Garrod, 1985). Here I shall simply note that desmosomes are symmetrical about the intercellular mid-line, the two halves of a desmosome being contributed by adjacent cells. Formation of a desmosome must therefore depend upon mutual recognition and adhesion between molecules on the surfaces of the two cells.

The major components of desmosomes are as follows. The plaque components are: (1) a pair of neutral proteins of M_r (by electrophoresis) 250 000 and 215 000 (desmoplakins I and II); (2) a neutral protein of 83 000 M_r; (3) a basic protein of 75 000 M_r (Franke *et al.* 1982; Mueller & Franke, 1983). The glycoproteins are: (1) a triplet of 175 000–164 000; (2) two bands of M_r 130 000 and 115 000 the former of which often appears as a doublet; and (3) a single band of 22 000 M_r (Gorbsky & Steinberg, 1981).

Gorbsky & Steinberg (1981) proposed that all the desmosomal glycoproteins are involved in desmosomal adhesion and suggested the collective name 'desmogleins' for them. However, the first evidence for involvement of a molecule in desmosomal adhesion was provided by ourselves, since univalent Fab' fragments of antibody against the 130 000 and 115 000 M_r glycoproteins inhibited desmosome formation in MDBK (Madin-Darby Bovine Kidney) cells (Cowin, Mattey & Garrod, 1984*b*). Similar results were not obtained with Fab' against the 175 000–164 000 M_r components and, indeed, none of our polyclonal antisera recognized the surface domain of this triplet in MDBK cells. (Since the 175 000–164 000 M_r components are glycoproteins, the existence of a surface domain seems almost certain.) We have therefore proposed the name desmocollins I and II for the 130 000 and 115 000 M_r components to denote their demonstrated function in desmosomal adhesion (Cowin *et al.* 1984*b*). We think that different names are desirable for the glycoprotein components because they are clearly different molecules, both antigenically (Cohen, Gorbsky & Steinberg, 1983; Cowin & Garrod, 1983), and in amino acid and sugar composition (Kaprell *et al.* 1985). It is possible that the 175 000–164 000 M_r component is also involved in cell adhesion, but the data presented by Gorbsky & Steinberg (1981) would be equally consistent with that of a transmembrane molecule with a small surface domain, primarily concerned with linking the adhesion molecules with the plaque (Cowin *et al.* 1984*b*). No information about the location and function of the 22 000 M_r component has yet been published.

DESMOSOMAL COMPONENTS IN DIFFERENT TISSUE AND ANIMAL SPECIES

Polyclonal antisera have been raised in guinea pigs, against desmosomal proteins and glycoproteins from bovine nasal epithelium obtained by preparative gel electrophoresis (Cowin & Garrod, 1983; see also Franke *et al.* 1981; Giudice, Cohen, Patel

& Steinberg, 1984). Fluorescent antibody studies of tissues from different animal species (man, cow, guinea pig, rat, chicken, lizard (*Lacerta viridis*), frog (*Rana pipiens*), axolotl and trout) revealed that the desmosomal antigens are widely distributed (Cowin & Garrod, 1983; Cowin *et al.* 1984a). The results suggested that desmosomal antigens are well conserved in the epidermis of mammals, birds, reptiles and anuran amphibians, since equally bright staining for all antigens was obtained. In non-epidermal epithelia, while staining for most antigens was as bright as that in the epidermis, staining for the desmocollins was conspicuously less bright. One possible explanation of this is that the desmocollins vary in composition between epidermal and non-epidermal tissues (see Cowin *et al.* 1984a, for detailed discussion).

Desmocollin-specific polyclonal antisera raised in mice confirm the difference between epidermal and non-epidermal epithelia, although not quite in the way we had expected (Parrish *et al.* 1986). They recognize only the suprabasal layers of epidermis and the arachnoid layer of the meninges, but no other epithelial tissues whatsoever. These antisera also stained meningiomas, raising the possibility of developing monoclonal reagents for the diagnosis of these tumours. This result demonstrates that there are indeed chemical differences between desmocollins in different tissues. In addition, Giudice *et al.* (1984), using monoclonal antibodies that recognize different epitopes of desmosomal glycoproteins, demonstrated differences between the 175 000–164 000 M_r glycoproteins and the desmocollins in bovine nasal, corneal and oesophageal epithelia.

We have carried out immunoblotting studies using polyclonal antisera on desmosome-enriched fractions from cells from different tissues and species (Suhrbier & Garrod, 1986). These were human foreskin keratinocytes, Madin-Darby bovine kidney cells (MDBK), Madin-Darby canine kidney cells (MDCK), chicken epidermis and frog epidermis. We found that desmosomal glycoproteins from various sources vary in apparent molecular weight, heterogeneity and antibody cross-reactivity. For example, bands reacting with antibody against bovine 175 000–164 000 M_r glycoprotein have M_r values of 175 000, 169 000 and 164 000 in bovine nasal epithelium, but 245 000, 230 000 and 210 000 in MDCK cells, while keratinocytes possess a single band of 190 000. In mammalian cells anti-desmocollin antibodies do not cross-react with bands recognized by anti-175 000–164 000 M_r antibodies. However, in chickens and frogs there are glycoprotein bands that react with both antibodies, as well as distinct desmocollin bands (for details refer to Suhrbier & Garrod, 1986). (Conservation of desmosomal plaque constituents is discussed by Franke *et al.* (1982), Mueller & Franke (1983), Giudice *et al.* (1985), Suhrbier & Garrod (1985).)

DESMOSOMAL CROSS-REACTIVITY: FORMATION OF DESMOSOMES BETWEEN DIFFERENT CELL TYPES

Desmosomes form between embryonic chick corneal epithelial cells and mouse epidermal cells (Overton, 1977). Furthermore, desmosome formation between cells of a metastatic oat cell carcinoma of the lung and liver parenchyma cells has been reported (Jesudason & Iseri, 1980). In view of the apparent conservation of desmosomal components, we wished to determine the capacity of a wider range of tissues and species for mutual desmosome formation. We have therefore made all binary combinations in culture between HeLa cells (human cervical carcinoma line), MDBK cells, MDCK cells, embryonic chick corneal epithelial cells and adult frog (*R. pipiens*) corneal epithelial cells (Mattey & Garrod, 1985). In every case mutual desmosome formation was obtained. Thus, irrespective of whether the cells were from man or the frog, from a simple (MDBK, MDCK) or a stratified (cornea) epithelium, from a cell line or a primary culture, from a normal cell or a neoplastic cell, the adhesive components of their desmosomes were sufficiently well conserved to participate in recognition and mutual binding.

In contrast, Overton (1974*b*) was unable to find evidence of mutual desmosome formation between embryonic chick cornea and liver cells, and between cornea and heart myocytes (see also Nicol & Garrod, 1982). Chick embryonic liver cells and myocytes possess very few desmosomes. However, the observation of Jesudason & Iseri (1980), described above, shows that hepatocytes can form desmosomes with other tissues.

The conclusion from this work is that, although there may be a few exceptions, cells from different tissues and animal species are capable of mutual desmosome formation. How can this conclusion be rationalized in terms of the variability of desmosomal glycoproteins demonstrated by fluorescent antibody staining and Western blotting?

Present evidence suggests that the biological activity of many glycoproteins is due to their protein components, while their carbohydrate moieties are thought to be important as sorting signals in glycoprotein routing, metabolic stability and cellular differentiation (Olden, Parent & White, 1982; Warren, Buck & Tuszyinski, 1978). This is probably true for desmosomal glycoproteins, since desmosomes can form in the absence of N-linked carbohydrates (King & Tabiowao, 1981; Overton, 1982 and see below). The most likely explanation of our results therefore is that they suggest that desmosomal adhesion is dependent upon a highly conserved protein domain in the desmosomal adhesion molecules, and that the variability between tissues and species arises because of differences in carbohydrate moieties, which may reflect differences in carbohydrate control mechanisms. Alternatively, the adhesion domain alone may be well conserved, the rest of the polypeptide showing divergence.

Why should desmosomal adhesive recognition be highly conserved? Probably because desmosomal adhesion is a cellular property fundamental to the organization of epithelia. Any alteration caused by mutation would tend to disrupt epithelial organization and would therefore be selected against.

DIFFERING ADHESIVE PROPERTIES OF DIFFERENT CELL TYPES: NUMBER AND DISTRIBUTION OF DESMOSOMES

In spite of the ability of their desmosomes to 'cross-react', the cells of different epithelia possess and, indeed, require different adhesive properties, as may be illustrated by the following considerations.

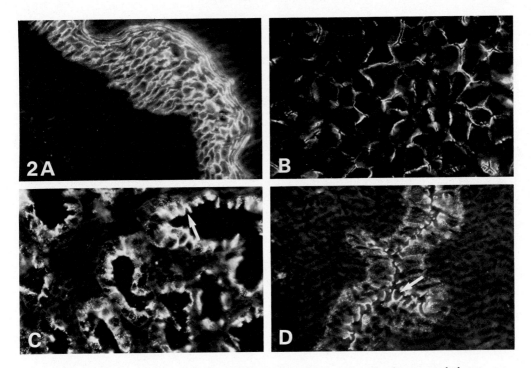

Fig. 2. Tissue sections stained with monoclonal antibody against the desmosomal plaque constituents, desmoplakins I and II, to illustrate differences in distribution and quantity between different tissues. A. Skin, showing punctate staining between lateral borders of basal cells and continuous all-round staining of cells in spinous and granular layers. Cornified squames are not stained by this antibody. B. Liver, showing punctate staining concentrated along bile canaliculi and interfaces between hepatocytes. C. Kidney tubules (cuboidal epithelium), showing concentration of staining at apico–lateral cell interfaces and diminishing towards the bases of the cells. Note that the luminal surfaces of the cells are unstained (arrow). D. Uterus, showing columnar epithelium with staining concentrated at the apico–lateral interfaces. Note that the luminal surfaces are again unstained (arrow). The antibody was raised and the photographs provided by Elaine Parrish. A–D, ×314.

Ultrastructural observations make it quite clear that the *number* and *distribution* of desmosomes differs between different tissues. Thus cells of the intermediate layers of stratified epithelia have numerous desmosomes distributed all around their surfaces, mediating all-round adhesion with other cells. In contrast, cells from simple epithelia have fewer desmosomes located, as is the case with other junctional types, on their lateral surfaces. Quantitative variations in desmosomes (number and size) between different layers of epidermis have been demonstrated, and similar studies on other tissues have been reviewed by White & Gohari (1984). This evidence has been greatly reinforced by recent studies of Franke and colleagues (Franke *et al.* 1981, 1982) and ourselves (Cowin & Garrod, 1983; Cowin *et al.* 1984*a*; Garrod, 1984), in which widely cross-reacting anti-desmosomal antibodies have enabled surveys of many tissues and cells, using immunofluorescence. Examples of simple and stratified epithelia stained with fluorescent anti-desmosomal antibodies are shown in Fig. 2.

The number of desmosomes possessed by a tissue may be directly related to its adhesiveness. Thus both Overton (1977), working with embryonic chick corneal epithelium and mouse epidermis, and Wiseman & Strickler (1981), working with chick embryonic heart of different ages, have shown that in sorting-out experiments the cells possessing the greater number of desmosomes adopted the internal position in aggregates of binary cell combinations. Adoption of the internal position suggests that cells are more adhesive than those that surround them (Steinberg, 1964).

The functional significance of variation in desmosome number may relate to the amount of stress a tissue is subjected to: tissues that have to resist stress require more desmosomes to link their intermediate filament cytoskeletons from cell to cell (Arnn & Staehelin, 1981; Garrod, 1985).

MODULATION OF DESMOSOME DISTRIBUTION VARIES BETWEEN DIFFERENT TYPES OF EPITHELIA

We have shown that cells in tissue culture can modulate the distribution of desmosomal components in order to achieve the characteristic patterns of simple or stratified epithelium, depending upon cell type.

MDBK cells are derived from bovine kidney tubule and in culture form a simple, polarized epithelium, each cell having a single row of desmosomes around its apico-lateral border. When MDBK cells are passaged their polarity is destroyed, their desmosomal plaques are internalized and their desmocollins can be removed by the action of trypsin and EDTA (Cowin *et al.* 1984*b*). When they are replated, the desmocollins initially reappear all over the upper surfaces of the cells, a process that is independent of intercellular contact. During a culture period of several days, however, polarity is re-acquired and the desmocollins become removed from the upper cell surfaces and confined to the lateral cell margins. Thus MDBK cells in culture exhibit a reorganization or modulation of adhesive molecules, generating this polarized arrangement of adhesive properties.

A different pattern of modulation is seen in stratified epithelia. Calcium-induced desmosome formation between keratinocytes in monolayer culture (Hennings *et al.* 1980; Jones *et al.* 1982; Hennings & Holbrook, 1983) has been followed with fluorescent antibody staining (Watt, Mattey & Garrod 1984; Garrod, 1985). In <0·1 mM-calcium the desmosomal components were diffusely distributed, but within 15 min of raising the calcium concentration to 1·8 mM all the molecules were concentrated at cell peripheries in the region of contact. At this stage the cells were still in monolayer, with desmosomes between their lateral surfaces. Stratification began after about 9 h in high concentrations of calcium. This was characterized by the appearance of desmosomes between the upper and lower surfaces of super-imposed cells, detectable by punctate staining with anti-desmosomal antibodies. We are not sure whether this process involves re-orientation of existing desmosomes, or breakdown and re-formation of desmosomes, though we have some preliminary evidence for the latter. (For details and photographs, see Watt *et al.* (1984).) The antigenic difference that we have demonstrated between the desmocollins of basal and suprabasal epidermal appears to be a consequence of stratification rather than a cause of it (Parrish *et al.* 1986). It could be associated with a difference in desmosomal stability in the different layers (see below). In this context the most important point is that formation of desmosomes between upper and lower surfaces of stratifying cells is a property that distinguishes stratified from simple epithelial cells.

The occurrence of desmosomal redistribution during morphogenesis *in vivo*, has been demonstrated in duct formation in the rat mammary gland (Dulbecco, Allen & Bowman, 1984). The epithelium of the duct consists of two layers, polarized cells with a luminal surface apically and myo-epithelial cells basally. In the early bud stages, microvillin and p80, markers of the apical cell surface, and desmoplakins are located together in the immature epithelial cells. In the two-layered ductal epithelium, however, the apical markers are present at the luminal surface, while the desmoplakins are concentrated at the interface between the apical cells and the myo-epithelial cells. The acquisition of the correct pattern of adhesive properties must be fundamental to the development and maintenance of epithelial structure. It is clear that different types of epithelial cells are able to regulate the distribution of desmosomes and desmosomal components in specific ways in order to achieve patterns appropriate to their tissues.

STABILITY OF DESMOSOMES

The capacity to modify adhesive contacts is necessary during development. In certain sites in adult organisms, such as intestinal crypts and the germinative layer of the epidermis, much cell rearrangement is also required. In other situations, such as the upper layers of the epidermis, the oesophagus and vaginal epithelium, firm linkages between cells are necessary (Revel, 1974). Variability in the stability of adhesive contacts, some being reversible, some more enduring, would thus seem a necessary requirement for a functional adhesion mechanism.

This idea was first raised in relation to desmosomes by Borysenko & Revel (1973), who showed that desmosomes of stratified squamous epithelia and glandular epithelia were insensitive to EDTA, whereas desmosomes of simple columnar epithelia were EDTA-sensitive. The former group of desmosomes were, however, disrupted by trypsin, while the latter were not. A third group of desmosomes, found in rat pancreas, were disrupted only by the detergent sodium deoxycholate. They suggested that the EDTA-resistant desmosomes were functionally stable, while those that were EDTA-sensitive were physiologically labile.

Our own data relating to desmosome stability come from calcium-switching experiments on keratinocytes (Watt *et al.* 1984), and MDCK and MDBK cells. I should first point out that MDCK cells exhibit rapid triggering of desmosome formation by low–high switching of calcium concentration, whereas MDBK cells show slow desmosome formation on calcium switching, requiring protein and RNA synthesis for production of the desmoplakins and 175 000–164 000 M_r glycoproteins (Mattey & Garrod, unpublished).

Once calcium-induced desmosome formation has taken place, the stability of desmosomes to calcium reduction changes with time and varies between the three cell types. Keratinocyte desmosomes may be disrupted by calcium depletion for up to 2 h after formation, but thereafter become resistant. MDCK cell desmosomes may be disrupted by calcium depletion for up to 3 days after formation but then acquire resistance. MDBK cell desmosomes do not become resistant to calcium depletion for at least 14 days after formation.

We are aware that calcium-switching may not truly parallel the *in vivo* situation but other environmental and, or, developmental triggers may be involved in controlling desmosome assembly and disassembly. Differential desmosomal stability may certainly provide a basis for adhesive differences between cell types.

THE MOLECULAR ROLE OF CALCIUM

We are beginning to unravel the molecular basis of calcium involvement in desmosomal adhesion (Suhrbier, Mattey & Garrod, unpublished observations). The desmosomal adhesion molecules, the desmocollins, are calcium protected: in the presence of 0.1 mM-calcium they are resistant to removal from the cell surface by 0.1% trypsin, but in the presence of EGTA they are rapidly removed by 0.0001% trypsin. Furthermore, trypsin digestion (0.1%) of desmosomal cores from bovine nasal epithelium yields a single soluble desmocollin fragment of M_r 42 000, which is digested in the presence of EGTA. Moreover, both the desmocollins and the 175 000–164 000 M_r desmosomal glycoproteins bind calcium. An essential point to note is that the calcium requirements for calcium protection and calcium-induced desmosome formation differ by at least an order of magnitude (approx. 0.1 mM and 1–2 mM respectively). Calcium-induced desmosome assembly and stability probably involve desmosomal carbohydrate, since cells may be induced to form stable desmosomes in low calcium medium by treatment with tunicamycin.

ADHESIVE DIFFERENCES WITH CELL ADHESION MOLECULES

Variation in the cellular distribution of cell adhesion molecules has been described. Thus, for example, N-CAM is concentrated at the end-feet of neuroepithelial cells in the optic nerve pathway, where it plays an important role in guidance of developing optic nerve fibres (Silver & Rutishauser, 1984), and at the nerve–muscle junction in developing mouse diaphragm (Rieger, Grumet & Edelman, 1985), while Ng-CAM is present on neuronal processes rather than cell bodies (Thiery *et al.* 1985). In developing optic retinal ganglian cells there is a differential distribution of the embryonic (E) and adult (A) forms of N-CAM within the same cells. The sialic-acid-rich E-form is present in the optic nerves in the 5–10 day chick embryo, while the sialic-acid-poor A-form is present in the retina (Schlosshauer, Schwarz & Rutishauser, 1984). The E-form of N-CAM has a lower binding affinity than the A-form (Edelman, 1983, 1984), conversion of the former to the latter providing a means of increasing cellular adhesiveness during development. In the case of N-CAM, variation in adhesiveness with time also occurs *via* down- or up-regulation of the molecule. Thus N-CAM disappears or decreases from skeletal muscle post-natally but reappears when regeneration of new synapses is required following denervation or disease (Moore & Walsh, 1985; Rieger *et al.* 1985). Reduction in the amount of N-CAM on the cell surface has also been shown to occur following viral transformation of embryonic chick retinal cells (Brackenbury, Greenberg & Edelman, 1984). A full discussion and summary of how variation or modulation of CAMs can generate differences in adhesive properties is given by Edelman (1984).

It has recently been reported that individual neural cell types express immuno-logically distinct forms of N-CAM (Williams, Goridis & Akeson, 1985). However, it is not known whether this is due to differences in glycosylation of N-CAM protein in different cells or to differences in the protein itself. Murray *et al.* (1984) reported that a N-CAM, cDNA probe detected only one N-CAM gene in the chick, but Goridis *et al.* (1985) reported that there are possibly three N-CAM genes in the mouse genome. Southern blot hybridization with an L-CAM probe suggested that there may be three distinct L-CAM genes in chick (Gallin, Prediger, Edelman & Cunningham 1985).

CONCLUSION

It seems that similar general principles may apply to adhesion mechanisms involving CAMs and intercellular junctions. Adhesive differences between cells may be qualitative, depending upon the presence of different molecular adhesion mech-anism. A single adhesion mechanism, present in many cell types, may give rise to adhesive differences because of variation in quantity, distribution, stability or affinity. It is important to determine how cells control these parameters.

I thank Dr Derek Mattey for his comments on the manuscript. This work was supported by the Cancer Research Campaign.

REFERENCES

ARMSTRONG, P. B. (1970). A fine structural study of adhesive cell junctions in heterotypic cell aggregates. *J. Cell Biol.* **47**, 197–210.

ARMSTRONG, P. B. (1971). Light and electron microscope studies of cell sorting in combination of chick embryo neural retina and retinal pigment epithelium. *Wilhelm Roux Arch. EntwMech. Org.* **168**, 125–141.

ARNN, J. & STAEHELIN, L. A. (1981). The structure and function of spot desmosomes. *Dermatology* **20**, 330–339.

BAKER, P. C. & SCHROEDER, T. E. (1967). Cytoplasmic filaments and morphogenetic movements in the Amphibian neural tube. *Devl Biol.* **15**, 432–450.

BERRY, M. N. & FRIEND, D. S. (1969). High-yield preparation of rat liver parenchymal cells. A biochemical and fine structural study. *J. Cell Biol.* **43**, 506–520.

BILLIG, D., NICOL, A., COWIN, P., MCGINTY, R., MORGAN, J. & GARROD, D. R. (1982). The cytoskeleton and substratum adhesion in chick embryonic corneal epithelial cells. *J. Cell Sci.* **57**, 51–71.

BOLLER, K., VESTWEBER, D. & KEMLER, R. (1985). Cell-adhesion molecule uvomorulin is localized in the intermediate junctions of adult intestinal epithelial cells. *J. Cell Biol.* **100**, 327–332.

BORYSENKO, J. Z. & REVEL, J. P. (1973). Experimental manipulation of desmosome structure. *J. Anat.* **137**, 403–422.

BRACKENBURY, R., GREENBERG, M. E. & EDELMAN, G. M. (1984). Phenotypic changes and loss of N-CAM-mediated adhesion in transformed embryonic chicken retinal cells. *J. Cell Biol.* **99**, 1944–1954.

BURGESS, D. R. (1982). Reactivation of intestinal epithelial brush border motility: ATP-dependent contraction via a terminal web contractile ring. *J. Cell Biol.* **95**, 853–863.

COHEN, S. M., GORBSKY, G. & STEINBERG, M. S. (1983). Immunochemical characterization of related families of glycoproteins in desmosomes. *J. biol. Chem.* **258**, 2621–2627.

COLE, G. J. & GLASER, L. (1984). Inhibition of embryonic neural retina cell–substratum adhesion with monoclonal antibody. *J. biol. Chem.* **259**, 4031–4034.

COWIN, P. & GARROD, D. R. (1983). Antibodies to epithelial desmosomes show wide tissue and species cross-reactivity. *Nature, Lond.* **302**, 148–150.

COWIN, P., MATTEY, D. L. & GARROD, D. R. (1984*a*). Distribution of desmosomal components in the tissues of vertebrates, studied by fluorescent antibody staining. *J. Cell Sci.* **66**, 119–132.

COWIN, P., MATTEY, D. L. & GARROD, D. R. (1984*b*). Identification of desmosomal surface components (desmocollins) and inhibition of desmosome formation by specific Fab'. *J. Cell Sci.* **70**, 41–60.

DAMSKY, C. H., KNUDSEN, K. & BUCK, C. A. (1984). Integral membrane proteins in cell–cell and cell–substratum adhesion. In *The Biology of Glycoproteins* (ed. R. Ivatt), pp. 1–64. New York: Plenum.

DAMSKY, C. H., RICHA, J., SOLTER, D., KNUDSEN, K. & BUCK, C. A. (1983). Identification and purification of a cell surface glycoprotein mediating intercellular adhesion in embryonic and adult tissues. *Cell* **34**, 455–466.

DOCHERTY, R. J., EDWARDS, J. G., GARROD, D. R. & MATTEY, D. L. (1984). Chick embryonic pigmented retina is one of a group of epithelial tissues that lack cytokeratins and desmosomes and have intermediate filaments composed of vimentin. *J. Cell Sci.* **71**, 61–74.

DULBECCO, R., ALLEN, W. R. & BOWMAN, M. (1984). Lumen formation and redistribution of intramembranous proteins during differentiation of ducts in the rat mammary gland. *Proc. natn. Acad. Sci. U.S.A.* **81**, 5763–5766.

EDELMAN, G. M. (1983). Cell adhesion molecules. *Science* **219**, 450–457.

EDELMAN, G. M. (1984). Modulation of cell adhesion during induction, histogenesis, and perinatal development of the nervous system. *A. Rev. Neurosci.* **7**, 339–377.

ELLISON, J. E. & GARROD, D. R. (1984). Anchoring filaments of the Amphibian dermal–epidermal junction traverse the basal lamina entirely from the plasma membrane of hemidesmosomes to the dermis. *J. Cell Sci.* **72**, 163–172.

EPSTEIN, M. L. & GILULA, N. B. (1977). A study of communication specificity between cells in culture. *J. Cell Biol.* **75**, 769–787.

FRANKE, W. W., MOLL, R., SCHILLER, D. L., SCHMID, E., KARTENBECK, J. & MUELLER, H. (1982). Desmoplakins of epithelial and myocardial desmosomes are immunologically and biochemically related. *Differentiation* **23**, 115–127.

FRANKE, W. W., SCHMID, E., GRUND, C., MUELLER, H., ENGELBRECHT, I., MOLL, R., STADLER, J. & JARASCH, E. D. (1981). Antibodies to high molecular weight polypeptides of desmosomes: specific localisation of a class of junctional proteins in cells and tissues. *Differentiation* **20**, 217–241.

GALLIN, W. J., PREDIGER, E. A., EDELMAN, G. M. & CUNNINGHAM, B. A. (1985). Isolation of a cDNA clone for the liver cell adhesion molecule (L-CAM). *Proc. nat. Acad. Sci. U.S.A.* **82**, 2809–2813.

GARROD, D. R. (1981). Adhesive interactions of cells in development: specificity, selectivity and cellular adhesive potential. *Fortschr. Zool.* **26**, 184–195.

GARROD, D. R. (1985). The adhesions of epithelial cells. In *Cellular and Molecular Control for Direct Cell Interactions in Developing Systems* (ed. H.-J. Marthy), NATO Advanced Studies Institute, series A. *Life Sci.* New York: Plenum (in press).

GARROD, D. R. & COWIN, P. (1985). Desmosome structure and function. In *Receptors in Tumour Biology* (ed. C. M. Chadwick). Cambridge University Press (in press).

GARROD, D. R. & NICOL, A. (1981). Cell behaviour and molecular mechanisms of cell adhesion. *Biol. Rev.* **56**, 199–242.

GIUDICE, G. J., COHEN, S. M., PATEL, N. H. & STEINBERG, M. S. (1984). Immunological comparison of desmosomal components from several bovine tissues. *J. Cell Biochem.* **26**, 35–45.

GORBSKY, G. & STEINBERG, M. S. (1981). Isolation of the intercellular glycoproteins of desmosomes. *J. Cell Biol.* **90**, 243–248.

GORIDIS, C., HIRN, M., SANTONI, M.-J., GENNARINI, G., DEAGOSTINI-BAZIN, H., JORDAN, B. R., KIEFER, M. & STEINMETZ, M. (1985). Isolation of mouse N-CAM-related cDNA: detection and cloning using monoclonal antibodies. *EMBO J.* **4**, 631–635.

HATTA, K., OKADA, T. S. & TAKEICHI, M. (1985). A monoclonal antibody disrupting calcium-dependent cell–cell adhesion of brain tissues: possible role of its target antigen in animal pattern formation. *Proc. natn. Acad. Sci. U.S.A.* 82, 2789–2793.

HEAYSMAN, J. E. M. & PEGRUM, S. M. (1973). Early contacts between fibroblasts. An ultrastructural study. *Expl Cell Res.* **78**, 71–78.

HENNINGS, H. & HOLBROOK, K. A. (1983). Calcium regulation of cell–cell contact and differentiation of epidermal cells in culture. An ultrastructural study. *Expl Cell Res.* **143**, 127–142.

HENNINGS, H., MICHAEL, D., CHENG, C., STEINERT, P., HOLBROOK, K. & YUSPA, S. H. (1980). Calcium regulation of growth and differentiation of mouse epidermal cells in culture. *Cell* **19**, 245–254.

HYAFIL, F., MORELLO, D., BABINET, C. & JACOB, F. (1980). A cell surface glycoprotein involved in the compaction of embryonal carcinoma cells and cleavage stage embryos. *Cell* **21**, 927–939.

JESUDASON, M. L. & ISERI, O. A. (1980). Host–tumor cellular junctions: an ultrastructural study of hepatic metastases in bronchogenic oat cell carcinoma. *Human Path.* **11**, 67–70.

JONES, J. C. R., GOLDMAN, A. E., STEINERT, P. M., YUSPA, S. & GOLDMAN, R. D. (1982). Dynamic aspects of the supramolecular organization of intermediate filament networks in cultured epidermal cells. *Cell Motil.* **2**, 197–213.

KAPPRELL, H.-P., COWIN, P., FRANKE, W. W., POSTINGL, H. & OPFERKUCH, H. J. (1985). Biochemical characterization of desmosomal proteins isolated from bovine muzzle epidermis: amino acid and carbohydrate composition. *Eur. J. Cell Biol.* **36**, 217–229.

KARFUNKEL, P. (1971). The role of microtubules and microfilaments in neurulation in *Xenopus*. *Devl Biol.* **25**, 30–56.

KING, I. A. & TABIOWO, A. (1981). Effect of tunicamycin on epidermal glycoprotein and glycosominoglycan synthesis *in vitro*. *Biochem. J.* **198**, 331–338.

KRUSE, J., KEILHAUER, G., FAISSNER, A., TIMPL, R. & SCHACHNER, M. (1985). The J1 glycoprotein – a novel nervous system cell adhesion molecule of the L2/HNK-1 family. *Nature, Lond.* **316**, 146–148.

MATTEY, D. L. & GARROD, D. R. (1985). Mutual desmosome formation between all binary combinations of human, bovine, canine, avian and amphibian cells: desmosome formation is not tissue or species specific. *J. Cell Sci.* **75**, 377–399.

McNUTT, M. S. & WEINSTEIN, R. S. (1973). Membrane ultrastructure at mammalian intercellular junctions. *Prog. Biophys. molec. Biol.* **26**, 45–101.

MIDDLETON, C. A. & PEGRUM, S. M. (1976). Contacts between pigmented retinal ephithelial cells in culture. *J. Cell Sci.* **22**, 371–383.

MOORE, S. E. & WALSH, F. S. (1985). Specific regulation of N-CAM/D2-CAM cell adhesion molecule during skeletal muscle development. *EMBO J.* **4**, 623–630.

MOSCONA, A. A. (1962). Analysis of cell recombinations in experimental synthesis of tissues *in vitro*. *J. cell. comp. Physiol.* **60** (suppl. I), 65–80.

MUELLER, H. & FRANKE, W. W. (1983). Biochemical and immunological characterization of desmoplakins I and II, the major polypeptides of the desmosomal plaque. *J. molec. Biol.* **163**, 647–671.

MUIR, A. R. (1967). The effects of divalent cations on the ultrastructure of the perfused rat heart. *J. Anat.* **101**, 239–261.

MURRAY, B. A., HEMPERLEY, J. J., GALLIN, W. J., MacGREGGOR, J. S., EDELMAN, G. M. & CUNNINGHAM, B. A. (1984). Isolation of cDNA clones for the chicken neural cell adhesion molecule (N-CAM). *Proc. natn. Acad. Sci. U.S.A.* **81**, 5584–5588.

NICOL, A. & GARROD, D. R. (1982). Fibronectin, intercellular junctions and the sorting-out of embryonic chick tissue cells in monolayer. *J. Cell Sci.* **57**, 357–372.

OCKLIND, C. & ÖBRINK, B. (1982). Intercellular adhesion of rat hepatocytes. Identification of a cell surface glycoprotein involved in the initial adhesion process. *J. biol. chem.* **257**, 6788–6795.

OLDEN, K., PARENT, J. B. & WHITE, S. L. (1982). Carbohydrate moieties of glycoproteins: a re-evaluation of their function. *Biochim. biophys. Acta* **650**, 209–232.

OVERTON, J. (1974a). Cell junctions and their development. *Prog. Surface Membr. Sci.* **8**, 161–208.

OVERTON, J. (1974b). Selective formation of desmosomes in chick cell reaggregates. *Devl Biol.* **39**, 210–225.

OVERTON, J. (1977). Formation of junctions and cell sorting in aggregates of chick and mouse cells. *Devl Biol.* **55**, 103–116.

OVERTON, J. (1982). Inhibition of desmosome formation with tunicamycin and with lectin in corneal cell aggregates. *Devl Biol.* **92**, 66–72.

PARRISH, E., GARROD, D. R., MATTEY, D. L., HAND, L., STEART, P. & WELLER, R. O. (1986). Mouse antisera specific for desmosomal adhesion molecules of suprabasal skin cells, meninges and meningioma. *Proc. natn. Acad. Sci. U.S.A.* (in press).

PITTS, J. D. (1978). Junctional communication and cellular growth control. In *Intercellular Junctions and Synapses, Receptors and Recognition,* series B, vol. 2 (ed. J. Feldman, N. B. Gilula & J. D. Pitts), pp. 61–79. London: Chapman and Hall.

RATHJEN, F. G. & RUTISHAUSER, U. (1984). Comparison of two cell surface molecules involved in neural cell adhesion. *EMBO J.* **3**, 461–465.

RATHJEN, F. G. & SCHACHNER, M. (1984). Immunocytological and biochemical characterization of a new neuronal cell surface component (L1 Antigen) which is involved in cell adhesion. *EMBO J.* **3**, 1–10.

REVEL, J.-P. (1974). Some aspects of cellular interactions in development. In *The Cell Surface in Development* (ed. A. A. Moscona), pp. 51–66. New York, London, Sydney, Toronto: John Wiley and Sons.

RIEGER, F., GRUMET, M. & EDELMAN, G. M. (1985). N-CAM at the vertebrate neuromuscular junction. *J. Cell Biol.* **101**, 285–293.

SCHLOSSHAUER, B., SCHWARZ, U. & RUTISHAUSER, U. (1984). Topological distribution of different forms of neural cell adhesion molecule in the developing chick visual system. *Nature, Lond.* **310**, 141–143.

SCHUBERT, D. & LA CORBIÈRE, M. (1985). Isolation of a cell-surface receptor for chick neural retina adhesions. *J. Cell Biol.* **100**, 56–63.

SEDAR, A. W. & FORTE, J. G. (1964). Effects of calcium depletion on the junctional complex between oxyntic cells of gastric glands. *J. Cell Biol.* **22**, 173–188.

SILVER, J. & RUTISHAUSER, U. (1984). Guidance of optic axons *in vivo* by a preformed adhesive pathway on neuroepithelial endfeet. *Devl Biol.* **106**, 485–499.

SKERROW, C. J. (1978). Intercellular adhesion and its role in epidermal differentiation. *Invest. Cell Path.* **1**, 23–37.

SPERRY, R. W. (1963). Chemoaffinity in the orderly growth of nerve fibre patterns and connections. *Proc. natn. Acad. Sci. U.S.A.* **50**, 703–710.

STAEHELIN, L. A. (1974). Structure and function of intercellular junctions. *Int. Rev. Cytol.* **39**, 191–283.

STEINBERG, M. S. (1964). The problem of adhesive selectivity in cellular interactions. In *Cellular Membranes in Development, 22nd Symp. Soc. Study of Development and Growth* (ed. M. Locke), pp. 321–366. New York: Academic Press.

SUHRBIER, A. & GARROD, D. R. (1985). An investigation of the molecular Components of desmosomes in epithelial cells of five vertebrates. *J. Cell Sci.* **81**, 223–242.

TAKEICHI, M., ATSUMI, T., YOSHIDA, C., UNO, K. & OKADA, T. S. (1981). Selective adhesion of embryonal carcinoma cells and differentiated cells by Ca^{2+}-dependent sites. *Devl Biol.* **87**, 340–350.

THIERY, J.-P., BRACKENBURY, R., RUTISHAUSER, U. & EDELMAN, G. M. (1977). Adhesion among neural cells of the chick embryo. II. Purification and characterisation of a cell adhesion molecule from neural retina. *J. biol. Chem.* **252**, 6841–6845.

THIERY, J.-P., DELOUVÉE, A., GRUMET, M. & EDELMAN, G. M. (1985). Initial appearance and regional distribution of the neuron–glial cell adhesion molecule in the chick embryo. *J. Cell Biol.* **100**, 442–456.

VESTWEBER, D., OCKLIND, C., GOSSLER, A., ODIN, P., ÖBRINK, B. & KEMLER, R. (1985). Comparison of two cell-adhesion molecules, uvomorulin and cell-CAM 105. *Expl Cell Res.* **157**, 451–461.

WARREN, L., BUCK, C. A. & TUSZYNSKI, G. P. (1978). Glycopeptide changes in malignant transformation: a possible role for carbohydrate in malignant behaviour. *Biochim. biophys. Acta* **516**, 97–127.

WATT, F. M., MATTEY, D. L. & GARROD, D. R. (1984). Calcium-induced reorganization of desmosomal components in cultured human keratinocytes. *J. Cell Biol.* **99**, 2211–2215.

WHITE, F. H. & GOHARI, K. (1984). Desmosomes in hamster cheek pouch epithelium: their quantitative characterization during epithelial differentiation. *J. Cell Sci.* **66**, 411–429.

WILLIAMS, R. K., GORIDIS, C. & AKESON, R. (1985). Individual cell types express immunologically distinct N-CAM forms. *J. Cell Biol.* **101**, 36–42.

WISEMAN, L. L. & STRICKLER, J. (1981). Desmosome frequency: experimental alteration may correlate with differential adhesion. *J. Cell Sci.* **49**, 217–223.

YOSHIDA-NORO, C., SUZUKI, N. & TAKEICHI, M. (1984). Molecular nature of the calcium-dependent cell–cell adhesion system in mouse teratocarcinoma and embryonic cells studied with monoclonal antibody. *Devl Biol.* **101**, 19–27.

J. Cell Sci. Suppl. 4, 239–266 (1986)
Printed in Great Britain © The Company of Biologists Limited 1986

THE GAP JUNCTION

JOHN D. PITTS AND MALCOLM E. FINBOW

Beatson Institute for Cancer Research, Garscube Estate, Bearsden, Glasgow G61 1BD, Scotland

INTRODUCTION

Intercellular communication is necessary in complex, differentiated organisms to coordinate the activities, differentiation and growth of the component cells. Two forms of cell–cell communication contribute to this coordination in metazoan animals. One form involves the secretion by cells of signal substances (e.g. neuro-transmitters, hormones, growth factors) into the extracellular fluids. Target cells, which may be immediately adjacent or in some distant tissue, respond appropriately if they have the right receptors. The other form of communication operates within the limiting plasma membranes of groups of cells coupled into integrated units by specialized junctions. These junctions are essentially sieve-like structures that permit free diffusion through all the coupled cytoplasms, of low molecular weight, water-soluble components. They are ubiquitous structures; all cells of metazoan animals appear to form these junctions, though in a few special cases they are lost in the terminal stages of differentiation. From their appearance in electron micrographs, these structures have been termed gap junctions.

THE STRUCTURE OF THE GAP JUNCTION CHANNEL

The structural unit of the gap junction is the connexon. Each connexon is 6–7 nm in diameter and is a hollow cylinder of protein that spans the plasma membrane and joins end-to-end with another connexon in the plasma membrane of an adjoining cell. The aligned, paired connexons form a continuous channel for direct cytoplasmic communication between the coupled cells. The channels do not appear to occur singly on the cell surfaces, except perhaps in early stages of junction assembly, but are clustered together in well-defined areas or plaques, which can be seen by thin-section and freeze-fracture electron microscopy (Figs 1, 2).

The size of individual gap junctions can vary from very small, containing just a few connexon pairs, to several square micrometres containing many thousands. The reason connexons cluster together into plaques is unknown but it would seem likely that such an arrangement is energetically favourable as it reduces to a minimum the area of unstably close apposition between two adjacent membranes. Connexons may interact with their partners in the neighbouring cell membrane and then migrate into clusters or, more likely, the clusters may provide focal points for assembly of connexon pairs. They may also be units for internalization during turnover (Larsen & Tung, 1978).

Gap junctions retain their characteristic, plaque-like structure in the presence of many detergents, 6 M-urea and alkali, properties that facilitate their purification from other membrane components. The connexons in isolated gap junctions are usually more tightly packed than in intact cells and display a characteristic quasi-crystalline hexagonal arrangement (Fig. 4), which has permitted the application of X-ray and electron diffraction techniques to determine the fine structure (Makowski, Caspar, Phillips & Goodenough, 1977; Caspar, Goodenough, Makowski & Phillips, 1977; Unwin & Zampighi, 1980; Unwin & Ennis, 1984). These analyses show the connexon is made of six similar, probably identical, subunits arranged axially around a 2 nm water-filled channel (Fig. 5). Each subunit appears to be a rod-like structure equivalent to 20000–30000 M_r protein but the resolution is not high enough to identify the exact size, the number of transmembrane domains present in each subunit or the nature of the protein secondary structure. However, it is known that each subunit is tilted at a slight angle to the long axis of the connexon. The subunits appear to be fixed where they meet in the space between the membranes but the angle of tilt, at least in isolated junctions, can be decreased (e.g. by the addition of Ca^{2+}), which results in a twisting movement and the closure of the channel at the cytoplasmic ends. Such a conformational change may form the basis of a mechanism for switching connexon channels *in situ* between open and closed states.

The characteristic 2–4 nm gap between the two membranes in the junctional plaques (Figs 1, 5) is the result of each connexon projecting 1–2 nm into the extracellular space. It is this separation or 'gap' that gave the name to the structure, and which distinguishes it from the 'tight' junctions (structures that provide seals between the lateral surfaces of cells in epithelial sheets), which otherwise can have a similar appearance in thin sections (Revel & Karnovsky, 1967). On the cytoplasmic faces of the junctions the connexons protrude very little, giving a somewhat feature-less surface (Hirokawa & Heuser, 1982). The isolated junctions, which retain the double membrane structure, are not only stable to chaotropic agents but also have an inherent resistance to proteases such as trypsin and collagenase (Goodenough, 1976), presumably because of the absence of sensitive peptide bonds on the accessible cytoplasmic surfaces. This property has been exploited in procedures for preparing pure fractions of gap junctions and has been an important criterion for choosing between different candidates for the gap junction protein. Only those proteins that survive, either whole or in part, protease treatment of intact gap junctions can be considered as potential junctional proteins.

Figs 1, 2. Thin-section and freeze-fracture micrographs of gap junctions between the columnar epithelial cells from the hepatopancreas of *Nephrops norvegicus* (Norway lobster). The characteristic 2–4 nm gap is clearly evident in the thin-section (Fig. 1) while the freeze-fracture replica (Fig. 2) shows the plaque-like structure of the gap junction. The connexon particles partition of the E-face in arthropods leaving corresponding P-face pits. Micrographs by courtesy of Dr N. J. Lane, Cambridge. Fig. 1, ×286000; Fig. 2, ×103000.

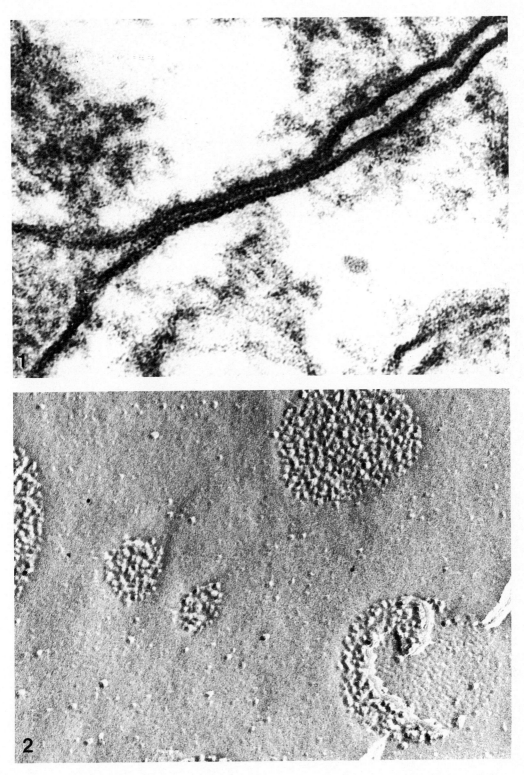

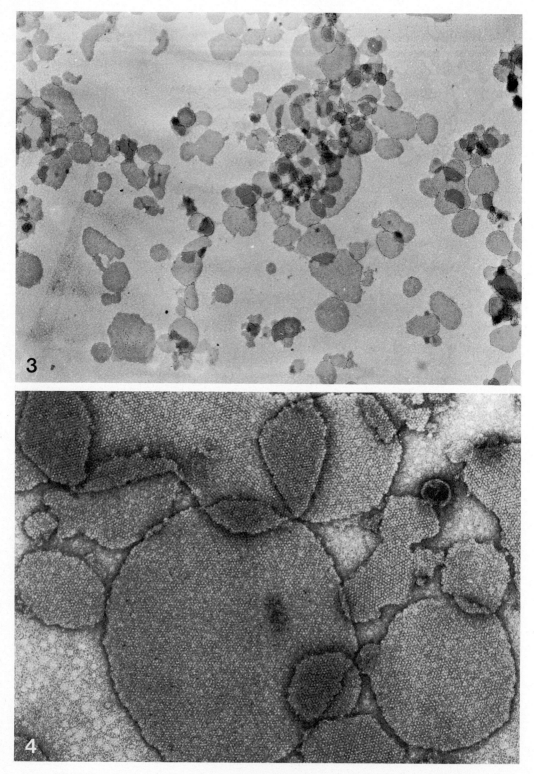

Figs 3, 4. Micrograph of negative stained preparation of isolated gap junctions prepared from the hepatopancreas of *N. norvegicus* (Norway lobster). The junctions were prepared by the method of Finbow *et al.* (1984) with the inclusion of a trypsin treatment step. Fig. 1, ×19750; Fig. 2, ×106000.

THE STRUCTURAL PROTEIN OF THE GAP JUNCTION

Even though the gap junction was one of the first membrane structures to be isolated (by Benedetti & Emmelot, 1967), the structural protein has only recently been identified. Over the years many different sized and seemingly unrelated proteins have been found in sodium dodecyl sulphate–polyacrylamide (SDS–PAGE) gel profiles of preparations seen by electron microscopy to contain junctions (for review, see Robertson, 1981). Only in 1979 did some consensus of opinion begin to emerge when in three separate laboratories a protein of M_r 27 000 was identified as a major component (Hertzberg & Gilula, 1979; Henderson, Eibl & Weber, 1979; Finbow, Yancey, Johnson & Revel, 1980). Since then considerable interest has been focused on this protein as a starting point for further research into the structure, regulation and function of the gap junction. It therefore came as something of a surprise when new evidence began to emerge that showed the junctional origin of a protein of M_r 16 000 (Finbow, Shuttleworth, Hamilton & Pitts, 1983). It was at first thought that this smaller protein might be a structurally important fragment of the 27 000 M_r protein, but recent work described below shows that this is not the case.

The 16 000 M_r protein was first found in gap junction preparations made from cultured cells but has since been shown to be the major component in gap junction preparations from a wide range of vertebrate sources. Gap junctions isolated from arthropod tissues contain a related though slightly larger protein of M_r 18 000 (Finbow *et al.* 1984).

The discovery of the 16 000 M_r protein came by chance when a new procedure was devised for the isolation of gap junctions from cultured cells (Finbow *et al.* 1983). Previously, gap junctions had been prepared in different laboratories (from mouse or rat, liver or heart) by variations of the original method in which plasma membranes are first isolated using the procedures devised by Neville (1960) and then extracted with detergents (e.g. Sarkosyl, deoxycholate, Triton X-100). The gap junctions are then pelleted along with other detergent-resistant material. Further fractionation is achieved by ultracentrifugation in sucrose density gradients. Extra steps have been introduced from time to time to remove contaminants. In some studies the plasma

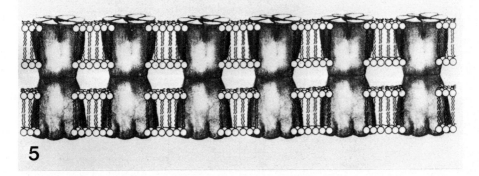

5

Fig. 5. An idealized view of a gap junction seen in cross-section. The figure was adapted and redrawn from Unwin & Henderson (1984).

membranes were treated with trypsin before detergent extraction but in others this step was replaced with one using chaotropic agents (e.g. urea).

The new procedure, because of the necessarily limited amount of starting material available from cell cultures, avoids the preliminary isolation of plasma membranes and instead starts with the direct solubilization of cell monolayers (or in later modifications, of crude tissue homogenates) in Triton X-100 under conditions where nuclei, cytoskeletal elements and other structural cell components remain intact. Soluble cell contents and membrane components (including gap junctions) not attached to the cytoskeleton are released and the junctions are further purified by their resistance to Sarkosyl, 6 M-urea and sometimes trypsin. This new approach has proved beneficial not only by increasing the yields of junctions but also by allowing gap junctions to be isolated from a very wide range of sources (i.e. different cultured cells and different tissues from different species and phyla). The resulting preparations are seen by electron microscopy to be rich in gap junctions and, particularly if a trypsin treatment step is included, to be of uniformly high quality (Figs 3, 4).

It is important to remember, however, that while electron microscopy can give an impression of purity it cannot be converted to a quantitative measure. Furthermore, micrographs of thin sections of pelletted preparations can be misleading, because differential rates of centrifugation result in stratification of different components in the pellet, producing junction-rich and junction-poor regions. Representative analyses can be made only by complete serial sectioning of pellets, but this is impractical for routine purposes. Also, at low magnification, when scanning the pellet the eye tends to pick out the strata containing the characteristic arrays of close-packed junctions. Analysis of negatively stained preparations can help to overcome this problem, but with this method there is a tendency for junctions to clump together, giving misleadingly rich, contaminant-free areas and there is also the possibility that non-junctional structures are adsorbed less efficiently to the grid support.

These problems with the initial identification of the gap junction protein are clearly illustrated by comparing the results of Hertzberg & Gilula (1979) with those of Fallon & Goodenough (1981). In both studies rodent liver was used as a source of junctions, similar isolation protocols were followed and both authors claim to have achieved near homogeneity as seen by electron microscopy of the final junction preparations. However, the SDS–PAGE profiles have no major bands in common. A similar situation has arisen with the isolation of junctions from heart (Kensler & Goodenough, 1980; Gros, Nicholson & Revel, 1983).

Lens is the only tissue that has consistently given preparations with the same gel profile. Lens junctions are similar in appearance to gap junctions from other tissues but lack the characteristic 'gap' and the particles seen in freeze-fractured preparations are much more loosely packed (Hertzberg, Anderson, Friedlander & Gilula, 1982). The membranes of lens fibres, however, are very rich in MIP26 ('main intrinsic protein' of lens, M_r 26 000) and this is always the most prominent band in junction preparations (e.g. see Goodenough, 1979). This clear picture with lens probably influenced the choice of a 27 000 M_r band in junction preparations from other tissues, but more recent work has shown that the 27 000 M_r protein in the liver is not related to MIP26 (Hertzberg *et al.* 1982) and it is now fairly widely accepted that the lens junctions are more likely to be involved in holding the transparent, crystallin filled lens fibres in close apposition to maintain the optical properties of the tissue than in intercellular communication. Lens fibres are coupled (Scheutze & Goodenough, 1982), so either the lens junctions perform both functions or communicating (liver-type) junctions are also present. If the two types are present the connexons may not congregate to form the typical plaques but may be dispersed among the particles of the other junctions.

It can be seen from the above discussion that any claim for the gap-junctional origin of a particular gel band must be accompanied by more than a subjective assessment of the purity of the final preparation based on electron microscopy. The only further criterion put forward in support of the 27 000 M_r protein is based on a correlation between the disappearance of morphologically identifiable gap junctions in the course of liver regeneration and a disappearance of isolatable 27 000 M_r protein (Finbow *et al.* 1980). There are many changes that occur during this complex process, so this apparent relationship may be fortuitous. Furthermore, other work has shown the 16 000 M_r protein also disappears at the same time (Finbow *et al.* 1983).

Several other criteria have provided additional support for the junctional origin of the 16 000 M_r protein (Finbow *et al.* 1983, 1984; John *et al.* unpublished results). The 16 000 M_r protein and the junctions are found in the same fractions when preparations are centrifuged to equilibrium in potassium iodide density gradients. The release of the protein from pelletable material (which includes the junctions) by increasing concentrations of SDS parallels the dissolution, observed by electron microscopy, of the gap-junctional structure. The disappearance of gap junctions from V79 cells after treatment with the phorbol ester TPA (Yancey *et al.* 1982) correlates with the disappearance of recoverable 16 000 M_r protein. The 16 000 M_r protein is immunologically related to the 18 000 M_r arthropod gap-junctional protein. A site-specific antibody raised to a synthetic peptide made according to the N-terminal sequence of the 16 000 M_r protein (determined in collaboration with Dr J. Walker, Cambridge) binds to gap junctions (visualized by protein-A-coated gold particles) and blocks junctional communication when injected into cells. This last observation is consistent with recent studies on Pronase accessibility of sites in isolated junctions, which have localized the N terminus of the 16 000 M_r protein to the cytoplasmic face (John *et al.* 1986).

Critics (Revel, Nicholson & Yancey, 1985; Hertzberg, 1985) of the 16 000 M_r protein have focused on the use of trypsin during isolation and on the size of the protein. The omission of a trypsin step does not change the major protein component produced by this method but endogenous proteolysis can never be entirely ruled out. The 16 000 M_r component may be derived from a larger protein (other than 27 000 M_r) and the issue will not be resolved until the appropriate complementary DNA has been fully sequenced. The 16 000 M_r component is, however, sufficient to maintain the characteristic, trypsin-resistant structure of the gap junction.

There is a difference between the estimated molecular weight of the 16 000 M_r protein and the mass of a subunit (20 000 to 30 000 M_r) calculated from X-ray and electron diffraction studies. This may be due to the known anomalous migration of very hydrophobic proteins in SDS–PAGE gels (e.g. the M_r of subunit 1 of cytochrome oxidase calculated from complete sequence data is 58 000 but its M_r from SDS–PAGE is only 38 000; Isaac, Jones & Leaver, 1985) or, and just as consistent with the diffraction data, each connexon subunit may contain the dimer of the 16 000 M_r protein (which migrates on SDS–PAGE gels with an M_r of 26 000).

In hindsight one can trace the reasons why the 16 000 M_r protein remained undetected in junctional preparations for so long. The original isolation studies of Goodenough (1974, 1976) used a trypsin treatment step but then solubilized the junctional fraction by heating in SDS before SDS–PAGE. Such preparations have now been shown (Finbow *et al.* 1986) to contain about equal amounts of the 16 000 M_r protein and the Goodenough 10 000 M_r protein (connexin) but because of heat-induced aggregation, the hydrophobic 16 000 M_r protein is converted to a state that is too large to enter the gel and only the 10 000 M_r band is resolved (solubilization without heating results in gels with both 10 000 M_r and 16 000 M_r bands). This phenomenon is illustrated in Fig. 6 by experiments in which the same mouse liver junction preparation has been solubilized in four different ways. Solubilization conditions most like those used by Goodenough (1976) were used for the sample shown in lane d.

This 10 000 M_r protein is not present in junction preparations made by the more recently devised method. Furthermore, when a plasma membrane preparation is divided into two equal parts and junctions isolated by the different procedures, the 10 000 M_r protein is present only in one of the final fractions but the 16 000 M_r protein is present in both (Fig. 7).

Further problems were caused in the earlier studies by the understandable but, as it turned out, probably mistaken concern about the possible dangers of proteolysis during isolation. Trypsin treatment was omitted, protease inhibitors were added and steps using chaotropic agents were introduced instead. Preparations made in this way contain more total protein and SDS–PAGE shows the presence of more different proteins, although the yield of gap junctions is probably unaffected. As a result, the 16 000 M_r protein appears only as a minor band in the presence of much larger amounts of the protease-sensitive 27 000 M_r protein.

The protease sensitivity of the 27 000 M_r protein, in contrast to the protease resistance of the gap-junctional structure, has always posed a dilemma. The 27 000 M_r protein can be considered as the junctional protein only if pieces large enough to maintain the plaque-like structure remain after trypsinization. The 10 000 M_r (and later the 16 000 M_r) protein was an obvious candidate for such a piece, although it seemed somewhat small. This criticism was apparently overcome when Nicholson *et al.* (1981) suggested, on the basis of multiple signals from sequence analysis, that the 10 000 M_r band was a mixture of peptides, one with the same N-terminal sequence as 27 000 M_r and another with a different sequence (and therefore possibly a more C-terminal fragment of 27 000 M_r). Subsequent work using two-dimensional

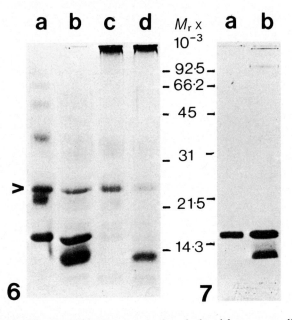

Figs 6, 7. SDS–PAGE of gap-junction preparations isolated from mouse liver.

Fig. 6 shows equal loadings of the same preparation solubilized in SDS sample buffer in 4 ways. In lanes a and b the samples were solubilized at room temperature, while in lanes c and d they were solubilized by heating to 100°C for 5 min; 2 % β-mercaptoethanol was included in the sample buffer during solubization for lanes b and d but not for a and c. The junction preparation used was isolated by the method of Goodenough (1976) as modified by Finbow *et al.* (1980) in which plasma membranes are first treated with trypsin and collagenase before extraction with Sarkosyl. The 16 000 M_r protein, which is present in similar abundance to the 10 000 M_r protein when the samples are solubilized at room temperature (lane b), is lost by boiling (due to heat-induced aggregation to multimeric forms too large to enter the gel; lanes c and d). The 10 000 M_r protein, but not the 16 000 M_r protein, is sensitive to β-mercaptoethanol, running as S–S bonded multimers in the absence of the reducing agent (lane a). Even when solubilized at room temperature a proportion of the 16 000 M_r protein runs as its SDS-stable dimeric form (lane a, arrow). The proportion of the dimeric (and higher multimeric forms) can be increased by controlled heating (Finbow *et al.* 1983).

Fig. 7 shows gap junction preparations made from equal amounts of a mouse liver plasma membrane preparation by either the same method as used for the samples shown in Fig. 6 (lane b) or by the new procedure described by Finbow *et al.* (1983) that was used to make the preparations shown in Figs 3, 4 (lane a). The 16 000 M_r protein is present in both preparations but the 10 000 M_r protein is lost from junction fractions made by the new procedure. Samples were solubilized at room temperature in the presence of 2 % β-mercaptoethanol.

peptide mapping has shown, however, that the 27 000 M_r, 10 000 M_r and 16 000 M_r proteins are unrelated (Finbow *et al.* 1986).

This combination of evidence in favour of the 16 000 M_r as the junctional protein is further supported by studies on the proteins of junctions isolated from different tissues and different species.

There do not appear to be different tissue forms of the 16 000 M_r junctional protein. Indistinguishable peptide maps are given by the 16 000 M_r protein isolated from purified junction preparations made from mouse liver, heart, kidney and brain (Buultjens, Finbow, Lane & Pitts, 1986). This is probably to be expected, as it is known that different cell types from different tissues are able to form fully functional gap junctions in culture (e.g. heart myocardial cells and ovarian granulosa cells; Lawrence, Beers & Gilula, 1978).

Some regions of the 16 000 M_r protein are conserved throughout the vertebrate phylum (Buultjens *et al.* 1986). As well as common antigenic sites there are also common tryptic peptides in digests of the mouse liver and *Xenopus* liver forms of the 16 000 M_r protein. Again, this is consistent with the functional studies showing that *Xenopus* cells can form operational gap-junction channels with mammalian cells in culture (Pitts, 1977).

The conservation of the junctional protein also extends to the arthropods. Gap junctions isolated from the hepatopancreas of the crustacean *Nephrops norvegicus* (Norway lobster) contain one major protein, M_r 18 000 (Finbow *et al.* 1984). This apparent molecular weight derived from SDS–PAGE is slightly larger than that for the 16 000 M_r vertebrate protein, which is consistent with the larger dimensions of the connexons of the arthropod gap junction (Perrachia, 1973). The junctional origin of the 18 000 M_r protein has been established independently using criteria based on morphological purity, isopycnic centrifugation, SDS solubilization and electron-microscopic (EM) immunological localization. The mouse liver 16 000 M_r and lobster hepatopancreas 18 000 M_r proteins have common antigenic determinants, although there are no common peptides in tryptic maps, indicating greater drift in primary sequence. However, there are peptides that co-migrate in tryptic digests of *Xenopus* 16 000 M_r and lobster 18 000 M_r proteins. These similarities show a high degree of conservation, not only of the general structure, but also of particular regions in the junctional protein, i.e. regions that are likely to be of functional importance. One such region lies on the cytoplasmic face where the sites that regulate junctional permeability are likely to be located. Evidence for such conservation of the cytoplasmic surface comes from experiments using antisera raised against isolated Norway lobster gap junctions (Buultjens, Finbow, Kam & Pitts, unpublished results). Antibodies in these sera bind strongly to the cytoplasmic faces of lobster gap junctions and to a lesser extent to the cytoplasmic faces of mouse junctions. They also inhibit junctional communication when injected into cultured rat liver cells. Another region of the junctional protein that is conserved (as indicated by interspecies junction formation) is the site involved in connexon–connexon interaction necessary for channel formation. The amino acids lining the channel may also be conserved to maintain the characteristic permeability properties of the junction.

PERMEABILITY OF THE JUNCTIONAL CHANNEL

Gap junctions are permeable to molecules and ions that are small enough to pass through the connexon channels. The specificity (i.e. exclusion limit) of the channel has been defined by different functional approaches, which have shown what types of molecule can pass between coupled cells, and by calculations based on the diameter of the channel as derived from the three-dimensional imaging techniques described above. These different approaches give consistent answers.

The functional analyses have been based on two different strategies. One stems from the discovery of metabolic cooperation by Subak-Sharpe, Burk & Pitts (1966, 1969) and uses a variety of genetic and biochemical techniques with mammalian cell cultures to show which normal cellular constituents are shared between coupled cells and which are not. Most cellular molecules are small (M_r less than about 600) and pass through the channels or are large (M_r greater than a few thousand) and do not (Pitts & Simms, 1977; Finbow & Pitts, 1981). Very few are in the critical size range near the exclusion limit, which has therefore been better defined by the other approach that uses the techniques of electrophysiology and is based on the original dye injection studies of Loewenstein & Kanno (1964). Fluorescent probes of different molecular size, shape and charge have been synthesized and injected into *Chironomus* salivary gland cells (which are conveniently large) and other arthropod and mammalian cell types. Observations to decide which of these synthetic probes can pass through junctions to surrounding cells provide a more complete permeability profile of the channel and this is consistent with the studies on the movement of endogenous molecules. The exclusion limit is about M_r 900 for mammalian cells (Flagg-Newton, Simpson & Lowenstein, 1979) and about M_r 1500 for arthropod cells (Simpson, Rose & Lowenstein, 1977). The expression of the limit in terms of molecular weight is convenient, but permeability is likely to be governed by the diameter of the hydrated molecules, and shape and possibly charge may play important roles, especially close to the cut-off point (Brink & Dewey, 1980).

The resolution of the three-dimensional imaging techniques is not yet sufficient to give an accurate measure of the channel diameter throughout the entire length of the connexon but the value seems to lie between 1·5 and 2·0 nm (Unwin & Zampighi, 1980). No information is yet available on the nature of the residues that line the channel, so it is not possible to estimate the effective space available for free movement of molecules through the channel. It might be expected, though, that the channel will have a hydrophilic surface that will be associated with a relatively immobile hydration shell. However, if the influence of such a shell is small, there is good agreement between the estimated dimensions of the channel and the sizes of the largest molecules that can be seen to pass through.

The rates of movement of ions and molecules between cells *via* gap junctions have been estimated in a variety of different systems. Single-channel recordings of junctional conductance have been made only very recently (Neyton & Trautman, 1985), using a somewhat indirect approach recording current flow through the last remaining channels during the final stages of uncoupling, but the value of 120 pS for the fully open state is similar to that obtained from earlier work on fully coupled cells (Sheridan *et al.* 1978). In these systems the non-junctional membrane, although it has a much lower specific conductance (about 10^4-fold), makes a significant and uncertain contribution to the measurements because of its much larger area and the number of junctional channels joining the cells has to be estimated from average values obtained by EM morphometric analysis using freeze-fracture methods. Such studies give conductance values of about 100 ps per channel. These values are high compared to those for some other transmembrane (cytoplasm to outside) channels but not unlike that obtained for the neuromuscular acetylcholine receptor channel (which has a smaller effective diameter but is about half the length), which has been calculated to be able to pass about 10^{10} $K^+ s^{-1}$.

The flux of small molecules through coupled cell populations should be a function of channel conductance and the number of junctional channels present between each cell. In most tissues (or cultures) this number is not known but direct measurements of the intercellular movement of various molecules show that it is normally enough to permit a functionally important level of communication. For example, the diffusion coefficient of the tracer dye lissamine rhodamine B (M_r 559) through the coupled cells of the epidermis of *Tenebrio* larvae is only an order of magnitude lower than that for the same dye through water (Safranyos & Caveney, 1985). In a qualitative analysis (Kam, Melville & Pitts, 1986) it has been shown that Lucifer Yellow (M_r 440) injected into one cell in the dermal layer of mouse skin (a tissue not thought of as particularly rich in gap junctions) migrates *via* the junctional pathway into more than 500 surrounding cells (involving movement of about 0·5 mm) in less than 5 min. In a cultured system, mixtures of two different mutant fibroblast cell lines, one unable to synthesize purine nucleotides and the other unable to synthesize thymine nucleotides, grow at the wild-type rate by mutual nucleotide exchange through gap junctions. The minimum rate of nucleotide transfer that must occur to permit this successful cross-feeding is in excess of 10^7 nucleotides per second per cell pair (Pitts *et al.* 1985) and presumably all other metabolites and small molecules are moving backwards and forwards between the cells at similar rates. From all these approaches, it is clear that the junctional pathway is not just a mechanism for slow 'leakage' between cells but a ubiquitous mechanism for rapid intercellular communication.

GATING OF THE JUNCTIONAL CHANNEL

An operational requirement of transmembrane channels is that they can be gated, that is switched between open and closed conformational states, and the connexon channel of the gap junction is no exception. It is generally believed that in the normal, resting state the junctional channels are open, allowing maximal cell–cell communication but in response to a number of treatments they can be rapidly and reversibly closed. Lowering of intracellular pH, increasing intracellular Ca^{2+}, large transjunctional voltages, retinoic acid and octanol can all result in loss of coupling. At present it is not clear whether any or all of these treatments induce true gating or whether they affect junctional permeability in some less-direct way.

The high-resolution imaging studies described above show that isolated gap junctions can adopt two different conformations, one apparently open and the other apparently closed. The change to the closed state, which is induced by free Ca^{2+}, appears to involve a simple twisting movement of the connexons, which results in a pinching of the channels at their cytoplasmic ends (Unwin & Ennis, 1984). It is not known if this kind of movement occurs *in situ* or if each connexon is able to operate independently from its partner in the adjacent cell membrane. The movement of the protein subunits is greatest at their cytoplasmic ends and least in the extracellular region where the connexons join, which suggests that independent closure is a possibility. Presumably the state of the connexon in a closed junction is similar to that of isolated connexons in the membrane before junction formation. Such precursor channels must be closed to prevent loss from cells of metabolites, ions and other important small cytoplasmic components.

The sensitivity to intracellular pH (Turin & Warner, 1977) appears to be a conserved feature of gap-junction channels, uncoupling having been demonstrated on intracellular acidification (by exposure to CO_2) of, for example, mouse liver hepatocytes and the crayfish septate axon. Voltage sensitivity (for review, see Spray *et al.* 1984) on the other hand, which appears to operate by an unrelated mechanism, is so far restricted to the junctions of amphibian and fish blastomeres and to certain 'rectifying electrical synapses' of specific neurones where current flow through gap junctions appears to be unidirectional. The response of the junctional channel to changes in transmembrane voltage is slow compared to the responses of other voltage-sensitive channels, but this may be explained in terms of difference in dipole moment of the channels.

Closure by increasing free intracellular Ca^{2+} was the first documented example of experimentally induced uncoupling (Rose & Loewenstein, 1975). As with the response to pH, the Ca^{2+} effect is seen in a wide variety of cell types but it is thought that quite large increases are usually necessary to inhibit junctional communication fully. These concentrations may be reached, however, when pancreatic acinar and lachrymal acinar cells uncouple in response to secretagogues (Iwatsuki & Petersen, 1978).

Intracellular acidification and increased intracellular Ca^{2+} probably occur when cells are damaged at times of tissue injury. The resulting closure of the junctions should isolate the dead and dying cells from their undamaged neighbours, preventing the otherwise general loss, *via* the damaged cells, of small ions and molecules from all the cytoplasm of the tissue compartment.

PATTERNS OF JUNCTIONAL COMMUNICATION

The discovery of specificity of gap junction formation led to the idea of communication compartments (Figs 8–11; Pitts, 1976) and the possibility that specific patterns of junctional communication could develop during embryogenesis and tissue differentiation.

The best-studied examples of specificity are in model systems in tissue culture. For example, mixed cultures of epithelial cells and fibroblasts show much greater levels of homologous cell communication compared to heterologous cell communication (Pitts & Burk, 1976; Fentiman, Taylor-Papadimitriou & Stoker, 1976). This preferential interaction is established very rapidly and is accompanied by a longer-term 'sorting-out', which is another property of such mixed cultures. Sorting-out results in islands of epithelial cells separated by channels of fibroblasts (Fig. 8). Within each epithelial island and within the fibroblast channels there is extensive (homologous) junctional communication but there is much reduced (heterologous) communication across the boundaries between the different domains.

This division of the population into communication compartments can be explained simply in terms of specificity of junction formation. Furthermore, the

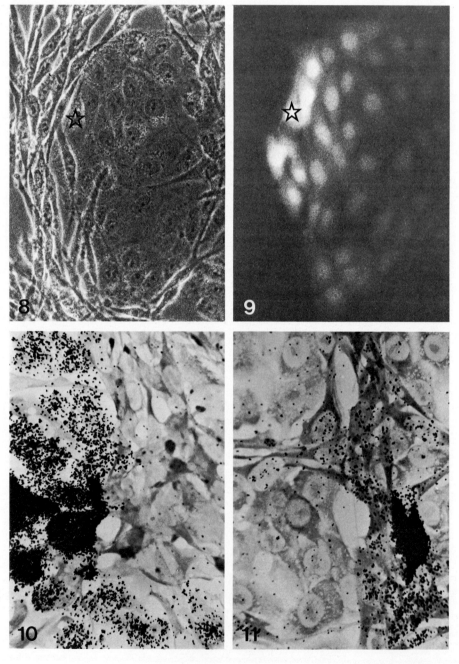

boundary effect resulting from the reduced frequency of heterologous junction formation is accentuated by the much higher frequency of homologous coupling on each side. Molecules diffusing slowly through the relatively few transboundary channels then disperse rapidly through the well-coupled population on the other side (Pitts & Kam, 1985).

The mechanism of specificity is unknown. It seems unlikely to be caused by differences in the junctional protein but seems instead to be due to other cell-surface determinants that affect the rates at which cells come sufficiently close together to permit interaction of the junctional channel precursors (which protrude only 1–2 nm from the membrane in the formed junction). These same membrane determinants may also be responsible for cell sorting. Despite considerable efforts, no clear relationship has been established between cell sorting in culture and the mechanisms of morphogenesis *in vivo* and it is therefore possible to consider that sorting results (coincidentally or by design) from the features that are primarily there to generate communication specificity rather than the other way round.

Various different mutant cell lines have been selected that show reduced rates of junction formation (for review, see Hooper & Subak-Sharpe, 1981). There is no evidence that these lack functionally normal junctional protein, as they form operational junctions but with lower frequency than the corresponding wild types. Complementation analysis has shown that different gene products are affected in different mutant lines, showing that different cell components can affect coupling (MacDonald, 1982). In a perhaps related way, the rate of junction formation in primary cultures derived from various types of tumour varies but is often less than that in cultures of normal cell counterparts (Morgan, Scott, Pitts & Frame, 1982). The range of variation (down to about 5%) is similar to the range seen in the different selected mutant lines. It seems possible, therefore, that the changes, either selected in the mutants or occurring during transformation in the tumour cells, are affecting various surface components, which in turn affect the process of junction formation.

Communication compartments superficially similar to those seen in culture have also been observed *in vivo*. Dye injection near the segmental boundary of fifth instar

Figs 8–11. Communication compartments in culture. Equal numbers of rat liver epithelial cells and hamster fibroblasts were mixed and grown together as described by Pitts & Kam (1985). The two cells types sort out into islands of epithelial cells separated by channels of fibroblasts.

Figs 8 and 9 are phase-contrast and fluorescence micrographs taken after injection of the fluorescent dye Lucifer Yellow into an epithelial cell (star) near an island–channel boundary. The dye spreads through the continuous communication compartment of the epithelial cell island *via* gap junctions but not detectably across the boundary into the fibroblast compartment.

Figs 10 and 11 are autoradiographs prepared after addition of either epithelial cells (Fig. 10) or fibroblasts (Fig. 11) prelabelled with [³H]uridine and then washed (so they contain [³H]uridine nucleotides and [³H]RNA but not [³H]uridine) to the sorted-out cultures. The uridine nucleotides pass first to homologous cells (a form of selective 'injection') and then spread through other cells in the same communication compartment but not detectably across the boundaries. For details of methods see Pitts & Kam (1985).

Figs 8 and 9 by courtesy of Dr E. Kam, Glasgow. Figs 8, 9 ×220; Figs 10, 11 ×300.

larvae of *Oncopeltus* shows dye spread in the same segment as the injected cell but not to the other side of the segmental border (Warner & Lawrence, 1982). This boundary, however, unlike those in the model systems, cannot be detected electro-physiologically. The situation is further complicated by more recent work, which concludes that the boundary is caused by the presence of a line of cells that are unable to form sufficient junctions either among themselves or with the cells of the adjacent segments to permit detectable dye transfer (Blennerhassett & Caveney, 1984).

Boundaries have also been reported, on the basis of similar experiments with dye injection, in the imaginal wing disc of *Drosophila* (Weir & Lo, 1984). It is suggested that these boundaries coincide with the boundaries of developmental compartments of the wing disc, but more recent work has produced contradictory results (Fraser & Bryant, 1985). The coincidence of communication and developmental compart-ments, if it does occur, would be interesting in several ways. It would permit the coordination of groups of cells that share a common developmental fate, it would permit the production of gradients of positional information within compartments, and it could be related to the observation that proliferative control operates within developmental compartments (Morata & Ripoll, 1975).

Dye injection methods have also been used to analyse the patterns of communi-cation in the early mouse embryo (Lo & Gilula, 1979). Junctional communication is first observed between all blastomeres at the eight-cell compaction stage, and all the cells appear to remain coupled until after differentiation of the trophoblast and inner cell mass. After this stage, in embryos implanted *in vitro*, all the cells of the inner cell mass appear to be coupled but dye does not spread to a detectable level into the trophoblast. It is not clear yet, however, whether this represents a boundary phenomenon or whether the absence of spread is due only to poor coupling among the trophoblast cells.

The methods available for analysing patterns of communication depend on insert-ing microelectrodes into cells in intact tissues. In order to identify which cell is being injected, the tissue must be transparent, but it is possible to obtain useful in-formation from blind injections. A recent analysis of junctional interactions in skin has been made using this approach (Kam *et al.* 1986). If Lucifer Yellow is used, the dye binds strongly to cellular (especially nuclear) material as it passes through the cells during the injection period and there is little subsequent movement after the injection is stopped. The distribution of dye in tissue fixed after injection is therefore a good indicator of the junctional pathways that were available in the live tissue. A three-dimensional picture of the dye spread can be obtained from serial sections. Blind injections are mostly intracellular, as most space inside tissue is intracellular. Extracellular injections do occur but can easily be recognized by the absence of intracellular staining (and the presence of extracellular staining) in the sections. This method shows that communication in the dermis is much more extensive than that in the epidermis. During a 5-min injection dye can spread during a dermal injection to more than 500 cells, while dye spread during epidermal injections is limited to a very few, closely packed cells. In new-born mouse skin there is no detectable transfer between the dermis and epidermis or *vice versa*, except at a few special sites. These sites are either in hair follicles close to the basal structures or, infrequently, in the non-follicular epidermis. It is possible that these latter sites, which are small, are regions where hair follicle development and dermal invasion are about to take place. The cells of developing sebaceous glands are coupled to each other but not to surrounding cells. Melanocytes and possibly Langerhan cells are not detectably coupled.

The small spreads in the epidermis could be delineating communication compartments, although at this stage it is difficult to be certain. If they are it is interesting that the size of the compartments (in new-born mouse skin), four to six basal cells with the few overlying cells of the next layers, is similar to that of proposed proliferative units that may play a role in growth control in skin (Mackenzie, 1975).

CONSEQUENCES OF GAP-JUNCTIONAL PERMEABILITY

The presence of gap junctions has a profound effect on the characteristics and behaviour of a cell population. A population of coupled cells is not just a collection of independent units; through gap junctions it becomes a form of syncytium (Pitts, 1980). The combined cytoplasm of all the cells forms a continuous aqueous compartment, which is separated by an uninterrupted hydrophobic barrier (mostly the lipid bilayer of the plasma membranes but completed by the walls of the channels where they cross the reduced gap between adjacent cells) from the continuous aqueous compartment of the extracellular space. The small intracellular molecules of such a coupled population can diffuse anywhere within the compartment but the intracellular macromolecules are relatively fixed in space because they remain in the cells (or the daughter cells after division) in which they are made.

As a direct result of this partial syncytial organization, changes in activity in any one cell can cause corresponding changes in neighbouring cells. For instance, in coupled excitable tissues, action potentials spread quickly and uniformly, with the gap junctions acting as electrotonic synapses. Such transmission is different from chemical synaptic transmission in two ways: there is no synaptic delay and transmission is bidirectional. Gap junctions in effect provide short-circuits between adjacent cells and are probably less sensitive to regulation than chemical synapses. In some tissues, such as heart, short-circuiting with minimum control provides an ideal mechanism for the spread of action potentials and contraction. Control of activity is by changes in the rate of initiation and not by changes in the intensity of contraction. Contraction in smooth muscle, in at least some cases, is similar but not in skeletal muscle. Short-circuiting in this tissue would produce unacceptable all-or-nothing responses and it is therefore not surprising that gap junctions are lost during the terminal stages of differentiation (Kalderon, Epstein & Gilula, 1977), so individually innervated fibres can be fired in appropriate numbers and combinations to produce the required tonicity.

Gap-junctional electrical synapses are also used in situations where the speed of response is paramount. For example, the neurones of the buccal ganglion of the mollusc *Navanax* (Baux, Simmoneau, Tauc & Segundo, 1978) are coupled by gap junctions to allow rapid, full dilation of the buccal cavity for the capture of prey. However, to swallow the prey, the neurones switch to chemical synaptic transmission to produce the required graded contractions (Bennett, Zimering, Spira & Spray, 1985). In this system it is not yet known how gap-junctional communication is turned off.

An inhibition of junctional transmission also occurs between the horizontal cells of the reptilian retina (Neyton, Piccolino & Gerschenfeld, 1985). GABA (γ-amino butyric acid) antagonists increase the extent of electrical and dye coupling between these cells by inhibiting the presynaptic dopaminergic neurones. The effect of dopamine on the horizontal cells appears to be mediated by an increase in cyclic AMP. Studies on the 16 000 M_r gap junction protein show, however, that it is not phosphorylated by cyclic-AMP-dependent kinase (Finbow, unpublished results), suggesting that control may operate through an effector protein. Whatever the detailed mechanism, the fact that junctional communication can be modulated by neurotransmitters has important implications for understanding the role of gap junctions in the central nervous system and other excitable tissues.

Electrical coupling resulting from the movement of current-carrying ions through gap junctions is also important in non-excitable tissues. It confers a stability on the resting potentials of cells by buffering transient changes caused by flickering between closed and open states of relatively small numbers of transmembrane ion channels in each cell (Petersen, 1985). This buffering may also be important in certain excitable tissues as well, such as the bag cell complex of the sea-hare *Aplysia californica* (Kaczmarek, Finbow, Revel & Strumwasser, 1979). These neuroendocrine cells secrete a hormone involved in reproduction and, being coupled by gap junctions, fire synchronously to release large pulses of hormone, which maximizes the response in the target tissue. Inopportune release of hormone by individual bag cells is probably suppressed by the buffering effect of surrounding cells on changes in ion concentrations. This ensures that hormone is released only at the most favourable times when input signals reach the appropriate threshhold.

In the same way as they behave as electrical units, coupled cell populations also behave as metabolic units. Intermediate metabolites form common pools shared by all the cells. This has an integrating effect and results in the coordinate control of cellular metabolic activity (Sheridan, Finbow & Pitts, 1979). The ensuing homeostatic effect means that the control mechanisms that operate on these enzymes in such cells need not be as precise as in cells that live independently.

Perhaps these simple advantages of homeostasis, integration and coordination were a sufficient driving force for the evolution of gap junctions. In this context it is interesting to note that intercellular junctions (plasmodesmata) with similar permeability properties but with quite different structure have evolved in plants (for review, see Gunning & Robards, 1976). In these junctions the plasma membranes of adjacent cells join to form a continuous tube through the intervening matrix of the cell walls. This tube is much wider than a gap-junctional channel but its permeability is very similar, probably due to the presence of an axially located plug-like blockage. An alternative way of achieving coordination, though one that brings with it inherent differences, is through the evolution of the true syncytial state, but in organisms (and tissues) that have adopted this organization all cellular independence has been surrendered and even nuclear division is synchronized.

Once the partial syncytial state produced by gap junctions had evolved, however, a pathway of intercellular communiction became available for other purposes.

The junctional pathway can be used for cross-feeding and for the support of cells that have lost particular metabolic functions. The original observations on metabolic cooperation between cultured cells (Subak-Sharpe *et al.* 1969) showed that mutant cells lacking hypoxanthine phosphoribosyl transferase activity (HPRT$^-$ cells) and so unable to incorporate exogenous hypoxanthine can do so when growing in contact with wild-type (HPRT$^+$) cells if the two cell types form intercellular junctions. This was subsequently shown to be due to the transfer of purine nucleotides through junctions from wild-type to HPRT$^-$ cells (Pitts, 1971; Pitts & Simms, 1977). Extensions of this work (Pitts, 1971) showed that mixed cultures of HPRT$^-$ cells and cells lacking thymidine kinase (TK$^-$ cells) can grow in HAT medium. This medium contains aminopterin (which blocks *de novo* purine nucleotide and TMP synthesis) along with hypoxanthine and thymidine, which provide exogenous sources and permit the normal growth of wild-type cells but not of either mutant cell type cultured alone. The growth of the mixed cultures depends on the HPRT$^-$ cells being fed purine nucleotides through junctions from the TK$^-$ cells and, reciprocally, the TK$^-$ cells being fed thymine nucleotides from HPRT$^-$ cells. Growth of the population is a 'tissue phenotype' (Pitts, 1980) in that it is a property of the cell mixture that is not expressed when either cell type is cultured separately. This interdependent growth also produces a form of self-regulatory growth control resulting, no matter what the starting proportions, in about equal numbers of the two cell types (Pitts, 1971). It is not yet known, however, if this form of growth regulation occurs *in vivo*.

Cross-feeding, however, does occur *in vivo*. Lesch-Nyhan hemizygotes have about equal proportions of HPRT$^-$ and HPRT$^+$ cells due to random X-inactivation, but as a result of intercellular nucleotide exchange *via* gap junctions the affected females are phenotypically normal (Migeon *et al.* 1968). In another example the mammalian oocyte loses the enzymic or transport activities necessary to incorporate a variety of precursors (it becomes a phenotypic 'mutant') but the metabolic deficiencies are overcome by the supply of metabolites through gap junctions from the surrounding cumulus cells (Moor, Smith & Dawson, 1980). Similar (but as yet undiscovered) situations may exist in other tissues because during evolution of differentiated phenotypes there is no pressure, if the cells are coupled, for any one cell type to retain a full complement of metabolic activities.

The concept of cross-feeding need not be limited to those situations where one or more cell type has lost some metabolic function. In some cases at least (Kam *et al.* 1986), capillary endothelial cells are coupled to the surrounding stromal cells providing a direct junctional pathway for supplying cells remote from the blood supply with nutrients (precursors or ready-made intermediate metabolites).

The junctional pathway is used for electrical signalling (as described above) and may also be used for developmental and proliferative signalling (see below). It also may be used for local signalling and the coordination of responses produced by intracellular messengers such as cyclic AMP or inositol phosphates. Experiments in model systems have shown that two different cell types (heart myoblasts and follicular cumulus cells), which each respond by cyclic-AMP-dependent mechanisms to different hormones, both respond in mixed culture to either hormone (Lawrence *et al.* 1978). Such sharing of second messengers may help to coordinate and amplify hormone-induced responses in tissues *in vivo*.

DEVELOPMENTAL AND PROLIFERATIVE SIGNALLING

The intercellular signalling mechanisms that control development, pattern formation, differentiation and tissue growth are mostly unknown but junctional communication has often been suggested as a likely candidate. As yet there is no direct evidence to substantiate such proposals but there are various reasons for considering the suggestion carefully.

In the examples described in previous sections it has been shown in model systems in culture that junctional communication can be involved in the intercellular control of cellular activity and cellular growth, that specificity of junction formation can produce complex patterns of communication and that gradients of small molecules can form within communication compartments (e.g. see Figs 9–11, 12).

Signalling *via* the junctional pathway differs in a number of important ways from signalling *via* the extracellular (humoral) pathway. The signal molecules must always be small (not informational) and can therefore act as triggers only to elicit preprogrammed responses in target cells. Unlike the humoral pathway of communication, the signal molecules do not require membrane transport or transduction mechanisms but can interact directly with intracellular receptors, which could be involved in the control of gene expression. The specificity of interaction may depend on the distribution of receptors within the cytoplasmic compartment of a coupled population but it is also governed by the specificity of junction formation and the consequent patterns of communication that develop. The use of an entirely intracellular pathway enables gradients of signal concentration to be established that are not affected by mechanical or thermal disturbances in the extracellular fluids or by changes in shape (and hence absolute positions of individual cells but not relative positions) of the coupled tissues (Fig. 12). The containment of the signals within physically separate communication compartments means that the same molecules can be used for different purposes (different preprogramming) in different compartments providing what might be important evolutionary economy.

Identifying the roles of gap junctions in development and growth requires new approaches. The use of specific inhibitors of junctional communication or the identification of the signal molecules are obvious possibilities.

The messenger molecules using the junctional pathway will probably be simple modifications of intermediate metabolites, as it is unlikely that complex biosynthetic

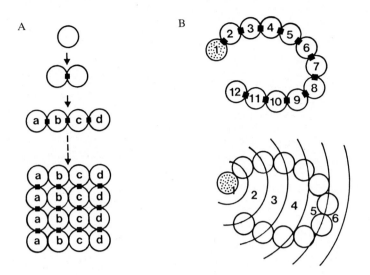

Fig. 12. A. Specificity of junction formation between cells following different differentiation pathways could result in the formation of communication compartments during development. B. The movement of molecules through a compartment *via* gap junctions can produce defined concentration gradients that are dependent only on the juxtaposition of the cells and not on the shape of the tissue. Gradients produced through the extracellular fluids are more ambiguous and are subject to disturbance by external forces causing fluid movement.

pathways will have evolved on the off-chance that the end-product will be a useful signal. Cyclic nucleotides and inositol phosphates may be representatives of a class of such signals, many or most of which are still unidentified. The failure to discover these molecules could be due to intrinsic difficulties. Operating within the confines of a coupled population, only very small amounts of signal would be required (a nM concentration in 1000 cells is equivalent to about 10^6 molecules, i.e. only fg amounts) and, because they cannot cross plasma membranes, they would have no effect when added back to tissues or cells; they would have to be microinjected into cells. As yet no one has looked for such signals with these difficulties in mind.

For functional investigations two classes of specific inhibitor are required, one that reacts with the surface receptors of the precursor connexons and blocks junction formation and one that reacts with the cytoplasmic faces of the channels and blocks permeability. Antibodies to different parts of the junctional protein could potentially provide inhibitors in both classes but although several have been found that interfere with junctional communication when injected into cells, none has been found that interferes with junction formation when added outside cells. Further efforts may produce inhibitory antibodies of this type, but it is possible that the surface receptors are highly conserved (cells from widely different vertebrate species form functional junctions in culture) and animals injected to raise antisera may be tolerant to these sites on the junctions from different species used as antigens.

Various antisera and affinity-purified antibody fractions inhibit junctional communication when injected into cells. Antisera raised in sheep by Hertzberg, Spray &

Bennett (1985) to rat liver gap junctions reduce the intercellular movement of Lucifer Yellow when injected into liver cells or superior cervical ganglion neurones. Antisera raised in rabbits to chicken liver gap junctions, to lobster hepatopancreas gap junctions and to the N-terminal synthetic peptide of the mouse liver 16 000 M_r protein conjugated to keyhole limpet haemocyanin, all block Lucifer Yellow transfer when injected into cultured cells of a rat liver line (John *et al.*, unpublished results). The serum raised by Hertzberg contains antibodies to the 16 000 M_r as well as to the 27 000 M_r protein and all these polyclonal antisera may contain other activities not detectable by Western blot analysis but present in sufficient quantities to reduce dye transfer. None of the injection methods (either using pressure or iontophoresis) delivers measured amounts of antibody. It may take only one antibody molecule per channel to inhibit transfer and as an average liver cell, for example, has only 10^5 channels joining it to all of its five or six neighbours (Revel, Yancey, Meyer & Nicholson, 1980), this could perhaps be provided by a low level of contaminating antibody in the serum. The best evidence to date that antibodies to the junctional protein do interfere with channel permeability is provided by the experiments with the site-specific antiserum.

It is not known how long the inhibition by antibodies lasts or what effects the antibodies have on cell growth and other activities. Now the reagents are available, these characteristics should soon be established, but in the meantime caution is required when interpreting the effects antisera have in the potentially much more interesting experiments where they have been injected into cells of early embryos.

The first of these studies used an antiserum raised by Gilula (unpublished data). Western blot analyses show that this antiserum contains activity to the rat liver 27 000 M_r protein and to a 54 000 M_r protein. It has been suggested that this 54 000 M_r protein is a biochemical precursor of the 27 000 M_r protein (Warner, Guthrie & Gilula, 1984) but this is now known, from the structure of the 27 000 M_r cDNA, to be incorrect (Dr D. Paul, Harvard Medical School, personal communication). It is not known if this serum contains anti-16 000 M_r protein activity. *Xenopus* oocytes contain detectable amounts of 27 000 and 54 000 M_r proteins and the 54 000 M_r (but not the 27 000) M_r protein can be detected in eight-cell and 16-cell embryos. Injections of the antiserum into a specific animal pole cell at the eight-cell stage (Warner *et al.* 1984) block dye and electrical coupling between that cell and its neighbours (80 % injections), while injections of control sera have less effect (blockage in 20 % injections). It is not known how long the inhibition lasts, but it is thought that injection of the antiserum does not have any immediate effect on cell division or survival (although no lineage studies have been undertaken to confirm this).

After injection, some of the embryos develop into tadpoles with a defective eye structure. Fate mapping with Texas Red dextran has shown that parts of this eye are normally derived from the cell that was chosen for injection, so the antiserum either interferes with communication involved in necessary determination events or it interferes with the expansion of the developmental clone that would normally populate the eye tissues. *Xenopus* embryos follow a mosaic form of development and defects in one cell or group of cells are not overcome by regulation of the rest of the embryo. Injection into the same cell of short mixed oligonucleotides, complementary to the deduced mRNA sequence of the $27\,000\,M_r$ protein, can also produce one-eyed tadpoles (unpublished observations of Gilula, quoted by Izant & Weintraub, 1985). However, in the course of experiments aimed at understanding the developmental function of homeobox containing genes (Dr E. De Robertis, Basel, personal communication), four-cell *Xenopus* embryos were injected with an antisense oligonucleotide (21 residues) to *Xenopus* homeobox or with a fusion protein of *Escherichia coli* β-galactosidase and a homeobox containing peptide. These injections produced some tadpoles lacking an eye, although embryos injected with other oligonucleotides or peptides (at lower concentration) did not show the defect. It is possible that the interference to normal eye development produced by these two agents is similar to that produced by the antiserum and antisense oligonucleotides to the $27\,000\,M_r$ protein, but it is also possible that all these results are due to non-specific toxicity, especially when concentrated oligonucleotides or proteins are injected. A more detailed analysis is required before this potentially important type of experiment can be properly interpreted.

There is no similar work aimed at establishing a role for junctional communication in proliferative control but there are some reasons for considering this possibility. Various growth control models have been proposed that explain how a cell population might regulate its terminal size by intercellular communication through junctions (Sheridan, 1976; Loewenstein, 1979). These models are basically variations on the same theme in that they work by enabling cells to assess the total volume of the coupled population or compartment. For instance, if cells make a small molecular weight control molecule for a short period at some time in the cell cycle, most likely just before commitment in early G_1, the final concentration of that molecule within the cell will depend on the number of other coupled cells into which it can diffuse. If progress through the cycle requires the activation of some protein by this molecule then the cell will divide only if its concentration reaches a high enough value. The final size of the population will be determined by the K_d of the protein for the control molecule, a value that can be altered by mutation. This should enable compartments of different sizes to evolve, a factor that may be important for morphogenesis. This type of model depends on the apparently natural asynchrony of cell division within tissues and has been discussed in detail by Loewenstein (1979).

The use of Minute mutations (Morata & Ripoll, 1975) to define accurately the boundaries of developmental compartments in the imaginal wing discs of *Drosophila* provides an example of a system in which this form of growth control might operate. When wild-type M^+/M^+ cells arise in a background of M/M^+ heterozygotes, they fill a much larger proportion of the developmental compartment than normal because they divide faster. However, the final size of the compartment is about the same, suggesting that growth is controlled at the level of the developmental compartment, which may also be a communication compartment (see above).

In skin, junctional communication in the epidermis is restricted, injected dye diffusing only into a small group of closely associated cells (Kam *et al.* 1986, and see above). These groups of cells are about the same size (five or six basal keratinocytes with a few overlying cells) as the proliferative units that have been suggested as elements of skin growth control (Mackenzie,1975). In situations like this there may be some overall growth control mechanism (perhaps humoral), with junctional communication involved in the local fine-tuning to coordinate proliferation and differentiation.

Analysis of primary cultures of human tumours has shown that some show a reduced frequency of homologous junction formation compared to normal cells (Morgan *et al.* 1982). This reduced frequency is similar to that seen between heterologous cells that show specificity and produce communication compartments. If the putative growth control signals can escape from such tumour cells only at the same reduced rate that they cross compartment boundaries, the signals will always reach the high concentrations needed to permit progress through the cell cycle and cell division.

Transformation of cells with a retrovirus carrying an *src* oncogene also reduces coupling and the use of temperature-sensitive strains has shown (Atkinson *et al.* 1981) that the reduction is related to the expression of active ppsrc60, a tyrosine kinase. Temperature-shift experiments show that the normal level of communication can be reduced to the transformed level over a period of about 15 min. This time scale is sufficiently long for the effect to be caused either by alteration of channel permeability or by loss of junctions. Other work, using cells transformed with cloned *src* DNA confirms that this gene is causing the effect but does not help to explain the mechanism (Chang *et al.* 1985).

There is now considerable evidence supporting a two-stage theory of chemical carcinogenesis. After initiation, some form of tumour promotion is necessary for the altered cells to express their transformed state. One of the most effective promotors is the phorbol ester TPA, which activates protein kinase C activity. TPA has also been shown to reduce junctional coupling between cells in culture and it has been suggested that the reduction in communication with surrounding cells could be a required step in the release of the initiated cell from normal growth control (Yotti, Chang & Trosko, 1979).

Now that more is known about the structure and chemistry of the gap junction, the reagents and techniques required for analysing functions are becoming available. These should lead to new discoveries and it will be interesting to see how well these agree with the various speculations that have appeared during the past 20 years, since the discovery of junctional communication.

The authors acknowledge the support of the Cancer Research Campaign.

REFERENCES

ATKINSON, M. M., MENKO, A. S., JOHNSON, R. G., SHEPPARD, J. R. & SHERIDAN, J. D. (1981). Rapid and reversible reduction of junctional permeability in cells infected with a temperature sensitive mutant of avian sarcoma virus. *J. Cell Biol.* **91**, 573–578.

BAUX, G., SIMMONEAU, M., TAUC, L. & SEGUNDO, J. P. (1978). Uncoupling of electrotonic synapses by calcium. *Proc. natn. Acad. Sci. U.S.A.* **75**, 4577–4581.

BENEDETTI, E. L. & EMMELOT, P. (1967). Hexagonal arrays of subunits in tight junctions separated from isolated rat liver plasma membranes. *J. Cell Biol.* **38**, 15–24.

BENNETT, M. V. L., ZIMERING, M. B., SPIRA, M. E. & SPRAY, D. C. (1985). Interactions of electrical and chemical synapses. In *Gap Junctions* (ed. M. V. L. Bennett & D. C. Spray). Cold Spring Harbor, NY: CSH Press (in press).

BLENNERHASSETT, M. G. & CAVENEY, S. (1984). Separation of developmental compartments by a cell type with a reduced junctional permeability. *Nature, Lond.* **309**, 361–364.

BRINK, P. R. & DEWEY, M. M. (1980). Evidence for fixed charge in the nexus. *Nature, Lond.* **285**, 101–102.

BUULTJENS, T. E. J., FINBOW, M. E., LANE, N. J. & PITTS, J. D. (1986). Tissue and species conservation of the vertebrate and arthropod forms of the gap junction protein. *J. Cell Sci.* (in press).

CASPAR, D. L. D., GOODENOUGH, D. A., MAKOWSKI, L. & PHILLIPS, W. C. (1977). Gap junction structures. *J. Cell Biol.* **74**, 605–628.

CHANG, C. C., TROSKO, J. E., KUNG, H.-J., BOMBICK, D. & MATSUMURA, F. (1985). Potential role of the src gene product in inhibition of gap junctional communication in NIH/3T3 cells. *Proc. natn. Acad. Sci. U.S.A.* **82**, 5360–5364.

FALLON, R. F. & GOODENOUGH, D. A. (1981). Five hour half-life of rat liver gap-junction protein. *J. Cell Biol.* **90**, 521–526.

FENTIMAN, I., TAYLOR-PAPADIMITRIOU, J. K. & STOKER, M. (1976). Selective contact dependent cell communication. *Nature, Lond.* **264**, 760–762.

FINBOW, M. E., BUULTJENS, T. J., KAM, E., SHUTTLEWORTH, J. & PITTS, J. D. (1985a). Comparison of the protein components present in vertebrate and arthropod gap junction preparations. In *Gap Junctions* (ed. M. V. L. Bennett and D. Spray). Cold Spring Harbor, NY: CSH Press (in press).

FINBOW, M. E., BUULTJENS, T. E. J., LANE, N. J., SHUTTLEWORTH, J. & PITTS, J. D. (1984). Isolation and characterization of arthropod gap junctions. *EMBO J.* **3**, 2271–2278.

FINBOW, M. E., BUULTJENS, T. E. J., JOHN, S., KAM, E. & PITTS, J. D. (1986). *Molecular Structure of the Gap Junctional Channel. CIBA Symp.* no. 125 (in press).

FINBOW, M. E. & PITTS, J. D. (1981). Permeability of junctions between animal cells: transfer of metabolites and a vitamin derived cofactor. *Expl Cell Res.* **131**, 1–13.

FINBOW, M. E., SHUTTLEWORTH, J., HAMILTON, A. E. & PITTS, J. D. (1983). Analysis of vertebrate gap junction protein. *EMBO J.* **2**, 1479–1486.

FINBOW, M. E., YANCEY, S. B., JOHNSON, R. & REVEL, J.-P. (1980). Independent lines of evidence suggesting a major gap junctional protein with a molecular weight of 26,000. *Proc. natn. Acad. Sci. U.S.A.* **77**, 970–974.

FLAGG-NEWTON, J., SIMPSON, I. & LOEWENSTEIN, W. R. (1979). Permeability of cell–cell membrane channels in mammalian cell junctions. *Science* **205**, 404–409.

FRASER, S. E. & BRYANT, P. J. (1985). Patterns of dye coupling in the imaginal wing dick of *Drosophila melanogaster. Nature, Lond.* **317**, 533–535.

GOODENOUGH, D. A. (1974). Bulk isolation of mouse hepatocyte gap junctions. *J. Cell Biol.* **61**, 557–563.

GOODENOUGH, D. A. (1976). *In vitro* formation of gap junction vesicles. *J. Cell Biol.* **68**, 220–231.

GOODENOUGH, D. A. (1979). Lens gap junctions: a structural hypothesis for non-regulated low-resistance intercellular pathways. *Invest. Ophthalmol.* **18**, 1104–1122.

GROS, B. D., NICHOLSON, B. J. & REVEL, J.-P. (1983). Comparative analysis of the gap junction protein from rat heart and liver. *Cell* **35**, 539–549.

GUNNING, B. E. S. & ROBARDS, A. W. (1976). *Intercellular Communication in Plants.* Berlin: Springer-Verlag.

HENDERSON, D., EIBL, H. & WEBER, K. (1979). Structure and biochemistry of mouse hepatocyte gap junctions. *J. molec. Biol.* **132**, 193–218.

HERTZBERG, E. L. (1984). A detergent independent procedure for the isolation of gap junctions from rat liver. *J. biol. Chem.* **259**, 9936–9943.

HERTZBERG, E. L. (1985). Antibody probes in the study of gap junctional communication. *A. Rev. Physiol.* **47**, 305–318.

HERTZBERG, E. L., ANDERSON, D. J., FRIEDLANDER, M. & GILULA, N. B. (1982). Comparative analysis of the major polypeptides from liver gap junctions and lens fiber junctions. *J. Cell Biol.* **92**, 53–59.

HERTZBERG, E. L. & GILULA, N. B. (1979). Isolation and characterization of gap junctions from rat liver. *J. biol. Chem.* **254**, 2138–2147.

HERTZBERG, E. L., SPRAY, D. C. & BENNETT, M. V. L. (1985). Reduction of gap junctional conductance by micro-injection of antibodies against the 27 kDa liver gap junction polypeptide. *Proc. natn. Acad. Sci. U.S.A.* **82**, 2412–2416.

HIROKAWA, N. & HEUSER, J. (1982). The inside and outside of gap junction membranes visualized by deep etching. *Cell* **30**, 395–406.

HOOPER, M. & SUBAK-SHARPE, J. H. (1981). Metabolic cooperation between cells. *Int. Rev. Cytol.* **69**, 45–105.

ISAAC, P. G., JONES, V. P. & LEAVER, C. P. (1985). The maize cytochrome *c* oxidase subunit I gene. *EMBO J.* **4**, 1617–1623.

IWATSUKI, N. & PETERSEN, O. H. (1978). Electrical coupling and uncoupling of exocrine acinar cells. *J. Cell Biol.* **79**, 533–545.

IZANT, J. G. & WEINTRAUB, H. (1985). Constitutive and conditional suppression of exogenous and endogenous genes by anti-sense RNA. *Science* **228**, 345–352.

KACZMAREK, L. K., FINBOW, M., REVEL, J. -P. & STRUMWASSER, F. (1979). The morphology and coupling of *Aplysia* bag cells within the abdominal ganglion and in cell culture. *J. Neurobiol.* **10**, 535–550.

KALDERON, N., EPSTEIN, M. L. & GILULA, N. B. (1977). Cell-to-cell communication and myogenesis. *J. Cell Biol.* **75**, 788–806.

KAM, E., MELVILLE, L. & PITTS, J. D. (1986). Patterns of junctional communication in skin. *J. invest. Derm.* (in press).

KENSLER, R. W. & GOODENOUGH, D. A. (1980). Isolation of mouse myocardial gap junctions. *J. Cell Biol.* **86**, 755–764.

LARSEN, W. J. & TUNG, H. N. (1978). Origin and fate of cytoplasmic gap junctional vesicles in rabbit granulosa cells. *Tiss. & Cell* **10**, 585–598

LAWRENCE, T. S., BEERS, W. H. & GILULA, N. B. (1978). Hormonal stimulation and cell communication in cocultures. *Nature, Lond.* **272**, 501–506.

LO, C. W. & GILULA, N. B. (1979). Gap junctional communication in the post-implantation mouse embryo. *Cell* **18**, 411–422.

LOEWENSTEIN, W. R. (1979). Junctional intercellular communication and the control of growth. *Biochim. biophys. Acta* **605**, 33–91.

LOEWENSTEIN, W. R. & KANNO, Y. (1964). Studies on an epithelial gland junction. *J. Cell Biol.* **22**, 565–586.

MACDONALD, C. (1982). Genetic complementation in hybrid cells derived from two metabolic cooperation defective mammalian cell lines. *Expl Cell Res.* **138**, 303–310.

MACKENZIE, I. C. (1975). Ordered structure of the epidermis. *J. invest. Derm.* **65**, 45–51.

MAKOWSKI, L., CASPAR, D. L. D., PHILLIPS, W. C. & GOODENOUGH, D. A. (1977). Gap junction structures. *J. Cell Biol.* **74**, 629–645.

MIGEON, B. R., KALOUSTIAN, V. M., NYHAN, W. L., YOUNG, W. J. & CHILDS, B. (1968). X-linked hypoxanthine-guanine phosphoribosyl transferase deficiency: heterozygote has two clonal populations. *Science* **160**, 425–427.

MOOR, R. M., SMITH, M. W. & DAWSON, R. M. C. (1980). Measurement of intercellular coupling between oocytes and cumulus cells using intracellular markers. *Expl Cell Res.* **126**, 15–29.

MORATA, G. & RIPOLL, P. (1975). Minutes: mutants of *Drosophila* autonomously affecting cell division rate. *Devl Biol.* **42**, 211–222.

MORGAN, D., SCOTT, K. G., PITTS, J. D. & FRAME, M. (1982). Junctional communication between human tumour cells in culture. *Eur. J. Cell Biol., Suppl. 1*, 31.

NEVILLE, D. M. (1960). The isolation of cell membrane fractions from rat liver. *J. biophys. biochem. Cytol.* **8**, 413–423.

NEYTON, J., PICCOLINO, M. & GERSCHENFELD, H. M. (1985). Neurotransmitter induced modulation of gap junctional permeability in retinal horizontal cells. In *Gap Junctions* (ed. M. V. L. Bennett & D. C. Spray). Cold Spring Harbor, NY: CSH Press (in press).

NEYTON, J. & TRAUTMANN, A. (1985). Single-channel currents of an intercellular junction. *Nature, Lond.* **317**, 331–335.

NICHOLSON, B. J., HUNKAPILLAR, M. W., GRIM, L. B., HOOD, L. E. & REVEL, J.-P. (1981). Rat liver gap junction protein: properties and partial sequence. *Proc. natn. Acad. Sci. U.S.A.* **78**, 7594–7598.

PERACCHIA, C. (1973). Low resistance junctions in crayfish. *J. Cell Biol.* **57**, 66–76.

PETERSEN, O. H. (1985). In *Gap Junctions* (ed. M. V. L. Bennett & D. C. Spray). Cold Spring Harbor, NY: CSH Press (in press).

PITTS, J. D. (1971). Molecular exchange and growth control in tissue culture. *Ciba Foundn. Symp. Growth Control in Cell Cultures,* 89–105.

PITTS, J. D. (1976). Junctions as channels of direct communication between cells. In *Developmental Biology of Plants and Animals* (ed. C. F. Graham & P. F. Wareing), pp. 96–110. Oxford: Blackwell.

PITTS, J. D. (1977). Direct communication between animal cells. In *International Cell Biology* (ed. B. R. Brinkley & K. R. Porter), pp. 43–49. New York: Rockefeller University Press.

PITTS, J. D. (1980). The role of junctional communication in animal tissues. *In Vitro* **16**, 1049–1056.

PITTS, J. D. & BURK, R. R. (1976). Specificity of junctional communication between animal cells. *Nature, Lond.* **264**, 762–764.

PITTS, J. D., FINBOW, M. E., BUULTJENS, T. E. J., KAM, E. & SHUTTLEWORTH, J. (1985). Junctional communication and communication compartments in development. In *Cellular and Molecular Control of Direct Cell Interactions in Developing Systems* (ed. H. J. Marthy). NATO/ASI Series. New York: Plenum (in press).

PITTS, J. D. & KAM, E. (1985). Communication compartments in mixed cell cultures. *Expl Cell Res.* **156**, 439–449.

PITTS, J. D. & SIMMS, J. M. (1977). Permeability of junctions between animal cells: intercellular transfer of nucleotoides but not macromolecules. *Expl Cell Res.* **104**, 153–163.

REVEL, J.-P. & KARNOVSKY, M. J. (1967). Hexagonal array of subunits in intercellular junctions between mouse heart and liver. *J. Cell Biol.* **33**, 87–102.

REVEL, J.-P., NICHOLSON, B. J. & YANCEY, S. B. (1985). Chemistry of gap junctions. *A. Rev. Physiol.* **47**, 263–279.

REVEL, J.-P., YANCEY, S. B., MEYER, D, J. & NICHOLSON, B. (1980). Cell junctions and intercellular communication. *In Vitro* **16**, 1010–1017.

ROBERTSON, D. (1981). Membrane structure. *J. Cell Biol.* **91**, 189s-204s.

ROSE, B. & LOEWENSTEIN, W. R. (1975). Permeability of cell junction depends on local cytoplasmic calcium activity. *Nature, Lond.* **254**, 250–252.

SAFRANYOS, R. G. A. & CAVENEY, S. (1985). Rates of diffusion of fluorescent molecules via cell-to-cell membrane channels in a developing tissue. *J. Cell Biol.* **100**, 736–747.

SCHUETZE, S. M. & GOODENOUGH, D. A. (1982). Dye transfer between cells of the embryonic chick lens becomes less sensitive to CO_2 treatment with development. *J. Cell Biol.* **92**, 694–705.

SHERIDAN, J. D. (1976). Cell coupling and cell communication during embryogenesis. In *The Cell Surface in Animal Embryogenesis* (ed. G. Poste & G. L. Nicholson), pp. 409–447. New York: Elsevier.

SHERIDAN, J. D., FINBOW, M. E. & PITTS, J. D. (1979). Metabolic interactions between animal cells through permeable intercellular junctions. *Expl Cell Res.* **123**, 111–117.

SHERIDAN, J. D., HAMMER, WILSON, M., PREUS, D. & JOHNSON, R. G. (1978). Quantitative analysis of low resistance junctions between cultured cells and correlation with gap junctional areas. *J. Cell Biol.* **76**, 532–544.

SIMPSON, I., ROSE, B. & LOEWENSTEIN, W. R. (1977). Size limit of molecules permeating the junctional membrane channel. *Science* **195**, 294–296.

SPRAY, D. C., WHITE, R. L., CAMPOS DE CARVALHO, A., HARRIS, A. L. & BENNETT, M. V. L. (1984). Gating of gap junction channels. *Biophys. J.* **45**, 219–230.

SUBAK-SHARPE, J. H., BURK, R. R. & PITTS, J. D. (1966). Metabolic cooperation by cell–cell transfer between genetically different mammalian cells in tissue culture. *Heredity* **21**, 342.

SUBAK-SHARPE, J. H. BURK, R. R. & PITTS, J. D. (1969). Metabolic cooperation between biochemically marked cells in tissue culture. *J. Cell Sci.* **4**, 353–367.

TURIN, L. & WARNER, A. E. (1977). Carbon dioxide reversibly inhibits ionic communication between cells of early amphibian embryo. *Nature, Lond.* **270**, 56–58.

UNWIN, N. & HENDERSON, R. (1984). The structure of proteins in biological membranes. *Scient. Am.* **250**, 56–66.

UNWIN, P. N. T. & ENNIS, P. D. (1984). Two configurations of a channel forming membrane protein. *Nature, Lond.* **307**, 609–613.

UNWIN, P. N. T. & ZAMPIGHI, (1980). Structure of the junction between communicating cells. *Nature, Lond.* **283**, 545–549.

WARNER, A. E., GUTHRIE, S. C. & GILULA, N. B. (1984). Antibodies to gap junctional protein selectively disrupt junctional communication in the early amphibian embryo. *Nature, Lond.* **311**, 127–131.

WARNER, A. E. & LAWRENCE, P. A. (1982). The permeability of gap junctions at the segmental border in insect epidermis. *Cell* **28**, 243–252.

WEIR, M. P. & LO, C. W. (1984). Gap-junctional communication compartments in the *Drosophila* wing imaginal disk. *Devl Biol.* **102**, 130–146.

YANCEY, S. B., EDENS, J. E., TROSKO, J. E., CHANG, C. C. & REVEL, J.-P. (1982). Decreased incidence of gap junctions between Chinese hamster V79 cells upon exposure to the tumour promotor 12-*O*-tetradecanoyl-phorbol 13-acetate. *Expl Cell Res.* **139**, 329–340.

YOTTI, L. P., CHANG, C. C. & TROSKO, J. E. (1979). Elimination of metabolic cooperation in Chinese hamster cells by a tumour promotor. *Science* **206**, 1089–1091.

J. Cell Sci. Suppl. 4, 267–286 (1986)
Printed in Great Britain © The Company of Biologists Limited 1986

BIOLOGY OF THE MACROPHAGE

SIAMON GORDON

Sir William Dunn School of Pathology, University of Oxford, Oxford OX1 3RE, UK

INTRODUCTION

The macrophage has a remarkable life history. In the mouse the first committed progenitors for macrophages appear on the fifth day of embryonic life (G. Shia, unpublished), but mature macrophages detected by the specific rat monoclonal antibody F4/80 (Austyn & Gordon, 1981; Gordon, Hirsch & Starkey, 1985) are first evident in the yolk sac on day 9 (L. Morris, unpublished). Subsequently macrophages appear in larger numbers in mesenchymal tissues (day 12 on), during organogenesis and progressively in foetal liver, spleen and bone marrow as haematopoietic activity shifts from one site to another. Except for the yolk sac the haematopoietic organs contain mature stellate macrophages that are closely associated with clusters of immature erythroid cells. The details of the distribution of macrophages during development and their functions in tissue growth and modelling are not known, but seeding of various sites such as gut, kidney and the central nervous system occurs from the time a circulation is established and continues after birth. In the retina (Hume, Perry & Gordon, 1983) and elsewhere throughout the central nervous system (Perry, Hume & Gordon, 1985) blood monocytes are recruited to dispose of senescent neurones and axons following programmed cell death during development. After phagocytosis of remnants, the macrophages extend elaborate plasma membrane processes and mature into microglia as shown in the plexiform layers of the retina, where a striking mosaic array of macrophages persists throughout adult life.

Mature macrophages are found in most tissues of the adult mouse, especially in haematopoietic and lymphoid organs (bone marrow, liver, spleen, lymph nodes) and in connective tissues (for reviews, see Hume & Gordon, 1985; Gordon *et al.* 1986). Macrophages occur in large numbers all the way down the lamina propria of the gut, in the epidermis and subcutaneous tissues and along other portals of entry (bronchoalveolar lining, genitourinary tract) (Hume, Perry & Gordon, 1984; Lee, Starkey & Gordon, 1985). Perhaps less well known is their presence in normal kidney (along the tubules in the medulla and as part of the juxta–glomerular complex, but not in the glomerular tuft) (Hume & Gordon, 1983), in several endocrine organs including adrenal and pituitary glands (Hume, Halpin, Charlton & Gordon, 1984), and in the reproductive tract (testis, ovary, uterus) where striking changes in macrophage activity occur during the reproductive cycle. The serosal cavities of normal mice all contain populations of 'resident cells'. These and other resident cells found in various sites in the absence of an extraneous inflammatory or infectious recruiting agent are relatively long-lived (weeks, even months) and are continuously replaced by fresh cells from blood and bone marrow, and possibly by low levels of local replication.

Steady-state production, recruitment and turnover of macrophages can be dramatically altered by an exogenous stimulus. A sterile inflammatory agent such as thioglycollate broth elicits an influx of 10-fold more macrophages into the peritoneal cavity, starting within 1 day and reaching a peak after 3–5 days. Rapidly growing pathogens such as *Listeria* monocytogenes (Lepay *et al.* 1985*b*) or *Plasmodium yoelii* (Lee, Crocker & Gordon, 1986), a murine blood-borne malarial parasite, evoke the accumulation of up to 10-fold more macrophages in organs such as liver and spleen within a week. Unlike the initial resident populations, which display relatively little microbicidal/parasiticidal activity and may even be selectively refractory to macrophage-activating lymphokines such as γ interferon (Lepay *et al.* 1985*a*), the newly recruited macrophages display vigorous respiratory-burst activity upon challenge and account for most of the defence against infection by oxidative killing (Gordon *et al.* 1986). Activation of macrophages by the products of specifically stimulated T lymphocytes, in particular γ interferon, represents a common, antigen-non-specific response to infection by many important intracellular pathogens (e.g. Mycobacteria, *Trypanosoma cruzi*) and its failure contributes to the immuno-pathology of diseases like leprosy and AIDS. The demands of infection and of the response to other inflammatory and injurious agents are met by increased production of macrophages in the bone marrow, increased emigration according to local need and accelerated turnover. Macrophages do not recirculate in normal or diseased states and most are disposed of locally by other macrophages or become trapped within lymph nodes.

Overall, the macrophages of the body are essential for host defence and repair, but perform other ill-defined functions in the economy of the organism, which transcend their well-known phagocytic and destructive capacities. Their widespread dispersal during early and adult life, versatile biosynthetic activities (Takemura & Werb, 1984) and remarkable responsiveness to local environmental influences (Mokoena & Gordon, 1986) endow these cells with the ability to interact with many cells and molecules of the body in health and disease. The aim of this review is to consider questions for further research in this area.

GROWTH, DIFFERENTIATION AND ACTIVATION

In the adult, macrophage precursors undergo several cycles of proliferation and differentiation in the bone marrow (approx. 8–10 days), circulate as monocytes for 1–2 days and enter tissues where terminal differentiation takes place. A satisfactory account of this process should explain the following: (1) stem cells are renewed during the life span of the animal and give rise to precursors for all haematopoietic lineages, including macrophages and granulocytes. (2) On demand there can be controlled production of one or several lineages, as appropriate. (3) Once initiated, differentiation is progressive and irreversible, but adaptation to various conditions demands a considerable degree of biosynthetic flexibility.

Possible solutions to some of these questions have emerged with the identification and purification of specific glycoproteins that control growth, differentiation and activation of macrophages and closely related haematopoietic cells in cell culture (Metcalf, 1984). These include Il-3 (multi-lineage), CSF-1, GM-CSF and G-CSF, which enhance macrophage growth, and interferons (α, β, γ), which tend to be growth-inhibitory (Trinchieri & Perussia, 1985). These cytokines act at several stages of macrophage differentiation, exert distinct but overlapping pleiotypic effects and bind to specific surface receptors, where known. Growth and some differentiation effects depend on continuous exposure of macrophages to the cytokine and are reversible, accounting for extrinsic control of primary macrophage proliferation. Malignant haemopoietic cell lines may be able to produce their own growth factors and in one case the product of an oncogene (*fms*) has been shown to be a receptor for CSF-1 (Sherr *et al.* 1985). Sources of cytokines include T lymphocytes, in some cases the only known source (γ interferon), whereas other factors that modulate macrophage functions can be produced by a variety of cells, including fibroblasts and possibly macrophages themselves. The molecules that control the earliest stages of stem-cell growth and differentiation have not been defined. Which, if any, of these cytokines are present in the haematopoietic/lymphoid microenvironment in the animal? There is little information available, but this could be forthcoming with new sensitive, specific antibody and gene probes. Factor production within the host can be stimulated by endotoxin, antigens and infectious agents, but little is known about the cells responsible and the regulatory circuits involved.

The cell culture system of Dexter (1982) illustrates an attempt to study the role of bone marrow stroma *in vitro*. A complex adherent cell layer, which is rich in macrophages and fibroblast-like cells, some laden with lipid, promotes cycling and, or, haematopoietic differentiation when recharged with stem cells. Curiously, although growth of macrophages and myeloid cells is prominent in these cultures, there is no free colony stimulating factor (CSF) activity, perhaps because of consumption by target cells. Another clue to the nature of the haematopoietic microenvironment may be the network of stellate macrophages with extensive processes found in adult bone marrow (Crocker & Gordon, 1985) and foetal liver (L. Morris, unpublished). These macrophages lie at the centre of clusters of proliferating haematopoietic cells and have been purified by collagenase digestion, unit gravity sedimentation and adherence to glass. After isolation, haematopoietic progenitors are not associated with mature stromal macrophages, unlike the intermediate stages of several series (erythroid, myeloid, monocytic), which proliferate vigorously and differentiate on the macrophage surface in the absence of exogenous growth factors. A novel lectin-like haemagglutinin is present on bone-marrow stromal macrophages and may be involved in cluster formation. Although absent in monocytes and peritoneal macrophages, a similar 'receptor' that binds non-opsonized sheep erythrocytes (ER) can be induced in these macrophages by a species-specific protein found in homologous plasma or serum (P. Crocker, unpublished). The possible significance of this macrophage receptor in haematopoietic cell interactions will be considered further below, here it indicates a possible role for stromal macrophages in controlling production of monocytes themselves.

An interesting feature of macrophage differentiation is the progressive decrease in the response to exogenous growth factors until the mature cells become refractory to growth stimuli, even though receptors for growth factors such as CSF-1 are present (Guilbert & Stanley, 1980). This programmed senescence results in G_0 arrest, which can be reversed by placing macrophage nuclei within the cytoplasm of a proliferating cell by heterokaryon formation (Gordon & Cohn, 1971). Mature or activated macrophages can also inhibit replication of younger cells (Hume & Gordon, 1984), perhaps through release of products such as prostaglandins and interferons.

As an *in vitro* model of differentiation, the macrophage offers some unusual opportunities for research. A bipotential precursor (CFU-C) gives rise to both macrophages and granulocytes, and commitment to each lineage can be controlled by the nature and concentration of CSF added to the culture (Metcalf, 1984). Improved yield and purity of the progenitors by FACS multiparameter analysis may make this a more feasible test-system. Bipotential myelomonocytic cell lines (e.g. HL60, Wehi 3) can retain the ability to differentiate along either lineage when treated with various agents (CSF, dimethyl sulphoxide, phorbol myristate acetate (PMA), interferon, vitamin D_3; Sachs, 1980; Nilsson, Ivhed & Forsbeck, 1985). Although more convenient, these artificial systems do not recapitulate differentiation in primary cells.

Mature macrophages can be readily isolated from the peritoneal cavity of the mouse in different functional states (resident, elicited, activated) (Ezekowitz & Gordon, 1984). Their phenotype is relatively stable *in vitro* and a variety of well-defined markers including surface antigens (F4/80) (Gordon *et al.* 1985), Fc and mannosyl, fucosyl receptors (MFR) (Stahl, Wileman & Shepherd, 1985), and secretory products such as lysozyme (Gordon, Todd & Cohn, 1974), plasminogen activator (Unkeless, Gordon & Reich, 1975) and complement (Colten *et al.* 1985) are now available for use in the study of gene expression in different macrophage populations. Some, but not all, features of macrophage differentiation within the animal can be reproduced in cell culture, e.g. recombinant γ interferon is able to reprogramme non-activated macrophages to express many of the hallmarks of activated cells, such as enhanced respiratory burst activity (Nathan, 1985), decrease of mannosyl, fucosyl receptors (Mokoena & Gordon, 1986), induction of Ia antigen and reversal of FcR isotype (Ezekowitz, Bampton & Gordon, 1983). The present studies imply that the considerable heterogeneity observed among macrophages *in vivo* results from selective modulation by various environmental influences acting on macrophages at different stages of their development, rather than from clonal diversification. Macrophage colonies are readily derived from bone marrow in cell culture thus providing a powerful tool for analysing diversity among independent clones (Hirsch, Austyn & Gordon, 1981). Study of various markers in this way supports the hypothesis that macrophages are clonally equivalent and that we are dealing with a single cell family, albeit a remarkably variable one. The evidence from the 'pan-macrophage' differentiation antigen such as F4/80 is consistent with this interpretation, although existence of F4/80 negative lineages, such as osteoclasts (Hume, Loutit & Gordon, 1984) and possibly dendritic cells (Steinman & Nussenzweig, 1980; Schuler & Steinman, 1985; Hume, Robinson, MacPherson & Gordon, 1983) that share some properties with *bona fida* macrophages (bone marrow origin, haematogenous distribution, other common antigens), leaves open the possibility that these have separated from macrophages at an early stage, like other granulocytic series, or have undergone extensive phenotypic modification *in vivo*.

Given the ease with which macrophages can be manipulated, we have learnt very little concerning mechanisms of cell-specific gene expression in the macrophage. Some proteins are unique to macrophages, others are synthesized by macrophages and a few other cells, e.g. complement (hepatocytes), lysozyme (oviduct), MFR (Hubbard, Wilson, Ashwell & Stukenbrok, 1979, liver endothelial cells), FcR (Unkeless, Fleit & Mellman, 1981) and complement receptors (Fearon, 1984, other haematopoietic cells). As genes for these markers are isolated they could provide insight into tissue-specific regulation. Finally, somatic cell hybridization and variant selection (Bloom *et al.* 1980) may compensate for the present dearth of cell mutants or inborn errors that involve macrophages. As in other systems, macrophage-specific traits can be extinguished by hybridization with different cells (Gordon, 1978, 1982), although the repressor elements have not been mapped or identified. Macrophage hybrids provide one method for capturing particular traits in long-term cell lines (Stahl & Gordon, 1982) and transformation by oncogenic viruses provides another (Franz *et al.* 1985).

CIRCULATION, RECRUITMENT AND MIGRATION

Like other haematopoietic cells, monocytes and macrophages are delivered to tissues *via* the circulation and afferent lymph, enter a wide variety of organs and connective tissue and, after crossing endothelial and epithelial surfaces, can be discharged into secretions (milk) and body cavities (gastrointestinal lumen, broncheoalveolar space etc.). Cell distribution is a controlled, non-random process – macrophages are motile and able to migrate readily along chemical gradients or remain fixed at particular sites. The defined waves of cell movement in the embryo and normal adult and the specific pattern of localization within the body imply a highly ordered route of migration. Parabiotic experiments (Volkman & Gowans, 1963) and adoptive transfer by transplantation of bone marrow point to blood-borne monocytes as the key cells involved in recruitment of macrophages to peripheral organs (Van Furth, 1980). Although forming a minor population in blood, monocytes are extremely active in a variety of cell-surface and biosynthetic responses, which control their interaction with other blood elements, endothelium and products reaching the circulation. Unlike blood lymphocytes, which leave the circulation only at specialized sites (high endothelium of post-capillary venules in lymphoid organs) and are able to recirculate, monocytes enter many tissues (at undefined sites) and do not recirculate. Emigration of monocytes occurs continually during development and adult life, and can be markedly enhanced at local sites by inflammation. It is doubtful whether granulocytes leave the bloodstream constitutively, in the absence of further stimuli to increase vascular permeability. Basophils/mast cells may constitute a similar, dual circulating and tissue pool of long-lived cells (Befus, Bieninstock & Denburg, 1985).

The question of macrophage distribution within tissues is complicated further by the fact that many cells do not actually leave the circulation, but adhere to the walls of vascular and lymphoid sinuses in organs such as liver (Kupffer cells), spleen, lymph nodes, and the pituitary and adrenal glands (Hume & Gordon, 1985). Endothelial macrophages are ideally situated to react with circulating ligands including pathogens, altered blood cells and various chemical mediators, as well as adjacent vascular cells. Authentic endothelial cells and endothelial macrophages share several traits constitutively or after induction (MFR, some FcR, angiotension-converting enzyme, Ia antigen expression) and influence one another through mediators such as interleukin-1 (Bevilacqua, Pober, Cotran & Gimbrone, 1985; Lee *et al.* 1986). The effects on the sinus-lining macrophage population of prolonged contact with circulating plasma (normal and abnormal) have hardly been explored. In cell culture monocytes exposed to homologous serum mature morphologically, acquire several receptors that mediate uptake of specific ligands (mannosyl, fucosyl-terminal glycoproteins (Mokoena & Gordon, 1985), transferrin (Andreessen *et al.* 1983) and immunoglobulins) and synthesize the haemagglutinin (ER) described above.

The signals that cause circulating monocytes to adhere to a sinusoidal wall or emigrate *via* endothelial cell junctions are unknown. Is a local substratum site revealed (? collagen, ? fibronectin), are activated plasma proteins (coagulation, complement) or surface changes on platelets or endothelial cells involved, and which monocyte plasma membrane receptors (? complement, ? fibronectin) participate in adhesion and emigration? The process could be initiated by the appearance of a new ligand at the site of localization, but it is also possible that new surface molecules are induced on monocytes from the time of initial exposure to plasma, thus providing a mechanism for programmed exit from the circulating pool after a defined interval. It is not known whether emigration is a random process occurring *via* small vessels (? post-capillary venules) in many tissues and whether in normal animals it is due to low levels of chemotactic agents such as leukotrienes or peptides derived from complement or fibronectin (Snyderman & Pike, 1984). The ability of monocytes to respond to products of cell injury has not been explained and could involve release of intracellular constituents similar to the potent chemotactic N-formylated peptides. Accumulation of macrophages at the distal end of degenerating axons is an early sign of proximal nerve injury (V. H. Perry, unpublished).

The route of cell migration within tissues can be reconstructed by analysing the distribution of F4/80[+] resident macrophages. Many remain associated with small blood vessels (gut and brain capillaries, choroid plexus) and arterioles (spleen, renal cortex), others move into interstitial connective tissue (smooth muscle, dermis, fat, muscle, nervous system, bone). A close physical association with epithelia is also apparent (Hume *et al.* 1984). F4/80[+] processes of macrophages spread beneath tubular epithelium, where they remain outside the basement membrane (renal medulla) or penetrate this to lie between epithelial cells (salivary gland, bile duct); macrophages may lie in the basal layers of a complex stratified epithelium (Langerhans cells of skin, cervix, trachea) or ramify throughout the full thickness of transitional epithelium in the bladder. These characteristic and often remarkably regular patterns of distribution presumably result from specific associations with epithelial cells (e.g. keratinocytes) and basement membrane constituents (? laminin, ? type IV collagen). If not immobilized, macrophages can escape across an epithelium or serosal surface as free cells.

Apart from the ligands and diffusible signals involved in these complex migrations, there should be surface molecules on the 'fixed' macrophage that are concerned with adhesion. Macrophages, including monocytes, express receptors for fibronectin (Bevilacqua, Amrani, Mosesson & Bianco, 1981; Hosein & Bianco, 1985) (the same tetrapeptide ligand as binds to fibroblasts; Wright & Meyer, 1985) and for laminin (Malinoff & Wisha, 1983). Unique, unidentified surface molecules must also be present to account for macrophage-specific adherence *in vitro*, which is highly resistant to trypsin and other proteinases. Further characterization of macrophage surface molecules may be useful in providing new markers to distinguish free from fixed macrophages and to identify molecules involved in different functions performed by these cells.

The effects of disease processes on mobilization, emigration and cell–cell interactions of macrophages have only just begun to be studied. Inflammation, infection and repair bring about changes in the nature of the cells involved (less-mature elicited or activated macrophages, which may be involved in specific interactions with activated platelets, T lymphocytes, endothelial cells, fibroblasts and the plasma products of injury), their distribution (granulomata, exudates) and functions (growth and migration, as well as enhanced cytocidal activity and tissue destruction). Perhaps less obvious, but also important is the recruitment of macrophages to lesions in major arteries (atherosclerosis), possibly as an early event in its pathogenesis, and to some tumours.

A major difficulty in further research is to develop methods of selective depletion of monocytes and macrophages in animals in order to define their role in complex physiological and disease processes. Specific cytotoxic antibodies or lectins that bind only to macrophages (e.g. ricin A chain) can be directed to mature sinus-lining macrophages *via* the blood stream, but are more difficult to target to other populations. Specific receptors for growth factors (CSF-1) may provide a means to destroy committed progenitors more selectively than X- or γ-irradiation. Another technical requirement is to develop refined methods for tracking monocytes and their end-products in tissues.

CELL SURFACE RECOGNITION

The multiplicity of potential ligands (cells, matrix, mediators, organisms) encountered by macrophages calls for a remarkable ability to discriminate among various cell-surface and soluble molecules and to respond appropriately. Several specific receptors, mostly glycoproteins, have been identified on macrophages, and their role in phagocytosis and receptor-mediated pinocytosis is known in some detail. I would like to consider recent findings that point to an unsuspected complexity of phagocytic recognition and extend this analysis to a problem that has received virtually no attention, namely specific interactions in which macrophages associate with other cells in a trophic, rather than purely destructive way.

Silverstein and his colleagues in an important series of experiments proposed the zipper hypothesis to account for opsonin(antibody, complement)-dependent phagocytosis (Silverstein, Steinman & Cohn, 1977). Receptor–ligand interactions in local segments of the plasma membrane mediate binding of a particle, but ingestion, which results from involvement of the contractile apparatus (actin and several other molecules), only proceeds if receptors interact sequentially around the full circumference of the target, guiding membrane flow before fusion. Apart from the role of ligand distribution on the surface of the particle, the macrophage receptors also vary in their ability to mediate engulfment. Fc receptors for certain immunoglobulin classes promote uptake in the cross-linked, multimeric state and can serve as ion channels in artificial lipid films (Young & Cohn, 1985). In contrast, receptors for cleaved third component of complement (CR1, CR3) exist in two distinct states, which mediate binding alone or also ingestion (Wright & Griffin, 1985). Studies by several groups have shown that CR activity depends on the physiological state of the macrophages (ingestion is observed in thioglycollate-elicited, but not resident peritoneal macrophages) and can be modulated by lymphokines, interaction with substratum (fibronectin) or pharmacologically active agents such as phorbol myristate acetate. Although different CRs have been isolated and characterized immunochemically, the details of receptor activation are unknown.

Studies by Wright & Silverstein (1984) have shown further that attachment and attempted phagocytosis are distinct processes. When macrophages spread on glass the zone of contact remains accessible to extracellular protein probes, whereas spreading on a specific ligand attached to the substratum creates a zone of exclusion to the probe (a 'black hole'), resembling the close apposition between macrophage and phagocytic target, and which probably reflects the involvement of receptors with the cytoskeleton. Macrophage receptors move through the plane of the membrane, become trapped on the ventral aspect of the cells in contact with bound ligand and are cleared from the dorsal surface (Michl, Pieczonka, Unkeless & Silverstein, 1979). Local interactions with fibronectin (Wright, Licht, Craigmyle & Silverstein, 1984) or laminin (Bohnsack et al. 1985), for which macrophages express distinct receptors, exert remote effects on the functions of other receptors, although the mechanisms of these indirect receptor-interactions are obscure.

How do macrophages interact with cells or organisms in the absence of specific antibody recognized directly (IgG, IgE Fc) or by activation of complement (IgM)? Many organisms, e.g. yeasts and microorganisms, activate the alternative pathway of complement directly, probably as a result of unique sugars on their surface, and others bind fibronectin, which might serve as a ligand in addition to its indirect effects on the function of other receptors. Direct sugar-specific recognition can also be mediated by the lectin-like MFR. These receptors are less well characterized, but expression by macrophages is known to vary with cell maturation (monocytes lack MFR, but acquire activity during cultivation in homologous serum) (Mokoena & Gordon, 1985) and can be markedly reduced by T lymphocyte products such as γ interferon. Naturally occurring ligands for MFR include mannan, a complex mannose-rich polymer found in yeast cell wall and zymosan, and poorly defined surface glycoproteins on parasites such as *Leishmania donovani* (Blackwell *et al.* 1985), an obligatory intracellular pathogen of macrophages. Study of uptake of these particles by macrophages has brought to light a remarkable synergy between MFR and CR3 (Ezekowitz, Sim, Hill & Gordon, 1984), in which sugar recognition proceeds directly (MFR) or *via* the alternative pathway for activation of complement (CR3). The receptors are distinct molecules, but a complex glycoprotein can react simultaneously with both receptors.

Here the previously unexplained, but well-known capacity of the macrophage to synthesize and secrete complement proteins, including the regulatory components of the alternative pathway, has been invoked to postulate an unusual local opsonization mechanism in which those targets that are efficient activators of macrophage-produced complement assemble the ligand iC3b on their surface and are then recognized by the cells' own CR3. Evidence for this hypothesis has been obtained by using several CR3-specific inhibitory monoclonal antibodies, including Mac-1 and M01, by biosynthetic labelling of macrophages and by demonstration of iC3b on the particle surface in the absence of an exogenous source of complement (Ezekowitz, Sim, MacPherson & Gordon, 1985). An alternative view holds that although macrophages can perform these complex functions, the undoubted involvement of the CR3 results from direct reaction with other ligands, as well as iC3b (Ross, Cain & Lachmann, 1985). Whatever the mechanism, these studies raise the possibility that neither the macrophage nor the target cell is passive in such an encounter. Control of binding as well as ingestion involves distinct macrophage receptors that can be controlled differentially or act in concert, whereas living targets provide not only potential ligands, but also display activities that can prevent the stable assembly of ligands such as iC3b on their surface (e.g. the decay-accelerating factor of certain erythrocytes) (Moore, Frank, Muller-Eberhard & Young, 1985). These studies point to a self-recognition (? sugar-dependent) discriminatory function of macrophages, which might have preceded the evolution of other humoral (antibody) and cellular (T lymphocyte) recognition mechanism. Primitive macrophage-like phagocytic cells in invertebrates use similar lectins (Vasta *et al.* 1982), some of which occur free in body fluids, and sugar-specific recognition could play a role in phagocytosis by protozoa (Brown, Bass & Coombs, 1975).

Let us return to the question of non-phagocytic interactions of macrophages and other cells. Induction of the immune response and activation of macrophages involve complex interactions between macrophages, lymphocytes and dendritic cells in which the role of different surface molecules of each cell type and the possible secretory interchanges (e.g. Il-1, Il-2 release) are poorly defined. Several T lymphocyte surface glycoproteins (T cell receptor, major histocompatibility complex (MHC) class I and II, CD3, CD4, CD8, CD2, LFA) (Williams & Barclay, 1985) play a role in antigen recognition and lymphocyte activation. Specific monoclonal antibodies directed against these molecules can inhibit immune cellular interactions, e.g. in the mixed leucocyte reaction and it is thought that they act on the T lymphocytes. Macrophages also express some of these molecules (MHC class I and II, CD4 (Jefferies, Green & Williams, 1985), LFA) and may provide additional sites of antibody action. Receptors for the T lymphocyte growth factor Il-2 are present on monocytes (Herrmann, Cannistra, Levine & Griffin, 1985), although nothing is known about their function in these cells. Other known macrophage antigens or receptors that could contribute directly or indirectly to immune cell interactions include CR3 and p150, 95 (ligand unknown, another member of the Mac-1/LFA family) (Sanchez-Madrid *et al.* 1983), the FcR for various immunoglobulin G (IgG) isotypes and fibronectin, and various lectin-like receptors, which may react with lymphocyte glycoproteins. There is no evidence of MHC class I-restricted interactions between macrophages and T lymphocytes and the possible role of induced macrophage Ia in immune cell interactions is a mystery.

One difficulty in defining the role of different cell types and surface molecules in these interactions has been the heterogeneity of the cell populations involved, and another the failure to appreciate the artefacts that arise in cell culture assays. The first problem can be overcome in part by using antigen-responsive T cell clones or hybridomas, although the important distinction between a secondary immune response and the more stringent primary response (Inaba & Steinman, 1984) must be kept in mind. Macrophage heterogeneity *in vivo* and phenotypic drift *in vitro* are illustrated by variable expression of the macrophage haemagglutinin (ER) described above. Apart from its presence on stromal macrophage in bone marrow, a similar receptor is expressed by resident Kupffer cells, some spleen and lymph-node macrophages, but not by monocytes and peritoneal macrophages (P. Crocker, unpublished). Although it is not known whether this receptor participates in macrophage–lymphocyte and, or, dendritic cell interactions, the broad distribution of potential ligands on haematopoietic cells, its presence on macrophages in lymphoid tissues and sites of immune inflammation, and its striking ability to mediate binding and growth, rather than phagocytosis of haematopoietic cells, make it or related molecules ideal candidates for lymphocyte–macrophage trophic interactions. Since ER$^+$ bone-marrow resident macrophages dedifferentiate rapidly when cultivated in the absence of the species-specific inducer protein (P. Crocker, unpublished), assay conditions have to be controlled with care.

Next, consider non-immune interactions between macrophages and other cells (haematopoietic cells, endothelium cells, epithelium, connective tissue, neurones) in a variety of physiological and pathological processes (growth, inflammation, repair, destruction). The complex nature of intercellular recognition and response can be illustrated by an analysis of macrophage–erythrocyte interactions. During erythropoiesis in foetal liver and adult bone marrow, developing erythroid stages cluster selectively to the processes of stromal macrophages, as noted already, and also bind selectively *in vitro* to macrophages in which the tissue macrophage haemagglutinin has been induced. The nature of the erythroid ligands (sialyl-lactose residues may be involved), and the structure and regulation of the macrophage receptors are currently under investigation (P. Crocker, unpublished). Progenitors, which are not initially bound by stromal macrophages (Crocker & Gordon, 1985), acquire the ability to do so during differentiation, perhaps by expressing an appropriate ligand. After further growth and differentiation on the surface of macrophages, mature erythrocytes detach and enter the bloodstream. This could involve loss or masking of the ligand. Whilst they retain maturing erythroid stages at their surface, the same stromal macrophages ingest red cell nuclei and damaged cells. Phagocytosis could be triggered by the appearance of new or altered ligands (undefined) and may involve 'activation' of ER for ingestion, as described for CR, or recruitment of other unidentified macrophage receptors working alone or in conjunction with ER, as described above for MFR and CR3. Resident bone-marrow macrophages express MFR, which is distinct from the ER, but lack Mac-1 antigen or CR3 activity and, although some cells express high levels of Ia antigen, these macrophages lack ER activity. There is a striking negative correlation *in situ* between ER, on the one hand, and CR3 and Ia, other potential haematopoietic cell adhesion molecules. It is possible that the failure to detect Mac-1 antigen on tissue macrophages reflects occupancy of the active site by ligand or down-regulation of the receptor. Further studies are needed with antibodies that react with the active binding sites as well as other epitopes of surface molecules that could be involved in adhesion to tissue macrophages.

The selective uptake of damaged erythrocytes by tissue macrophages is further evident in peripheral organs (spleen red pulp, liver) where large numbers of senescent erythrocyte are destroyed continuously. The mechanism of recognition remains unknown, although various hypotheses have been put forward involving desialylation of erythrocyte glycoproteins, unmasking of determinants, activation of complement and formation of autoantibodies (Kay, 1981). Although the macrophage receptors have not been identified, it is likely that the cells will express a tissue-resident cell phenotype similar to that of other sinus-lining macrophages, and that binding and control of ingestion will follow the principles described above. In addition to control of ingestion, macrophage plasma membrane receptors can also initiate extracellular cytolysis. Receptors vary markedly in their ability to mediate such responses, as discussed further below, and the expression of particular receptors (Ezekowitz, Bampton & Gordon, 1983) and coupling to various secretory responses is profoundly altered by macrophage activation.

These observations indicate that there is considerable heterogeneity among macrophage populations and individual macrophages in interacting with cells of the erythroid series. Virtually nothing is known about interactions between macrophages and other cells. An important goal will be to develop suitable *in vitro* models for future experiments in which both the macrophage population and the interacting cells are adequately defined. Some of the class-specific, rather than antigen-specific, mechanisms by which macrophages recognize foreign or altered host ligands apply to soluble as well as particle-bound ligands. Apart from receptors, as already noted, that also mediate pinocytosis (Fc, CR, MFR), macrophages express receptors for lipo-proteins (Fogelman *et al.* 1985), for modified sugars (non-enzymically glycosylated proteins) (Vlassara, Brownlee & Cerami, 1984) and for various peptides, hormones, neurotransmitters and pharmacological agents (reviewed by Mokoena & Gordon, 1986). The role of receptor clustering, mobility and cooperation in fluid phase *versus* particle recognition has not been adequately studied. Finally, the full repertoire of macrophage discriminatory functions has obviously not been defined. There is little evidence that macrophages can distinguish directly between denatured and native proteins, malignant and normal cells or virus-infected and uninfected cells, all of which have been postulated.

SECRETORY RESPONSES

It is only over the last 15 years that the macrophage has been recognized as a major secretory cell. This neglect arose because macrophages do not on the whole store large amounts of preformed product in granules, unlike other leucocytes, but respond to particular stimuli by new synthesis or by generating active species from less-obvious precursor pools in membrane. Further, macrophages produce relatively small amounts of many products of which only lysozyme is produced in relative bulk; in other cases, e.g. complement biosynthesis, the contribution of the macrophage is overshadowed by that of the hepatocyte. However, evidence that macrophage products can reach high local concentrations at extravascular sites and that released activities can be amplified by extracellular proteolytic cascades (Gordon & Ezekowitz, 1985) supports the concept that macrophages constitute a significant and unusually responsive dispersed secretory 'organ'. The range of macrophage biological activities involved in host defence, inflammation, metabolic regulation and growth control has stimulated much recent interest in producing pure 'monokines' by recombinant DNA techniques (interleukin 1 (Lomedico *et al.* 1984; March *et al.* 1985), cachectin/tumour necrosis factor (Pennica *et al.* 1984), α/β interferons (Pestka, 1983)), thus facilitating further studies on product heterogeneity, binding to target-cell receptors and mechanisms of action. At the same time there has been a great deal of interest in studying activation of the oxidative burst by which toxic oxygen products are generated and in defining diverse metabolites derived from arachidonates. Here I consider mainly how secretory responses are regulated in macrophages, with emphasis on the role of the plasma membrane and cell surface interactions.

Research on biosynthesis and secretory pathways in macrophages is in its infancy. Some of the problems posed, e.g. the range and selectivity of response induced by an external agonist, the variability that results from macrophage heterogeneity, and product sorting and control of membrane flow during secretion and endocytosis (Steinman, Mellman, Muller & Cohn, 1983), are formidable. It is generally assumed that release of products is a function of living macrophages and in several cases the recombinant gene sequence has confirmed the presence of membrane transfer signals. The apparent absence of a signal sequence in the interleukin-1 gene raises interesting questions in this regard.

Secretion of several proteins by macrophages is influenced by specific cytokines (γ interferon, CSF) and glucocorticoids (Werb, 1980), which sometimes act antagonistically to control cell activation (for review, see Werb, Banda, Takemura & Gordon, 1986). Several neutral proteinase activities (plasminogen activator, elastase, collagenase) are increased (γ interferon) or reduced (glucocorticoids) in parallel, although other potential proteolytic enzymes (factor B) are enhanced by both regulators (T. Mokoena, unpublished). Secretion of lysozyme, a constitutive product, is unaffected by these agents, whilst other products are controlled independently. For example, γ interferon also induces synthesis of a novel thromboglobulin-like chemotactic protein by macrophages (Luster, Unkeless & Ravetch, 1985), but inhibits release of apolipoprotein E, whereas glucocorticoids induce release of an angiotensin-converting enzyme and of macrocortin, an inhibitor of phospholipase activity in target cells. Regulation of protein secretion, and analogous changes in expression of plasma membrane antigens and receptors occurs at stages of biosynthesis and intracellular transport that have not yet been defined. However, it is clear that sets of genes involved in cell differentiation and activation are coordinately and selectively regulated in macrophages following the interaction of each agonist with its receptors. As noted above, different cytokines exert distinct, but overlapping pleiotypic effects on macrophage products. Colony-stimulating factors that act on macrophages are highly specific, presumably because only macrophages or closely related cells bear receptors for these ligands, whereas others, including γ interferon, act on many cell types, although their effects on macrophages may be unique.

Can the same macrophages synthesize and secrete all these different products? There has been no adequate clonal survey to establish this point and cell lines may express only a partial phenotype. Macrophages in different sites show interesting differences in secretion of complement proteins (Colten *et al.* 1985), presumably reflecting differences in cell maturation and in their response to the local environment. Similarly, different macrophage populations taken from the same site show marked heterogeneity in secretory profile. Some products are associated with resident macrophages (prostaglandins, apolipoprotein E) and are lost after cell stimulation, others (neutral proteinase and respiratory-burst activities) are only released by elicited or activated cells, whereas lysozyme is secreted constitutively by all macrophages. It is useful to distinguish products secreted continuously in culture (lysozyme) from those whose release depends on a surface-active stimulus such as endotoxin or PMA (respiratory burst, arachidonates, procoagulant). Macrophages may acquire the ability to generate a product (e.g. toxic O_2 molecules) only after a prior priming stimulus (γ interferon). It is also important to distinguish between rapid, early release following degranulation or activation of a plasma membrane system and the cells' ability to resynthesize a product *in vitro*, which may depend on a specific inducer.

There is little information on the nature of the molecules involved in direct generation of products from macrophage membranes. The substrates (O_2, plasma membrane arachidonates) are rapidly converted to labile highly reactive products by poorly defined enzymic reactions. Release of these products is very different from conventional vesicular secretory pathways. Activation of neutral proteinases such as plasminogen activator provides another instructive example of the complex control of secretory activity in macrophages (Gordon & Ezekowitz, 1985). Some macrophages store, release or bind a specific inhibitor of this urokinase-like enzyme (Vassalli, Dayer, Wohlwend & Belin, 1984; Vassalli, Baccini & Belin, 1985), which can however be activated by an appropriate stimulus to the macrophages (e.g. cytokines, lectins *in vitro*; cell activation *in vivo*). Further specific proteolytic cleavages occur at the cell surface or extracellularly, involving other zymogens (plasminogen), inhibitors (anti-plasmin, α_2-macroglobulin) and potential substrates (fibrin, fibronectin) and generate potent proteolytic enzymes (plasmin) and biologically active peptides. Similar complex cellular and plasma membrane interactions underlie macrophage-induced coagulation and may involve novel enzymes and phospholipid activators (Edgington *et al.* 1985).

As already noted, macrophages are able to assemble components and regulators of the alternative complement pathway on a suitable surface as a functional opsonic unit. High concentrations of reactants may be produced in a sealed-off zone of contact between phagocyte and target. Other examples of self-production of potential ligands include fibronectin, α_2-macroglobulin and apolipoprotein E, with the possibility of positive and negative feedback regulation of macrophage secretion and endocytosis.

How does the interaction between plasma membrane receptors and ligands control distinct macrophage secretory responses? Receptors differ in this regard (ligation of FcR, but not CR, triggers a respiratory burst (Wright & Silverstein, 1983; Yamamoto & Johnston, 1984) and arachidonate release (Aderem, Wright, Silverstein & Cohn, 1985)) and various enzyme reactions (NADPH oxidase, phospholipase A_2) can be activated separately. The key events occur at the plasma membrane, independent of internalization (Rouzer, Scott, Kempe & Cohn, 1980), although there may be mobilization of receptors and other constituents from intracellular pools. Membrane mass may be added at specific sites of surface interaction by degranulation and secretion by macrophages could also be targeted by orientation of the Golgi complex and microtubule organizing centre (Kupfer, Dennert & Singer, 1985). The subsequent interactions between receptors and signal-transducing molecules are unknown, and may vary among different leucocytes. Monoclonal antibodies provide probes for identifying molecules involved in stimulus–response coupling and to study cross-linking and formation of specialized microdomains within the plasma membrane. We have recently identified a novel proteolipid antigen, which may be involved in signal transduction in myelo-monocytic cells (Berton *et al.* 1986). Engagement of other macrophage surface molecules including Ia could regulate the synthesis and selective release of macrophage products such as interleukin-1 (Palacios, 1985).

Products generated by macrophages account for many of the local and systemic effects observed in inflammation and immunity. The destructive effects of respiratory-burst products and neutral proteinases have received a great deal of attention, but these and other macrophage products also influence cells, matrix and plasma constituents in other ways. Recently, there has been a revival of interest in the hormone-like actions of macrophage-derived products such as interleukin-1 (Durum, Schmidt & Oppenheim, 1985; Kampschmidt, 1984) and cachectin (Beutler *et al.* 1985) on a wide range of cellular targets (hepatocytes, endothelium, lymphoid cells, thermogulatory centres in the hypothalamus, adipocytes). It is not yet clear to what extent molecular heterogeneity underlies the remarkably diverse reactivities attributed to these substances. These and other proteins released by macrophages (e.g. angiogenesis factor, fibroblast growth factor, erythropoietin, GM-CSF) are potential mediators of tissue growth and repair. Their regulation by environmental conditions such as hypoxia (Knighton *et al.* 1983), biochemical characterization and mechanism of action are important subjects for further study.

The role of the macrophage in controlling growth of other cells is likely to be more complex than simply serving as a source of growth factor. In performing trophic cellular interactions, macrophages could display various ligands on their surface (? including growth factors themselves; Kurt-Jones, Beller, Mizel & Unanue, 1985), endocytose and metabolize important molecules (e.g. transferrin, lipoproteins, glucocorticoids, neuropeptides), and release products that control the target cells' response. These and other short-range interactions could play a central role in tissue homeostasis. If growth restraints imposed by macrophages were lost or the target cells escaped their influence, interactions with macrophages could promote the emergence of abnormal clones of proliferating cells at an early stage in oncogenesis. Far from immune elimination of nascent tumours, the surface-binding and secretory capabilities of macrophages could then enhance tumour growth, reflecting the dual contributions of macrophages to defence and trophic functions.

I thank Dr Paul Crocker for many stimulating discussions and Elwena Gregory and Pam Woodward for typing the manuscript. Supported by a grant from the Medical Research Council, UK.

REFERENCES

ADEREM, A. A., WRIGHT, S. D., SILVERSTEIN, S. C. & COHN, Z. A. (1985). Ligated complement receptors do not activate the arachidonic acid cascade in resident peritoneal macrophages. *J. exp. Med.* **161**, 617–622.
ANDREESSEN, R., OSTERHOLZ, J., BROSS, K. J., SCHULZ, A., ALBRECHT LUCKENBACH, G. & LOHR, G. W. (1983). Cytotoxic effector cell function at different stages of human monocyte–macrophage maturation. *Cancer Res.* **43**, 5931–5936.
AUSTYN, J. M. & GORDON, S. (1981). F4/80, a monoclonal antibody directed specifically against the mouse macrophage. *Eur. J. Immun.* **11**, 805–815.
BEFUS, A. D., BIENINSTOCK, J. & DENBURG, J. A. (1985). Mast cell differentiation and heterogeneity. *Immun. Today* **6**, 281–284.

BERTON, G., ROSEN, H., EZEKOWITZ, R. A. B., BELLAVITTE, P., SERRA, M. C., ROSSI, F. & GORDON, S. (1986). Monoclonal antibodies to a particulate superoxide forming system stimulate a respiratory burst in intact guinea pig neutrophils. *Proc. natn. Acad. Sci., U.S.A.* (in press).

BEUTLER, B., MAHONEY, J., LE TRANG, N., PEKALA, P. & CERAMI, A. (1985). Purification of cachectin, a lipoprotein–lipase-suppressing hormone secreted by endotoxin-induced RAW264.7 cells. *J. exp. Med.* **161**, 984–995.

BEVILACQUA, M. P., AMRANI, D., MOSESSON, M. W. & BIANCO, C. (1981). Receptors for cold-insoluble globulin (plasma fibronectin) on human monocytes. *J. exp. Med.* **153**, 42–60.

BEVILACQUA, M. P., POBER, J. S., COTRAN, R. S. & GIMBRONE, M. A. JR (1985). Effects of mononuclear phagocytes and their secretory products on vascular endothelium. In *Mononuclear Phagocytes. Characteristics, Physiology and Function* (ed. R. van Furth), pp. 747–752. Dordrecht, Boston, Lancaster: Martinus Nijhoff.

BLACKWELL, J. M., EZEKOWITZ, R. A. B., ROBERTS, M. B., CHANNON, J. Y., SIM, R. B. & GORDON, S. (1985). Macrophage complement and lectin-like receptors bind *Leishmania* in the absence of serum. *J. exp. Med.* **162**, 324–331.

BLOOM, B. R., DIAMOND, B., NEWMAN, W., SCHNECK, J., PISCATELLO, J., DAMANI, G., ROSEN, N., MUSCHEL, R. & ROSEN, O. (1980). Genetic and functional studies of continuous macrophage-like cell lines. In *Mononuclear Phagocytes. Functional Aspects* (ed. R. van Furth), pp. 941–967. The Hague, Boston, London: Martinus Nijhoff.

BOHNSACK, J. F., KLEINMAN, H. K., TAKAHASHI, T., O'SHEA, J. J. & BROWN, E. J. (1985). Connective tissue proteins and phagocytic cell function. Laminin enhances complement and Fc-mediated phagocytosis by cultured human macrophages. *J. exp. Med.* **161**, 912–923.

BROWN, R. C., BASS, H. & COOMBS, J. P. (1975). Carbohydrate binding proteins involved in phagocytosis by *Acanthamoeba. Nature, Lond.* **254**, 434–435.

COLTEN, H. R., COLE, F. S., SACKSTEIN, R. & AUERBACH, J. S. (1985). Tissue and species specific regulation of complement biosynthesis in mononuclear phagocytes. In *Mononuclear Phagocytes. Characteristics, Physiology and Function* (ed. R. van Furth), pp. 147–154. Dordrecht, Boston, Lancaster: Martinus Nijhoff.

CROCKER, P. R. & GORDON, S. (1985). Isolation and characterization of resident stromal macrophages and haematopoietic cell clusters from mouse bone marrow. *J. exp. Med.* **162**, 993–1014.

DEXTER, T. M. (1982). Stromal cell-associated haemopoiesis. *J. cell. Physiol.* (Suppl.) **1**, 87.

DURUM, S. K., SCHMIDT, J. A. & OPPENHEIM, J. J. (1985). Interleukin 1: an immunological perspective. *A. Rev. Immun.* **3**, 263–288.

EDGINGTON, T. S., HELIN, H., GREGORY, S. A., LEVY, G., FAIR, D. S. & SCHWARTZ, B. S. (1985). Cellular pathways and signals for the induction of biosynthesis of initiators of the coagulation protease cascade by cells of the monocyte lineage. In *Mononuclear Phagocytes. Characteristics, Physiology and Function* (ed. R. van Furth), pp. 687–696. Dordrecht, Boston, Lancaster: Martinus Nijhoff.

EZEKOWITZ, R. A. B., BAMPTON, M. & GORDON, S. (1983). Macrophage activation selectively enhances expression of Fc receptors for IgG2a. *J. exp. Med.* **157**, 807.

EZEKOWITZ, R. A. B. & GORDON, S. (1984). Alterations of surface properties by macrophage activation. Expression of receptors for Fc and mannose-terminal glycoproteins and differentiation antigens. In *Contemporary Topics in Immunobiology* (ed. D. O. Adams & M. G. Hanna, Jr), vol. 18, pp. 33–56. New York: Plenum.

EZEKOWITZ, R. A. B., SIM, R., HILL, M. & GORDON, S. (1984). Local opsonisation by secreted macrophage complement components. Role of receptors for complement in uptake of zymosan. *J. exp. Med.* **159**, 244–260.

EZEKOWITZ, R. A. B., SIM, R. B., MACPHERSON, G. G. & GORDON, S. (1985). Interaction of human monocytes, macrophages and polymorphonuclear leukocytes with zymosan *in vitro*. Role of type 3 complement receptors and macrophage-derived complement. *J. clin. Invest.* **76**, 2368–2376.

EARON, D. T. (1984). Cellular receptors for fragments of the third component of complement. *Immun. Today* **5**, 105–110.

FOGELMAN, S. M., VAN LENTEN, B. J., HOKOM, M., SEAGER, J., WONG, H., NAVAB, M., SHAPIRO, S., HABERLAND, M. E. & EDWARDS, P. A. (1985). In *Mononuclear Phagocytes. Characteristics, Physiology and Function* (ed. R. van Furth), pp. 803–809. Dordrecht, Boston, Lancaster: Martinus Nijhoff.

FRANZ, T., LOHLER, J., FUSCO, A., PRAGNELL, I., NOBIS, P., PADUA, R. & OSTERTAG, W. (1985). Transformation of mononuclear phagocytes *in vitro* and malignant histiocytosis caused by a novel murine spleen focus-forming virus. *Nature, Lond.* **315**, 149–151.

GORDON, S. (1978). Regulation of enzyme secretion by mononuclear phagocytes: Studies with macrophage plasminogen activator and lysozyme. *Fedn Proc. Fedn Am. Socs exp. Biol.* **37**, 2754–2758.

GORDON, S. (1982). Receptor-mediated endocytosis in macrophage cell hybrids. In *Phagocytosis – Past and Future* (ed. M. Karnovsky & L. Bolis), pp. 287–293. New York: Academic Press.

GORDON, S. & COHN, Z. (1971). Macrophage–melanocyte heterokaryons. II. The activation of macrophage DNA synthesis. Studies with inhibitors of RNA synthesis. *J. exp. Med.* **133**, 321.

GORDON, S., CROCKER, P. R., LEE, S.-H., MORRIS, L. & RABINOWITZ, S. (1986). Trophic and defence functions of murine macrophages. In *Host-resistance Mechanisms to Infectious Agents, Tumours and Allografts* (ed. R. M. Steinman & R. J. North). New York: Rockefeller University Press (in press).

GORDON, S., CROCKER, P., MORRIS, L., LEE, S.-H., PERRY, V. H. & HUME, D. (1986). Localisation and function of tissue macrophages. In *Biochemistry of Macrophages. Ciba Fdn Symp.* 118, pp. 54–67. London: Pitman.

GORDON, S. & EZEKOWITZ, R. A. B. (1985). Macrophage neutral proteinases. Nature, regulation and role. In *The Reticuloendothelial System. A Comprehensive Treatise*, vol. 7B (ed. S. M. Reichard & J. P. Filkins), pp. 95–141. New York: Plenum.

GORDON, S., HIRSCH, S. & STARKEY, P. (1985). Differentiation antigens of mouse macrophages and polymorphonuclear leukocytes. In *Mononuclear Phagocytes. Characteristics, Physiology and Function* (ed. R. van Furth), pp. 3–8. Dordrecht, Boston, Lancaster: Martinus Nijhoff.

GORDON, S., STARKEY, P., HUME, D., EZEKOWITZ, A., HIRSCH, S. & AUSTYN, J. (1985). Plasma membrane markers to study differentiation, activation and localisation of murine macrophages. Ag F4/80 and the mannosyl fucosyl receptor. *Handbook of Experimental Immunology*, 4th edn (ed. D. M. Weir, L. A. Herzenberg & L. A. Herzenberg), pp. 43.1–43.14. Oxford: Blackwell Scientific.

GORDON, S., TODD, J. & COHN, Z. A. (1974). *In vitro* synthesis and secretion of lysozyme by mononuclear phagocytes. *J. exp. Med.* **139**, 1228–1248.

GUILBERT, L. J. & STANLEY, E. R. (1980). Specific interaction of murine colony-stimulating factor with mononuclear phagocytic cells. *J. Cell Biol.* **84**, 153–159.

HERRMANN, F., CANNISTRA, S. A., LEVINE, H. & GRIFFIN, J. D. (1985). Expression of interleukin 2 receptors and binding of interleukin 2 by gamma interferon-induced human leukemic and normal monocytic cells. *J. exp. Med.* **162**, 1111–1115.

HIRSCH, S., AUSTYN, J. M. & GORDON, S. (1981). Expression of the macrophage-specific antigen F4/80 during differentiation of mouse bone marrow cells in culture. *J. exp. Med.* **154**, 713–725.

HOSEIN, B. & BIANCO, C. (1985). Monocyte receptors for fibronectin characterised by a monoclonal antibody that interferes with receptor activity. *J. exp. Med.* **162**, 157–170.

HUBBARD, A. L., WILSON, G., ASHWELL, G. & STUKENBROK, H. (1979). An electron microscopic and autoradiographic study of the carbohydrate recognition system in rat liver. *J. Cell Biol.* **83**, 47.

HUME, D. A. & GORDON, S. (1983). The mononuclear phagocyte system of the mouse defined by immunohistochemical localisation of antigen F4/80. Identification of resident macrophages in renal medullary and cortical interstitium and the juxtaglomerular complex. *J. exp. Med.* **157**, 1704–1709.

HUME, D. A. & GORDON, S. (1984). The correlation between plasminogen activator activity and thymidine incorporation in mouse bone marrow derived macrophages. Opposing actions of colony stimulating factor, phorbol myristate acetate, dexamethasone and prostaglandin E. *Expl Cell Res.* **150**, 347–355.

HUME, D. A. & GORDON, S. (1985). The mononuclear phagocyte system of the mouse defined by immunohistochemical localisation of antigen F4/80. In *Mononuclear Phagocytes. Characteristics, Physiology and Function* (ed. R. van Furth), pp. 9–17. Dordrecht, Boston, Lancaster: Martinus Nijhoff.

HUME, D. A., HALPIN, D., CHARLTON, H. & GORDON, S. (1984). The mononuclear phagocyte system of the mouse defined by immunohistochemical localisation of antigen F4/80. Macrophages of endocrine organs. *Proc. natn. Acad. Sci. U.S.A.* **81**, 4174–4177.

HUME, D. A., LOUTIT, J. F. & GORDON, S. (1984). The mononuclear phagocyte system of the mouse defined by immunohistochemical localization of antigen F4/80. Macrophages of bone and associated connective tissue. *J. Cell Sci.* **66**, 189–194.

HUME, D. A., PERRY, V. H. & GORDON, S. (1983). The histochemical localisation of a macrophage-specific antigen in developing mouse retina. Phagocytosis of dying neurons and differentiation of microglial cells to form a regular array in the plexiform layers. *J. Cell Biol.* **97**, 253–257.

HUME, D. A., PERRY, V. H. & GORDON, S. (1984). The mononuclear phagocyte system of the mouse defined by immunohistochemical localisation of antigen F4/80. Macrophages associated with epithelia. *Anat. Rec.* **210**, 503–572.

HUME, D. A., ROBINSON, A. P., MACPHERSON, G. G. & GORDON, S. (1983). The immunohisto-chemical localisation of antigen F4/80. The relationship between macrophages, Langerhans cells, reticular cells and dendritic cells in lymphoid and hematopoietic organs. *J. exp. Med.* **158**, 1522–1536.

INABA, K. & STEINMAN, R. M. (1984). Resting and sensitized T lymphocytes exhibit distinct stimulatory (antigen-presenting cell) requirements for growth and lymphokine release. *J. exp. Med.* **160**, 1717.

JEFFERIES, W. A., GREEN, J. R. & WILLIAMS, A. F. (1985). Authentic T helper CD4 (W3/25) antigen on rat peritoneal macrophages. *J. exp. Med.* **162**, 117–127.

KAMPSCHMIDT, R. F. (1984). The numerous postulated biological manifestations of Il-1. *J. Leuk. Biol.* **36**, 341.

KAY, M. M. B. (1981). Isolation of the phagocytosis-inducing IgG binding antigen in senescent somatic cells. *Nature, Lond.* **289**, 491–494.

KNIGHTON, D. R., HUNT, T. K., SCHEUENSTUL, W. H., HALLIDAY, B. J., WERB, Z. & BANDA, M. J. (1983). Oxygen tension regulates the expression of angiogenesis factor by macrophages. *Science* **221**, 1283–1285.

KUPFER, A., DENNERT, G. & SINGER, S. J. (1985). The reorientation of the Golgi apparatus and the microtubule-organizing center in the cytotoxic effector cell is a prerequisite in the lysis of bound target cells. *J. molec. Cell. Immun.* **2**, 37–50.

KURT-JONES, E. A., BELLER, D. I., MIZEL, S. B. & UNANUE, E. R. (1985). Identification of a membrane associated interleukin 1 in macrophages. *Proc. natn. Acad. Sci. U.S.A.* **82**, 1204.

LEE, S.-H., CROCKER, P. & GORDON, S. (1986). Macrophage plasma membrane and secretory properties in murine malaria. Effects of *Plasmodium yoelii* infection on macrophages in the liver, spleen and blood. *J. exp. Med.* **163**, 54–74.

LEE, S.-H., STARKEY, P. & GORDON, S. (1985). Quantitative analysis of total macrophage content in adult mouse tissues. Immunochemical studies with monoclonal antibody F4/80. *J. exp. Med.* **161**, 475–489.

LEPAY, D. A., NATHAN, C. F., STEINMAN, R. M., MURRAY, H. W. & COHN, Z. A. (1985a). Murine Kupffer cells. Mononuclear phagocytes deficient in the generation of reactive oxygen intermediates. *J. exp. Med.* **161**, 1079.

LEPAY, D. A., STEINMAN, R. M., NATHAN, C. F., MURRAY, H. W. & COHN, Z. A. (1985b). Liver macrophages in murine listeriosis. Cell-mediated immunity is correlated with an influx of macrophages capable of generating reactive oxygen intermediates. *J. exp. Med.* **161**, 1503.

LOMEDICO, P. A., GABLER, U., HELLMANN, C. P., DAKOVICH, M., GIRI, J. G., PAN, Y. C. E., COLLIER, K., SEMIONOV, R., CHUA, A. O. & MIZEL, S. B. (1984). Cloning and expression of murine Il-1 cDNA in *E. coli. Nature, Lond.* **312**, 458.

LUSTER, A. D., UNKELESS, J. C. & RAVETCH, J. V. (1985). Interferon transcriptionally regulates an early-response gene containing homology to platelet proteins. *Nature, Lond.* **315**, 672.

MALINOFF, H. L. & WISHA, M. S. (1983). Isolation of a cell surface receptor protein for laminin from murine fibrosarcoma cells. *J. Cell Biol.* **96**, 1475–1478.

MARCH, C. J., MOSLEY, B., LARSEN, A., CERRETTI, D. P., BRAEDT, G., PRICE, V., GILLES, S., HENNEY, C. S., KRONHEIM, S. R., GRABSTEIN, K., CONLON, P. J., HOPP, T. P. & COSMAN, D. (1985). Cloning, sequence and expression of two distinct human interleukin complementary DNAs. *Nature, Lond.* **315**, 641–647.

METCALF, D. (1984). *The Haematopoietic Colony Stimulating Factors*, pp. 1–493. Amsterdam: Elsevier Science Publishers.

MICHL, J., PIECZONKA, M. M., UNKELESS, J. C. & SILVERSTEIN, S. C. (1979). Effects of immobilized immune complexes on Fc and complement-receptor function in resident and thioglycollate-elicited mouse peritoneal macrophages. *J. exp. Med.* **150**, 607–621.

MOKOENA, T. & GORDON, S. (1985). Activation of human macrophages. Modulation of mannosyl, fucosyl receptors for endocytosis by lymphokine, gamma and alpha interferons and dexamethasone. *J. clin. Invest.* **75**, 624–631.

MOKOENA, T. & GORDON, S. (1986). Role of the macrophage in inflammatory responses in man. In *Subcellular Pathology: A Biochemical Approach to Organelle Damage* (ed. T. J. Peters). Andover, Hampshire: Chapman & Hall (in press).

MOORE, J. G., FRANK, M. M., MULLER-EBERHARD, H. J. & YOUNG, H. S. (1985). Decay-accelerating factor is present on paroxysmal nocturnal hemoglobinuria erythroid progenitors and lost during erythropoiesis *in vitro. J. exp. Med.* **162**, 1182–1192.

NATHAN, C. F. (1985). Regulation of macrophage oxidative metabolism and antiparasitic activity. In *Mononuclear Phagocytes. Characteristics, Physiology and Function* (ed. R. van Furth), pp. 411–420. Dordrecht, Boston, Lancaster: Martinus Nijhoff.

NILSSON, K., IVHED, I. & FORSBECK, K. (1985). Induced differentiation on human malignant hematopoietic cell lines. In *Gene Expression During Normal and Malignant Differentiation* (ed. C. C. Andersson, C. G. Gahmberg & P. Ekblom), pp. 57–72. London: Academic Press.

PALACIOS, R. (1985). Monoclonal antibodies against human Ia antigens stimulate monocytes to secrete interleukin 1. *Proc. natn. Acad. Sci. U.S.A.* **82**, 6652–6656.

PENNICA, D., NEDUSIN, G. E., HAYFLICK, J. S., SEEBURG, P. H., DERYNEK, R., PALLADINO, M. A., KOHR, W. J., AGARWAL, B. B. & GOEDDEL, D. V. (1984). Human tumour necrosis factor: precursor structure, expression and homology to lymphotoxin. *Nature, Lond.* **312**, 724–729.

PERRY, V. H., HUME, D. A. & GORDON, S. (1985). Immunohistochemical localisation of macrophages and microglia in the adult and developing mouse brain. *Neuroscience* **15**, 313–326.

PESTKA, S. (1983). The human interferons – from protein purification and sequence to cloning, and expression in bacteria: before, between and beyond. *Archs Biochem. Biophys.* **221**, 1.

ROSS, G. D., CAIN, J. A. & LACHMANN, P. J. (1985). Membrane complement receptor type three (CR3) has lectin-like properties analogous to bovine conglutinin and functions as a receptor for zymosan and rabbit erythrocytes as well as a receptor for iC3b. *J. Immun.* **134**, 3307–3315.

ROUZER, C. A., SCOTT, W. A., KEMPE, J. & COHN, Z. A. (1980). Prostaglandin synthesis by macrophage requires a specific receptor–ligand interaction. *Proc. natn. Acad. Sci. U.S.A.* **77**, 4279.

SACHS, L. (1980). Constitutive uncoupling of pathways of gene expression that control growth and differentiation in myeloid leukemia: A model for origin and progression of malignancy. *Proc. natn. Acad. Sci. U.S.A.* **77**, 6152–6156.

SANCHEZ-MADRID, F., NAGY, J. A., ROBBINS, E., SIMON, P. & SPRINGER, T. A. (1983). Characterisation of a human leukocyte differentiation antigen family with distinct alpha subunits and a common beta subunit; the lymphocyte-function associated antigen (LFA-1), the C3bi complement receptor (OKM1/Mac1) and the P150, 95 molecule. *J. exp. Med.* **158**, 1785–1803.

SCHULER, G. & STEINMAN, R. M. (1985). Murine epidermal Langerhans cells mature into potent immunostimulatory dendritic cells *in vitro. J. exp. Med.* **161**, 526–546.

SHERR, C. J., RETTENMIER, C. W., SACCA, R., ROUSSEL, M. F., LOOK, A. T. & STANLEY, E. R. (1985). The c-*fms* proto-oncogene product is related to the receptor for the mononuclear phagocyte growth factor CSF-1. *Cell* **41**, 665–676.

SILVERSTEIN, S. C., STEINMAN, R. M. & COHN, Z. A. (1977). Endocytosis. *A. Rev. Biochem.* **46**, 669–722.

SNYDERMAN, R. & PIKE, M. C. (1984). Chemoattractant receptors on phagocytic cells. *A. Rev. Immun.* **2**, 257–281.

STAHL, P. D. & GORDON, S. (1982). Expression of a mannosyl-fucosyl receptor for endocytosis on cultured primary macrophages and their hybrids. *J. Cell Biol.* **93**, 49–56.

STAHL, P. D., WILEMAN, T. E. & SHEPHERD, V. L. (1985). The mannose receptor of macrophages: a current perspective. In *Mononuclear Phagocytes. Characteristics, Physiology and Function* (ed. R. van Furth), pp. 59–65. Dordrecht, Boston, Lancaster: Martinus Nijhoff.

STEINMAN, R. M., MELLMAN, J. S., MULLER, W. A. & COHN, Z. A. (1983). Endocytosis and the recycling of the plasma membrane. *J. Cell Biol.* **96**, 1–28.

STEINMAN, R. M. & NUSSENZWEIG, M. C. (1980). Dendritic cells: features and functions. *Immun. Rev.* **53**, 127.

TAKEMURA, R. & WERB, Z. (1984). Secretory products of macrophages and their physiologic functions. *Am. J. Physiol.* **246** (Cell Physiol. 15) C1–C9.

TRINCHIERI, G. & PERUSSIA, B. (1985). Immune interferon: a pleiotropic lymphokine with multiple effects. *Immun. Today* **6**, 131.

UNKELESS, J. C., FLEIT, H. & MELLMAN, I. S. (1981). Structural aspects and heterogeneity of immunoglobulin Fc receptors. *Adv. Immun.* **31**, 247–270.

UNKELESS, J. C., GORDON, S. & REICH, E. (1974). Secretion of plasminogen activator by stimulated macrophages. *J. exp. Med.* **139**, 834–850.

VAN FURTH, R. (1980). Cells of the mononuclear phagocyte system. Nomenclature in terms of sites and conditions. In *Mononuclear Phagocytes. Functional Aspects* (ed. R. V. Furth), pp. 1–30. The Hague, Boston, London: Martinus Nijhoff.

VASSALLI, J. D., BACCINO, D. & BELIN, D. (1985). A cellular binding site for the M_r 55,000 form of the human plasminogen activator urokinase. *J. Cell Biol.* **100**, 86.

VASSALLI, J. D., DAYER, J. M., WOHLWEND, A. & BELIN, D. (1984). Concomitant secretion of prourokinase and of a plasminogen activator-specific inhibitor by cultured human monocytes–macrophages. *J. exp. Med.* **159**, 1653–1668.

VASTA, G. R., SULLIVAN, J. T., CHENG, T. C., MARCHALONIS, J. J. & WARR, G. W. (1982). A cell membrane-associated lectin of the oyster hemocyte. *J. Inverteb. Path.* **40**, 367–377.

VLASSARA, H., BROWNLEE, M. & CERAMI, A. (1984). Accumulation of diabetic rat peripheral nerve myelin by macrophages increases with the presence of advanced glycosylation end product. *J. exp. Med.* **160**, 197–207.

VOLKMAN, A. & GOWANS, J. L. (1963). The origin of macrophages from bone marrow in the rat. *Br. J. exp. Path.* **46**, 62–70.

WERB, Z. (1980). Hormone receptors and hormonal regulation of macrophage physiological functions. In *Mononuclear Phagocytes. Functional Aspects* (ed. R. Van Furth), p. 809. The Hague, Boston, London: Martinus Nijhoff.

WERB, Z., BANDA, M. J., TAKEMURA, R. & GORDON, S. (1986). Secreted proteins of resting and activated macrophages. In *Handbook of Experimental Immunology*, 4th edn (ed. D. M. Weir, L. A. Herzenberg & L. A. Herzenberg), pp. 47.1–47.28. Oxford: Blackwell Scientific Publications.

WILLIAMS, A. F. & BARCLAY, A. N. (1985). Glycoproteins of the lymphocyte surface and their purification by antibody affinity chromatography. In *Handbook of Experimental Immunology*, 4th edn (ed. D. M. Weir, L. A. Herzenberg & L. A. Herzenberg). Oxford: Blackwell Scientific Publications (in press).

WRIGHT, S. D. & GRIFFIN, F. M. JR (1985). Activation of phagocytic cells' C3 receptors for phagocytosis. *J. Leuk. Biol.* **38**, 327–339.

WRIGHT, S. D., LICHT, M. R., CRAIGMYLE, L. S. & SILVERSTEIN, S. C. (1984). Communication between receptors for different ligands on a single cell: Ligation of fibronectin receptors induces a reversible alteration in the function of complement receptors on cultured human monocytes. *J. Cell Biol.* **99**, 336–339.

WRIGHT, S. D. & MEYER, B. C. (1985). Fibronectin receptor of human macrophages recognizes the sequence Arg-Gly-Asp-Ser. *J. exp. Med.* **162**, 762–767.

WRIGHT, S. D. & SILVERSTEIN, S. C. (1983). Receptors for C3b and C3bi promote phagocytosis but not the release of toxic oxygen from human phagocytes. *J. exp. Med.* **158**, 2016–2023.

WRIGHT, S. D. & SILVERSTEIN, S. C. (1984). Phagocytosing macrophages exclude proteins from the zones of contact with opsonized targets. *Nature, Lond.* **309**, 359.

YAMAMOTO, K. & JOHNSTON, R. B. JR (1984). Dissociation of phagocytosis from stimulation of the oxidative metabolic burst in macrophages. *J. exp. Med.* **159**, 405–416.

YOUNG, J. D.-E. & COHN, Z. A. (1985). Nature of transmembrane signal associated with binding to the macrophage. In *Mononuclear Phagocytes. Characteristics, Physiology and Function* (ed. R. Van Furth), pp. 399–406. Dordrecht, Boston, Lancaster: Martinus Nijhoff.

J. Cell Sci. Suppl. 4, 287–318 (1986)
Printed in Great Britain © The Company of Biologists Limited 1986

NUCLEAR TRANSPLANTATION IN EGGS AND OOCYTES

J. B. GURDON

Cancer Research Campaign Molecular Embryology Unit, Department of Zoology, University of Cambridge, Downing Street, Cambridge CB2 3EJ, England

HISTORICAL BACKGROUND

Nuclear transplantation involves the replacement of the nucleus of one cell with that of another. The original purpose of this technique was to test whether the nucleus of a somatic cell can replace the zygote nucleus of a fertilized egg, and so determine whether cell differentiation and morphogenesis are accompanied by stable changes in the genome. The need for such a test was evident since Weismann's (1892) germ-plasm hypothesis in which it was supposed that genetic determinants are segregated into different cells as development proceeds. The technique of nuclear transfer was first achieved in single-celled organisms, such as *Acetabularia* (Hammerling, 1934) and *Amoeba* (Comandon & De Fonbrune, 1939). The delayed-nucleation experiment of Spemann (1938) showed that nuclei are genetically equivalent up to at least the eight-cell stage in amphibia, but was not able to test the reasonable possibility that nuclei might change at later stages when cells begin to differentiate.

The first successful nuclear transfer experiment in animals was achieved in 1952 by Briggs & King who obtained normal feeding stage larvae from transplanted blastula nuclei of *Rana pipiens*. This was soon followed by the discovery that nuclei transplanted from the mesoderm or endoderm of *R. pipiens* late gastrulae can no longer support normal development (King & Briggs, 1955). This result and much subsequent nuclear transfer work with *R. pipiens* and the axolotl (e.g. see Briggs & King, 1957, 1960; Briggs, Signoret & Humphrey, 1964), led to the suggestion that as cells differentiate their nuclei undergo restrictions in developmental capacity reflecting some kind of nuclear differentiation. The next significant step came from the serial nuclear transplantation experiments of King & Briggs (1956), which showed that the developmental restrictions of individual *Rana* gastrula nuclei differ from each other and are stable over many nuclear divisions. The nature of these developmental restrictions was greatly clarified by detailed chromosome analyses carried out over several years. It became evident that nuclear-transplant embryos that develop abnormally most often have microscopically visible chromosome abnormalities, which are not present in the donor nuclei (Briggs, King & Di Berardino, 1960; Briggs *et al.* 1964; Di Berardino & King, 1965), and that these chromosome defects are a sufficient explanation for the developmental abnormalities observed. It was clear that these developmental and chromosomal abnormalities are not a direct reflection of the properties of somatic nuclei but rather a consequence of the inability of those nuclei to accelerate their replication cycle to coincide with the exceptionally rapid pace imposed by eggs.

Well before this level of understanding had been reached, the first nuclear transfer results were obtained with *Xenopus*, this species being easier to rear to sexual maturity than *Rana*. Two significant results came from these early experiments (Fischberg, Gurdon & Elsdale, 1958; Gurdon, Elsdale & Fischberg, 1958). First, nuclear transplant embryos were reared to sexually mature individuals, demonstrating that the transplanted nuclei were totipotent, rather than pluripotent as shown by the production of larvae. Second, sexually mature frogs were obtained from transplanted nuclei of endoderm cells of tail-bud larvae, a very different result from that obtained in *Rana*. Nuclear transfers from the endoderm of *Xenopus* were pursued, and culminated in the finding that fertile adult nuclear-transplant frogs could be obtained from nuclei from the intestine of feeding larvae (Gurdon, 1962c; Gurdon & Uehlinger, 1966). Although the proportion of intestinal nuclei shown by nuclear transfer to be pluripotent or totipotent was small, these results generated the interpretation (see Gurdon, 1962c) that cell differentiation does not require or depend upon any irreversible change in nuclear genetic material, a view contrasting with that generated at that time by work on *R. pipiens*. This interpretation was reinforced several years later by transplanting nuclei from the terminally differentiated, keratinized skin cells of adult foot web (Gurdon, Laskey & Reeves, 1975); these yielded feeding-stage tadpoles (but not adults) and therefore contained pluripotential nuclei.

The purpose of this article is to review the conclusions that can be drawn from nuclear transfer experiments, to examine their validity, and to consider the prospects for further work in this field.

NUCLEAR TRANSFER PROCEDURE

The procedure for transplanting nuclei in amphibia, as first used successfully by Briggs & King (1952), is as follows. Donor cells are dissociated, and a single cell sucked into a micropipette of such a size that the cell is ruptured but its nucleus is still surrounded by cytoplasm. The whole broken cell is injected into an unfertilized egg that has been enucleated, and if necessary activated. The egg should then develop by division of the transplanted nucleus, which has therefore replaced the nuclear material normally present in the zygote.

The technique involves three main steps: the preparation of donor cells, the preparation of recipient eggs, and the transplantation procedure itself (Fig. 1). Eggs of amphibia, unlike those of mammals, do not need to be fertilized before nuclear transfer, and only the egg's chromosomes, which are present near the animal pole on the second meiotic metaphase spindle, have to be removed or destroyed. This is done either manually with a needle (*Rana*) or by ultraviolet irradiation (*Xenopus*). In the case of Anura (*Rana, Xenopus*), unfertilized eggs do not need activation beyond what is already achieved by penetration with an injection pipette. In Urodeles

(*Ambystoma, Pleurodeles*), the additional activation stimulus required is provided, usually before enucleation, by an electric shock.

To prepare nuclei for injection, donor cells are dissociated in a calcium-free medium supplemented with EDTA, or trypsin for more differentiated tissues, and maintained in a medium containing serum albumin, spermine, or other components found to improve results. The nuclear transfer step requires a micropipette made with great precision. It must be small enough to rupture a cell sucked into it; it must also be large enough and must have a sufficiently smooth contour on its opening not to disperse the cytoplasm, which protects the nucleus from the adverse effects of all

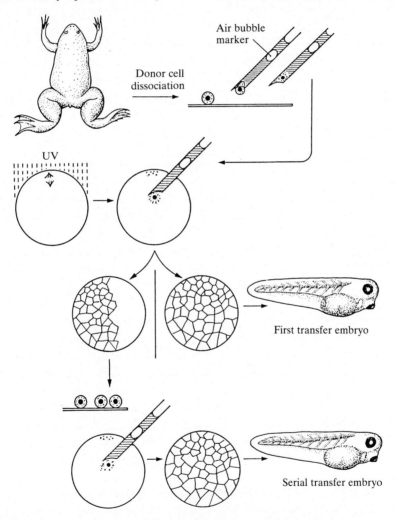

Fig. 1. Nuclear transfer procedure for *Xenopus*, illustrated with transfers from adult foot skin cells. Nuclear transfers from specialized cells often yield a substantial number of partially cleaved blastulae, which can be used, as shown here, as a source of nuclei for serial transfers. The nuclear transfer procedure for other amphibian species differs from that shown mainly by the method of enucleation (UV, ultraviolet irradiation, in this figure) and in some cases by the inclusion of an egg activation step.

media so far used. It must also have a point sharp enough not to damage the recipient egg. Such a pipette, whose tip resembles that of a hypodermic needle, is made with a microforge. Since the tip of the pipette cannot be seen once it is in an egg, an air bubble is used to monitor ejection of the nucleus.

This procedure requires considerable practice for the best results. Detailed requirements differ for each species used, and these are described in the following papers: *Rana*: King (1966); *Xenopus*: Gurdon (1977); *Ambystoma*: Signoret, Briggs & Humphrey (1962); *Pleurodeles*: Signoret & Picheral (1962).

NORMAL DEVELOPMENT OF NUCLEAR-TRANSPLANT EMBRYOS

The most conclusive outcome of a nuclear-transplant experiment is the development of a normal adult frog that is fertile, and which carries a genetic marker proving its derivation from the transplanted nucleus and not from the recipient egg pronucleus. Fertile adults, carrying a genetic marker, have been most readily obtained in *Xenopus*, and are listed in Table 1, to exemplify the cell types from which they have been obtained. It can be seen that nuclei of endoderm and of intestine at the stage when its cells are first differentiated (feeding stage) have yielded fertile adult frogs. The same is true of other *Xenopus* cell types, including hatched tadpole epidermis and presumptive neural-fold brain cells (Table 1). In *R. pipiens* adults have been obtained from transplanted blastula nuclei (Table 1). All of these cases provide direct evidence for the totipotency of nuclei during cell differentiation, as discussed in detail at the end of this section. The success of nuclear transplantation with the nuclei of embryonic cells has made it possible to produce clones of genetically identical animals from the nuclei of one embryo (Gurdon, 1962*d*; McKinnell, 1962; Gallien & Aimar, 1966). Such multiple identical twins are all the same sex, they accept each other's skin grafts, and differ only in the detailed speckling of their skin and in growth rate if crowded. No-one has yet obtained a normal adult nuclear-transplant frog from the transplanted cell nucleus of another *adult* frog. A very small number of nuclear transfer larvae from adult skin started feeding, the longest survivor dying just after metamorphosis (Gurdon, 1974, page 23).

Many nuclear-transplant embryos that fail to become fertile adults nevertheless develop far enough to give valuable information about the developmental capacity of transplanted nuclei. One such level of development is a heart-beat larva, in which all major cell types, including muscle, nerve, blood, lens, etc., are fully functional and are furthermore organized into morphogenetically normal tissues and organs (Fig. 2B,C). The only obvious defect in such larvae is that they fail to feed or grow, eventually becoming oedematous and dying. Transplanted nuclei that promote development this far are usually described as pluripotential. An earlier stage at which it is also useful to assess nuclear-transplant embryo development is the muscular response stage (Fig. 2A). In *Xenopus*, this is reached 2 days after fertilization or nuclear transfer, and reflects the formation of sufficiently normal muscle and nerve for lateral body movements to take place spontaneously and after stimulation.

Table 1. *Adult nuclear-transplant frogs and their cell type of origin*

Source of transplanted nuclei	Degree of normality demonstrated	Nuclear marker	Reference
Xenopus endoderm (st. 8–30, blastula → heart-beat)	4 fertile females	1-*nu*	Gurdon (1962*a*)
	80 fertile males	1-*nu*	Gurdon (1962*a*)
Xenopus intestine (st. 33–41, hatched and swimming)	18 fertile females	1-*nu*	Gurdon (1962*a*)
	2 fertile males	1-*nu*	Gurdon (1962*a*)
Xenopus intestine (st. 45–47, feeding)	4 fertile females	1-*nu*	Gurdon & Uehlinger (1966)
	1 fertile male	1-*nu*	Gurdon & Uehlinger (1966)
Xenopus neural cells (st. 20–21, closed neural folds)	4 metamorph.	1-*nu*	Simnett (1964)
Xenopus larval epidermis (st. 36–42)	3 fertile adults	1-*nu*	Brun & Kobel (1972)
Xenopus cultured cells (st. 40, epithelium)	3 metamorph.	1-*nu*	Gurdon & Laskey (1970)
R. pipiens blastula	47 metamorph.	Kandiyohi	McKinnell (1962)
R. nigromaculata subspecies (blastula)	1 metamorph.	Subspecies	Sambuichi (1957)
P. waltlii (blastula)	22 males	—	Gallien & Aimar (1966)
	13 females	—	Gallien & Aimar (1966)
P. waltlii (tailbud)	14 metamorph.	—	Aimar (1972)

The majority of larvae that complete metamorphosis (metamorph. above) become sexually mature adults, if maintained for 1–2 years.

Macroscopic and histological examination shows the presence of differentiated muscle cells organized into characteristic blocks of myotomes. As seen in Table 2, heart-beat stage larvae have been obtained with transplanted nuclei taken from all adult cell types that have been well tested in *Xenopus* and from many terminally specialized cell types including skin, muscle and melanophore. With *R. pipiens*, such larvae have also been obtained from transplanted nuclei of adult erythrocytes (Table 2). The proportion of nuclear transplants reaching the heart-beat larval stage is small, though their significance is clear when the donor cell population has been well characterized. A substantially higher proportion of embryos derived from the same donor nuclei reach the muscular response stage (Table 2). Even though many of these embryos become abnormal before reaching the heart-beat stage, the formation of functional and histologically normal muscle cells from the nuclei of such cells as adult skin and erythrocytes demonstrates a dramatic change in gene expression.

Before drawing definitive conclusions from these experiments, certain possible reservations about their interpretation and validity need discussion.

Egg enucleation and genetic markers of donor nuclei

It is essential to be sure that there has been no contribution of the recipient egg chromosomes to nuclear-transplant embryo development. The most direct and convincing evidence comes from the use of genetic markers. In *Xenopus*, the 1-*nu* nucleolar mutation (Elsdale, Gurdon & Fischberg, 1960) can be seen from the gastrula stage onwards, and the a^P albino mutant (Hoperskaya, 1975) in a stage 40 swimming tadpole and thereafter. In *Rana*, where genetic markers visible at early stages of development are not yet available, evidence for non-participation of the egg nucleus has depended on finding the egg nucleus in sectioned egg jellies containing an exovate (Di Berardino & Hoffner, 1983). In the best cases, this has been coupled with the use of triploid donor nuclei (McKinnell, Deggins & Labat, 1969; Di Berardino, Mizell, Hoffner & Friesendorf, 1983). In all nuclear-transplant experiments, it is normal practice to show that fertilized eggs subjected to enucleation treatment yield haploids, i.e. that the egg nucleus has been eliminated. However, in the absence of other evidence this is not completely convincing, especially if conclusions are drawn from a very small proportion of total nuclear transplants; cases of this kind (Muggleton-Harris & Pezzella, 1972) are not included in Table 1.

The most widely used genetic marker in nuclear-transplant experiments is the 1-*nu* mutant of *Xenopus*. How reliable is this? Extensive tests were reported by Gurdon *et al.* (1975) to show that a 1-*nu* diploid chromosome set does not arise by

---

Fig. 2. Examples of muscular response and heart-beat nuclear transplant larvae. A. 2-Day abnormal larva, with well-organized functional myotomes, and capable of swimming movements. B. 4-Day larva, not completely normal as seen by small eyes and heart oedema; it has a beating heart, with circulating blood cells, and swims actively. C. A histological section through an eye of a heart-beat stage larva, derived in this case from the transplanted nucleus of an adult epidermal skin cell. All figures are of *X. laevis*. C is from Gurdon *et al.* (1975).

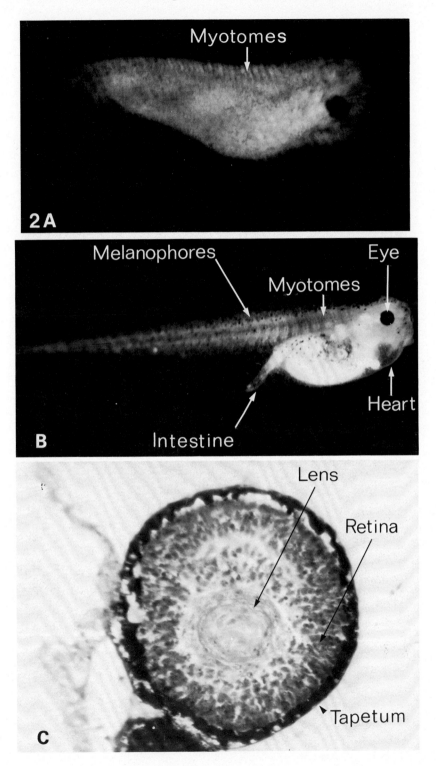

Table 2. Nuclear transfers from differentiated and adult cells

Species	Nuclear stage	Donor tissue	Evidence of differentiated donor cells	% Total transfers[*] reaching stage of:		Genetic marker	Reference
				Muscular response	Heart-beat		
X. laevis	Tailbud (st. 26)	Muscle	Elongated cells with myofibril	4·5	2	1-nu a^P	Gurdon et al. (1984)
	Hatched (st. 35–40)	Cultured melanophore	Pigmented	1	0·5	—	Kobel et al. (1973)
	Feeding (st. 45)	Intestine	Epithelial cells	20	7	1-nu	Gurdon (1962c)
	Feeding (st. 46–57)	Intestine	Epithelial cells	1·5	1·5	—	Marshall & Dixon (1977)
	Adult	Lung, kidney heart	—	8	4	1-nu	Laskey & Gurdon (1970)
	Adult	Foot skin	Keratin antibody	4·5	3	1-nu	Gurdon et al. (1975)
	Adult	Spleen	Immunogen antibody	6	2	1-nu	Wabl et al. (1975)
	Adult	Intestinal epithelium	Location of crest cells	0·5	0·35	—	McAvoy et al. (1975)
	Adult	Erythroblasts	Oval red cell	0·5	0·8	1-nu	Brun (1978)
R. pipiens	Adult	Male germ cells	Cell size	2	1	—	Di Berardino & Hoffner (1971)
	Adult	Erythrocytes	Cell shape	8·5	4·5	—	Di Berardino & Hoffner (1983)

* Includes the results of serial transfers when these have been carried out.

the combined effects of ultraviolet irradiation of the egg pronucleus and a doubling of its chromosome set. In recent work, the albino mutation was used in conjunction with the 1-*nu* marker (Gurdon, Brennan, Fairman & Mohun, 1984). 2-*nu* nuclei are sometimes seen in 1-*nu* embryos, but when investigated these have turned out to be tetraploid cells (Gurdon, 1959) and therefore to be valid derivatives of the transplanted nucleus, which must have undergone a doubling in some somatic cells.

The differentiated state of donor cells

The proportion of nuclear-transplant embryos that develop normally or nearly so is small, and it is essential to be sure that these are not derived from a minority of non-specialized cells that differ from the well-characterized majority. Ideally, the specialized characteristics of individual donor cells can be seen under a microscope, and only such cells taken for nuclear transfer, as has been done for melanocytes (Kobel, Brun & Fischberg, 1973), erythrocytes (Di Berardino & Hoffner, 1983), and spindle-shaped muscle cells (Gurdon *et al.* 1984). When donor cells cannot be individually recognized, it is necessary to have a fairly homogeneous donor cell population, and to determine what proportion of these cells are not of the differentiated kind. For adult skin cells and lymphocytes, this has been done with antibodies and a simple statistical assessment used to prove that the embryos reaching a certain stage of development could not have come from the small minority of donor cells that did not react with antibody (Gurdon *et al.* 1975; Wabl, Brun & Du Pasquier, 1975). Under one or other of these conditions just discussed, there is no doubt about the differentiated state of the donor cells from which tadpoles were obtained.

Is new gene activity required for nuclear-transplant embryo development?

Amphibian eggs contain a large store of maternal mRNA (Rosbash & Ford, 1974), and we must consider the possibility that development as far as the muscular response stage, and perhaps even to the heart-beat larval stage, could be achieved by the use of maternal components and might not depend on gene activity by transplanted nuclei. All information at present available strongly indicates the specific requirement of nuclear gene activity if development is to proceed beyond the late blastula stage. Thus nuclear-transplant hybrids between species die at this stage (see below), and the earliest cell types to differentiate, such as muscle, make their proteins from newly transcribed nuclear genes (Mohun *et al.* 1984). Therefore, it seems clear that all stages of development beyond a late blastula are a meaningful test of the genetic activity of transplanted nuclei.

Cancer nuclei

A final comment on the transplantation of cancer cell nuclei is justified. All experiments have been carried out using the Lucké adenocarcinoma, a herpes virus induced and transplantable epithelial cancer of *R. pipiens* kidney. Since the first experiments of King & McKinnell (1960), nuclear transfer results have steadily improved; King & Di Berardino (1965) and McKinnell *et al.* (1969) have all obtained muscular response, and in a few cases heart-beat, larvae from adeno-carcinoma nuclear transfers. In the last of these papers, triploid donor nuclei were used to provide direct evidence of successful recipient egg enucleation. No tumours were observed in the nuclear-transplant embryos, though it would have been surprising if they had appeared so early in development. A crucial question of interpretation in these experiments is whether the larvae were derived from the transfer of nuclei from true cancer cells or from non-cancerous cells present in the tumour. McKinnell *et al.* (1976) argue convincingly that the donors of nuclear-transplant tadpoles were epithelial and not stromal or blood cells. Di Berardino *et al.* (1983) selected only epithelial cells of Lucké tumours for nuclear transfer, and obtained larvae that died somewhere between the muscular response and feeding stage; but even in this case it is hard to eliminate entirely the possibility that non-cancerous epithelial cell nuclei gave the best development. In conclusion, it seems very likely, though not conclusively proved, that nuclei from at least one kind of cancer cell can promote nuclear-transplant embryo development to about the same extent as the nuclei of normal adult cells.

Conclusion

In summary, the following conclusions can be drawn from the extent to which transplanted nuclei promote normal development. Totipotency, or the ability to promote the formation of fertile adult frogs, has been demonstrated for the nuclei of many kinds of embryonic cells and for one source of differentiated cells of early larvae. Pluripotency, as judged by the development of heart-beat larvae has been documented for the nuclei of all cell types thoroughly tested, including terminally specialized adult cells, though only in a small proportion of total nuclear transfers. A higher proportion of nuclei from specialized cells promote development to the muscular response than to the heart-beat stage. A substantial change in nuclear gene activity is demonstrated by the development of muscular response stage (motile) embryos. All these conclusions rest on experiments in which the differentiated state of donor cells has been established, and in which recipient egg enucleation is documented, usually with a genetic marker.

ABNORMAL DEVELOPMENT OF NUCLEAR-TRANSPLANT EMBRYOS

Most nuclear-transplant embryos develop abnormally, not only in post-blastula stages that depend on nuclear gene expression, but also during early cleavage before gene transcription has started. We now ask to what extent we can account for these abnormalities and whether they give useful information about the nuclei of dif-ferentiating cells.

Nuclear-transplant abnormalities occur most frequently, and are most severe, when nuclei are taken from the more differentiated and least actively dividing cells. This result was first described in *R. pipiens* (King & Briggs, 1955; Briggs & King, 1957), and has been subsequently confirmed in all other species tested (e.g. see Gurdon, 1960, for *Xenopus*; Briggs *et al.* 1964, for axolotl; Picheral, 1962; Aimar,

1972, for *Pleurodeles*). The effect is most pronounced in *R. pipiens* and least in *Xenopus* (Fig. 3), though later experiments of Hennen (1970) with *Rana* endoderm nuclei, using improved procedures, gave results equivalent to those typical of *Xenopus*. Nuclear transfers from germ cells, by definition totipotent, develop more normally than those from endoderm nuclei (8% larvae *versus* 0%) though less normally than those from blastula nuclei (55% larvae); these results of Smith (1965) with *R. pipiens* argue that the reduction in nuclear transfer success is more likely to be due to a lower donor cell division rate than to loss of nuclear totipotency.

Nuclear-transplant abnormalities are propagatable and stable. It was first found by King & Briggs in 1956 and confirmed in all subsequent work that serial nuclear-transfer clones tend to be morphologically homogeneous within each clone, but substantially different between clones (Fig. 4). This implies that there are stable differences between the nuclei that populate a first-transfer embryo; since all of these nuclei were derived from a single originally transplanted nucleus, the stable differences evidently arose after the first transfer, but were little if at all enhanced during serial transfer. The developmental defects are alleviated neither by parabiosis

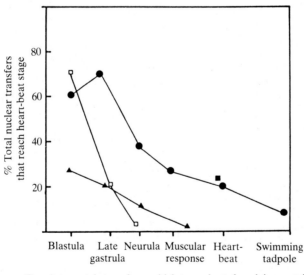

Fig. 3. Nuclear transplant embryo development in relation to increasing donor stage (endoderm nuclei). (●—●) *X. laevis* (Gurdon, 1960); (□—□) *R. pipiens* (Briggs & King, 1957); (■) *R. pipiens* (Hennen, 1970); (▲—▲) *Pleurodeles* (Aimar, 1972).

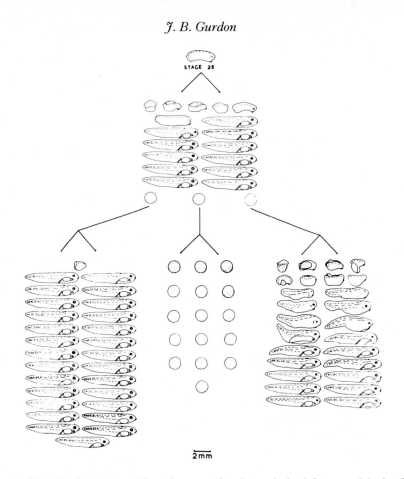

Fig. 4. Variation between serial nuclear transfer clones derived from nuclei of a first transfer embryo. Endoderm nuclei were transplanted from a muscular response, stage 25, embryo. When the resulting embryos had become late blastulae, three were used to provide nuclei for serial transfers. All other first-transfer embryos, and all serial transfer embryos, were allowed to develop to the feeding larva stage if they were able. Most of the normal larvae shown would have become frogs if maintained. Two of the serial transfer clones developed very uniformly within each clone but very differently between clones. (From Gurdon, 1960.)

(fusion) with normal embryos (Briggs *et al.* 1960), nor by allowing a transplanted nucleus to fuse with the haploid nucleus of a non-enucleated egg thereby creating triploid embryos (Subtelny, 1965); thus the deficiencies of nuclei in abnormal embryos are 'rescued' neither by circulating components of embryos nor by a normal set of chromosomes.

Chromosome abnormalities

The basis of these stable nuclear changes is now known to lie in chromosomal aberrations that arise after the first transfer of somatic nuclei. Though early results described chromosome defects in only the most abnormal embryos (King & Briggs, 1956), subsequent more detailed studies have shown that all embryos dying before the feeding stage have visibly abnormal chromosomes, that the most severe developmental abnormalities have the most severe chromosomal defects, and hence that chromosome abnormalities are a sufficient explanation for the developmental abnormalities (Di Berardino & King, 1965; Briggs *et al.* 1964; Di Berardino & Hoffner, 1970; Aimar, 1972). This at once provides an explanation for the irreversibility of nuclear-transplant embryo defects observed in serial nuclear transfer experiments.

A particularly interesting feature of these chromosomal defects is that they occur not only at the first mitosis after nuclear transfer (Briggs *et al.* 1960; Gurdon, 1962*c*), but continue to take place during many mitoses thereafter (Briggs *et al.* 1964). For example, fragments of chromosomes without centromeres (which means that they must have arisen in the last few divisions) are seen in late blastulae, at least 12 divisions after the original nuclear transfer (Fig. 5). It seems that major chromosome defects occur at the first post-transfer mitosis, a situation readily

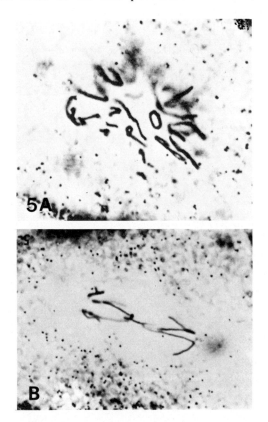

Fig. 5. Abnormal chromosomes in nuclear transplant embryos. Each figure shows an abnormal chromosome set in nuclear-transplant embryos of *R. pipiens*. The stained squash preparations were made from blastulae, about 10 divisions after nuclear transfer. If chromosome abnormalities were to arise only at the first division after nuclear transfer, the ring chromosome and acentromeric fragments (A) would have been lost by the 10th division. Chromosomes that do not separate properly at division (B) are usually lost before the next mitosis. (From Briggs *et al.* (1964).)

understandable in view of the gross disparity in division rate between donor cells and recipient egg. What is unexpected and unexplained is the continued shedding of chromosome fragments long after the transplanted nucleus has been forced to adopt the cell division cycle of an egg.

The key question that now arises is whether the chromosomal and developmental abnormalities of nuclear-transplant embryos bear any relationship to the tissue origin of the transplanted nuclei. Embryos prepared from transplanted endoderm nuclei first show defects in their ectoderm and mesoderm (Briggs & King, 1957); this is probably due to the later differentiation of endoderm compared to other germ layers and the same defects are also observed in embryos derived from ectodermal and mesodermal nuclei. Di Berardino & King (1967) made a detailed study of over 1200 nuclear transfers from neural nuclei; these yielded only four embryos with normal chromosome sets, and three of these had deficiencies in their mesoderm and endoderm; but even these had histologically and morphogenetically recognizable mesoderm and endoderm tissues such as muscle, notochord and gut. In all other work involving several species, no relationship has been observed between the nature of the developmental abnormalities and the tissue of origin of the transplanted nuclei (e.g. see Gurdon, 1962c; and Simnett, 1964, for *Xenopus*; Aimar, 1972, for *Pleurodeles*). It is important to recognize this point. Readers should not be confused by the description of developmental abnormalities as being "consistent with the donor tissue of origin". This situation is expected for endoderm nuclei (see above) but is not significant unless nuclei of different origins can be shown to give different kinds of abnormality.

Conclusion and prospects

The simplest interpretation of abnormal nuclear-transplant embryo development, at the present time, is the following. All abnormal development is attributable to chromosome aberrations that occur soon after the transfer of a somatic cell nucleus to an egg, and to a lesser extent in subsequent cell divisions. The more differentiated, and the less active in cell division, are donor cells, the more abnormal are the chromosomal, and hence developmental, defects. There is no evidence that these defects are related to the cell type from which nuclei are taken. As Briggs *et al.* (1964) pointed out, the chromosomal changes that follow nuclear transfer, like those that can occur in cell culture, need to be understood or controlled, before full advantage can be taken of this experimental system.

Future work on the developmental capacity of transplanted nuclei is likely to concentrate on attempts to obtain adult animals from the nuclei of adult cells, and to increase the proportion of transplanted nuclei from differentiated cells that yield larvae. A way has to be found of derepressing the chromatin of somatic nuclei so that replication can be completed within the first cell cycle of the egg. The simplest concept is that, as development proceeds, non-specific repressors such as histones become tightly associated with all chromosomal DNA that has not already been bound by gene-specific transcription factors (Brown, 1984). Two experimental approaches have given some encouragement. One is to add spermine to the nuclear transfer medium; this has dramatically improved nuclear transfer results with *R. pipiens* endoderm nuclei (Hennen, 1970). The other is to transplant nuclei to *R. pipiens* meiotic oocytes, thereby giving them some 24 h of exposure to cytoplasm before they are required to replicate (Di Berardino & Hoffner, 1983). Spermine has a more beneficial effect in *Rana* than in *Xenopus*, whose eggs appear to have stronger natural derepressing properties, and so to yield more normal nuclear transfer results. Since spermine has already been used in all recent *Xenopus* work, some additional procedures are needed. One that does not make much difference is to transplant nuclei synchronized at different stages of the cell cycle (McAvoy, Dixon & Marshall, 1975; Ellinger, 1978; von Beroldingen, 1981). If a means can be found of substantially improving nuclear transfer results, this would be important in its own right, and might also suggest the nature of the developmental mechanisms that restrict replication and, perhaps, transcription of somatic nuclei.

NUCLEAR TRANSFERS BETWEEN DIFFERENT SPECIES

Enucleated eggs of one species, when fertilized with sperm of another, develop as androgenetic haploids in which all of the genetic material is of one (paternal) species, and all of the cytoplasm is of the other (maternal) species. Nucleocytoplasmic combinations of this kind are useful for showing the earliest time of nuclear gene expression as well as the longest lasting cytoplasmic effects, and hence the relative contribution of nucleus and cytoplasm to normal development. They also show how far cytoplasmic signals that regulate nuclear activity are species specific. Fertilization cannot be achieved between distantly related species, and nuclear transplantation, which has no such limitations, has opened up a more extensive analysis of nucleo-cytoplasmic interactions.

Nuclear transfers between members of the same species (subspecies, strain or other variant) develop entirely normally, becoming fertile adults. In contrast, the nucleus of one species with the cytoplasm of another is nearly always lethal; the more distantly related the species, the earlier does development arrest (Fig. 6). The general rule is that nuclear transfers between any amphibian species (even between *Urodeles* and *Anura*) will form a regularly cleaved late blastula. However, more distant combinations, such as an insect or mammalian nucleus in frog egg cytoplasm, do not permit more than a few replications, development being arrested as irregular blastulae (Brun, 1973).

For assessing the contribution of nucleus and cytoplasm to early development, the most informative nuclear transfers are those between closely related forms, in which distinguishing characteristics are known, and in which development is normal enough for these to show. Gene expression in nuclear-transplant hybrids has been reviewed by Gallien (1979), who cites previous work. The main conclusions are these. The only cytoplasmic or maternally determined characteristics of nuclear-transplant embryos are those directly attributable to components of the egg. These include pigmentation derived from the unfertilized egg, and the size of the pre-feeding embryo, itself determined by the size of the egg; both properties can still be

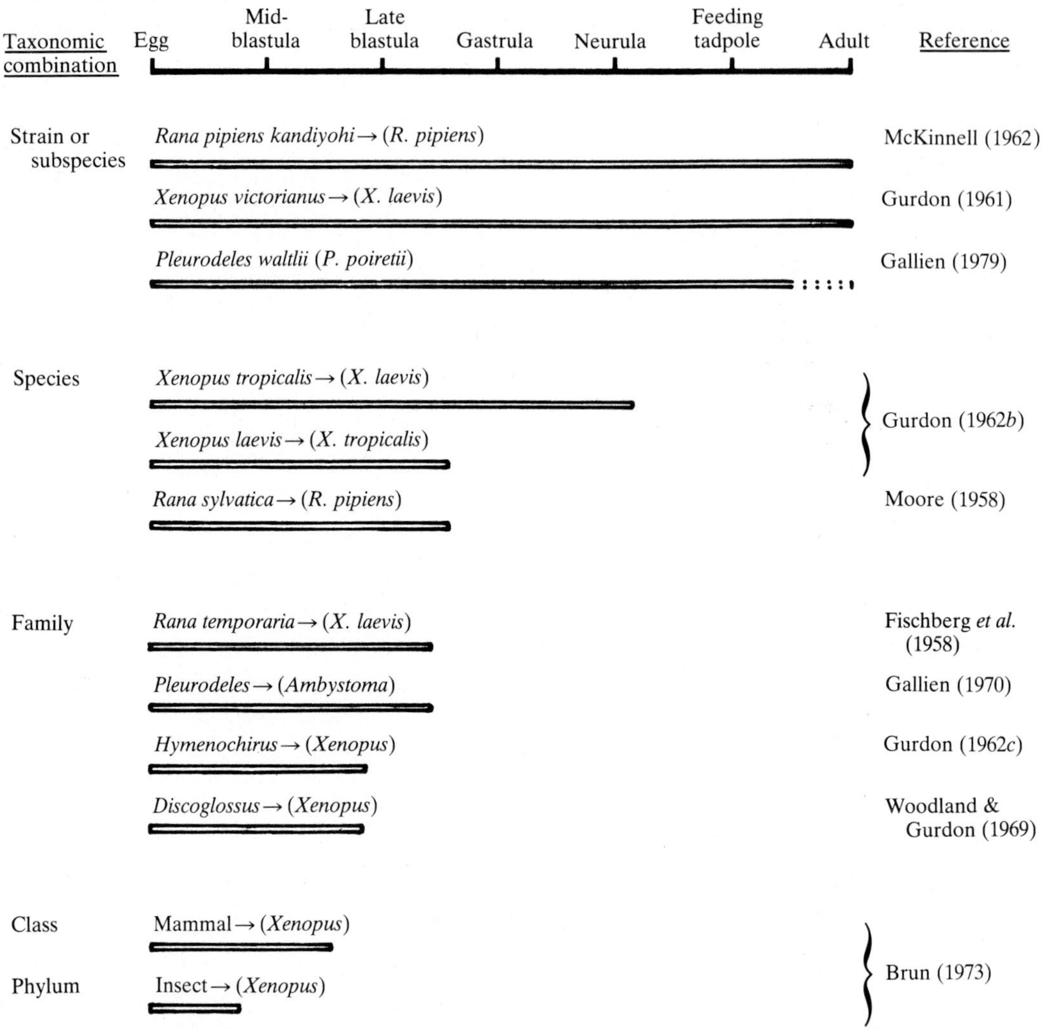

Taxonomic combination	Egg	Mid-blastula	Late blastula	Gastrula	Neurula	Feeding tadpole	Adult	Reference

Strain or subspecies

Rana pipiens kandiyohi → (*R. pipiens*)   McKinnell (1962)

Xenopus victorianus → (*X. laevis*)   Gurdon (1961)

Pleurodeles waltlii (*P. poiretii*)   Gallien (1979)

Species

Xenopus tropicalis → (*X. laevis*)

Xenopus laevis → (*X. tropicalis*)   Gurdon (1962*b*)

Rana sylvatica → (*R. pipiens*)   Moore (1958)

Family

Rana temporaria → (*X. laevis*)   Fischberg *et al.* (1958)

Pleurodeles → (*Ambystoma*)   Gallien (1970)

Hymenochirus → (*Xenopus*)   Gurdon (1962*c*)

Discoglossus → (*Xenopus*)   Woodland & Gurdon (1969)

Class   Mammal → (*Xenopus*)

Phylum   Insect → (*Xenopus*)   Brun (1973)

Fig. 6. Developmental arrest of hybrid nuclear-transplant embryos. The greater the taxonomic difference between nucleus and cytoplasm, the earlier in development does arrest take place, and the more severe are chromosome abnormalities. Brackets signify an enucleated and unfertilized egg.

seen several days after fertilization. However, there is no persistent effect of egg cytoplasm in viable intraspecific combinations; even when a nucleus of one sub-species was serially transplanted three times (a total of 45 replications) into eggs of another subspecies, and the progeny of the resulting nuclear-transplant frogs examined, no cytoplasmic effect was seen (Gurdon, 1961). In nearly all respects, the characteristics of embryos are determined entirely by the expression of nuclear genes. Furthermore, the activation of genes takes place at the same stage in development as it does in normally fertilized eggs of the nuclear species (e.g. lactate dehydrogenase isozymes in *Pleurodeles*; Gallien, Aimar & Guillet, 1973). The earliest nuclear gene expression in a nuclear-transplant hybrid has been described for certain proteins that were seen at the late blastula and early gastrula stages in a *Pleurodeles/Ambystoma* combination (Aimar, Desvaux & Chalumeau-le-Foulgoc, 1976). The observation that nuclear-transplant hybrids between distantly related species are arrested at the late blastula stage (Fig. 6) reinforces the conclusion that new gene activity not only takes place but is already necessary at this very early stage.

The results of nuclear transfers between species that are not closely related are hard to interpret on account of the chromosomal abnormalities that commonly arise. Soon after the technique of nuclear transplantation was established, some surprising results were described by Moore (1958, 1960). An enucleated egg of *Rana sylvatica* was fertilized with *R. pipiens* sperm. When nuclei from the resulting blastula were back-transferred to enucleated eggs of their own *R. pipiens* type, all of the resulting embryos arrested by the early gastrula stage. This result was interpreted, at the time, as incorporation of genetic material during replication in foreign cytoplasm (Moore, 1962). However, Hennen (1963) repeated the *Rana* experiments, and found that back-transfers were arrested at all developmental stages from a late blastula to abnormal larvae, and that the developmental abnormalities of the back-transfer embryos were correlated with chromosomal abnormalities. Evidently, nuclear replication in the cytoplasm of a foreign species (but not subspecies) causes chromosome, and hence developmental, abnormalities. Why this should be so is obscure, though it is known that abnormal chromosomes can be easily induced by injecting adult liver nuclear proteins into normal fertilized eggs of *R. pipiens* (Markert & Ursprung, 1963; Ursprung & Markert, 1963).

Nuclear transfers between closely related species may escape chromosomal damage and are potentially informative. For example, Hennen (1965, 1972, 1974) found that nuclei of *Rana palustris* in cytoplasm of *R. pipiens* develop as abnormal neurulae, and yet back-transfers of these nuclei to their own *R. palustris* cytoplasm develop normally. The developmental arrest of the *palustris–pipiens* combination is not therefore due to chromosome defects; it could result from either the failure of the cytoplasm of one species to activate genes of the other or from an incompatibility of gene products of one species with the cytoplasm of the other. Either situation would be of value if it turns out that some genes or gene products function correctly and others not at all, since this could provide a means of investigating the activation or activity of *individual* genes operative in early development. It has indeed been found that some genes are more inhibited than others in a lethal nucleocytoplasmic combination (Woodland & Gurdon, 1969). This approach could be seen as a partial substitute for mutants that are hard to collect in amphibia; its main benefit will be felt when the activation of many different genes can be accurately probed as is now beginning to be done (Sargent & Dawid, 1983; Mohun *et al.* 1984).

TRANSFER OF NUCLEI TO GROWING OOCYTES AND TO OOCYTES IN MEIOTIC DIVISION

Somatic cell nuclei can be injected into oocytes (the growing egg cells present in an amphibian ovary), or into oocytes undergoing meiotic division, i.e. those that have been released from the ovary through a hormone effect and are passing along the oviduct. Nuclei injected into these kinds of oocytes soon conform in morphology to that of the host cell nuclei or chromosomes (Gurdon, 1968), as they also do when injected into eggs. Whether deposited in the cytoplasm of an oocyte or in its nucleus (germinal vesicle), somatic nuclei gradually enlarge; they usually develop prominent nucleoli if of amphibian, but not of mammalian, origin (Fig. 7A). In contrast, somatic nuclei injected into oocytes in meiotic division are soon resolved into condensed chromosomes on multiple spindles (Fig. 7B). In contrast again, the same kind of nuclei injected into eggs undergo a massive and rapid swelling, as do sperm nuclei, but nucleoli do not appear until later (Fig. 7C).

The most important consequence and advantage of injecting somatic nuclei into oocytes is that they do not divide, nor do their genes increase in number. A single nucleus transplanted into an egg will have increased to 10^4 nuclei in 7 h, whereas 500 somatic nuclei injected into an oocyte will still be 500 nuclei after several days. Another major difference between eggs and oocytes is that an egg, once activated by injection, will always proceed through embryonic development as far as it can. In contrast, an ovarian oocyte shows no visible response to numerous injected nuclei, and can be maintained in culture, in a metabolically active but unchanged state, for as long as 3 weeks. The main value of injecting somatic nuclei into oocytes is to study changes in gene expression unaccompanied by cell division or DNA replication (see next section).

CHANGES IN GENE EXPRESSION INDUCED BY NUCLEAR TRANSFER

The fact that transplanted nuclei of terminally differentiated cells can lead to the formation of feeding-stage tadpoles demonstrates the important point that genes rendered inactive in the course of cell differentiation can be re-expressed after nuclear transfer. This is not an obvious result, since cell differentiation is remarkably stable. There is no known way of converting a keratinized skin cell into a blood cell, or muscle cell into a lens cell. Yet the transplanted nuclei of skin and muscle cells generate cells of totally different kinds, including blood, lens, etc. The nature of these induced changes is of considerable interest, since they may throw light on the mechanisms regulating genes in specialized cells.

Nuclear transfers to eggs

How soon after transplantation do changes in nuclear activity take place? The first change is DNA synthesis; this is initiated in nuclei from all cell types including adult erythrocytes within 1 h of injection into eggs (Graham, Arms & Gurdon, 1966; Leonard, Hoffner & Di Berardino, 1982). This is not a traumatic response to nuclear isolation or injection since the ability to induce DNA synthesis is absent from oocytes and is acquired during the maturation process (Gurdon, 1967a).

Changes in transcription are also evident very soon after nuclear transfer. It has been known since the work of Bachvarova & Davidson (1966) that no nuclear RNA

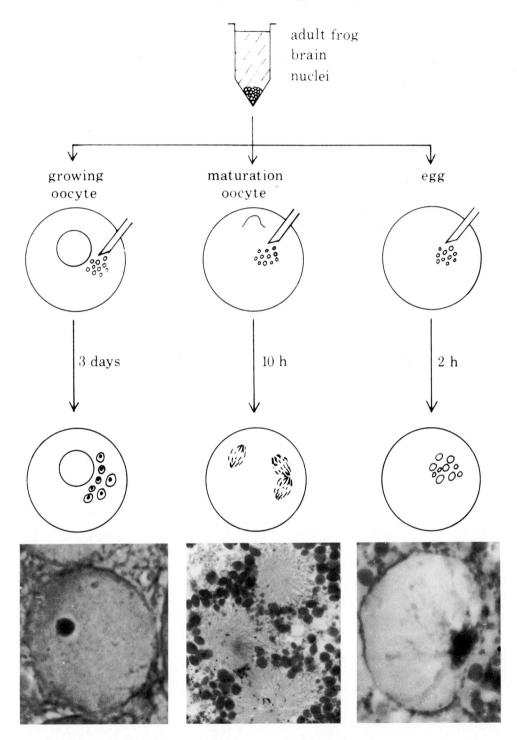

Fig. 7. Changes in adult brain nuclei injected into oocytes or eggs. About 300 adult *Xenopus* brain nuclei were injected into each oocyte or egg, which was incubated for the time stated. The same kind of injected nuclei undergo substantial changes in morphology and activity to conform to that characteristic of the host cell to whose cytoplasm they are exposed. (From Graham *et al.* (1966), Gurdon (1968), and Gurdon (1977).)

synthesis is detectable in *Xenopus* embryos for the first few hours after fertilization. It starts suddenly at about the 12th division as the cell cycle lengthens at the so-called mid-blastula transition (Newport & Kirschner, 1982). When a neurula endoderm nucleus, very active in RNA synthesis, is transplanted to an egg, no [^{3}H]uridine incorporation into RNA is detected by autoradiography 1 h later (Gurdon, 1967*b*; Gurdon & Woodland, 1969), though the same procedure shows massive incorporation of [^{3}H]thymidine into DNA over the same period. Thus a major switch from transcription to replication takes place almost immediately after nuclear transfer.

When transcription recommences at the mid-blastula transition, do transplanted nuclei adopt an embryonic pattern of RNA synthesis or do they resume the transcriptional activity of their original tissue? As far as current analysis permits, it is clear that the former is the case. Using sucrose gradients and column chromatography, it was clear that transplanted nuclei follow the same sequence of nucleic acid activation events as normal embryos reared from fertilized eggs; these include a synthesis of high molecular weight (non-ribosomal, but at that time undefined) RNA in mid-blastulae (stage 8), followed by 4 S (believed to be transfer) RNA synthesis in late blastulae, followed in turn by 18 S and 28 S RNA synthesis during gastrula and neurula stages (Gurdon & Brown, 1965; Gurdon & Woodland, 1969). Current methods of analysis are more sensitive, and synthesis of these classes of RNA can now be detected at earlier stages of development than by older methods (review by Woodland & Old, 1984). Nevertheless, the rates of synthesis of these classes of RNA relative to each other and to DNA clearly differ in blastulae and early gastrulae compared to later stages; in all experiments nuclear transplant embryos change their pattern of synthesis to coincide exactly with that of fertilized controls at the same stage.

More recently it has been possible to confirm these results with more precision and in respect of single kinds of regulated genes. Oocyte-type 5 S genes are not transcribed in somatic cells except very briefly at the late blastula stage (Wakefield & Gurdon, 1983; Wormington & Brown, 1983). Embryos prepared from transplanted nuclei of neurulae, in which 5 S^{ooc} genes are inactive, transcribe these genes briefly as they pass through the late blastula stage (Wakefield & Gurdon, 1983). Of genes that show cell-type specific expression, one of the earliest to be expressed in *Xenopus*, and one for which a cloned probe is available, is a muscle-specific actin gene first expressed at the late gastrula stage and only in prospective myotome cells (Mohun *et al.* 1984). Nuclear-transplant embryos prepared from muscle cell nuclei show inactivation of muscle actin gene transcription as soon as measurements can be made (mid-blastula), and reactivation of it at the normal stage (late gastrula) (Gurdon *et al.* 1984) (Fig. 8). In conclusion, it is evident that nuclei transplanted to eggs undergo rapid changes in the expression of all genes whose transcription has been measured.

Nuclear transfers to oocytes

We can ask whether the reprogramming of gene expression seen in somatic nuclei transplanted to eggs depends upon DNA replication; perhaps genes in the originally transferred nucleus remain repressed, and only new genes formed by DNA synthesis are expressed. This can be tested by transplanting multiple nuclei into oocytes in which no nuclear division takes place. As mentioned above, somatic nuclei injected

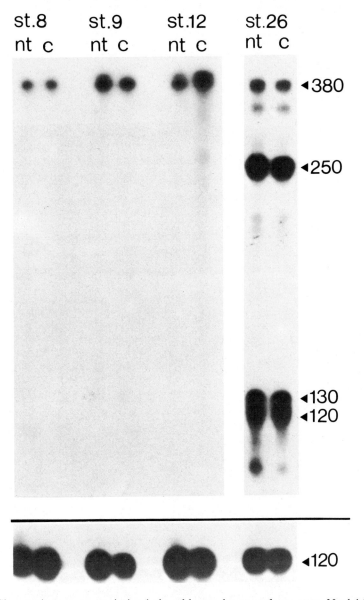

Fig. 8. Changes in gene transcription induced by nuclear transfer to eggs. Nuclei from differentiated muscle cells of a *Xenopus* muscular response embryo were transplanted to enucleated eggs. When these had reached the mid-blastula (stage 8), late blastula (stage 9), mid-gastrula (stage 12), or muscular response (stage 26) stages, representative samples (nt) and controls (c) were frozen and RNA extracted. Part of each embryo was analysed by S_1 nuclease protection for muscle actin gene transcripts (250, 130, 120); another part of each embryo was analysed independently with a probe for 5 S gene transcripts (120), as a measure of the amount of maternal 5 S RNA and hence of total material in each sample. (From Gurdon *et al.* (1984).)

GENE ACTIVATION IN OOCYTES

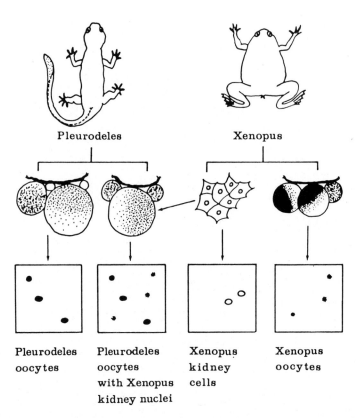

Fig. 9. Changes in gene expression induced by injecting nuclei into oocytes. The nuclei of cultured *Xenopus* kidney cells were injected into oocytes of *Pleurodeles*, and the labelled proteins of the injected oocytes analysed by two-dimensional gel electrophoresis. The diagrams of the two-dimensional gel results show only the most abundant two or three newly synthesized proteins. (Based on De Robertis & Gurdon (1977).)

into oocytes enlarge and are very active in RNA synthesis, as seen autoradiographically, for up to a few weeks. Changes in gene expression induced by oocytes were first seen with HeLa nuclei; of 25 proteins synthesized by HeLa cells but not by *Xenopus* oocytes, 22 were extinguished and three were expressed in oocytes containing HeLa nuclei (Gurdon, De Robertis & Partington, 1976*a*; De Robertis, Partington, Longthorne & Gurdon, 1977). Direct evidence that an oocyte causes injected nuclei to switch to an oocyte type of gene expression came from experiments in which *Xenopus* kidney cell nuclei were injected into oocytes of another amphibian, *Pleurodeles*. This was done because several oocyte-specific proteins of *Xenopus* differ, by two-dimensional gel analysis, from the oocyte specific proteins of *Pleurodeles*. It was found that kidney nuclei in oocytes ceased synthesizing kidney-specific proteins, but started to synthesize oocyte-specific proteins (De Robertis & Gurdon, 1977; see Fig. 9). These changes take place in nuclei deposited in the cytoplasm of an oocyte, and relatively slowly (3–5 days) compared to events in eggs and embryos. A similar type of experiment has been carried out with oocyte-type 5 S genes (Korn & Gurdon, 1981) and with another class of repetitive genes called OAX (Wakefield, Ackerman & Gurdon, 1983). In each case, these genes are inactive in somatic cells, but are extensively transcribed when somatic nuclei containing these genes are injected into oocytes. Using lactate dehydrogenase (LDH) and alcohol dehydrogenase (ADH) isozyme assays, Etkin (1976) found that liver nuclei injected into oocytes adopted an oocyte pattern of expression.

To date all results mentioned emphasize the rapid effect of egg or oocyte cytoplasm on nuclear gene activity. There are, however, two apparent exceptions. 5 S^{ooc} genes are activated by the oocytes of most females, as mentioned above, but not by oocytes of certain 'non-activating' females (Korn & Gurdon, 1981). This seems to be due to individual variation in the amount of activating substance in oocytes (Korn, personal communication). The injection of 500 nuclei, with 40 000 5 S^{ooc} genes each, seems to exceed the activating capacity of some oocytes, since each of these genes is individually repressed in somatic cells (Gurdon, Dingwall, Laskey & Korn, 1982), though all oocytes have sufficient activating substance to de-repress their own endogenous 5 S genes during oogenesis. The activation of 5 S genes by oocytes is not therefore a real exception to the general rule.

The other apparent exception to the rule of cytoplasmic dominance comes from experiments on the maternal effect o mutant of the axolotl, in which fertilized eggs laid by a homozygous mutant (o/o female) fail to activate RNA synthesis as usual at the mid-blastula stage and die as early gastrulae (Briggs, 1972). Brothers (1976) found that enucleated mutant eggs (of a o/o female) are arrested in development if injected with a mid-blastula (pre-activation) nucleus, but develop normally with a post-activation (late blastula) nucleus. Once a nucleus has undergone activation, this state is inherited in o/o eggs, as deduced from the following experiment (Brothers, 1976). A post-activation +/+ nucleus was transplanted to o/o eggs, which were grown to a pre-activation stage, when serial nuclear transfers were made to other o/o eggs. These embryos were able to develop normally, indicating that the activated state of the original +/+ nucleus can be propagated through several o/o embryos in which activation does not take place. Unfortunately, confirmation of these remarkable results seems to be precluded by the loss of the o mutant stock (Malacinski, personal communication). If the interpretation of these results is correct, this would be a unique situation in which transplanted nuclei are not rapidly reprogrammed by egg cytoplasm.

In conclusion, gene expression by transplanted nuclei appears to be fully under the control of the surrounding cytoplasm, an influence exerted within a few hours or less in eggs. The huge volume excess of cytoplasm over nucleus in eggs may account for the rapidity and strength of cytoplasmic control, which is also evident, though less clearly, in hybrid somatic cells. The cytoplasmic effect seems not to require DNA synthesis or cell division, as is also the case with hybrid somatic cells (Blau, Chiu & Webster, 1983).

The clear objective of this type of work is to understand at the molecular level how components of egg and oocyte cytoplasm regulate nuclear or gene activity. It seems essential to simplify the assay for cytoplasmic effects, ideally to the point of analysing the transcription of a single gene or type of gene. However, even the most sensitive assays cannot detect less than 10^5 molecules of a gene transcript, and it is therefore highly desirable to be able to work with cloned genes. While it is undesirable to inject more than a few hundred nuclei, it is easy to inject 10^8 copies of a cloned gene into an egg or oocyte, and extensive work of this kind has been done over the last 10 years (review by Gurdon & Melton, 1981). If injected genes come under correct regulation, it is a matter of technology to define 'cis-acting' sequences required for their regulation, and so work towards identifying cytoplasmic components that interact with these sequences. If genes are not correctly transcribed after injection, this opens up the possibility of rescue or complementation analysis, by co-injecting extracts of cells in which the genes work correctly (Weisbrod, Wickens, Whytock & Gurdon, 1982; Korn, Gurdon & Price, 1982; Galli, Hofstetter, Stunnenberg & Birnstiel, 1983). Oocytes are particularly favourable cells for this type of analysis, since fairly large amounts of crude cell extract can be injected into the cytoplasm, from where appropriate molecules migrate into the nucleus (references just cited above). Eventually it will be necessary to develop cell-free systems in which genes or nuclei respond meaningfully enough to cytoplasmic preparations to permit these to be fractionated and to identify active components.

STRUCTURAL CHANGES AND PROTEIN MIGRATION IN NUCLEI UNDERGOING CHANGES IN GENE EXPRESSION

The magnitude and rapidity of changes in gene activity undergone by transplanted nuclei encourage special interest in the molecular mechanisms involved. Nothing detailed can be said in this respect, except that some events that follow nuclear transfer suggest processes likely to be involved. One event is a dramatic swelling that occurs within an hour of nuclear transfer to eggs, and within a few days of transfer to oocytes. The enlargement can reach 50-fold in eggs and in oocytes (Subtelny & Bradt, 1963; Graham *et al.* 1966), as seen in Fig. 7, and the use of nuclei with prelabelled DNA shows that the chromatin of the injected nuclei is dispersed throughout the enlarged nuclei (Gurdon, 1976). In this respect nuclei transplanted to eggs simulate the natural behaviour of a sperm nucleus after fertilization.

The other apparently significant event associated with nuclear transfer is an exchange of proteins between nucleus and cytoplasm. By prelabelling the proteins of donor nuclei or recipient cytoplasm, a loss of acidic proteins is observed in nuclei injected into eggs (Gurdon, 1970; Gurdon & Woodland, 1969; Leonard *et al.* 1982) or into oocytes (Gurdon, Partington & De Robertis, 1976b), and both acidic and basic proteins migrate from the cytoplasm into injected nuclei.

The enlargement and chromatin dispersion seen in somatic nuclei injected into oocytes might be regarded as a non-specific effect of manipulation and could involve a gross derangement of chromatin structure. Some of these possibilities have been tested by injecting nuclei containing labelled core histones, as well as by reisolating injected nuclei and looking for changes in structure (Weisbrod *et al.* 1982). Such tests have shown that the reprogramming of somatic nuclei in oocytes is not accompanied by a general displacement of core histones or of the non-histone protein group known as HMG proteins. Furthermore chromatin assembled *in vitro* with an incorrect 145 base-pair nucleosome spacing is not corrected after injection to the normal 200 base-pair spacing (which is in fact formed by injecting purified DNA). These results argue that reprogramming in oocytes does not involve a general destruction or gross rearrangement of chromatin structure, but rather a more specific and perhaps physiological change. As more is learnt about the structure of chromatin and as methods are developed for correctly assembling chromatin *in vitro* with known labelled components, experiments along the lines of those just described above should provide a fruitful route towards an analysis of molecular changes associated with nuclear transfer.

The swelling and chromatin dispersion described above take place in eggs and in oocytes whether DNA or RNA synthesis is induced. Presumably, oocyte and egg cytoplasm contains chromatin decondensing factors that remove H1 histone and other components, so that genes are responsive to specific cytoplasmic signals. Some of the cytoplasmic proteins that enter transplanted nuclei may help to direct subsequent nuclear activity. It is interesting that similar events to those just described also take place in hybrid cells when changes in DNA synthesis, RNA synthesis, or gene expression are induced (Ringertz & Savage, 1976).

NUCLEAR TRANSFER IN GROUPS OTHER THAN AMPHIBIA

Nuclei have been successfully transplanted in many species, including *Amoeba*, ciliates, *Acetabularia*, *Neurospora* (for references, see Gurdon, 1964), and perhaps in fish and ascidians (Tung *et al.* 1973, 1977). In some of these cases, nuclear markers have not been used, and in none have nuclei been taken from differentiated cells. These results do not therefore extend conclusions reached with amphibia. More extensive experiments have been carried out with insects and mammals.

Two nuclear transfer procedures have been used in insects. In one, multiple donor nuclei and associated cytoplasm are sucked out of an embryo and injected into another genetically different (host) embryo at a syncytial (pre-cellular) stage. Parts of the resulting mosaic embryos are then transferred to an adult abdomen for growth, and subsequently to a larval abdomen, for metamorphosis into adult structures. In all such work (e.g. see Zalokar, 1973; Okada, Kleinman & Schneiderman, 1974; Santamaria, 1975) it is found that nuclei from preblastoderm and even early blastoderm stages can participate in all kinds of adult differentiation, including the formation of gametes, irrespective of their normal developmental fate. The transplanted nuclei seem to conform to the type of differentiation expected of the host region in which they are deposited, and are therefore influenced by host cytoplasmic factors as in amphibia. The only work to give a different result is that of Kauffman (1980), who found that groups of 10–20 nuclei, and associated cytoplasm, give their own type of (anterior) differentiation when transferred to other (posterior) regions of a host. A possible explanation for this discordant result is that nuclei were transferred to much later (late pre-blastoderm) hosts, and may have been cellularized with their own cytoplasm soon after transfer, thus escaping the cytoplasmic control factors of the host. None of these experiments provides a rigorous test of nuclear potentiality for development, since host cells are always present in an embryo, and could compensate for deficiencies in the transplanted nuclei.

The other design of nuclear transfer experiment in insects is close to that used for amphibia, and involves the injection of one or a few nuclei into an unfertilized egg. Though not enucleated, it is assumed that the egg pronucleus does not fuse with the injected nuclei. In work of this kind (Geyer-Duszynska, 1967; Illmensee, 1972, 1973, 1976; Schubiger & Schneiderman, 1971) larvae have been obtained from five different regions of an early gastrula, no differences in survival or types of defects being observed between nuclei from the various regions. These experiments, assuming no egg-nucleus participation, clearly establish pluripotentiality of early gastrula nuclei. Totipotency has not been demonstrated since none of the nuclear-transplant larvae became adults.

Success with nuclear transplantation in mammals was first described by Illmensee & Hoppe (1981), and Hoppe & Illmensee (1982), who reported that an inner cell mass nucleus can support early development of a one-cell mouse egg, subsequently enucleated. Recently, McGrath & Solter (1984*b*) have carried out a detailed investigation of nuclear transfers in mice, and found that transplanted nuclei from one-cell and two-cell stages can support blastocyst formation by enucleated eggs, but nuclei from four-cell and later stages cannot. They suggest that the results of Illmensee & Hoppe may depend on persistent and functional fragments of the host egg pronuclei. Since it is known that each of the first four cells of a mouse egg can form an embryo (Kelly, 1977), nuclei must be totipotent at this stage and yet unable to cooperate harmoniously with the cytoplasm of a one-cell embryo. The special difficulty that seems to afflict nuclear transplantation in mammals may well be connected with the surprising requirement for both maternal and paternal genomes for normal mouse development, and with the very early transcriptional activity of the genome (see McGrath & Solter, 1984*a*). These special properties apply to mouse and probably other mammalian development, but not to the great majority of eggs of other species.

It will be interesting to see whether future nuclear transfer experiments with invertebrate and other species give results similar to those with amphibia, and whether they are affected by chromosomal damage. If results resemble those in mice, where even an eight-cell nucleus cannot replace the zygote nucleus, this could open a way of identifying gene products required for early development. Some mouse genes start to be actively transcribed at the two-cell stage; the injection of two-cell RNA, together with an eight-cell nucleus into a one-cell egg might be informative.

The author is grateful to S. Brennan, S. Cascio, R. A. Laskey, T. J. Mohun and J. O. Thomas for comments on the manuscript.

REFERENCES

AIMAR, C. (1972). Analyse par la greffe nucleaire des proprietes morphogenetiques des noyaux embryonnaires chez *Pleurodeles waltlii* (amphibien urodele); application a l'etude de la gemellarite experimentale. *Annls Embryol. Morphogen.* **5**, 5–42.

AIMAR, C., DESVAUX, F. X. & CHALUMEAU-LE-FOULGOC, M. TH. (1976). Protein synthesis in lethal nucleocytoplasmic hybrids between the species *Pleurodeles waltlii* Michahelles and *Ambystoma mexicanum* Shaw (urodele amphibians) obtained by nuclear grafting. *J. exp. Zool.* **197**, 265–274.

BACHVAROVA, R. & DAVIDSON, E. H. (1966). Nuclear activation at the onset of amphibian gastrulation. *J. exp. Zool.* **163**, 285–296.

BLAU, H. M., CHIU, C.-P. & WEBSTER, C. (1983). Cytoplasmic activation of human nuclear genes in stable heterokaryons. *Cell* **32**, 1171–1180.

BRIGGS, R. (1972). Further studies on the o gene in the Mexican Axolotl. *J. exp. Zool.* **181**, 271–280.

BRIGGS, R. & KING, T. J. (1952). Transplantation of living nuclei from blastula cells into enucleated frogs' eggs. *Proc. natn. Acad. Sci. U.S.A.* **38**, 455–463.

BRIGGS, R. & KING, T. J. (1957). Changes in the nuclei of differentiating endoderm cells as revealed by nuclear transplantation. *J. Morph.* **100**, 269–312.

BRIGGS, R. & KING, T. J. (1960). Nuclear transplantation studies on the early gastrula (*Rana pipiens*). *Devl Biol.* **2**, 252–270.

BRIGGS, R., KING, T. J. & DI BERARDINO, M. A. (1960). Development of nuclear-transplant embryos of known chromosome complement following parabiosis with normal embryos. *Symp. Germ Cell Dev.* (Inst. Intern. d'Embryologie), pp. 441–477. Pavia: Fondaz A. Baselli.

BRIGGS, R., SIGNORET, J. & HUMPHREY, R. R. (1964). Transplantation of nuclei of various cell-types from neurulae of *Ambystoma mexicanum*. *Devl Biol.* **10**, 233–246.

BROTHERS, A. J. (1976). Stable nuclear activation dependent on a protein synthesized during oogenesis. *Nature, Lond.* **260**, 112–115.

BROWN, D. D. (1984). The role of stable complexes that repress and activate eucaryotic genes. *Cell* **37**, 359–365.

BRUN, R. (1973). Mammalian cells in *Xenopus* eggs. *Nature, Lond.* **243**, 26–27.

BRUN, R. (1978). Developmental capacities of *Xenopus* eggs provided with erythrocyte or erythroblast nuclei from adults. *Devl Biol.* **65**, 271–284.

BRUN, R. & KOBEL, H. R. (1972). Des grenouilles metamorphosees obtenues par transplantation nucleaire a partir du prosencephale et de l'epiderme larvaire de *Xenopus laevis*. *Revue suisse Zool.* **79**, 961–965.

COMANDON, J. & DE FONBRUNE, P. (1939). Greffe nucleaire totale, simple ou multiple, chez une Amibe. *C.r. Séanc. Soc. Biol.* **130**, 744–748.

DE ROBERTIS, E. M. & GURDON, J. B. (1977). Gene activation in somatic nuclei after injection into amphibian oocytes. *Proc. natn. Acad. Sci. U.S.A.* **74**, 2470–2474.

DE ROBERTIS, E. M., PARTINGTON, G. A., LONGTHORNE, R. F. & GURDON, J. B. (1977). Somatic nuclei in amphibian oocytes: evidence for selective gene expression. *J. Embryol. exp. Morph.* **40**, 199–214.

DI BERARDINO, M. A. & HOFFNER, N. (1970). Origin of chromosomal abnormalities in nuclear transplants – a reevaluation of nuclear differentiation and nuclear equivalence in amphibians. *Devl Biol.* **23**, 185–209.

DI BERARDINO, M. A. & HOFFNER, N. (1971). Development and chromosomal constitution of nuclear-transplants derived from male germ cells. *J. exp. Zool.* **176**, 61–72.

DI BERARDINO, M. A. & HOFFNER, N. (1983). Gene reactivation in erythrocytes: nuclear transplantation in oocytes and eggs of *Rana*. *Science* **219**, 862–864.

DI BERARDINO, M. A. & KING, T. J. (1965). Transplantation of nuclei from the frog renal adenocarcinoma. II. Chromosomal and histologic analysis of tumour nuclear-transplant embryos. *Devl Biol.* **11**, 217–242.

DI BERARDINO, M. A. & KING, T. J. (1967). Development and cellular differentiation of neural nuclear-transplants of known karyotype. *Devl Biol.* **15**, 102–128.

DI BERARDINO, M. A., MIZELL, M., HOFFNER, N. & FRIESENDORF, D. G. (1983). Frog larvae cloned from nuclei of pronephric adenocarcinoma. *Differentiation* **23**, 213–217.

ELLINGER, M. S. (1978). The cell cycle and transplantation of blastula nuclei in *Bombina orientalis*. *Devl Biol.* **65**, 81–89.

ELSDALE, T. R., GURDON, J. B. & FISCHBERG, M. (1960). A description of the technique for nuclear transplantation in *Xenopus laevis*. *J. Embryol. exp. Morph.* **8**, 437–444.

ETKIN, L. D. (1976). Regulation of lactate dehydrogenase (LDH) and alcohol dehydrogenase (ADH) synthesis in liver nuclei, following their transfer into oocytes. *Devl Biol.* **52**, 201–209.

FISCHBERG, M., GURDON, J. B. & ELSDALE, T. R. (1958). Nuclear transplantation in *Xenopus laevis*. *Nature, Lond.* **181**, 424.

GALLI, G., HOFSTETTER, H., STUNNENBERG, H. G. & BIRNSTIEL, M. L. (1983). Biochemical complementation with RNA in the *Xenopus* oocyte: a small RNA is required for the generation of 3′ histone mRNA termini. *Cell* **34**, 823–828.

GALLIEN, C. L. (1970). Recherches sur la greffe nucleaire interspecifique dans le genre *Pleurodeles*. *Annls Embryol. Morph.* **3**, 145–192.

GALLIEN, C.-L. (1979). Expression of nuclear and cytoplasmic factors in ontogenesis of amphibian nucleocytoplasmic hybrids. *Int. Rev. Cytol.* (Suppl.) **9**, 189–219.

GALLIEN, L. & AIMAR, C. (1966). Isojumeaux multiples obtenus chez le Triton *Pleurodeles waltlii* Michah. par greffe nucleaire. *C.r. hebd. Séanc. Acad. Sci., Paris* **262**, 567–569.

GALLIEN, C.-L., AIMAR, CH. & GUILLET, F. (1973). Nucleocytoplasmic interactions during ontogenesis in individuals obtained by intra- and interspecific nuclear transplantation in the genus *Pleurodeles* (urodele amphibian). *Devl Biol.* **33**, 154–170.

GEYER-DUSZYNSKA, I. (1967). Experiments on nuclear transplantation in *Drosophila melanogaster*. Preliminary report. *Revue suisse Zool.* **74**, 614–616.

GRAHAM, C. F., ARMS, K. & GURDON, J. B. (1966). The induction of DNA synthesis by frog egg cytoplasm. *Devl Biol.* **14**, 349–381.

GURDON, J. B. (1959). Tetraploid frogs. *J. exp. Zool.* **141**, 519–544.

GURDON, J. B. (1960). The developmental capacity of nuclei taken from differentiating endoderm cells of *Xenopus laevis*. *J. Embryol. exp. Morph.* **8**, 505–526.

GURDON, J. B. (1961). The transplantation of nuclei between two subspecies of *Xenopus laevis*. *Heredity* **16**, 305–315.

GURDON, J. B. (1962*a*). Adult frogs derived from the nuclei of single somatic cells. *Devl Biol.* **4**, 256–273.

GURDON, J. B. (1962*b*). The transplantation of nuclei between two species of *Xenopus*. *Devl Biol.* **5**, 68–83.

GURDON, J. B. (1962*c*). The developmental capacity of nuclei taken from intestinal epithelium cells of feeding tadpoles. *J. Embryol. exp. Morph.* **10**, 622–640.

GURDON, J. B. (1962*d*). Multiple genetically-identical frogs. *J. Hered.* **53**, 4–9.

GURDON, J. B. (1963). Nuclear transplantation in Amphibia and the importance of stable nuclear changes in cellular differentiation. *Q. Rev. Biol.* **38**, 54–78.

GURDON, J. B. (1964). The transplantation of living cell nuclei. *Adv. Morphogen.* **4**, 1–43.

GURDON, J. B. (1967*a*). On the origin and persistence of a cytoplasmic state inducing nuclear DNA synthesis in frogs' eggs. *Proc. natn. Acad. Sci. U.S.A.* **58**, 545–552.

GURDON, J. B. (1967*b*). Nuclear transplantation and cell differentiation. In *Cell Differentiation* (ed. A. V. S. de Reuck & J. Knight), pp. 65–74. *CIBA Fdn Symp.* London: Churchill.

GURDON, J. B. (1968). Changes in somatic cell nuclei inserted into growing and maturing amphibian oocytes. *J. Embryol. exp. Morph.* **20**, 401–414.

GURDON, J. B. (1970). Nuclear transplantation and the control of gene activity in development. *Proc. R. Soc.* B **176**, 303–314.

GURDON, J. B. (1974). *The Control of Gene Expression in Animal Development*. Oxford and Harvard University Presses.

GURDON, J. B. (1976). Injected nuclei in frog oocytes: fate, enlargement, and chromatin dispersal. *J. Embryol. exp. Morph.* **36**, 523–540.

GURDON, J. B. (1977). Methods for nuclear transplantation in Amphibia. In *Methods in Cell Biology* (ed. G. & J. Stein), vol. 16, pp. 125–139. New York: Academic Press.

GURDON, J. B., BRENNAN, S., FAIRMAN, S. & MOHUN, T. J. (1984). Transcription of muscle-specific actin genes in early *Xenopus* development: nuclear transplantation and cell dissociation. *Cell* **38**, 691–700.

GURDON, J. B. & BROWN, D. D. (1965). Cytoplasmic regulation of ribosomal RNA synthesis and nucleolus formation in developing embryos of *Xenopus laevis*. *J. molec. Biol.* **12**, 27–35.

GURDON, J. B., DE ROBERTIS, E. M. & PARTINGTON, G. A. (1976a). Injected nuclei in frog oocytes provide a living cell system for the study of transcriptional control. *Nature, Lond.* **260**, 116–120.

GURDON, J. B., DINGWALL, C., LASKEY, R. A. & KORN, L. J. (1982). Developmental inactivity of 5 S RNA genes persists when chromosomes are cut between genes. *Nature, Lond.* **299**, 652–653.

GURDON, J. B., ELSDALE, T. R. & FISCHBERG, M. (1958). Sexually mature individuals of *Xenopus laevis* from the transplantation of single somatic nuclei. *Nature, Lond.* **182**, 64–65.

GURDON, J. B. & LASKEY, R. A. (1970). The transplantation of nuclei from single cultured cells into enucleate frogs' eggs. *J. Embryol. exp. Morph.* **24**, 227–248.

GURDON, J. B., LASKEY, R. A. & REEVES, O. R. (1975). The developmental capacity of nuclei transplanted from keratinized skin cells of adult frogs. *J. Embryol. exp. Morph.* **34**, 93–112.

GURDON, J. B. & MELTON, D. A. (1981). Gene transfer in amphibian eggs and oocytes. *A. Rev. Genet.* **15**, 189–218.

GURDON, J. B., PARTINGTON, G. A. & DE ROBERTIS, E. M. (1976b). Injected nuclei in frog oocytes: RNA synthesis and protein exchange. *J. Embryol. exp. Morph.* **36**, 541–553.

GURDON, J. B. & UEHLINGER, V. (1966). "Fertile" intestine nuclei. *Nature, Lond.* **210**, 1240–1241.

GURDON, J. B. & WOODLAND, H. R. (1969). The influence of the cytoplasm on the nucleus during cell differentiation, with special reference to RNA synthesis during amphibian cleavage. *Proc. R. Soc.* B **173**, 99–111.

HAMMERLING, J. (1934). Uber Genomwirkungen und Formbildungsfahigkeit bei *Acetabularia*. *Arch. EntwMech. Org.* **132**, 424–462.

HENNEN, S. (1963). Chromosomal and embryological analyses of nuclear changes occurring in embryos derived from transfers of nuclei between *Rana pipiens* and *Rana sylvatica*. *Devl Biol.* **6**, 133–183.

HENNEN, S. (1965). Nucleocytoplasmic hybrids between *Rana pipiens* and *Rana palustris*. I. Analysis of the developmental properties of the nuclei by means of nuclear transplantation. *Devl Biol.* **11**, 243–267.

HENNEN, S. (1970). Influence of spermine and reduced temperature on the ability of transplanted nuclei to promote normal development in eggs of *Rana pipiens*. *Proc. natn. Acad. Sci. U.S.A.* **66**, 630–637.

HENNEN, S. (1972). Morphological and cytological features of gene activity in an amphibian hybrid system. *Devl Biol.* **29**, 241–249.

HENNEN, S. (1974). Back-transfer of late gastrula nuclei of nucleocytoplasmic hybrids. *Devl Biol.* **36**, 447–451.

HOPERSKAYA, O. (1975). The development of animals homozygous for a mutation causing periodic albinism (a^p) in *Xenopus laevis*. *J. Embryol. exp. Morph.* **34**, 253–264.

HOPPE, P. C. & ILLMENSEE, K. (1982). Full-term development after transplantation of partheno-genetic nuclei into fertilized mouse eggs. *Proc. natn. Acad. Sci. U.S.A.* **79**, 1912–1916.

ILLMENSEE, K. (1972). Developmental potencies of nuclei from cleavage, preblastoderm, and syncytial blastoderm transplanted into unfertilized eggs of *Drosophila melanogaster*. *Wilhelm Roux Arch. EntwMech. Org.* **170**, 267–298.

ILLMENSEE, K. (1973). The potentialities of transplanted early gastrula nuclei of *Drosophila melanogaster*. Production of their imago descendants by germ-line transplantation. *Wilhelm Roux Arch. EntwMech. Org.* **171**, 331–343.

ILLMENSEE, K. (1976). Nuclear and cytoplasmic transplantation in *Drosophila*. In *Insect Development* (ed. P. A. Lawrence), pp. 76–96. London: Blackwell Scientific.

ILLMENSEE, K. & HOPPE, P. C. (1981). Nuclear transplantation in *Mus musculus*: developmental potential of nuclei from preimplantation embryos. *Cell* **23**, 9–18.

KAUFFMAN, S. A. (1980). Heterotopic transplantation in the syncytial blastoderm of *Drosophila*: evidence for anterior and posterior nuclear commitments. *Wilhelm Roux Arch. EntwMech. Org.* **189**, 135–145.

KELLY, S. J. (1977). Studies on the developmental potential of 4- and 8-cell stage mouse blastomeres. *J. exp. Zool.* **200**, 365–376.

KING, T. J. (1966). Nuclear transplantation in amphibia. In *Methods in Cell Physiol.* vol. 11, pp. 1–36. New York: Academic Press.

KING, T. J. & BRIGGS, R. (1955). Changes in the nuclei of differentiating gastrula cells, as demonstrated by nuclear transplantation. *Proc. natn. Acad. Sci. U.S.A.* **41**, 321–325.

KING, T. J. & BRIGGS, R. (1956). Serial transplantation of embryonic nuclei. *Cold Spring Harbor Symp. quant. Biol.* **21**, 271–290.

KING, T. J. & DI BERARDINO, M. A. (1965). Transplantation of nuclei from the frog renal adenocarcinoma. I. Development of tumor nuclear-transplant embryos. *Ann. N.Y. Acad. Sci.* **126**, 115–126.

KING, T. J. & MCKINNELL, R. G. (1960). An attempt to determine the developmental potentialities of the cancer cell nucleus by means of transplantation. In *Cell Physiology of Neoplasia* (ed. R. W. Cumley, M. Abbott & J. McCay), *14th Symp. Fundamental Cancer Res., 1960*, pp. 591–617. Austin: University of Texas Press.

KOBEL, H. R., BRUN, R. B. & FISCHBERG, M. (1973). Nuclear transplantation with melanophores, ciliated epidermal cells, and the established cell-line A-8 in *Xenopus laevis*. *J. Embryol. exp. Morph.* **29**, 539–547.

KORN, L. J. & GURDON, J. B. (1981). The reactivation of developmentally inert 5S genes in somatic nuclei injected into *Xenopus* oocytes. *Nature, Lond.* **289**, 461–465.

KORN, L. J., GURDON, J. B. & PRICE, J. (1982). Oocyte extracts reactivate developmentally inert *Xenopus* 5S genes in somatic nuclei. *Nature, Lond.* **300**, 354–355.

LASKEY, R. A. & GURDON, J. B. (1970). Genetic content of adult somatic cells tested by nuclear transplantation from cultured cells. *Nature, Lond.* **228**, 1332–1334.

LEONARD, R. A., HOFFNER, N. J. & DI BERARDINO, M. A. (1982). Induction of DNA synthesis in amphibian erythroid nuclei in *Rana* eggs following conditioning in meiotic oocytes. *Devl Biol.* **92**, 343–355.

MARKERT, C. L. & URSPRUNG, H. (1963). Production of replicable persistent changes in zygote chromosomes of *Rana pipiens* by injected proteins from adult liver nuclei. *Devl Biol.* **7**, 560–577.

MARSHALL, J. A. & DIXON, K. E. (1977). Nuclear transplantation from intestinal epithelial cells of early and late *Xenopus laevis* tadpoles. *J. Embryol. exp. Morph.* **40**, 167–174.

MCAVOY, J. W., DIXON, K. E. & MARSHALL, J. A. (1975). Effects of differences in mitotic activity, stage of cell cycle, and degree of specialization of donor cells on nuclear transplantation in *Xenopus laevis*. *Devl Biol.* **45**, 330–339.

MCGRATH, J. & SOLTER, D. (1984a). Completion of mouse embryogenesis requires both the maternal and paternal genomes. *Cell* **37**, 179–183.

MCGRATH, J. & SOLTER, D. (1984b). Inability of mouse blastomere nuclei transferred to enucleated zygotes to support development *in vitro*. *Science* **226**, 1317–1319.

MCKINNELL, R. G. (1962). Intraspecific nuclear transplantation in frogs. *J. Hered.* **53**, 198–207.

MCKINNELL, R. G., DEGGINS, B. A. & LABAT, D. D. (1969). Transplantation of pluripotential nuclei from triploid frog tumours. *Science* **165**, 394–396.

MCKINNELL, R. G., STEVEN, L. M. JR & LABAT, D. D. (1976). Frog renal tumours are composed of stroma, vascular elements and epithelial cells: what type nucleus programs for tadpoles with the cloning procedure? In *Progress in Differentiation Research* (ed. N. Muller-Berat), pp. 319–330. Amsterdam: North-Holland.

MOHUN, T. J., BRENNAN, S., DATHAN, N., FAIRMAN, S. & GURDON, J. B. (1984). Cell type-specific activation of actin genes in the early amphibian embryo. *Nature, Lond.* **311**, 716–721.

MOORE, J. A. (1958). The transfer of haploid nuclei between *Rana pipiens* and *Rana sylvatica*. *Expl Cell Res.* (Suppl.) **6**, 179–191.

MOORE, J. A. (1960). Serial back-transfers of nuclei in experiments involving two species of frogs. *Devl Biol.* **2**, 535–550.

MOORE, J. A. (1962). Nuclear transplantation and problems of specificity in developing embryos. *J. cell. comp. Physiol.* **60** (Suppl. 1), 19–34.

MUGGLETON-HARRIS, A. L. & PEZZELLA, K. (1972). The ability of the lens cell nucleus to promote complete embryonic development through to metamorphosis and its applications to ophthalmic gerontology. *Expl Geront.* **7**, 427–431.

NEWPORT, J. & KIRSCHNER, M. (1982). A major developmental transition in early *Xenopus* embryos: II. Control of the onset of transcription. *Cell* **30**, 687–696.

OKADA, M., KLEINMAN, I. A. & SCHNEIDERMAN, H. A. (1974). Chimeric *Drosophila* adults produced by transplantation of nuclei into specific regions of fertilized eggs. *Devl Biol.* **39**, 286–294.

PICHERAL, B. (1962). Capacites des noyaux de cellules endodermiques embryonnaires a organizer un germe viable chez l'urodele, *Pleurodeles waltlii*. *C.r. hebd. Séanc. Acad. Sci. Paris* **255**, 2509–2511.

RINGERTZ, N. R. & SAVAGE, R. E. (1976). *Cell Hybrids*. New York, London: Academic Press.

ROSBASH, M. & FORD, P. J. (1974). Polyadenylic acid containing RNA in *Xenopus laevis* oocytes. *J. molec. Biol.* **85**, 87–101.

SAMBUICHI, H. (1957). The roles of the nucleus and the cytoplasm in development. I. An intersubspecific frog developed from a combination of *Rana nigromaculata* subspecies. *J. Sci. Hiroshima Univ. Ser.* B **17**, 33–41.

SANTAMARIA, P. (1975). Transplantation of nuclei between eggs of different species of *Drosophila*. *Wilhelm Roux Arch. EntwMech. Org.* **178**, 89–98.

SARGENT, T. D. & DAWID, I. B. (1983). Differential gene expression in the gastrula of *Xenopus laevis*. *Science* **222**, 135–139.

SCHUBIGER, M. & SCHNEIDERMAN, H. A. (1971). Nuclear transplantation in *Drosophila melanogaster*. *Nature, Lond.* **230**, 185–186.

SIGNORET, J., BRIGGS, R. & HUMPHREY, R. R. (1962). Nuclear transplantation in the Axolotl. *Devl Biol.* **4**, 134–164.

SIGNORET, J. & PICHERAL, B. (1962). Transplantation de noyaux chez *Pleurodeles waltlii* Michah. *C.r. hebd. Séanc. Acad. Sci., Paris* **254**, 1150–1151.

SIMNETT, J. D. (1964). The development of embryos derived from the transplantation of neural ectoderm cell nuclei in *Xenopus laevis*. *Devl Biol.* **10**, 467–486.

SMITH, L. D. (1965). Transplantation of the nuclei of primordial germ-cells into enucleated eggs of *Rana pipiens*. *Proc. natn. Acad. Sci. U.S.A.* **54**, 101–107.

SPEMANN, H. (1938). *Embryonic Development and Induction*. New Haven, Conn.: Yale University Press.

SUBTELNY, S. (1965). On the nature of the restricted differentiation-promoting ability of transplanted *Rana pipiens* nuclei from differentiating endoderm cells. *J. exp. Zool.* **159**, 59–92.

SUBTELNY, S. & BRADT, C. (1963). Cytological observations on the early developmental stages of activated *Rana pipiens* eggs receiving a transplanted blastula nucleus. *J. Morph.* **112**, 45–59.

TUNG, T. C., TUNG, Y. F. Y., LUH, T. Y., TUNG, S. M. & TU, M. (1973). Transplantation of nuclei between two subfamilies of teleosts (goldfish-domesticated *Carassius auratus*, and Chinese bitterling *Rhodeus sinensis*). *Acta zool. sin.* **19**, 201–212.

TUNG, T. C., WU, S. C., YEH, Y. F., LI, K. S. & HSU, M. C. (1977). Cell differentiation in ascidian studied by nuclear transplantation. *Scient. Sin.* **20**, 222–233.

URSPRUNG, H. & MARKERT, C. L. (1963). Chromosome complements of *Rana pipiens* embryos developing from eggs injected with protein from adult liver cells. *Devl Biol.* **8**, 309–321.

VON BEROLDINGEN, C. H. (1981). The developmental potential of synchronized amphibian cell nuclei. *Devl Biol.* **81**, 115–126.

WABL, M. R., BRUN, R. B. & DU PASQUIER, L. (1975). Lymphocytes of *Xenopus laevis* have the gene set for promoting tadpole development. *Science* **190**, 1310–1312.

WAKEFIELD, L., ACKERMAN, E. & GURDON, J. B. (1983). The activation of RNA synthesis by somatic nuclei injected into Amphibian oocytes. *Devl Biol.* **95**, 468–475.

WAKEFIELD, L. & GURDON, J. B. (1983). Cytoplasmic regulation of 5 S RNA genes in nuclear-transplant embryos. *EMBO J.* **2**, 1613–1619.

WEISBROD, S., WICKENS, M. P., WHYTOCK, S. & GURDON, J. B. (1982). Active chromatin of oocytes injected with somatic cell nuclei or cloned DNA. *Devl Biol.* **94**, 216–229.

WEISMANN, A. (1892). *Das Keimplasma. Eine Theorie der Vererbung*. Jena: G. Fischer. (Translation in English, 1893. London: Walter Scott Publ.)

WOODLAND, H. R. & GURDON, J. B. (1969). RNA synthesis in an amphibian nuclear-transplant hybrid. *Devl Biol.* **20**, 89–104.

WOODLAND, H. R. & OLD, R. W. (1984). In *Developmental Control in Animals and Plants* (ed. C. F. Graham & P. F. Wareing), pp. 476–479. Oxford: Blackwell Scientific.

WORMINGTON, W. M. & BROWN, D. D. (1983). Onset of 5 S RNA gene regulation during *Xenopus* embryogenesis. *Devl Biol.* **99**, 248–257.

ZALOKAR, M. (1973). Transplantation of nuclei into the polar plasm of *Drosophila* eggs. *Devl Biol.* **32**, 189–193.

J. Cell Sci. Suppl. 4, 319–336 (1986)
Printed in Great Britain © The Company of Biologists Limited 1986

THE REGULATION OF THE DIFFERENTIAL EXPRESSION OF THE HUMAN GLOBIN GENES DURING DEVELOPMENT

D. J. WEATHERALL

MRC Molecular Haematology Unit, Nuffield Department of Clinical Medicine, University of Oxford, John Radcliffe Hospital, Oxford, UK

INTRODUCTION

Although a great deal is known about the structure and molecular pathology of the human haemoglobin genes it is still not clear how their differential expression during normal development is regulated. As well as being of considerable interest to developmental geneticists, this problem has important practical implications. Variability in the expression of the foetal globin genes plays a major role in modifying the clinical course of some of the common genetic disorders of adult haemoglobin production. If it were possible to prevent the switching off of foetal haemoglobin production after the neonatal period, or to reactivate it even partially, we would have an extremely valuable approach to the management of these conditions, which are globally the commonest single gene disorders.

Here I shall summarize what has been learnt from the experimental systems that are being used to study the regulation of the developmental changes in globin gene expression. It will be possible to touch on only those areas that seem to be of particular promise for future work. Several recent reviews cover human haemoglobin genetics and the developmental biology of haemoglobin in more detail (Wood & Weatherall, 1983; Collins & Weissman, 1984; Orkin & Kazazian, 1984; Weatherall, Higgs, Wood & Clegg, 1984; Weatherall & Wainscoat, 1985); original references to much of the experimental work described here will be found in these articles.

THE ORGANIZATION OF THE HUMAN GLOBIN GENES

The structures of the different haemoglobins that are synthesized during embryonic, foetal and adult life are summarized in Fig. 1. They are all tetramers consisting of two pairs of unlike peptide chains, each associated with a haem molecule. Normal adults have a major haemoglobin, haemoglobin A ($\alpha_2\beta_2$), and a minor component called haemoglobin A_2 ($\alpha_2\delta_2$). The main haemoglobin in foetal life is haemoglobin F, which has α chains combined with γ chains ($\alpha_2\gamma_2$). It is a mixture of two different molecular forms that differ only by one amino acid in their γ chains, glycine or alanine at position 136; the γ chains that make up these two types of foetal haemoglobin are thus referred to as $^G\gamma$ and $^A\gamma$. In embryonic life there is yet another series of haemoglobins in which the α chains are replaced by ς chains and the γ and β chains by ε chains.

As shown in Fig. 1 the globin genes are organized in two families, an α-like gene cluster on chromosome 16 and a β-like cluster on chromosome 11. Within each complex the genes, together with several inactive pseudogenes, are all in the same 5' to 3' orientation and are arranged in the order in which they are expressed at different stages of development. However, comparison with other vertebrate species suggests that it is unlikely that there is any general relationship between gene order and developmental expression.

The β-like genes are distributed over approximately 60 kb (10^3 bases) and are arranged in the order $5'-\varepsilon-{}^G\gamma-{}^A\gamma-\psi\beta-\delta-\beta-3'$. The α-like genes form a smaller cluster on chromosome 16, in the order $5'-\varsigma-\psi\varsigma-\psi\alpha-\alpha2-\alpha1-3'$. The $\psi\beta$, $\psi\varsigma$ and $\psi\alpha$ genes are pseudogenes. The position of the introns is shown in Fig. 1. The 5' flanking regions of each of the genes contain two regions of homology. One, the ATA box, is 20–30 base-pairs (bp) upstream from the RNA initiation site; the other, the CCAAT box, is 70–90 bp upstream from this site. Each α gene is located within a region of homology approximately 4 kb long, interrupted by two small non-homologous regions. The exons and the first introns of the two α globin genes have identical sequences. The two ς genes are also highly homologous. Like the $\alpha1$ and $\alpha2$ genes, the ${}^G\gamma$ and ${}^A\gamma$ genes appear to be virtually identical, reflecting a process of gene matching during evolution. In fact, the ${}^G\gamma$ and ${}^A\gamma$ genes on one chromosome are identical in the region 5' to the centre of the large intron, yet show greater divergence in a 3' direction. At the boundary between the conserved and divergent regions there is a block of simple sequence, which may be a 'hotspot' for the initiation of recombination events that lead to unidirectional gene conversion.

Several classes of repetitive sequences have been identified in the $\varepsilon\gamma\delta\beta$ globin gene cluster. There are single *Alu* repeat sequences upstream from the γ globin genes and

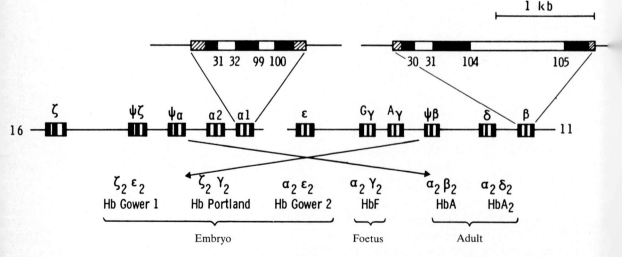

Fig. 1. The genetic control of human haemoglobin.

from the β genes, and inverted pairs of *Alu* sequences upstream from the ε and δ genes and downstream from the β globin gene. The three inverted pairs are orientated tail to tail with about 800 bp of non-repetitive DNA between them. The second major class of repeat sequences belongs to the *Kpn* family. One copy lies downstream from the β globin gene; another between the ε and γ genes. The latter region, over 6 kb in length, has been sequenced and at the end near the γ globin gene has strong homology with the retrovirus long-terminal repeat (see Collins & Weissman, 1984).

Table 1. *The globin gene switches during normal human development*

$$\varsigma \to \alpha1 \text{ and } \alpha2$$
$$\varepsilon \to {}^{G}\gamma \text{ and } {}^{A}\gamma$$
$${}^{G}\gamma \text{ and } {}^{A}\gamma \to \delta \text{ and } \beta$$
$$\text{Foetal } {}^{G}\gamma/{}^{A}\gamma \to \text{adult } {}^{G}\gamma/{}^{A}\gamma$$

GLOBIN GENE EXPRESSION DURING HUMAN DEVELOPMENT (Table 1)

The embryonic haemoglobins are synthesized mainly during the period when erythropoiesis is confined to the yolk sac. Throughout the rest of foetal life the liver and spleen are the main sources of red cell production, although the marrow starts to produce red cells during the second trimester and becomes the major erythropoietic site during later foetal life.

Recently, the patterns of globin chain production at very early stages of embryonic development, during the transition from yolk sac (primitive) to hepatic (definitive) erythropoiesis, have been analysed (Peschle *et al.* 1984, 1985). During the 4th to 5th week ς and ε chains and very small quantities of γ chains are synthesized. During the 6th to 7th week α, ς, ε, ${}^{G}\gamma$ and ${}^{A}\gamma$ chains are produced by the remaining primitive erythroblasts, and α, ε, ${}^{G}\gamma$ and ${}^{A}\gamma$ chains by the definitive line. By the 7th to 8th week ε and ς chain synthesis is no longer detectable and the main globin chains synthesized are α, ${}^{G}\gamma$ and ${}^{A}\gamma$; β chain production is just detectable at this time and gradually increases so that at about 10 weeks it constitutes about 10 % of total non-α chain production. Thus there appears to be a slight asynchrony in the switch from ς to α compared with ε to γ chain production; the $\varsigma \to \alpha$ chain transition is completed slightly earlier.

From the 10th to the 33rd week of gestation the main globin chains produced are α, ${}^{G}\gamma$, ${}^{A}\gamma$ and β. Assessment of the output of the two linked α globin genes by mRNA analysis suggests that they are expressed in the ratio $\alpha2/\alpha1$ of $1{\cdot}5{-}3{\cdot}0/1$ throughout foetal life (Liebhaber & Kan, 1981; Orkin & Goff, 1981); this does not change during development and is the same as that observed in normal adults. The relative rates of ${}^{G}\gamma$ and ${}^{A}\gamma$ chain production are also constant throughout foetal life at a ${}^{G}\gamma/{}^{A}\gamma$ ratio of approximately 3/1 (Nute, Pataryas & Stamatoyannopoulos, 1973). Between the 32nd and 36th week of gestation the relative rate of β chain synthesis increases and that of γ chain production declines, so that at birth β chain synthesis constitutes approximately 50% of non-α chain synthesis. After birth the level of γ chain production declines steadily and that of β chain production increases; at the end of the first year γ chain synthesis reaches the low level characteristic of adult life. During the first few months of life the $^G\gamma/^A\gamma$ ratio changes from 3/1 to 2/3 (Schroeder *et al.* 1972). Delta chain production has been observed as early as 32 weeks gestation; δ chain activation lags behind that of β chains, and the adult β/δ chain synthesis ratio is only reached at about 4–6 months after birth.

Although there has been extensive debate about the intercellular distribution of different haemoglobins during development it is now believed that the transition from embryonic to foetal and foetal to adult haemoglobin production occurs within the same erythrocyte populations. This conclusion is also consistent with recent studies of the patterns of γ and β chain production in red cell colonies grown from foetal and neonatal blood. It is also clear that the type of globin chains produced at different stages of development is not related to the site of erythropoiesis; both ς and ε chains are synthesized in both primitive and definitive cell lines (Peschle *et al.* 1984, 1985) and the switchover from γ to β chain production occurs synchronously throughout the liver, spleen and bone marrow during the later stages of foetal development (Wood & Weatherall, 1973; Wood *et al.* 1979). Furthermore, the transition from γ to β chain synthesis is related closely to gestational age and not to birth; premature infants continue to synthesize relatively high levels of γ chains until about 40 weeks gestation (Bard, 1975).

Thus the various developmental haemoglobin transitions occur within the same cell populations, are synchronized between the changing sites of erythropoiesis during development, and are closely related to the gestational age of the foetus. These changes in haemoglobin constitution are associated with other developmental modifications of the red cell, particularly the switching on of one of the carbonic anhydrase isozymes and several alterations in surface antigens.

FOETAL HAEMOGLOBIN PRODUCTION IN NORMAL ADULTS

Normal adults produce small amounts of haemoglobin F, which range from 0·3 to 0·8% of the total haemoglobin. Analysis of the intercellular distribution suggests that this is confined to a small population of adult red cells, which for this reason are called F cells, although they also include large amounts of haemoglobin A. The relative proportion of F cells is remarkably constant in different individuals and appears to be genetically determined, though how many genes are involved is not clear. The relative number of F cells increases during rapid regeneration of the marrow after periods of transient aplasia. Studies of disorders such as polycythaemia vera or chronic myeloid leukaemia suggest that F cells are not clonally derived but arise from the same stem cell pool as adult haemoglobin-containing red cells; the apparent restriction of γ chain production to a small proportion of adult red cells may be an artefact of the methods used to assess the intercellular distribution of foetal and adult haemoglobin (see Wood & Weatherall, 1983).

THE REGULATION OF GLOBIN GENE EXPRESSION DURING DEVELOPMENT

Because so little is known about the developmental regulation of gene expression, and the lack of good experimental models with which to investigate this problem, our current approaches to the analysis of gene switching are, of necessity, indirect. Areas of study that are providing some information on this question are summarized in Table 2.

Table 2. *Methods used to analyse the regulation of globin genes during development*

(1) Methylation state and DNase I sensitivity of the globin genes
(2) Mutations associated with persistent γ chain synthesis
(3) Haemopoietic-cell transplantation across developmental stages
(4) Gene expression in colony systems *in vitro*
(5) Gene expression in neoplastic cell lines
(6) Transgenic mice
(7) Manipulation of gene switching *in vivo*

Changes in globin gene structure during development

Several aspects of the structure of the globin gene complexes have been studied in an attempt to understand the mechanism of the differential expression of their constituent loci during development. Comparisons of the primary sequences of the individual genes and their flanking regions have shown that, in general, they rapidly lose homology upstream and downstream of the transcribed sequences except in the case of those that have diverged recently. However, interspecies comparisons have not identified any sequences either 5′ or 3′ to the structural genes that might be candidates for regulation of their differential expression during development. I shall return to some very recent studies of globin gene mutations that are relevant to this question in a later section. There is no evidence that there are any major rearrangements of the globin gene clusters at different stages of human development.

The globin genes are hypomethylated in tissues in which they are expressed and are differentially methylated at different stages of development. It appears that at all stages of ontogeny the β-like globin genes show a strong correlation between their methylation state and expression. Similarly, there is a strong tissue and age-dependent relationship between their differential sensitivity to nuclease digestion. DNase I hypersensitive sites have been found 5′ to the $^G\gamma$, $^A\gamma$, δ and β genes in foetal liver haemopoietic tissue but only 5′ to the δ and β genes in adult haemopoietic tissues. These changes are presumably due to alterations in chromatin structure, both around the cluster reflecting its potential expression in erythroid cells, and within a cluster as each gene is activated at different times during development (Collins & Weissman, 1984).

5-Azacytidine, a cytidine analogue that is incorporated into DNA but cannot be methylated, appears to be able to activate γ gene expression in adult animals and in humans (DeSimone, Heller, Hall & Zwiers, 1982; Ley *et al.* 1982). Demethylation of the γ chain genes was observed in erythroid cells after azacytidine treatment of humans and experimental animals, although this was also true of the ε genes in the case of humans, yet the latter were not expressed. These studies also suggest that hypomethylation may be necessary for expression. I shall return to this question later.

Table 3. *Mutations associated with persistent haemoglobin F production*

(1) Sickle cell anaemia and β thalassaemia
(2) Hereditary persistence of foetal haemoglobin (HPFH)
Deletion
Non-deletion
linked to β globin gene cluster
unlinked to β globin gene cluster

Mutations associated with persistent γ chain synthesis in adult life

The mutations that are characterized by persistent foetal haemoglobin production are summarized in Table 3. The most important are the β thalassaemias and β chain haemoglobin disorders such as sickle cell anaemia, and a family of conditions that are characterized by persistent foetal haemoglobin synthesis without any major haematological abnormalities, hereditary persistence of foetal haemoglobin (HPFH). Gene-analysis studies of HPFH have shown that the condition can be divided into deletion and non-deletion forms. More recently it has been found that the latter group can be subdivided into conditions in which the genetic determinants are linked to the β globin gene cluster and those in which they segregate independently from the cluster.

Sickle cell anaemia and β thalassaemia. The factors that are involved in the production of elevated levels of foetal haemoglobin in the blood of individuals with these conditions are extremely complex. Haemoglobin F protects against sickling. In β thalassaemia, cells that produce γ chains are at an advantage since the latter combine with excess α chains; red cell precursor destruction in this disorder results from the deleterious effect of excess α chains that accumulate due to defective β chain synthesis. Thus in both of these disorders red cell precursors or mature red cells that have the capacity for producing γ chains undergo intense selection, either in the marrow or in the peripheral blood. On the other hand, it is equally clear that genetic factors are also involved in haemoglobin F production in these conditions. In some individuals with sickle cell anaemia or β thalassaemia, in whom unusually high levels of haemoglobin F afford protection from the effects of the disease, it is possible to find normal or heterozygous family members with increased levels of haemoglobin F. Thus it appears that a gene (or genes) for heterocellular HPFH (see below) is segregating in these families. This is not always the case, however.

Another approach to this problem has been developed recently. Scattered throughout the β globin gene cluster there are a number of restriction fragment length polymorphisms (RFLPs), which can be used as genetic markers for following mutations of the β globin genes (Antonarakis, Boehm, Giardina & Kazazian, 1982). It has been found that particular arrangements of these RFLPs (haplotypes) may be associated with an unusually high production of haemoglobin F in individuals with sickle cell anaemia or β thalassaemia (Wainscoat *et al.* 1985*a*). This suggests that there may be a genetic determinant within or linked to the β globin gene cluster, which, since these haplotypes are not associated with increased haemoglobin F production in symptomless heterozygotes, results in an unusually high level of γ chain production in states of increased erythropoiesis. The only clue to the nature of this determinant is the recent observation that an alteration in the relative amount of $^G\gamma$ to $^A\gamma$ chain production in individuals with sickle cell anaemia, and possibly an increased capacity for γ chain synthesis, may be associated with a single base change, C→T, at position -158 in the $^G\gamma$ globin gene (Gilman & Huisman, 1984). I shall return to the significance of this finding in a later section.

The $\delta\beta$ thalassaemias and deletion forms of HPFH. These conditions are all characterized by long deletions of the $\gamma\delta\beta$ globin gene cluster. Their rather daunting nomenclature is explained in the legend to Fig. 2. They constitute a spectrum of disorders in which absent β chain production is compensated by persistent γ chain synthesis. If compensation is more or less complete the condition is haematologically normal and is called HPFH; if there is less efficient γ chain synthesis, and hence unbalanced globin chain production, the condition is called $\delta\beta$ thalassaemia. However, in all these disorders there is an absolute increase in γ chain production in adult life that cannot be accounted for by cell selection. This suggests that the deletions that cause them must be responsible for the high output of γ chains.

The different deletions that produce $\delta\beta$ thalassaemia and HPFH are summarized in Fig. 2. A question of major interest is whether a comparison of their site and size can explain the difference in phenotype between HPFH and $\delta\beta$ thalassaemia and hence tell us anything about the position of putative regulatory regions in the $\gamma\delta\beta$ gene cluster. A comparison of particular interest is the $5'$ extent of the deletions that cause either $(\delta\beta)^\circ$ thalassaemia or $(\delta\beta)^\circ$ HPFH in Black populations (Fig. 2). These deletions end within 1 kb of each other in the *Alu* repeat region $5'$ to the δ globin gene. The deletion that causes HPFH ends in the middle of the upstream *Alu* repeat while that which causes $\delta\beta$ thalassaemia ends 1 kb downstream from the latter in the other *Alu* repeat (see Collins & Weissman, 1984). Is this region involved in the regulation of γ and β chain synthesis during development? While this may be the case, the fact is that both these deletions cause considerably elevated levels of γ chain production in adult life; the difference between them is only a matter of degree. Furthermore, a Greek family has recently been described in which homozygotes have the clinical picture of a mild form of β thalassaemia and heterozygotes have either normal or marginally elevated haemoglobin F levels, and yet this condition results from a deletion that removes the entire region occupied by the *Alu* repeat sequences (Wainscoat *et al.* 1985*b*).

Another interpretation of these different phenotypes is that they do not depend directly on the region of DNA that is deleted but rather on the particular sequences that are brought into apposition to the β globin gene complex by the deletion.

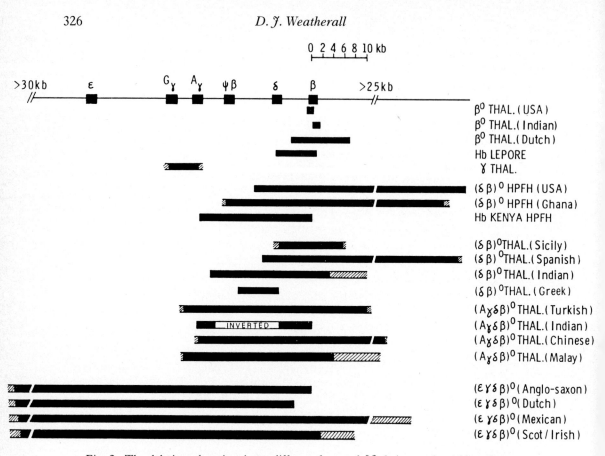

Fig. 2. The deletions that give rise to different forms of $\delta\beta$ thalassaemia and hereditary persistence of foetal haemoglobin (HPFH). $(\delta\beta)°$, $(^A\gamma\delta\beta)°$ etc. indicate that these conditions are characterized by an absence of δ and β, or $^A\gamma$, δ and β chain production. THAL means that persistent γ chain production is insufficient to compensate for lack of β chains and hence that the condition has a thalassaemic phenotype. The country or nationality in which the lesion was first described is added to define the particular mutation. References to original descriptions are given by Collins & Weissman (1984) and Weatherall & Wainscoat (1985).

Perhaps, it has been argued, in some forms of HPFH sequences are brought in from 3' to the β globin gene complex that act as *cis* enhancers, thus allowing expression of the foetal genes in adult life (Collins & Weissman, 1984). However, as shown in Fig. 2, the 3' ends of all these deletions are different; do they all contain rather similar enhancer sequences? This seems unlikely, and perhaps the most attractive hypothesis to explain the phenotypic variability of these deletions is that the $\gamma\delta\beta$ globin gene cluster is organized into two chromatin domains, one surrounding the foetal genes, the other flanking the δ and β genes, both with distinct 5' and 3' borders. Interference with any of these domain boundaries may prevent activation of the adult domain and leave the foetal genes unrepressed. This hypothesis was discussed in detail by Bernards & Flavell (1980). Additional deletion mutations of the $\gamma\delta\beta$ globin gene cluster are being mapped in an attempt to clarify these issues. However, because they all cause such a major disruption of the gene complex, their

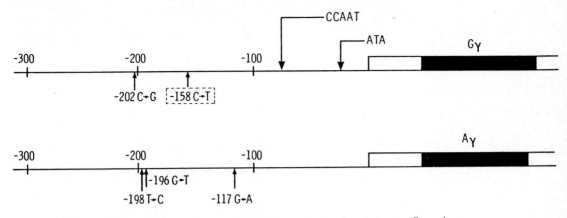

Fig. 3. The non-deletion forms of HPFH due to lesions involving the $^G\gamma$ or $^A\gamma$ genes.

study may be of limited value for providing information about gene control during normal development.

Non-deletion HPFH. Because these conditions are not associated with major disruptions of the β globin gene cluster they are of much greater potential interest for analysing the regulation of gene expression during development. As mentioned earlier, the genetic determinants for some of these conditions map within or near the β gene complex while others segregate independently from the β globin gene markers and hence must be at a considerable distance away on chromosome 11 or even on another chromosome.

Some well-defined forms of non-deletion HPFH in which the genetic determinants are within the β globin gene cluster are summarized in Fig. 3. In the $^G\gamma\beta^+$ variety of HPFH, which has been found exclusively in Black populations, heterozygotes produce approximately 20 % haemoglobin F of the $^G\gamma$ type and there is β chain production in *cis*. Sequence analyses of the $^A\gamma$ gene and of the *Alu* repeat region 5' to the δ gene have shown no abnormality (Jones, Goodbourn, Old & Weatherall, 1985; Dr Oliver Smithies, personal communication). However, a single point mutation (C→G) has been identified 202 base-pairs 5' to the CAP site of the $^G\gamma$ gene (Collins *et al.* 1984). A related disorder, called Greek HPFH, in which heterozygotes produce approximately 15 % foetal haemoglobin in adult life has also been analysed at the molecular level. The sequence of the $^A\gamma$ globin genes showed no abnormalities except for a single change, G→A at position −117, i.e. 117 bases 5' to the CAP site (Collins *et al.* 1985; Gelinas *et al.* 1985). This change has been found in two unrelated heterozygotes. In a similar disorder observed in Italy a single base change, G→T, has been found at position −196 in the $^A\gamma$ gene (Giglioni *et al.* 1984). This has also been observed in a Chinese individual with a similar phenotype (Dr G. Stamatoyannopoulos, personal communication).

In the British form of non-deletion HPFH (Weatherall *et al.* 1975*a*) homozygotes have about 20 % haemoglobin F, which is mainly of the $^A\gamma$ variety; heterozygotes have between 3 and 10 % haemoglobin F. We have studied several heterozygotes for this condition at birth and followed their pattern of haemoglobin F production during the first year of life (Wood *et al.* 1982). The $^G\gamma/^A\gamma$ chain production ratio is normal at birth but the rate of decline of haemoglobin F production is retarded and the adult pattern of predominantly $^A\gamma$ chain synthesis appears during the first few months of life. These observations suggest that the primary defect in this condition affects a regulatory region involved in the neonatal suppression of $^A\gamma$ chain production; when the $^G\gamma$ and $^A\gamma$ loci are fully activated in foetal life the expression of the genes is normal. Recently, we have sequenced the $^G\gamma$ and $^A\gamma$ genes from an individual homozygous for this condition; both genes are normal except for a T→C change at position −198 in the $^A\gamma$ gene (Tate *et al.* unpublished data).

These interesting new forms of HPFH are summarized in Fig. 3. They appear to result from a series of single base changes clustered 5′ to the $^G\gamma$ or $^A\gamma$ genes, upstream from the CCAT and ATA boxes. In view of the developmental history of foetal haemoglobin production in the British variety, it is possible that these mutations alter DNA/protein interactions that are involved in the neonatal suppression of γ gene synthesis.

Finally, there are non-deletion HPFH-like conditions associated with relatively low levels of haemoglobin F production in heterozygotes. Although some of them may be caused by determinants that map within the β globin gene cluster (Old *et al.* 1982) several families have now been reported in which this is not the case (Gianni *et al.* 1983). This is the first evidence for the existence of genes that influence globin chain synthesis that are not linked to the globin gene cluster. Currently, linkage studies are being carried out to attempt to determine the chromosomal location of these putative regulatory regions. Recently, we have established a linkage for a form of HPFH of this type to a restriction fragment length polymorphism defined by a mini-satellite probe (Jeffreys, Wilson & Thein, 1985).

Haemopoietic cell transplantation between developmental stages

The pattern of switching between foetal and adult haemoglobin is similar in sheep and man, and thus it has been possible to perform interdevelopmental stage haemopoietic cell transfer studies in this species (Wood *et al.* 1985). The rationale for these experiments was as follows. Foetal haemopoietic cells, obtained from liver and bone marrow, can be transplanted into irradiated lambs in which the switch from foetal to adult haemoglobin synthesis is already complete. If the transplanted cells switch over to adult haemoglobin synthesis immediately, it would imply that switching is determined mainly by the microenvironment of the erythroid progenitors in the bone marrow. If, on the other hand, switching occurs in the donor cells at about the same time as it would had the cells remained in the foetus, this would point to the existence of an intrinsic regulatory mechanism or 'developmental clock' within the foetal haemopoietic stem cells. Finally, if the transplanted cells continue to produce foetal haemoglobin indefinitely, it suggests that gene switching is under the control of a regulatory mechanism that is only present at a particular time during foetal development and hence had been bypassed by the transplantation.

Given the technical difficulty of these studies, the results of a large number of experiments are now reasonably consistent (Wood *et al.* 1985). Foetal haemopoietic cells transplanted into newborn animals continue to synthesize foetal haemoglobin and then gradually switch over to adult haemoglobin production. The timing of the transition is related to the gestational age of the foetus from which the donor cells were obtained, although it may be accelerated very slightly in the recipient. In the converse experiment, adult bone marrow cells transplanted into a foetus synthesize predominantly adult haemoglobin, implying that once the switch has occurred it is irreversible. To date, the results of these transplant experiments are compatible with a 'developmental clock mechanism' for the regulation of foetal globin gene expression.

Gene expression in neoplastic cell lines

The notion that analysis of gene expression in haematological neoplasms might provide some useful models for studying the developmental genetics of haemoglobin is not new. It has been known for some time that infants with juvenile chronic myeloid leukaemia (JCML) revert to a pattern of red cell protein production that is very similar to that observed late in foetal life (Weatherall, Edwards & Donohoe, 1968; Weatherall *et al.* 1975*b*). Their haemoglobin consists predominantly of Hb F with a marked reduction of Hb A_2 and carbonic anhydrase, another protein that is switched on during the later part of foetal development. Unfortunately it has not been possible to establish JCML cells in culture.

There are, however, several established cell lines that are of potential interest for studying the developmental genetics of haemoglobin. The main stimulus to these studies came from the observation that a mouse erythroleukaemic cell line (MEL), first established by Charlotte Friend, when induced by dimethyl sulphoxide, haem or other agents, undergoes terminal erythroid differentiation and synthesizes haemoglobin, in this case of the adult variety (Marks & Rifkind, 1978). The human cell line K562 was originally derived from a patient with transforming chronic granulocytic leukaemia (CGL) (Lozzio & Lozzio, 1975). Although there are slight variations between different K562 lines, most of them synthesize predominantly ε and ς chains with smaller amounts of α and γ chains when induced with haem or other agents (Rutherford, Clegg & Weatherall, 1979). No β chain production has been found in these cells. The β globin genes are intact, have a normal structure and are expressed normally when cloned and transferred to COS cells. Curiously, of the two α genes, only $\alpha 1$ is expressed in K562 cells (D. R. Higgs, unpublished observation).

Another line, in this case derived from a patient with erythroleukaemia and called Human Erythroleukaemia Line (HEL), after induction, produces mainly $^A\gamma$ and $^G\gamma$ chains with some α but no β chains (Martin & Papayannopoulou, 1982). Another human leukaemia cell population that synthesized only haemoglobin F was also derived from an adult patient with transforming CGL, but a permanent line could not be established (Potter *et al.* 1984).

Thus it appears that some adult-derived leukaemia cell lines can be induced to express their embryonic and, or, foetal globin genes. There does not appear to be any structural abnormality of the later-developmental globin genes, which are not expressed in these cells; in a sense they appear to be 'frozen' at an early developmental stage, similar to JCML cells described earlier. Hence they offer a useful model for chromosome or gene transfer experiments for defining the possible role of *trans*-acting regulatory factors that might be involved in the expression of globin genes during development.

Intact chromosome or gene transfer experiments

A number of experiments have been carried out that have asked whether there is any evidence for developmental-stage-specific *trans* regulation of the $\varepsilon\gamma\delta\beta$ globin gene complex. The interpretation of these studies is based on the assumption that some of the mouse or human malignant cell lines that can be induced to produce adult or foetal haemoglobin, described above, are 'fixed' at specific developmental stages. It has been found that if chromosome 11, cosmids containing the human β, γ and ε genes, or plasmids containing the β genes alone, are inserted into mouse erythroleukaemia (MEL) cells there is a significant increase in β globin gene expression after induction of haemoglobin synthesis, whereas there is no increase in the expression of the γ or ε genes (Willing, Nienhuis & Anderson, 1979; Wright, De Boer, Grosveld & Flavell, 1983). Similarly, when intact human chromosomes 16 are transferred into MEL cells there is expression of the α globin genes but not of the embryonic ζ globin genes (Zeitlin & Weatherall, 1984). Furthermore, if chromosome 16 of K562 cells, in which the embryonic globin genes are active, is transferred into MEL cells, no ζ gene expression is observed (Anagnou *et al.* 1985).

Recently, chromosome 11 derived from the human cell line HEL has been transferred into MEL cells (Papayannopoulou *et al.* 1985). As mentioned earlier, HEL cells synthesize embryonic and foetal non-α chains but do not produce adult β globin chains. After transfer, the β globin genes were activated, suggesting that they are transcriptionally competent and thus that they may be responding to a positive *trans*-acting element within the MEL environment. Presumably they fail to express in the HEL environment because of the absence of this factor or the presence of a *trans*-acting inhibitor of β globin gene expression.

The results of these experiments suggest that, if it is assumed that MEL cells are 'adult' in character, they lack the appropriate stage-specific developmental *trans* regulatory factors that are required for the expression of the embryonic or foetal globin genes but produce *trans*-acting factors capable of supporting α and β gene expression. However, other data have not all been consistent with this interpretation. The α globin genes, when part of chromosome 16, show induction, as does the β globin gene on chromosome 11, but when α globin genes are introduced into MEL cells as part of a cosmid or plasmid they are expressed at a high level, independent of induction. This behaviour contrasts with that of the β globin genes, which still show induction dependence when introduced in either a cosmid or plasmid. Nevertheless, this is a promising approach to the definition of *trans* regulators and it should be possible to expand these studies provided that a source of embryonic or foetal recipient cells can be obtained for similar transfer experiments.

Gene expression in colony systems in vitro

There is an extensive literature on the differential expression of the γ and β globin genes in clonal colonies derived from BFU–Es and CFU–Es, erythroid progenitor cells which can be defined by their size and time of appearance in culture *in vitro*. This work is summarized in the published accounts of three recent conferences on gene switching (Stamatoyannopoulos & Nienhuis, 1979, 1981, 1983).

The expression of the foetal and adult globin genes in colonies reflects the stage of maturation of the individuals from which the progenitors were obtained. Colonies derived from foetuses produce predominantly γ chains, whereas those obtained from adults synthesize mainly β chains although there is always a higher proportion of γ chains produced in adult-derived colonies than is present in adult red cells. Both γ and β chain genes are expressed in the same colonies and there is a continuum in the relative proportion of γ and β chain production in BFU–Es obtained from newborns at different gestational ages. The latter argues against there being specific stem cell populations that are programmed for foetal or adult globin chain synthesis.

A variety of modifications of experimental conditions, particularly those that affect the growth of colonies, can change the relative expression of γ and β globin genes in erythroid colonies. This may be because the relative expression of γ and β genes is related to the maturity of the progenitors. At least in some species there appears to be asynchrony of γ and β gene expression during colony maturation, with γ genes expressed earlier than β genes. Recent experiments in which the absoute amount of γ and β chain accumulation in colonies has been estimated suggest that this may not always be the case, particularly in human BFU–Es. However, when absolute levels of haemoglobin accumulated per cell are calculated, the amount *in vitro* is always considerably below that obtained *in vivo*. Thus the attention that has been paid to the higher proportion of haemoglobin F in adult BFU–Es has not yet been demonstrated to have any bearing on globin gene regulation *in vivo*.

Perhaps the most interesting observation relating to the regulation of gene switching that has arisen from studies of erythroid colonies is that the expression of the γ genes in both adult BFU–Es and those from individuals with various genetic conditions associated with persistent γ chain production, including deletion HPFH, can be 'switched off' by a factor that is present in foetal sheep sera. This has led to the development of a model in which switching occurs when the appropriate receptors for this putative inhibitory factor are expressed during the later stages of foetal development.

Several other models of the regulation of the γ and β globin genes have been derived from analyses of the pattern of globin gene expression in colonies. For example, it has been suggested that programming may reflect a 'decision' by early progenitors to move to terminal differentiation in which γ chain production is more likely, rather than to go through further divisions and differentiation steps that make β gene expression more probable. This stochastic model of differentiation has been extended to encompass the regulation of foetal and adult globin gene expression during *in vivo* development. However, the *in vitro* colony model has not provided any clear insights into how these different pathways of differentiation might be mediated or regulated.

In vivo *modification of γ globin gene expression*

As mentioned earlier, the administration of agents such as 5-azacytidine, which cause hypomethylation of genes, is associated with a modest increase in γ chain production in patients with sickle cell anaemia or β thalassaemia (Ley *et al.* 1982; Charache *et al.* 1983). Since this effect can be obtained with cytotoxic agents that do not cause hypomethylation of DNA it has been suggested that the effect on γ chain production results from perturbations of the patterns of erythroid maturation (Letvin *et al.* 1985). It is possible that both mechanisms play a role.

CONCLUSIONS

Clearly, it is impossible to synthesize the diverse information outlined in this review and provide a coherent model for the regulation of globin gene expression during normal human development. One of the great difficulties in this field is uncertainty about whether the mutations that are associated with persistent γ chain production, or for that matter the experimental models that have been used to study the differential expression of the foetal and adult globin genes, have any real relevance to the normal globin gene switching mechanism. They may have, but only with respect to a limited part of what must be an extremely complex multi-step regulatory system.

The consistent changes in chromatin and the methylation state of the β globin gene cluster that are associated with activation of the different gene loci at various stages of development provide an anatomical explanation for the activity of these loci but tell us nothing about how these changes are mediated. However, the gene or chromosome transfer experiments suggest that there may be developmental-stage-specific *trans* factors involved in the regulation of these genes, presumably by interacting with chromatin. This is a very promising area for further work although, since all these experiments rely on the expression of genes in neoplastic cell lines, the results have to be interpreted with particular caution. Equally interesting is the possibility that the 'upstream' mutations, which have been found recently in some varieties of non-deletion HPFH, will provide a clue as to the site of interactions between chromatin and regulatory proteins. Thus at least we have some indications of what might be the most productive area of investigation for trying to characterize the mechanisms of regulation at the chromosomal level. Similarly, recent successes with the expression of 'foreign' globin genes in transgenic mice point the way to how we might learn more about the tissue specificity of globin gene expression (Chada *et al.* 1985).

This may be as far as we can go in the immediate future. The central question remains, however. How is the differential expression of the globin genes during development actually timed? All we know at the moment is that it is related fairly closely to gestational age and that it is not tissue dependent. The only experimental data relating to this question, derived from the sheep transplant model, suggest that there may be a 'developmental clock' built into the haemopoietic stem cell. Here we have a serious conceptual difficulty because there is no obvious model with which to analyse time-related events; none of the forms of HPFH is, strictly speaking, a heterochronic mutation. That is, these conditions are not characterized by a change in the *time* of globin gene switching; in the only form of non-deletion HPFH that has been studied during the period of switching the timing of the transition from foetal to adult haemoglobin production was completely normal; there was a delay in the *rate of decline* of foetal haemoglobin production suggesting that the mutation involved the mechanism of adult suppression of γ chain production (Wood *et al.* 1982; Tate *et al.* unpublished data).

One of the main difficulties in designing experiments to ask questions about the timing of events during development is the lack of any clear concept of how the process might be mediated. One possibility, that should be amenable to investigation, is that differential globin gene expression is related to the number of haemopoietic stem cell divisions. A clock based on such a mechanism is feasible; in the mouse it has been estimated that there may only be a limited number of haemopoietic stem cell divisions during foetal development. However, our preliminary experiments in sheep suggest that the foetal haemopoietic stem cell is extremely resistant to perturbation by agents such as busulphan, and that chronic hypertransfusion of the foetus, which might be expected to reduce the number of stem cell divisions, has very little effect on the timing of the transition from foetal to adult haemoglobin (W. G. Wood & C. Bunch, unpublished observations).

Clearly, our current understanding of the developmental genetics of haemoglobin is at an extremely rudimentary stage. However, it is apparent that there are several promising areas for further work and that the globin gene model may still have something to offer to developmental biology.

REFERENCES

ANAGNOU, N. P., YUAN, T. Y., LIM, E., HELDER, J., WIEDER, S., GLAISTER, D., MARKS, B., WANG, A., COLBERT, D. & DEISSEROTH, A. (1985). Regulatory factors specific for adult and embryonic globin genes may govern their expression in erythroleukemia cells. *Blood* **65**, 705–712.

ANTONARAKIS, S. E., BOEHM, C. D., GIARDINA, P. J. V. & KAZAZIAN, H. H. (1982). Non random association of polymorphic restriction sites in the β-globin gene complex. *Proc. natn. Acad. Sci. U.S.A.* **79**, 137–141.

BARD, H. (1975). The postnatal decline of hemoglobin F synthesis in normal full-term infants. *J. clin. Invest.* **55**, 395–398.

BERNARDS, R. & FLAVELL, R. A. (1980). Physical mapping of the globin gene deletion in hereditary persistence of foetal haemoglobin (HPFH). *Nucl. Acids Res.* **8**, 1521–1534.

CHADA, K., MAGRAM, J., RAPHAEL, K., RADICE, G., LACEY, E. & COSTANTINI, F. (1985). Specific expression of a foreign β-globin gene in erythroid cells of transgenic mice. *Nature, Lond.* **314**, 377–380.

CHARACHE, S., DOVER, G., SMITH, K., TALBOT, C. C., MOYER, M. & BOYER, S. H. (1983). Treatment of sickle cell anemia with 5-azacytidine results in increased fetal hemoglobin production and is associated with nonrandom hypomethylation of DNA around the γ-δ-β-globin gene complex. *Proc. natn. Acad. Sci. U.S.A.* **80**, 4842–4846.

COLLINS, F. S., BOEHM, C. D., WABER, P. G., STOECKERT, C. J., WEISSMAN, S. M., FORGET, B. G. & KAZAZIAN, H. H. (1984). Concordance of a point mutation 5' to the $^{G}\gamma$ globin gene with $^{G}\gamma\beta^{+}$ hereditary persistence of fetal hemoglobin in the Black population. *Blood* **64**, 1292–1296.

COLLINS, F. S., METHERALL, J. E., YAMAKAWA, M., PAN, J., WEISSMAN, S. M. & FORGET, B. G. (1985). A point mutation in the $^{A}\gamma$-globin gene promoter in Greek hereditary persistence of fetal haemoglobin. *Nature, Lond.* **313**, 325–326.

COLLINS, F. S. & WEISSMAN, S. M. (1984). The molecular genetics of human hemoglobin. *Prog. Nucl. Acid Res. molec. Biol.* **31**, 315–462.

DESIMONE, J., HELLER, P., HALL, L. & ZWIERS, D. (1982). 5-azacytidine stimulates fetal hemoglobin synthesis in anemic baboons. *Proc. natn. Acad. Sci. U.S.A.* **79**, 4428–4431.

GELINAS, R., ENDLICH, B., PFEIFFER, C., YAGI, M. & STAMATOYANNOPOULOS, G. (1985). G to A substitution in the distal CCAAT box of the $^{A}\gamma$-globin gene in Greek hereditary persistance of fetal haemoglobin. *Nature, Lond.* **313**, 323–325.

GIANNI, A. M., BREGNI, M., CAPPELLINI, M. D., FIORELLI, G., TARAMELLI, R., GIGLIONI, B., COMI, P. & OTTOLENGHI, S. (1983). A gene controlling fetal hemoglobin expression in adults is not linked to the non-α globin cluster. *EMBO J.* **2**, 921–925.

GIGLIONI, B., CASINI, C., MANTOVANI, R., MERLI, S., COMI, P., OTTOLENGHI, S., SAGLIO, G., CAMASCHELLA, C. & MAZZA, U. (1984). A molecular study of a family with Greek hereditary persistance of fetal hemoglobin and β-thalassemia. *EMBO J.* **3**, 2641–2645.

GILMAN, J. G. & HUISMAN, T. H. J. (1984). A mutation 158 base pairs 5' to the $^{G}\gamma$ gene is associated with elevated $^{G}\gamma$ production. *Blood* **64**, 62.

JEFFREYS, A. J., WILSON, V. & THEIN, S. L. (1985). Hypervariable "minisatellite" regions in human DNA. *Nature, Lond.* **314**, 67–73.

JONES, R. W., GOODBOURN, S. E. Y., OLD, J. M. & WEATHERALL, D. J. (1985). The sequence of the $^{A}\gamma$ globin gene in a $^{G}\gamma\beta^{+}$ type of hereditary persistence of fetal haemoglobin. *Br. J. Haemat.* **59**, 357–362.

LETVIN, N. L., LINCH, D. C., BEARDSLEY, P., MCINTYRE, K. W., MILLER, B. A. & NATHAN, D. G. (1985). Influence of cell cycle phase-specific agents on simian fetal hemoglobin synthesis. *J. clin. Invest.* **75**, 1999–2005.

LEY, T. J., DESIMONE, J., ANAGNOU, N. P., KELLER, G. H., HUMPHRIES, R. K., TURNER, P. H., YOUNG, N. S., HELLER, P. & NIENHUIS, A. W. (1982). 5-azacytidine selectivity increases γ-globin synthesis in a patient with β-thalassemia. *New Engl. J. Med.* **307**, 1469–1475.

LIEBHABER, S. A. & KAN, Y. W. (1982). Different rates of mRNA translation balance the expression of the two human α-globin loci. *J. biol. Chem.* **257**, 11 852–11 855.

LOZZIO, C. B. & LOZZIO, B. B. (1975). Human chronic myelogenous leukemia cell line with positive Philadelphia chromosome. *Blood* **45**, 321–334.

MARKS, P. A. & RIFKIND, R. A. (1978). Erythroleukemic differentiation. *A. Rev. Biochem.* **47**, 419–448.

MARTIN, P. & PAPAYANNOPOULOU, T. (1982). HEL cells: A new human erythroleukemia cell line with spontaneous and induced globin expression. *Science* **216**, 1233–1235.

NUTE, P. E., PATARYAS, H. A. & STAMATOYANNOPOULOS, G. (1973). The $^{G}\gamma$ and $^{A}\gamma$ hemoglobin chains during human fetal development. *Am. J. hum. Genet.* **35**, 271–276.

OLD, J. M., AYYUB, H., WOOD, W. G., CLEGG, J. B. & WEATHERALL, D. J. (1982). Linkage analysis of non-deletion hereditary persistence of fetal hemoglobin using DNA polymorphisms. *Science* **215**, 981–982.

ORKIN, S. H. & GOFF, S. C. (1981). The duplicated human α-globin genes: their relative expression as measured by RNA analysis. *Cell* **24**, 345–351.

ORKIN, S. H. & KAZAZIAN, H. H. (1984). The mutation and polymorphism of the human β-globin gene and its surrounding DNA. *A. Rev. Genet.* **18**, 131–171.

PAPAYANNOPOULOU, T., LINDSLEY, D., KURACHI, S., LEWISON, K., HEMENWAY, T., MELIS, M., ANAGNOU, N. P. & NAJFELD, V. (1985). Adult and fetal human globin genes are expressed following chromosomal transfer into MEL cells. *Proc. natn. Acad. Sci. U.S.A.* **82**, 780–784.

PESCHLE, C., MIGLIACCIO, A. R., MIGLIACCIO, G., PETRINI, M., CALANDRINI, M., RUSSO, G., MASTROBERARDINO, G., PRESTA, M., GIANNI, A. M., COMI, P., GIGLIONI, B. & OTTOLENGHI, S. (1984). Embryonic→fetal Hb switch in humans: Studies on erythroid bursts generated by embryonic progenitors from yolk sac and liver. *Proc. natn. Acad. Sci. U.S.A.* **81**, 2416–2420.

PESCHLE, C., MAVILIO, F., CARÈ, A., MIGLIACCIO, G., MIGLIACCIO, A. R., SAMOGGIA, P., PETTI, S., GUERRIERO, R., MARINUCCI, M., LAZZARO, D., RUSSO, G. & MASTROBERARDINO, G. (1985). Haemoglobin switching in human embryos: asynchrony of $\zeta \to \alpha$ and $\varepsilon \to \gamma$ switches in primitive and definitive erythropoietic lineages. *Nature, Lond.* **313**, 235–237.

POTTER, C. G., BUNCH, C., POTTER, A. C., BUCKLE, V., DERRY, S., WOOD, W. G. & WEATHERALL, D. J. (1984). Erythroid differentiation in CGL cells from a patient with blast crisis. *Leuk. Res.* **8**, 713–721.

RUTHERFORD, T. R., CLEGG, J. B. & WEATHERALL, D. J. (1979). K562 human leukaemic cells synthesise embryonic haemoglobin in response of haemin. *Nature, Lond.* **280**, 164–165.

SCHROEDER, W. A., SHELTON, J. R., SHELTON, J. B., APELL, G., HUISMAN, T. H. J. & BOUVER, N. G. (1972). World-wide occurrence of nonallelic genes for the γ-chain of human foetal haemoglobin in newborns. *Nature, new Biol.* **240**, 273–274.

STAMATOYANNOPOULOS, G. & NIENHUIS, A. W. (1979). *Cellular and Molecular Regulation of Hemoglobin Switching.* New York: Grune and Stratton.

STAMATOYANNOPOULOS, G. & NIENHUIS, A. W. (1981). *Hemoglobins in Development and Differentiation.* New York: A. R. Liss.

STAMATOYANNOPOULOS, G. & NIENHUIS, A. W. (1983). *Globin Gene Expression and Hematopoietic Differentiation.* New York: Alan R. Liss.

WAINSCOAT, J. S., THEIN, S. L., HIGGS, D. R., BELL, J. I., WEATHERALL, D. J., AL-AWAMY, B. & SERJEANT, G. (1985*a*). A genetic marker for elevated levels of haemoglobin F in homozygous sickle cell disease. *Br. J. Haemat.* **60**, 261–268.

WAINSCOAT, J. S., THEIN, S. L., WOOD, W. G., WEATHERALL, D. J., TZOTOS, S., KANAVAKIS, E., METAXATOU-MAVROMATI, A. & KATTAMIS, C. (1985*b*). A novel deletion in the β globin gene complex. *Ann. N.Y. Acad. Sci.* **445**, 20–27.

WEATHERALL, D. J., CARTNER, R., CLEGG, J. B., WOOD, W. G., MACRAE, I. & MACKENZIE, A. (1975*a*). A form of hereditary persistence of fetal haemoglobin characterised by uneven cellular distribution of haemoglobin F and the production of haemoglobins A and A$_2$ in homozygotes. *Br. J. Haemat.* **29**, 205–220.

WEATHERALL, D. J., CLEGG, J. B., WOOD, W. G., CALLENDER, S. T., SHERIDAN, B. L. & PRITCHARD, J. (1975*b*). Foetal erythropoiesis in human leukaemia. *Nature, Lond.* **257**, 710–712.

WEATHERALL, D. J., EDWARDS, J. A. & DONOHOE, W. T. A. (1968). Haemoglobin and red cell enzyme changes in juvenile chronic myeloid leukaemia. *Br. med. J.* **1**, 679–681.

WEATHERALL, D. J., HIGGS, D. R., WOOD, W. G. & CLEGG, J. B. (1984). Genetic disorders of human haemoglobin as models for analysing gene regulation. *Phil. Trans. R. Soc. Lond.* B **307**, 247–259.

WEATHERALL, D. J. & WAINSCOAT, J. S. (1985). The molecular pathology of thalassaemia. In *Recent Advances in Haematology*, 4th edn (ed. A. V. Hoffbrand), pp. 63–88. Edinburgh: Churchill Livingstone.

WILLING, M. C., NIENHUIS, A. W. & ANDERSON, W. F. (1979). Selective activation of human β- but not γ-globin gene in human fibroblast X mouse erythroleukaemia cell hybrids. *Nature, Lond.* **277**, 534–538.

WOOD, W. G. & BUNCH, C. (1983). Fetal-to-adult hemopoietic cell transplantation: Is hemoglobin synthesis gestational age-dependent? In *Globin Gene Expression and Hematopoietic Differentiation* (ed. G. Stamatoyannopoulos & A. W. Nienhuis), pp. 511–521. New York: Alan R. Liss.

WOOD, W. G., BUNCH, C., KELLY, S., GUNN, Y. & BRECKON, G. (1985). Haemoglobin switching: evidence for a developmental clock. *Nature, Lond.* **314**, 320–323.

WOOD, W. G., MACRAE, I. A., DARBRE, P. D., CLEGG, J. B. & WEATHERALL, D. J. (1982). The British type of non-deletion HPFH: characterisation of developmental changes *in vivo* and erythroid growth *in vitro*. *Br. J. Haemat.* **50**, 401–414.

WOOD, W. G., NASH, J., WEATHERALL, D. J., ROBINSON, J. S. & HARRISON, F. A. (1979). The sheep as an animal model for the switch from fetal to adult hemoglobins. In *Cellular and Molecular Regulation of Hemoglobin Switching* (ed. G. Stamatoyannopoulos & A. W. Nienhuis), pp. 153–167. New York: Grune and Stratton.

WOOD, W. G. & WEATHERALL, D. J. (1973). Haemoglobin synthesis during human foetal development. *Nature, Lond.* **244**, 162–165.

Wood, W. G. & Weatherall, D. J. (1983). Developmental genetics of the human haemoglobin. *Biochem. J.* **215**, 1–10.

Wright, S., De Boer, E., Grosveld, F. G. & Flavell, R. A. (1983). Regulated expression of the human β-globin gene family in murine erythroleukaemia cells. *Nature, Lond.* **305**, 333–336.

Zeitlin, H. C. & Weatherall, D. J. (1983). Selective expression within the human α globin gene complex following chromosome-dependent transfer into diploid mouse erythroleukaemia cells. *Molec. Biol. Med.* **1**, 489–500.

J. Cell Sci. Suppl. 4, 337–356 (1986)
Printed in Great Britain © The Company of Biologists Limited 1986

CELL MINGLING DURING MAMMALIAN EMBRYOGENESIS

R. L. GARDNER

Sir William Dunn School of Pathology, South Parks Road, Oxford OX1 3RE, UK

INTRODUCTION

Genetic mosaics produced by selective chromosome loss or X-ray induced mitotic recombination have been studied extensively in *Drosophila* (for review, see Gehring, 1978). A consistent finding is that clonally related cells tend to remain in contiguity throughout development in this arthropod. Use of exogenous molecules such as horseradish peroxidase (HRP) to label single cells in the early embryo of the leech has revealed that clones also exhibit coherent growth in this invertebrate (Weisblat, Kim & Stent, 1984). Using essentially the same approach, Kominami (1983) found that little intermingling of cells occurred in the starfish embryo up to the early bipinnaria larval stage, except in the migratory mesenchyme that originates during gastrulation. Exhaustive lineage studies have shown that spatial relationships between cells are also largely conserved during development of the nematode worm, *Caenorhabditis elegans* (Sulston, Schierenberg, White & Thompson, 1983). Investigations using various extrinsic cell markers lead to the conclusion that growth is coherent during early development in the mouse as well (Mintz, 1965; Garner & McLaren, 1974; Kelly, 1979; Balakier & Pedersen, 1982; Gearhart, Shaffer, Musser & Oster-Granite, 1982; Ziomek & Johnson, 1982; Surani & Barton, 1984; Fein, 1985). However, this pattern of growth is evidently not maintained in the mouse, and seems to be succeeded by more generalized cell mingling than is observed in any of the invertebrates mentioned earlier.

The aim of this article is to try to assess the extent to which cells mingle during mammalian embryogenesis, and to consider some of the factors that may contribute to the occurrence of this phenomenon. However, before proceeding further, it is pertinent to discuss ways of producing genetic mosaicism in mammals, because it is from studying mice and humans exhibiting such mosaicism that the relevant data have been obtained. In practice, experimental chimaeras and X-inactivation mosaics are the two types of organism with which this article will be mainly concerned. The chimaeras are normally produced by combining cells from two genotypically dissimilar types of preimplantation embryo (Tarkowski, 1961; Mintz, 1962; Gardner, 1968; Kelly, 1975), although cells of up to four different genotypes have been shown to participate in normal development (Petters & Markert, 1980). There are several points worth noting about such organisms. First, the stage at which mosaicism was initiated is known precisely and can be varied to some extent. Second, mosaicism can be produced in all tissues of the conceptus or in specific subsets of them (Gardner,

1984*a*). Third, allelic differences at suitable loci anywhere in the genome can be exploited as cell markers for studying the distribution of mosaicism. Finally, the proportions of the two constituent cell populations can be varied to some extent. This is important because unbalanced mosaicism is often more informative than balanced mosaicism (Whitten, 1978), particularly when a single cell of one genotype is introduced into an embryo of the opposite genotype (Gardner & Lyon, 1971; Kelly, 1975). Nevertheless, production of chimaeras inevitably entails some perturbation of development and, in general, result in organisms composed of cells that are more disparate genetically than X-inactivation mosaics.

Obviously, no intervention is necessary in the production of X-inactivation mosaicism, other than ensuring that female embryos are heterozygous at an appropriate marker locus on the X chromosome. The range of potential marker loci is obviously limited, but can be extended to some extent by exploiting X-autosome translocations. However, the pattern of inactivation of genes that have been trans-located to the X chromosome is not necessarily identical to that of native X-linked genes (Cattanach & Isaacson, 1967; Simpson, McLaren, Chandler & Tomonari, 1984). Apart from the shortage of marker genes on the X chromosome, there is also persisting uncertainty as to when X-inactivation takes place (see West, 1982, for review), particularly in the primitive ectoderm or epiblast from which the foetus originates (Gardner, Lyon, Evans & Burtenshaw, 1985). Furthermore, balanced mosaicism is the rule in derivatives of the primitive ectoderm, because inactivation seems to be random with respect to the two X chromosomes in this tissue (West, 1982). It is not clear at present whether the non-random inactivation that occurs in the trophectoderm and primitive endoderm (Takagi & Sasaki, 1975; West, Papaioannou, Frels & Chapman, 1978; Papaioannou & West, 1981; Papaioannou, West, Bucher & Linke, 1981) entails the paternally inherited X chromosome being switched off in most or all cells in these lineages (West, 1982). The distinction is important because vey unbalanced mosaicism would be produced on the one hand, and no mosaicism on the other. This issue merits closer investigation because of the prospect of being able to undertake strictly clonal studies in these extraembryonic tissues if, at least occasionally, the maternally inherited X chromosome was in-activated in just one cell.

It is evident from the foregoing discussion that chimaerism constitutes a richer and more versatile source of genetic mosaicism than X-inactivation. Nevertheless, in view of possible artifacts in chimaeras, due to such factors as size regulation (Rands, 1985) and the often marked genetic disparity between their component cells, comparative studies using both types of organism are desirable whenever practicable.

MOSAICISM IN THE PRIMITIVE ECTODERM AND FOETUS

Primitive ectoderm

If coherent clonal growth persisted without interruption throughout mammalian development, both chimaeras and X-inactivation mosaics would be expected to consist of large blocks of tissue that were composed entirely of cells belonging to one

or other of the constituent populations. In practice this has not been observed in the case of either type of organism, regardless of whether they have been examined pre- or post-natally. Pigmentation mosaicism in the coat and skin is a useful indicator of the extent of distribution of the two cell populations in chimaeras because cutaneous melanocytes originate from neural crest tissue that extends along each side of the neuraxis in the early postimplantation embryo (Rawles, 1947). Such mosaicism has been studied in large numbers of chimaeras produced by embryo aggregation, and is particularly striking when one genotype is albino and the other wild type. It usually takes the form of alternating, bilaterally asymmetrical transverse stripes or patches of variable width that are discernible on the head, trunk and tail (Mintz, 1967; McLaren, 1976*a*). Interestingly, similar patterns of widespread pigmentation mosaicism were also seen in most of a series of 80 chimaeras obtained by injecting single fifth day primitive ectoderm cells into genetically dissimilar host blastocysts (see Fig. 1; and Gardner *et al.* 1985).

The reason for singling out pigmentation mosaicism is that it provides particularly graphic evidence of the widespread distribution of clonally related cells within the foetal primordium. Studies using chromosomal polymorphisms and other genetic markers that can be used to detect chimaerism in additional tissues lead to the same conclusion (see McLaren, 1976*a*, for review). Again, the most impressive evidence comes from the analysis of chimaeras produced by transplanting a few or, preferably, one cell between genetically dissimilar blastocysts (Ford, Evans & Gardner, 1975; Gardner *et al.* 1985; and unpublished data).

Hence, clonal descendants of inner cell mass (ICM) cells that contribute to the foetus are evidently widely distributed by the time the embryonic axis has formed on the eighth day of gestation. It is difficult to see how this can be accomplished without substantial disruption of coherent clonal growth, unless clones form long bands or stripes that are consistently oriented with their long axis approximately parallel to that of the future foetus. While such an orientation of clones in the early post-implantation ectoderm seems most improbable, there are at present no data that enable it to be discounted. However, if, as is much more likely, the pigmentation patterns in chimaeras reflect extensive dispersal of clonally related cells, the question arises as to when this takes place. The most probable time is immediately after implantation because it is during this period that the ectoderm is rapidly transformed from a solid cluster of cells into a monolayer (Snell & Stevens, 1966; Poelmann, 1975). Since this process is accompanied by the formation of a central proamniotic cavity, it is not difficult to envisage how cells that were originally contiguous might become widely separated at this stage (Fig. 2). Once conversion of this tissue into a columnar epithelium has taken place, there would seem to be less scope for extensive dissemination of cells, except in the primitive streak region (Snell & Stevens, 1966). However, as discussed later, several other factors may contribute to cell mingling during subsequent development of this tissue.

Fig. 1. A mouse chimaera obtained from a blastocyst that had been injected with a single primitive ectoderm cell. Note that the darker donor pigmentation is present on the head, trunk and tail.

Detailed analysis of the distribution of mosaicism within, as opposed to between, various organs and tissues have also been undertaken both in chimaeras and X-inactivation mosaics. It is clear from the results of these investigations that cell mingling does not occur as a single isolated episode in the ectoderm before its axiation, but extends well into the period of organogenesis. The next section provides a brief survey of some of the principal evidence on which this conclusion is based.

Selected organs and tissues

Retinal pigment epithelium. The melanocytes that comprise this epithelium originate within the optic cup itself rather than from the neural crest (Coulombre,

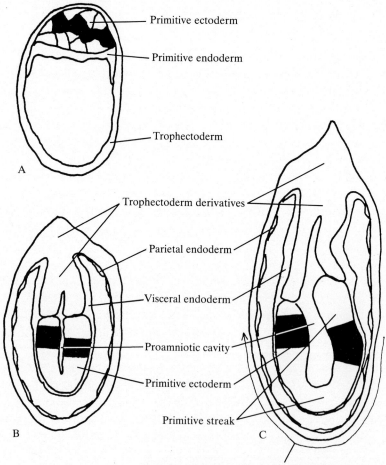

Fig. 2. Diagrammatic mid-sections of implanting blastocyst (A), early egg cylinder (B), and primitive streak stage (C) post-implantation embryo of the mouse to show how an initially coherent cluster of primitive ectoderm cells (black) might become dispersed along the embryonic axis as a result of formation of the pro-amniotic cavity.

1979), unlike those occurring in other parts of the eye and elsewhere. Since these melanocytes do not secrete their melanin granules (McLaren, 1976*a*), albino *versus* wild-type pigmentation constitutes an ideal *in situ* marker for studying mosaicism at the cellular level in this tissue. Furthermore, analysis can be undertaken relatively early in the development of the eye because all cells of the epithelium express pigment by the 13th day of gestation in wild-type foetuses (West, 1976*a*). Finally, mosaicism can readily be produced in the tissue in X-inactivation mosaics as well as in chimaeras by generating females that are homozygous autosomally for albino but carry a corresponding wild-type allele inserted in one of their two X chromosomes (Cattanach, 1961). Melanocytes in which the rearranged X chromosome is active will therefore be pigmented, while most if not all of those in which this chromosome is inactive will be phenotypically albino (Cattanach & Isaacson, 1967).

Deol & Whitten (1972) were the first to compare patterns of albino *versus* wild-type pigmentation in sections and whole-mount preparations of the epithelia from several post-natal chimaeras and X-inactivation mosaics. On finding that pigmented patches were consistently smaller and more numerous in mosaic than chimaeric specimens, they suggested that X-inactivation occurs at a relatively late stage of development in the epithelial precursor cells. However, as pointed out by West (1976*a*), these workers did not take into account the relative proportions of the two types of melanocytes, which are consistently more disparate in the chimaeras than the mosaics. When allowance was made for this difference, similar estimates of mean coherent clone size were obtained for the epithelia in the two types of organism. The mean size of such clones on the 13th day of gestation was estimated to be approximately one cell, implying extremely fine-grained mosaicism at this stage of development. Since corresponding estimates for the adult were only about fourfold higher, growth of the epithelium may depend more on enlargement and flattening than division of cells in the mouse, as in the chick embryo (Coulombre, 1955; Zimmerman, 1975).

Two additional points of interest have emerged from another investigation of this tissue in chimaeras that were examined around the time of weaning (Sanyal & Zeilmaker, 1977). First, a striking positive correlation in the relative proportions of albino *versus* pigmented melanocytes was found between the two retinal pigment epithelia, but not the choroids, in individual chimaeras. This suggests that the two optic cups are derived from a common pool of precursor cells. Second, indications of overall sectoring of mosaicism were discernible in some specimens of the epithelium, despite a high degree of local intermingling of wild-type and albino melanocytes. Hence, although mosaicism is obviously very fine-grained in this tissue, it may not be strictly random in distribution (Sanyal & Zeilmaker, 1977). Nevertheless, large coherent clones certainly cannot exist in the region of the central nervous system from which the optic cups develop. A similar conclusion seems to be warranted for the cerebellum or, more precisely, the precursors of the Purkinje cells that differentiate within this component of the brain (Mullen, 1981; Oster-Granite & Gearhart, 1981).

Gut and liver. Ponder and his colleagues have developed an *in situ* genetic marker than can be used to visualize mosaicism in large intact sheets of chimaeric intestinal mucosa (Schmidt, Wilkinson & Ponder, 1984; Ponder, Festing & Wilkinson, 1985a; see Fig. 3). They found that, even in specimens with markedly unbalanced representation of epithelial cells of the two genotypes, the minor component is widely distributed in patches that are generally relatively small (Schmidt, Garbutt, Wilkinson & Ponder, 1985a). This work will not be considered further here because it is discussed in some detail in a later section.

As in the case of the retinal pigment epithelium, mosaicism in the liver can be studied by means of *in situ* markers in both chimaeras and X-inactivation mosaics. The existence of a thermolabile variant of the lysosomal enzyme β-glucuronidase in the mouse (see Green, 1981) has been exploited in studies on chimaeric liver (Condamine, Custer & Mintz, 1971; West, 1976b), and heterozygosity for mutant alleles of X-linked ornithine carbamoyl transferase in both man and mouse for examining mosaic specimens (Ricciutti, Gelehrter & Rosenberg, 1976; Wareham, Howell, Williams & Williams, 1983). Relatively fine-grained mosaicism is apparent in sections of both chimaeric and mosaic liver stained histochemically for the appropriate enzyme. However, West's (1976b) study of chimaeric mouse liver is the only one in which an attempt was made to determine the mean size and approximate number of coherent clones. He concluded that adult liver comprises either several million small regular coherent clones or a smaller number of irregularly shaped ones. Extensive and accurate reconstruction from serial sections would be needed to discriminate between these alternatives. However, regardless of the outcome of such an exercise, it is evident that extensive cell mingling takes place at some stage during hepatogenesis.

Somites and skeletal muscle. Using allozymes of glucose phosphate isomerase (GPI) that can be distinguished electrophoretically as cell markers, Gearhart & Mintz (1972) detected mosaicism in 30 out of 38 individual somites isolated from day 8–9 p.c. aggregation chimaeras. Although the ratio of the two allozymes varied considerably among the somites, it tended to be similar in sequences of two to three that were immediate neighbours *in vivo*. These workers also analysed the extrinsic muscles of the eye, as examples of distinct and relatively small somite derivatives, in postnatal chimaeras. All 33 such muscles from the eyes of four unequivocal coat chimaeras that were analysed contained cells of both genotypes. The electrophoretograms of 22 muscles showed heterodimeric GPI molecules in addition to the two parental types of homodimers, thereby establishing that some of their constituent fibres had arisen by fusion of myoblast of both genotypes (see Mintz & Baker, 1967). The lack of hybrid enzyme in the remaining third of the muscles suggests that there is either some degree of spatial segregation of myoblasts of the two genotypes or preferential fusion of those of like genotype. Application of an *in situ* marker to chimaeric specimens of these muscles earlier in their development would be the simplest way of distinguishing between these alternatives.

Epidermis. Pieces of epidermis approximately $0 \cdot 5$–1 mm^2 from 28 adult chimaeras produced by aggregating morula or transplanting entire ICMs between blastocysts

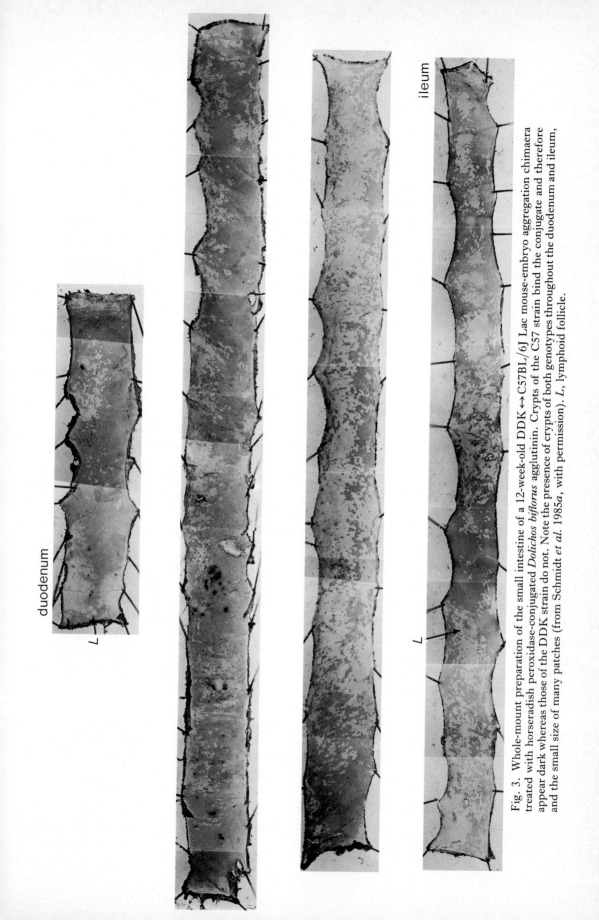

duodenum

ileum

Fig. 3. Whole-mount preparation of the small intestine of a 12-week-old DDK ↔ C57BL/6J Lac mouse-embryo aggregation chimaera treated with horseradish peroxidase-conjugated *Dolichos biflorus* agglutinin. Crypts of the C57 strain bind the conjugate and therefore appear dark whereas those of the DDK strain do not. Note the presence of crypts of both genotypes throughout the duodenum and ileum, and the small size of many patches (from Schmidt *et al.* 1985*a*, with permission). *L*, lymphoid follicle.

were analysed for mosaicism using the GPI marker mentioned earlier (Iannaccone, Gardner & Harris, 1978). Both allozymes were detected in all except 39 out of 495 samples. Gartler *et al.* (1971) analysed single scalp-hair follicles for mosaicism in human females who were heterozygous for electrophoretically distinguishable allozymes of X-linked glucose-6-phosphate dehydrogenase. Since no enzyme activity could be detected in the dermal papillae of such follicles, they were scoring only the epidermal components. They estimated that patch size was of the order of 1 mm^2 in adult epidermis and approximately 50-fold smaller at 3 months of gestation, when follicular development is initiated. Such estimates are necessarily very approximate because they assume, for example, that the patches are regular in shape and that there is commensurate growth of follicular and interfollicular epidermis. It is only when use of *in situ* markers is extended to this tissue that the validity of these assumptions can be tested. Nonetheless, the data are consistent with a phase of extensive mingling of epidermal precursor cells until the stage of initiation of follicular development.

It is apparent from this brief survey that studies on both chimaeras and X-inactivation mosaics provide evidence that considerable cell mingling occurs during the development of derivatives of all three classical germ layers. Furthermore, this is the case not only for obviously three-dimensional structures like the liver and skeletal muscle, but also for those that remain as essentially two-dimensional epithelia throughout most of, if not their entire, development. Indications that this situation may indeed prevail throughout the foetus were afforded by detailed examination of the distribution of sex-chromatin-positive cells in an XY/XXY human abortus, aged approximately 3 months (Klinger & Schwarzacher, 1962). This is not an ideal marker because the sex chromatin body is not detectable in all XXY cells and some XY cells may exhibit bodies with which it can be confused. Nevertheless, the authors noted that the sex chromatin mosaic pattern was on a 'micro' scale throughout the entire foetus. This was in sharp contrast to the situation in the amnion, where sex-chromatin-positive patches of between 0·2 and 5·0 mm were discernible in both the epithelial and connective tissue layers. As discussed later, a relatively large patch size is also typical of mosaicism in certain extraembryonic tissues of the mouse conceptus.

Aspects of primitive ectoderm development

The extensive cell mingling that occurs in foetal lineages has yet to be elucidated. Detailed information on patterns of mosaicism in the primitive ectoderm and its embryonic derivatives would be particularly illuminating in this respect. However, no such data are available at present either for chimaeras or X-inactivation mosaics, despite the availability of increasing numbers of *in situ* cell markers (West, 1984). Nevertheless, it is worth considering some of the factors that may contribute to the mixing and dispersal of clones in the primitive ectoderm during its postimplantation phase of development.

First, as noted earlier, the conversion of the tissue from a compact cluster of cells into an epithelial vesicle that takes place during formation of the proamniotic cavity is likely to cause major disruption of the continuity of clones (see Fig. 2), particularly since it is accompanied by a rapid increase in cell number (McLaren, 1976b; Snow, 1976). Second, marked regional differences in the frequency of mitoses have been detected once the primitive streak has formed. Following the consolidation of this gastrulation centre, Poelmann (1980) recorded a consistently higher mitotic index for lateral than for frontal ectoderm. Snow (1977), on the basis of analysis of serially sectioned material, has provided evidence for the existence of a proliferative zone slightly anterior to the distal tip of the ectoderm. This zone, which seems to comprise less than 10 % of the tissue at $6\frac{1}{2}$–$7\frac{1}{2}$ days p.c., was estimated to have a substantially shorter mean cell cycle time than elsewhere. Its significance has yet to be clearly established, although there is circumstantial evidence that it may contribute cells to the definitive ectoderm (Snow & Bennett, 1978).

The third and perhaps most striking feature of early postimplantation development of the primitive ectoderm is cell death. Cellular degeneration is more conspicuous in the primitive ectoderm than in any other part of the early conceptus, and can account for up to 10–20 % of cells in this tissue (Snow & Bennett, 1978; Poelmann, 1980). It is first seen transiently in the blastocyst before implantation (El-Shershaby & Hinchliffe, 1974; Copp, 1978), where, according to Handyside & Hunter (1984), it occurs mainly in the ICM rather than the trophectoderm. It is evident throughout the ICM-derived primitive ectoderm but shows regional differences in prevalence, being more common in areas with a lower mitotic index than in those with a higher one (Poelmann, 1980). Poelmann (1980) claims, furthermore, that degenerating cells often occur in small groups in the ectoderm that have roughly the same location in different embryos. However, no morphogenetic role has been ascribed to cell death in either the ectoderm or ICM. In addition, it is not clear how long degenerating cells persist in an identifiable form. In the absence of such information, the 'dead cell' indices obtained in the foregoing studies cannot be used to estimate the scale on which cell death takes place in the ectoderm. That this tissue can withstand a very substantial reduction in cell number is evident from experiments involving maternal administration of mitomycin C (Snow & Tam, 1979).

A fourth and more contentious aspect of ectoderm development concerns the occurrence of non-cycling cells. Poelmann (1980) argued that such cells were present in relatively large numbers in 7th day ectoderm, particularly in the frontal region of the tissue. However, failure of cells to incorporate [^{3}H]thymidine during a 2 h period of labelling *in vivo* does not constitute compelling evidence that they have ceased to cycle. Lengthening of G_1 and, or, G_2 could equally well account for such findings, particularly since no unlabelled cells were found in an earlier investigation in which embryos were exposed to [^{3}H]thymidine for longer (Solter, Skreb & Damjanov, 1971). All ectoderm cells in 8th day embryos evidently synthesize DNA (Beddington, 1981), so that failure to do so on the previous day may herald degeneration (Poelmann, 1980).

Finally, the process of gastrulation involves a complex sequence of alterations in spatial relationships between cells that are still only partially understood. The loss of epithelial organization of the ectoderm in the primitive streak (Spiegelman, 1976;

Batten & Haar, 1979) is likely to facilitate cell mixing in the nascent mesoderm. In addition, it has been found that the definitive endoderm of the foetus also originates from the primitive ectoderm (Gardner & Rossant, 1979; Gardner, 1982, 1985*a*), although where and when it does so remain uncertain (Beddington, 1985). Hence, in the upheavals attending gastrulation there is considerable scope for cell mixing both in the populations of cells that leave the primitive ectoderm to establish the mesodermal and endodermal germ layers, and in the one left behind that must re-establish continuity as the definitive ectoderm.

STUDIES ON MOSAICISM *IN SITU*

Perhaps the most surprising aspect of cell mingling in mammalian embryogenesis is that it occurs in cell monolayers as well as thicker tissue masses. It is true that considerable relative movement of cells during the course of a few hours can be demonstrated in certain monolayers maintained *in vitro* (e.g. see Garrod & Steinberg, 1975). Nevertheless, according to Honda *et al.* (1984), the mobility of cells is likely to be limited in cases in which elaborate intercellular junctional complexes that are characteristic of many types of epithelia are present. However, the relevance of these findings *in vitro* to the situation *in vivo* is uncertain, except possibly for mitotically inactive tissues like the retinal pigment epithelium, because they are based on analysis of non-dividing cell populations. Obviously, the ideal way of investigating epithelial growth would be by obtaining time-lapse records of living material *in vivo*. In the absence of means of achieving this, it is instructive to see what can be learnt about cell movement in growing epithelia by examining mosaic specimens using *in situ* cell markers. The postnatal intestinal epithelium and certain extraembryonic tissues of the conceptus are particularly convenient for such studies because of the availability of cell markers that enable them to be examined as whole-mount preparations.

Intestinal epithelium

Ponder and his colleagues devised a method for isolating large intact sheets of intestinal mucosa (Schmidt *et al.* 1984). On exposing such preparations to per-oxidase-conjugated *Dolichos biflorus* agglutinin (DBA) they found that the lectin binds to the surface of all epithelial cells of the small intestine and colon (with the possible exception of the ~1 % of entero-endocrine cells) in most but not all strains of mice that were tested (Ponder *et al.* 1985*a,b*). Whether DBA binding does or does not occur seems to be determined by alternative alleles at a single genetic locus (Ponder *et al.* 1985*a*). The genotypic specificity of lectin binding in chimaeric intestinal epithelium was established by use of H-2 antigens as independent *in situ* cell markers (Ponder *et al.* 1983, 1985*b*).

The principal novel finding made by Ponder *et al.* (1985*b*) using the DBA conjugate was that each intestinal crypt is invariably composed of cells of one or other genotype in chimaeric epithelium. Using allozymes of phosphoglycerate kinase as markers, these workers demonstrated that the absence of mosaicism in individual crypts was also the case in X-inactivation mosaics. It is therefore difficult to escape the conclusion that each crypt is normally of clonal derivation, at least from an early stage *post-partum*. Since crypts evidently proliferate by fission during postnatal growth of the intestine (Potten, Chwalinski & Khokhar, 1982), groups of adjacent ones may constitute a clone.

In an analysis of mosaicism in the intestinal epithelium using the DBA marker, patch size was expressed in terms of the number of contiguous crypts rather than cells of like genotype (Fig. 3). Patches of the minor component in preparations showing markedly unbalanced chimaerism were distributed widely but evidently non-randomly (Schmidt *et al.* 1985*a,b*). Furthermore, they were typically small, a large number consisting of individual crypts, and very few of many crypts. This resulted in a marked skewing in a plot of patch-size frequency that was found to fit a negative binomial rather than a geometric distribution (Schmidt *et al.* 1985*a*). This implies that, contrary to what has been assumed in most previous analyses of mosaicism, clone sizes are not normally distributed around the mean. Schmidt *et al.* (1985*a*) suggest that differential rates of proliferation of crypts, possibly exaggerated by the presence of genotypically dissimilar cells in chimaeras, may be an important factor in accounting for the observed distribution of patch size in the intestinal epithelium. In view of the fact that Whitten (1978) has also questioned whether mean patch size is a reliable statistic for evaluating mosaicism, it would be interesting to examine frequency distributions of patch size in other tissues in which individual cells rather than groups of cells constitute the basic proliferative unit.

Ponder and his colleagues have also used the DBA marker to visualize the continual cell movements that take place during turnover of the intestinal epithelium much more clearly than hitherto (Schmidt *et al.* 1985*c*). The migratory pathways stand out strikingly in mosaic regions of chimaeric intestine where individual villi receive cells from crypts of both genotypes. Such villi exhibit stripes of cells of variable width that typically extend from base to tip in more or less straight lines. The narrowest stripes, which presumably represent the contribution from a single crypt, may be interrupted distally, particularly in the duodenum rather than the ileum. Schmidt *et al.* (1985*c*) suggest that this may be due to the shedding of cells sub-apically, and that its more common occurrence in the duodenum than in the ileum may account for the typical tapering of villi in the former region. Evidently, the process of cell renewal in the intestinal epithelium entails directed movements of coherent sheets of cells generated in the crypts with very little mingling in the villi. Hence, once the epithelium has attained its definitive state, little if any clonal mixing seems to occur. Presumably, the major upheavals occur prenatally during the period when it builds up to a stratified tissue up to eight cells thick and then via secondary lumen formation and concomitant cell death, is converted into a monolayer (Trier & Moxey, 1979). It would be most instructive to extend analysis of mosaicism back to this period in order to understand how the basic pattern is established.

Extraembryonic membranes

The analysis of patterns of mosaicism in certain extraembryonic tissues is simplified by the fact that, unlike various epithelia of foetal origin including that of the intestine, they are monolayers throughout their existence. Mosaicism can be visualized readily in these tissues by exploiting a recently discovered null mutation at the *Mod-1* locus coding for cytoplasmic malic enzyme (Lee *et al.* 1980*a,b*; Johnson *et al.* 1981). Conditions of fixation and histochemical staining have been defined that give excellent discrimination between homozygous mutant and wild-type cells in the parietal endoderm, visceral yolk sac endoderm and amniotic mesoderm in whole-mount preparations (Gardner, 1984*b*, 1985*b*). Such preparations are less satisfactory for studying mosaicism in the mesoderm of the visceral yolk sac because it is multi-layered, and in the ectoderm of the amnion due to relatively intense staining of wild-type cells in the adjacent mesoderm.

So far, the *Mod-1* marker has been used mainly to study chimaerism produced by transplanting single primitive endoderm cells between blastocysts. The majority of the transplanted cells form clones that, despite varying considerably in size, are readily detected in the extraembryonic endoderm to which they are invariably confined later in development. Most of these clones are found in the parietal endoderm only, the remainder spanning both the parietal and visceral endoderm. They consistently yield strikingly different patterns of mosaicism in these two monolayers. Despite marked regional differences in abundance, the clonal descendants of the donor cell show extensive intermingling with host cells wherever they occur in the parietal endoderm (Fig. 4B). Indeed, in only one of a series of fields from several specimens that have been analysed did the pattern of mosaicism exhibit a marginally significant departure from that expected on the basis of random association of donor and host cells. This was the case both for fields in which the donor cells were in the majority as well as those in which they made a more modest contribution (Gardner, 1985*b*).

In striking contrast to their distribution in the parietal endoderm, clonal descendants of transplanted primitive endoderm cells that colonize the visceral endoderm show very little intermingling with host cells (Fig. 4B). In this layer donor cells occur almost exclusively in one or more irregularly shaped coherent patches, both in cloning experiments and in others entailing injection of multiple primitive endoderm or early ICM cells into blastocysts (Gardner, 1984*b*, 1985*b*). The patches tend to be both more numerous and smaller when present more distally than elsewhere, suggesting that fairly extensive re-modelling may take place in this region during formation of the definitive foetal endoderm and, or, subsequent expansion of

---

Fig. 4. A. Part of a histochemically stained chimaeric whole-mount preparation of parietal endoderm from a 12th day mutant conceptus that received a single wild-type primitive endoderm cell at the blastocyst stage. Note the extensive intermingling of wild-type cells that have stained for malic enzyme activity and mutant cells than have not. B. Chimaerism in the proximal visceral yolk sac endoderm of a mutant conceptus injected with a daughter pair of wild-type early ICM cells at the blastocyst stage. The donor cells are almost entirely segregated from the non-staining mutant host cells (from Gardner, 1984*b*).

the visceral yolk sac. Nevertheless, rarely are individual cells of one genotype entirely surrounded by those of the other in chimaeric specimens of visceral endoderm. When such cells are encountered, they almost invariably lie close to a patch boundary.

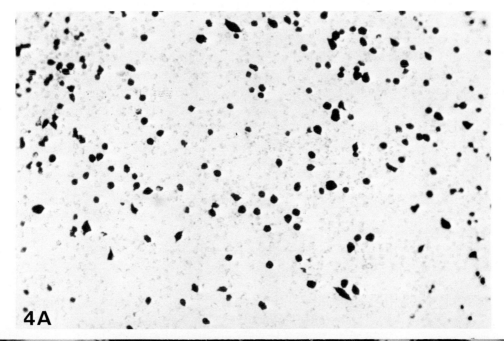

4A

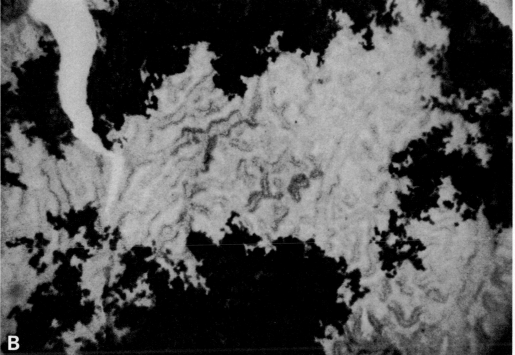

B

Chimaerism can be produced in the amnion by injecting single primitive ecto-derm cells into blastocysts, although these cells have a considerably lower cloning efficiency than their endodermal counterparts (Gardner *et al.* 1985). Progeny of the transplanted cells are often discernible in both the mesoderm and ectoderm of chimaeric amnia where, as in the case of the visceral endoderm, they are typically arranged in coherent patches (Gardner, 1985*b*; and unpublished observations). However, as well as being generally smaller, patches in both layers of the amnion tend to be more widespread and numerous than in visceral endoderm. These differences are presumably attributable to the fact that the amnion develops approximately 3 days later than this endoderm layer (Snell & Stevens, 1966), and originates from the primitive ectoderm in which coherent growth is not maintained. Patches in amniotic ectoderm bear no obvious spatial relationship to those in the adjacent mesoderm layer, and those whose boundaries are clearly discernible are not consistently larger than mesodermal ones. Since cell size is similar in the two layers, it appears that coherent growth is initiated at approximately the same stage in both. This is contrary to what might have been anticipated because, while the mesoderm layer originates from cells that appear to have undergone extensive rearrangement during gastrulation, the ectoderm layer is evidently formed by epithelial extension (Snell & Stevens, 1966).

The patterns of mosaicism observed in the different extraembryonic monolayers cannot be attributed to their selective colonization by donor cells that differ in clonal growth characteristics. This is demonstrated most convincingly by the fact that these patterns are also seen in cases where clonal descendants of single early ICM cells colonize all four tissues in the same conceptus (Gardner, 1984*b*, 1985*b*). Further-more, the almost total segregation of donor and host cells in the visceral endoderm and amnion is unlikely to be simply an artifact of chimaerism due to genotypic differences between them. Any such effect of genotype would obviously have to be tissue-specific because there are evidently no constraints on cell mingling in the parietal endoderm. Many of the experiments discussed above were done on embryos from mutant and wild-type mice derived from the same random-bred strain. It is therefore very improbable that clear-cut genetic differences between donor and host cells would have been conserved except at the *Mod-1* locus itself or loci closely linked to it. It is difficult to see how presence *versus* absence of cytoplasmic malic enzyme could affect cell mingling other than by an effect on cell viability. It is clear from the results of reciprocal blastocyst-injection experiments that mutant cells are not inferior to wild type in either cloning efficiency or clone size, and that they yield similar patterns of chimaerism (Gardner, 1984*b*, 1985*b*).

Hence, it is not unreasonable to assume that the spatial arrangement of donor and host cells in the various tissues is a valid index of their normal pattern of growth. Both the amniotic ectoderm and the visceral endoderm display the morphological characteristics of specialized epithelia (Padykula, Deren & Wilson, 1966; Scott, Ream & Pendergrass, 1982). It is therefore perhaps not surprising that they show strict coherent clonal growth. It is likely that the shapes of patches are determined primarily by the distribution and orientation of mitoses in these tissues. Indeed, even the presence of occasional isolated cells in the boundary regions between patches could be explained thus, rather than by active cellular migration (Lewis, 1973). The arrangement of cells in the parietal endoderm is entirely different, since this layer is discontinuous throughout its existence (Jollie, 1968; Enders, Given & Schlafke, 1978; Poelmann & Mentink, 1982; Hogan & Newman, 1984; Cockroft, 1985). However, there seems to be considerable variability in the extent of discontinuity, particularly in younger specimens (cf. fig. 2 of Poelmann & Mentink, 1982; and fig. 6b of Cockroft, 1985). It remains to be established whether this reflects regional or temporal differences in organization of the tissue (Cockroft, 1985), or its susceptibility to distortion during isolation and fixation. Nevertheless, gaps clearly exist between parietal endoderm cells, and specialized junctions have not been identified where they make contact (Jollie, 1968). There is obviously much greater scope for relative movement of cells in such a layer than in a continuous epithelium. The mesoderm of the amnion is also said to be discontinuous (Scott, Beam & Pendergrass, 1982). Therefore, it is perhaps surprising that cell mingling does not also occur in this layer. However, the amnia studied by Scott *et al.* (1982) were recovered on the 13th day of gestation. This is somewhat later than any of the chimaeric specimens that have been examined to date. Preliminary observations indicate that mesoderm cells form an almost uninterrupted layer in younger amnia (author's unpublished findings), although the nature of their intercellular contacts has not been elucidated.

CONCLUSIONS

In primitive endoderm cloning experiments, the donor contribution to the visceral endoderm may consist of a single large coherent patch (Gardner, 1985b). Hence, dispersal and mingling of clonally related cells does not take place in every tissue of the conceptus during early post-implantation development, although the situation in trophectoderm derivatives has not been elucidated. The extremely fine-grained mosaicism observed in the parietal endoderm is explicable in terms of the tenuous links and conspicuous gaps between its constituent cells. Consideration has been given to several factors that might contribute to breakdown of coherent growth in the primitive ectoderm, but too little is known at present about its morphogenesis to enable their relative importance to be assessed. As noted earlier, detailed analysis of patterns of mosaicism at sequential stages in development of this tissue using an *in situ* marker would be very informative, particularly if this could be coupled with the initiation of clones somewhat later than hitherto. In addition, more detailed knowledge of the growth kinetics of the tissue is needed, with as much emphasis being placed on quantifying spatial and temporal patterns of the death of cells as on their replication. Finally, examination of cell mingling in other developing organisms that are more amenable to observation in the living state might be very instructive. Recent application of *in situ* cell marking techniques to amphibian and teleost embryos has revealed that breakdown of coherent growth is not peculiar to mammals among vertebrates (Kimmel & Law, 1985; Jacobson & Klein, 1985). Interestingly, in these organisms too, it is around the time of gastrulation that clones tend to lose coherence. One very attractive prospect in using these lower vertebrate embryos is the possibility of monitoring clones repeatedly by the combined use of a fluorescent intracellular tracer and an imaging-intensifying device (see Kimmel & Law, 1985). Hitherto, the information obtained from *in situ* cell marking experiments has been limited to the initial location of the marked cell and the ultimate position of its surviving clonal descendants at analysis.

I thank Dr G. H. Schmidt for Fig. 3, and Dr Rosa Beddington, Miss Judy Green and Mrs Jo Williamson for help in preparing the manuscript. The support of the Royal Society and the Imperial Cancer Research Fund is gratefully acknowledged.

REFERENCES

BALAKIER, H. & PEDERSEN, R. A. (1981). Allocation of cells to inner cell mass and trophectoderm lineages in preimplantation mouse embryos. *Devl Biol.* **90**, 352–362.
BATTEN, B. E. & HAAR, J. L. (1979). Fine structural differentiation of germ layers in the mouse at the time of mesoderm formation. *Anat. Rec.* **194**, 125–142.
BEDDINGTON, R. S. P. (1981). An autoradiographic analysis of the potency of embryonic ectoderm in the 8th day postimplantation mouse embryo. *J. Embryol. exp. Morph.* **64**, 87–104.
BEDDINGTON, R. S. P. (1985). The analysis of tissue fate and prospective potency in the egg cylinder. In *Experimental Approaches to Mammalian Embryonic Development* (ed. J. Rossant & R. A. Pedersen). Cambridge University Press (in press).
CATTANACH, B. M. (1961). A chemically-induced variegated-type position effect in the mouse. *Z. VererbLehre* **92**, 165–182.
CATTANACH, B. M. & ISAACSON, J. H. (1967). Controlling elements in the mouse X chromosome. *Genetics* **57**, 331–346.
COCKROFT, D. L. (1985). Regional and temporal differences in the parietal endoderm of the mid-gestation mouse embryo. *J. Anat.* (in press).
CONDAMINE, H., CUSTER, R. P. & MINTZ, B. (1971). Pure-strain and genetically mosaic liver tumors histochemically identified with the β-glucuronidase marker in allophenic mice. *Proc. natn. Acad. Sci. U.S.A.* **68**, 2032–2036.
COPP, A. J. (1978). Interaction between inner cell mass and trophectoderm of the mouse blastocyst. I. A study of cellular proliferation. *J. Embryol. exp. Morph.* **48**, 109–125.
COULOMBRE, A. J. (1955). Correlations of structural and biochemical changes in the developing retina of the chick. *Am. J. Anat.* **96**, no. 1; 153–189.
COULOMBRE, A. J. (1979). Roles of the retinal pigment epithelium in the development of ocular tissues. In *Retinal Pigment Epithelium* (ed. K. M. Zinn & M. F. Marmor), pp. 53–57. Cambridge, Mass., U.S.A.: Harvard University Press.
DEOL, M. S. & WHITTEN, W. K. (1972). Time of X chromosome inactivation in retinal melanocytes of the mouse. *Nature, new Biol.* **238**, 159–160.
EL-SHERSHABY, A. M. & HINCHLIFFE, J. R. (1974). Cell redundancy in the zona-intact pre-implantation mouse blastocyst: a light and electron microscope study of dead cells and their fate. *J. Embryol. exp. Morph.* **31**, 643–654.
ENDERS, A. C., GIVEN, R. L. & SCHLAFKE, S. (1978). Differentiation and migration of endoderm in the rat and mouse at implantation. *Anat. Rec.* **190**, 65–78.
FEIN, A. (1985). Cell lineage evaluation in preimplantation mouse embryos by intracellular injection of IgG. *Gynecol. obstet. Invest.* **19**, 107–112.
FORD, C. E., EVANS, E. P. & GARDNER, R. L. (1975). Marker chromosome analysis of two mouse chimaeras. *J. Embryol. exp. Morph.* **33**, 447–457.
GARDNER, R. L. (1968). Mouse chimaeras obtained by the injection of cells into the blastocyst. *Nature, Lond.* **220**, 596–597.
GARDNER, R. L. (1982). Investigation of cell lineage and differentiation in the extraembryonic endoderm of the mouse embryo. *J. Embryol. exp. Morph.* **68**, 175–198.

GARDNER, R. L. (1984*a*). Mammalian chimeras – future perspectives. In *Chimeras in Developmental Biology* (ed. N. M. Le Douarin & A. McLaren), pp. 431–443. London: Academic Press.

GARDNER, R. L. (1984*b*). An *in situ* cell marker for clonal analysis of development of the extraembryonic endoderm in the mouse. *J. Embryol. exp. Morph.* **80**, 251–288.

GARDNER, R. L. (1985*a*). Regeneration of endoderm from primitive ectoderm in the mouse embryo: fact or artifact? *J. Embryol. exp. Morph.* **88**, 303–326.

GARDNER, R. L. (1985*b*). Clonal analysis of early mammalian development. *Phil. Trans. R. Soc. Lond.* B **312**, 163–178.

GARDNER, R. L. & LYON, M. F. (1971). X-chromosome inactivation studied by injection of a single cell into the mouse blastocyst. *Nature, Lond.* **231**, 385–386.

GARDNER, R. L., LYON, M. F., EVANS, E. P. & BURTENSHAW, M. D. (1985). Clonal analysis of X-chromosome inactivation and the origin of the germ line in the mouse embryo. *J. Embryol. exp. Morph.* **88**, 349–363.

GARDNER, R. L. & ROSSANT, J. (1979). Investigation of the fate of 4·5 day *post-coitum* mouse inner cell mass cells by blastocyst injection. *J. Embryol. exp. Morph.* **52**, 141–152.

GARNER, W. & MCLAREN, A. (1974). Cell distribution in chimaeric mouse embryos before implantation. *J. Embryol. exp. Morph.* **32**, 495–503.

GARROD, D. R. & STEINBERG, M. S. (1975). Cell locomotion within a contact inhibited monolayer of chick embryonic liver parenchyma cells. *J. Cell Sci.* **18**, 405–425.

GARTLER, S. M., GANDINI, E., HUTCHINSON, H. T., CAMPBELL, B. & ZECHHI, G. (1971). Glucose-6-phosphate dehydrogenase mosaicism: utilization in the study of hair follicle variegation. *Ann. hum. Genet.* **35**, 1–7.

GEARHART, J. D. & MINTZ, B. (1972). Clonal origins of somites and their muscle derivatives: evidence from allophenic mice. *Devl Biol.* **29**, 27–37.

GEARHART, J., SHAFFER, R. M., MUSSER, J. M. & OSTER-GRANITE, M. L. (1982). Cell lineage analyses of preimplantation mouse embryos after blastomere injection with horseradish peroxidase. *Ped. Res.* **16**, 111a.

GEHRING, W., ed. (1978). *Genetic Mosaics and Cell Differentiation: Results and Problems in Cell Differentiation,* vol. 9. Berlin: Springer-Verlag.

GREEN, M. D., ed. (1981). *Genetic Variants and Strains of the Laboratory Mouse.* Stuttgart: Gustav Fischer Verlag.

HANDYSIDE, A. & HUNTER, S. (1984). Cell division in the inner cell mass of the mouse blastocyst is restricted before implantation. *J. Embryol. exp. Morph.* **82 Suppl.**, 64.

HOGAN, B. L. M. & NEWMAN, R. (1984). A scanning electron microscope study of the extraembryonic endoderm of the 8th day mouse embryo. *Differentiation* **26**, 138–143.

HONDA, H., KODAMA, R., TAKEUCHI, T., YAMANAKA, H., WATANABE, K. & EGUCHI, G. (1984). Cell behaviour in a polygonal sheet. *J. Embryol. exp. Morph.* **83 Suppl.**, 313–327.

IANNACCONE, P. M., GARDNER, R. L. & HARRIS, H. (1978). The cellular origin of chemically induced tumours. *J. Cell Sci.* **29**, 249–269.

JACOBSON, M. & KLEIN, S. L. (1985). Analysis of clonal restriction of cell mingling in *Xenopus. Phil. Trans. R. Soc. Lond.* B **312**, 57–65.

JOHNSON, F. M., CHASALOW, F., LEWIS, S. E., BARNETT L. & LEE, C.-Y. (1981). A null allelle at the Mod-1 Locus of the mouse. *J. Hered.* **72**, 134–136.

JOLLIE, W. P. (1968). Changes in the fine structure of the parietal yolk sac of the rat placenta with increasing gestational age. *Am. J. Anat.* **122**, 513–532.

KELLY, S. J. (1975). Studies of potency of the early cleavage blastomeres of the mouse. In *The Early Development of Mammals. 2nd Symp. Br. Soc. Devl Biol.* (ed. M. Balls & A. E. Wild), pp. 97–105. Cambridge University Press.

KELLY, S. J. (1979). Investigation into the degree of cell mixing that occurs between the 8-cell stage and the blastocyst stage of mouse development. *J. exp. Zool.* **207**, 121–130.

KIMMEL, C. B. & LAW, R. D. (1985). Cell lineage of zebrafish blastomeres. III. Clonal analyses of the blastula and gastrula stages. *Devl Biol.* **108**, 94–101.

KLINGER, H. P. & SCHWARZACHER, H. G. (1962). XY/XXY and sex chromatin cell distribution in a 60 mm human foetus., *Cytogenetics* **1**, 266–290.

KOMINAMI, T. (1983). Establishment of embryonic axes in larvae of the starfish, *Asterina pectinifera. J. Embryol. exp. Morph.* **75**, 87–100.

LEE, C-Y., LEE, S-M., LEWIS, S. & JOHNSON, F. M. (1980a). Identification and biochemical analysis of mouse mutants deficient in cytoplasmic malic enzyme. *Biochemistry* **19**, 5098–5103.

LEE, C-Y., CHASALOW, F., LEE, S-M., LEWIS, S. & JOHNSON, F. M. (1980b). A null mutation of cytoplasmic malic enzyme in mice. *Mol. cell. Biochem.* **30**, 143–149.

LEWIS, J. (1973). The theory of clonal mixing during growth. *J. theor. Biol.* **39**, 47–54.

McLAREN, A. (1976a). *Mammalian Chimaeras*. Cambridge University Press.

McLAREN, A. (1976b). Growth from fertilization to birth in the mouse. In *Embryogenesis in Mammals*: *Ciba Fdn Symp.* 40 (new series) (ed. K. Elliott & M. O'Connor), pp. 47–51. Amsterdam: Elsevier.

MINTZ, B. (1962). Formation of genotypically mosaic mouse embryos. *Am. Zool.* **2**, 432 (Abstr. 310).

MINTZ, B. (1965). Experimental genetic mosaicism in the mouse. In *Preimplantation Stages of Pregnancy: Ciba Fdn Symp.* (ed. G. E. W. Wolstenholme & M. O'Connor), pp. 194–207. London: Churchill.

MINTZ, B. (1967). Gene control of mammalian pigmentary differentiation. I. Clonal origin of melanocytes. *Proc. natn. Acad. Sci. U.S.A.* **58**, 344–351.

MINTZ, B. & BAKER, W. W. (1967). Normal mammalian muscle differentiation and gene control of isocitrate dehydrogenase synthesis. *Proc. natn. Acad. Sci. U.S.A.* **58**, 592–598.

MULLEN, R. J. (1981). Mosaicism in the central nervous system of mouse chimeras. In *The Clonal Basis of Development* (ed. S. Subtelny & I. M. Sussex), pp. 83–101. New York: Academic Press.

OSTER-GRANITE, M. L. & GEARHART, J. (1981). Cell lineage analysis of cerebellar Purkinje cells in mouse chimeras. *Devl Biol.* **85**, 199–208.

PADYKULA, H. A., DEREN, J. J. & WILSON, T. H. (1966). Development of structure and function in the mammalian yolk sac. I. Developmental morphology and vitamin B_{12} uptake of the rat yolk sac. *Devl Biol.* **13**, 311–348.

PAPAIOANNOU, V. E. & WEST, J. D. (1981). Relationship between the parental origin of the X chromosomes, embryonic cell lineage and X chromosome expression in mice. *Genet. Res.* **37**, 183–197.

PAPAIOANNOU, V. E., WEST, J. D., BUCHER, T. & LINKE, I. M. (1981). Non-random X-chromosome expression in early mouse development. *Devl Genet.* **2**, 305–315.

PETTERS, R. M. & MARKERT, C. L. (1980). Production and reproductive performance of hexaparental and octaparental mice. *J. Hered.* **71**, 70–74.

POELMANN, R. E. (1975). An ultrastructural study of implanting mouse blastocysts: coated vesicles and epithelium formation. *J. Anat.* **119**, 421–434.

POELMANN, R. E. (1980). Differential mitosis and degeneration patterns in relation to the alterations in the shape of the embryonic ectoderm of early postimplantation mouse embryos. *J. Embryol. exp. Morph.* **55**, 33–51.

POELMANN, R. E. & MENTINK, M. M. T. (1982). Parietal yolk sac in early gestation mouse embryos: structure and function. *Biblthca anat.* **22**, 123–127.

PONDER, B. A. J., FESTING, M. F. W. & WILKINSON, M. M. (1985a). An allelic difference determines reciprocal patterns of expression of binding sites for *Dolichos biflorus* lectin in inbred strains of mice. *J. Embryol. exp. Morph.* **87**, 229–239.

PONDER, B. A. J., SCHMIDT, G. H., WILKINSON, M. M., WOOD, M. J., MONK, M. & REID, A. (1985b). Derivation of mouse intestinal crypts from single progenitor cells. *Nature, Lond.* **313**, 689–691.

PONDER, B. A. J., WILKINSON, M. M. & WOOD, M. (1983). H-2 antigens as markers of cellular genotype in chimaeric mice. *J. Embryol. exp. Morph.* **76**, 83–93.

POTTEN, C. S., CHWALINSKI, S. & KHOKHAR, M. T. (1982). Spatial interrelationships in surface epithelia: their significance in proliferation control. In *The Functional Integration of Cells in Animal Tissues: 5th Symp. Br. Soc. Cell Biol.* (ed. J. D. Pitts & M. E. Finbow), pp. 285–300. Cambridge University Press.

RANDS, G. F. (1985). Cell allocation in half and quadruple-sized preimplantation mouse embryos. *J. exp. Zool.* **236**, 67–70.

RAWLES, M. E. (1947). Origin of pigment cells from the neural crest in the mouse embryo. *Physiol. Zool.* **20**, 248–266.

RICCIUTTI, F. C., GELEHRTER, T. D. & ROSENBERG, L. E. (1976). X-chromosome inactivation in human liver: confirmation of X-linkage of ornithine transcarbamylase. *Am. J. hum. Genet.* **28**, 332–338.

SANYAL, S. & ZEILMAKER, G. H. (1977). Cell lineage in retinal development of mice studied in experimental chimaeras. *Nature, Lond.* **265**, 731–733.

SCHMIDT, G. H., GARBUTT, D. J., WILKINSON, M. M. & PONDER, B. A. J. (1985a). Clonal analysis of intestinal crypt populations in mouse aggregation chimaeras. *J. Embryol. exp. Morph.* **85**, 121–130.

SCHMIDT, G. H., WILKINSON, M. M. & PONDER, B. A. J. (1984). A method for the preparation of large intact sheets of intestinal mucosa: application to the study of mouse aggregation chimeras. *Anat. Rec.* **210**, 407–411.

SCHMIDT, G. H., WILKINSON, M. M. & PONDER, B. A. J. (1985b). Detection and characterization of spatial pattern in chimaeric tissue. *J. Embryol. exp. Morph.* **88**, 219–230.

SCHMIDT, G. H., WILKINSON, M. M. & PONDER, B. A. J. (1985c). Cell migration pathway in the intestinal epithelium: an *in situ* marker system using mouse aggregation chimaeras. *Cell* **40**, 425–429.

SCOTT, J. N., REAM, L. J. & PENDERGRASS, P. B. (1982). Developmental changes in the mouse amnion: A SEM study. *J. submicrosc. Cytol.* **14** (4), 607–612.

SIMPSON, E., McLAREN, A., CHANDLER, P. & TOMONARI, K. (1984). Expression of H-Y antigen by female mice carrying Sxr[1]. *Transplantation* **37**, 17–21.

SNELL, G. D. & STEVENS, L. C. (1966). Early embryology. In *Biology of the Laboratory Mouse,* 2nd edn (ed. E. L. Green), pp. 205–245. New York: McGraw-Hill.

SNOW, M. H. L. (1976). Embryo growth during the immediate postimplantation period. In *Embryogenesis in Mammals: Ciba Fdn Symp.* 40 (new series) (ed. K. Elliott & M. O'Connor), pp. 53–66. Amsterdam: Elsevier.

SNOW, M. H. L. (1977). Gastrulation in the mouse: growth and regionalization of the epiblast. *J. Embryol. exp. Morph.* **42**, 293–303.

SNOW, M. H. L. & BENNETT, D. (1978). Gastrulation in the mouse: assessment of cell populations in the epiblast of t^{w18}/t^{w18} embryos. *J. Embryol. exp. Morph.* **47**, 39–52.

SNOW, M. H. L. & TAM, P. P. L. (1979). Is compensatory growth a complicating factor in mouse teratology? *Nature, Lond.* **279**, 555–557.

SOLTER, D., SKREB, N. & DAMJANOV, I. (1971). Cell cycle analysis in the mouse egg-cylinder. *Expl Cell Res.* **64**, 331–334.

SPIEGELMAN, M. (1976). Electron microscopy of cell associations in T-locus mutants. In *Embryogenesis in Mammals: Ciba Fdn Symp.* 40 (new series) (ed. K. Elliott & M. O'Connor), pp. 199–220. Amsterdam: Elsevier.

SULSTON, J. E., SCHIERENBERG, E., WHITE, J. G. & THOMSON, J. N. (1983). The embryonic cell lineage of the nematode *Caenorhabditis elegans*. *Devl Biol.* **100**, 64–119.

SURANI, M. A. H. & BARTON, S. C. (1984). Spatial distribution of blastomeres is dependent on cell division order and interactions in mouse morulae. *Devl Biol.* **102**, 335–343.

TAKAGI, N. & SASAKI, M. (1975). Preferential inactivation of the paternally derived X-chromosomes in the extraembryonic membranes of the mouse. *Nature, Lond.* **256**, 640–642.

TARKOWSKI, A. K. (1961). Mouse chimaeras developed from fused eggs. *Nature, Lond.* **190**, 857–860.

TRIER, J. S. & MOXEY, P. C. (1979). Morphogenesis of the small intestine during fetal development. In *Development of Mammalian Absorptive Processes: Ciba Fdn Symp.* 70 (new series) (ed. K. Elliott & J. Whelan), pp. 3–20. Amsterdam: Excerpta medica.

WAREHAM, K. A., HOWELL, S., WILLIAMS, D. & WILLIAMS, E. D. (1983). Studies of X-chromosome inactivation with an improved technique for ornithine carbamoyl transferase. *Histochem. J.* **15**, 363–371.

WEISBLAT, D. A., KIM, S. Y. & STENT, G. S. (1984). Embryonic origins of cells in the leech *Helobdella triserialis*. *Devl Biol.* **104**, 65–85.

WEST, J. D. (1976a). Clonal development of the retinal epithelium in mouse chimaeras and X-inactivation mosaics. *J. Embryol. exp. Morph.* **35**, 445–461.

WEST, J. D. (1976b). Patches in the livers of chimaeric mice. *J. Embryol. exp. Morph.* **36**, 151–161.

WEST, J. D. (1982). X chromosome expression during mouse embryogenesis. In *Genetic Control of Gamete Production and Function* (ed. P. G. Crosignani & B. L. Rubin), pp. 49–91. New York: Academic Press.

WEST, J. D. (1984). Cell markers. In *Chimaeras in Developmental Biology* (ed. N. Le Douarin & A. McLaren), pp. 39–67. New York: Academic Press.

WEST, J. D., PAPAIOANNOU, V. E., FRELS, W. I., & CHAPMAN, V. M. (1978). Preferential expression of the maternally derived X chromosome in extraembryonic tissues of the mouse. In *Genetic Mosaics and Chimeras in Mammals* (ed. L. B. Russell), pp. 361–377. New York: Plenum Press.

WHITTEN, W. K. (1978). Combinatorial and computer analysis of random mosaics. In *Genetic Mosaics and Chimeras in Mammals* (ed. L. B. Russell), pp. 445–463. New York: Plenum Press.

ZIMMERMAN, J. (1975). The initiation of melanogenesis in the chick retinal pigment epithelium. *Devl Biol.* **44**, 102–118.

ZIOMEK, C. A. & JOHNSON, M. H. (1982). The roles of phenotype and position in guiding the fate of 16-cell mouse blastomeres. *Devl Biol.* **91**, 440–447.

J. Cell Sci. Suppl. 4, 357–381 (1986)
Printed in Great Britain © The Company of Biologists Limited 1986

HIERARCHICAL INDUCTIONS OF CELL STATES: A MODEL FOR SEGMENTATION IN *DROSOPHILA*

HANS MEINHARDT

Max-Planck-Institut für Entwicklungsbiologie, 7400 Tübingen, FRG

INTRODUCTION

As a rule, models do not have a good reputation in the field of developmental biology. They are mostly regarded as questionable speculations. Real understanding is believed to result only from a complete experimental determination of the system, including the detection and characterization of the molecules involved. However, pattern formation is a system property and the investigation of the molecules participating in this process alone will not reveal how the spatial organization is achieved. It would certainly be a major step if it could be experimentally determined that the accumulation of a particular substance at a particular position at a particular stage leads to the formation of a particular structure. But even then we would gain little insight into how this local accumulation has been generated. For this reason, most information about pattern formation has been obtained using a different approach: from perturbations of normal development. The subsequent changes in pattern provide an inroad into the system properties of the underlying pattern-forming system. Important concepts in developmental biology have been found in this way; for instance, that of the embryonic organizer and induction (Spemann, 1938) or that of positional information (Wolpert, 1969). By consideration of hypo-thetical mechanisms (models) possible molecular interactions can be found that are compatible with the observations. If these models are formulated in a mathematically precise way, the danger that the postulated and the actual properties of a model will disagree is much reduced. In addition, the comparison between model and experiment becomes more rigorous. If a model is in general successful, the discrepancies between model and experiment are especially valuable, since they enable an improvement of the paradigm to be made. We have proposed several models for a variety of developmental situations (Gierer & Meinhardt, 1972; Meinhardt & Gierer, 1980; see Meinhardt, 1982, for a review). Among these are models for the generation of gradients and of stripe-like distributions, which will be used as elements in the model to be proposed.

In the present paper, an attempt is made to formulate a model for a complex pattern-forming event: the segmentation of insects. The formation of the metameric pattern is an important step in the development of higher organisms, since in this process the primary anterior–posterior pattern is laid down. Insect segmentation has been studied intensively in order to approach this problem experimentally. The particular experimental basis for the model to be proposed (the perturbations in the sense mentioned above) are mutations affecting segment formation in *Drosophila* (Nüsslein-Volhard, 1977; Nüsslein-Volhard & Wieschaus, 1980). As shown below in detail, the richness of the observations rules out many mechanisms that appear reasonable, but which turn out to be incompatible with the data.

Four major classes of mutant phenotypes have been found (Fig. 1). (1) The (maternal) co-ordinate mutants that lead, for instance, to the bicaudal (double-abdomen) phenotype. (2) The gap mutants that show a contiguous pattern deletion of about seven segments. (3) The pair-rule mutants in which structures around the borders of every second segment are lost, thus forming half the normal number of segments. (4) The segment polarity mutants in which homologous pattern elements are lost in every segment and in which the remaining patterns show mirror-image duplications. The different classes of mutant phenotypes indicate that segmentation is achieved by a superimposition of several pattern-forming events.

Saturation mutagenesis experiments in *Drosophila* have shown that at least 25 genes are involved in segmentation and new classes of mutant phenotypes are not to be expected (Nüsslein-Volhard, Wieschaus & Jürgens, 1982). Four of these genes have already been cloned (Knipple *et al.* 1985; Poole, Kauver, Drees & Kornberg, 1985; Laughon & Scott, 1984; Ish-Horowicz, Howard, Pinchin & Ingham, 1985). By themselves neither the mutant phenotypes nor the sequence of the base-pairs of the genes involved in segmentation provide a direct understanding of how segments are formed.

The model proposed is capable of explaining the segmentation of both normal and mutant *Drosophila* embryos. It is based upon a few, molecularly feasible, interactions. The details of the model will certainly have to be modified according to the rapidly accumulating molecular data, but we hope that it provides a framework for understanding the experimental data.

FOUR STEPS IN THE FORMATION OF SEGMENTS

The basic proposal is that segmentation in insects is achieved in four major steps (Fig. 2). A gradient controls the overall anterior–posterior pattern. Under its influence, four cardinal (and two marginal) regions are determined. The border between any two cardinal regions acts as an organizing region for the initiation of the first truly periodic pattern, the double segments. The double-segment pattern results from the sevenfold repetition of four cell states. By an inductive process, these give rise to the periodic pattern of individual segments that results from periodic repetition of (at least) three cell states. According to this view, the formation of segments begins with a simple pattern (the gradient) and reaches the complex pattern by passing through a hierarchical series of intermediate patterns. Each pattern is more complex or has a higher spatial frequency than that by which it has been induced. In the segmentation mutants, only the pattern at the level of single segments is directly observable. For this reason I start with an analysis of what gives rise to single segments and of what determines their polarity. On the basis of this analysis I try to reconstruct the next pattern in the hierarchy: the double-segment pattern, which controls the pattern formation of single segments, and so on, unravelling the hierarchy of pattern-forming events in this way.

FORMATION OF THE PERIODIC PATTERN IS THE PRIMARY EVENT

Insect segmentation results from the superimposition of two patterns: on the one hand, a periodic pattern of segments separated by segment borders and, on the other hand, a sequential pattern of different segmental identities. From the phenotypes of *Drosophila* embryos that carry a deletion of the bithorax gene complex (Lewis, 1978) or a mutation in the *Pc* locus (Denell & Frederick, 1983), we know that the number of segments remains unchanged even if most segments have the same identity. Two essential conclusions can be drawn from these observations. First, the formation of a segment border does not depend on the juxtaposition of cells with two different segmental identities, for instance, of mesothoracic and metathoracic cells. Second, the formation of the correct number of segments is not achieved by a sequential addition of segments until the last segment, in *Drosophila* the eighth abdominal segment, is formed. Since in normal development the sequential and the periodic patterns are in perfect register, and since the periodic pattern of segments and segment borders remains intact even if the sequential pattern of segmental identities is abolished, we must conclude that the formation of the periodic pattern is the primary event. In other words, the genes that control particular segmental identities (for instance, the genes of the bithorax gene complex) must be at least partly under the control of the periodic pattern and not, for instance, under the direct control of a primary gradient. This view is supported by the phenotypes of the bithorax mutations. They cause a reproducible but incorrect activation of segment identities in relation to the unchanged periodic pattern. A particular segmental identity is activated too anteriorly or too posteriorly in comparison to the wild-type pattern but the shifts are particular units (segments or compartments) of the periodic pattern.

SEGMENTATION: THE PERIODIC PATTERN OF A QUANTITY OR A QUALITY?

Each segment of an insect body has a clearly defined anterior–posterior polarity. According to a well-known model for segmentation, the periodic pattern of segments results from a sawtooth-like distribution of a morphogen, i.e. from a periodically changing *quantity*. The concentration rises continuously over the length of a segment and shows an abrupt jump from high to low concentrations at the segment borders. Such a model accounts for many transplantation experiments with insect epidermis (see Lawrence, 1970).

On the other hand, very early in *Drosophila* development, cells of future (thoracic) segments segregate into anterior (A) or posterior (P) developmental pathways (Garcia-Bellido, Ripoll & Morata, 1973). The borders between the resulting anterior and posterior compartments are sharp. The decision between both pathways is all-or-nothing, no graded transition between A and P exists. This suggests that the pattern

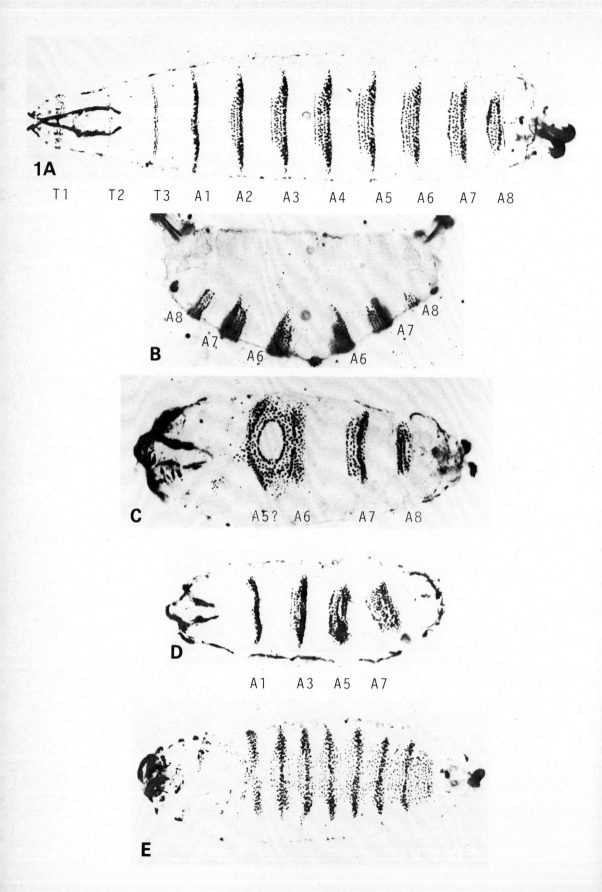

1A

T1   T2   T3   A1   A2   A3   A4   A5   A6   A7   A8

B

A8   A7   A6   A6   A7   A8

C

A5? A6   A7   A8

D

A1   A3   A5   A7

E

of segmentation results from the periodic pattern of different *qualities*. The model proposed is based on this stipulation.

MOLECULAR REQUIREMENTS FOR THE GENERATION OF CELL STATES

Compartmentalization is assumed to result from the position-dependent activation of selector genes (Garcia-Bellido, 1975). Their pattern of activation must consist of narrow stripes, 1–2 cells wide in the anterior–posterior direction and about 100 cells wide in the dorsal–ventral direction (Lohs-Schardin, Cremer & Nüsslein-Volhard, 1979). Our previous analysis permits predictions as to how the network of molecular interactions for the activation of selector genes is presumably constructed to enable stripe formation to occur (Meinhardt & Gierer, 1980). A periodic stripe-like activation of genes results if: (1) a set of genes exists (one gene for each stripe type, e.g. A or P) that directly or indirectly have an autocatalytic feedback on their own activation such that a gene, once turned on, will remain on; (2) the genes of the set compete locally with each other so that in a particular cell only one gene of the set will win the competition, while the other, alternative genes become suppressed; (3) the local activity of one gene depends on the activity of other genes of the set in the neighbourhood, i.e. the genes of the set activate each other over some distance. A pattern in the form of narrow stripes of different cell states is an especially stable configuration, since in stripes the long boundaries between different cell states permit an efficient mutual stabilization. The narrowness of a stripe ensures that no cell in a particular state is too remote from the other cell states required for its stabilization. The long-range activation of cell states may be realized molecularly by long-range self-inhibition of cell states, since in competing systems, a self-inhibition is equivalent to help for the competitors (see Appendix).

If in a particular cell a particular gene of a set is activated, we will term this cell as being in a particular cell state. If more than two cell states are involved, the mechanism outlined above is able to generate periodic sequences of cell states that possess polarity. For this, the mutual activation must be cyclic. For instance, a gene A activates gene B at long range, B activates C and C activates A. No wave-like prepattern, such as postulated in other models (Kauffman, Shymko & Trabert, 1978; Russell, 1985), is required for the periodic activation of genes.

We expect that genes involved in the formation of cell states are not cell-autonomous, since a mutation would not only cause the loss of a particular cell state but also a loss of help for the neighbouring cell states. Further, since the genes of the

Fig. 1. Examples of the four classes of mutations affecting segmentation in *Drosophila* (Nüsslein-Volhard, 1977; Nüsslein-Volhard & Wieschaus, 1980). A. Wild-type embryo. B. The coordinate mutant *bicaudal*: a mirror-image embryo with two abdomen. C. *Krüppel*, a gap mutant: a single region of about seven segments is missing (T1–A4). D. *hairy*, a pair-rule mutant: homologous pattern elements around every second segment border are deleted; the remaining denticle belts indicate the maintenance of the polarity. E. *gooseberry*, a segment polarity mutant. Certain pattern elements are deleted in every segment, the remaining pattern of each segment is duplicated. The polarity of the segments is lost. (Negatives of dark field photographs, kindly provided by Christiane Nüsslein-Volhard.)

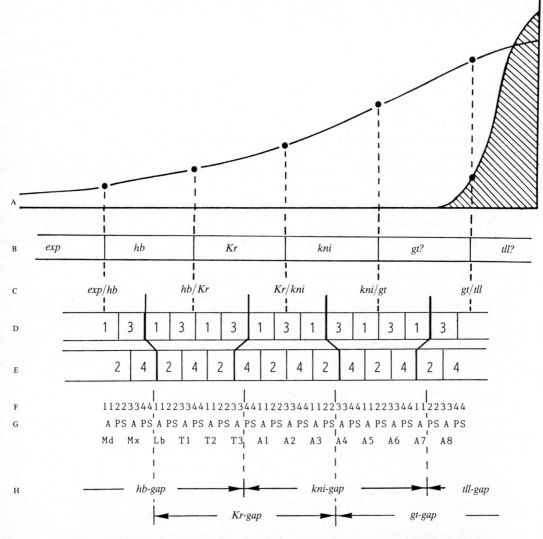

Fig. 2. The hierarchy of pattern forming events in the formation of segments. According to the model proposed, the primary anterior–posterior gradient (A) is assumed to activate four position-dependent cardinal genes (B) (*hb, Kr, kni* and possibly *gt*). Two further genes are activated at both margins (*exp* = expected, and possibly *tll*) (C). The borders between these cardinal region (*hb/Kr*...) organize a portion of 3·5 segments (enframed) of the two binary sequences ... 131 ... (D) and ... 242... (E). Both sequences are out of register. F. A sevenfold repetition of four cell states (... 1234 ...) represents the double-segment pattern. It results from the ... 131 ... and ... 242 ... sequence either by merging or by induction. A tentative assignment of the 1, 2, 3 and 4 cell states and pair-rule loci is given in Fig. 5. G. Each 1234 sequence induces two SAP sequences (see Fig. 4), the pattern of individual segments. H. The predicted gap sizes if one of the cardinal genes is lost. The actual gaps can be somewhat smaller due to an elongation of the 1234 sequences from both margins.

set compete with each other, the elimination of one competitor would lead to an enlargement of the regions in which the remaining genes are active. Many of the pair-rule mutations are not cell-autonomous (Ish-Horowicz *et al.* 1985; Wakimoto, Turner & Kaufman, 1984), in agreement with this model.

HIERARCHICAL INDUCTION OF CELL STATES

A sequence of cell states, once activated, can give rise to other and more complicated sequences by inductive processes. Induction should describe the turning on of genes required for a particular cell state by one or several other active cell states. A possible mechanism of generating more complex sequences requires cooperative interaction of two cell states at their boundary. For instance, a doubling of the periodicity will occur, if a sequence ... ABAB ... exists, and A and B together induce X of a ... XYX ... sequence, since each A state gives rise to two A–B borders. The result would be a sequence ... YXYXYXY .... In the following process of frequency doubling, the polarity of a sequence is maintained. If a four-member sequence ... DABCDA ... exists and D and A together, as well as B and C together, induce X, A induces Y and B induces Z, the resulting pattern consists of two sequences with three members each (XYZXYZ) occupying the same space formerly occupied by one ABCD sequence. This mechanism will be used for the transition of the double-segment to the single-segment pattern (see Fig. 10, Appendix). If the X, Y and Z genes have a stronger autocatalysis and compete *via* the same repressor as the ABCD genes, the activation of the XYZ sequence leads to the inactivation of the ABCD sequence. So, the induction of a new pattern can lead to erasure of the inducing pattern. On the other hand, different sequences of cell states can co-exist if the corresponding genes do not compete with each other. Applications and computer simulations of these pattern-forming mechanisms are given in the Appendix.

THE THREEFOLD SUBDIVISION OF SEGMENTS

In a periodic pattern of two cell states ... APAPAP ... , neither the position of the segment borders nor the polarity of the segments would be determined: it could be .../AP/AP/AP/... or ... A/PA/PA/P .... For this reason, I have proposed that segmentation results from the repetition of (at least) three cell states, to be called S, A and P (Meinhardt, 1982, 1984). The A and P regions would correspond to the well-known anterior and posterior compartments. The third cell state S is assumed to occupy the anterior-most portion of each segment and forms mainly the larval denticle belts. A sequence of three (or more) structures always has a defined polarity. According to this model, a segment border is formed whenever P and S cells are juxtaposed (... P/SAP/SAP/S ...). The juxtaposition between A and P is used in a similar manner to induce new structures: the A–P border is a prerequisite for the formation of legs and wings (Meinhardt, 1982, 1983).

The loss of any one of the three states would lead to an alternating pattern of the remaining two. We expect three basic types: ... SASASA ... , ... S/P/S/P/S/P ... and ... APAP .... All three patterns are symmetric, since each cell state would have the same neighbour on both sides. This loss of polarity fits well with the phenotypes of the segment polarity mutations mentioned above. In terms of the model, if state A is lost, the sequence .../S/P/S/P... remains. Since in the larvae the denticle belts presumably correspond to the hypothetical S region, while the naked regions belong to the A and P regions (Fig. 3), we would expect the same number of denticle belts (S) but twice the normal number of segment borders (P/S and S/P). This is what is observed in the mutation *patch* (Fig. 3; Nüsslein-Volhard & Wieschaus, 1980).

According to a widely accepted view, pattern duplications occur by intercalation along the 'shortest route' when a majority of the positional values are missing (French, Bryant & Bryant, 1976). According to the model I propose, duplications in the segment polarity mutants have a different origin, since two of the three positional values (i.e. more than half) remain present. Apparent duplications result from a loss of any of the three cell states, since all three are required for the development of polarity. No intercalation and thus no additional cell proliferation is expected to be involved in this duplication, a prediction that should be testable.

Direct support for the proposal that a third cell state separates the P and the A cells of two adjacent segments can be derived from an experiment described by Bohn (1974). He removed epidermal cells close to the anterior metathoracic segment border in cockroaches. After wound healing, he observed the formation of a supernumerary leg. In terms of the model, this corresponds to the removal of an S region (.../SAP/$_S$AP/... = .../SAPAP/...; the region lost is written as a subscript). This leads to a new P–A confrontation, which creates the prerequisite for leg formation (Meinhardt, 1984).

In summary, we postulate that segmentation results from the periodic repetition of (at least) three states, in contrast to the assumption that a pre-established segment is later subdivided into an anterior and a posterior compartment. The segment border is the product of the confrontation of two of the three cell states.

THE FOURFOLD SUBDIVISION OF DOUBLE SEGMENTS

If we assume that there are 14 segments and each segment consists of three stripes, the determination of 42 stripes altogether would be required. Such a detailed pattern can hardly be generated in a single step under the control of a morphogen gradient. The interactions between earlier, coarser subdivisions of the embryo are expected to generate this complexity by inductive processes. A candidate is the double-segment pattern discovered by Nüsslein-Volhard & Wieschaus (1980) with the pair-rule mutations. These mutations show periodic pattern deletions around the border of every second segment. Either posterior parts of the even-numbered and anterior parts of the odd-numbered segments are deleted, or *vice versa*. Thus, mutant phenotypes show half the normal number of segments and those segments that remain have normal polarity (except in *runt*). These mutations suggest a transient formation of a periodic pattern with a repeat length corresponding to two segments.

The explanation of these phenotypes requires the assumption of at least four cell states per double segment, for the following reason. If there were an alternation of

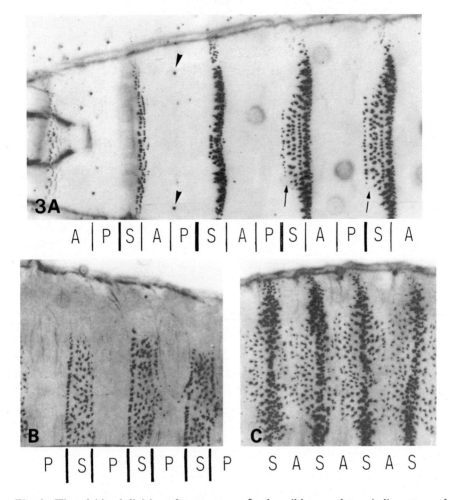

Fig. 3. Threefold subdivision of segments. A. In the wild-type, the periodic pattern of segments is indicated by the alternation of denticle belts and naked regions. The denticle belt forms the anterior third of a segment. The segment border is located between the first and second denticle row (arrows). The Keilin's organs (black dots, indicated by arrowheads) indicate the A–P border (Struhl, 1984). According to the model, segmentation results from the reiteration of three cell states … P/SAP/S …; the S region is assumed to form the denticle belt, the A and P regions together the naked region. A segment border is formed at P/S juxtaposition (thin denticles). The heavy denticles result from an S–A juxtaposition. Thus, the internal polar structure of a band is organized from the borders with the two (different) neighbouring regions. In the thoracic segments, the denticle belts seems to be restricted to the S–A border. B. The mutation *patch* (Nüsslein-Volhard & Wieschaus, 1980). According to the model, it results from a loss of the A cell states. In agreement, the remaining … S/P/S … sequence is a symmetrical pattern with twice the number of segment borders. The belts have thin denticles only. C. In the mutation *gooseberry*, the P state is presumably lost. (This prediction is in agreement with the observation of Martinez-Arias & Ingham (1985).) No segment borders but heavy denticles are formed. The precise location of the S–A border is not known. (Photographs kindly supplied by C. Nüsslein-Volhard.)

only two states, even (E) and odd (O) (i.e. a sequence ... OEOE ...) the loss of any one state would lead to the loss of the periodic character. In a three-state model, the loss of any one state would lead, as mentioned above, to symmetrical patterns, in contrast to the known phenotypes of the pair-rule mutants. Thus, we must assume (at least) four cell states (to be called 1, 2, 3 and 4) as the basic building blocks of a double segment. After the loss of one of the four elements, the remaining three elements still possess an unambiguous polarity, in agreement with the pair-rule phenotypes. For instance, if cell state 2 is lost, the (polar) sequence ... 134134... remains.

Each double segment has to direct the formation of two normal segments. In terms of the model, each ... 1234... sequence has to induce two ... SAP ... sequences. A possible mode is shown in Fig. 4: state 1 induces state A, state 2 induces S, and 1 and 2 together induce P. In a similar way states 3 and 4 induce the second APS sequence. In the following, I will show that this model provides a straightforward explanation of the main pattern alterations found in the pair-rule mutants. For example, if state 2 is lost due to a mutation ($... 341_234 ...$), the P and the S region of every other segment would be lost ($... AP/SA_{P/S}AP/S ... = ... AP/SAAP/S ...$). S is lost because it is directly induced by the state 2, and a P is lost because it is induced by the cooperation of states 1 and 2. Since S is assumed to form essentially the denticle belt, and A and P the naked region, we expect a normal-sized denticle belt (S) separated by a large

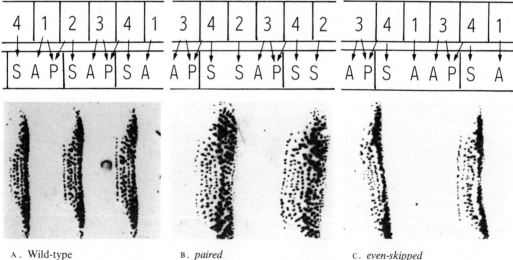

A. Wild-type   B. *paired*   C. *even-skipped*

Fig. 4. The double-segment (1234) to single segment (SAP) transformation and the pair-rule phenotypes. According to the model, one double segment consisting of a 1234 sequence gives rise to two SAP sequences. A possible mode is shown in A: 1 induces A, 2 induces S, and 1 and 2 together induce P. In a similar way 3 and 4 give rise to the second APS sequence. B. In *paired*, it is assumed that cell state 1 is substantially reduced or lost, and a sequence ... 342342... remains. Each second AP region is lost, which leads to the omission of a segment border and to the fusion of two denticle belts. C. In *even-skipped*, cell state 2 is assumed to be reduced or lost: the result is an omission of the P/S region and thus of a segment border in every second segment.

naked region (AAP). This is the phenotype of a weak allele of *even-skipped* (Fig. 4). (Possible reasons why in strong alleles of *even-skipped* the periodic character is lost will be discussed below.) An analogous phenotype, shifted by one segment, is expected if state 4 is lost.

If state 1 (or 3) is lost a deletion of the states A and P, i.e. the naked region, of every second segment will result ($\ldots 34_1234 \ldots = AP/S_{AP}/SAP/S \ldots = \ldots AP/SSAP/S \ldots$). The expected phenotype is a broad denticle belt (SS) of approximately the same size as the remaining naked region (AP). This corresponds to the phenotype of the mutation *paired*. In agreement with the model, the weaker allele *paired*[2] reveals that the loss of pattern elements starts in the naked region, and that pairs of two denticle belts fuse (Nüsslein-Volhard & Wieschaus, 1980).

The model describes correctly essential features of the pair-rule mutants. Two frames of deletions exist for both even- and odd-numbered segments. According to the model, a loss of state 1 or of state 2 leads to a deletion of the same segment borders (A1/A2, A3/A4 ...), but with different pattern deletions surrounding those borders, either $\ldots S_{AP}/S \ldots$ or $\ldots SA_{P/S}AP$. The alternative segment borders (... T3/A1, A2/A3 ...) are deleted if state 3 or 4 is lost and again, two different frames of deletion exist. The borders of pattern deletion do not coincide with segment borders. According to the model, primarily only two thirds of a segment are removed when one of the four cell states is missing. Thus, the resulting pattern cannot span from one segment border to the next. A deletion $P_{/SAP}/S = P/S$ should not occur. Since the pattern around the segment border results from a cooperative interaction of P and S cells, the loss of the one part, for instance the P state in a S_{AP}/S deletion, would lead to a complete loss of a border. The isolated formation of the pattern on one side of the border only should not occur.

From inspection of the phenotypes of the pair-rule mutants it has been concluded that a complete segment equivalent is lost, while the model predicts that only two thirds of a segment are deleted. The assumption of the threefold subdivision of segments reconciles both views. After deletion of two of the three cell states, two regions of the same type merge (S–S or A–A). Since the border in between is normally invisible and since the structure within a region (and thus its polarity) is determined by both neighbours, an ... SAAP ... pattern or an SSAP ... would be very similar to the normal SAP pattern, thus mimicking the deletion of a complete segment equivalent. There is, however, some evidence that composite bands are formed in the pair-rule mutants. For instance, Ish-Horowicz *et al.* (1985) and Nüsslein-Volhard & Weischaus (1980) have shown for *h* and *prd* with homoeotic *Ubx* transformations that the first abdominal denticle belt is in its anterior part of A1 character and in its posterior part of A2 character.

In situ hybridization experiments have shown that the pair-rule gene *fushi tarazu* (*ftz*) is transcribed in seven regularly spaced bands at the early blastoderm stage. Each band and interspace has the width of one future segment (Hafen, Kuroiwa & Gehring, 1984). Later in development, the regions of *ftz* activity shrink while interspaces extend (Martinez-Arias & Lawrence, 1985). The transcription of *hairy* (*h*) takes place in similar bands and combined *h* and *ftz* transcriptions have shown

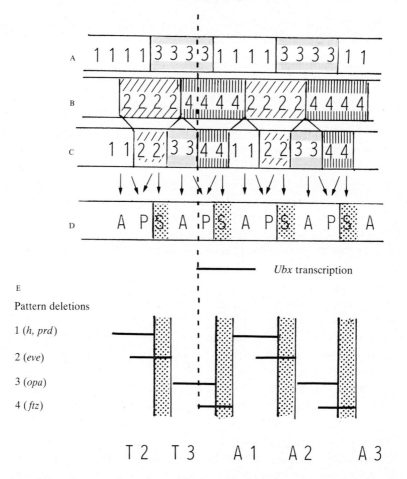

Fig. 5. Tentative assignments of the 1234 double-segment pattern (A–C) to the pair-rule loci. If we assume that cell state 1 is generated by *hairy* (*h*) and/or *paired* (*prd*), 2 by *even-skipped* (*eve*), 3 by *odd-paired* (*opa*) and 4 by *fushi tarazu* (*ftz*), we obtain a scheme compatible with the *in situ* hybridization experiments of Ish-Horowicz *et al.* (1985): the fourth *hairy* band begins one cell posterior to the P compartment of T3 (D, visualized by the *Ubx* transcription) while the third *ftz* band begins one cell anterior to it. A simultaneous *in situ* hybridization with a *ftz* and a *hairy* probe shows six regions in which *ftz/hairy* transcriptions overlap (4/1) while the first *hairy* and the seventh *ftz* band are isolated (see Fig. 2). This scheme is also compatible with the pair-rule phenotypes. The expected deletions are indicated by bars (E).

that the anterior-most *h* and the posterior-most *ftz* band are isolated, while between these extremes six bands exist in which *h* and *ftz* transcription partly overlap (Ish-Horowicz *et al.* 1985).

These findings can be integrated into the following scheme (Figs 2, 5). The first pattern of pair-rule gene activity consists of two sequences, each of which has two members (... 1313 ... and ... 2424 ...). Both are out of register. These two sequences give rise to the double-segment pattern proper, the 1234 sequence, either by merging or by an inductive process (in the latter case, the genes of the ... 131 ... and ... 242 ...

sequences on the one hand, and of the ... 1234 ... sequence on the other, would not be identical). A merging is necessarily connected with a shrinkage of the regions (see also computer simulations in Fig. 9, Appendix). A pattern such as that observed in the *h/ftz* hybridization experiment would indicate that *h* is involved in the generation of state 1, *ftz* in the generation of state 4. The observation that the (parasegmental) *Ubx* transcription starts one cell posterior to the third *ftz* band and one cell anterior to the fourth *h* band (Ish-Horowicz *et al.* 1985) enables us to determine the register of the 1234 SAP pattern (Fig. 5) and a tentative assignment of the *even-skipped* locus to state 2 and of the *odd-paired* locus to state 3 (Fig. 5). In general, the expected and observed pattern deletions are in agreement.

In *even-skipped* or *hairy* mutants, the pair-rule phenotype is expressed only if some gene function remains. In strong phenotypes the periodic character of the pattern disappears (Nüsslein-Volhard, Kluding & Jürgens, 1985; Ish-Horowicz *et al.* 1985). According to the model, a minimum gene function could be required for the merging mentioned above. If state 2 (*even-skipped*) is completely lost, the periodic pattern of the ... 242 ... sequence is lost, since state 2 can no longer compete with state 4, so that 4 (*ftz*) would become active in the whole area. The remaining pattern would be the ... 131 ... pattern. But since both 1 and 3 induce the same cell states (A of the SAP pattern) the (symmetrical) periodic pattern would be invisible. However, from the model, we expect that a periodic pattern would still exist. A possibility would be that the *hairy* and *odd-paired* loci are turned on alternatively.

The mutations in the locus *runt* are different from the other pair-rule mutations in that they cause symmetrical patterns. Experiments with gynandromorph embryos (which are partly *runt*, partly wild-type) have shown that *runt* is essentially cell-autonomous (Gergen & Wieschaus, 1985). That means that cells affected by *runt* obtain the same information as they would obtain in the wild-type embryo, but react differently. In terms of the SAP pattern, the runt pattern consists presumably of an ... P/SS/PAAP/SS/PA ... pattern instead of the normal P/SAP/SAP/SAP/S pattern (the patterns affected by *runt* are underlined). This would occur if state 3 behaved like state 2 and state 4 behaved like state 1. An explanation of why this (and only this) transformation into a symmetrical pattern occurs cannot at present be given.

The transition from double to single segments requires a particular cell state belonging to the single-segment sequence to be turned on at two positions in the double-segment pattern. For instance, the P state is activated by the 1/2 *and* by the 3/4 border. These two P-state activations need not be completely equivalent. This may be the reason why the mutation *engrailed* is expressed differently in every second segment (Nüsslein-Volhard & Wieschaus, 1980). The *engrailed* gene is active in the posterior compartment (Lawrence & Morata, 1976; Kornberg, Siden, O'Farrel & Simon, 1985).

In summary, the assumption of a fourfold subdivision of double segments is consistent with the pair-rule mutations since: (1) the pattern deletions lead to half the normal number of segments, due to the loss of every other segment border; (2) the remaining segments still have normal polarity; (3) pattern deletions never coincide with segment borders; and (4) two different frames of pattern deletion exist for both the even-numbered and the odd-numbered segments.

THE FORMATION OF CARDINAL REGIONS UNDER THE CONTROL OF A MONOTONIC GRADIENT

Previous work has shown that many experiments concerned with the overall anterior–posterior pattern of the insect embryo can be explained by the assumption of a monotonic gradient (see below). How can the spacing of a periodic pattern be under the control of a monotonic gradient? A link must be found between the primary anterior–posterior gradient and the periodic ... 1234 ... double-segment pattern.

The clue to this question can be found in the gap mutants discovered by Nüsslein-Volhard & Wieschaus (1980), in which a coherent region of about seven segments is missing. Three gap loci have been described: *hunchback* (*hb*), *Krüppel* (*Kr*) and *knirps* (*kni*). In *Krüppel*, the gap ranges from the first thoracic segment to the fourth abdominal segment (T1–A4, assuming that the inverted segment is A5, see Fig. 1c), in *knirps*, the missing segments are A1–A7. Thus, these gap mutants show a substantial overlap in the areas they affect. For instance, A1–A4 is missing in *Kr* and *kni*. There are several maternal mutants that behave similarly to the *knirps* mutation (Lehmann, 1985). So, a crude regionalization may already occur under the influence of maternal genes. The displacement between different gap regions is about 3·5 segments. For instance, the *hb* gap ends with T3, the next but one gap, *kni*, ends with A7, resulting in a shift of seven segments per two gap loci.

I propose that the wild-type function of the gap genes is to subdivide the embryo coarsely into a few cardinal regions, which, in turn, organize the double-segment pattern discussed above. The phenotypes of the gap mutations provide some hints of how this takes place. A straightforward explanation for the overlap of the gaps would be that it is not the cardinal regions themselves, but the borders between two cardinal regions, that control the formation of the double-segment pattern. Imagine a series of cardinal regions, I, II, III, IV ... . If, for instance, the II region is lost, the I/II and the II/III border would be lost. To explain the gap size and the displacement between the gaps mentioned above, I assume that each cardinal region has an extension of 3·5 segments and that each border organizes about 3·5 segments (see Fig. 2). Thus the model predicts that the region in which the gap gene is transcribed (3·5 segments, Fig. 2) is about half as wide as the affected region, the gap. This prediction has been found to be true. *In situ* hybridization experiments with the *Kr* gene (Knipple *et al.* 1985) show an early band of *Kr* activity, which is three to four segments wide. This is much smaller than the gap of seven segments caused by a loss of *Kr*. Also, the predicted location of the primary *Kr* transcript is correct: it begins with the T2 region and ends in the anterior A2 region (Fig. 2). If the assignment of the pair-rule genes and the 1234 pattern (Fig. 5) is correct, the model predicts further that the anterior *Kr* border is centered over a *ftz* band, while the posterior *Kr* border is in register with a *ftz* off–on border. Pertinent experimental data are not yet available.

An extension of the cardinal regions corresponding to four segments appears more reasonable and would also be compatible with the *Krüppel* data. However, the positions of the gaps predicted by such a model do not agree with the observations. The reason why the extension of a cardinal region corresponds to a non-integral multiple of a segment length (3·5) may be as follows. This facilitates the initiation of the ...131... and ...242... sequence with a half-segment phase shift, since the anterior border of a cardinal region would be in register with one sequence (e.g. ...131...) and the posterior border in register with the other (...242...).

To make the gap mutations fit a regular scheme, I have to postulate two additional loci that cause, if mutated, a deletion of the posterior-most segments. One of these 'gaps' should begin with A5, the other with A8 (Fig. 2). A comparison with known mutations suggests that the former gap may be related to mutations in the locus *giant* (*gt*), the latter to mutations in the locus *tailless* (*tll*) (Wieschaus, Nüsslein-Volhard & Jürgens, 1984; Jürgens, Wieschaus, Nüsslein-Volhard & Kluding, 1984). Mutations in the *tll* locus have not been classified as gap mutations since they delete marginal and not internal pattern elements. A second marginal region (*exp* in Fig. 2) is expected at the anterior egg pole. On the assumption that each cardinal border organizes about 3·5 segments, the expected gaps agree well with those experimentally observed: in *hunchback* the anterior segments up to T3; in *Krüppel* from T1 to the denticle band of A4 (assuming that the reversed segment is A5); in *kni*, A1–A7; in *tll*, A8 to *telson* and in *gt*, A5 and posterior segments.

Experimental evidence exists to show that the sequence of cardinal regions also determines the polarity of the double-segment pattern, and that the polarity of the double-segment pattern is not under the control of the primary gradient. In several gap mutations, some of the remaining segments close to the border of the gap show a polarity reversal. It is reasonable to assume that the (maternally determined) gradient remains unchanged, whether a (zygotic) gap mutatation is present or not. The polarity reversals that occasionally occur suggest that the polarity of the segments is not under the control of the (unchanged) primary gradient but results normally from the sequence of cardinal regions. If a cardinal region is missing, this transmission of polarity may fail. The transmission of polarity is presumably also the reason why the borders between the cardinal regions, and not the cardinal regions themselves, organize the double-segment pattern. The asymmetry of a border between two regions of gene expression contains polarity information while a region of gene activity alone does not. According to the model, one reason for a polarity reversal would be an incorrect merging of the 131–242 sequence, leading to a 2143 instead of a 1234 sequence, the former having reversed polarity. For the transmission of polarity a particular cardinal border must activate at least the genes coding for two neighbouring regions (see Fig. 9, Appendix).

THE PRIMARY ANTERIOR–POSTERIOR GRADIENT

How is the sequence of cardinal regions determined? The phenotype of the *bicaudal* mutation restricts conceivable mechanisms. In eggs laid by a *Drosophila* female that carries the *bicaudal* mutation, embryos develop with high frequency the double-abdomen malformation: instead of head and thorax, a second abdomen is formed, resulting in a symmetrical embryo (Nüsslein-Volhard, 1977; and Fig. 1B). Double-abdomen embryos can be induced in other insects by a variety of manipulations (see Sander, 1976), indicating a general instability that can lead to a switch to the symmetrical pattern. The bicaudal phenotype rules out the assumption that the terminal regions (head and abdomen) are fixed in the egg by maternal determinants and that the remaining regions are filled in by intercalation, since in the *bicaudal* embryo both terminal regions are the same and no intercalation would be possible. Also, a mechanism with three predetermined regions (anterior, central and posterior) is unlikely, since then one would always expect the same central pattern element at the plane of symmetry. This is in contrast to the observed variability. The *bicaudal* phenotype also argues against models of segmentation based on standing waves in the egg, since the number of segments is reduced in bicaudal embryos. The altered number of segments also indicates that the bicaudal phenotype does not result from a homoeotic transformation of anterior into posterior segments. These problems are resolved if one assumes that the anterior–posterior axis is organized by a gradient that has its high point at the posterior egg pole. The gradient can be generated by the interaction of a short-ranging autocatalytic 'activator' and its long-ranging antagonist, the inhibitor (Gierer & Meinhardt, 1972; Meinhardt, 1977). The smoothly graded inhibitor is a candidate for the morphogen. The inhibitor would therefore have two functions: first, to restrict the area in which autocatalysis can take place, i.e. to restrict the source area; and second, to provide positional information. Low concentration of inhibitor would cause head structures and high concentration would lead to abdominal structures.

The gradient model and its generation by autocatalysis and long-range inhibition provide a straightforward explanation for the occurrence of the bicaudal phenotype. Inhibition emanating from the posterior egg pole may become too weak at the anterior pole to suppress the onset of autocatalysis. A second source would then appear at the anterior pole. The result would be symmetrical positional information, which would determine abdominal structures at both ends (Fig. 6). The model agrees with the observation that the plane of mirror symmetry in *bicaudal* embryos occurs at a structure that is not in the middle but located more posteriorly in the wild-type. If each egg pole carries a morphogen source, the morphogen concentration in the centre is elevated. Therefore, we expect that the plane of symmetry is formed by structures that normally form in the posterior half of the egg. The expected shallower gradient in bicaudal embryos would also have the consequence that fewer segments are determined, in agreement with observation.

From the analysis given above it can be concluded that the gradient does not determine the sequence of segments directly, but that it organizes the relatively coarse pattern of cardinal regions, and that the mutual interactions of the cardinal regions lead to segmentation proper. This reconciles the gradient model with observations by Vogel (1977, 1978). He concluded on the basis of his careful ligation experiments that insect segmentation is controlled by short-range inductive processes of at least three cytoplasmatic determinants and not by a gradient. In terms of the model I propose, the segments formed after a ligation depend not only on the change in the gradient but also on whether the ligation interrupts the juxtaposition of particular cardinal regions. For instance, Vogel (1977) found that ligation at a particular position leads to an especially large gap comprising the first abdominal segments. That is the region organized (according to our model) by the *Kr/kni* border (Fig. 2).

Occasionally, asymmetrical *bicaudal* embryos are formed (see Fig. 8, Appendix). In the extreme case, only head structures are replaced by abdominal structures. Such a pattern appears to contradict any gradient model. However, a symmetrical pattern of segmentation will result only if the switch from the polar to symmetrical pattern

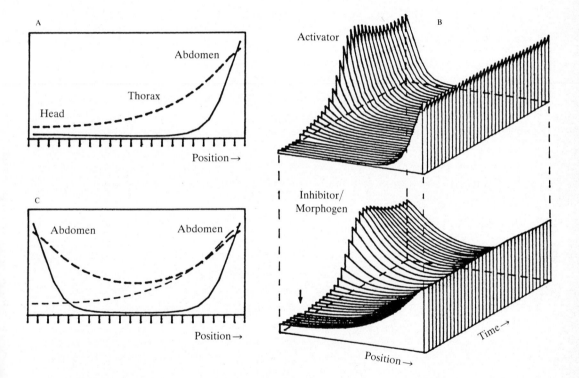

Fig. 6. A gradient model for the overall organization and the formation of a double-abdomen (*bicaudal*) embryo. A. The normal pattern is assumed to be under the control of a gradient, which has its high point at the posterior pole (Meinhardt, 1977). The gradient is generated by a short-ranging autocatalytic substance, the activator (——) and its long-ranging antagonist, the inhibitor (– – –). The inhibitor acts in addition as a morphogen by activating the cardinal genes (see Figs 2, 7, 8). B. If the inhibition at the anterior pole becomes too low (arrow), a second activator maximum can appear. C. A symmetrical morphogen distribution results, which corresponds to the *bicaudal* phenotype (see Fig. 1B). In the centre, the concentration rises, which leads to the formation of more posterior structures at the plane of symmetry, in comparison to the central structures found in the fate map of the wild-type.

takes place early enough so that all cells (or nuclei) can still respond to the changed signal. In the head region the difference between the old and the new signal is highest. During a critical period only here could a reprogramming of an anterior into a posterior cardinal region be possible. A simulation of the resulting asymmetrical pattern of cardinal regions is shown in Fig. 8 (Appendix). In the beetle *Callosobruchus*, van der Meer (1984) found partial double abdomens, restricted to one side of the embryo or to a narrow stripe. I expect that in these cases only the cells in the affected region were still able to respond to the changed positional information and formed a new pattern of cardinal regions. In the remaining embryo, the wild-type pattern is formed despite the fact that an overall change of positional information has taken place. In these cells the determination of the cardinal regions was no longer reversible.

DISCUSSION

In the model described above, I have shown that a reliable subdivision of a large area into a precise number of repetitive subunits (segments) can be achieved by several hierarchically ordered sequences of cell states coupled to each other by overlapping inductive interactions. The first step involves the generation of an overall anterior–posterior gradient, which determines the cardinal regions. Through cooperative interactions at their boundaries the embryo becomes subdivided into repetitive sequences of four cell states (termed 1, 2, 3 and 4). Each 1234 sequence corresponds to a double-segmental unit. Finally, each double-segment becomes subdivided into two single segments. Each segment consists of (at least) three cell states (termed P, S and A).

On the assumption that each cell state corresponds to the activation of a gene, four distinct classes of mutant phenotypes are expected. A change in the gradient can lead to symmetrical patterns or to a loss of the terminal regions (Nüsslein-Volhard *et al*. 1982; Nüsslein-Volhard, 1977). The loss of any cardinal region would lead to a large and unique gap of about seven segments, as seen in the gap mutants. The loss of any of the four cell states of the double-segment pattern would cause the omission of structures around every second segment border in two major frames of deletion, as seen in the pair-rule mutants. The loss of any of the three cell states of which a single segment is composed would produce a symmetrical pattern, in agreement with the segment polarity mutants. The details of this model should be approached with caution. For instance, the assignment of particular loci to particular functions in the model is certainly premature. It is done here to illustrate the general idea. These details will certainly have to be changed in the light of forthcoming experiments showing the mutual dependence of the gene activities.

For several problems, the model cannot at present provide an unambiguous answer. For instance, is the merging of the two sequences essential or does the SAP induction occur from the …131…–…242… pattern? Are the genes of the …1313… and …2424… sequence really the same as in those of the …1234… sequence? (if not, the …1234… sequence would result from an induction, not from a merging). What is the function of *runt*? Why do so many loci exist that seem to be involved in the P region (*hh, ci*^D*, gsb, fused, wg*; Nüsslein-Volhard & Wieschaus, 1980; Martinez-Arias & Ingham, 1985)? Why do all these mutants have slightly different phenotypes? Why does a mutation of a gene that is certainly involved in the P state, *engrailed*, not lead to mirror-image patterns?

The activation of the homoeotic genes, responsible for the identity of the segments, has not yet been incorporated in the model. I expect that the cardinal genes play an essential role in this process. However, a straightforward combinational scheme is not possible, since any pair-rule gene is active at two positions in a particular cardinal region (see Fig. 2). This ambiguity can be resolved if the distances to neighbouring cardinal regions are used as additional clues.

The model proposed differs in many aspects from other models (Kauffman, Shymko & Trabert, 1978; Russell, 1985). It is not a standing-wave mechanism, so the model can easily be applied to insects in which the embryo proper is formed very asymmetrically in the egg, e.g. close to the posterior pole (Krause, 1939). The subdivisions we assume are, as a rule, not binary but involve three or four elements. Periodic patterns with three or more elements necessarily have an intrinsic polarity. Except for the primary gradient, no separation between positional information, on the one hand, and the activation of genes on the other, is assumed. The spatial periodic pattern of gene activity results directly from the interactions of the genes and not from a wave-like prepattern.

In many insect species, the segments are formed sequentially in an anterior–posterior order (see Sander, 1976). This may be a more elementary form of segmentation. Only a fraction of the molecular machinery postulated in the model is required for those insects, i.e. a single threshold and the mutual activation mechanism. For instance, if a field grows at the posterior end and the 1234 pattern-forming system is active, new cell states are added in the correct order whenever the last cell state becomes too large. So, minor changes in the model are sufficient to account for the two modes of segmentation that appear to be very different. According to this view, the global subdivision into cardinal regions, as seen in *Drosophila*, is a means by which time-consuming sequential segment formation can be substituted by a more rapid simultaneous segment formation.

APPENDIX

Computer simulations

Some computer simulations demonstrate that the model proposed is indeed able to generate a pattern of segmentation. In these simulations, the mechanism of long-range activation and of space-dependent gene activation has been used. Mathematical formulations of these types of interaction can be found elsewhere (Meinhardt & Gierer, 1980; Meinhardt, 1982). They have the form of coupled differential equations. These equations describe the concentration change per time unit, for instance, of a gene product as a function of the concentration of the other substances involved.

In the computer simulations, the time course of a pattern is calculated by integration of these equations. Starting from some initial condition (as a rule a uniform distribution) a concentration change in a short time interval is calculated and added to the momentary concentration. In this way, one obtains the concentration at a somewhat later time, which permits the calculation of the next change, and so on. In this Appendix, some of the many intermediate patterns and the final patterns are shown in a graphical form. The density of dots indicates the concentrations of gene products. Examples of computer programs for such calculations have been published (Meinhardt, 1982).

Common to all of these simulations is the assumption that the genes have a positive feedback on their own expression, i.e. that they are autocatalytic. Further, the genes of a set (I–VI, 1–4 or SAP) compete with each other so that in a particular cell only one of the genes can remain active.

For the gradient-dependent activation of the cardinal genes (Figs 7, 8) it is assumed that the morphogen enhances the cardinal gene activation in a monomolecular

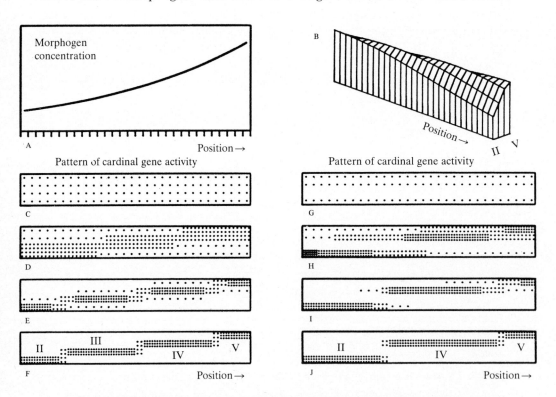

Fig. 7. Regional activation of the cardinal genes II … V under control of the gradient. The gradient (A) provides space-dependent advantages (B) for particular genes. C–F. Stages in the activation: a particular cardinal gene (II–V, corresponding to *hb, Kr, kni* and perhaps *gt*) wins the competition in a particular region and loses in others. The density of dots indicates gene activity. Regions in which particular cardinal genes are active develop. At the borders, an abrupt switch from one gene activity to the next takes place. G–J. Pattern of cardinal gene activities if gene III is lost by a mutation. Regions II and IV extend into the area in which gene II is normally active.

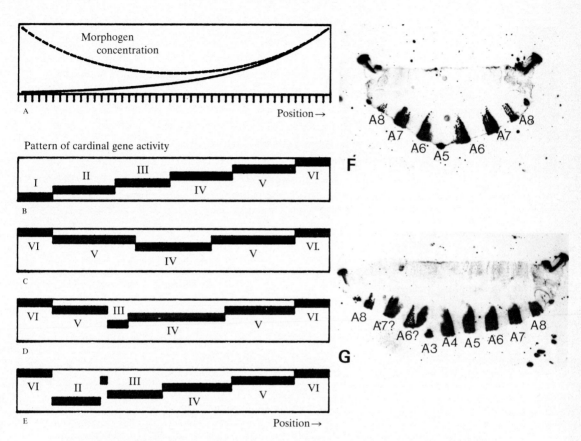

Fig. 8. Double-abdomen formation: symmetrical and asymmetrical patterns of cardinal gene activation. A. Polar and symmetrical morphogen distribution (see Fig. 6). B. A normal (polar) pattern of cardinal gene activity. C. If the switch to symmetrical pattern occurs early, the resulting pattern of cardinal gene activation is also symmetrical. D,E. Asymmetrical patterns of cardinal gene activity can arise if the switch to symmetrical pattern occurs when the activation of cardinal genes is in progress. Only the anterior-most cells may switch to different gene activities, since on the anterior side, the difference between old and new positional information is highest. F,G. For comparison, a normal (F) and an asymmetrical (G) *bicaudal* embryo (Nüsslein-Volhard, 1977). Note that the pattern discontinuity in G is not repaired by intercalation.

form but inhibits in a bimolecular form. The activation and inhibition are balanced for the different cardinal genes at different morphogen concentrations. This leads to a smooth gradient-dependent optimum for each cardinal gene (Fig. 7B). Owing to the competition, particular cardinal genes become fully activated in regions surrounding these optima and become suppressed elsewhere, despite the fact that no thresholds exist. This becomes clearly visible in the simulation in which one of the cardinal genes is lost (Fig. 7G–J). Both neighbouring genes extend into the region in which the affected gene is normally active.

Fig. 8 shows the pattern of the cardinal gene activities, on the assumption that a switch from polar to symmetrical positional information has occurred (see Fig. 6).

The result can be an asymmetrical pattern, in agreement with the asymmetrical phenotypes observed occasionally in *bicaudal* embryos.

In the simulation of the 1234 double-segment pattern, in addition to autocatalysis and competition, it is assumed that genes that code for neighbouring regions have some cross-activation, resulting, for instance, from the physical similarity of the molecules. Further, the area in which a particular gene is active is restricted by a long-ranging self-inhibitory substance. (In competing systems, long-range self-inhibition is equivalent to long-range help by a competitor.) Both features, cross-activation and self-limitation, provide that system with self-organizing properties. Partially organized sequences that occasionally show polarity reversal can appear under the influence of random fluctuations. To obtain a regular and reproducible pattern, the ...412341... pattern must be initiated at pre-determined points. According to the model, these points are the borders of the cardinal regions. In the

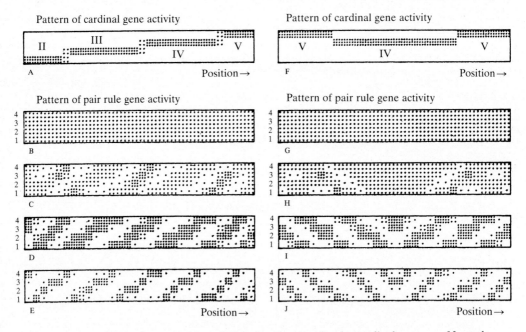

Fig. 9.   Stages in the activation of the pair-rule genes by the cardinal genes. A. Normal pattern of the cardinal genes (II–V, see Fig. 7). B–C. The borders between cardinal genes activate the pair-rule genes (1–4). For instance, the II/III border activates a 341 sequence. These are the first regions of increased gene activities (C). The polarity residing in the sequence of cardinal genes is transmitted. D. If states 1 and 3 compete *via* the same repressor and this repressor is different from the repressor by which states 2 and 4 compete, the 1 and 3 regions as well as the 2 and 4 regions are complementary. The phase shift is achieved only by the mode of ...131... and ...242... induction at the borders of the cardinal regions. If the 131 and 242 sequences compete *via* a common repressor (or if both repressors have a physical similarity), both sequences merge. The extension of an active region shrinks in such a way that in a particular cell only one of the 1, 2, 3 or 4 genes would be active. Such merging would stabilize the phase shift between both sequences. F. If the pattern of the cardinal genes is symmetrical (*bicaudal* phenotype, Figs 6, 8) the resulting 1234 pattern (G–J) is a mirror image too. The polarity resident in the cardinal borders is transferred to the pattern of pair-rule genes.

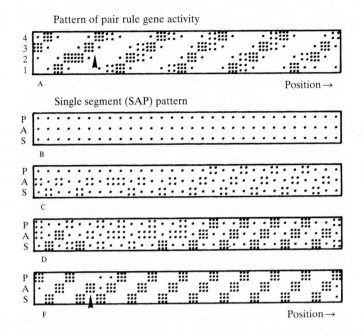

Fig. 10. Induction of the single-segment pattern (cell states S, A and P) by the double-segment pattern (1234 pattern, see also Fig. 4). A. The pattern of pair-rule gene activity (see Fig. 9). B–F. Stages in the activation of the SAP pattern. The S, the A and the P cell states are activated at two different positions of the 1234 pattern: A at 1 and 3, S at 2 and 4, and P at the 1/2 and 3/4 borders. The result is a doubling of the spatial frequency such as is required for the double segment to single segment transition. If not enough cells carry a particular activation in the double-segment pattern the resulting single-segment pattern may contain a locally symmetrical pattern (arrowheads). In the real system, too-narrow regions of gene activities are expected if the autocatalysis of a gene is reduced due to a mutation.

simulation (Fig. 9) it has been assumed that, for instance, the II/III border activates the genes 3, 4 and 1 (corresponding to the *hb/Kr* border, Fig. 2). Cell state 3 has to appear at the anterior side, 1 at the posterior side of the border and 4 to be centred over the border. This is achieved by an activation of gene 4 if II *and* III molecules are present in equally high amounts, 3 is activated by a higher concentration of II and a lower (but non-zero) concentration of III, and so on. In this way, the polarity is transmitted from the sequence of cardinal genes to the double-segment pattern. This is clearly visible in the double-segment pattern formed under the influence of a symmetrical pattern of cardinal gene activity (*bicaudal* phenotype, Fig. 9F–J). Both cardinal borders have opposite polarities (V/IV *versus* IV/V) and the resulting double-segment pattern has opposite polarity in the anterior and posterior halves.

The simulations are not yet a perfect translation of the model. In the simulation, a region smaller than 3·5 segments is directly initiated by a cardinal border. The remaining segments are formed by the elongation of these incipient sequences. In the real system, such an elongation seems to be suppressed, otherwise a gap would be filled with time from both sides.

The simulation of the conversion of the double-segment pattern into the single-segment pattern (Fig. 10) is based on a similar mechanism. Since this process requires a frequency doubling, each element of the single-segment pattern is activated at two different positions in the double-segment pattern (see Fig. 4).

I thank Herbert Jäckle, Gerd Jürgens, Ruth Lehmann, Christiane Nüsslein-Volhard and Eric Wieschaus for many critical discussions of their published and unpublished results. I thank Jonathan Raper for a critical reading of the manuscript. The photographs of the mutants have been kindly provided by Christiane Nüsslein-Volhard.

REFERENCES

BOHN, H. (1974). Extent and properties of the regeneration field in the larval legs of cockroaches (*Leucophaea maderae*). I. Extirpation experiments. *J. Embryol. exp. Morph.* **31**, Part 3, 557–572.

DENELL, R. E. & FREDERICK, R. D. (1983). Homoeosis in *Drosophila*: A description of the polycomb lethal syndrome. *Devl Biol.* **97**, 34–47.

FRENCH, V., BRYANT, P. J. & BRYANT, S. V. (1976). Pattern regulation in epimorphic fields. *Science* **193**, 969–981.

GARCIA-BELLIDO, A. (1975). Genetic control of wing disc development in *Drosophila*. In *Cell Patterning. Ciba Fdn Symp.* vol. 29, pp. 161–182. Amsterdam: Associated Scientific Publishers.

GARCIA-BELLIDO, A., RIPOLL, P. & MORATA, G. (1973). Developmental compartmentalization of the wing disk of *Drosophila*. *Nature, new Biol.* **245**, 251–253.

GERGEN, J. P. & WIESCHAUS, E. F. (1985). The localized requirements for a gene affecting segmentation in *Drosophila*: Analysis of larvae mosaic for *runt*. *Devl Biol.* **109**, 321–335.

GIERER, A. & MEINHARDT, H. (1972). A theory of biological pattern formation. *Kybernetik* **12**, 30–39.

HAFEN, E., KUROIWA, A. & GEHRING, W. J. (1984). Spatial distribution of transcripts from the segmentation gene *fushi tarazu* during *Drosophila* embryonic development. *Cell* **37**, 833–841.

ISH-HOROWICZ, D., HOWARD, K. R., PINCHIN, S. M. & INGHAM, P. W. (1985). Molecular and genetic analysis of the *hairy* locus in *Drosophila*. *Cold Spring Harbour Symp. quant. Biol.* **50** (in press).

JÜRGENS, G., WIESCHAUS, E., NÜSSLEIN-VOLHARD, C. & KLUDING, H. (1984). Mutations affecting the pattern of the larval cuticle in *Drosophila melanogaster*. II. Zygotic loci on the third chromosome. *Wilhelm Roux Arch. EntwMech. Org.* **193**, 283–295.

KAUFFMAN, S. A., SHYMKO, R. M. & TRABERT, K. (1978). Control of sequential compartment formation in *Drosophila*. *Science* **199**, 259–270.

KNIPPLE, D. C., SEIFERT, E., ROSENBERG, U. B., PREISS, A. & JÄCKLE, H. (1985). Spatial and temporal patterns of *Krüppel* gene expression in early *Drosophila* embryos. *Nature, Lond.* **317**, 40–44.

KORNBERG, T., SIDEN, I., O'FARREL, P. & SIMON, M. (1985). The engrailed locus of *Drosophila*: In situ localization of transcripts reveals compartment-specific expression. *Cell* **40**, 45–53.

KRAUSE, G. (1939). Die Eitypen der Insekten. *Biol. Zbl.* **59**, 495–536.

LAUGHON, A. & SCOTT, M. P. (1984). Sequence of a *Drosophila* segmentation gene: protein structure homology with DNA-binding proteins. *Nature, Lond.* **310**, 25–31.

LAWRENCE, P. A. (1970). Polarity and patterns in the postembryonic development of insects. *Adv. Insect Physiol.* **7**, 197–266.

LAWRENCE, P. A. & MORATA, G. (1976). Compartments in the wing of *Drosophila*: a study of the *engrailed* gene. *Devl Biol.* **50**, 321–337.

LEHMANN, R. (1985). Regionsspezifische Segmentierungsmutanten bei *Drosophila melanogaster* Meigen. Dissertation, University of Tübingen.

LEWIS, E. B. (1978). A gene complex controlling segmentation in *Drosophila*. *Nature, Lond.* **276**, 565–570.

LOHS-SCHARDIN, M., CREMER, C. & NÜSSLEIN-VOLHARD, C. (1979). A fate map for the larval epidermis of *Drosophila melanogaster*: Localized cuticle defects following irradiation of the blastoderm with an ultraviolet laser microbeam. *Devl Biol.* **73**, 239–255.

MARTINEZ-ARIAS, A. & INGHAM, P. W. (1985). The origin of pattern duplications in segment polarity mutants of *Drosophila melanogaster*. *J. Embryol. exp. Morph.* **87**, 129–135.

MARTINEZ-ARIAS, A. & LAWRENCE, P. A. (1985). Parasegments and compartments in the *Drosophila* embryo. *Nature, Lond.* **313**, 639–642.

MEINHARDT, H. (1977). A model for pattern formation in insect embryogenesis. *J. Cell Sci.* **23**, 117–139.

MEINHARDT, H. (1982). *Models of Biological Pattern Formation*. London: Academic Press.

MEINHARDT, H. (1983). Cell determination boundaries as organizing regions for secondary embryonic fields. *Devl Biol.* **96**, 375–385.

MEINHARDT, H. (1984). Models for positional signalling, the threefold subdivision of segments and the pigmentation pattern of molluscs. *J. Embryol. exp. Morph.* **83 Supplement**, 289–311.

MEINHARDT, H. & GIERER, A. (1980). Generation and regeneration of sequences of structures during morphogenesis. *J. theor. Biol.* **85**, 429–450.

NÜSSLEIN-VOLHARD, C. (1977). Genetic analysis of pattern formation in the embryo of *Drosophila melanogaster*. *Wilhelm Roux Arch. EntwMech. Org.* **183**, 249–268.

NÜSSLEIN-VOLHARD, C., KLUDING, H. & JÜRGENS, G. (1985). Genes affecting the segmental subdivision of the *Drosophila* embryo. *Cold Spring Harb. Symp. quant. Biol.* **50** (in press).

NÜSSLEIN-VOLHARD, C. & WIESCHAUS, E. (1980). Mutants affecting segment number and polarity in *Drosophila*. *Nature, Lond.* **287**, 795–801.

NÜSSLEIN-VOLHARD, C., WIESCHAUS, E. & JÜRGENS, G. (1982). Segmentierung bei *Drosophila* – Eine genetische Analyse. *Verh. dt. Zool. Ges.* 91–104.

NÜSSLEIN-VOLHARD, C., WIESCHAUS, E. & KLUDING, H. (1984). Mutations affecting the pattern of the larval cuticle in *Drosophila melanogaster*. I. Zygotic loci on the second chromosome. *Wilhelm Roux Arch. devl Biol.* **193**, 267–282.

POOLE, S. J., KAUVAR, L. M., DREES, B. & KORNBERG, T. (1985). The *engrailed* locus of *Drosophila*: Structural analysis of an embryonic transcript. *Cell* **40**, 37–43.

RUSSELL, M. A. (1985). Positional information in insect segments. *Devl Biol.* **108**, 269–283.

SANDER, K. (1976). Formation of the basic body pattern in insect embryogenesis. *Adv. Insect Physiol.* **12**, 125–238.

SPEMANN, H. (1938). *Embryonic Development and Induction*. New Haven: Yale University Press.

STRUHL, G. (1984). Splitting of the *Bithorax* complex of *Drosophila*. *Nature, Lond.* **308**, 454.

VAN DER MEER, J. M. (1984). Parameters influencing reversal of segment sequence in posterior egg fragments of *Callosobruchus* (Coleoptera). *Wilhelm Roux Arch. devl Biol.* **193**, 339–356.

VOGEL, O. (1977). Regionalisation of the segment-forming capacities during early embryogenesis in *Drosophila melanogaster*. *Wilhelm Roux Arch. EntwMech. Org.* **182**, 9–32.

VOGEL, O. (1978). Pattern formation in the egg of the leafhopper *Euscelis plebejus* Fall. (Homeoptera): Developmental capacities of fragment isolated from the polar egg region. *Devl Biol.* **67**, 357.

WAKIMOTO, B. T., TURNER, F. R. & KAUFMAN, T. C. (1984). Defects in embryogenesis in mutants associated with the *Antennapedia* gene complex of *Drosophila melanogaster*. *Devl Biol.* **102**, 147–172.

WIESCHAUS, E., NÜSSLEIN-VOLHARD, C. & JÜRGENS, G. (1984). Mutations affecting the pattern of the larval cuticle in *Drosophila melanogaster*. III. Zygotic loci on the X-chromosome and fourth chromosome. *Wilhelm Roux Arch. devl Biol.* **193**, 296–307.

WOLPERT, L. (1969). Positional information and the spatial pattern of cellular differentiation. *J. theor. Biol.* **25**, 1–47.

J. Cell Sci. Suppl. 4, 383–416 (1986)
Printed in Great Britain © The Company of Biologists Limited 1986

DNA MAINTENANCE AND ITS RELATION TO HUMAN PATHOLOGY

F. GIANNELLI

Paediatric Research Unit, United Medical Schools of Guy's & St Thomas's Hospitals, Guy's Hospital Medical School, 7th Floor, Guy's Tower, London Bridge SE1 9RT, UK

INTRODUCTION

The evolution of life bears witness to the pliability of DNA. This molecule has changed and diversified not simply by base changes but also by duplication and expansion of coding and non-coding sequences, reshuffling of elemental units of function and interaction of segments by processes that involve DNA repair functions. Furthermore, as the genomes increased in complexity and, redundancy, in the form of di- or poly-ploidy, became the rule, the transmission of genetic information from one generation to the next had to rely on regular processes of matching, reassorting and segregation (i.e. meiosis and sexual reproduction), which also require DNA repair. Such repair, therefore, is an essential part of life in its widest possible sense. Commonly, however, DNA repair is seen as a process that ensures correct DNA copying and forms a last line of defence by reversing or removing damage that the cell has failed to prevent.

DNA repair functions are present in virtually all organisms either as corrective activities in DNA polymerases or as independent enzymes or both. Thus, for example, a small genome, bacteriophage T4, which relies on host cell functions for its expression, codes for its own pyrimidine dimer repairing enzyme. This stresses the importance of DNA repair and suggests that individual solutions may be required to optimize its adaptive value. In fact if the survival of a species depends upon the ability of its genome to adapt to changing environments a fine balance must exist between the forces that stimulate and those that suppress DNA change. Therefore, the DNA repair processes of different organisms should vary in detail even if they follow the same schemes dictated by both the structure of DNA and the environmental agents that have acted on DNA during evolution. Furthermore, in higher organisms one can distinguish germ line and soma. The former, immortal and responsible for the propagation of the species, may need special devices to maintain its DNA.

In the last 20 years an enormous amount of information has been published on the DNA repair of different organisms and especially *Escherichia coli* and man. Many reviews of different aspects of this topic are available, but Friedberg (1985) has most impressively waded through existing information to provide a comprehensive, critical and extremely clear picture of DNA repair in both prokaryotes and eukaryotes. I shall consider the role of DNA stability in human pathology. Space, however, does not allow a complete and systematic review. I shall therefore present a personal view.

DNA DAMAGE AND REPAIR

DNA is subject to both spontaneous degradation and exogenous damage. The former, which comprises base loss, base deamination, and strand breakage at sites of base loss, is due to the instability of the components of the DNA molecule and is easily repaired except for the deamination of 5-methylcytosine to thymine, which may cause hotspots of G to A transitions (Lindahl & Nyberg, 1972, 1974; Lindahl & Karlström, 1973; Lindahl, 1979; Coulondre *et al.* 1978). Spontaneous DNA damage may also result from attack by endogenous reactive chemicals produced during cell metabolism, such as oxygen radicals. Reactive oxygen species are known to occur in mammalian cells. Thus, for example, singlet oxygen has been demonstrated in both the lens and retina of the mammalian eye. Superoxide radicals (O_2^-) are formed by single electron addition in almost all aerobic cells and stimulation of some cells (phagocytes) may lead to bouts of O_2^- production as part of normal physiological responses (Babior, 1978). One further electron addition converts O_2^- into the peroxide ion or O_2^- converts to hydrogen peroxide by dismutation ($2O_2^- + 2H^+ \rightarrow H_2O_2 + O_2$).

Chance *et al.* (1979) calculated that 82 nmol of H_2O_2 are produced per gram of tissue per min in perfused livers isolated from normally fed rats. In the presence of transition metals H_2O_2, or $O_2^- + H_2O_2$ may convert into the highly reactive hydroxyl radicals (OH·). While these act at the site of formation, H_2O_2 and O_2^- are less reactive and may act away from their site of production. O_2^-, however, may cross the cell membranes only through special channels. Singlet oxygen, superoxide, hydroxyl and hydroperoxy radicals may initiate lipid peroxidation and this may cause, especially in the presence of transition metals, a chain reaction that yields lipid peroxy and alkoxy radicals. These, possibly together with icosanoids, released from arachidonic acid after phospholipase activation by lipid peroxides (Bus & Gibson, 1979; Parente, 1982), may represent or generate chromosomal-breaking or clasto-genic factors detectable in the sera of some patients or the culture medium of some mammalian cell lines (Emerit & Cerutti, 1984). The amount of DNA damage caused by the endogenous toxic species mentioned above is unclear. Mammalian cells are rich in enzymic and non-enzymic radical scavenging systems and the most dangerous chemical reactions are confined in specialized organelles, e.g. mitochondria and peroxisomes, but there is evidence that the homeostasis between radical generation and dissipation can be altered, causing cellular injury (Hochstein, 1983).

Most spontaneous DNA alterations are due to misincorporation of nucleotides during DNA synthesis. In *E. coli*, fidelity of replication is achieved in multiple steps. Base-pairing secures accuracy to one misincorporation in 10^{-1} to 10^{-2}; base selection and editing by DNA polymerases increase this to 10^{-5} to 10^{-6}; accessory proteins to 10^{-7} and, finally, post replicative mismatch repair to 10^{-10} (Radman *et al.* 1981).

The mechanisms of replication fidelity in eukaryotes are less clear. Mammalian DNA polymerases do not have editing functions and therefore accessory proteins may make a greater contribution to fidelity than in *E. coli*. However, Grosse *et al.* (1983) observe that purified α-polymerase produces, *in vitro*, stable errors; that is, misincorporations followed by further synthesis at a frequency of 10^{-4} to 10^{-5}. They suggest that this result makes proof-reading by an independent exonuclease unlikely and propose that a powerful mismatch correction must take place to reduce the error rate to the 10^{-9} to 10^{-11} level observed *in vivo*.

DNA may also be damaged by both chemical and physical environmental agents, which cause a great variety of lesions (see Friedberg, 1985, for a review).

Such spontaneous and induced DNA damage is repaired by reversal or excision. Reversal usually involves the action of a single enzyme and is free, or relatively free, of errors. Examples are: (1) the enzymic photoreactivation of pyrimidine dimers (Sutherland, 1974); (2) the repair of O^6-alkylguanine and other oxygen alkylations by transmethylases (Schendel & Robins, 1978; Olsson & Lindahl, 1980; Harris *et al.* 1983); (3) the direct rejoining of single-strand breaks; (4) the insertion of purines into apurinic sites (Livneh & Sperling, 1981; Deutsh & Linn, 1979). In man the biological importance of enzymic photoreactivation and purine insertion is uncertain and the direct ligation of strand breaks is possible only in the minority of lesions that have appropriate ends. There is no doubt, however, that the reversal of O^6-alkylguanine is important since the mutagenic potency of simple alkylating agents is correlated to their reactivity with the oxygen in position 6 of guanine (Roberts, 1980). Mammalian cells lacking methyl transferases do not repair O^6-methylguanine, do not reactivate N-methyl-N'-nitro-N-nitrosoguanidine (MNNG)-treated adenovirus 5 and are abnormally sensitive to MNNG or crosslinking agents producing O^6-alkylguanine intermediates (Yarosh, 1985; Brent *et al.* 1985; Gibson *et al.* 1985).

Excision repair has distinct, but related, enzymic pathways (Friedberg, 1985). Some inappropriate and damaged bases are excised by specific N-glycosylases with the formation of a base-free site. Mammalian N-glycosylases for uracil, hypoxanthine and 3-methyladenine have been identified (see Friedberg, 1985). The excision of bulky lesions occurs by a different pathway, best understood in *E. coli*, where an enzyme formed by the products of the *uvr A*, *B* and *C* genes cleaves damaged strands on both sides of the lesion (e.g. 7 base-pairs 5' and 3 or 4 base-pairs 3' of pyrimidine dimers). DNA repair synthesis then replaces the damaged segment and ligase restores the continuity of the DNA strand. In man several genes seem to be involved in the initiation of this excision repair but its biochemistry is still unclear. Both DNA polymerases α and β seem to contribute to DNA repair synthesis and form patches of 30–100 nucleotides (see Friedberg, 1985). Two ligases may complete repair (Soderhall & Lindahl, 1975).

Finally, mammalian cells are capable of mismatch repair as indicated by experiments in which they are transfected with mismatch-containing DNA. For example, Miller *et al.* (1976) transfected heteroduplexes of polyoma viruses differing at four positions and observed concordant or independent correction of differences, respectively, less than 90 base-pairs or more than 600 base-pairs apart.

Schemes of DNA repair in man must consider the complexities of chromatin and nuclear organization. There is evidence that: (1) the distribution of different DNA lesions may be affected both by the primary DNA sequence and the chromatin organization; (2) repair is influenced by the location of lesions and the functional state of the chromatin; and (3) nucleosome structure is modified during repair (see Bohr & Hanawalt, 1984; Bohr et al. 1985). Furthermore, poly(ADP-ribose) polymerase, an enzyme that modifies many nuclear proteins is involved in repair (Shall, 1984).

Damage that is not repaired before DNA replication may become fixed by miscopying or result in the break down of DNA replication and cell death. However, there are damage tolerance systems that aim to ensure the completion of DNA replication and a second chance to repair. So far, such systems in human cells are poorly understood. Also unclear is whether DNA damage induces new repair pathways or modulates constitutive ones (see Friedberg, 1985, for details).

XERODERMA PIGMENTOSUM (XP)

It is impossible to discuss DNA repair in man without referring to XP, not only because this was the first disease attributed to a DNA repair defect (Cleaver, 1968) but also because it is the only one with fairly well understood metabolic defects. The clinical and cell biological aspects of the disease have been repeatedly reviewed (Pawsey et al. 1979; Lehmann, 1982; Cleaver, 1983; Kraemer & Slor, 1984). It is an autosomal recessive disorder, with an incidence of 1 in 65 000–250 000 characterized by sun sensitivity causing freckling, dryness, atrophy, telangiectasia and finally cancer of the exposed skin and actinic damage to the eye. Slowly progressive neurological complications affect more than 15 % of the patients. These are due to neurone loss and include mental deterioration, choreoathetosis, ataxia, spasticity, reduced or absent tendon reflexes, extensor plantar reflexes and sensorineural deafness. A total of 80–90 % of the patients with the clinical features of the disease are clearly defective in excision repair while the remainder shows difficulties in replicating damaged DNA and are called XP-variants.

XP is genetically very heterogeneous as, to date, nine complementation groups have been described and designated A–I (de Weerd-Kastelein et al. 1972, 1974; Kraemer et al. 1975; Arase et al. 1979; Keijzer et al. 1979; Moshell et al. 1983; Fisher et al. 1985).

Groups A, C and D are the most frequent in Europe and group A is the most frequent in Japan. The patients of group A usually show a severe disease with neurological complications, those of group C seldom have such complications and those of group D tend to develop neurological complications later than group A. Group E consists of three kindreds with a mild disease (de Weerd-Kastelein et al. 1974; Fujiwara et al. 1985b). Group F comprises three Japanese kindreds and one

European patient also with a mild disease (Arase *et al.* 1979; Fujiwara *et al.* 1985*a*; Giannelli, Avery & Magnus, unpublished). Five patients with different clinical features fall into group G (Keijser *et al.* 1979; Arlett *et al.* 1980; Giannelli, Avery & Hawk, unpublished). Groups B and H are represented by single patients with clinical features overlapping those of Cockayne syndrome (Robbins *et al.* 1974; Moshell *et al.* 1983); and finally group I is represented by two siblings with neurological complications (Fisher *et al.* 1985). The cells of patients from all these complementation groups have been shown to have clear deficits in DNA repair synthesis after 254 nm ultraviolet irradiation, removal of sites sensitive to enzymic probes specific for pyrimidine dimers and, or, incision of DNA damaged by 254 nm ultraviolet irradiation (Fornace *et al.* 1976; Tanaka *et al.* 1977; Cook *et al.* 1978; Paterson *et al.* 1981; Fujiwara, 1985*a,b*; Zelle & Lohman, 1979; Moshell *et al.* 1983; Fisher *et al.* 1985). Clearly, therefore, XP patients are defective in the incision of DNA-containing pyrimidine dimers and many genes must be involved in this repair step in man. However, the precise number of such genes is unknown, not only because further XP complementation groups may be discovered but also because complementation between some of the nine known groups may result from intra- rather than intergenic complementation and thus define different alleles rather than different loci. This possibility has been excluded for groups A, C and D on two counts: firstly, because cells of these groups complement one another as well as they are complemented by normal cells in heteropolykaryons where the degree of complementation is a linear function of the dose of wild-type alleles; intragenic complementation, which occurs in the absence of normal gene products by the interaction of defective molecules, could not be so efficient. Secondly, because the gene products defective in the three complementation groups turn over at different rates. In fact, the product of the *XP-A* locus is present in excess in normal cells, turns over rapidly and seems to diffuse freely within the cell; the products of the *XP-C* and *D* loci are not in marked excess in the cell cytoplasm, do not readily diffuse out of the nucleus and turn over slowly; the product of the *XP-D* locus turns over more slowly than that of the *XP-C* locus. There are also suggestions of interactions between such gene products (Giannelli *et al.* 1973, 1982*c*; Giannelli & Pawsey, 1976). Some of the above conclusions have been confirmed recently by the microinjection of protein or mRNA fractions into XP cells, which was performed to develop biological assays for the products of the XP loci (De Jonge *et al.* 1983; Legerski *et al.* 1984).

The example of *E. coli*, in which three proteins are needed to initiate excision repair of bulky DNA lesions, and the great complexity of the mammalian chromosomes, justify the apparent need of several proteins to initiate the repair of bulky lesions in man. Such proteins could combine to form a larger complex as suggested by the observation of a very large protein catalysing the excision of pyrimidine dimers in calf thymus (Waldstein *et al.* 1979) or, possibly, by the large size calculated for the hypothetical complex by tentatively applying the target theory to data on the inactivation of the pyrimidine dimer incising activity by methyl-methane sulphonate (Cleaver, 1982). The function of such a complex may extend beyond the identification of the lesion and incision of the DNA. For example, some experiments suggest that chromatin modification may be required to initiate repair because extracts of normal cells attack pyrimidine dimers in chromatin while those of XP cells from groups A, C and D attack dimers only in purified DNA (Mortelmans *et al.* 1976; Kano & Fujiwara, 1983). If excision repair is organized in space and occurs at the nuclear 'matrix' (McCready & Cook, 1984), factors may also be required to attain such order. Furthermore, XP mutations may affect different components of the time course of excision repair or the excision of pyrimidine dimers from different regions of the chromatin. Thus group F cells are deficient in the fast component of excision repair (Zelle *et al.* 1980; Fujiwara *et al.* 1985*a*) and the residual excision of group C seems directed to transcriptionally active and matrix-associated regions (Mansbridge & Hanawalt, 1983; Bohr *et al.* 1985; Mullenders *et al.* 1984). This suggests that some factor may facilitate the repair of lesions in subfractions of the genome. Finally, XP cells are sensitive to different mutagens and unable to excise a variety of bulky adducts. This indicates that the specificity of the human activity incising damaged DNA is broad. Cleaver & Gruenert (1984) have suggested that different XP mutations may have slight differential effects on such broad specificity. Therefore, the picture is emerging of a repair complex with components that may subtly influence its function.

In contrast to XP, the metabolic defect of XP-variant is poorly understood. DNA repair synthesis and excision of pyrimidine dimers seem normal but DNA synthesis soon after 254 nm u.v. irradiation of cells in culture results in strands of abnormally low molecular weight; a phenomenon that can be enhanced by high concentrations of caffeine in the culture medium (Lehmann *et al.* 1975). The precise cause of such abnormal response is not known but could be a defect in mechanisms for the tolerance of DNA damage. XP and XP-variant are clinically indistinguishable and their cells are sensitive to the same agents. Therefore, it would be attractive to think that they have a deficit in common such as, for example, an inability by XP-variant cells to deal with DNA damage near replication forks. However, there is only very indirect evidence in favour of such an idea (Moustacchi *et al.* 1979) and only a few results have suggested the possibility of a subtle defect in excision repair by detecting in XP-variant cells a slight excess of DNA strand breakage during the recovery from 254 and 313 nm u.v. irradiation (Fornace *et al.* 1976; Netrawali & Cerutti, 1979).

OTHER DISEASES WITH CLEAR HYPERSENSITIVITY TO DNA-DAMAGING TREATMENTS

The literature on the DNA repair defects of man abounds in claims and counter-claims of cellular hypersensitivity to DNA-damaging treatments, but whenever a disease is clearly associated with abnormal cellular responses the evaluation of such responses should have become part of routine diagnostic procedures. So far this applies only to Cockayne (CS) and Bloom (BS) syndromes, ataxia-telangiectasia (AT) and Fanconi anaemia (FA), where, respectively, sensitivity to 254 nm u.v. radiation, spontaneous levels of sister chromatid exchanges, X-ray sensitivity and sensitivity to bifunctional alkylating agents have been used for postnatal, and even prenatal, diagnosis (Kawai *et al.* 1983; Lehmann *et al.* 1985; German, 1979; Giannelli *et al.* 1982*a*; Cox *et al.* 1978; Auerbach *et al.* 1981; Shipley *et al.* 1984).

These four autosomal recessive diseases have been extensively reviewed (Guzzetta, 1972; Lehmann, 1982; German, 1979; Polani, 1981; Bridges & Harnden, 1982). Their clinical features are summarized in Table 1 and their most interesting cell biological features are outlined below.

CS cells

These cells are hypersensitive to the cytotoxic effects of short wavelength u.v. radiations (250–315 nm) but no DNA repair defect has been clearly identified (Mayne *et al.* 1982). The most remarkable consequence of u.v. irradiation in CS cells is a marked, prolonged inhibition of synthesis of DNA and RNA (Lehmann *et al.* 1979; Mayne & Lehmann, 1982), and this together with the observation that inhibitors of DNA repair may prevent the recovery of RNA synthesis after u.v. irradiation has led Mayne (1984) to suggest that CS cells may be defective in the repair of actively transcribed DNA. If this were true CS and XP of group C could have reciprocal defects. The idea that the XP and CS mutations might involve overlapping metabolic pathways is made attractive by the report of two XP patients with features of CS (i.e. complementation group B and H). These patients therefore merit special mention. XP cells of group B and H show the excision-repair defect pathognomonic of XP. This is generally sufficient to cause the marked and prolonged inhibition of synthesis of DNA and RNA also observed in CS and, therefore, it is impossible to establish if the patients are homozygous only for an XP mutation or for both an XP and CS mutation. In fact they could be: (1) CS phenocopies, (2) defective in an XP factor contributing to the metabolic pathway impaired in CS, or (3), less likely, homozygous double mutants. In view of the rarity of the XP and CS mutations, the probability of the latter event (barring parental consanguinity) is below 10^{-10} and consanguinity has not been reported for the parents of either patient. So far, two complementation groups have been described in CS (Lehmann, 1982).

BS cells

These cells may show sensitivity to u.v. radiations (250–315 nm) but this is less constant and obvious than in CS (Giannelli *et al.* 1977; Krepinski *et al.* 1980; Smith & Paterson, 1981; Zbinden & Cerutti, 1981) and some authors have put more emphasis on the sensitivity to other DNA-damaging agents such as ethylmethane sulphonate and mitomycin C (Arlett & Lehmann, 1978; Krepinski *et al.* 1979; Ishizaki *et al.* 1981; Hook *et al.* 1984). Specific defects of DNA repair have not been detected but unscheduled DNA synthesis after 254 nm u.v. radiation is abnormally high and sensitive to aphidicolin inhibition (Giannelli *et al.* 1981, 1982*b*), and an anomalous pattern of cell cycle variations in DNA repair activity has also been claimed (Gupta & Sirover, 1984). The principal feature of BS cells is their pattern of spontaneous chromosomal aberrations and, in particular, the symmetrical quadri-radials (attributable to exchanges between homologous chromosomes at homologous

Table 1. *Clinical features of Cockayne syndrome, Bloom syndrome, ataxia-telangiectasia and Fanconi anaemia*

Cockayne syndrome	Bloom syndrome	Ataxia-telangiectasia	Fanconi anaemia
Autosomal recessive	Autosomal recessive	Autosomal recessive	Autosomal recessive
Rare	? $1/10^6$ newborns gentiles, more frequent in Ashkenazi Jews	$1/50\,000$–$30\,000$ newborns	$1/350\,000$ newborns
Cachectic dwarfism	Birth weight <2 kg	Progressive ataxia/athetosis (early onset)	Pancytopenia
Progressive mental deterioration	Adult height $1\cdot45$ m in ♂♂	Progressive telangiectasia (late onset: eyes, face, etc.)	Bone-marrow hyper- then hypo- and then aplastic
Pepper–salt choroidoretinitis	Sunlight sensitivity	Foetal thymus, impaired T cells	Birth weight below $2\cdot5$ kg
Optic atrophy	Progressive telangiectatic erythema	Low IgA	50 % growth retarded
Intracranial calcifications	Immune deficiency (low immunoglobulins, impaired B cells)	High α foetoprotein	50 % skeletal malformations (thumb, radius, etc.)
Extensive atheroma	Small testes	Hypoplastic ovaries	50 % microcephaly
Progeric appearance	Prone to infection and malignancies	Clinical X-ray sensitivity	20 % mental defective, 7 % deaf
Sunlight sensitivity		Prone to sinopulmonary infections	Kidney malformations
		Prone to myeloproliferative disease and other cancers	Hypogenital
			Skin café-au-lait spots and melanosis
			Infection- and cancer-prone

sites) and the many-fold excess of sister chromatid exchanges (SCE). Such exchanges are strictly coupled with DNA replication and the symmetrical quadriradials, which spare the X chromosome, may also be favoured by difficulties at DNA synthesis with consequent interaction of synchronously replicating chromosome regions (i.e. homologous regions except those of the X chromosome; Giannelli, 1970). Therefore, the chromosomal aberrations of BS, parralleled by high rates of spontaneous mutations (Gupta & Goldstein, 1980; Warren *et al.* 1981; Vijayalaxmi *et al.* 1983), suggest a defect that finds its expression at DNA replication. Slow elongation of new DNA chains has been reported (Hand & German, 1975, 1977; Giannelli *et al.* 1977; Kapp, 1982) but not in all situations (Ockey, 1979). Several authors have reported changes in the frequency of SCE in either BS cells or their partners in co-cultivation experiments and have argued the case for SCE inducing factors released from, or SCE reducing factors absorbed by the BS cells (Tice *et al.* 1978; Van Buul *et al.* 1978; Rudiger *et al.* 1980). Others, however, see no change (Shonberg & German, 1980; Shiraishi *et al.* 1981). West *et al.* (1981) have found a 30 % decrease of SCE in BS cells as the temperature of incubation is lowered from 39 to 32 °C while the minimum incidence of SCE in normal cells is at the physiological temperature of 37·5 °C. They have then suggested that incubation at a low temperature might alleviate the difficulties in DNA replication that occur in BS cells. Such results, however, could also be consistent with the free-radical hypothesis of Emerit & Cerutti (1981), which postulates that BS cells deal inadequately with oxygen radicals produced during normal metabolism. In this case, low incubation temperatures could slow down metabolism and reduce the rate of free radical production. However, the hypothesis of Emerit & Cerutti is based on rather indirect evidence; namely, the detection in ultrafiltrates of BS cell culture medium or in the serum of two BS patients of a chromosome-breaking agent inactivatable by superoxide dismutase (Emerit & Cerutti, 1981; Emerit *et al.* 1982). Such a factor, however, does not reproduce the characteristic chromosomal features of BS, i.e. the many-fold increase of SCE and symmetrical quadriradials.

Support for the idea that BS cells may have problems at DNA replication may come from the report of Shiraishi *et al.* (1983) that the SCEs in BS cells labelled with bromodeoxyuridine (BrdUrd) occur mostly (i.e. 12:1) during the second of the two replication cycles necessary to detect SCE and hence when the template DNA contains BrdUrd. This is a very unusual finding, because in normal cells SCEs occur with equal frequency during both DNA replications irrespective of the labelling procedure (Herreros & Giannelli, 1967; Shiraishi *et al.* 1983), and could, therefore. suggest that the replication machinery of BS cells is unusually sensitive to modifications of the DNA template.

AT cells

These cells are very sensitive to the cytotoxic and clastogenic action of X-rays and of some radiomimetic drugs. Recent results suggest problems in the repair of DNA strand breaks but there is no firm evidence of specific biochemical defects (Cox *et al.* 1984). The best case for a defect of DNA repair in AT still rests, therefore, on the observation that the survival of AT cells does not increase, in contrast to the norm, when they are irradiated at very low dose rates or kept in a growth arrested state so as to favour DNA repair (Cox, 1982). Another consistent feature of AT cells is the paradoxical radioresistance of their DNA synthesis and, especially, of their replicon initiation (Houldsworth & Lavin, 1980; Edwards & Taylor, 1980; Painter & Young, 1980; de Wit *et al.* 1981). This suggests that inhibition of replicon initiation in normal cells may be an active process of adaptive value. Therefore, it has been proposed that failure of DNA synthesis inhibition may prevent adequate DNA repair in AT cells. However, the abnormal response of AT cells to ionizing radiations cannot be due simply to the failure to inhibit replicon initiation, because AT cells do not repair potential lethal damage when kept in growth-arrested states. A related but less-specific hypothesis suggests that anomalies in chromatin structure and organization account for the phenotype of AT cells (Painter, 1982). Complementation tests based on the assay of DNA synthesis inhibition have suggested the possibility of several complementation groups (Murnane & Painter, 1982; Jaspers & Bootsma, 1982) as have other assays also (Chen *et al.* 1984).

FA cells

These cells may show 'spontaneous' chromosome breakage and are very sensitive to the cytotoxic and clastogenic action of bifunctional alkylating agents such as mitomycin C or diepoxybutane and to treatments capable of causing DNA crosslinks (e.g. psoralens plus 365 nm u.v. radiation). However, defects in the repair of interstrand DNA crosslinks have not been consistently demonstrated (Fujiwara *et al.* 1977*b*; Fornace *et al.* 1979; Kaye *et al.* 1980; Fujiwara, 1982) and a variety of different defects has been claimed in controversial or unconfirmed reports. Few authors have suggested a defect in the neutralization of oxygen radicals on the grounds that the chromosomes of FA cells may show hypersensitivity to hyperbaric oxygen and to ^2H_2O or benefit from treatment with enzymes that act on oxygen radicals (Nordenson, 1977; Jonjie *et al.* 1981, 1983; Nagasawa & Little, 1983), but hyperbaric oxygen does not cause detectable DNA breakage in the FA cells (Seres & Fornace, 1982) and the specificity of the beneficial effects of radical scavengers on FA cell cultures has been questioned (Raj & Heddle, 1980). Cell hybridization experiments indicate also that this disease is genetically heterogeneous (Duckworth-Rysiecki *et al.* 1985).

SEARCHES FOR DNA REPAIR DEFECTS BASED ON SPECIFIC AETIOPATHOGENETIC HYPOTHESES

XP and the diseases mentioned above have been used as models for hypotheses on the pathological consequences of DNA repair defects. Thus, for example, Robbins (1978, 1983), after observing a close correlation in XP patients between the severity of neurological complications and the cellular sensitivity to 254 nm u.v. irradiation, elaborated the theory that DNA damage from endogenous or exogenous sources is the cause of primary degenerations of excitable tissues. He sought evidence for such a theory in several inheritable or non-inheritable degenerative diseases and reported in its support survival studies suggesting hypersensitivity to X-rays and MNNG in cell lines (usually EB virus-transformed lymphocitoid cells) derived from individuals affected by tuberous sclerosis, familial dysautonomia, Huntington disease, olivo-ponto cerebellar atrophy, sporadic autonomic neurodegeneration (Shy-Drayer S.), Usher syndrome, retinitis pigmentosa, Alzheimer disease, Parkinson disease, infantile spinal muscular atrophy, myotonic muscular atrophy and Duchenne, Becker muscular dystrophy (Moshell *et al.* 1980; Robbins *et al.* 1980, 1984, 1985; Scudiero *et al.* 1981, 1982).

Similarly, Kidson *et al.* (1983) take XP and AT as models to suggest that some aspects of the development and differentiation of the nervous and immune systems are controlled by genes concerned with general DNA replication, repair and recombination. In support of this idea, he and his collaborators examined the radiosensitivity of primary degenerative neurological diseases such as Huntington disease, amyotrophic lateral sclerosis, Parkinson dementia and multiple sclerosis (Chen *et al.* 1981; Gipps & Kidson, 1981; Kidson *et al.* 1983). Kidson *et al.* (1983) summarized their observations, claiming that: in none of the diseases they examined is cellular radiosensitivity a constant feature; when present, such sensitivity appears to be inherited in a dominant fashion and, at least in multiple sclerosis, it is not necessarily associated with the development of the disease.

The results of Robbins' and Kidson's groups seem to be in partial disagreement and they both are at variance with reports of normal radiosensitivity in some of the diseases they analysed (Brennan & Lewis, 1983; Arlett, 1980; Evans *et al.* 1982). In fact, Robbins (1983) remarked that the cellular radiosensitivity of patients with neuronal and neuromuscular degenerative disease is less pronounced than that of AT heterozygotes. This raises doubts on the significance and aetiological role of the alleged hypersensitivities, since it is still unclear whether AT heterozygotes differ significantly from the general population in their cellular radiosensitivity (Bridges & Harnden, 1982; Kinsella *et al.* 1982; Natarajan *et al.* 1982; Nagasawa *et al.* 1985).

The concept that DNA damage is important to carcinogenesis has stimulated investigations on syndromes with predisposition to malignancy or inheritable forms of cancer. Positive results have been reported in some conditions such as: Rothmund-Thomson (Smith & Paterson, 1982), basal cell naevus syndrome, retino-blastoma, familial polyposis coli and Gardner syndrome, and familial malignant melanoma. However, the results on these conditions, reported from different laboratories, vary both in their substance and their interpretation. Thus, for example, while Chan & Little (1983) emphasized the hypersensitivity to irradiation of fibroblasts from patients with basal cell naevus syndrome, Featherstone *et al.* (1983) found normal cell survival and considered the excess of damage in chromosomes irradiated in G_0 phase too slight to be of aetiological importance. Controversial and often negative results have accumulated on familial retinoblastoma (e.g. see Weichselbaum *et al.* 1985; Cox & Masson, 1980; Morten *et al.* 1981; Ejima *et al.* 1982; Gainer & Kinsella, 1983). The fibroblasts of patients with familial polyposis coli and Gardner syndrome have also yielded variable results with a number of chemical mutagens (Little *et al.* 1980; Hori *et al.* 1980; Barfknecht & Little, 1982; Akamatsu *et al.* 1983; Kopelovich, 1983; Miyaki *et al.* 1982; Henson *et al.* 1983; Domoradzki *et al.* 1984). Interesting, recent data suggest hypermutability to 4-nitro-quinoline-1-oxide and u.v. light in fibroblasts from patients with familial cutaneous malignant melanoma or dysplastic naevus syndrome (Howell *et al.* 1984; Kraemer *et al.* 1984b), but the exact cause of such hypermutability is not known.

Immune deficiency has also been considered a criterion for defining populations that may harbour defects of DNA repair, and the most notable find in this population is a patient with hypogammaglobulinemia, marked IgA deficiency, lymphocytes unresponsive to mitogenic stimulation, dwarfism, modest mental retardation and lack of secondary sexual characteristics at 18 years of age. The fibroblasts of this patient have shown sensitivity to many DNA-damaging agents and metabolic responses suggesting a defect in DNA ligase (Henderson *et al.* 1985). Abnormal responses to DNA-damaging agents have been reported in the lymphocytes of patients with diseases associated with abnormal immune responses or immune status, such as, for example, rheumatoid arthritis and lupus erythematosus (Harris *et al.* 1982). However, the lymphocytes are very seriously involved in the pathological processes of such diseases and, therefore, the results they provide are more likely to be a consequence of the pathological process than the expression of a constitutional defect. In fact it cannot be stressed too much that lymphocytes freshly sampled from patients are not a good test system for the detection of constitutional defects of DNA repair, since they are a complex, heterogeneous cell population with variable admixture of subtypes and physiologically very susceptible to environmental stimuli and accumulating environmental damage, to such an extent (at least in a subset of lymphocytes) as to be used to assess long-past and cumulative radiation damage (Sasaki and Miyata, 1968; Dolphin *et al.* 1973).

Difficulties may also result from the use of transformed cell lines since these have abnormal physiology and may show alterations in easily measurable DNA repair functions (Ayres *et al.* 1982; Yarosh, 1985; Gantt *et al.* 1984). In general, the excessive frequency of discrepancies among the reports of cell hypersensitivity in human diseases suggests not only biological heterogeneity of the experimental material but also a poor understanding and hence a poor control of the experimental factors that influence the survival of human cultured cells after DNA-damaging treatments.

DEFECTS IN THE DISSIPATION OF OXYGEN-FREE RADICALS

It is interesting to note that as attempts to identify the DNA repair defects of CS, BS, AT and FA were providing unsatisfactory results attention turned to processes that may affect DNA integrity in a less-direct way; for example, alterations of nucleotide pools, NAD^+ metabolism and defects of oxygen radical dissipation. This underlines the fact, too often overlooked, that sensitivity to DNA-damaging treatments does not necessarily imply a primary defect of DNA repair or replication. The suggestion, however, of a defect in NAD^+ supply in CS (Fujiwara *et al.* 1982) has not been confirmed (Mayne *et al.* 1984) and the possibility of nucleotide pool defects in BS (Taylor *et al.* 1983) deserves further study. Of greater concern is the neutralization of oxygen-related free radicals because, as indicated in the Introduction, respiration and other metabolic processes fundamental to the life of the cell may generate free radicals, which may cause endogenous damage whenever the ingenious physical and chemical defence systems of the cell are overcome. Normal levels of superoxide dismutase have been found in AT (Brown & Harnden, 1978), but the hypothesis of defective neutralization of oxygen radicals has taken some hold in FA, although the evidence in its favour is controversial (see above). The hypothesis of a similar defect in BS has been already discussed briefly. This hypothesis was based on the isolation, from BS cell culture medium, of a clastogenic factor (CF) that could be inactivated by superoxide dismutase. A similar factor has also been detected, in higher concentration, in tissue culture medium and serum of AT patients (Shaham *et al.* 1980), and in the serum of patients with diseases with abnormal immune status such as rheumatoid arthritis, scleroderma and lupus erythematosus (Emerit, 1980). The precise nature and origin of CFs is not known but, as mentioned earlier, various oxidative insults could result in reactive compounds of sufficient stability to act as CFs. Are, therefore, CFs a primary product of the metabolic defect causing the disease or a secondary consequence of the pathological process? Inflammation *in vivo* and cell death *in vitro* could represent, for example, trivial sources of CF. Cell release and cell-dependent accumulation into the medium of chromophores that increase photodynamic reactions could also result in free radicals and CFs, unless the cultures and media are shielded from light.

A good candidate for the title of disease due to or associated with a primary defect(s) in the dissipation of oxygen radicals is actinic reticuloid (AR). This is a disease of late onset (30–50 years) that affects predominantly males. Although the patients may not be aware of their sun or light sensitivity, monochromatic light tests readily establish abnormal skin responses to u.v. light of medium and long wavelength and sometimes even to parts of the visible spectrum. The cardinal hystological feature is a dense dermal lymphohistiocytic infiltrate with a tendency to invade the epidermis as seen in mycosis fungoides, a malignant reticulosis. However, AR does not seem to be a malignant neoplastic condition and the skin lesions regress if nursed in the dark (Magnus, 1964, 1976). AR fibroblasts irradiated in complete culture medium with long-wavelength u.v. radiations (320–400 nm; peak = 365 nm) show massive cytopathic changes with nuclear pycnosis or karyolysis, and cytoplasmic loss 24 h after doses that have no effect on normal cells and cells from other photodermatoses such as XP, XP-variant, CS and BS. Such cytopathic effects are so general and quick to appear as to suggest that the cells die from membrane damage rather than DNA damage, even though excessive single-strand DNA breakage is observed in AR cells after doses 5- to 10-fold lower than those necessary for marked cytopathic effects (Giannelli *et al.* 1983; Botcherby *et al.* 1984). In our conditions of irradiation, electron spin resonance detects generation of radicals (Botcherby, Davies, Tomasi & Giannelli, unpublished). Radical scavengers reduce both cytopathic effects and DNA damage. Furthermore, the DNA breakage induced by u.v.-A in AR cells is brought down to normal levels by the addition of few units of catalase to the irradation medium while the cytopathic effects can be reduced by larger doses of the enzyme. Superoxide dismutase, on the contrary, has detrimental effects on DNA breakage and little effect on cell inactivation, presumably because it dismutates O_2^- generated in the medium into H_2O_2, which can more easily cross the cell membrane and damage DNA either directly or indirectly. On the other hand, the net effect of such dismutation on membrane damage can be expected to be small (Botcherby & Giannelli, unpublished). Irradiation of AR cells in medium conditioned by normal fibroblasts and, *vice versa*, irradiation of the latter cells in medium conditioned by the former does not alter the response of either cell type, thus indicating that AR cells do not release photosensitizers in the culture medium (Botcherby *et al.* 1984). These observations have suggested to us the following hypothesis for the pathogenesis of AR. The cells of AR patients poorly neutralize oxygen radicals or their conversion products and, therefore, u.v.-A-induced radicals cause excessive cellular and tissue damage. This acts as a leucotactic stimulus and results in the lymphohistiocytic infiltrates characteristic of the disease. The infiltrating cells, by producing further radicals, as part of their physiological response, cause further tissue damage and establish a vicious circle responsible for the chronic character of the lesions (Giannelli *et al.* 1983).

Our irradiation system would seem to produce a stress capable of revealing hypersensitivity to reactive oxygen species. We have therefore examined its effect on BS cells and the results have been negative (Botcherby *et al.* 1984; Botcherby & Giannelli, unpublished). On the contrary, we have detected hypersensitivity to u.v.-A irradiation in complete medium in a family showing transmission of a newly recognized dermatological syndrome associated with high incidence of internal cancer (Atherton, Botcherby, Marimo, Francis & Giannelli, unpublished).

DNA REPAIR AND CANCER

Most of the interest in the DNA repair defects of man is due to their possible contribution to carcinogenesis. Thus XP, CS, BS, AT and FA have been frequently used as models for the discussion of human carcinogenesis. XP seems to provide support for the mutational theory of cancer as it shows correlations between proneness to actinic cancer, failure to excise DNA lesions, such as pyrimidine dimers of demonstrable carcinogenic potential (Hart *et al.* 1977), and a high rate of *in vitro* cell transformation and mutation per unit dose of u.v. irradiation (Maher & McCormick, 1984). However, the idea that the actinic cancers of XP are due to the accumulation of single gene mutations is too simplistic, even if recent work begins to define a discrete number of genes particularly important to the control of cell growth and malignancy (Bishop, 1985). Thus, Bridges (1981) noted that both XP and CS cells are hypermutable to u.v. radiations, while only the first is clearly prone to actinic cancers. He also reviewed the evidence for the local and systemic effects of DNA-damaging treatments on immune defences and came to the conclusion that actinic DNA damage exerts its carcinogenic action largely in a pseudo-promotional manner by inhibiting immune control.

Cairns (1981), argued that point mutations and environmental mutagens (except sunlight) do not contribute much to human carcinogenesis. Important to his thesis is the consideration that XP patients, whose cells cannot repair DNA damaged by many mutagens, do not show high incidence of common internal cancers while BS patients with efficient repair clearly do. Cairns consequently stressed the role of chromosomal instability and considered genetic transposition a more likely cause of cancer than single gene mutations. Whether Cairns' comparison of XP and BS is totally fair is still uncertain, since more extensive reviews of the literature suggest increased risk of internal cancer in XP (Kraemer *et al.* 1984*a*), while the metabolic defect of BS is unclear. However, if we consider XP, BS, AT and FA, we note that although only the cells of the first two are hypermutable in single gene mutation assays they all show 'spontaneous' or 'induced' chromosome fragility and proneness to cancer. XP shows excessive chromosome damage after u.v. irradiation, AT shows high levels of X-ray-induced chromosomal breakage, possibly leading to deletions and hemizygosity for large chromosomal regions, and also somatic cell clones with specific chromosomal rearrangements (Taylor, 1982). In FA the frequently observed triradials and asymmetrical quadriradials may lead to deficiency or duplications that would unmask recessive mutations and alter gene expression by gene dose and position effects. Finally, the symmetrical quadriradials often observed in BS may result in daughter cells with balanced genomes but homozygous for large chromosomal regions as previously discussed by Giannelli (1982). The importance of such events is best illustrated (as explained below) by recent discoveries in retinoblastoma and other embryonal cancers, i.e. Wilms tumours, rhabdomyosarcoma and hepatoblastoma (Michalopoulos *et al.* 1985; Orkin, 1984; Sparkes, 1984; Cavanée *et al.* 1983, 1985; Koufos *et al.* 1985).

Predisposition to retinoblastoma may be dominantly inherited and the predisposed individuals show a high risk of bilateral multifocal disease. Knudson (1971) argued that such pattern could be explained if two mutations were necessary for the development of retinoblastoma as, in this case, inheritance of one mutation would enable the risk of the two required mutational changes to be realized independently in several somatic cells. The predisposing mutation in retinoblastoma or the other embryonal cancers mentioned above appears to be a recessive change that results in malignancy when it is followed by an additional event that causes hemi- or homozygosity for the predisposing mutation in the appropriate somatic cell. This has been demonstrated by studies of DNA, enzymic and chromosomal markers, which have clearly indicated that hemi- or homozygosity for the relevant chromosomal regions may be caused by chromosomal non-disjunction or by somatic recombination of the type that may be associated with symmetrical quadriradials. It is interesting to note, in this context, that lymphoblastoid lines from BS patients may or may not show the chromosomal phenotype characteristic of the patient, but only the former appear abnormally prone to malignant transformation (Shiraishi *et al.* 1985).

DNA-repair studies in various syndromes with familial predisposition to cancer have given inconsistent or negative results, and therefore the case for a significant contribution of DNA repair defects to cancer morbidity in man still rests largely and uncomfortably on retrospective epidemiological evidence of high incidences of cancer in heterozygotes for AT and FA and possibly XP (Swift, 1977; Swift & Chase, 1979). Such heterozygotes represent a significant proportion of the general population (1–3 %) and could contribute significantly to cancer morbidity. However, early conclusions on the cancer incidence of FA heterozygotes have been retracted (Swift *et al.* 1980) and those on AT and XP heterozygotes still await confirmation from prospective studies.

DNA REPAIR AND AGEING

Deterioration of the genetic information of the cell or infidelity of its transcription and translation have been considered as likely causes of 'intrinsic' cellular ageing and, therefore, DNA-repair functions have been looked at in relation to this process. Various approaches have been followed: clinical syndromes of precocious ageing such as Hutchinson-Gilford progeria and Werner syndrome have been examined for DNA-repair defects with essentially negative, though controversial, results (Regan & Setlow, 1974; Little *et al.* 1975; Bradley *et al.* 1976; Brown *et al.* 1978, 1980; Fujiwara *et al.* 1977*a*; Gebhart *et al.* 1985). Changes in the level of some repair functions during the life of different mammals or during the life of their cells in culture have been examined. Early results tabulated by Williams & Dearfield (1981) and later reports do not provide clear evidence, at least in man, for an age-related decline of DNA repair *in vivo* or *in vitro* (Liu *et al.* 1982; Hall *et al.* 1982; Sognier & Hittelman, 1983; Nette *et al.* 1984).

A positive correlation between the DNA-repair synthesis induced by 254 nm u.v. light and the life-span of various mammalian species has been reported, though not without exceptions (Hart & Setlow, 1974; Kato *et al.* 1980; Francis *et al.* 1981; Hall *et al.* 1984), and, in any event, the level of DNA-repair synthesis of cells cultured from individuals of different species may not truly reflect their repair efficiency. The observation that the evolution of non-coding DNA in hominoids is slower than in more primitive primates and eutherians could indicate better DNA maintenance at least in the germ line of hominoids but differences in generation time could also explain such an observation (Goodman, 1976; Neel, 1983; Goodman *et al.* 1984).

DNA MAINTENANCE IN THE GERM LINE

It is well established that some mutations of yeast and *Drosophila* impair both DNA repair in somatic cells and meiosis. In contrast, little is known about the molecular physiology and pathology of human and, more generally, mammalian recombination, meiosis and gametogenesis. Some patients with XP, AT, BS and FA show hypogonadism but this could well be a secondary effect of the disease. If the quality of meiosis and gametogenesis were impaired by mild defects in DNA repair such as those that may exist in heterozygotes for XP or for any other mutation affecting DNA metabolism, such defects could contribute to human pathology subtly and yet much more substantially than suggested by their effect on somatic cells, as their consequences would propagate by hereditary transmission. In fact a retrospective epidemiological study claims a higher incidence of specific and different malformations in the offsprings of heterozygotes for AT, FA and XP (Welshimer & Swift, 1982). This important and intriguing finding must now be verified by prospective studies.

The nature of the germ line and its relevance to hereditary stability (yet within evolutionary variation) suggests that special strategies may exist for the maintenance of its DNA, and much has been written about the possible rejuvenating and correcting properties of recombination, meiosis and gametogenesis (see Martin, 1977; Medvedev, 1981; Bernstein *et al.* 1984). However, the DNA at meiosis undergoes additional manipulations and this may carry specific risks. Thus, the direct comparison of somatic and meiotic mutation rates in *Saccharomyces cerevisiae* suggests a higher mutation rate at meiosis (Magni & Sora, 1969; Auerback, 1976). Furthermore, a number of human gene mutations or indeed variations in the length of repeated sequences have been attributed to errors at recombination, such as unequal crossing over. Is, therefore, DNA maintenance inferior in the germline to that in somatic cells? Or, conversely, are the potential risks of recombination and meiosis offset by more effective DNA screening and correcting ability? Direct evidence on this point is not available because we cannot compare the yield of mutations per somatic or germ cell replication *in vivo*. The estimate of the mutation rate of cultured male fibroblasts to 6-thioguanine resistance and that of the germ line mutation rate for the Lesch–Nyhan disease, which refer both to severe defects at the hypoxanthine–guanine phosphoribosyl transferase locus (HGPRT), are, respectively, 3×10^{-6} to 10^{-5} per gene per cell division and 2×10^{-6} per gene per gamete per generation (Albertini & De Mars, 1973; Wald, 1984). Therefore, the mutation rate per cell division could be much lower in the germ line, as female germ cells undergo 30 cell divisions prior to meiosis and male germ cells 380–540 in a man of 28–35 years of age (Vogel & Rathenberg, 1975). It is reasonable, however, to suspect that growth *in vitro* increases the mutation rate of fibroblasts and we do not know how efficiently the Lesch–Nyhan mutation is selected against before, at or after fertilization.

Germ cell and gamete selection could be a key factor in the accurate transmission of genetic information (Cohen, 1975). Medvedev (1981) emphasized the opportunities for selection at the haploid stage of gametogenesis. Such opportunities, however, do not seem to apply to the human situation. In fact, female gametogenesis seems carefully to avoid the genetic effects of haploidy. The oocytes undergo the early stages of the first meiotic prophase in foetal life and come to rest in the dictyate state. They have then a tetraploid DNA content and their homologous chromosomes, each consisting of two chromatids, remain closely associated to one another until ovulation and fertilization 13–50 years later. Furthermore, fertilization takes place before expulsion of the second polar body and, so, while the female complement is still diploid. Thus at no time is a female germ cell haploid. Haploidy is the normal state for the spermatozoa but there is little evidence of nuclear gene expression in the sperm (Bellvé & O'Brien, 1983; Stern *et al.* 1983). What features of gametogenesis and fertilization may then be important to maintain the integrity of the genetic message?

I propose the following. In female gametogenesis, economy of both cell replication and usage limits replicational errors while securing an excess of germ cells (i.e. 2×10^6 at birth, $0 \cdot 5 \times 10^6$ at puberty against 500 that mature during sexual life). Very many oocytes die (so called prenatal and postnatal atresia) and therefore germ cell selection may occur. This, however, cannot operate on the new gene assortments caused by recombination because they segregate after fertilization. Attention may therefore focus on other features of gametogenesis and especially on the extraordinary physical proximity of homologous chromosomes during the long dictyate stage. This phenomenon, is very poorly understood but could be of fundamental importance. It is possible, for example, that it favours postrecombinational matching of homologous sequences and gene conversion. This could cause changes in the ratio of alleles (e.g. $2:2$ to $3:1$) at different heterozygous loci in different oocytes. Selection could then exploit such inequalities. In fact, since such oocytes are genically active, detrimental mutations of genes controlling general cellular functions could be selected against during the long interval between the beginning of meiosis and ovulation. The oocyte would thus avoid the harsh selection that would operate on haploid gametes, while using a long period of genetic expression and postmeiotic gene conversion to select against detrimental recessive or codominant mutations on a locus-by-locus basis. Similarly, such a process could act against mutations occurring during the long life of the oocyte, especially if sequence matching occurred repeatedly over the life of this cell. Thus, for example, if one of the four copies of a wild-type gene undergoes a mutational change, selection would begin to operate unless matching with one of the three wild-type alleles remaining reverses the change. The strength of phenotype selection would increase geometrically if the mutation gains further hold by gene conversion (e.g. from $1:3$ to $2:2$ mutant to wild-type sequences). However, repeated matching with gene conversion should have a $3:1$ chance of reconstituting the wild-type state even if each gene conversion event is totally random. There is experimental evidence that the immature, arrested oocytes of various mammals are extremely resistant to mutation induction by radiations (Russell, 1977; Cox & Lyon, 1975; Ehling & Favor, 1984) though showing species differences in their sensitivity to killing, possibly correlated to chromosomal organization (Baker, 1971). It appears also that gene conversion at the major histocompatibility complex of the mouse occurs preferentially if not exclusively in oogenesis (Loh & Baltimore, 1984).

In male gametogenesis uneconomical cell replication provides as many as 10^8 sperm for each ferilization event and accurate DNA replication is important. One may wonder whether the lower and accurately controlled testicular temperature may play a part (Reanney & Pressing, 1984). Of particular interest, however, is the opportunity for sperm selection at fertilization. As mentioned earlier, nuclear gene expression is shut down in spermatozoa and therefore selection should be based on other criteria. I suggest that mitochondrial gene function is used as an indirect yardstick of genetic wellbeing. This seems feasible not only because mitochondrial function is essential to sperm motility, but also because different facts concur to suggest that mitochondrial DNA damage could be a sensitive measure of the genetic damage suffered by the male gamete. Thus, the 10-fold faster evolution and the much poorer repair of mitochondrial relative to nuclear DNA suggest that the former DNA damage may become more readily fixed than the latter, while the 8- to 10-fold reduction in mitochondrial DNA during gametogenesis suggests that the re- dundancy of mitochondria may be low enough in sperms to permit the expression of mitochondrial DNA damage (Brown *et al.* 1979; Clayton *et al.* 1974; Lansman & Clayton, 1975; Hecht *et al.* 1984). The efficiency of such indirect selection could vary with the degree of genetic damage and be lower at high damage levels, thus contributing to the non-linear increase with age of the mutation rate in males (Vogel & Rathenberg, 1975). The greater risk of genome miscopying and the indirect method of selection would be consistent with the higher rate of single gene mutations in male than in female gametogenesis (Vogel & Rathenberg, 1975).

CONCLUSIONS AND FUTURE PROSPECTS

It is now clear that it is very difficult to identify the DNA repair defects of man. Physicochemical assays of DNA damage monitor the fate of majority lesions while the relevant biological effects investigated may be due to minority lesions or to damage in small fractions of the genome. Sensitivity to a DNA-damaging agent does not clearly indicate the DNA repair pathway, if any, that is faulty. Cells with clear hypersensitivities do not show clear DNA repair defects (e.g. AT, CS and FA cells), while others, with enzyme defects unrelated to DNA metabolism, may show de- fective repair (e.g. glutathione synthetase deficiency and reduced repair of u.v. irradiation-induced potentially lethal damage; Deschavanne *et al.* 1984). There are still too few enzymic and antibody probes to provide sensitive and specific tests for the precise study of the removal of DNA lesions.

Some human repair enzymes (e.g. some N-glycosylases and O^6-guanine methyl- transferase) have been isolated but inherited defects of such enzymes have not been detected.

In XP, the only disease with a clearly identified metabolic defect, a multi- component enzyme complex is involved and one is faced with the hard task of identifying its different units and determining their separate and combined activities.

The gradual appreciation of the influence on DNA replication and repair of relatively unrelated metabolic pathways, such as those that regulate the levels of nucleotide pools and NAD^+ concentration, is important but further advance is hampered by the lack of suitable human mutants. Reports of proteins induced by DNA damage or produced in abnormal amounts by patients with XP and BS are interesting, but again their significance is still uncertain (Miskin & Ben-Ishai, 1981; Mallick *et al.* 1982; Schorpp *et al.* 1984; Kenne & Ljungquist, 1984).

The importance of redox reactions in the activations of chemical DNA-damaging agents, the intermediacy of free radicals in the action of physical and some chemical

DNA-damaging agents and the endogenous DNA damage that could be caused by oxygen-related free radicals suggest that the complex mechanisms for the containment and dissipation of free radicals may play an important role in the control of DNA stability and cellullar wellbeing.

Recently, the advances of molecular biology have opened new avenues for the study of DNA repair in man and other organisms. Thus a fervour for investigations based on new methodological approaches has begun to bear its fruits. For example, the combined use of sequencing, enzymic probes and detailed gene analysis has led to the demonstration that the u.v. light-induced lesion, called the 6–4 pyrimidine photoproduct may be a major mutagenic lesion (Lippke *et al.* 1981; Haseltine, 1983). The ability to probe specific, highly amplified, expressed genes has permitted the comparison of pyrimidine dimer repair in expressed and non-expressed mammalian DNA sequences (Bohr *et al.* 1985). The development of transfection procedures and genetically engineered shuttle vectors capable of growing in both mammalian cells and *E. coli* have permitted the use of not only viral but also laboratory constructed replicons to study homologous and non-homologous DNA recombination, repair and both direct and indirect mutagenesis in mammalian cells (Kucherlapati *et al.* 1984; De Saint Vincent & Wahl, 1983; Shapira *et al.* 1983; Subramani & Rubnitz, 1985; Lin *et al.* 1984; Cox *et al.* 1984; Ashman & Davidson, 1984; Calos *et al.* 1983; Miller *et al.* 1984; Wake *et al.* 1984; Sarkar *et al.* 1984). However the events occurring on such exogenous replicons may not adequately represent those occurring in the normal genome. In fact the transfected DNA undergoes extensive damage and degradation and shows mutation rates four orders of magnitude higher than those of cellular genes.

Of particular importance is the development of procedures for the cloning of repair genes. Many such genes of *E. coli* have been cloned and their products characterized (see Friedberg, 1985, for a review). Progress in yeast has also been substantial as at least seven DNA repair genes have been cloned and at least partially characterized (Higgins *et al.* 1983, 1984; Naumovski & Friedberg, 1983; Naumovski *et al.* 1985; Kupiek & Simchen, 1984; Yasui & Langeveld, 1985; Schild *et al.* 1984; Reynolds *et al.* 1985*a,b*; Yan & Friedberg, 1984; Weiss & Friedberg, 1985).

More complex and, therefore, less successful has proved the cloning of human DNA repair genes, but a valid approach has been developed. This is as follows: segments of human DNA are ligated to a selectable gene marker before transfection into a DNA repair-deficient mammalian cell line (e.g. a Chinese hamster ovary (CHO) derivative). Cells that have taken up and express the selectable gene can be isolated and tested for resistance to an appropriate DNA-damaging agent. Any cell that has become resistant by the integration and expression of a transfected gene should contain human DNA. This can be easily tested by hybridization to probes specific for human dispersed repetitive DNA sequences. The human DNA from a resistant cell clone, presumably containing the gene of interest, can then be purified by a second cycle of transfection. Thus DNA is extracted from the resistant cloned cells and transfected into repair-deficient CHO cells. If these become repair-proficient by the expression of a transfected gene they are likely to contain only the human DNA of interest. A genomic DNA library from such a second-cycle transformant may be used to isolate the human DNA. Unique sequences from such a human DNA can then be used to identify or hybrid-select the corresponding messenger RNA or complementary DNA and to assign the cloned DNA to the appropriate chromosome or chromosomal region. In this way a human gene, which corrects the hypersensitivity to u.v. and mitomycin C (MMC) and the incision defect of a CHO cell line, has been identified, partly characterized and assigned to chromosome 19 (Westerveld *et al.* 1984; Rubin *et al.* 1985).

The transfection of human DNA into human cells has not led yet to the isolation of DNA repair genes as this presents additional difficulties (e.g. the identification of the donor DNA). Recently, however, Okayama & Berg (1985) have developed a vector, for the transduction of cDNA clone libraries into mammalian cells, that should facilitate considerably experiments of the type outlined above. In fact, this vector should overcome or reduce the difficulties due to the complexity of the human genome, the size of the human genes, and their expression after integration. The vector has also been designed to facilitate identification and recovery of the foreign DNA. The main problem in this case is the quality of the cDNA libraries.

This augurs well for the future, but of course the function and biological importance of any human gene isolated can be assessed only when individuals mutant for the gene are available. It follows, therefore, that a serious limitation to the above approach is the variety of CHO or other cellular mutants that are true analogues of defects found in man or, conversely, of the variety of patient-derived human cell lines with defects of DNA repair that can be used as recipients of mammalian repair genes. The isolation of human repair genes seems necessary to unravel the complexities of human DNA repair pathways and its academic importance cannot be overstated. Less clear are the immediate practical benefits that could be derived from such endeavours. These refer to the genetic counselling of diseases with DNA repair defects and to the identification of individuals predisposed to cancer. According to current schemes, if a relevant DNA repair gene had been cloned, and if probes capable of detecting intra- and perigenic restriction fragment length polymorphisms (RFLP) were available, they could be used to follow the segregation of defective genes in families and to diagnose at least a proportion of the carriers or affected individuals in the family (see Brownlee, 1986, this volume). However, in the genetic counselling of rare autosomal recessive diseases such as XP, AT, FA, CS and BS the identification of carriers is strictly necessary only when individuals at risk marry a blood relative as, otherwise, the chance of marrying a heterozygote for the same defect is very low. Very important, on the contrary, is prenatal diagnosis because parents of a patient, at each new pregnancy, have a 1 in 4 risk of producing an affected child. Direct prenatal diagnostic tests are already available for such diseases (Ramsay *et al.* 1974; Giannelli *et al.* 1982*a*; Auerbach *et al.* 1981; Shipley *et al.* 1984; Lehmann *et al.* 1985), but the analysis of the familial segregation of DNA polymorphisms could be a useful addition.

Very important would also be the identification of heterozygotes for DNA repair defects if these individuals were prone to cancer. However, current methods of DNA diagnosis based on the detection of RFLP or on the use of mutation-specific probes are not likely to be very helpful because, in practice, they may diagnose directly only those mutations that have been favoured and fixed in the population by natural selection. Other mutations, which cause the vast majority of the serious, rare genetic defects, such as those relevant to this discussion, are usually identified indirectly by their family specific pattern of cosegregation with linked RFLPs. In this case, it is essential to know the polymorphic marker associated with the mutations of the affected individuals in each family. However, in rare autosomal recessive conditions and especially those with a high degree of genetic heterogeneity, such as XP and possibly also AT, FA and CS, only a very small minority of heterozygotes may have an affected relative. Therefore, effective screening for such individuals will have to be based on the direct assay of genes or their products or on indirect functional assays rather than DNA polymorphisms.

There is no doubt that we are approaching a time of great progress in the understanding of DNA repair in man through the isolation of repair genes and the identification of their products. This, however, will require not only the application of recombinant DNA technology but also the development of suitable functional and enzymic assays and, most of all, the identification of a more complete range of natural mutants and cell lines with well-defined genomes.

I am grateful to Professor P. E. Polani for stimulating discussions. The work was supported by the Cancer Research Campaign and the Spastics Society.

REFERENCES

AKAMATSU, N., MIYAKI, M., SUZUKI, K., ONO, T. & ASAKI, M. S. (1983). Mechanism of increased susceptibility to 4-nitroquinoline-1-oxide in cultured skin fibroblasts from patients with familial polyposis coli. *Mutat. Res.* **120**, 173–180.

ALBERTINI, R. J. & DE MARS, R. (1973). Somatic cell mutation – Detection and quantification of X-ray induced mutation in cultured, diploid human fibroblasts. *Mutat. Res.* **18**, 199–222.

ARASE, S., KOZUKA, T., TANAKA, K., IKENAGA, M. & TAKEBE, H. (1979). A sixth complementation group in xeroderma pigmentosum. *Mutat. Res.* **59**, 143–146.

ARLETT, C. F. (1980). Presymptomatic diagnosis of Huntington's disease. *Lancet* **i**, 540.

ARLETT, C. F., HARCOURT, S. A., LEHMANN, A. R., STEVENS, S., FERGUSON-SMITH, M. A. & MOSLEY, W. N. (1980). Studies on a new case of xeroderma pigmentosum (XP 3BR) from complementation group G with cellular sensitivity to ionising radiation. *Carcinogenesis* **1**, 745–751.

ARLETT, C. F. & LEHMANN, A. R. (1978). Human disorders showing increased sensitivity to the induction of genetic damage. *A. Rev. Genet.* **12**, 95–115.

ASHMAN, C. R. & DAVIDSON, R. L. (1984). High spontaneous mutation frequency in shuttle vector sequences recovered from mammalian cellular DNA. *Molec. cell. Biol.* **4**, 2266–2272.

AUERBACH, A. D., ALDER, B. & CHAGANTI, R. S. K. (1981). Prenatal and postnatal diagnosis and carrier detection of Fanconi anemia by a cytogenetic method. *Pediatrics* **67**, 128–135.

AUERBACH, C. (1976). *Mutation Research*. London: Chapman & Hall.

AYRES, K., SKLAR, R., LARSON, K., LINDGREN, V. & STRAUSS, B. (1982). Regulation of the capacity for O^6-methylguanine removal from DNA in human lymphoblastoid cells studied by cell hybridization. *Molec. cell. Biol.* **2**, 904–913.

BABIOR, B. M. (1978). Oxygen-dependent microbial killing by phagocytes. *N. Engl. J. Med.* **298**, 721–725.

BAKER, T. G. (1971). Comparative aspects of the effects of radiation during oogenesis. *Mutat. Res.* **11**, 9–22.

BARFKNECHT, T. R. & LITTLE, J. B. (1982). Abnormal sensitivity of skin fibroblasts from familial polyposis patients to DNA alkylating agents. *Cancer Res.* **2**, 1249–1254.

BELLVÉ, A. R. & O'BRIEN, D. A. (1983). The mammalian spermatozoon: structure and temporal assembly. In *Mechanisms and Control of Animal Fertilization* (ed. J. F. Hartmann), pp. 55–137. New York, London: Academic Press.

BERNSTEIN, H., BYERLY, H. C., HOPF, F. A. & MICHOD, R. E. (1984). Origin of sex. *J. theor. Biol.* **110**, 323–351.

BISHOP, J. M. (1985). Viral oncogenes. *Cell* **42**, 23–38.

BOHR, V. & HANAWALT, P. (1984). Factors that affect the initiation of excision repair in chromatin. In *RNA Repair and Its Inhibition* (ed. A. Collins, C. S. Downes & R. T. Johnson), pp. 109–125. Oxford: IRL Press.

BOHR, V. A., SMITH, C. A., OKUMOTO, D. S. & HANAWALT, P. C. (1985). DNA repair in an active gene: removal of pyrimidine dimers from the DHFR gene of CHO cells is much more efficient than in the genome overall. *Cell* **40**, 359–369.

BOTCHERBY, P. K., MAGNUS, I. A., MARIMO, B. & GIANNELLI, F. (1984). Actinic recticuloid – An idiopathic photodermatosis with cellular sensitivity to near ultraviolet radiation. *Photochem. Photobiol.* **39**, 641–649.

BRADLEY, M. O., ERICKSON, L. C. & KOHN, K. W. (1976). Normal DNA strand rejoining and absence of DNA crosslinking in progeroid and aging human cells. *Mutat. Res.* **37**, 279–292.

BRENNAN, S. & LEWIS, P. D. (1983). Studies of cellular radiosensitivity in hereditary disorders of nervous system and muscle. *J. Neurol. Neurosurg. Psychiat* **46**, 1143–1145

BRENT, T. P., HOUGHTON, P. J. & HOUGHTON, J. A. (1985). O^6-Alkylguanine–DNA alkyltransferase activity correlates with the therapeutic response of human rhabdomyosarcoma xenographs to 1-(2-chloroethyl)-3-(trans-4-methylcyclohexyl)-1-nitrosourea. *Proc. natn. Acad. Sci. U.S.A.* **82**, 2985–2989.

BRIDGES, B. A. (1981). How important are somatic mutations and immune control in skin cancer? Reflections on xeroderma pigmentosum. *Carcinogenesis* **2**, 471–472.

BRIDGES, B. A. & HARNDEN, D. G. (1982). *Ataxia-Telangiectasia – A Cellular and Molecular Link between Cancer, Neuropathology and Immune Deficiency*. Chichester: Wiley.

BROWN, K. W. & HARNDEN, D. G. (1978). Erythrocyte superoxide dismutase in ataxia-telangiectasia and Fanconi anaemia. *Lancet* **ii**, 1260–1261.

BROWN, W. M., GEORGE, M. JR & WILSON, A. C. (1979). Rapid evolution of animal mitochondrial DNA. *Proc. natn. Acad. Sci. U.S.A.* **76**, 1967–1971.

BROWN, W. T., FORD, J. P. & GERSHEY, E. L. (1980). Variation of DNA repair in progeria cells unrelated to growth conditions. *Biochem. biophys. Res. Commun.* **97**, 347–353.

BROWN, W. T., LITTLE, J. B., EPSTEIN, J. & WILLIAMS, J. R. (1978). DNA repair defect in progeric cells. In *Genetic Effects on Aging* (ed. D. Bergsma, D. F. Harrison & N. W. Paul), pp. 417–430. New York: Liss.

BROWNLEE, G. (1986). The molecular genetics of haemophilia A and B. *J. Cell Sci. Suppl. 4*, 445–458.

BUS, J. S. & GIBSON, J. E. (1979). Lipid peroxidation and its role in toxicology. In *Reviews in Biochemical Toxicology,* vol. I (ed. E. Hodgson, J. R. Bend & R. M. Philpot), pp. 125–149. New York, Oxford: Elsevier/North Holland.

CAIRNS, J. (1981). The origin of human cancers. *Nature, Lond.* **289**, 353–357.

CALOS, M. P., LEBKOSKI, J. S. & BOTCHAN, M. R. (1983). High mutation frequency in DNA transfected into mammalian cells. *Proc. natn. Acad. Sci. U.S.A.* **80**, 3015–3019.

CAVENÉE, W. K., DRYJA, T. P., PHILLIPS, R. A., BENEDICT, W. F., GODBOUT, R., GALLIE, B. L., MURPHREE, A. L., STRONG, L. C. & WHITE, R. L. (1983). Expression of recessive alleles by chromosomal mechanisms in retinoblastoma. *Nature, Lond.* **305**, 779–784.

CAVENÉE, W. K., HANSEN, M. F., NORDENSKJOLD, M., KOCK, E., MAUMENEE, I., SQUIRE, J. A., PHILLIPS, R. A. & GALLIE, B. L. (1985). Genetic origin of mutations predisposing to retinoblastoma. *Science* **228**, 501–503.

CHAN, G. L. & LITTLE, J. B. (1983). Cultured diploid fibroblasts from patients with Nevoid Basal Cell Carcinoma Syndrome are hypersensitive to killing by ionizing radiation. *Am. J. Path.* **111**, 50–55.

CHANCE, B., SIES, H. & BOVERIS, A. (1979). Hydroperoxide metabolism in mammalian organs. *Physiol. Rev.* **59**, 527–605.

CHEN, P., IMRAY, F. P. & KIDSON, C. (1984). Gene dosage and complementation analysis of ataxia telangiectasia lymphoblastoid cell lines assayed by induced chromosome aberrations. *Mutat Res.* **129**, 165–172.

CHEN, P., KIDSON, C. & IMRAY, F. P. (1981). Huntington's Disease: implications of associated cellular radiosensitivity. *Clin. Genet.* **20**, 331–336.

CLAYTON, D. A., DODA, J. N. & FRIEDBERG, E. C. (1974). The absence of a pyrimidine dimer repair mechanism in mammalian mitochondria. *Proc. natn. Acad. Sci. U.S.A.* **71**, 2777–2781.

CLEAVER, J. E. (1968). Defective repair replication of DNA in xeroderma pigmentosum. *Nature, Lond.* **218**, 652–656.

CLEAVER, J. E. (1982). Inactivation of ultraviolet repair in normal and xeroderma cells by methyl methane sulfonate. *Cancer Res.* **42**, 860–863.

CLEAVER, J. E. (1983). Xeroderma pigmentosum. In *The Metabolic Basis of Inherited Disease* (ed. J. B. Stanbury, J. R. Wyngarden, D. S. Fredrickson, J. L. Goldstein & M. S. Brown), pp. 1227–1248. New York, London: McGraw Hill.

CLEAVER, J. E. & GRUENERT, D. C. (1984). Repair of psoralen adducts in human DNA: Differences among xeroderma pigmentosum complementation groups. *J. invest. Derm.* **82**, 311–315.

COHEN, J. (1975). Gamete redundancy – wastage or selection? In *Gamete Competition in Plants and Animals* (ed. D. L. Mulcahy), pp. 99–112. Amsterdam: North-Holland.

COOK, P. R., BRAZELL, I. A., PAWSEY, S. A. & GIANNELLI, F. (1978). Changes induced by ultraviolet light in the superhelical DNA of lymphocytes from subjects with xeroderma pigmentosum and normal controls. *J. Cell Sci.* **29**, 117–127.

COULONDRE, C., MILLER, J. H., FARABAUGH, P. J. & GILBERT, W. (1978). Molecular basis of base substitution hotspots in *Escherichia coli. Nature, Lond.* **274**, 775–780.

COX, B. D. & LYON, M. F. (1975). X-ray induced dominant lethal mutations in mature and immature oocytes of guinea pigs and golden hamsters. *Mutat. Res.* **28**, 421–436.

COX, R. (1982). A cellular description of the repair defect in ataxia telangiectasia. In *Ataxia-telangiectasia: A Cellular and Molecular Link between Cancer, Neuropathology and Immune Deficiency* (ed. B. A. Bridges & D. G. Harnden), pp. 141–153. Chichester: Wiley.

COX, R., HOSKING, G. P. & WILSON, J. (1978). Ataxia telangiectasia: the evaluation of radiosensitivity in cultured skin fibroblasts as a diagnostic test. *Archs Dis. Childh.* **53**, 386–390.

COX, R. & MASSON, W. K. (1980). Radiosensitivity in cultured human fibroblasts. *Int. J. Radiat. Biol.* **38**, 575–576.

COX, R., MASSON, W. K., DEBENHAM, P. G. & WEBB, M. B. T. (1984). The use of recombinant DNA plasmids for the determination of DNA repair and recombination in cultured mammalian cells. *Br. J. Cancer* **49**, 67–72.

DE JONGE, A. J. R., VERMEULEN, W., KLEIN, W., BERENDS, F. & BOOTSMA, D. (1983). Microinjection of human cell extracts corrects xeroderma pigmentosum defect. *EMBO J.* **2**, 637–641.

DE SAINT VINCENT, B. R. & WAHL, G. M. (1983). Homologous recombination in mammalian cells mediates formation of a functional gene from two overlapping gene fragments. *Proc. natn. Acad. Sci. U.S.A.* **80**, 2002–2006.

DESCHAVANNE, P. J., CHAVAUDRA, N., DEBIEU, D. & MALAISE, E. P. (1984). Reduced PLD repair ability in glutathione synthetase deficient human fibroblasts after UV irradiation. *Int. J. Radiat. Biol.* **46**, 375–382.

DEUSTCH, W. A. & LINN, S. (1979). DNA binding activity from cultured human fibroblasts that is specific for partially depurinated DNA and that inserts purines into apurinic sites. *Proc. natn. Acad. Sci. U.S.A.* **76**, 141–144.

DE WEERD-KASTELEIN, E. A., KEIJZER, W. & BOOTSMA, D. (1972). Genetic heterogeneity of xeroderma pigmentosum demonstrated by somatic cell hybridization. *Nature, new Biol.* **238**, 80–83.

DE WEERD-KASTELEIN, E. A., KEIJZER, W. & BOOTSMA, D. (1974). A third complementation group in xeroderma pigmentosum. *Mutat. Res.* **22**, 87–91.

DE WIT, J., JASPERS, N. G. J. & BOOTSMA, D. (1981). The rate of DNA synthesis in normal human and ataxia telangiectasia cells after exposure to X-irradiation. *Mutat. Res.* **80**, 221–226.

DOLPHIN, G. W., LLOYD, D. C. & PURROTT, R. J. (1973). Chromosome aberration analysis as a dosimetric technique in radiological protection. *Health Phys.* **25**, 1–7.

DOMORADZKI, J., PEGG, A. E., DOLAN, M. E., MAHER, V. M. & MCCORMICK, J. J. (1984). Correlation between O^6-methylguanine–DNA methyltransferase activity and resistance of human cells to the cytotoxic and mutagenic effect of N-methyl-N'-nitro-N-nitrosoguanidine. *Carcinogenesis* **5**, 1641–1647.

DUCKWORTH-RYSIECKI, G., CORNISH, K., CLARKE, C. A. & BUCKWALD, M. (1985). Identification of two complementation groups in Fanconi anaemia. *Somat. Cell molec. Genet.* **11**, 35–41.

EDWARDS, M. J. & TAYLOR, A. M. R. (1980). Unusual levels of (ADP-ribose)n and DNA synthesis in ataxia telangiectasia cells following γ-ray irradiation. *Nature, Lond.* **287**, 745–747.

EHLING, U. H. & FAVOR, J. (1984). Recessive and dominant mutations in mice. In *Mutation, Cancer and Malformation* (ed. E. H. Y. Chu & W. M. Generoso), pp. 389–428. New York, London: Plenum.

EJIMA, Y., SASAKI, M. S., UTSUMI, H., KANEKO, A. & TANOOKA, H. (1982). Radiosensitivity of fibroblasts from patients with retinoblastoma and chromosome-13 anomalies. *Mutat. Res.* **103**, 177–184.

EMERIT, I. (1980). Chromosomal instability in collagen disease. *Z. Rheumat.* **39**, 84–90.

EMERIT, I. & CERUTTI, P. (1981). Clastogenic activity from Bloom Syndrome fibroblast cultures. *Proc. natn. Acad. Sci. U.S.A.* **78**, 1868–1872.

EMERIT, I. & CERUTTI, P. (1984). Icosanoids and chromosome damage. In *Icosanoids and Cancer* (ed. H. Thaler-Dao, A. Crastes de Paulet & R. Paoletti), pp. 127–138. New York: Raven Press.

EMERIT, I., CERUTTI, P. A., LEVY, A. & JALBERT, P. (1982). Chromosome breakage factor in the plasma of two Bloom's syndrome patients. *Hum. Genet.* **61**, 65–67.

EVANS, H. J., VIJAYALAXMI & NEWTON, M. S. (1982). The response of cells from patients with Huntington's Chorea to mutagen-induced chromosome damage. *Ann. hum. Genet.* **46**, 177–185.

FEATHERSTONE, T., TAYLOR, A. M. R. & HARNDEN, D. G. (1983). Studies on the radiosensitivity of cells from patients with basal cell naevus syndrome. *Am. J. hum. Genet.* **35**, 58–66.

FISHER, E., KEIJZER, W., THIELMANN, H. W., POPANDA, O., BOHNERT, E., EDLER, L., JUNG, E. G. & BOOTSMA, D. (1985). A ninth complementation group in xeroderma pigmentosum, XP I. *Mutat. Res.* **145**, 217–225.

FORNACE, A. J. JR, KOHN, K. W. & KANN, H. E. JR (1976). DNA single-strand breaks during repair of UV damage in human fibroblasts and abnormalities of repair in xeroderma pigmentosum. *Proc. natn. Acad. Sci. U.S.A.* **73**, 39–43.

FORNACE, A. J. JR, LITTLE, J. B. & WEICHSELBAUM, R. R. (1979). DNA repair in Fanconi's anemia fibroblast cell strain. *Biochim. biophys. Acta* **561**, 99–109.

FRANCIS, A. A., LEE, W. H. & REGAN, J. A. (1981). The relationship of DNA excision repair of ultraviolet induced lesions to the maximum life span of mammals. *Mech. Ageing Dev.* **16**, 181–189.

FRIEDBERG, E. C. (1985). *DNA Repair*. New York: Freeman.

FUJIWARA, Y. (1982). Defective repair of mitomycin C crosslinks in Fanconi's anaemia and loss in confluent normal human and xeroderma pigmentosum cells. *Biochim. biophys. Acta* **699**, 217–225.

FUJIWARA, Y., GOTO, K. & KANO, Y. (1982). Ultraviolet hypersensitivity of Cockayne's syndrome fibroblasts – Effects of nicotinamide adenine dinucleotide and poly(ADP-ribose) synthesis. *Expl Cell Res.* **139**, 207–215.

FUJIWARA, Y., HIGASHIKAWA, T. & TATSUMI, M. (1977a). A retarded rate of DNA replication and normal level of DNA repair in Werner's syndrome fibroblasts in culture. *J. cell. Physiol.* **92**, 365–374.

FUJIWARA, Y., TATSUMI, M. & SASAKI, M. S. (1977b). Cross-link repair in human cells and its possible defect in Fanconi's anemia cells. *J. molec. Biol.* **113**, 635–649.

FUJIWARA, Y., UEHARA, Y., ICHIHASHI, M. & NISHIOKA, K. (1985a). Xeroderma pigmentosum complementation group F: more assignments and repair characteristics. *Photochem. Photobiol.* **41**, 629–634.

FUJIWARA, Y., UEHARA, Y., ICHIHASHI, M., YAMAMOTO Y. & NISHIOKA, K. (1985b). Assignment of 2 patients with xeroderma pigmentosum to complementation group E. *Mutat. Res.* **145**, 55–61.

GAINER, H. ST. C. & KINSELLA, A. R. (1983). Analysis of spontaneous, carcinogen-induced and promoter-induced chromosomal instability in patients with hereditary retinoblastoma. *Int. J. Cancer* **32**, 449–453.

GANTT, R., TAYLOR, W. G., CAMALIER, R. F. & STEPHENS, E. V. (1984). Repair of DNA–protein cross-links in an excision repair-deficient human cell line and its simian virus 40-transformed derivative. *Cancer Res.* **44**, 1809–1812.

GEBHART, E., SCHINZEL, M. & RUPRECHT, K. W. (1985). Cytogenetic studies using various clastogens in two patients with Werner Syndrome and control individuals. *Hum. Genet.* **70**, 324–327.

GERMAN, J. (1979). Bloom's syndrome. VIII. Review of clinical and genetic aspects. In *Genetic Diseases among Ashkenazi Jews* (ed. R. M. Goodman & A. G. Motulsky), pp. 121–139. New York: Raven Press.

GIANNELLI, F. (1970). *Human Chromosomes DNA Synthesis* (ed. L. Beckman & M. Hauge). Basel: Karger. (Monographs in Hum. Genet. no. 5.)

GIANNELLI, F. (1982). The repair of genetic damage and its relevance to human health. In *Paediatric Research: A Genetic Approach* (ed. M. Adinolfi, P. Benson, F. Giannelli & M. Seller), pp. 47–75. London: Heinemann.

GIANNELLI, F., AVERY, J. A., PEMBREY, M. E. & BLUNT, S. (1982*a*). Prenatal exclusion of ataxia-telangiectasia. In *Ataxia-telangiectasia: A Cellular and Molecular Link Between Cancer, Neuropathology and Immune Deficiency* (ed. B. A. Bridges & D. G. Harnden), pp. 393–400. Chichester: Wiley.

GIANNELLI, F., BENSON, P. F., PAWSEY, S. A. & POLANI, P. E. (1977). Ultraviolet light sensitivity and delayed DNA-chain maturation in Bloom's syndrome fibroblasts. *Nature, Lond.* **265**, 466–469.

GIANNELLI, F., BOTCHERBY, P. K. & AVERY, J. A. (1982*b*). The effect of aphidicolin on the rate of DNA replication and unscheduled DNA synthesis of Bloom syndrome and normal fibroblasts. *Hum. Genet.* **60**, 357–359.

GIANNELLI, F., BOTCHERBY, P. K., MARIMO, B. & MAGNUS, I. A. (1983). Cellular hypersensitivity to UV-A: a clue to the aetiology of actinic reticuloid. *Lancet* **i**, 88–91.

GIANNELLI, F., CROLL, P. M. & LEWIN, S. A. (1973). DNA repair synthesis in human heterokaryons formed by normal and UV-sensitive fibroblasts. *Expl Cell Res.* **78**, 175–185.

GIANNELLI, F. & PAWSEY, S. A. (1976). DNA repair synthesis in human heterokaryons III. The rapid and slow complementing varieties of xeroderma pigmentosum. *J. Cell Sci.* **20**, 207–213.

GIANNELLI, F., PAWSEY, S. A. & AVERY, J. A. (1982*c*). Differences in the patterns of complementation of the more common groups of xeroderma pigmentosum. Possible implications. *Cell* **29**, 451–458.

GIANNELLI, F., PAWSEY, S. A. & BOTCHERBY, P. K. (1981). Tendency to high levels of UVR-induced unscheduled DNA synthesis in Bloom syndrome. *Mutat. Res.* **81**, 229–241.

GIBSON, N. W., ZLOTOGORSKI, C. & ERICKSON, L. C. (1985). Specific DNA repair mechanisms may protect some human tumor cells from DNA interstrand cross-linking by chloro-ethylnitrosoureas but not from cross-linking by other anti-tumor alkylating agents. *Carcinogenesis* **6**, 445–450.

GIPPS, E. & KIDSON, C. (1981). Ionising radiation sensitivity in multiple sclerosis. *Lancet* **i**, 947.

GOODMAN, M. (1976). Towards a genealogical description of the primates. In *Molecular Anthropology: Genes and Protein in Evolutionary Ascent of Primates* (ed. M. Goodman & R. E. Tashian), pp. 321–353. New York: Plenum.

GOODMAN, M., KOOP, B. F., CZELUSNIAK, J., WEISS, M. L. & SLIGHTOM, J. L. (1984). The η-globin gene. Its long evolutionary history in the β-globin gene family of mammals. *J. molec. Biol.* **180**, 803–823.

GROSSE, F., KRAUSS, G., KNILL-JONES, J. W. & FERSHT, A. R. (1983). Accuracy of DNA polymerase-α in copying natural DNA. *EMBO J.* **2**, 1515–1519.

GUPTA, P. K. & SIROVER, M. A. (1984). Altered temporal expression of DNA repair in hypermutable Bloom's syndrome cells. *Proc. natn. Acad. Sci. U.S.A.* **81**, 757–761.

GUPTA, R. S. & GOLDSTEIN, S. (1980). Diphtheria toxin resistance in human fibroblast cell strains from normal and cancer-prone individuals. *Mutat. Res.* **73**, 331–338.

GUZZETTA, F. (1972). Cockayne–Neil–Dingwall Syndrome. In *Handbook of Clinical Neurology*, vol. 13 (ed. P. J. Vinken & G. W. Bruyn), pp. 431–440. Amsterdam: North Holland.

HALL, J. D., ALMY, R. E. & SCHERER, K. L. (1982). DNA repair in cultured human fibroblasts does not decline with donor age. *Expl Cell Res.* **139**, 351–359.

HALL, K. Y., HART, R. W., BENIRSCHKE, A. K. & WALFORD, R. L. (1984). Correlation between ultraviolet-induced DNA repair in primate lymphocytes and fibroblasts and species maximum achievable life span. *Mech. Ageing Dev.* **24**, 163–173.

HAND, R. & GERMAN, J. (1975). A. retarded rate of DNA chain growth in Bloom's syndrome. *Proc. natn. Acad. Sci. U.S.A.* **72**, 758–762.

HAND, R. & GERMAN, J. (1977). Bloom's syndrome: DNA replication in cultured fibroblasts and lymphocytes. *Hum. Genet.* **38**, 297–306.

HARRIS, A. L., KARRAN, P. & LINDAHL, T. (1983). O^6-methylguanine–DNA methyltransferase of human lymphoid cells: structural and kinetic properties and absence in repair-deficient cells. *Cancer Res.* **43**, 3247–3252.

HARRIS, G., ASBERY, L., LANCEY, P. D., DENNAN, A. M. & HYLTON, W. (1982). Defective repair of O^6-methylguanine in autoimmune diseases. *Lancet* **ii**, 952–956.

HART, R. W. & SETLOW, R. B. (1974). Correlation between deoxyribonucleic acid excision repair and life-span in a number of mammalian species. *Proc. natn. Acad. Sci. U.S.A.* **71**, 2169–2173.

HART, R. W., SETLOW, R. B. & WOODHEAD, A. D. (1977). Evidence that pyrimidine dimers in DNA can give rise to tumors. *Proc. natn. Acad. Sci. U.S.A.* **74**, 5574–5578.

HASELTINE, W. A. (1983). Site specificity of ultraviolet light induced mutagenesis. In *Cellular Responses to DNA Damage* (ed. E. C. Friedberg & B. A. Bridges), pp. 3–22. New York: Liss.

HECHT, N. B., LIEM, H., KLEENE, K. C., DISTEL, R. J. & HO, S. M. (1984). Maternal inheritance of the mouse mitochondrial genome is not mediated by a loss or gross alteration of the paternal mitochondrial DNA or by methylation of the oocyte mitochondrial DNA. *Devl Biol.* **102**, 452–461.

HENDERSON, L. M., ARLETT, C. F., HARCOURT, S. A., LEHMANN, A. R. & BROUGHTON, B. C. (1985). Cells from an immunodeficient patient (46 BR) with a defect in DNA ligation are hypomutable but hypersensitive to the induction of sister chromatid exchanges. *Proc. natn. Acad. Sci. U.S.A.* **82**, 2044–2048.

HENSON, P., FORNACE, A. J. JR & LITTLE, J. B. (1983). Normal repair of ultraviolet induced DNA damage in a hypersensitive strain of fibroblasts from a patient with Gardner's syndrome. *Mutat. Res.* **112**, 383–395.

HERREROS, B. & GIANNELLI, F. (1967). Spatial distribution of old and new chromatid subunits and frequency of chromatid exchanges in induced human lymphocytes endoreduplications. *Nature, Lond.* **216**, 286–288.

HIGGINS, D. R., PRAKASH, S., REYNOLDS, P. & PRAKASH, L. (1983). Molecular cloning and characterisation of the *RAD 1* gene of *Saccharomyces cerevisiae*. *Gene* **26**, 119–126.

HIGGINS, D. R., PRAKASH, L., REYNOLDS, P. & PRAKASH, S. (1984). Isolation and characterisation of the *RAD 2* gene of *Saccharomyces cerevisiae*. *Gene* **30**, 121–128.

HOCHSTEIN, P. (1983). Futile redox cycling: implications for oxygen radical toxicity. *Fundam. appl. Toxicol.* **3**, 215–217.

HOOK, G. J., KWOK, E. & HEDDLE, J. A. (1984). Sensitivity of Bloom syndrome fibroblasts to mitomycin C. *Mutat. Res.* **131**, 223–230.

HORI, T., MURATA, M. & UTSUNOMIJA, J. (1980). Chromosome aberrations induced by N-methyl-N'-nitro-N-nitrosoguanidine in cultured skin fibroblasts from patients with adenomatosis coli. *Gann* **71**, 628–633.

HOULDSWORTH, J. & LAVIN, M. F. (1980). Effect of ionising radiation on DNA synthesis in ataxia-telangiectasia cells. *Nucl. Acids Res.* **8**, 3709–3720.

HOWELL, J. N., GREENE, M. H., CORNER, R. C., MAHER, V. M. & McCORMICK, J. J. (1984). Fibroblasts from patients with hereditary cutaneous malignant melanoma are abnormally sensitive to the mutagenic effect of simulated sunlight and 4-nitroquinoline-1-oxide. *Proc. natn. Acad. Sci. U.S.A.* **81**, 1179–1183.

ISHIZAKI, K., YAGI, T., INOUE, M., NIKAIDO, O. & TAKEBE, H. (1981). DNA repair in Bloom's syndrome fibroblasts after UV irradiation or treatment with mitomycin C. *Mutat. Res.* **80**, 213–219.

JASPERS, N. G. J. & BOOTSMA, D. (1982). Genetic heterogeneity in ataxia telangiectasia studied by cell fusion. *Proc. natn. Acad. Sci. U.S.A.* **79**, 2641–2644.

JONJIE, H., ARWERT, F., ERIKSSON, A. W., DE KONING, H. & OOSTRA, A. B. (1981). Oxygen-dependence of chromosomal aberrations in Fanconi's anaemia. *Nature, Lond.* **290**, 142–143.

JONJIE, H., OOSTRA, A. B. & WANAMARTA, A. H. (1983). Cytogenetic toxicity of D_2O in human lymphocyte cultures. Increased sensitivity in Fanconi's anemia. *Experientia* **39**, 782–784.

KANO, Y. & FUJIWARA, Y. (1983). Defective thymine dimer excision from xeroderma pigmentosum chromatin and its characteristic catalysis by cell-free extracts. *Carcinogenesis* **4**, 1419–1424.

KAPP, L. N. (1982). DNA fork displacement rates in Bloom's Syndrome fibroblasts. *Biochim. biophys. Acta* **696**, 226–227.

KATO, H., HARADA, M., TSUCHIYA, K. & MORIWAKI, K. (1980). Absence of correlation between DNA repair in ultra-violet irradiated mammalian cells and life span of the donor species. *Jap. J. Genet.* **55**, 99–108.

KAWAI, K., IKENAGA, M., OHTANI, H., FUKUCHI, K. I., YAMAMURA, K. I. & KUMAHARA, Y. (1983). Rapid procedures for prenatal diagnosis of Cockayne syndrome. *Jap. J. hum. Genet.* **28**, 223–229.

KAYE, J., SMITH, C. A. & HANAWALT, P. C. (1980). DNA repair in human cells containing photoadducts of 8-methoxypsoralen or angelicin. *Cancer Res.* **40**, 696–702.

KEIJZER, W., JASPERS, M. G. J., ABRAHAMS, P. J., TAYLOR, A. M. R., ARLETT, C. F., ZELLE, B., TAKEBE, J., KINMONT, P. D. S. & BOOTSMA, D. (1979). A. seventh complementation group in excision-deficient xeroderma pigmentosum. *Mutat. Res.* **62**, 183–190.

KENNE, K. & LJUNGQUIST, S. (1984). A DNA-recombinogenic activity in human cells. *Nucl. Acids Res.* **12**, 3057–3068.

KIDSON, C., CHEN, P., IMRAY, F. P. & GIPPS, E. (1983). Nervous system disease associated with dominant cellular radiosensivity. In *Cellular Responses to DNA Damage* (ed. E. C. Friedberg & B. A. Bridges), pp. 721–729. New York: Liss. (UCLA *Symp. Mol. Cell. Biol.*, New Series, vol. 11).

KINSELLA, T. J., MITCHELL, J. B., McPHERSON, S., RUSSO, A. & TVETZE, F. (1982). *In vitro* X-ray sensitivity in ataxia telangiectasia homozygote and heterozygote skin fibroblasts under oxic and hypoxic conditions. *Cancer Res.* **42**, 3950–3956.

KNUDSON, A. G. JR (1971). Mutation and cancer: statistical study of retinoblastoma. *Proc. natn. Acad. Sci. U.S.A.* **42**, 820–823.

KOPELOVICH, L. (1983). Skin fibroblasts from humans predisposed to colon cancer are not abnormally sensitive to DNA damaging agents. *Cell Biol. Int. Rep.* **7**, 369–375.

KOUFOS, A., HANSEN, M. F., COPELAND, N. G., JENKINS, N. A., LAMPKIN, B. C. & CAVENÉE, W. K. (1985). Loss of heterozygosity in three embryonal tumours suggest a common pathogenetic mechanism. *Nature, Lond.* **316**, 330–334.

KRAEMER, K. H., DE WEERD-KASTELEIN, E. A., ROBBINS, J. H., KEIJZER, W., BARRETT, S. F., PETINGA, R. A. & BOOTSMA, D. (1975). Five complementation groups in xeroderma pigmentosum. *Mutat. Res.* **33**, 327–340.

KRAEMER, K. H., LEE, M. M. & SCOTTO, J. (1984a). DNA repair protects against cutaneous and internal neoplasia: evidence from xeroderma pigmentosum. *Carcinogenesis* **5**, 511–514.

KRAEMER, K. H. & SLOR, H. (1984). Xeroderma pigmentosum. *Clin. Derm.* **2**, 33–69.

KRAEMER, K. H., UM, K. II, PERERA, M. I. R., GREENE, M. & WATERS, H. L. (1984b). Dysplastic nevus syndrome: ultraviolet hypermutability in association with increased melanoma susceptibility. *Photochem. Photobiol.* **39** (Suppl.) 51S.

KREPINSKI, A. B., HEDDLE, J. A. & GERMAN, J. (1979). Sensitivity of Bloom's syndrome lymphocytes to ethylmethane sulfonate. *Hum. Genet.* **50**, 151–156.

KREPINSKI, A. B., RAINBOW, A. J. & HEDDLE, J. A. (1980). Studies on the ultraviolet light sensitivity of Bloom's syndrome fibroblasts. *Mutat. Res.* **69**, 357–368.

KUCHERLAPATI, R. S., EVES, E. M., SONG, K-Y., MORSE, B. S. & SMITHIES, O. (1984). Homologous recombination between plasmids in mammalian cells can be enhanced by treatment of input DNA. *Proc. natn. Acad. Sci. U.S.A.* **81**, 3153–3157.

KUPIEK, M. & SIMCHEN, G. (1984). Cloning and mapping of the RAD 50 gene of *Saccharomyces cerevisiae. Molec. gen. Genet.* **193**, 525–531.

LANSMAN, R. A. & CLAYTON, D. A. (1975). Selective nicking of mammalian mitochondrial DNA *in vivo*: photosensitization by incorporation of 5-bromo-deoxyuridine. *J. molec. Biol.* **99**, 761–776.

LEGERSKI, R. J., BROWN, D. B., PETERSON, C. A. & ROBBERSON, D. L. (1984). Transient complementation of xeroderma pigmentosum cells by microinjection of poly(A)$^+$ RNA. *Proc. natn. Acad. Sci. U.S.A.* **81**, 5676–5679.

LEHMANN, A. R. (1982). Xeroderma pigmentosum, Cockayne syndrome and ataxia-telangiectasia: Disorders relating DNA repair to carcinogenesis. *Cancer Surv.* **1**, 93–118.

LEHMANN, A. R., FRANCIS, A. J. & GIANNELLI, F. (1985). Prenatal diagnosis of Cockayne's syndrome. *Lancet* **i**, 486–488.

LEHMANN, A. R., KIRK-BELL, S., ARLETT, C. F., HARCOURT, S. A., DE WEERD-KASTELEIN, E. A. & BOOTSMA, D. (1975). Xeroderma pigmentosum cells with normal levels of excision repair have a defect in DNA synthesis after UV-irradiation. *Proc. natn. Acad. Sci. U.S.A.* **72**, 219–223.

LEHMANN, A. R., KIRK-BELL, S. & MAYNE, L. (1979). Abnormal kinetics of DNA synthesis in ultraviolet-irradiated cells from patients with Cockayne's syndrome. *Cancer Res.* **39**, 4238–4241.

LIN, F.-L., SPERLE, K. & STERNBERG, N. (1984). Model for homologous recombination during transfer of DNA into mouse L cells: role for DNA ends in the recombination process. *Molec. cell. Biol.* **4**, 1020–1034.

LINDAHL, T. (1979). DNA glycosylases, endonucleases for apurinic/apyrimidinic sites and base excision repair. In *Progress in Nucleic Acid Research and Molecular Biology,* vol. 22 (ed. W. E. Cohn), pp. 135–192. New York, London: Academic Press.

LINDAHL, T. & KARLSTRÖM, O. (1973). Heat-induced depyrimidination of deoxyribonucleic acid in neutral solution. *Biochemistry* **12**, 5151–5154.

LINDAHL, T. & NYBERG, B. (1972). Rate of depurination of native deoxyribonucleic acid. *Biochemistry* **11**, 3610–3618.

LINDAHL, T. & NYBERG, B. (1974). Heat-induced deamination of cytosine residues in deoxyribonucleic acid. *Biochemistry* **13**, 3405–3410.

LIPPKE, J. A., GORDON, L. K., BRASH, D. E. & HASELTINE, W. A. (1981). Distribution of UV light-induced damage in a defined sequence of human DNA: detection of alkaline-sensitive lesions at pyrimidine nucleotide-cytidine sequences. *Proc. natn. Acad. Sci. U.S.A.* **78**, 3388–3392.

LITTLE, J. B., EPSTEIN, J. & WILLIAMS, J. R. (1975). Repair of DNA strand breaks in progeric fibroblasts and human diploid cells. In *Molecular Mechanisms for Repair of DNA,* part B (ed. P. C. Hanawalt & R. B. Setlow), pp. 793–800. New York: Plenum. (Basic Life Sciences, vol. 5)

LITTLE, J. B., NOVE, J. & WEICHSELBAUM, R. R. (1980). Abnormal sensitivity of diploid fibroblasts from a family with Gardner's Syndrome to the lethal effects of X-irradiation, ultraviolet light and mitomycin C. *Mutat. Res.* **70**, 241–250.

LIU, S.-C., PARSONS, C. S. & HANAWALT, P. C. (1982). DNA repair response in human epidermal keratinocytes from donors of different age. *J. invest. Derm.* **79**, 330–335.

LIVNEH, Z. & SPERLING, J. (1981). DNA base-insertion enzymes (insertases). In *The Enzymes,* 3rd edn, vol. 14, *Nucleic Acids,* part A (ed. P. D. Boyer), pp. 549–563. New York, London: Academic Press.

LOH, D. Y. & BALTIMORE, D. (1984). Sexual preference of apparent gene conversion events in MHC genes of mice. *Nature, Lond.* **309**, 639–640.

MAGNI, G. E. & SORA, S. (1969). Relationship between recombination and mutation. In *Mutation as a Cellular Process* (ed. G. E. W. Wolstenholme & R. M. O'Connor), pp. 186–198. London: Churchill.

MAGNUS, I. A. (1964). Studies with a monochromator in the common idiopathic photodermatoses. *Br. J. Derm.* **76**, 245–264.

MAGNUS, I. A. (1976). *Dermatological Photobiology, Clinical and Experimental Aspects*. Oxford, Blackwell.

MAHER, V. M. & McCORMICK, J. J. (1984). Role of DNA lesions and repair in the transformation of human cells. *Pharmac. Ther.* **25**, 395–408.

MALLICK, U., RAHMSDORF, H. J., YAMAMOTO, N., PONTA, H., WEGNER, R. D. & HERRLICH, P. (1982). 12-O-tetradecanoylphorbol 13-acetate-inducible proteins are synthesised at an increased rate in Bloom syndrome fibroblasts. *Proc. natn. Acad. Sci. U.S.A.* **79**, 7886–7890.

MANSBRIDGE, J. N. & HANAWALT, P. C. (1983). Domain-limited repair of DNA in ultraviolet irradiated fibroblasts from xeroderma pigmentosum complementation group C. In *Cellular Responses to DNA Damage* (ed. E. C. Friedberg & B. A. Bridges), pp. 195–207. New York: Liss. (UCLA *Symp. Mol. Cell. Biol.,* New Series, vol. 11).

MARTIN, R. (1977). A. possible genetic mechanism of ageing, rejuvenation and recombination in germinal cells. In *Human Cytogenetics* (ed. R. S. Sparks, D. E. Comings & C. F. Fox), pp. 355–377. New York: Academic Press. (ICN-UCLA *Symp. Mol. Cell. Biol.,* vol 7).

MAYNE, L. V. (1984). Inhibitors of DNA synthesis (Aphidicolin and araC/HU prevent the recovery of RNA synthesis after UV-irradiation. *Mutat. Res.* **131**, 187–191.

MAYNE, L. V., BROUGHTON, B. C. & LEHMANN, A. R. (1984). The ultra-violet sensitivity of Cockayne Syndrome cells is not a consequence of reduced cellular NAD content. *Am. J. hum. Genet.* **36**, 311–319.

MAYNE, L. V. & LEHMANN, A. R. (1982). Failure of RNA synthesis to recover after UV irradiation: an early defect in cells from individuals with Cockayne's Syndrome and xeroderma pigmentosum. *Cancer Res.* **42**, 1473–1478.

MAYNE, L. V., LEHMANN, A. R. & WATERS, R. (1982). Excision repair in Cockayne syndrome. *Mutat. Res.* **106**, 179–189.

McCREADY, S. J. & COOK, P. R. (1984). Lesions induced in DNA by ultraviolet light are repaired at the nuclear cage. *J. Cell Sci.* **70**, 189–196.

MEDVEDEV, Z. A. (1981). On the immortality of the germ line: genetic and biochemical mechanism. A review. *Mech. Ageing Dev.* **17**, 331–359.

MICHALOPOULOS, E. E., BEVILACQUA, P. J., STOKOE, N., POWERS, V. E., WILLARD, H. F. & LEWIS, W. T. (1985). Molecular analysis of gene deletion in Aniridia-Wilms tumor association. *Hum. Genet.* **70**, 157–162.

MILLER, J. H., LEBROWSKI, J. S., GREISEN, K. S. & CALOS, M. P. (1984). Specificity of mutations induced in transfected DNA by mammalian cells. *EMBO J.* **3**, 3117–3121.

MILLER, L. K., COOKE, B. E. & FRIED, M. (1976). Fate of mismatched base-pair regions in polyoma heteroduplex DNA during infection of mouse cells. *Proc. natn. Acad. Sci. U.S.A.* **73**, 3073–3077.

MISKIN, R. & BEN-ISHAI, R. (1981). Induction of plasminogen activator by UV light in normal and xeroderma pigmentosum fibroblasts. *Proc. natn. Acad. Sci. U.S.A.* **78**, 6236–6240.

MIYAKI, M., AKAMATSU, N., ONO, T., TONOMURA, A. & UTSUNOMIYA, J. (1982). Morphologic transformation and chromosomal changes induced by chemical carcinogens in skin fibroblasts from patients with familial adenomatosis coli. *J. natn. Cancer Inst.* **4**, 563–571.

MORTELMANS, K., FRIEDBERG, E. C., SLOR, H., THOMAS, G. & CLEAVER, J. E. (1976). Defective thymine dimer excision by cell-free extracts of xeroderma pigmentosum cells. *Proc. natn. Acad. Sci. U.S.A.* **73**, 2757–2761.

MORTEN, J. E. N., HARNDEN, D. G. & TAYLOR, A. M. R. (1981). Chromosome damage in G_0 X-irradiated lymphocytes from patients with hereditary retinoblastoma. *Cancer Res.* **41**, 3635–3638.

MOSHELL, A. N., GANGES, M. B., LUTZNER, M. A., COON, H. G., BARRETT, S. F., DUPUY, J-M. & ROBBINS, J. H. (1983). A. new patient with both xeroderma pigmentosum and Cockayne syndrome establishes the new xeroderma pigmentosum complementation group H. In *Cellular Responses to DNA Damage* (ed. E. C. Friedberg & B. A. Bridges), pp. 209–213. New York : Liss. (UCLA *Symp. Mol. Cell. Biol.*, New Series, Vol. 11).

MOSHELL, A. N., TARONE, R. E., BARRETT, S. F. & ROBBINS, J. H. (1980). Radiosensitivity in Huntington's disease: implications for pathogenesis and presymptomatic diagnosis. *Lancet* **i**, 9–11.

MOUSTACCHI, E., EHMANN, U. K. & FRIEDBERG, E. C. (1979). Defective recovery of semi-conservative DNA synthesis in xeroderma pigmentosum following split-dose ultraviolet irradiation. *Mutat. Res.* **62**, 159–171.

MULLENDERS, L. H. F., VAN KESTEREN, A. C., BUSSMANN, C. J. M., VAN ZEELAND, A. A. & NATARAJAN, A. T. (1984). Preferential repair of nuclear matrix associated DNA in xeroderma pigmentosum complementation group C. *Mutat. Res.* **141**, 75–82.

MURNANE, J. P. & PAINTER, R. B. (1982). Complementation of the defects in DNA synthesis in irradiated and unirradiated ataxia telangiectasia cells. *Proc. natn. Acad. Sci. U.S.A.* **79**, 1960–1963.

NAGASAWA, H., LATT, S. A., LALANDE, M. E. & LITTLE, J. B. (1985). Effects of X-irradiation on cell-cycle progression, induction of chromosomal aberrations and cell killing in ataxia telangiectasia (AT) fibroblasts. *Mutat. Res.* **148**, 71–82.

NAGASAWA, H. & LITTLE, J. B. (1983). Suppression of cytotoxic effect of mitomycin-C by superoxide dismutase in Fanconi's anaemia and dyskeratosis congenita fibroblasts. *Carcinogenesis* **4**, 795–798.

NATARAJAN, A. T., MEIJERS, M., VAN ZEELAND, A. A. & SIMONS, J. W. I. M. (1982). Attempts to detect ataxia telangiectasia (AT) heterozygotes by cytogenetical techniques. *Cytogenet. Cell Genet.* **33**, 145–151.

NAUMOVSKI, L., CHU, G., BERG, P. & FRIEDBERG, E. C. (1985). *RAD 3* gene of *Saccharomyces cerevisiae*: nucleotide sequence of wild type and mutant alleles, transcript mapping and aspects of gene regulation. *Molec. cell. Biol.* **5**, 17–26.

NAUMOVSKI, L. & FRIEDBERG, E. C. (1983). A DNA repair gene required for the incision of damaged DNA is essential for viability in *Saccharomyces cerevisiae*. *Proc. natn. Acad. Sci. U.S.A.* **80**, 4818–4821.

NEEL, J. V. (1983). Frequency of spontaneous and induced 'point' mutations in higher eukaryotes. *J. Hered.* **74**, 2–15.

NETRAWALI, M. S. & CERUTTI, P. A. (1979). Increased near-ultraviolet induced DNA fragmentation in xeroderma pigmentosum variants. *Biochem. biophys. Res. Commun.* **87**, 802–810.

NETTE, E. G., XI, Y.-P., SUN, Y.-K., ANDREWS, A. D. & KING, D. W. (1984). A correlation between ageing and DNA repair in human epidermal cells. *Mech. Ageing Dev.* **24**, 283–292.

NORDENSON, I. (1977). Effect of superoxide dismutase and catalase on spontaneously occurring chromosome breaks in patients with Fanconi's anaemia. *Hereditas* **86**, 147–150.

OCKEY, C. H. (1979). Quantitative replicon analysis of DNA synthesis in cancer-prone conditions and the defects in Bloom's syndrome. *J. Cell Sci.* **40**, 125–144.

OKAYAMA, H. & BERG, P. (1985). Bacteriophage lambda vector for transducing a cDNA clone library into mammalian cells. *Molec. cell. Biol.* **5**, 1136–1142.

OLSSON, M. & LINDAHL, T. (1980). Repair of alkylated DNA in *Escherichia coli*. Methyl group transfer from O^6-methylguanine to a protein cysteine residue. *J. biol. Chem.* **255**, 10569–10571.

ORKIN, S. H. (1984). Wilms' tumour: molecular evidence for the role of chromosome 11. *Cancer Surv.* **3**, 465–477.

PAINTER, R. B. (1982). Structural changes in chromatin as the basis for radiosensitivity in ataxia telangiectasia. *Cytogenet. Cell Genet.* **33**, 139–144.

PAINTER, R. B. & YOUNG, B. R. (1980). Radiosensitivity in ataxia-telangiectasia: a new explanation. *Proc. natn. Acad. Sci. U.S.A.* **77**, 7315–7317.

PARENTE, L. (1982). Study on the effect of superoxide dismutase on arachidonic acid metabolism. *Prostaglandins* **23**, 725–730.

PATERSON, M. C., SMITH, B. P. & SMITH, P. J. (1981). Measurement of enzyme-sensitive sites in UV or γ-irradiated human cells using *Micrococcus luteus* extracts. In *DNA Repair: A Laboratory Manual of Research Procedures,* vol. 1 (A) (ed. E. C. Friedberg & P. C. Hanawalt), pp. 99–111. New York: Dekker.

PAWSEY, S. A., MAGNUS, I. A., RAMSAY, C. A., BENSON, P. F. & GIANNELLI, F. (1979). Clinical, genetic and DNA repair studies on a consecutive series of patients with xeroderma pigmentosum. *Q. Jl Med.* **48**, 179–210.

POLANI, P. E. (1981). Chromosomes and chromosomal mechanisms in the genesis of maldevelopment. In *Maturation and Development: Biological and Psychological Perspectives* (ed. K. J. Connolly & H. F. R. Prechtl), pp. 50–72. London: Heinemann. (*Clinics in devl Med.,* no. 77/78).

RADMAN, M., DOHET, C., BOURGINGNON, M.-F., DOUBLEDAY, O. P. & LECOMTE, P. (1981). High fidelity devices in the reproduction of DNA. In *Chromosome Damage and Repair* (ed. E. Seeberg & K. Kleppe), pp. 431–445. New York: Plenum. (NATO advanced study institute series A, vol. 40).

RAJ, A. S. & HEDDLE, J. A. (1980). The effect of superoxide dismutase, catalase and L-cysteine on spontaneous and on mitomycin-C induced chromosomal breakage in Fanconi's anemia and normal fibroblasts as measured by the micronucleus method. *Mutat. Res.* **78**, 59–66.

RAMSAY, C. A., COLTART, R. M., BLUNT, S., PAWSEY, S. A. & GIANNELLI, F. (1974). Prenatal diagnosis of xeroderma pigmentosum. Report of the first successful case. *Lancet* **ii**, 1109–1112.

REANNEY, D. C. & PRESSING, J. (1984). Temperature as a determinative factor in the evolution of genetic systems. *J. molec. Evol.* **21**, 72–75.

REGAN, J. D. & SETLOW, R. B. (1974). DNA repair of human progeroid cells. *Biochem. biophys. Res. Commun.* **59**, 858–864.

REYNOLDS, P., HIGGINS, D. R., PRAKASH, L. & PRAKASH, S. (1985*a*). The nucleotide sequence of the *RAD 3* gene of *Saccharomyces cerevisiae*: a potential adenine nucleotide binding amino acid sequence and a nonessential acidic carboxyl terminal region. *Nucl. Acids Res.* **13**, 2357–2372.

REYNOLDS, P., WEBER, S. & PRAKASH, L. (1985*b*). *RAD 6* gene of *Saccharomyces cerevisiae* encodes a protein containing a tract of 13 consecutive aspartates. *Proc. natn. Acad. Sci. U.S.A.* **82**, 168–172.

ROBBINS, J. H. (1978). Significance of repair of human DNA: evidence from studies of xeroderma pigmentosum. *J. natn. Cancer Inst.* **61**, 645–655.

ROBBINS, J. H. (1983). Hypersensitivity to DNA-damaging agents in primary degenerations of excitable tissue. In *Cellular Responses to DNA Damage* (ed. E. C. Friedberg & B. A. Bridges), pp. 671–700. New York : Liss. (UCLA *Symp. Mol. Cell. Biol.,* New Series, vol. 11).

ROBBINS, J. H., KRAEMER, K. H., LUTZNER, M. L., FESTOFF, B. W. & COON, H. G. (1974). Xeroderma pigmentosum: an inherited disease with sun sensitivity, multiple cutaneous neoplasms, and abnormal DNA repair. *Ann. intern. Med.* **80**, 221–248.

ROBBINS, J. H., MOSHELL, A. N., SCARPINATO, R. G. & TARONE, R. E. (1980). Cells from patients with olivoponto cerebellar atrophy and familial dysautonomia are hypersensitive to ionising radiation. *Clin. Res.* **28**, 290A.

ROBBINS, J. H., OTSUKA, F., TARONE, R. E., POLINSKY, R. J., BRUMBACK, R. A. & LEE, L. E. (1985). Parkinson's disease and Alzheimer's disease: hypersensitivity to X-rays in cultured cell lines. *J. Neurol. Neurosurg. Psychiat.* **48**, 916–923.

ROBBINS, J. H., SCUDIERO, D. A., OTSUKA, F., TARONE, R. E., BRUMBACK, R. A., WIRTSCHAFTER, J. D., POLINSKY, R. J., BARRETT, S. F., MOSHELL, A. N., SCARPINATO, R. G., GANGES, M. B., NEE, L. E., MEYER, S. A. & CLATTERBUCK, B. E. (1984). Hypersensitivity to DNA-damaging agents in cultured cells from patients with Usher's syndrome and Duchenne muscular dystrophy. *J. Neurol. Neurosurg. Psychiat.* **47**, 391–398.

ROBERTS, J. J. (1980). Cellular responses to carcinogen-induced DNA damage and the role of DNA repair. *Br. med. Bull.* **36**, 25–31.

RUBIN, J. S., PRIDEAUX, V. R., WILLARD, H. F., DULHANTY, A. M., WHITMORE, G. F. & BERNSTEIN, A. (1985). Molecular cloning and chromosomal localization of DNA sequences associated with a human DNA repair gene. *Molec. cell. Biol.* **5**, 398–405.

RUDIGER, H. W., BARTRAM, C. R., HARDER, W. & PASSARGE, E. (1980). Rate of sister chromatid exchange in Bloom's syndrome fibroblasts reduced by cocultivation with normal fibroblasts. *Am. J. hum. Genet.* **32**, 150–157.

RUSSELL, W. L. (1977). Mutation frequencies in female mice and the estimation of genetic hazards of radiation in women. *Proc. natn. Acad. Sci. U.S.A.* **74**, 3523–3527.

SARKAR, S., DASGUPTA, U. B. & SUMMERS, W. C. (1984). Error-prone mutagenesis detected in mammalian cells by a shuttle vector containing the *sup F* gene of *Escherichia coli. Molec. cell. Biol.* **10**, 2227–2230.

SASAKI, M. S. & MIYATA, H. (1968). Biological dosimetry in atomic bomb survivors. *Nature, Lond.* **220**, 1189–1193.

SCHENDEL, P. F. & ROBINS, P. E. (1978). Repair of O^6-methylguanine in adapted *Escherichia coli. Proc. natn. Acad. Sci. U.S.A.* **75**, 6017–6020.

SCHILD, D., JOHNSTON, J., CHANG, C. & MORTIMER, R. K. (1984). Cloning and mapping of *Saccharomyces cerevisiae* photoreactivation gene *PHR I. Molec. cell. Biol.* **4**, 1864–1870.

SCHORPP, M., MALLICK, U., RAHMSDORF, L. & HERRLICH, P. (1984). UV-induced extracellular factor from human fibroblasts communicates the UV response to non-irradiated cells. *Cell* **37**, 861–868.

SCUDIERO, D. A., MEYER, S. A., CLATTERBUCK, B. E., TARONE, R. E. & ROBBINS, J. H. (1981). Hypersensitivity to *N*-methyl-*N*'-nitro-*N*-nitrosoguanidine in fibroblasts from patients with Huntington's disease, familial dysautonomia and other primary neuronal degenerations. *Proc. natn. Acad. Sci. U.S.A.* **78**, 6451–6455.

SCUDIERO, D. A., MOSHELL, A. N., SCARPINATO, R. G., MEYER, S. A., CLATTERBUCK, B. E., TARONE, R. E. & ROBBINS, J. H. (1982). Lymphoblastoid lines and skin fibroblasts from patients with tuberous sclerosis are abnormally sensitive to ionising radiation and to a radiomimetic chemical. *J. invest. Derm.* **78**, 234–238.

SERES, D. S. & FORNACE, A. J. JR (1982). Normal response of Fanconi's anemia cells to high concentrations of O_2 as determined by alkaline elution. *Biochim. biophys. Acta* **698**, 237–242.

SHAHAM, M., BECKER, Y. & COHEN, M. M. (1980). A. diffusable clastogenic factor in ataxia telangiectasia. *Cytogenet. Cell Genet.* **27**, 155–161.

SHALL, S. (1984). ADP-ribose in DNA repair: a new component of DNA excision repair. *Adv. Radiat. Biol.* **11**, 1–69.

SHAPIRA, U., STACHELEK, J. L., LETSOU, A., SOODAK, L. K. & LISKAY, R. M. (1983). Novel use of synthetic oligonucleotide insertion mutants for the study of homologous recombination in mammalian cells. *Proc. natn. Acad. Sci. U.S.A.* **80**, 4827–4831.

SHIPLEY, J., RODECK, C. H., GARRETT, C., GALBRAITH, J. & GIANNELLI, F. (1984). Mitomycin-C induced chromosome damage in fetal blood cultures and prenatal diagnosis of Fanconi's anaemia. *Prenatal Diagn.* **4**, 217–221.

SHIRAISHI, Y., MATSUI, S. I. & SANDBERG, A. A. (1981). Normalization by cell fusion of sister-chromatid exchange in Bloom syndrome lymphocytes. *Science* **212**, 820–822.

SHIRAISHI, Y., YOSIDA, T. H. & SANDBERG, A. A. (1983). Analyses of bromodeoxyuridine-associated sister chromatid exchanges (SCEs) in Bloom syndrome based on cell fusion : single and twin SCEs in endoreduplication. *Proc. natn. Acad. Sci. U.S.A.* **80**, 4369–4373.

SHIRAHISHI, Y., YOSIDA, T. H. & SANDBERG, A. A. (1985). Malignant transformation of Bloom syndrome B-lymphoblastoid cell lines by carcinogens. *Proc. natn. Acad. Sci. U.S.A.* **82**, 5102–5106.

SHONBERG, S. & GERMAN, J. (1980). Sister chromatid exchange in cells metabolically coupled to Bloom's syndrome cells. *Nature, Lond.* **284**, 72–74.

SMITH, P. J. & PATERSON, M. C. (1981). Abnormal responses to mid-ultraviolet light of cultured fibroblasts from patients with disorders featuring sunlight sensitivity. *Cancer Res.* **41**, 511–518.

SMITH, P. J. & PATERSON, M. C. (1982). Enhanced radiosensitivity and defective DNA repair in cultured fibroblasts derived from Rothmund Thomson syndrome patients. *Mutat. Res.* **94**, 213–228.

SODERHALL, S. & LINDAHL, T. (1975). Mammalian DNA ligases. Serological evidence for two separate enzymes. *J. biol. Chem.* **250**, 8438–8444.

SOGNIER, M. A. & HITTELMAN, W. N. (1983). Loss of repairability of DNA interstrand crosslinks in Fanconi's anaemia cells with culture age. *Mutat. Res.* **108**, 383–393.

SPARKES, R. S. (1984). Cytogenetics of retinoblastoma. *Cancer Surv.* **3**, 479–496.

STERN, L., KLEENE, K. C., GOLD, B. & HECHT, N. B. (1983). Gene expression during mammalian spermatogenesis. III Changes in populations of mRNA during spermiogenesis. *Expl Cell Res.* **143**, 247–255.

SUBRAMANI, S. & RUBNITZ, J. (1985). Recombination events after transient infection and stable integration of DNA into mouse cells. *Molec. cell. Biol.* **5**, 659–666.

SUTHERLAND, B. M. (1974). Photoreactivating enzyme from human leukocytes. *Nature, Lond.* **248**, 109–112.

SWIFT, M. (1977). Malignant neoplasms in heterozygous carriers of genes for certain autosomal recessive syndromes. In *Genetics of Human Cancer: Progress in Cancer Research and Therapy,* vol. 3 (ed. J. J. Mulvihill, R. W. Miller & J. F. Fraumeni), pp. 209–215. New York: Raven Press.

SWIFT, M., CALDWELL, R. J. & CHASE, C. (1980). Reassessment of cancer predisposition of Fanconi anemia heterozygotes. *J. natn. Cancer Inst.* **65**, 863–867.

SWIFT, M. & CHASE, C. (1979). Cancer in families with xeroderma pigmentosum. *J. natn. Cancer Inst.* **62**, 1415–1421.

TANAKA, K., HAYAKAWA, H., SEKIGUCHI, M. & OKADA, Y. (1977). Specific action of the T4 endonuclease V. on damaged DNA in xeroderma pigmentosum cells *in vivo. Proc. natn. Acad. Sci. U.S.A.* **74**, 2958–2962.

TAYLOR, A. M. R. (1982). Cytogenetics of ataxia-telangiectasia. In *Ataxia-telangiectasia: a Cellular and Molecular Link Between Cancer, Neuropathology and Immune Deficiency* (ed. B. A Bridges & D. G. Harnden), pp. 53–81. Chichester: Wiley.

TAYLOR, M. W., KOTHARI, R. M., HOLLAND, G. D., MARTINEZ-VALDEZ, H. & ZEIGE, G. (1983). A comparison of purine and pyrimidine pools in Bloom's syndrome and normal cells. *Cancer Biochem. Biophys.* **7**, 19–25.

TICE, R., WINDLER, G. & RARY, J. M. (1978). Effect of co-cultivation on sister-chromatid exchange frequencies in Bloom's syndrome and normal fibroblast cells. *Nature, Lond.* **273**, 538–540.

VAN BUUL, P. P. W., NATARAJAN, A. T. & VERDEGAAL-IMMERZEEL, E. A. M. (1978). Suppression of the frequencies of sister-chromatid exchange in Bloom's syndrome fibroblasts by co-cultivation with Chinese hamster cells. *Hum. Genet.* **44**, 187–189.

VIJAYALAXMI, EVANS, H. J., RAY, J. H. & GERMAN, J. (1983). Bloom's syndrome: evidence for an increased mutation frequency *in vivo*. *Science* **221**, 851–853.

VOGEL, F. & RATHENBERG, R. (1975). Spontaneous mutations in man. In *Advances in Human Genetics,* vol. 5 (ed. H. Harris & K. Hirschhorn), pp. 223–318. New York, London: Plenum.

WAKE, C. T., GUDEWICZ, T., PORTER, T., WHITE, A. & WILSON, J. H. (1984). How damaged is the biologically active subpopulation of transfected DNA? *Molec. cell. Biol.* **4**, 387–398.

WALD, N. J. (1984). *Antenatal and Neonatal Screening.* Oxford University Press.

WALDSTEIN, E. A., PELLER, S. & SETLOW, R. B. (1979). UV-endonuclease from calf thymus with specificity toward pyrimidine dimers in DNA. *Proc. natn. Acad. Sci. U.S.A.* **76**, 3746–3750.

WARREN, S. T., SCHULTZ, R. A., CHANG, C.-C., WADE, M. H. & TROSKO, J. E. (1981). Elevated spontaneous mutation rate in Bloom syndrome fibroblasts. *Proc. natn. Acad. Sci. U.S.A.* **78**, 3133–3137.

WEICHSELBAUM, R. R., TOMKINSON, K. & LITTLE, J. B. (1985). Repair of potentially lethal x-ray damage in fibroblasts derived from patients with hereditary and D-deletion retinoblastoma. *Int. J. Radiat. Biol.* **47**, 445–456.

WEISS, W. A. & FRIEDBERG, E. C. (1985). Molecular cloning and characterization of the yeast RAD 10 gene and expression of RAD 10 protein in *E. coli. EMBO J.* **4**, 1575–1582.

WELSHIMER, K. & SWIFT, M. (1982). Congenital malformation and developmental disabilities in ataxia-telangiectasia, Fanconi anemia, and xeroderma pigmentosum families. *Am. J. hum. Genet.* **34**, 781–793.

WEST, J., LYTTLETON, M. J. & GIANNELLI, F. (1981). Effect of incubation temperature on the frequency of sister chromatid exchange in Bloom's syndrome lymphocytes. *Hum. Genet.* **59**, 204–207.

WESTERVELD, A., HOEIJMAKERS, J. A. J., VAN DUIN, M., DE WIT, J., ODIJK, H., WOOD, R. D. & BOOTSMA, D. (1984). Molecular cloning of a human DNA repair gene. *Nature, Lond.* **310**, 425–429.

WILLIAMS, J. R. & DEARFIELD, K. L. (1981). DNA damage and repair in ageing mammals. In *CRC Handbook of Biochemistry in Aging* (ed. J. R. Florini, R. C. Aldeman & G. S. Roth), pp. 25–48. Boca Raton, Florida: CRC Press.

YAN, G. E. & FRIEDBERG, E. C. (1984). Molecular cloning and nucleotide sequence analysis of the *Saccharomyces cerevisiae* RAD 1 gene. *Molec. cell. Biol.* **4**, 2161–2169.

YAROSH, D. B. (1985). The role of O^6-methylguanine–DNA methyltransferase in cell survival, mutagenesis and carcinogenesis. *Mutat. Res.* **145**, 1–16.

YASUI, A. & LANGEVELD, S. A. (1985). Homology between the photoreactivation genes of *Saccharomyces cerevisiae* and *Escherichia coli. Gene* **36**, 349–355.

ZBINDEN, I. & CERUTTI, P. (1981). Near-ultraviolet sensitivity of skin fibroblasts of patients with Bloom's syndrome. *Biochem. biophys. Res. Commun.* **98**, 579–587.

ZELLE, B., BERENDS, F. & LOHMAN, P. H. M. (1980). Repair of ultraviolet radiation damage in xeroderma pigmentosum cell strains of complementation group E and F. *Mutat. Res.* **73**, 157–169.

ZELLE, B. & LOHMAN, P. H. M. (1979). Repair of UV-endonuclease-susceptible sites in the seven complementation groups of xeroderma pigmentosum A through G. *Mutat. Res.* **62**, 363–368.

J. Cell Sci. Suppl. 4, 417–430 (1986)
Printed in Great Britain © The Company of Biologists Limited 1986

ONCOGENES

C. J. MARSHALL

Chester Beatty Laboratories, Institute of Cancer Research: Royal Cancer Hospital, Fulham Road, London SW3 6JB, UK

INTRODUCTION

In the last few years the study of oncogenes has considerably advanced our understanding of the molecular mechanisms leading to cancer. Oncogenes may be defined as genes in which alterations to expression or coding potential are essential steps in neoplastic transformation. Much of the impetus for the study of oncogenes is derived from the farsightedness of those virologists who studied transforming viruses and argued that the ways in which these viruses caused transformation would mimic mechanisms in tumours where there was no viral involvement. Since the field of oncogene research has been extensively reviewed (see, e.g. Bishop, 1985; Varmus, 1984; Marshall, 1985), it is not the purpose of this review to catalogue the accumulated evidence for the role of oncogenes in tumorigenesis. I wish to discuss the viewpoint that oncogenes encode proteins that are intimately concerned in the control of cell proliferation *via* growth factors, their receptors, and mechanisms that may be involved in the transduction of signals from receptors.

That such a relationship might exist became initially apparent from observations that some oncogene proteins encoded a tyrosine kinase activity like the receptors for growth factors such as insulin, somatomedin C and platelet-derived growth factor (PDGF). More-direct links arose from the demonstrations that a viral oncogene (v-*sis*) (Doolittle *et al.* 1983; Waterfield *et al.* 1983) was derived from a normal cellular gene that encodes a chain of the platelet-derived growth factor and that a second viral oncogene (v-*erb*B) is a truncated form of the gene encoding the epidermal growth factor receptor (Downward *et al.* 1984). Subsequent evidence has shown that two more oncogenes, v-*fms* and *neu*, are probably derived from genes that encode growth factor receptors (Sherr *et al.* 1985; Schechter *et al.* 1985).

Analysis of the biochemical properties of the proteins encoded by viral oncogenes and their cellular counterparts enables them to be classified into distinct groups (Table 1). These groups are growth factors, tyrosine kinases, serine kinases, GTP binding, nuclear localized and finally those with unknown properties. While cellular oncogenes were initially recognized as being the cellular homologues of viral oncogenes, it is clear that there are also genes that could function as oncogenes that have not been associated with viral oncogenesis. These genes include those recognized by functional assays similar to those that identified the homologues of viral oncogenes, e.g. N-*ras*, *neu*. But also include those that encode growth factors and their receptors. These molecules may be proposed as potential oncogenes on the basis of their biological properties.

GROWTH FACTORS, RECEPTORS AND ONCOGENES

Although there are now examples in which growth factors appear to be produced by the same cells on which they act (Seifert, Schwartz & Bowen-Pope, 1984; Walker, Bowen-Pope & Reidy, 1984), in other cases growth factors are produced and exported by one cell type to act on another. Clearly, one way in which cell proliferation control can be interfered with is for there to be an uncontrolled synthesis of the growth factor by the target cell itself. Such a mechanism is termed 'autocrine' and has the result that the cells no longer require a growth factor to be supplied externally (Sporn & Todaro, 1980). However, this is only one point for alterations in the pathway of growth-factor-stimulated cell proliferation. Alterations may occur in receptors so that they no longer need to bind growth factors to generate a mitogenic signal. Cells may become more sensitive to, or independent of, growth factors by either changes in the receptors or in effector molecules after the immediate ligand–receptor interaction. Finally, cells may begin to synthesize receptors that they do not normally make and thereby respond to a different set of growth factors. All of these mechanisms could result in altered proliferation signals and some specific examples will now be discussed in detail.

Table 1. *Classification of oncogene proteins*

Growth factor	*Sub-cellular localization of protein*		
sis	Extracellular/membrane (PDGF)		
Tyrosine kinase			
src	Plasma membrane		
yes	Plasma membrane		
fes/fps	Plasma membrane		
ros	Plasma membrane		
abl	Plasma membrane		
fgr	Plasma membrane		
fms	Plasma membrane (CSF-1 receptor)		
erbB	Plasma membrane (EGF receptor)		
neu	Plasma membrane		
met	Plasma membrane		
Serine kinase			
raf/mil	Cytoplasm		
mos	Cytoplasm		
GTP binding			
N, H, K-ras	Plasma membrane		
Nuclear		*Unknown*	
myc	Nuclear	ets	
myb	Nuclear	erbA	
fos	Nuclear	ski	
p53	Nuclear		

*Autocrine stimulation of growth PDGF/c-*sis, TGFα*, bombesin*

Platelet-derived growth factor is a potent mitogen for connective tissue cells such as fibroblasts, smooth muscle and glial cells (Ross, Glomsett, Kariya & Harker, 1974; Scher, Shepard, Antoniades & Stiles, 1979; Heldin, Westermark & Wasteson, 1971). Other cell types do not appear to express PDGF receptors and so cannot respond to PDGF. While PDGF has to be supplied exogenously to stimulate the growth of most connective tissue cells, it now appears that PDGF is found not only in platelets but also in normal cells such as the cytotrophoblast (Goustin *et al.* 1985) and cultured aortic smooth muscle cells from neonatal rats (Seifert, Schwartz & Bowen-Pope, 1984). Thus in these situations there may be a natural autocrine stimulation of growth. The demonstration that v-*sis* encodes a molecule highly related to PDGF (Doolittle *et al.* 1983; Waterfield *et al.* 1983) was the first direct evidence of how oncogenes might be linked to growth control. Before these observations were made, Eva *et al.* (1982) had shown that connective tissue tumours such as sarcomas and glioblastomas expressed c-*sis*, whereas normal tissue did not. Thus these tumour cells appear to synthesize a mitogen to which they can respond. While it has become clear that v-*sis* is derived from a gene that encodes the B chain of PDGF (Chiu *et al.* 1984), the origin of the A chain is still not resolved.

The mechanism by which c-*sis* expression is activated in tumour cells has not been analysed. However, it is clear that when a c-*sis* cDNA is expressed in NIH-3T3 cells from a foreign promoter, it is sufficient to transform the cells morphologically and cause anchorage-independent growth (Clarke *et al.* 1984). This result presents a paradox because high levels of PDGF supplied exogenously do not result in anchorage-independent growth of NIH-3T3 cells. Thus it is the internal synthesis of PDGF-like molecules that leads to transformation. While insertion into membranes *via* a leader sequence appears to be essential for transformation (Hannink & Donoghue, 1984), in some systems secretion into the medium does not (Robbins, Leal, Pierce & Aaronson, 1985). However, in other experiments secretion of the v-*sis* PDGF-like product appears to be essential for the maintenance of the transformed phenotype because addition to the medium of antibodies against PDGF results in partial phenotypic reversion (Johnsson, Betsholtz, Heldin & Westermark, 1985). Since both the *sis* product and the PDGF receptor are synthesized in the endoplasmic reticulum and pass to the Golgi apparatus, it is possible that the critical interaction between growth factor and receptor may occur before they reach the cell membrane.

While the production of c-*sis*/PDGF by sarcomas and glioblastomas could clearly function as an autocrine loop, it is unclear why certain tumour types such as some carcinomas (Bowen-Pope, Vogel & Ross, 1984) and lymphomas should synthesize PDGF-like molecules. Epithelial and lymphoid cells do not appear to express PDGF receptors and therefore cannot respond to the growth factor they are synthesizing. Expression of c-*sis* in such tumours may reflect disturbances in gene regulation following a neoplastic transformation and have no functional significance. However, a more exciting prospect is that these tumour cells produce PDGF-like molecules in order to influence surrounding stromal cells with PDGF receptors, perhaps to produce other growth factors necessary for tumour growth.

Although v-*sis* is the only viral oncogene that has been shown to be derived from a cellular gene encoding a growth factor, two other autocrine systems in tumours have been described in some detail. These systems are the production of transforming growth factor α (TGFα) by a number of tumour types and of bombesin in small cell carcinomas of the lung.

TGFα is a peptide that is structurally related to epidermal growth factor (EGF) and is released from virally transformed rodent fibroblasts (v-*ras*, v-*abl*, v-*mos*, v-*fes* transformants) and from human carcinomas (Todaro, Delarco & Cohen, 1976; Todaro, Fryling & Delarco, 1980). TGFα acts *via* the EGF receptor, thus only cells that express this receptor are susceptible to TGFα and a diagnostic characteristic of cells expressing high levels of TGFα is down-regulation of the EGF receptor. The mechanism by which some transformed cells express TGFα remains obscure. TGFα is not detectable in most normal adult tissues, with the possible exception of platelets (Assoian, Grotendorst, Miller & Sporn, 1984), and appears to be synthesized for only a short period of embryogenesis (Twardzik, Ranchalis & Todaro, 1982). Even in tumours the levels of TGFα mRNA expression appear to be very low (Derynck *et al.* 1984). Although the observation that rodent fibroblasts transformed with viral or cellular *ras* genes release TGFα suggests that human tumours that harbour a mutant transforming *ras* gene might express TGFα, this does not seem to be true. Two human tumour cell lines (RD, rhabdomyosarcoma; EJ, bladder carcinoma) with activated *ras* genes do not make detectable TGFα (B. Ozanne & C. J. Marshall, unpublished results), thus the presence of a *ras* oncogene in a tumour is not synonymous with TGFα production. While it has been possible to show by cell growth in serum-free medium that the release of TGFα functions as an autocrine in virally transformed rodent cells (Kaplan, Andersson & Ozanne, 1982), this has not yet been demonstrated in human tumour systems.

However, in a second human tumour growth factor system, autocrine stimulation has clearly been demonstrated. Cutita *et al.* (1985) have shown that in small cell carcinoma of the lung where bombesin-like peptides are produced by the tumour cells, cell growth can be inhibited both *in vitro* and *in vivo* by antibodies against bombesin. Not only do these results show an autocrine stimulation of growth, but also that antibodies against growth factors or their receptors may be of use therapeutically.

Alterations to growth factor receptors

The demonstration that a growth factor gene might function as an oncogene was the first direct indication of how oncogenes might be linked to growth control. The next step was to show that a second viral oncogene, v-*erb*B, was derived from the cellular gene encoding a growth factor receptor (Downward *et al.* 1984). A number of mechanisms have now been described by which activation of a growth factor receptor could lead to that molecule functioning as a transforming protein. These mechanisms are structural modifications of receptor protein, overexpression and possibly abnormal or ectopic expression. In different cases, such modifications may lead to independence from exogenous growth factor or increase sensitivity to growth factors.

To date, the only clear examples of a structural modification of a growth factor receptor leading to transformation are the ways in which viruses affect the *erb* B locus to cause erythroblastosis in chickens. This locus is either transduced by the two avian erythroblastosis viruses ES4 or AEV-H or disrupted by the insertion of a non-transforming virus (Nilsen *et al.* 1985). In both situations the result is the ectopic expression in erythroblasts of a modified EGF receptor truncated at the amino terminus. Truncation results in loss of the ligand binding domain and leads to constitutive activation of the biochemical activity of the EGF receptor. Why such an activated EGF receptor should function as an oncogene in erythroblasts remains unanswered. The EGF receptor is not expressed in normal erythroblasts so transformation cannot result from the cells being provided with an activated form of a receptor that they normally use. Presumably other growth-factor receptor systems in erythroblasts must generate similar biochemical signals to the EGF receptor, probably involving tyrosine kinase activity, and it is the ectopic and unregulated generation of these signals that results in transformation. Although such considerations provide an explanation of how truncated EGF receptors could cause transformation, they do not adequately account for why transformation is targeted to erythroblasts.

To date, N-terminal truncated forms of the EGF receptor similar to v-*erb*B have not been identified in human tumours. Truncated forms of the EGF receptor are found in human tumours, but here the truncation is before the transmembrane region so that cells secrete an amino-terminal EGF-binding fragment (Ullrich *et al.* 1984). Since such molecules lack a transmembrane region and cytoplasmic catalytic domain, they are unlikely to function directly as transforming proteins. Rather than truncation, overexpression of a presumably normal EGF receptor appears to be involved in human tumours. A sizeable fraction of glioblastomas (Libermann *et al.* 1985) and a majority, of perhaps all, of squamous cell carcinomas express high levels of EGF receptors (Ozanne *et al.* 1985; B. Ozanne, personal communication). Such tumour cells have between 10^6 and 15×10^6 receptors compared with 10^5 receptors in normal cells. At least in some cases overexpression of the receptors results from receptor gene amplification (Libermann *et al.* 1985; B. Ozanne, personal communication). How overexpression of the receptor acts as a transforming event remains unclear. One possibility is that when large amounts of the receptor are present, the background 'firing' of the receptor occurs at a sufficiently high level for cells to be triggered into mitosis. Alternatively, high levels of the receptor may sensitize cells to very low levels of growth factor. In this context it is intriguing that some cells with high levels of the EGF receptor produce TGFα (Derynck *et al.* 1984; B. Ozanne, personal communication). Thus these cells may be driven by an autocrine loop, but an autocrine loop that involves a sensitization to growth factor by expressing high levels of the receptor.

Although the truncation of the EGF receptor appears to generate a viral oncogene in the case of v-*erb*B, in a second example of a viral oncogene, v-*fms,* constitutive activation of the receptor by truncation may not be involved. The c-*fms* gene appears to encode the receptor for CSF-1, the growth factor for mononuclear phagocytic cells (Sherr *et al.* 1985). Structural studies suggest that v-*fms,* unlike v-*erb*B, retains an extensive N-terminal external domain and therefore may retain the ligand binding domain. However, the fact that fibroblasts, the target cell for v-*fms* transformation, produce CSF-1 suggests that the mechanism of transformation may be for cells to be provided with the receptor for a growth factor that the cells normally make but do not respond to. This would imply that v-*fms*-expressing cells need to be exposed to CSF-1 to be transformed.

A third example of how oncogenes may bypass growth factor requirements is provided by v-*abl*. Infection of IL3-dependent mast cells (Pierce *et al.* 1985) or an IL3, GM-CSF-dependent myeloid cell line (Cook *et al.* 1985) results in factor-independent cells. This factor independence does not appear to arise from an autocrine stimulation of growth resulting from the v-*abl* gene stimulating the cells to produce factors. Neither is factor independence the consequence of an increased level of receptors. While it has not yet been demonstrated that the c-*abl* protein is part or the whole of a receptor, transformation by v-*abl*, like v-*erb*B, may involve a constitutively activated tyrosine kinase activity. Thus growth factor independence appears to result from the v-*abl* protein mimicking a growth factor signal.

Secondary messenger systems after growth factor stimulation: the role of nuclear oncoproteins

Four viral oncogenes (v-*myc,* v-*myb,* v-*fos* and v-*ski*) and their cellular homologues encode proteins that are localized in the nucleus (Bishop, 1985). A fifth protein, p53, which was initially recognized because it complexed with the simian virus 40 (SV40) large T antigen (Rotter & Wolf, 1985) is also nuclear and appears to be able to function as an oncogene (Jenkins, Rudge & Currie, 1984; Parada *et al.* 1984; Eliyahu *et al.* 1984). In three of these genes that have been studied, c-*fos,* c-*myc* and p53, expression as judged by RNA levels appears to be elevated following the stimulation of quiescent fibroblasts (Kelly, Cochran, Stiles & Leder, 1983; Greenberg, & Ziff, 1984; Kruijer, Cooper, Hunter & Verma, 1984; Muller, Bravo, Burkhardt & Curran, 1984; Reich & Levine, 1984). However, the kinetics of induction vary for the three genes. The induction of c-*fos* is very rapid, reaching a peak within 30 min and then rapidly falling away (Greenberg & Ziff, 1984; Kruijer *et al.* 1984; Muller *et al.* 1984); c-*myc* reaches a peak level of RNA expression at around 2 h post-stimulation and then falls away after 4 h (Kelly *et al.* 1983), while p53 expression reaches a peak 18–24 h after stimulation (Reich & Levine, 1984). Furthermore, there appear to be differences in the way these levels of changed RNA expression are achieved. For c-*fos* the control appears to be transcriptional (Greenberg & Ziff, 1984), while for c-*myc* there may be both a transcriptional and a post-transcriptional component at the level of mRNA stability (Blanchard *et al.* 1985).

While the kinetics and mechanism of induction may vary, both the mRNAs and proteins encoded for c-*fos*, c-*myc* and p53, are all characterized by having short half-lives of the order of 20–25 min (Ramsay, Evan & Bishop, 1984; Reich & Levine, 1984; Klempanauer, Symonds, Evan & Bishop, 1984; Dani *et al.* 1984). The induction kinetics and the short half-lives have been used to argue that the nuclear proteins function as effectors to link events at the cell surface to nuclear events, such as changes in gene transcription and the initiation of DNA synthesis. The constitutive expression of c-*myc* relieves, at least partially, the requirement for growth factors (Armelin *et al.* 1984; Rapp *et al.* 1985) or sensitizes cells to growth factors (Roberts *et al.* 1985). Furthermore, it has been shown in some cases that the relaxation of growth factor requirements is not a result of the cells producing growth factors but is bypassing the need for growth factor stimulation (Rapp *et al.* 1985). At present there is no clear indication of how the nuclear proteins act as a link between nucleus and membrane, but one obvious mechanism is that they somehow affect the expression of other genes.

The elevated level of expression of c-*myc* following mitogenic stimulation of quiescent cells led to the idea that c-*myc* expression might be regulated during the cell cycle (Kelly *et al.* 1983). It was also argued that alterations to the expression of c-*myc* in the cell cycle might be a common consequence of the varied changes to the c-*myc* gene that result from specific chromosome translocations in B-lymphoid cells. Subsequent experiments, however, have convincingly shown that in exponentially growing cells, the level of c-*myc* expression at both the RNA and protein levels remains constant throughout the cell cycle (Hann, Thompson & Eisenman, 1985; Thompson, Challoner, Neiman & Groudine, 1985). These observations in the cell cycle of growing cells raise the question of why there is a pulse of elevated *myc* RNA following stimulation of quiescent cells. Although this question is not fully resolved, some experiments do suggest that the level of *myc* expression is somewhat lower in quiescent cells (Keath, Kelakar & Cole, 1984*a*). However, the rise in c-*myc* RNA following stimulation appears to be much higher (up to 40-fold) than the few-fold difference in levels between quiescent and growing cells. One explanation of the elevated RNA levels is that following stimulation there is a requirement for a more rapid turnover of c-*myc* protein, perhaps because c-*myc* protein functions as a nuclear message system. As far as the other nuclear proteins, c-*myb*, c-*fos* and p53, are concerned, there is at present no strong indication as to whether their expression is regulated in the cell cycle.

Nuclear oncoproteins and cell immortilization

The observation that some malignant cell lines with alterations to c-*myc* genes also contained mutant transforming *ras* genes (Murray *et al.* 1983) led to the idea that there might be an interaction between the two oncogenes. Experimental support for this idea was obtained when it was shown that non-established rat embryo cell strains could be converted into established tumorigenic cell lines if they were transfected with both a *ras* and a *myc* oncogene (Land, Parada & Weinberg, 1983). Transfection with *myc* or *ras* on its own was insufficient to produce a tumorigenic cell line, although it was shown that a *ras* oncogene on its own could result in morphological transformation, but the cells still retained a finite lifespan (Land *et al.* 1983; Newbold & Overell, 1983). It was later shown that transfection with a *myc* oncogene on its own could lead to immortalization without morphological transformation or tumorigenicity. These experiments led to the idea that there were two classes of oncogenes, exemplified by *myc* and *ras*, that cooperated to produce a fully malignant cell. Subsequent experiments have shown that both the *myc* and p53 genes can immortalize embryo fibroblasts and cooperate with *ras* genes to produce a transformed cell (Parada *et al.* 1984; Jenkins *et al.* 1984; Eliyahu, Michalovitz & Oren, 1985). Thus the oncogenes that code for nuclear proteins appear to be immortalizing genes and to cooperate with *ras*. The mechanism by which these gene products lead to immortalization and cooperation remains unclear, although one possible explanation is that the nuclear proteins may sensitize cells to the effects of growth factors (Balk, Riley, Gunther & Morris, 1985; Roberts *et al.* 1985). In spite of the clear-cut evidence for cooperation between oncogenes, recent evidence argues that there may not be a functional division between the effects of the transforming *ras* genes and those of the genes encoding nuclear transforming proteins. Such arguments rest on the observation that under appropriate circumstances of high-level expression *ras* genes can immortalize cells (Spandidos & Wilkie, 1984), a *fos* oncogene can both immortalize and make cells tumorigenic (Jenuwein, Muller, Curran & Muller, 1985), and the introduction of *myc* or p53 genes into established non-tumorigenic cell lines leads to the cells becoming tumorigenic (Keath, Caimi & Cole, 1984*b*; Eliyahu *et al.* 1985). Thus, while two oncogenes may be better than one, in the right conditions one oncogene may be sufficient to render cells tumorigenic.

WHAT IS THE ROLE OF THE *ras* ONCOGENES?

Although it is clear how genes encoding growth factors, their receptors and perhaps secondary nuclear message systems after growth factor–receptor interaction could function as oncogenes, it is not clear how the major class of oncogenes detected in human tumours fits into such a scheme. The *ras* genes form a family of at least three (Shimizu *et al.* 1983; Chang *et al.* 1982; Hall, Marshall, Spurr & Weiss, 1983) and maybe more (Madaule & Axel, 1985) genes that are altered in about 10–20% of most human tumour types (see Marshall, 1985). Five sites, amino acids 12, 13, 59, 61 and 63, in the p21–188/189 amino acid *ras* protein molecules are known to be positions at which single amino acid substitutions can lead to transforming activity (Fasano *et al.* 1984). Mutations at three of these sites, amino acids 12, 13 and 61 (Tabin *et al.* 1982; Yuasa *et al.* 1983; Bos *et al.* 1985), have been identified in human malignancies. However, the mechanism by which these mutations result in neoplastic activity are unclear. The p21 *ras* proteins do not appear to be either growth factors or growth factor receptors, but it is known that the p21 *ras* proteins are located on the inner surface of the cell membrane, bind GTP and have a GTPase activity. Localization at the inner surface of the cell membrane is dependent on palmitation at the C terminus and is essential for transformation (Willumsen *et al.* 1984). Mutations of either Gly12 to valine, or Ala59 to threonine, both of which lead to transforming activity, result in a reduction of GTPase activity (Gibbs, Sigal, Poe & Scolnick, 1984; McGrath, Capon, Goeddel & Levinson, 1984; Sweet *et al.* 1984). Together with significant sequence homology to G proteins (Hurley *et al.* 1984; Tanabe *et al.* 1985), these observations suggest that the p21 *ras* proteins may be part of a family of G proteins. The known G proteins are involved in mediating interactions between cell surface receptors and effector enzymes (Gilman, 1984). These effector enzymes may be adenylate cyclase (Gilman, 1984), cyclic GMP phosphodiesterase (Tanabe *et al.* 1985), or possibly phosphodiesterases involved in the breakdown of phosphoinositols (Cockcroft & Gomperts, 1985). Furthermore, different G proteins may exert stimulating or inhibitory effects on effector enzymes. Although the idea that p21 *ras* proteins function in a homologous way to G proteins is attractive, this hypothesis lacks experimental support. First, the receptors with which *ras* interacts have not been identified, although there is some evidence that there may be an interaction with the EGF receptor (Kamata & Feramisco, 1984). Second, the effector enzymes have not been identified. Finally, the G proteins have a three-subunit structure with 41, 26 and $10 \times 10^3 M_r$ components, which does not correspond to the single-subunit structure of p21 *ras*. Although evidence from yeast suggests that in this organism *ras* is part of the adenylate cyclase system (Broek *et al.* 1985; Toda *et al.* 1985), there is some evidence to suggest that this does not appear to be the case in vertebrate cells (Beckner, Hatton & Shih, 1985). At present the clearest evidence that p21 *ras* may be involved in mediating growth factor signals is provided by experiments in which antibodies against the *ras* proteins have been injected into cells. If antibodies are injected into quiescent cells following serum stimulation, the stimulated cells do not make DNA (Mulcahy, Smith & Stacey, 1985). In addition these experiments suggest that p21 *ras* is involved in an event that occurs up until late G_1 and commits the cell to S phase. We are therefore left in a situation in which there are strong circumstantial arguments that the p21 *ras* molecules interact with growth factor receptors, but there is no direct evidence that this is the case.

CONCLUSIONS

In this review I have emphasized the way in which alterations to genes encoding growth factors or their receptors leads these genes to function as oncogenes and to maintain the transformed phenotype. Although such observations have given us a central theme for investigating the role of oncogenes, much remains to be answered. The major question is to understand the role of these oncogene products for which we have no known function. This includes both the serine kinases and tyrosine kinases, which have not been attributed to a receptor function. In spite of some promising leads, the role of p21 *ras* proteins remains ill-defined. But perhaps most intractable at present is the role of those oncogenes whose products are nuclear. The shared characteristics of these proteins, such as short half-lives, induction after quiescence and ability to immortalize, suggest that they all do something similar; however, we have no clear evidence of what that is. It is likely that much of the understanding of the functions of oncogenes will come from areas that a short time ago would not have seemed closely connected to transforming genes. These areas include the metabolism of phosphoinositols, protein kinase C, cyclic AMP metabolism, ion fluxes and many other aspects of cell physiology. In addition, it can be argued that the mechanism of oncogenesis by the production of a transforming protein that has to be present to transform the cell is only part of the picture of oncogenesis. There is evidence suggesting that there is another class of transformation events that operate in a different mode by deleting some functions essential to normal cell behaviour (Murphree & Benedict, 1984; see Harris, 1986, this volume). How such mechanisms operate and possibly interact with the products of transforming proteins remains to be elucidated.

REFERENCES

ARMELIN, H. A., ARMELIN, M. C. S., KELLY, K., STEWART, T., LEDER, P., COCHRAN, B. H. & STILES, C. D. (1984). Functional role for c-*myc* in mitogenic response to platelet-derived growth factors. *Nature, Lond.* **310**, 655–660.

ASSOIAN, R. K., GROTENDORST, G. R., MILLER, D. M. & SPORN, M. B. (1984). Cellular transformation by the coordinated action of three peptide growth factors from human platelets. *Nature, Lond.* **309**, 804.

BALK, S. D., RILEY, T. M., GUNTHER, H. S. & MORISI, A. (1985). Heparin treated, v-*myc* transformed chicken heart mesenchymal cells assume a normal morphology but are hypersensitive to epidermal growth factor (EGF) and brain fibroblast growth factor (bFGF); cells transformed by the v-Ha-*ras* oncogene are refractory to EGF and bFGF but are hypersensitive to insulin-like growth factors. *Proc. natn. Acad. Sci. U.S.A.* **82**, 5781–5785.

BECKNER, S. K., HATTON, S. & SHIH, T. Y. (1985). The *ras* oncogene product is not a regulatory component of adenylate cyclase. *Nature, Lond.* **317**, 71–72.

BISHOP, J. M. (1985). Viral oncogenes. *Cell* **42**, 23–38.

BLANCHARD, J.-M., PIECHACZYK, M., DANI, C., CHAMBARD, J.-C., FRANCHI, A., POUYSSEGUR, J. & JEANTEUR, P. (1985). c-*myc* gene is transcribed at high rate in G_0-arrested fibroblasts and is post-transcriptionally regulated in response to growth factors. *Nature, Lond.* **317**, 443–445.

BOS, J. L., TOKSOZ, D., MARSHALL, C. J., VERLAAN DE VRIES, M., VEENEMAN, G. H., VAN DER EB, A., VAN BOOM, J. H., JANSSEN, J. W. G. & STEENVOORDEN, A. C. M. (1985). Amino-acid substitutions at codon 13 of the N-*ras* oncogene in human acute myeloid leukaemia. *Nature, Lond.* **315**, 726–730.

BOWEN-POPE, D. F., VOGEL, A. & ROSS, R. (1984). Production of platelet-derived growth factor-like molecules and reduced expression of platelet-derived growth factor receptors accompany transformation by a wide spectrum of agents. *Proc. natn. Acad. Sci. U.S.A.* **81**, 2396–2400.

BROEK, D., SAMIY, N., FASANO, O., FUJIYAMA, A., TAMANOI, F., NORTHUP, J. & WIGLER, M. (1985). Differential activation of yeast adenylate cyclase by wild type and mutant RAS proteins. *Cell* **41**, 763–769.

CHANG, E. H., GONDA, M. A., ELLIS, R. W., SCOLNICK, E. M. & LOWY, D. R. (1982). Human genome contains four genes homologous to transforming genes of Harvey and Kirsten murine sarcoma virsuses. *Proc. natn. Acad. Sci. U.S.A.* **79**, 4848–4852.

CHIU, I.-M., REDDY, E. P., GIVOL, D., ROBBINS, K. C., TRONICK, S. R. & AARONSON, S. A. (1984). Nucleotide sequence analysis identifies the human c-*sis* proto-oncogene as a structural gene for platelet-derived growth factor. *Cell* **37**, 123–129.

CLARKE, M. F., WESTIN, E., SCHMIDT, D., JOSEPHS, S. F., RATNER, L., WONG-STAAL, F., GALLO, R. C. & REITZ, M. S. (1984). Transformation of NIH-3T3 cells by a human c-*sis* cDNA clone. *Nature, Lond.* **308**, 464–467.

COCKCROFT, S. & GOMPERTS, B. D. (1985). Role of guanine nucleotide binding protein in the activation of polyphosphoinositide phosphodiesterase. *Nature, Lond.* **314**, 534–536.

COOK, W. D., METCALF, D., NICOLA, N. A., BURGESS, A. W. & WALTER, F. (1985). Malignant transformation of a growth factor-dependent myeloid cell line by Abelson virus without evidence of an autocrine mechanism. *Cell* **41**, 677–683.

CUTITA, F., CARNEY, D. N., MULSHINE, J., MOODY, T. W., FEDORKO, J., FISCHLER, A. & MINNA, J. D. (1985). Bombesin-like peptides can function as autocrine growth factors in human small-cell lung cancer. *Nature, Lond.* **316**, 823–826.

DANI, C. H., BLANCHARD, J. M., PIECHAEZYK, M., SABOUTY, S., EL, S., MARTY, L. & JEANTEUR, P. H. (1984). Extreme instability of *myc* mRNA in normal and transformed human cells. *Proc. natn Acad. Sci. U.S.A.* **81**, 7046–7050.

DERYNCK, R., ROBERTS, A. B., WINKLER, M. E., CHEN, E. Y. & GOEDDEL, D. V. (1984). Human transforming growth factor α: Precursor structure and expression in *E. coli. Cell* **38**, 287–297.

DICORLETO, P. E. & BOWEN-POPE, D. F. (1983). Cultured endothelial cells produce a platelet-derived growth factor like protein. *Proc. natn. Acad. Sci. U.S.A.* **80**, 1919.

DOOLITTLE, R. F., HUNKAPILLER, M. W., HOOD, L. E., DEVARE, S. R., ROBBINS, K. C., AARONSON, S. A. & ANTONIADES, H. N. (1983). Simian sarcoma virus *onc* gene, v-*sis*, is derived from the gene (or genes) encoding a platelet-derived growth factor. *Science* **221**, 275–277.

DOWNWARD, J., YARDEN, Y., MAYES, E., SCRACE, G., TOTTY, N., STOKWELL, P., ULLRICH, A., SCHLESSINGER, J. & WATERFIELD, M. D. (1984). Close similarity of epidermal growth factor receptor and v-*erb*B oncogene protein sequence. *Nature, Lond.* **307**, 521–527.

Eliyahu, D., Michalovitz, D. & Oren, M. (1985). Overproduction of p53 antigen makes established cells highly tumorigenic. *Nature, Lond.* **316**, 158–160.

ELIYAHU, D., RAZ, A., GRUSS, P., GIVOL, D. & OREN, M. (1984). Participation of p53 cellular tumour antigen in transformation of normal embryonic cells. *Nature, Lond.* **312**, 646–649.

EVA, A., ROBBINS, K. C., ANDERSEN, P. R., SRINIVASAN, A., TRONICK, S. R., REDDY, E. P., ELMORE, N. W., GALEN, A. T., LAUTENBERGER, J. A., PAPAS, T. S., WESTIN, E. H., WONG-STAAL, F., GALLO, R. C. & AARONSON, S. A. (1982). Cellular genes analogous to retroviral *onc* genes are transcribed in human tumour cells. *Nature, Lond.* **295**, 116–119.

FASANO, O., ALDRICH, T., TAMANOI, F., TAPOROWSKY, E., FURTH, M. & WIGLER, M. (1984). Analysis of the transforming potential of the human H-*ras* gene by random mutagenesis. *Proc. natn. Acad. Sci. U.S.A.* **81**, 4008–4012.

GIBBS, J. B., SIGAL, I. S., POE, M. & SCOLNICK, E. M. (1984). Intrinsic GTPase activity distinguishes normal and oncogenic *ras* p21 molecules. *Proc. natn. Acad. Sci. U.S.A.* **81**, 5704–5708.

GILMAN, A. G. (1984). G Proteins and dual control of adenylate cyclase. *Cell* **36**, 577–579.

GOUSTIN, A. S., BETSHOLTZ, C., PFEIFER-OHLSSON, S., PERSSON, H., RYDNERT, J., BYWATER, M., HOLMGREN, G., HELDIN, C.-H., WESTERMARK, B. & OHLSSON, R. (1985). Coexpression of the *sis* and *myc* proto-oncogenes in developing human placenta suggests autocrine control of trophoblast growth. *Cell* **41**, 301–312.

GREENBERG, M. E. & ZIFF, E. B. (1984). Stimulation of 3T3 cells induces transcription of the c-*fos* proto-oncogene. *Nature, Lond.* **311**, 433–438.

HALL, A., MARSHALL, C. J., SPURR, N. & WEISS, R. A. (1983). The transforming gene in two human sarcoma cell lines is a new member of the *ras* gene family located on chromosome one. *Nature, Lond.* **303**, 396–400.

HANN, S. R., THOMPSON, C. B. & EISENMAN, R. N. (1985). c-*myc* oncogene protein synthesis is independent of the cell cycle in human and avian cells. *Nature, Lond.* **314**, 366–369.

HANNINK, M. & DONOGHUE, D. J. (1984). Requirement for a signal sequence in biological expression of the v-*sis* oncogene. *Science* **226**, 1197–1199.

HARRIS, H. (1986). The genetic analysis of malignancy. *J. Cell Sci. Suppl. 4,* 431–444.

HELDIN, C.-H., WESTERMARK, B. & WASTESON, A. (1981). Specific receptors for platelet-derived growth factor on cells derived from connective tissue and glia. *Proc. natn. Acad. Sci. U.S.A.* **78**, 3664–3668.

HURLEY, J. B., SIMON, M. J., TEPLOW, D. B., ROBISHAW, J. D. & GILMAN, A. G. (1984). Homologies between signal transducing G-proteins and *ras* gene products. *Science* **226**, 860–862.

JENKINS, J. R., RUDGE, K. & CURRIE, G. A. (1984). Cellular immortalization by a c-DNA encoding the transformation associated phosphoprotein p53. *Nature, Lond.* **312**, 651–654.

JENUWEIN, T., MULLER, D., CURRAN, T. & MULLER, R. (1985). Extended lifespan and tumorigenicity of non-established mouse connective tissue cells transformed by the *fos* oncogene of FBR-MuSV. *Cell* **41**, 629–637.

JOHNSSON, A., BETSHOLTZ, C., HELDIN, C.-H. & WESTERMARK, B. (1985). Antibodies against platelet-derived growth factor inhibit acute transformation by simian sarcoma virus. *Nature, Lond.* **317**, 438–440.

KAMATA, T. & FERAMISCO, J. R. (1984). Epidermal growth factor stimulates guanine nucleotide binding activity and phosphorylation of *ras* oncogene proteins. *Nature, Lond.* **310**, 147–150.

KAPLAN, P. L., ANDERSSON, M. & OZANNE, B. (1982). Transforming growth factor(s) production enables cells to grow in the absence of serum: an autocrine system. *Proc. natn. Acad. Sci. U.S.A.* **79**, 485–489.

KEATH, E. J., CAIMI, P. G. & COLE, M. D. (1984*b*). Fibroblast lines expressing activated c-*myc* oncogenes are tumorigenic in nude mice and syngeneic animals. *Cell* **39**, 339–348.

KEATH, E. J., KELEKAR, A. & COLE, M. D. (1984*a*). Transcriptional activation of the translocated c-*myc* oncogene in mouse plasmacytomas: Similar RNA levels in tumor and proliferating normal cells. *Cell* **37**, 521–528.

KELLY, K., COCHRAN, B. H., STILES, C. D. & LEDER, P. (1983). Cell-specific regulation of the c-*myc* gene by lymphocyte mitogens and platelet-derived growth factors. *Cell* **35**, 603–610.

KLEMPANAUER, K.-H., SYMONDS, G., EVAN, G. & BISHOP, J. M. (1984). Subcellular localization of proteins encoded by oncogenes of avian myeloblastosis virus and avian leukaemia virus E26 and by the chicken c-*myc* gene. *Cell.* **37**, 537–547.

KRUIJER, W., COOPER, J. A., HUNTER, T. & VERMA, I. M. (1984). Platelet-derived growth factor induces rapid but transient expression of the c-*fos* gene and protein. *Nature, Lond.* **312**, 711–716.

LAND, H., PARADA, L. F. & WEINBERG, R. A. (1983). Tumorigenic conversion of primary embryo fibroblasts requires at least two co-operating oncogenes. *Nature, Lond.* **304**, 596–602.

LIBERMANN, T. A., NASBAUM, M. R., RAZON, N., KRIS, R., LAX, I., SOREQ, H., WHITTLE, N., WATERFIELD, M. D., ULLRICH, A. & SCHLESSINGER, J. (1985). Amplification, enhanced expression and possible rearrangement of EGF receptor gene in primary human brain tumours of glial origin. *Nature, Lond.* **313**, 144–147.

MADAULE, P. & AXEL, R. (1985). A novel *ras*-related gene family. *Cell* **41**, 31–40.

MARSHALL, C. J. (1985). Human oncogenes. In *RNA Tumor Viruses*, 2nd edn and supplement (ed. R. A. Weiss, N. Teich, H. E. Varmus & J. E. Coffin), chap. 12, pp. 488–558. New York: Cold Spring Harbor Laboratory Press.

MCGRATH, J. P., CAPON, D. J., GOEDDEL, D. V. & LEVINSON, A. D. (1984). Comparative biochemical properties of normal and activated human p21 *ras* protein. *Nature, Lond.* **310**, 644–649.

MULCAHY, L. S., SMITH, M. R. & STACEY, D. W. (1985). Requirement for *ras* proto-oncogene function during serum-stimulated growth of NIH-3T3 cells. *Nature, Lond.* **313**, 241–243.

MULLER, R., BRAVO, R., BURKHARDT, J. & CURRAN, T. (1984) Induction of c-*fos* gene and protein by growth factors precedes activation of c-*myc*. *Nature, Lond.* **312**, 716–720.

MURPHREE, A. L. & BENEDICT, W. F. (1984). Retinoblastoma: clues to human oncogenesis. *Science* **223**, 1028–1033.

MURRAY, M. J., CUNNINGHAM, J. M., PARADA, L. F., DAUTRY, F., LEIBOWITZ, P. & WEINBERG, R. A. (1983). The HL60 transforming sequences: a *ras* oncogene co-existing with altered *myc* genes in hematopoietic tumors. *Cell* **33**, 749–757.

NEWBOLD, R. F. & OVERELL, R. W. (1983). Fibroblast immortality is a prerequisite for transformation by EJ c-Ha-*ras* oncogene. *Nature, Lond.* **304**, 648–651.

NILSEN, T. W., MARONEY, P. A., GOODWIN, R. G., ROTTMAN, F. M., CRITTENDEN, L. B., RAINES, M. A. & KUNG, H.-J. (1985). c-*erb*-B activation in ALV-induced erythroblastosis: novel RNA processing and promoter insertion result in expression of an amino-truncated EGF receptor. *Cell* **41**, 719–726.

OZANNE, B., SHUM, A., RICHARDS, C. S., CASSELLS, D., GROSSMAN, D., TRENT, J., GUSTERSON, B. & HENDLER, F. (1985). Evidence for an increase of EGF receptors in epidermoid malignancies. *Cancer Cells* (ed. J. Feramisco, B. Ozanne & C. D. Stiles), pp. 41–46. New York: Cold Spring Harbor Laboratory Press.

PARADA, L. F., LAND, H., WEINBERG, R. A., WOLF, D. & ROTTER, V. (1984). Cooperation between gene encoding p53 tumour antigens and *ras* in cellular transformation. *Nature, Lond.* **312**, 649–651.

PIERCE, J. H., DIFIORE, P. B., AARONSON, S. A., POTTER, M., PUMPHREY, J., SCOTT, A. & IHLE, J. N. (1985). Neoplastic transformation of mast cells by Abelson-MuLV: Abrogation of IL-3 dependence by a non-autocrine mechanism. *Cell* **41**, 685–693.

RAMSAY, G., EVAN, G. I. & BISHOP, J. M. (1984). The protein encoded by the human proto-oncogene c-*myc*. *Proc. natn. Acad. Sci. U.S.A.* **81**, 7742–7746.

RAPP, U. R., CLEVELAND, J. L., BRIGHTMAN, K., SCOTT, A. & IHLE, J. N. (1985). Abrogation of IL-3 and IL-2 dependence by recombinant murine retrovirus expressing v-*myc* oncogenes. *Nature, Lond.* **317**, 434–438.

REICH, N. C. & LEVINE, A. J. (1984). Growth regulation of a cellular tumour antigen, p53, in non-transformed cells. *Nature, Lond.* **308**, 199–201.

ROBBINS, K. C., LEAL, F., PIERCE, J. H. & AARONSON, S. A. (1985). The v-*sis*/PDGF-2 transforming gene product localises to cell membranes but is not a secretory protein. *EMBO J.* **4**, 1783–1792.

ROBERTS, A. B., ANZANO, M. A., WATERFIELD, L. M., ROCHE, N. S., STERN, D. F. & SPORN, M. B. (1985). Type β transforming growth factor: a bifunctional regulator of cellular growth. *Proc. natn. Acad. Sci. U.S.A.* **82**, 119–123.

ROSS, R., GLOMSETT, J., KARIYA, B. & HARKER, L. (1974). Platelet dependent serum factor that stimulates the proliferation of arterial smooth muscle cells *in vitro*. *Proc. natn. Acad. Sci. U.S.A.* **71**, 1207.

ROTTER, V. & WOLF, D. (1985). Biological and molecular analysis of p53 cellular-encoded tumor antigens. *Adv. Cancer Res.* **43**, 113–141.

SCHECHTER, A. L., STERN, D. F., VAIDYANATHAN, L., DECKER, S. J., DREBIN, J. A., GREEN, M. I. & WEINBERG, R. A. (1984). The *neu* oncogene: an *erb*-B-related gene encoding a 165,000 M_r tumor antigen. *Nature, Lond.* **312**, 513–516.

SCHER, C. D., SHEPARD, R. C., ANTONIADES, H. N. & STILES, C. D. (1979). Platelet-derived growth factor and the regulation of the mammalian fibroblast cell cycle. *Biochim. biophys. Acta* **560**, 217.

SEIFERT, R. A., SCHWARTZ, S. M. & BOWEN-POPE, D. F. (1984). Developmentally regulated production of platelet-derived growth factor-like molecules. *Nature, Lond.* **311**, 669–671.

SHERR, C. J., RETTENMIER, C. W., SACAA, R., ROUSSEL, M. F., LOOK, A. T. & STANLEY, E. R. (1985). The c-*fms* proto-oncogene product is related to the receptor for the mononuclear phagocyte growth factor, CSF-1. *Cell* **41**, 665–676.

SHIMIZU, K., GOLDFARB, M., SUARD, Y., PERUCHO, M., LI, Y., KAMATA, T., FERAMISCO, J., STAVNEZER, E. & WIGLER, M. H. (1983). Three human transforming genes are related to the viral *ras* oncogenes. *Proc. natn. Acad. Sci. U.S.A.* **80**, 2112–2116.

SPANDIDOS, D. A. & WILKIE, N. M. (1984). Malignant transformation of early passage cells by a single mutated human oncogene. *Nature, Lond.* **310**, 508–511.

SPORN, M. B. & TODARO, C. J. (1980). Autocrine secretion and malignant transformation of cells. *N. Engl. J. Med.* **303**, 878.

SWEET, R. W., YOKOYAMA, S., KAMATA, T., FERAMISCO, J. R., ROSENBERG, M. & GROSS, M. (1984). The product of *ras* is a GTPase and T24 oncogenic mutant is deficient in this activity. *Nature, Lond.* **311**, 273–275.

TABIN, C. J., BRADLEY, S. M., BARGMANN, C. I., WEINBERG, R. A., PAPAGEORGE, A. G., SCOLNICK, E. M., DHAR, R., LOWY, D. R. & CHANG, E. H. (1982). Mechanism of activation of a human oncogene. *Nature, Lond.* **300**, 143–149.

TANABE, T., NAKADA, T., NISHIKAWA, Y., SUGIMOTO, K., SUZUKI, H., TAKAHASHI, H., NODA, M., HAGA, T., ICHIYAMA, A., KANGAWA, K., MINAMINO, N., MATSUO, H. & NUMA, S. (1985). Primary structure of the α-subunit of transducin and its relationship to *ras* proteins. *Nature, Lond.* **315**, 242–245.

THOMPSON, C. B., CHALLONER, P. B., NEIMAN, P. E. & GROUDINE, M. (1985). Levels of c-*myc* oncogene mRNA are invariant throughout the cell cycle. *Nature, Lond.* **307**, 363–366.

TODA, T., UNO, I., ISHIKAWA, T., POWERS, S., KATAOKA, T., BROEK, D., BROACH, J., MATSAMOTO, K. & WIGLER, M. (1985). In yeast RAS proteins are controlling elements of the cyclic AMP pathway. *Cell* **40**, 27–36.

TODARO, C. J., DELARCO, J. E. & COHEN, S. (1976). Transformation by murine and feline sarcoma viruses specifically blocks binding of epidermal growth factor to cells. *Nature, Lond.* **264**, 26.

TODARO, G. J., FRYLING, C. M. & DELARCO, J. E. (1980). Transforming growth factors produced by certain human tumor cells: polypeptides that interact with epidermal growth factor receptors. *Proc. natn. Acad. Sci. U.S.A.* **77**, 5258.

TWARDZIK, D. R., RANCHALIS, J. E. & TODARO, G. J. (1982). Mouse embryonic transforming growth factors related to those isolated from tumour cells. *Cancer Res.* **42**, 590–593.

ULLRICH, A., COUSSENS, L., HAYFLICK, J. S., DULL, T. J., GRAY, A., TAM, A. W., LEE, Y., YARDEN, Y., LIBERMANN, T. A., SCHLESSINGER, J., DOWNWARD, J., MAYES, E. L. V., WHITTLE, N., WATERFIELD, M. D. & SEEBURG, P. H. (1984). Human epidermal growth factor receptor cDNA sequence and aberrant expression of the amplified gene in A431 epidermoid carcinoma cells. *Nature, Lond.* **309**, 418–425.

VARMUS, H. E. (1984). The molecular genetics of cellular oncogenes. *A. Rev. Genet.* **18**, 553–612.

WALKER, L. N., BOWEN-POPE, D. F. & REIDY, M. A. (1984). Secretion of platelet-derived growth factor (PDGF)-like activity by arterial smooth muscle cells is induced as a response to injury. *J. Cell Biol.* **99**, 416(a).

WATERFIELD, M. D., SCRACE, G. T., WHITTLE, N., STROOBANT, P., JOHNSON, A., WASTESON, A., WESTERMARK, B., HELDIN, C.-H., HUANG, J. S. & DEUEL, T. F. (1983). Platelet-derived growth factor is structurally related to the putative transforming protein p28^{Sis} of simian sarcoma virus. *Nature, Lond.* **304**, 35–39.

WILLUMSEN, B. M., CHRISTENSEN, A., HUBBERT, N. L., PAPAGEORGE, A. G. & LOWY, D. R. (1984). The p21 *ras* C-terminus is required for transformation and membrane association. *Nature, Lond.* **310**, 583–586.

YUASA, Y., SRIVASTAVA, S. K., DUNN, C. Y., RHIM, J. S., REDDY, E. P. & AARONSON, S. A. (1983). Acquisition of transforming properties by alternative point mutations within c-*has*/*bas* human proto-oncogene. *Nature, Lond.* **303**, 775–779.

J. Cell Sci. Suppl. 4, 431–444 (1986)
Printed in Great Britain © *The Company of Biologists Limited 1986*

THE GENETIC ANALYSIS OF MALIGNANCY

HENRY HARRIS

Sir William Dunn School of Pathology, University of Oxford, Oxford OX1 3RE, UK

INTRODUCTION

The term malignancy defines a complex cellular phenotype that is conventionally divided into three stages: (1) progressive multiplication *in vivo*; (2) loss of co-aptation resulting in the movement of cells away from the growing tumour into the surrounding tissues (invasion); and (3) the generation of secondary deposits elsewhere in the body (metastasis). Metastasis presupposes invasion, but progressive (and destructive) growth may occur without either. In a clinical context a tumour would not be classified as malignant unless it showed at least some evidence of invasion; but a malignant tumour may or may not metastasize. Essentially nothing is known about the genetic determinants of invasiveness. In large part this is due to the absence of any satisfactory experimental model for the study of this parameter. Systems involving the penetration of cells into avian and other embryonic membranes (Armstrong, Quigley & Sidebottom, 1982; Basson & Sidebottom, unpublished), or into artificial deposits of collagen, gelatin or other semi-solid matrices *in vitro*, have not proved reliable predictors of invasiveness (Basson & Sidebottom, 1985).

The analysis of metastasis has moved a little further, but is still at a very early stage. For several years the issue was confused by the use of inappropriate methods, notably the scoring of colonies developing in the lungs or other organs after intravenous injection of cell suspensions. It is now clear, and has indeed been so for many years, that the potential of tumour cells to colonize organs after intravenous injection does not predict metastatic potential under natural conditions (Stackpole, 1981). A beginning has been made in the genetic analysis of metastasis by somatic cell hybridization, and it has been shown that the genetic determinants of progressive growth can be segregated from those that determine metastasis (Sidebottom & Clark, 1983; Clark & Sidebottom, 1984, 1985); but as yet no cultural characteristic *in vitro* or no biochemical marker has been found that consistently cosegregates with metastatic potential. A claim has been made that metastatic potential can be conferred on non-metastatic cells by transfection with preparations of DNA from metastatic cells (Bernstein & Weinberg, 1985); and there is one study that suggests that transfection of epithelial tumour cells by a c-H-*ras* oncogene may enhance their ability to produce metastases (Eccles, Marshall, Vousden & Purvies, 1985). However, neither of these reports contains any information about karyoptic changes induced by the transfection and selection procedures used, so that it is not yet possible to assess how specific or how direct the effect produced by the transfected genes might be. In any case, the data so far available do not permit a review of metastasis in genetic terms. We are therefore reduced to a consideration of progressive cell multiplication *in vivo*. On this subject there is a rich and interesting genetic literature, and it is this that will form the basis of the present article.

The genetic analysis of progressive cell multiplication *in vivo* falls into four categories based on different, but overlapping, methodologies: (1) the study of 'hereditary' tumours (tumours for which a predisposition is inherited); (2) somatic cell hybridization; (3) cytogenetic investigations; and (4) the study of oncogenes (defined in the present context as cellular genes showing substantial homology with the genes of retroviruses). The conclusions drawn from the study of hereditary tumours and those reached by somatic cell hybridization are in substantial agreement. These conclusions are supported by some of the cytogenetic studies, and they are not actually contradicted by any; but they are contradicted by the interpretation given to many of the studies on oncogenes. One aim of the present article is to suggest that these latter interpretations may be inadequate; another is to present a model in which the results obtained with all four methodologies can be accommodated.

HEREDITARY TUMOURS

The idea that malignancy might be a consequence of recessive mutations in somatic cells appears first to have been suggested in 1969 on the basis of cell fusion experiments in which the malignant phenotype was found to be suppressed when malignant cells were fused with non-malignant ones (Harris *et al.* 1969). In 1971, Ohno argued, on theoretical grounds, that the malignant phenotype was much more likely to be generated in somatic cells by recessive mutations than by dominant ones and proposed that these recessive mutations might be unmasked by genetic events that rendered them hemizygous, commonly by a loss, in aneuploid cells, of the homologous chromosome bearing the unaffected allele (Ohno, 1971). In the same year, a specific version of this general model was proposed by Knudson (1971) to account for the incidence pattern of retinoblastoma. This tumour exists in two forms, one sporadic and another in which the predisposition to form the tumour is inherited in an autosomally dominant fashion. Knudson postulated that the genetic locus involved was the same in the two forms of the disease, but that in the heritable form one of the alleles was already mutated in the germ line. A single somatic mutation involving the homologous locus in the unaffected chromosome would then be enough to generate the tumour in the predisposed individual, whereas both alleles would have to be inactivated by two separate genetic events in the sporadic cases. This model, essentially based on homozygosity or hemizygosity of recessive mutations, accommodated the incidence data reasonably well and prompted a search for more direct supporting evidence. This was in due course obtained.

It is now clear from evidence based on both cytogenetic analysis and the analysis of a genetically linked enzyme polymorphism that Knudson's model is essentially correct (Sparkes *et al.* 1983; Benedict *et al.* 1983; Cavenée *et al.* 1985). The locus involved maps to band q14 on the long arm of chromosome 13. In the cases where predisposition is heritable, the cells of the affected individual often show a visible deletion in this region, and even when no deletion is visible, evidence based on enzyme polymorphism suggests the presence of a submicroscopic deletion. Tumours arising in such individuals show either homozygosity for the mutated allele, or hemizygosity caused either by a secondary deletion in the previously unaffected allele or by elimination of the whole of the unaffected chromosome 13. An essentially similar situation is found in the sporadic cases of the disease, in which the two genetic events generating homozygosity or hemizygosity of the recessive mutation must both have been somatic. Knudson & Strong (1972) further suggested that the model proposed for retinoblastoma might also be applicable to Wilms's tumour and, indeed, quite generally, to all cancers for which a heritable predisposition can be demonstrated. In the case of Wilms's tumour, the prediction has again been fulfilled: a deletion in band p13 on chromosome 11 is found in the germ line, and this recessive lesion becomes homozygous or hemizygous in the tumours (Koufos *et al.* 1984; Orkin, Goldman & Sallan, 1984; Fearon, Vogelstein & Feinberg, 1984). Recent work has revealed a similar situation in oat cell (small cell) carcinoma of the lung, where the homozygous deletions are in band p14 on chromosome 3 (Minna, 1985), and in hepatoblastoma and rhabdomyosarcoma, where the deletions, as in Wilms's tumour, are in chromsome 11 (Koufos *et al.* 1985). It seems very likely that similar homozygous genetic defects will be found in other tumours in which there is an overt inherited predisposition, for example, familial renal carcinoma (Pathak, Strong, Ferrell & Trindade, 1982) and several malignancies of the nervous system; but Knudson (1985) argues that there may be a cryptic genetic component in many other tumours for which an inherited predisposition has not yet been recognized. If so, then homozygosity or hemizygosity of recessive mutations might be a much more general mechanism for generating the malignant phenotype than originally envisaged. Recent work on the *lethal(2)giant larvae* mutation in *Drosophila melanogaster* has revealed that the malignant tumours of presumptive adult brain cell centres and imaginal discs that arise in this condition are determined by homozygosity or hemizygosity of recessive mutations (deletions or mutational insertions) at the *l(2)gl* locus (Mechler, McGinnis & Gehring, 1985). It is clear that retinoblastoma and Wilms's tumour are not to be regarded as special cases. Three important general conclusions can be drawn from this work: (1) malignancy can be determined by mutational events at a single locus; (2) the number of genetic events involved need not exceed two, the minimum number required to generate homozygosity or hemizygosity at that locus; and (3) the mutations are recessive and engender loss of function, not gain in function. What this function might be will be discussed at a later stage.

SOMATIC CELL HYBRIDIZATION

The overall results obtained by somatic cell hybridization are in complete agreement with the conclusion that progressive multiplication of cells *in vivo* involves a loss of some cell function, not a gain of function. It is now well established that when malignant cells, defined by their ability to generate progressive tumours in genetically compatible hosts, are fused with diploid fibroblasts of the same species, the resulting hybrid cells, so long as they retain certain specific chromosomes donated by the diploid parent cell, are unable to generate such tumours. When these particular chromosomes are eliminated, however, the ability to multiply progressively *in vivo* reappears in the hybrid cell, and it is once more able to generate a progressive tumour. This phenomenon, commonly described as the suppression of malignancy or tumorigenicity, has been extensively studied in several laboratories and has been shown to apply to crosses between malignant and non-malignant cells in the mouse, hamster and man. (For reviews, see Miller & Miller, 1983; Sager, 1985.) Apparent exceptions to this rule arise from two sources: (1) the relevant chromosomes derived from the diploid parent cell are eliminated early so that the clones are already malignant segregants of the original hybrid cells when they are first examined (in some cases there is strong selection pressure against certain chromosomes derived from the diploid cell); and (2), less frequently, the malignant parent cells contain more than two gene sets or multiple copies of some of the autosomes. (The significance of this will become apparent when the role of gene dosage in the suppression of malignancy is discussed below). While the terms 'dominance' and 'recessiveness' are not easy to apply in a genetically rigorous fashion to experiments with hybrid cells, an acceptable operational description of the overall findings would be that, in this kind of test, the genetic determinants of the malignant phenotype are recessive to those determining the normal phenotype.

Cytogenetic analysis of this phenomenon has revealed that in hybrids between malignant and diploid mouse cells, the chromosomes 4 derived from the diploid parent cell have a decisive role in suppressing the malignant phenotype (Jonasson, Povey & Harris, 1977). This is true for a wide range of different kinds of malignant cells, including tumour cells bearing and expressing retroviral oncogenes. The locus involved appears to map to the lower part of the upper half of chromosome 4, but this assignment remains to be confirmed and further refined. The critical role played by a single diploid chromosome in suppressing the malignant phenotype and, in particular, the assignation of the operative locus to chromosome 4 in mouse hybrids is strongly reinforced by a similar analysis in crosses between normal diploid human fibroblasts and anchorage-independent hamster cells transformed by exposure to a chemical carcinogen. In these crosses, a locus that maps to human chromosome 1 is apparently responsible for the suppression of the transformed phenotype (Stoler & Bouck, 1985). Since human chromosome 1 shares a large area of homology with mouse chromosome 4 (Lalley, Francke & Minna, 1978), it seems probable that the same genetic mechanism is operative in the two species. Further evidence for the role of human chromosome 1 in the suppression of tumorigenicity comes from crosses between a human fibrosarcoma (HT1080) and normal human diploid fibroblasts (Benedict, Weissman, Mark & Stanbridge, 1984). In this case, suppression occurs despite the fact that the fibrosarcoma carries a transforming N-*ras* oncogene. There is also evidence that, in crosses between a human cervical carcinoma cell line and normal diploid human fibroblasts, suppression of tumorigenicity is again determined by a single chromosome (in this case chromosome 11), but the cytogenetic analysis remains uncertain since no markers were available to permit discrimination between the chromosomes derived from the tumour cell and those derived from the diploid fibroblast (Stanbridge, Flandermeyer, Daniels & Nelson-Rees, 1981).

A detailed cytogenetic study of the suppression of tumorigenicity in a particularly informative set of intraspecific mouse hybrids, in which the parental origin of all the chromosomes 4 in the cells could be assigned with certainty, has provided strong evidence for the conclusion that this suppression is subject to gene dosage effects: it is reinforced by an increase in the number of diploid chromosomes 4 in the hybrids and it may be overcome by an increase in the number of chromosomes 4 derived from the malignant parent cell (Evans *et al.* 1982). It is for this reason that suppression of tumorigenicity may not be observed in some crosses between diploid cells and aneuploid or subtetraploid malignant cells in which multiple copies of many autosomes may be found. Similar gene dosage effects for human chromosome 1 have been described in hybrids between diploid human fibroblasts and human fibrosarcoma cells, where, again, tumorigenicity was found to be suppressed when the fibroblasts were crossed with near-diploid sarcoma cells but not when they were crossed with near-tetraploid cells (Benedict *et al.* 1984).

The observations made on hybrid cells are thus in accord with those made on retinoblastoma and other hereditary tumours: the malignant phenotype appears to be generated by recessive mutations at a particular locus and appears to be suppressed by the product of the homologous normal locus. Knudson (1985) calls such homologous loci 'anti-oncogenes', but the function of these genes is not, of course, to suppress cancer any more than the function of oncogenes is to induce it. 'Anti-oncogenes' are simply normal cellular genes carrying out normal cellular functions. But what might these functions be? Recent histological studies on hybrids in which malignancy has been suppressed have been especially informative in this regard. It has been shown that when a normal diploid cell is fused with a malignant one, it suppresses the malignant phenotype by imposing on the hybrid cell its own pattern of terminal differentiation. When tumour cells are fused with diploid fibroblasts, the hybrid cells, when injected into the animal, assume an increasingly elongated fibrocytic morphology, synthesize a collagenous extracellular matrix, as normal fibroblasts do in forming scar tissue, and stop multiplying (Stanbridge & Ceredig, 1981; Harris, 1985). But segregants from which the specific suppressive chromosome derived from the diploid fibroblast has been eliminated, do not assume an elongated fibrocytic morphology, do not synthesize any stainable collagenous extracellular matrix and continue to multiply. Similarly, hybrids in which malignancy is suppressed by fusion of the tumour cells with normal diploid keratinocytes undergo squamous differentiation and keratinization *in vivo*, whereas malignant segregants derived from these hybrids do not (Peehl & Stanbridge, 1982). In the suppression of malignancy by cell fusion we are thus dealing with an imposed pattern of terminal differentiation bringing cell multiplication to a stop. But this encourages the conclusion that the tumour cells themselves continue to multiply progressively *in vivo* because they cannot execute the pattern of terminal differentiation that is proper to them. In other words, the recessive defect that generates progressive cell multiplication *in vivo* is a defect of differentiation. In cell fusion experiments, this defect may be overcome either by the imposition of a foreign pattern of terminal differentiation on the malignant cell, as occurs when non-fibroblastic tumour cells are fused with normal fibroblasts, or by the restoration of the malignant cell's own pattern of terminal differentiation. The latter effect has been observed with anaplastic fibrosarcoma cells, which do not synthesize an extracellular matrix *in vivo*, but which can be induced to do so and to undergo terminal fibrocytic differentiation when fused with normal diploid cells of a non-fibroblastic type (Harris, 1985). The relationship between terminal differentiation and progressive cell multiplication *in vivo* is discussed further below.

CYTOGENETIC INVESTIGATIONS

The role of homozygous or hemizygous deletions in the genesis of hereditary tumours has already been considered; but cytogenetic studies have revealed, in certain other malignant tumours, two other types of chromosome abnormality that are thought to involve quite different genetic mechanisms: translocations and gene amplifications. While a wide variety of translocations may be found sporadically in many malignant tumours, some malignancies of the haemopoietic system are characterized by the consistent presence of specific translocations involving constant chromosome regions. These translocations have been intensively studied in both mouse and man and have been reviewed recently by Rowley (1984) and Klein & Klein (1985). The biological interest of these translocations has been immensely enhanced by the realization that the break-points involve bands in which known oncogenes have been located and in three cases (two human, one murine) it has been demonstrated that the translocation moves an oncogene to a new site. The human cases are Burkitt's lymphoma, in which the *myc* gene on chromosome 8 is trans-located to the vicinity of one of the three immunoglobulin loci on chromosomes 14, 2 or 22, and chronic myeloid leukaemia, in which the *abl* gene on chromosome 9 is translocated to chromosome 22. In the mouse, plasmacytomas show essentially homologous translocations to those seen in Burkitt's lymphoma: the *myc* gene on chromosome 15 is moved to the vicinity of immunoglobulin gene loci on chromo-somes 12 or 6. Since nothing is known of the function of the genetic area to which the *abl* gene is translocated in chronic myeloid leukaemia, most investigations have so far centred on the *myc* translocations in Burkitt's lymphoma and mouse plasmacytoma.

An attractive idea proposed by Klein was that the translocation of the *myc* gene to an immunoglobulin gene region, where a high level of transcription was operative, would impose a higher than normal level of transcription on the translocated gene, and that this would ensure continued stimulation of cell multiplication. In its simplest form, however, this idea has become untenable. Although a higher than normal level of transcription was claimed for some Burkitt's lymphoma cell lines (Erickson *et al.* 1983), it was not clear that the appropriate normal controls had been chosen or, indeed, what they should be; and other reports on different cell lines soon showed that an enhanced level of transcription of the translocated *myc* gene was by no means the rule, either in Burkitt's lymphoma or in mouse plasmacytoma (Klein & Klein, 1985). Nucleotide sequence determination then revealed that, in some cases, the translocated *myc* gene had undergone mutation, rearrangement or partial deletion; but usually no structural change could be detected in the translocated gene. These findings reduced the original model to a suggestion that perhaps the translocated gene, although specifying a normal product, was not regulated properly. If so, then it would have to be assumed that the transcription of the translocated gene was regulated by *cis*-acting mechanisms, for example, changes in chromosome structure. Evidence in support of this view was provided by the claim that only the translocated gene was transcribed in Burkitt's lymphoma, while the untranslocated homologue was silent (Nishikura *et al.* 1983). However, almost at once it was shown, in a different Burkitt's lymphoma cell line, that the untranslocated *myc* gene was transcribed (Rabbitts, Forster, Hamlyn & Baer, 1984), although apparently at a lower level than the translocated gene (Feo *et al.* 1985). On the other hand, it has been shown, in experiments in which Burkitt's lymphoma cells were fused with fibroblasts, that, like several other oncogenes that have been tested in this way, transcription of the translocated *myc* gene can be regulated by *trans*-acting elements (Nishikura *et al.* 1984).

Despite the hazards inherent in generating models from such variable data, it is worth considering what the genetic consequences of these different claims might be. If the translocated *myc* gene is mutated or structurally altered in such a way as to make it unlikely that a normal functional gene product is made, and the untranslocated gene is silent (because it, too, carries a cryptic mutation, or for any other reason), then the cell is without a functional *myc* gene and is formally equivalent to a cell that has undergone a homozygous or hemizygous recessive mutation. If the product of the translocated gene is functionally normal, then the variability found in the rate of transcription of this gene makes it unlikely that an elevated level of the *myc* gene product can be the essential determinant of the malignant phenotype. If the product of the translocated gene is abnormal, but is in some way functional, while that of the untranslocated gene remains normal, then the consequences would depend on whether the abnormal gene product interfered with the action of the normal product. If it did, then one would expect to observe dosage effects of various kinds. But all these models are called into question by recent data on the behaviour of the *myc* protein itself. It has been shown that the level, rate of synthesis and rate of turnover of the *myc* protein is no different in Burkitt's lymphoma cells carrying a translocated *myc* gene than in chronic leukaemia cells carrying no translocated or amplified *myc* gene (Hann, Thompson & Eisenman, 1985). Moreover, the levels of *myc* protein do not vary significantly throughout the cell cycle, as might be expected if the *myc* gene were involved in stimulating the entry of the cells into the phase of DNA synthesis. This study on the *myc* protein is supported by an independent study showing a similar lack of variation of *myc* messenger RNA throughout the cell cycle (Thompson, Chaloner, Neiman & Groudine, 1985). Nonetheless, it is difficult to avoid the conclusion that the *myc* translocation in Burkitt's lymphomas and in mouse plasmacytomas must confer some selective advantage on these particular cells, as it would otherwise be difficult to explain its consistent presence. What this selective advantage might be and how it operates are at the moment unclear. One idea that appears not to have been considered is that the importance of the *myc* translocations might lie not in their effects on the *myc* gene, but in their effects on the further differentiation of the antibody-forming cell. The possibility seems worth exploring that the *myc* translocations act by impeding the progress of the antibody-forming cell into its normal fully differentiated state, the non-dividing memory cell. It remains an open question whether the translocation is involved in initiating the process that leads to malignancy or whether it takes place at a later stage in the growth of the tumours conferring such a strong selective advantage that cells bearing it become the dominant, or even exclusive, cell type. There is, in any case, nothing in the studies on Burkitt's lymphomas or mouse plasmacytomas that provides convincing evidence of a genetically dominant mode of action for the cytogenetic abnormalities found in this form of malignancy.

Many examples have been described of gene amplification in malignant tumours, both in the form of supernumerary chromosomes and as tandem expansions of particular genes commonly identified in cytological preparations as homogeneously staining regions. Among the genes that may be amplified in this way are a number of oncogenes. For example, amplification of c-*myc* has been described in some breast carcinomas (Capon *et al.* 1983; Kozbor & Croce, 1984), colon carcinoma (Alitalo *et al.* 1983), neuroblastoma (Schwab *et al.* 1983), retinoblastoma (Lee, Murphree & Benedict, 1984) and leukaemia (Nowell *et al.* 1983); and amplification of either c-*myc* or n-*myc* has been found in some 20 % of human lung cancer cell lines (Little *et al.* 1983). However, in no case is amplification of a particular oncogene invariably or consistently associated with any particular kind of malignant tumour. Nor is gene amplification limited to malignant cells: amplification of an unmodified c-H-*ras* oncogene has recently been demonstrated in normal diploid human fibroblasts during their limited replicative life-span *in vitro* (Srivastava, Norris, Schmooker-Reis & Goldstein, 1985). It is therefore very unlikely that amplification of oncogenes is the initiating event in the generation of the malignant tumour. Most of the evidence bearing on this point suggests that this amplification is a later effect of selection pressure applied to the growing cell population. How the amplified onco-gene confers a selective advantage is not at all clear, but it seems that the selection pressure is not limited to malignant cells multiplying *in vivo* but can operate on normal diploid cells growing *in vitro*.

ONCOGENES

There is now a massive literature, punctuated by excited editorials from *Nature*, on the occurrence and behaviour of cellular genes that show homology with retroviral genes, and the subject is constantly being reviewed. Only one aspect of this literature will be considered in any depth here: the evidence that some of these oncogenes act to produce malignancy in a genetically dominant fashion. The question is of great theoretical importance, for the experiments in which morphological transformation *in vitro* or tumorigenicity *in vivo* are conferred on non-transformed and non-tumorigenic cells by transfection of oncogenes constitute the only substantial body of work that appears to contradict the conclusions reached from the study of hereditary tumours and from somatic cell hybridization. Because clones of transformed and sometimes tumorigenic cells arise in populations of untransformed cells after transfection with identifiable genes taken from malignant cells, the assumption is commonly made that these genes must be operating in a dominant fashion. This assumption is precarious. To begin with, it overlooks the complexity of the changes that may be produced in the recipient cells by the transfection and subsequent selection procedures. If it were certain that the only change produced in the genotype of the recipient cell by the transfection procedure was the addition of a single copy of the transfected oncogene, then the conclusion that this gene acted in a dominant fashion would, at least provisionally, be plausible. But it is, in fact, certain that this is not the case. Karyological investigation of clones transformed by transfected oncogenes invariably shows that the karyotype of the transformed cells differs substantially from that of the untransformed cells (Gilbert, Evans & Harris, unpublished). The recipient cells have not only received the oncogene, they have in the process also undergone other, often multiple, genetic changes. Against this background of complex modifications in genotype, conclusions about the dominance of the mode of action of the transfected gene are meaningless, unless it can be shown that these complex modifications are irrelevant. To do this, it would be necessary to back-select against the transfected oncogene and demonstrate that all clones that have eliminated the transfected oncogene have reverted to a non-transformed and non-tumorigenic phenotype. A systematic investigation of this question is at present being undertaken (Gilbert & Harris, unpublished); but, in the interim, it is of interest to consider the available evidence.

It has been claimed that if NIH3T3 cells are transformed by transfection with an N-*ras* oncogene, the continued presence of the oncogene is required to maintain the transformed phenotype (Murray *et al.* 1983); but this assumption is based on the analysis of a single flat revertant in which the transfected oncogene was not found. On the other hand, in a more extensive set of experiments, it has been shown that flat revertants of NIH3T3 cells transformed by the K-*ras* oncogene may or may not retain the transfected gene (Noda, Selinger, Scolnick & Bassin, 1983); and there is evidence that such revertants may retain and express the K-*ras* oncogene but still be resistant to its transforming action (Norton *et al.* 1984). Moreover, it has been shown that the lymphomas produced by the Abelson virus eliminate the Abelson virus genes on continued growth *in vivo*, but remain tumorigenic (Grunwald *et al.* 1982). This is also true for tumours induced by the avian leukosis virus (Payne *et al.* 1981), and for Chinese hamster fibroblasts transformed and rendered tumorigenic by transfection with the c-H-*ras* oncogene (Lau *et al.* 1985). In all these cases the results support the view that the transfected oncogene acts in an indirect way by inducing stable secondary changes in the genotype of the recipient cell, a mechanism that has been dubbed 'hit and run'. But even if this were not the case, the evidence for a dominant mode of action of mutated or transfected oncogenes would still be weak. It has been shown in three different malignant tumours carrying mutated K-*ras* oncogenes (from colon (Capon *et al.* 1983), bladder and lung (Santos *et al.* 1984)) that the cells in each case have eliminated the normal unmutated K-*ras* allele, a hemizygous state obviously reminiscent of the findings in hereditary tumours. And even in the prototype case, transformation of NIH3T3 cells by transfection with the H-*ras* oncogene, it appears that the normal mouse allele is only transcribed at a very low level in the transfected cells (Capon *et al.* 1983), a situation that may not be very different from that previously discussed in the section dealing with *myc* translocations in Burkitt's lymphoma. It is, in any case, clear that the expression of at least some oncogenes can be suppressed when malignant cells bearing them are fused with non-malignant cells (Marshall, 1980; Dyson, Quade & Wyke, 1982; Benedict *et al.* 1983; Dyson, Cook, Searle & Wyke, 1985; Craig & Sager, 1985).

Perhaps enough has been said to convince the reader that the case for a genetically dominant mode of action for oncogenes has yet to be established; but whatever the formal genetic situation may turn out to be, the mode of action of these genes in generating tumours remains a fascinating subject. In a recent paper, the suggestion has been made that mutated, or otherwise functionally abnormal oncogenes, may act by impeding the process of terminal differentiation in the cell (Harris, 1985). A good deal of evidence already exists that at least some of the normal cellular homologues of oncogenes are involved in a critical way in various forms of differentiation (Jacob, 1983). In a recent study with the c-*fos* oncogene, it has been shown that transfection of the normal mouse or human gene into an embryonic carcinoma cell line that does not normally differentiate *in vitro* can induce various elements of the differentiated state (Müller & Wagner, 1984; Rüther, Wagner & Müller, 1985). If one supposes that the normal cellular homologue of an oncogene acts to initiate a particular programme of differentiation, or is involved in that programme in some decisive way, then it is not difficult to envisage that a mutated or otherwise functionally abnormal form of that gene might impede that programme of differentiation, especially if it is present in a hemizygous or homozygous condition, or if, for some reason, the altered gene product were made in much greater amounts than the normal product. In the case of transfection experiments, an aberrant effect might in some cases be achieved even with a structurally normal gene, for any one such gene might be involved in only one specific programme of differentiation (for example, the *erb* gene in erythropoiesis), but it might be transfected to a cell of a quite different lineage (for example, the NIH3T3 fibroblast). This could have the consequence that the recipient cell's own programme of differentiation might be impaired by the operation of quite inappropriate signals. This idea finds experimental support in several experimental systems in which it has been shown that a variety of different oncogenes introduced into the cell do indeed impede the process of differentiation. For example, transformation of fibroblastic cells by Rous sarcoma virus (Arbogast *et al.* 1977; Vaheri *et al.* 1978), by simian virus 40 (Krieg *et al.* 1980; Trüeb, Lewis & Carter, 1985) or by transfection with the H-*ras* or v-*mos* oncogene (Liau, Yamada & de Crombrugghe, 1985; Schmidt, Setoyama & de Crombrugghe, 1985) produces in all cases a severe impairment of the production of one or more components of the extracellular matrix. Transfection of bronchial epithelial cells by the H-*ras* oncogene renders them incapable of undergoing squamous differentiation (Yoakum *et al.* 1985); and several different oncogenes similarly impair the differentiation of myogenic cells (Falcone, Tato & Alemà, 1985). The great attraction of the idea that the genesis of malignancy is causally linked to a defect in the process of normal differentiation is that it can accommodate without conflict all the evidence provided by the four different categories of investigation that have been discussed: the data from hereditary tumours, somatic cell hybridization, cytogenetics and oncogenes. But one is still entitled to ask how the defect in the process of differentiation induces progressive cell multiplication *in vivo*.

DIFFERENTIATION AND CELL MULTIPLICATION

The least taxing approach to this question is to assume that cells, both prokaryotic and eukaryotic, are so constituted that they will continue to multiply, given an adequate supply of nutrients and co-factors, until the process of differentiation induces them to stop. Continuous multiplication is, in this model, envisaged as the natural steady state, and cessation of multiplication a restriction imposed on the system. Any event that produces a stable heritable block to the process of differentiation would then *ipso facto* result in continuous cell multiplication. This model is not contradicted by the observed effects of growth factors, for it is perfectly plausible to regard growth factors as agents that do impede the process of differentiation, perhaps, in some cases, by preventing the exit of cells from the cycle of DNA synthesis. These ideas have been discussed in greater detail elsewhere (Harris, 1985). If they are true, they make the prospect of finding agents that might discriminate between the multiplication of malignant cells and that of their normal homologues rather remote, but they should encourage the search for physiologically tolerable agents that can induce the terminal differentiation of malignant cells.

REFERENCES

ALITALO, K., SCHWAB, M., LIN, C. C., VARMUS, H. E. & BISHOP, J. M. (1983). Homogeneously staining chromosomal regions contain amplified copies of an abundantly expressed cellular oncogene (c-*myc*) in malignant neuroendocrine cells from a human colon carcinoma. *Proc. natn. Acad. Sci. U.S.A.* **80**, 1707–1711.

ARBOGAST, B. W., YOSHIMURA, M., KEFALIDES, N. A., HOLTZER, H. & KAJI, A. (1977). Failure of cultured chick embryo fibroblasts to incorporate collagen into their extracellular matrix when transformed by Rous sarcoma virus. *J. biol. Chem.* **252**, 8863–8868.

ARMSTRONG, P. B., QUIGLEY, J. P. & SIDEBOTTOM, E. (1982). Transepithelial invasion and intramesenchymal infiltration of the chick embryo chorioallantois by tumor cell lines. *Cancer Res.* **42**, 1826–1837.

BASSON, C. T. & SIDEBOTTOM, E. (1985). An *in vitro* study of tumour invasion to compare metastatic and non-metastatic cells. In *Treatment of Metastasis: Problems and Prospects* (ed. K. Hallam & S. A. Eccles), pp. 243–246. London: Taylor and Francis.

BENEDICT, W. F., MURPHREE, A. L., BANERJEE, A., SPINA, C. A., SPARKES, M. C. & SPARKES, R. (1983). Patient with 13 chromosome deletion: evidence that the retinoblastoma gene is a recessive cancer gene. *Science* **219**, 973–975.

BENEDICT, W. F., WEISSMAN, B. E., MARK, C. & STANBRIDGE, E. J. (1984). Tumorigenicity of human HT1080 fibrosarcoma × normal fibroblast hybrids: chromosome dosage dependency. *Cancer Res.* **44**, 3471–3479.

BERNSTEIN, S. C. & WEINBERG, R. A. (1985). Expression of the metastatic phenotype in cells transfected with human metastatic tumor DNA. *Proc. natn. Acad. Sci. U.S.A.* **82**, 1726–1730.

CAPON, D. J., SEEBURG, P. H., McGRATH, J. P., HAYFLICK, J. S., EDMAN, U., LEVINSON, A. D. & GOEDDEL, D. V. (1983). Activation of Ki-*ras* 2 gene in human colon and lung carcinomas by two different point mutations. *Nature, Lond.* **304**, 507–513.

CAVENÉE, W. K., HANSEN, M. F., NORDENSKJOLD, M., KOCK, E., MAUMENEE, I., SQUIRE, J. A., PHILLIPS, R. A. & GALLIE, B. L. (1985). Genetic origin of mutations predisposing to retinoblastoma. *Science* **228**, 501–503.

CLARK, S. R. & SIDEBOTTOM, E. (1984). Selection of metastatic variants on the basis of clonal morphology *in vitro*. *Invasion, Metastasis 4* (suppl. 1), 1–11.

CLARK, S. R. & SIDEBOTTOM, E. (1985). Heterogeneity, stability and selection in metastatic cells. In *Treatment and Metastasis: Problems and Prospects* (ed. K. Hallam & S. A. Eccles), pp. 393–396. London: Taylor and Francis.

CRAIG, R. W. & SAGER, R. (1985). Suppression of tumorigenicity in hybrids of normal and oncogene-transformed CHEF cells. *Proc. natn. Acad. Sci. U.S.A.* **82**, 2062–2066.

DYSON, P. J., COOK, P. R., SEARLE, S. & WYKE, J. A. (1985). The chromatin structure of Rous sarcoma proviruses is changed by factors that act in *trans* in cell hybrids. *EMBO J.* **4**, 413–420.

DYSON, P. J., QUADE, K. & WYKE, J. A. (1982). Expression of the ASV *src* gene in hybrids between normal and virally transformed cells: specific suppression occurs in some hybrids but not others. *Cell* **30**, 491–498.

ECCLES, S. A., MARSHALL, C. J., VOUSDEN, K. & PURVIES, H. P. (1985). Enhanced spontaneous metastatic capacity of mouse mammary carcinoma cells transfected with c-H-*ras*. In *Treatment of Metastasis: Problems and Prospects* (ed. K. Hallam & S. A. Eccles), pp. 385–389. London: Taylor and Francis.

ERIKSON, J., AR-RUSHDI, A., DRWINGA, H. L., NOWELL, P. C. & CROCE, C. M. (1983). Transcriptional activation of the translocated c-*myc* oncogene in Burkitt lymphoma. *Proc. natn. Acad. Sci. U.S.A.* **80**, 820–824.

EVANS, E. P., BURTENSHAW, M. D., BROWN, B. B., HENNION, R. & HARRIS, H. (1982). The analysis of malignancy by cell fusion. IX. Re-examination and clarification of the cytogenetic problem. *J. Cell Sci.* **56**, 113–130.

FALCONE, G., TATO, F. & ALEMÀ, S. (1985). Distinctive effects of the viral oncogenes *myc, erb, fps* and *src* on the differentiation program of quail myogenic cells. *Proc. natn. Acad. Sci. U.S.A.* **82**, 426–430.

FEARON, E. R., VOGELSTEIN, B. & FEINBERG, A. P. (1984). Somatic deletion and duplication of genes on chromosome 11 in Wilms' tumours. *Nature, Lond.* **309**, 176–178.

FEO, S., AR-RUSHDI, A., HUEBNER, K., FINAN, J., NOWELL, P. C., CLARKSON, B. & CROCE, C. M. (1985). Suppression of the normal mouse c-*myc* oncogene in human lymphoma cells. *Nature, Lond.* **313**, 493–495.

GRUNWALD, D. J., DALE, B., DUDLEY, J., LAMPH, W., SUGDEN, B., OZANNE, B. & RISSER, R. (1982). Loss of viral gene expression and retention of tumorigenicity by Abelson lymphoma cells. *J. Virol.* **43**, 92–103.

HANN, S. R., THOMPSON, C. B. & EISENMAN, R. N. (1985). c-*myc* oncogene protein synthesis is independent of the cell cycle in human and avian cells. *Nature, Lond.* **314**, 366–369.

HARRIS, H. (1985). Suppression of malignancy in hybrid cells: the mechanism. *J. Cell Sci.* **79**, 105–117.

HARRIS, H., MILLER, O. J., KLEIN, G., WORST, P. & TACHIBANA, T. (1969). Suppression of malignancy by cell fusion. *Nature, Lond.* **223**, 363–368.

JACOB, F. (1983). Expression of embryonic characters by malignant cells. *Ciba Fdn Symp.* vol. 96, pp. 4–27. London: Pitman.

JONASSON, J., POVEY, S. & HARRIS, H. (1977). The analysis of malignancy by cell fusion. VII. Cytogenetic analysis of hybrids between malignant and diploid cells and of tumours derived from them. *J. Cell Sci.* **24**, 217–254.

KLEIN, G. & KLEIN, E. (1985). Evolution of tumours and the impact of molecular oncology. *Nature, Lond.* **315**, 190–195.

KNUDSON, A. G. (1971). Mutation and cancer: statistical study of retinoblastoma. *Proc. natn. Acad. Sci. U.S.A.* **68**, 820–823.

KNUDSON, A. G. (1985). Hereditary cancer, oncogenes and antioncogenes. *Cancer Res.* **45**, 1437–1443.

KNUDSON, A. G. & STRONG, L. C. (1972). Mutation and cancer: a model for Wilms' tumour of the kidney. *J. natn. Cancer Inst.* **48**, 313–324.

KOUFOS, A., HANSEN, M. F., COPELAND, N. G., JENKINS, N. A., LAMPKIN, B. C. & CAVENÉE, W. K. (1985). Loss of heterozygosity in three embryonal tumours suggests a common pathogenic mechanism. *Nature, Lond.* **316**, 330–334.

KOUFOS, A., HANSEN, M. F., LAMPKIN, B. C., WORKMAN, M. L., COPELAND, N. G., JENKINS, N. A. & CAVENÉE, W. K. (1984). Loss of alleles at loci on human chromosome 11 during genesis of Wilms' tumour. *Nature, Lond.* **309**, 170–172.

KOZBOR, D. & CROCE, C. M. (1984). Amplification of the c-*myc* oncogene in one of five human breast carcinoma cell lines. *Cancer Res.* **44**, 438–441.

KRIEG, T., AUMAILLEY, M., DESSAU, W., WIESTNER, M. & MÜLLER, P. (1980). Synthesis of collagen by human fibroblasts and their SV40 transformants. *Expl Cell Res.* **125**, 23–30.

LALLEY, P. A., FRANCKE, U. & MINNA, J. D. (1978). Homologous genes for enolase, phosphogluconate dehydrogenase, phosphoglucomutase and adenylate kinase are syntenic on mouse chromosome 4 and human chromosome 1p. *Proc. natn. Acad. Sci. U.S.A.* **75**, 2382–2386.

LAU, C. C., GADI, I. M., KALVONJIAN, S., ANISOWICZ, A. & SAGER, R. (1985). Plasmid-induced 'hit-and-run' tumorigenesis in Chinese hamster embryo fibroblast (CHEF) cells. *Proc. natn. Acad. Sci. U.S.A.* **82**, 2839–2843.

LEE, W.-H., MURPHREE, A. L. & BENEDICT, W. F. (1984). Expression and amplification of the N-*myc* gene in primary retinoblastoma. *Nature, Lond.* **309**, 458–460.

LIAU, G., YAMADA, Y. & DE CROMBRUGGHE, B. (1985). Coordinate regulation of the levels of Type 111 and Type 1 collagen mRNA in most but not all mouse fibroblasts. *J. biol. Chem.* **260**, 531–536.

LITTLE, C. D., NAU, M. M., CARNEY, D. N., GAZDAR, A. F. & MINNA, J. D. (1983). Amplification and expression of the c-*myc* oncogene in human lung cancer cell lines. *Nature, Lond.* **306**, 194–195.

MARSHALL, C. J. (1980). Suppression of the transformed phenotype with retention of the viral '*src*' gene in cell hybrids between Rous sarcoma virus-transformed rat cells and untransformed mouse cells. *Expl Cell Res.* **127**, 373–384.

MECHLER, B. M., McGINNIS, W. & GEHRING, W. J. (1985). Molecular cloning of *lethal(2)giant larvae*, a recessive oncogene of *Drosophila melanogaster*. *EMBO J.* **4**, 1551–1557.

MILLER, D. A. & MILLER, O. (1983). Chromosomes and cancer in the mouse: studies in tumors, established cell lines, and cell hybrids. *Adv. Cancer Res.* **39**, 153–182.

MÜLLER, R. & WAGNER, E. F. (1984). Differentiation of F9 teratocarcinoma stem cells after transfer of c-*fos* proto-oncogenes. *Nature, Lond.* **311**, 438–442.

MURRAY, M. J., CUNNINGHAM, J. M., PARADA, L. F., DAUTRY, F., LEBOWITZ, P. & WEINBERG, R. A. (1983). The HL-60 transforming sequence: a *ras* oncogene coexisting with altered *myc* genes in hematopoietic tumors. *Cell* **33**, 749–757.

NISHIKURA, K., AR-RUSHDI, A., ERIKSON, J., WATT, R., ROVERA, G. & CROCE, C. M. (1983). Differential expression of the normal and of the translocated human c-*myc* oncogenes in B cells. *Proc. natn. Acad. Sci. U.S.A.* **80**, 4822–4826.

NISHIKURA, K., AR-RUSHDI, A., ERIKSON, J., DEJESUS, E., DUGAN, D. & CROCE, C. M. (1984). Repression of rearranged μ gene and translocated c-*myc* in mouse 3T3 cells × Burkitt lymphoma cell hybrids. *Science* **224**, 399–402.

NODA, M., SELINGER, Z., SCOLNICK, E. M. & BASSIN, R. H. (1983). Flat revertants isolated from Kirsten sarcoma virus-transformed cells are resistant to the action of specific oncogenes. *Proc. natn. Acad. Sci. U.S.A.* **80**, 5602–5606.

NORTON, J. D., COOK, F., ROBERTS, P. C., CLEWLEY, J. P. & AVERY, R. J. (1984). Expression of Kirsten murine sarcoma virus in transformed nonproducer and revertant NIH/3T3 cells: evidence for cell-mediated resistance to a viral oncogene in phenotypic reversion. *J. Virol.* **50**, 439–444.

NOWELL, P., FINAN, J., FAVERA, R. D., GALLO, R. C., AR-RUSHDI, A., ROMANCZUKI, H., SELDEN, J. R., EMANUAL, B. S., ROVERA, G. & CROCE, C. M. (1983). Association of amplified oncogene c-*myc* with an abnormally banded chromosome 8 in a human leukaemia cell line. *Nature, Lond.* **306**, 494–497.

OHNO, S. (1971). Genetic implication of karyological instability of malignant somatic cells. *Physiol. Rev.* **51**, 496–526.

ORKIN, S. H., GOLDMAN, D. S. & SALLAN, S. E. (1984). Development of homozygosity for chromosome 11p markers in Wilms' tumour. *Nature, Lond.* **309**, 172–174.

PATHAK, S., STRONG, L. C., FERRELL, R. E. & TRINDADE, A. (1982). Familial renal cell carcinoma with a 3;11 chromosome translocation limited to tumor cells. *Science* **217**, 939–941.

PAYNE, G. S., COURTNEIDGE, S. A., CRITTENDEN, L. B., FADLY, A. M., BISHOP, J. M. & VARMUS, H. E. (1981). Analysis of avian leukosis virus DNA and RNA in bursal tumors: viral gene expression is not required for maintenance of the tumor state. *Cell* **23**, 311–322.

PEEHL, D. M. & STANBRIDGE, E. J. (1982). The role of differentiation in the suppression of tumorigenicity in human hybrid cells. *Int. J. Cancer* **30**, 113–120.

RABBITTS, T. H., FORSTER, A., HAMLYN, P. & BAER, R. (1984). Effect of somatic mutation within translocated c-*myc* genes in Burkitt's lymphoma. *Nature, Lond.* **309**, 592–597.

ROWLEY, J. D. (1984). Biological implications of consistent chromosome rearrangements in leukemia and lymphoma. *Cancer Res.* **44**, 3159–3168.

RÜTHER, U., WAGNER, E. F. & MÜLLER, R. (1985). Analysis of the differentiation-promoting potential of inducible c-*fos* genes introduced into embryonal carcinoma cells. *EMBO J.* **4**, 1775–1781.

SAGER, R. (1985). Genetic suppression of tumor formation. *Advan. Cancer Res.* **44**, 43–68.

SANTOS, E., MARTIN-ZANCA, D., REDDY, E. P., PIEROTTI, M. A., DELLA PORTA, G. & BARBACID, M. (1984). Malignant activation of a K-*ras* oncogene in lung carcinoma but not in normal tissue of the same patient. *Science* **223**, 661–664.

SCHMIDT, A., SETOYAMA, C. & DE CROMBRUGGHE, B. (1985). Regulation of a collagen gene promoter by the product of viral *mos* oncogene. *Nature, Lond.* **314**, 286–289.

SCHWAB, M., ALITALO, K., KLEMPNAUER, K.-H., VARMUS, H. E., BISHOP, J. M., GILBERT, F., BRODEUR, G., GOLDSTEIN, M. & TRENT, J. (1983). *Nature, Lond.* **305**, 245–248.

SIDEBOTTOM, E. & CLARK, S. R. (1983). Cell fusion segregates progressive growth from metastasis. *Br. J. Cancer* **47**, 399–406.

SPARKES, R. S., MURPHREE, A. L., LINGUA, R. W., SPARKES, M. C., FIELD, L. L., FUNDERBURK, S. J. & BENEDICT, W. F. (1983). Gene for hereditary retinoblastoma assigned to human chromosome 13 by linkage to esterase D. *Science* **219**, 971–973.

SRIVASTAVA, A., NORRIS, J. S., SCHMOOKER-REIS, R. J. & GOLDSTEIN, S. (1985). c-H-*ras* 1 proto-oncogene amplification and overexpression during the limited replicative life-span of normal human fibroblasts. *J. biol. Chem.* **260**, 6404–6409.

STACKPOLE, C. W. (1981). Distinct lung-colonizing and lung-metastasizing cell populations in B16 mouse melanoma. *Nature, Lond.* **289**, 798–800.

STANBRIDGE, E. J., FLANDERMEYER, R. R., DANIELS, D. W. & NELSON-REES, W. A. (1981). Specific chromosome loss associated with the expression of tumorigenicity in human cell hybrids. *Somat. Cell Genet.* **7**, 699–712.

STANBRIDGE, E. J. & CEREDIG, R. (1981). Growth-regulatory control of human cell hybrids in nude mice. *Cancer Res.* **41**, 573–580.

STOLER, A. & BOUCK, N. (1985). Identification of a single chromosome in the normal human genome essential for suppression of hamster cell transformation. *Proc. natn. Acad. Sci. U.S.A.* **82**, 570–574.

THOMPSON, C. R., CHALLONER, P. B., NEIMAN, P. E. & GROUDINE, M. (1985). Levels of c-*myc* oncogene mRNA are invariant throughout the cell cycle. *Nature, Lond.* **314**, 363–366.

TRÜEB, B., LEWIS, J. B. & CARTER, W. G. (1985). Translatable mRNA for GP140 (a subunit of Type VI collagen) is absent in SV40 transformed fibroblasts. *J. Cell Biol.* **100**, 638–641.

VAHERI, A., KURKINEN, M., LEHTO, V.-P., LINDER, E. & TIMPL, R. (1978). Codistribution of pericellular matrix proteins in cultured fibroblasts and loss in transformation: Fibronectin and procollagen. *Proc. natn. Acad. Sci. U.S.A.* **75**, 4944–4948.

YOAKUM, G. H., LECHNER, J. F., GABRIELSON, E. W., KORBA, B. E., MALAN-SHIBLEY, L., WILLEY, J. C., VALERIO, M. G., SHAMSUDDIN, A. M., TRUMP, B. F. & HARRIS, C. C. (1985). Transformation of human bronchial epithelial cells transfected by Harvey *ras* oncogene. *Science* **227**, 1174–1179.

J. Cell Sci. Suppl. 4, 445–458 (1986)
Printed in Great Britain © The Company of Biologists Limited 1986

THE MOLECULAR GENETICS OF HAEMOPHILIA A AND B

G. G. BROWNLEE

Sir William Dunn School of Pathology, University of Oxford, South Parks Road, Oxford OX1 3RE, UK

INTRODUCTION

Haemophilia has been known since biblical times as an inherited bleeding condition, as boys born into families known to have the disease were excluded from ritual circumcision in the third century AD (quoted by McKee, 1983). The pattern of inheritance whereby males were affected, whereas females were not (although they could transmit the disease to future generations), intrigued the 19th century biologists and was not adequately explained until the genetic basis of sex was understood. The clinical symptoms of the disease can be very serious and were life-threatening before replacement therapy was available. Internal bleeding occurred into muscles and joints, often without obviously following any trauma and patients could die of massive internal haemorrhage. Haemophilia A and B pose identical clinical pictures and both show a similar X-linked pattern of inheritance. Their differential diagnosis depends on laboratory clotting tests and they were first clearly distinguished in 1952. Subsequent work showed that the former condition involved defects in the protein factor VIIIC and the latter in factor IX. Both proteins function in the middle phase of the intrinsic clotting cascade (Fig. 1). Haemophilia A is the commoner disease, occurring in Caucasians in approximately one in 5000 males, and is also referred to as classical haemophilia. Haemophilia B occurs in approximately 1 in 30 000 males and is also known as Christmas disease, after the name of a patient, Stephen Christmas, in whom the disease was characterized early on.

Between 1960 and 1980 the methods of analysing the sequence of amino acids in proteins that had been pioneered by Sanger and his colleagues on insulin were applied to the proteins of the clotting cascade, including the factor IX protein. By 1979 the entire amino acid sequence of the bovine factor IX was known (Katayama *et al.* 1979) and there was evidence suggesting that a rather similar sequence might be present in humans. This was a considerable feat of work because of the low yield (about $5 \mu g \, ml^{-1}$ of the protein) in plasma. But this basic knowledge of protein structure was not as easily obtained for factor VIIIC, partly because of its minute yield in plasma, but also because its high molecular weight and instability made it particularly difficult to characterize. In fact, factor VIIIC exists as a minor component of the high molecular weight complex referred to as factor VIII, and the bulk of this complex is composed of another protein, the von Willebrand factor.

In this short review, I will briefly describe and discuss the advances made since 1980 that have enabled the genes for factor VIIIC and IX to be isolated by recombinant DNA methods. I will then describe progress in the uses of such gene probes in clinical diagnosis of carriers, as well as their use for studying the molecular pathology of the disease and the production of genetically engineered protein.

CLONING AND CHARACTERIZATION OF THE GENES FOR FACTORS VIIIC AND IX

In the period between 1970 and 1980, considerable advances were made in the purification of messenger RNA from highly specialized cells, such as the α and β globin mRNA from reticulocytes. It became possible to clone these highly enriched mRNA preparations, first by making complementary DNA, or cDNA, copies of the mRNA, and then subsequently converting this material to double-stranded DNA *in vitro* and cloning in plasmid or in phage λ vectors propagated in the bacterium, *Escherichia coli*. Subsequently, these cDNA clones could be characterized and used to isolate and study the gene organization. For clotting factor IX, a different approach was necessary as its messenger RNA was present in extremely low concentrations in liver. Nevertheless, using the approach of synthesizing short oligonucleotide probes based on a knowledge of the amino acid sequence of portions of the protein, the problem became soluble. We synthesized oligonucleotide probe mixtures for several regions of the bovine factor IX sequence to enable the isolation

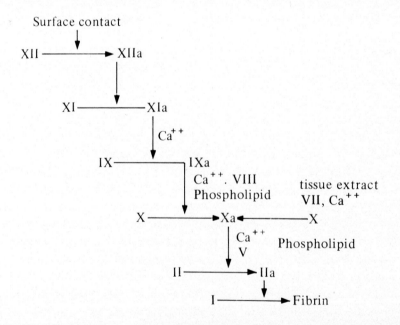

Fig. 1. The clotting cascade. The intrinsic pathway is shown from top left to bottom right. The extrinsic pathway (activation of X by activated VII) is also shown. This is a simplified version showing the main features, but it omits feedback loops and a step, e.g. factor VIIa activation of IX, interconnecting the two pathways (from Austen & Rhymes, 1975, with permission).

of an initial short cDNA probe from bovine liver (Choo, Gould, Rees & Brownlee, 1982). Others used essentially the same principles, although the details differed slightly (Kurachi & Davie, 1982; Jaye *et al.* 1983). These initial cDNA clones were then used as probes in order to isolate both human genomic and cDNA clones establishing the nature of the gene structure as about a 34×10^3 base long region of DNA split into eight coding regions or exons of varying length, which are interrupted by seven non-coding regions or introns (Anson *et al.* 1984). Subsequently, the entire gene sequence has been established by Davie and co-workers (Yoshitake *et al.* 1985).

For factor VIIIC a variation on the method of using oligonucleotide probes was used. Because there was some uncertainty as to which tissue to use as a source of mRNA in the preparation of factor VIIIC-containing cDNA libraries of clones, both groups who successfully cloned and characterized the factor VIIIC gene chose to isolate the initial clone from a short section of the factor VIIIC gene. It turned out to be extremely long and complicated and is about 186×10^3 bases in length, and boasts 26 introns. The mRNA codes for a mature glycoprotein of 2332 amino acids in length. This gene is the largest known to date and occupies approaching $0 \cdot 1 \%$ of the total length of the X chromosome (Gitschier *et al.* 1984; Toole *et al.* 1984).

DIAGNOSIS OF CARRIERS AND PRENATAL DIAGNOSIS OF AFFECTED INDIVIDUALS

When girls in known haemophiliac families reach child-bearing age, they naturally wish to know the risk of having an affected son. Girls have, on average, a 50 % chance of carrying the defective gene, assuming they inherit this from their mother. Traditional methods of carrier detection in such girls rely on the measurement of the concentration of factors VIIIC and IX in plasma. On average, the value in carriers is half that in normal individuals, but unfortunately the diagnostic value of such measurements is limited because of the wide spread of actual values among both normal individuals and carriers. The range of values in carriers is explained by lyonization, i.e. the random inactivation of one X chromosome early in embryonic life, resulting in the fact that the factor-VIII- or IX-producing cells in an individual carrier may be strongly biased in favour of one or other of the paternal or maternal chromosomes.

Although of some value, these classical methods of diagnosis of carriers are thought to have an error-rate of, on average, 17 % in haemophilia A and a somewhat similar rate in haemophilia B (see review by Giannelli, 1986; Barrow, Miller, Reisner & Graham, 1982; Graham, Flyer, Elston & Kasper, 1979). Prenatal diagnosis of affected males, in contrast, is reliable so long as a foetal blood sample can be obtained from the foetal circulation (umbilical vein) uncontaminated with maternal blood (see Mibashan, Giannelli, Pembrey & Rodeck, 1986). A simple clotting assay clearly distinguishes affected from normal individuals. The disadvantage of this procedure is that it requires a skilled gynaecologist to carry out this operation. Furthermore, foetal blood sampling cannot easily be carried out before the 19th or 20th week in pregnancy, when a termination, if desired, is a reasonably unpleasant experience for the mother.

Cloned DNA probes derived from parts of the gene for factors VIIIC or IX offer an alternative and more reliable method of diagnosing carriers. Such clones can also be used for prenatal diagnosis at an early stage in pregnancy, using chorionic trophoblast or amniotic cell samples. Such procedures have been pioneered for the antenatal diagnosis of sickle cell anaemia and some forms of thalassaemia. In these cases, gene probes can identify the mutation directly causing the gene defect (reviewed by Weatherall, 1982). In contrast, haemophilia A and B gene defects are not fixed and maintained in the population by virtue of heterozygote advantage (as is believed to be the case for sickle cell anaemia). Hence mutations are believed (see below) to be caused by a variety of defects of recent and independent origin. For this reason, it is not practical to develop mutation-specific probes for every affected pedigree, so that an *indirect* diagnosis relying on genetic linkage to a polymorphism identified within or very close to a gene becomes the method of choice. Polymorphisms in DNA can be detected by different methods, but those that result in the appearance of one or other of two bands of differing size in a restriction enzyme digest of DNA on an agarose gel are the easiest to work with experimentally. These polymorphisms are referred to as restriction fragment length polymorphisms (RFLP). Three distinct such RFLPs have been identified and used for carrier diagnosis in haemophilia B pedigrees (Giannelli *et al.* 1984; Winship, Anson, Rizza & Brownlee, 1984; Giannelli, 1986). Two such polymorphisms are known at present for haemophilia A (Gitschier *et al.* 1985a; Antonarakis *et al.* 1985).

One current limitation of the linkage analysis with RFLPs is that the frequencies of these polymorphisms in the general population, which appear to mimic that in the affected pedigrees, is such that carrier diagnosis is possible as yet on an average of only 68 % of known Caucasian haemophilia B pedigrees and about 50 % of Caucasian haemophilia A pedigrees. Moreover, as the assays are indirect, they rely on the availability of blood samples not only from the potential carrier under investigation but also from a known patient within the pedigree, preferably a brother, as well as from the mother and father. Fig. 2 illustrates the example of such an RFLP linkage study taken from Winship *et al.* (1984). The person under investigation III_3 was shown to have a genotype a_1a_1. Given the genotypes of her mother (a_1a_2), father (a_1) and affected brother (a_1), we concluded she must be a carrier. If she had been a_1a_2, we would have excluded her as a carrier. The chances of error in this method, omitting issues like paternity and technical errors in the assay due to mixing up samples, are the chance that recombination occurred in the female oocyte at meiosis between the actual disease mutation (somewhere in the factor IX gene) and the RFLP (also located and at a known position within the factor IX gene). Recombination probably occurs non-randomly in chromosomes and we do not know whether this is more frequent or less frequent than average near the factor IX locus; but for the purposes of argument, if we assume there is a possibility of three crossovers per X chromosome and that the X chromosome is 200×10^6 bases long, and

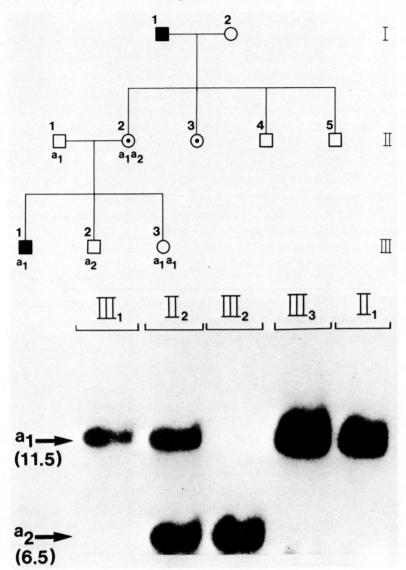

Fig. 2. Carrier diagnosis (below) of a haemophilia B pedigree (above) using an *Xmn*I RFLP in the factor IX gene and a subgenomic probe VIII that gives a_1 ($11\cdot5\times10^3$ base) and a_2 ($6\cdot5\times10^3$ base) alleles (from Winship *et al.* 1984, with permission).

knowing the maximum distance between the polymorphism and gene defect cannot be more than 30×10^3 bases, there will be an even chance of the linkage being broken in the ratio of $30\times3:200\times10^3$ or $\simeq1$ in 2×10^3 times. In percentage terms this is $0\cdot05\%$ chance. For such reasons, we concluded that the indirect linkage analysis with intragenic RFLPs is $99\cdot9\%$ accurate for factor IX (Winship *et al.* 1984). For factor VIIIC with a gene of approximately five times the length of the factor IX gene, the corresponding value is $99\cdot7\%$. In the clinical situation, where families and carriers may be counselled, one must remember that this is an average probability and only an approximate calculation, and that there must be a chance, as more families are counselled as a result of these new methods of analysis, that cases will arise in which the linkage is broken and therefore a wrong diagnosis is made.

More distantly related RFLP markers, e.g. anonymous DNA probes, have been advocated by some experimentalists for carrier and prenatal diagnosis, particularly in the case of factor VIII (Gitschier *et al.* 1985*a*) in which few intragenic RFLPs are known to date. However, a problem with these markers, e.g. DX13 and St14, at a close, but still uncertain (Janco *et al.* 1986), distance from the disease locus, is that the recombination fraction is not known with sufficient accuracy to make them as reliable diagnostically as specific gene probes. Only if and when 200 to 300 total meioses are studied and the recombination fraction is shown to be less than 1 % would I advocate their use clinically.

If obligatory carriers fail to show heterozygosity for any of the known gene-specific polymorphisms, of course, no accurate information is forthcoming for potential carriers – a situation hardly reassuring for the family under investigation, as they would have to fall back on classical diagnostic methods or somewhat less-reliable diagnostic markers such as DX13 or St14 in the case of haemophilia A. One may calculate that if 95 % of all families with haemophilia A or B are to be counselled, a knowledge of at least five different gene-specific RFLPs will be required even if we assume that (1) each RFLP is distributed in the haemophiliac population at the theoretical maximum frequency of 50 %, and (2) each RFLP segregates independently. In practice, not all RFLPs are favourably distributed and because of the tendency of adjacent regions of DNA to be inherited in a linked way some of the RFLPs will not be distributed independently of each other in the population at large. This *linkage disequilibrium* can severely reduce the value of additional RFLPs (as shown for the *Xmn*I polymorphism in factor IX; Winship *et al.* 1984) when information from a *Taq*I RFLP is already known. Because of such difficulties, which have also been described for the β-globin locus (Weatherall, 1982), a realistic estimate of the number of RFLPs required in order to 'catch' 95 % of the affected pedigrees is nearer seven to ten. This value will be difficult to achieve in the short term, but in the medium term, say the next 3–5 years, it should be possible. Of course, a highly polymorphic 'minisatellite' type of sequence such as that occurring near the α-globin locus (Weatherall, Higgs, Wood & Clegg, 1984) would be extremely valuable, but to date there is no evidence of this near the factor VIIIC or IX loci. The current position on factor IX is that a fourth RFLP involving an *Mnl*I RFLP is under investigation in Oxford (P. R. Winship, personal communication). Similarly, I am sure that further RFLPs will be found in the much longer factor VIIIC gene. So far, only a few prenatal diagnoses have been performed on foetal chorionic villi or amniotic samples using RFLPs in haemophilia A and B, but as the modern techniques for carrier diagnosis become more available and potential carriers in affected families find out their status, I predict an increasing demand for such antenatal information.

MOLECULAR DEFECTS IN HAEMOPHILIA A AND B

Evidence of heterogeneity exists in both haemophilia A and B as there is variation in the clinical severity of the disease in different pedigrees, as well as variation in laboratory tests of clotting activity and the antigen concentration measured in samples of blood taken from different patients. We therefore expect a wide range of molecular defects and indeed a precedent for this exists in the variety of mutations already known in the haemoglobin disorders (Weatherall *et al.* 1984). Haemophilia patients may be conveniently subdivided into those patients in whom protein is present as detected by immunological methods, referred to as antigen positive, and those in whom it is absent, referred to as antigen negative. The former might be expected to have point mutations in that region of the gene encoding amino acid residues of the protein and studies of such patients can clearly pinpoint critical functional regions. The latter are more likely to be mutants involving deletions of reasonably large regions of the molecule or critical point mutations involved in the biosynthesis of mRNA (e.g. splice junction sequences), or of protein. Critical point mutations involved in protein synthesis might be changes in the translation initiation or termination codons, or indeed the introduction of such nonsense codons in incorrect coding positions, or mutations affecting protein secretion and maturation. A small subgroup of patients of the antigen negative subgroup are referred to as 'inhibitor' patients because they have specific anti-factor-VIIIC or -IX antibodies in their plasma, which arise in response to therapy with injected normal clotting factors.

Only a few defects of patients have been characterized fully at the molecular level using recombinant DNA methods and the results are summarized in Table 1. (For completion, I include one factor IX antigen positive patient, factor IX$_{Chapel Hill}$ (Noyes *et al.* 1983), whose defect has been characterized by a study of the abnormal protein using the methods of amino acid sequencing.) An antigen positive patient, haemophilia B$_{Oxford 3}$, has been investigated by recombinant DNA methods (Bentley *et al.* unpublished data) and this patient possesses a point mutation at an amino acid in the propeptide precursor domain of the protein, specifically at amino acid −4, (i.e. 4 amino acids preceding the N-terminal tyrosine of the mature factor IX), which results in an abnormally long factor IX protein with an N-terminal extension of 18 amino acids accumulating in plasma. This material is inactive in clotting for reasons that are unknown. Nevertheless, it clearly shows the need for accurate protein processing, which is obviously critically dependent on the arginine residue at amino acid −4 and defines a processing intermediate that has not previously been characterized. Another antigen positive patient, factor IX$_{Alabama}$, has been characterized as a change at amino acid 47, which affects calcium binding (Davis *et al.* 1984, and personal communication). Among the factor IX antigen negative patients, two patients, haemophilia B$_{Oxford 1 and 2}$, from independent pedigrees have been shown to have a defect in different splice–donor junction sequences. One is at the G-T donor at the 3′ end of exon f (exon f is the sixth of the 8 coding regions of the gene), which is changed to T-T (Fig. 3; and Rees, Rizza & Brownlee, 1985). The other involves the G-T at the 3′ end of exon c (the third of the 8 coding regions of the gene), which

Table 1. *Characterized molecular defects in haemophilia*

Subgroup	Haemophilia B		Haemophilia A	
	Patient	Defect	Patient	Defect
Antigen positive	Factor IX$_{Alabama}$	Asp → Gly (47)	—	—
	Factor IX$_{Chapel\ Hill}$	Arg → His (145)		
	Haemophilia B$_{Oxford\,3}$	Arg → Gln (−4)		
Antigen negative	Haemophilia B$_{Oxford\,1}$	G-T → T-T, donor splice junction of exon f	H22	Arg (2307) → TGA, chain termination giving truncated protein
	Haemophilia B$_{Oxford\,2}$	G-T → G-G, donor splice junction of exon c	H51	Deletion of 22×10^3 bases of last exon (no. 26) and extending 3' to the gene, giving truncated (2282 amino acid long) protein
Inhibitors	4 patients from independent pedigrees in UK	Partial and complete gene deletions; exact length of deletion not known	Family A	80×10^3 base deletion within gene
			Family B	Arg (1941) → TGA, chain termination giving truncated protein
			H2	Arg (2209) → TGA, chain termination giving truncated protein
			H96	Deletion of 39×10^3 bases within gene, excising exons 23–25

The numbers in parentheses refer to the amino acid residues of the protein.

is changed to G-G (P. R. Winship, unpublished). These mutations are very reminiscent of the kind of defect that occurs in the β-globin gene in β^0 thalassaemias (Weatherall *et al.* 1984) and it is instructive to note how critical a single point mutation in a vital processing pathway can be, causing as it does clinically severe haemophilia in both affected patients.

The third group of patients, which have been studied in detail in haemophilia B and less extensively in haemophilia A, are those that produce inhibitors. We argued that the reason these patients made antibodies was that their immune system had not been made tolerant to normal factor IX and therefore such patients were likely to have gene deletions. Of course, critical point mutations involving RNA processing or nonsense mutations affecting translation may also have the same effect as gene deletion by preventing normal protein synthesis. Of the six known UK patients, five had evidence of partial or complete gene deletion (Giannelli *et al.* 1983; Peake, Furlong & Bloom, 1984). Presumably, the one non-deletion inhibitor patient described by Giannelli *et al.* (1983) has a critical point mutation elsewhere. Other examples of factor IX inhibitor patients are under study and three Italian patients seem to have at least partial gene deletions whereas an Australian patient may be of the non-deletion type. In haemophilia A, four inhibitor patients have been characterized in detail. Only one (family A, Table 1) has an extensive gene deletion estimated as greater than 80×10^3 bases. The others either have much shorter deletions near the 3' end of the gene (patient H96) or point mutations generating an aberrant stop codon, which would effectively produce a truncated factor VIIIC protein in family B and patient H2 (Gitschier *et al.* 1985*b*; Antonarakis *et al.* 1985). The postulate still remains valid, however, that the basic reason for the development of the inhibitor status, a clinical complication second only in importance to AIDS contamination of concentrates, is the same in both haemophilia A and B, i.e. that the patient's tolerance has not been induced to critical epitopes of the protein (Giannelli *et al.* 1983). However, the position of these critical epitopes in the protein, and the probable differences in detail in the development of tolerance to factor VIIIC and IX remain unknown. Two other clinically severe haemophilia A patients H22 and H51 (see Table 1) have been characterized at the molecular level. One is caused by another point mutation, generating an aberrant translation stop codon, and a second is caused by a short deletion at the 3' terminus of the gene (Gitschier *et al.* 1985*b*). Neither is an inhibitor patient, but Giannelli & Brownlee (1986) note that the probable effect of these latter two mutations on the protein would be expected to be

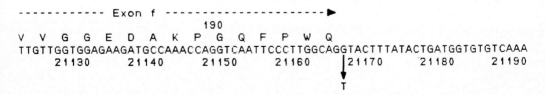

Fig. 3. Sequence surrounding the 3' end of exon f of the normal factor IX gene showing the G $\rightarrow$ T mutation in haemophilia B$_{Oxford 1}$. One-letter symbols are used for the amino acids (from Rees *et al.* 1985, with permission).

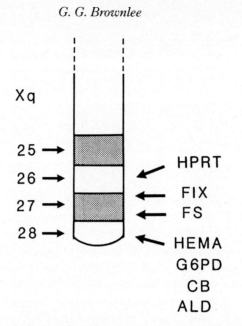

Fig. 4. Diagram of the terminal section of the long arm of the human X chromosome showing some disease loci. For abbreviations, see the text. HPRT is the locus for hypoxanthine guanine phosphoribosyl transferase.

less than the mutations discussed above in the two patients with inhibitors. To date no patients have been described with defects in the promoter or in the A-A-U-A-A-A polyadenylation region of the gene.

Further studies of antigen positive patients should give valuable information about the critical regions for function in both the factor VIIIC and the factor IX molecules. Factor IX and its activated form IXa have to interact with at least five other molecules in the middle stage in the intrinsic clotting pathway, so we must expect many parts of the molecule to be critical for function and, or, correct folding of the protein. Similar arguments apply to factor VIIIC, although in this case we suspect that the central carbohydrate-rich portion of this very large molecule is less important functionally than the rest of the molecule, as it has diverged extensively in amino acid sequence among mammals (Orr *et al.* 1985).

REGIONAL LOCALIZATION ON THE X CHROMOSOME

Fig. 4 shows the localization of the factor IX locus (labelled FIX) to band q27 near to the tip of the long arm of the X chromosome. The localization was discovered using cloned factor IX probes (e.g. see Boyd *et al.* 1984) and has been more recently refined to band q27.1 by *in situ* hybridization to extended early metaphase chromosomes (V. J. Buckle, personal communication). The short cytogenetic distance from the locus at q27.3 for mental retardation with macro-orchidism associated with fragility (FS) is clear. Unfortunately, however, there is still too much recombination (20 %) between the factor IX locus and the FS for the factor IX probes to have any real value in carrier diagnosis of this rather common and depressing disease (e.g. see Choo *et al.* 1984). The haemophilia A locus (HEMA) is known to be closely linked to a group of three other markers; glucose-6-phosphate dehydrogenase (G6PD), colour blindness (CB) and adrenoleukodystrophy (ALD), but again the recombinational fraction between haemophilia A and FS is too great for the factor VIII probes to be useful in diagnosis of the mental retardation syndrome. Many other anonymous gene markers are now known for this region of the X chromosome, but those that have been tested so far are no closer to the FS locus than factor IX. A closely linked probe or a specific gene probe is urgently needed.

GENETICALLY ENGINEERED FACTORS VIIIC AND IX

Haemophilia A and B patients need regular injections of factors VIIIC and IX if haemorrhage is to be avoided and controlled. Unfortunately, there is risk of viral contamination introduced in the donor blood used for these preparations, which has not been completely removed in the purification procedure. Recently, AIDS has superseded hepatitis B and the non-A, non-B hepatitis as the most hazardous complication of therapy. Although the AIDS virus is fortunately rather heat-labile, we do not yet know how successful the heat treatment (instituted in 1985) will be and whether other viruses might appear from time to time that cannot be so easily inactivated. It is therefore highly desirable to produce the required proteins from a genetically engineered source non-contaminated with viruses. This should in addition give a well-standardized product and manufacturers would no longer need to rely on blood donors for their starting material.

The ability to produce factor VIII *in vitro* from cloned DNA was first described late in 1984 by two genetic engineering companies (Wood *et al.* 1984; Toole *et al.* 1984). They introduced modified cDNA clones into mammalian cells, i.e. kidney cells or T lymphoma cells, and showed that biologically active factor VIIIC was secreted into the medium, as assayed by highly specific *in vitro* tests. In 1985, three papers, including one from my own laboratory, reported similar successes with factor IX, also in mammalian cells (Anson, Austen & Brownlee, 1985; de la Salle *et al.* 1985; Busby *et al.* 1985). Both liver and kidney cells successfully produced active material, although the specific activity of the factor IX protein was higher in the liver cell, presumably reflecting the fact that this cell tissue had correctly modified and processed the factor IX. As liver is the tissue in which factor IX is normally synthesized, it might be expected to be appropriate for correct expression and production of factor IX that is indistinguishable from the raw material. Nevertheless, in all these studies, of both factor VIIIC and IX, minute yields of product are reported. One of the best yields of approaching 1 μg of factor IX per ml of medium was reported in one of the papers on factor IX (Busby *et al.* 1985). Even with this, I estimate it would be necessary to culture hundreds of thousands of litres of cells to obtain enough material for the UK requirement of 50 g of factor IX for one year. Given that purification of proteins on a large scale necessarily entails losses, it is clear that more efficient small-scale synthesis has to be developed before an investment in a large-scale industrial process is made. Fortunately, there is an indication that a protein related to factor IX (the anti-coagulant protein C) can be successfully produced in high yields in Chinese hamster ovary cells using recombinant DNA methods. In these cells the protein C gene copy number can be amplified by linkage of the clone to the gene for dihydrofolate reductase followed by growth of cells in methotrexate. Thus it may be possible to produce cell lines giving at least 10 times more factor IX. For factor VIIIC, there is a similar requirement for maximization of the yields of genetically engineered material on a small scale.

I estimate that it will be 3–5 years before the necessary industrial processes for factors VIIIC and IX will be developed and the material adequately characterized and tested for clinical application to human beings. Nevertheless, the product should be safer, free of viruses, and, I suggest, will supersede traditional products made from blood with all their inherent problems.

I thank the Medical Research Council for support.

REFERENCES

ANSON, D. S., AUSTEN, D. E. G. & BROWNLEE, G. G. (1985). Expression of active human clotting factor IX from recombinant DNA clones in mammalian cells. *Nature, Lond.* **315**, 683–686.

ANSON, D. S., CHOO, K. H., REES, D. J. G., GIANNELLI, F., GOULD, K., HUDDLESTON, J. A. & BROWNLEE, G. G. (1984). Gene structure of human anti-haemophilic factor IX. *EMBO J.* **3**, 1053–1064.

ANTONARAKIS, S. E., WABER, P. G., KITTUR, S. D., PATEL, A. S., KAZAZIAN, H. H., JR, MELLIS, M. A., COUNTS, R. B., STAMATOYANNOPOULOS, G., BOWIE, E. J. W., FASS, D. N., PITTMAN, D. D., WOSNEY, J. M. & TOOLE, J. J. (1985). Hemophilia A: detection of molecular defects and of carriers by DNA analysis. *N. Eng. J. Med.* Oct. 3, 842–848.

AUSTEN, D. E. G. & RHYMES, I. L. (1975). *A Laboratory Manual of Blood Coagulation*. Oxford: Blackwell Scientific.

BARROW, E. S., MILLER, C. H., REISNER, H. M. & GRAHAM, J. B. (1982). Genetic counselling in haemophilia by discriminant analysis 1975–1980. *J. med. Genet.* **19**, 26.

BOYD, Y., BUCKLE, V. J., MUNRO, E. A., CHOO, K. H., MIGEON, B. R. & CRAIG, I. W. (1984). Assignment of the haemophilia B (factor IX) locus to the q26–qter region of the X chromosome. *Ann. hum. Genet.* **48**, 145–152.

BUSBY, S., KUMAR, A., JOSEPH, M., HALFPAP, L., INSLEY, M., BERKNER, K., KURACHI, K. & WOODBURY, R. (1985). Expression of active human factor IX in transfected cells. *Nature, Lond.* **316**, 271–273.

CHOO, K. H., GEORGE, G., FILBY, G., HALLIDAY, J. L., LEVERSHA, M., WEBB, G. & DANKS, D. M. (1984). Linkage analysis of X-linked mental retardation with and without fragile X using factor IX gene probe. *Lancet* **ii** Aug., 349.

CHOO, K. H., GOULD, K. G., REES, D. J. G. & BROWNLEE, G. G. (1982). Molecular cloning of the gene for human antihaemophilic factor IX. *Nature, Lond.* **299**, 178–180.

DAVIS, L. M., MCGRAW, R. A., GRAHAM, J. B., ROBERTS, H. R. & STAFFORD, D. W. (1984). Identification of the genetic defect in factor IX$_{Alabama}$·DNA sequence reveals a Gly substitution for Asp46. *Blood* **64** (Suppl. 1), 262a.

DE LA SALLE, H., ALTENBURGER, W., ELKAIM, R., DOTT, K., DIETERLE, A., DRILLIEN, R., CASENAVE, J.-P., TOLSTOSHEV, P. & LECOCQ, J.-P. (1985). Active γ-carboxylated human factor IX expressed using recombinant DNA techniques. *Nature, Lond.* **316**, 268–270.

GIANNELLI, F. (1986). The contribution of gene specific probes to the genetic counselling of families segregating for haemophilia B (factor IX deficiency). In *Bari Int. Conf. on Factor VIII/von Willebrand Factor – Biological and Clinical Advances* (ed. N. Ciavarella, Z. Ruggieri & T. S. Zimmerman). Milan: Wichtig (in press).

GIANNELLI, F. & BROWNLEE, G. G. (1986). *Nature, Lond.* (in press).

GIANNELLI, F., CHOO, K. H., REES, D. J. G., BOYD, Y., RIZZA, C. R. & BROWNLEE, G. G. (1983). Gene deletions in patients with haemophilia B and anti-factor IX antibodies. *Nature, Lond.* **303**, 181–182.

GIANNELLI, F., CHOO, K. H., WINSHIP, P. R., ANSON, D. S., REES, D. J. G., FERRARI, N., RIZZA, C. R. & BROWNLEE, G. G. (1984). Characterisation and use of an intragenic polymorphic marker for detection of carriers of haemophilia B (factor IX deficiency). *Lancet* **i**, 239–241.

GITSCHIER, J., DRAYNA, D., TUDDENHAM, E. G. D., WHITE, R. I. & LAWN, R. M. (1985*a*). Genetic mapping and diagnosis of haemophilia A achieved through a BclI polymorphism in the factor VIII gene. *Nature, Lond.* **314**, 738–740.

GITSCHIER, J., WOOD, W. I., GORALKA, T. M., WION, K. L., CHEN, E. Y., EATON, D. H., VEHAR, G. A., CAPON, D. J. & LAWN, R. M. (1984). Characterization of the human factor VIII gene. *Nature, Lond.* **312**, 326–330.

GITSCHIER, J., WOOD, W. I., TUDDENHAM, E. G. D., SHUMAN, M. A., GORALKA, T. M., CHEN, E. Y. & LAWN, R. M. (1985*b*). Detection and sequence of mutations in the factor VIII gene of haemophiliacs. *Nature, Lond.* **315**, 427–430.

GRAHAM, J. B., FLYER, P., ELSTON, R. C. & KASPER, C. K. (1979). Statistical study of genotype assignment (carrier detection) in haemophilia B. *Thromb. Res.* **15**, 69.

JANCO, R. L., PHILLIPS, J. A., ORLANDO, P., DAVIES, K. E., OLD, J. & ANTONARAKIS, S. E. (1986). Carrier testing in haemophilia A. *Lancet* **i**, 148.

JAYE, M., DE LA SALLE, H., SCHAMBER, F., BALLAND, A., KOHLI, V., FINDELI, A., TOLSTOSHEV, P. & LECOCQ, J.-P. (1983). Isolation of a human anti-haemophilic factor IX cDNA clone using a unique 52-base synthetic oligonucleotide probe deduced from the amino acid sequence of bovine factor IX. *Nucl. Acids Res.* **11**, 2325–2335.

KATAYAMA, K., ERICSSON, L. H., ENFIELD, D. L., WALSH, K. A., NEURATH, H., DAVIE, E. W. & TITANI, K. (1979). Comparison of amino acid sequence of bovine coagulation factor IX (Christmas factor) with that of other vitamin K-dependent plasma proteins. *Proc. natn. Acad. Sci. U.S.A.* **76**, 4990–4994.

KURACHI, K. & DAVIE, E. W. (1982). Isolation and characterization of a cDNA coding for human factor IX. *Proc. natn. Acad. Sci. U.S.A.* **79**, 6461–6464.

MCKEE, P. A. (983). Haemostasis and disorders of blood coagulation. In *The Metabolic Basis of Inherited Disease,* 5th edn (ed. J. B. Stanbury, J. B. Wyngaarden, D. S. Fredrickson, J. L. Goldstein & M. S. Brown), pp. 1531–1560. New York: McGraw-Hill.

MIBASHAN, R. S., GIANNELLI, F., PEMBREY, M. E. & RODECK, C. H. (1986). The antenatal diagnosis of clotting disorders. In *Advanced Medicine,* vol. 20 (ed. M. J. Brown). London: Pitman (in press).

NOYES, C. M., GRIFFITH, M. J., ROBERTS, H. R. & LUNDBLAD, R. L. (1983). Identification of the molecular defect in factor IX (Chapel Hill): Substitution of histidine for arginine at position 145. *Proc. natn. Acad. Sci. U.S.A.* **80**, 4200–4202.

ORR, E., WOZNEY, J., BUECKER, J., PITTMAN, D., KAUFMAN, R. & TOOLE, J. (1985). "Spacer" function implied for the heavily glycosylated region of factor VIII. *Thromb. Haemostas.* **54**, 54.

PEAKE, I. R., FURLONG, B. L. & BLOOM, A. L. (1984). Carrier detection by gene analysis in a family with haemophilia B (factor IX deficiency). *Lancet* **i**, 242.

REES, D. J. G., RIZZA, C. R. & BROWNLEE, G. G. (1985). Haemophilia B caused by a point mutation in a donor splice junction of the human factor IX gene. *Nature, Lond.* **316**, 643–645.

TOOLE, J. J., KNOPF, J. L., WOSNEY, J. M., SULTZMAN, L. A., BUECKER, J. L., PITTMAN, D. D., KAUFMAN, R. J., BROWN, E., SHOEMAKER, C., ORR, E. C., AMPHLETT, G. W., FOSTER, B. W., COU, M. L., KNUTSON, G. J., FASS, D. N. & HEWICK, R. M. (1984). Molecular cloning of a cDNA encoding human anti-haemophilic factor. *Nature, Lond.* **312**, 342–347.

WEATHERALL, D. J. (1982). *The New Genetics and Clinical Practice.* London: Nuffield Provincial Hospitals Trust.

WEATHERALL, D. J., HIGGS, D. H., WOOD, W. G. & CLEGG, J. B. (1984). Genetic disorders of human haemoglobin as models for analysing gene regulation. *Phil. Trans. R. Soc. Lond.* B **307**, 247–259.

WINSHIP, P. R., ANSON, D. S., RIZZA, C. R. & BROWNLEE, G. G. (1984). Carrier detection in haemophilia B using two further intragenic restriction fragment length polymorphisms. *Nucl. Acids Res.* **12**, 8861–8872.

Wood, W. I., Capon, D. J., Simonsen, C. C., Eaton, D. L., Gitschier, J., Keyt, B., Seeburg, P. H., Smith, D. H., Hollingshead, P., Wion, K. L., Delwart, E., Tuddenham, E. G. D., Vehar, G. A. & Lawn, R. M. (1984). Expression of active human factor VIII from recombinant DNA clones. *Nature, Lond.* **312**, 330–337.

Yoshitake, S., Schach, B. G., Foster, D. C., Davie, E. W. & Kurachi, K. (1985). Nucleotide sequence of the gene for human factor IX (antihaemophilic factor B). *Biochemistry* **24**, 3736.